Harmonic Materials in Tonal Music Part I

Answer Cover

Note: To create the Answer Cover, tear out the entire page at the perforation and fold to size, or cut keyboard portion off along dotted line.

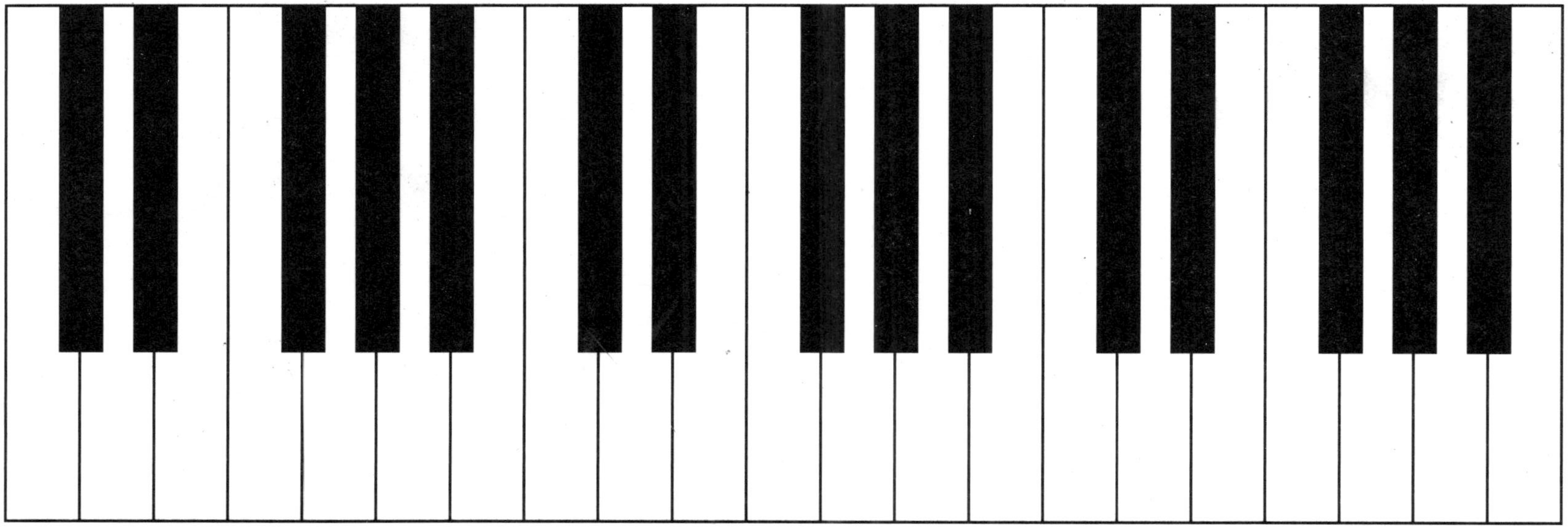

Harmonic Materials in Tonal Music

A Programed Course

Part I

TENTH EDITION

Revised by

Greg A Steinke

Independent Composer/Musician

based on materials
originally created by

Paul O. Harder

Late, of Michigan State University

Prentice Hall

Upper Saddle River   London   Singapore
Toronto   Tokyo   Sydney   Hong Kong   Mexico City

Editor-in-Chief: Sarah Touborg
Executive Editor: Richard Carlin
Project Manager: Sarah Holle
Editorial Assistant: Emma Gibbons
Director of Marketing: Tim Stookesberry
Senior Marketing Manager: Kate Mitchell
Marketing Assistant: Jennifer Lang
Senior Managing Editor: Mary Rottino
Production Editor: Emilcomp/Prepare
Project Management Liaison: Joe Scordato
Senior Operations Supervisor: Brian Mackey
Cover Designer: Margaret Kenselaar
Creative Director: Jayne Conte
Cover Photo: Jane Burton/Dorling Kindersley Media Library
Manager, Cover Visual Research and Permissions: Karen Sanatar
Composition: Emilcomp/Prepare
Full-Service Management: Emilcomp/Prepare
Printer/Binder: Bind-Rite Graphics
Cover Printer: Coral Graphics
Recording Engineer/Performer: Margaret Mayer

Credits and acknowledgments borrowed from other sources and reproduced, with permission, in this textbook appear on appropriate page within text. Musical examples completed using *NoteWriter*™, *NoteAbilityPro*™, and *Finale 2008*™.

Library of Congress Cataloging-in-Publication Data

Greg A Steinke
Harmonic Materials in Tonal Music: a programed course/Greg A Steinke, based on material originally created by Paul O. Harder. — 10th ed.
p. cm.
Includes bibliographical references and index.
ISBN 0-205-62971-7
1. Harmony–Programed instruction. I. Steinke, Greg A,

MT50.H26 2010
781.2'5077—dc22 2008036055

10 9 8 7 6 5 4 3 2 1

Prentice Hall
is an imprint of

PEARSON

www.pearsonhighered.com

ISBN-10: 0-205-62971-7
ISBN-13: 978-0-205-62971-8

Contents

About the Authors v
Preface to the Tenth Edition vii
Preface to the Fifth Edition viii
How to Use This Text ix
An Important Perspective for the Study of Harmony xi

1.0

Some Definitions **1**
Summary 14
Mastery Frames 15
Supplementary Activities for Chapters 1.0–3.0 18
Supplementary Assignments 19

2.0

The Structure of Tonality **23**
Summary 41
Mastery Frames 43
Supplementary Assignments 45

3.0

Triads in Root Position: Doubling and Spacing **49**
Summary 75
Mastery Frames 77
Supplementary Assignments 79

4.0

Triads in Root Position: Voice Leading **83**
Summary 114
Mastery Frames 115
Supplementary Activities 116
Supplementary Assignments 117

5.0

Triads in First and Second Inversion **121**
Summary 162
Mastery Frames 163
Supplementary Activities 164
Supplementary Assignments 165

6.0

Introduction to Seventh Chords and the Dominant Seventh **169**
Summary 196
Mastery Frames 197
Supplementary Activities 200
Supplementary Assignments 201

7.0

Phrase Structure and Cadences **207**
Summary 234
Mastery Frames 235
Supplementary Activities 236
Supplementary Assignments 237

8.0

Nonharmonic Tones **241**
Summary 285
Summary of Nonharmonic Tones 286
Mastery Frames 289
Supplementary Activities 290
Supplementary Assignments 291

9.0

Harmonic Progression **295**
Summary 320
Mastery Frames 321
Supplementary Activities 322
Supplementary Assignments 323

10.0

The Technique of Harmonization **327**
Summary 346
Mastery Frames 347
Supplementary Activities 348
Supplementary Assignments 349

Appendix A: Chord Symbols **353**
Appendix B: Piano Styles **357**
Appendix C: Glossary of Terms **369**
Appendix D: Orchestration Chart; Note/Octave, MIDI Charts **375**
Bibliography for Further Study **379**
Index of Musical Examples **385**
Subject Index **387**
Notes and Staff Paper **391**

About the Authors

Dr. Paul O. Harder (1923–1986) received a Master of Music degree in Music Theory from the Eastman School of Music, University of Rochester, where he performed as oboist with the Rochester Philharmonic Orchestra. Later, as a fellowship student at the University of Iowa, he received his Ph.D. in Music Composition. He studied composition with Mlle. Nadia Boulanger at the École des Beaux Arts de Fontainebleau, France, and at the Royal Academy of Music in Copenhagen, Denmark.

Dr. Harder held the post of Chairman of Music Theory at Michigan State University before becoming Assistant Vice President and Professor of Music at California State University, Stanislaus. He was a Professor Emeritus at Michigan State University.

In addition to approximately fifty compositions for a variety of media including orchestra, band, chorus, and chamber groups, Dr. Harder was the author of *Harmonic Materials in Tonal Music,* Parts I and II, through the fifth edition; *Basic Materials in Music Theory,* through the sixth edition; *Music Manuscript Techniques,* Parts I and II; *Bridge to Twentieth Century Music,* through the first edition; and as co-author (with H. Owen Reed), *Basic Contrapuntal Techniques.* All were published by Allyn & Bacon (see the Bibliography).

Dr. Greg A Steinke (b. 1942) holds a Bachelor of Music degree from Oberlin Conservatory, a Master of Music degree from Michigan State University, a Master of Fine Arts degree from the University of Iowa, and a Doctor of Philosophy degree from Michigan State University.

Dr. Steinke retired in June 2001 as Chair of the Art and Music Departments, Associate Dean for Undergraduate Studies, and holder of the Joseph Naumes Endowed Chair in Music at Marylhurst University in Oregon. Formerly, he was Dean of the College of Fine Arts and Professor of Music at Millikin University, Director of the School of Music and Professor of Music at Ball State University, Assistant Director of the School of Music at the University of Arizona, Chairman of the Music Department at San Diego State University, Director of the School of Music at the University of Idaho, Chairman of the Music Department at Linfield College, and a faculty member at Northern Arizona University, The Evergreen State College, California State University, Northridge, and the University of Maryland. Currently, he is a freelance composer, writer, oboist, and conductor.

Dr. Steinke is the author of numerous articles, has done the revisions to Paul Harder's *Basic Materials in Music Theory* (seventh through twelfth editions), *Harmonic Materials in Tonal Music,* (sixth through tenth editions), *Bridge to Twentieth Century Music* (revised edition), and, with H. Owen Reed, *Basic Contrapuntal Techniques* (revised edition, Alfred Music). He holds membership in a number of professional organizations and served for nine years (three terms, 1988–97) as the President and National Chairman of the Society of Composers, Inc. Professor Steinke is active as a composer of chamber and symphonic music with a number of published works, as a speaker on interdisciplinary arts, and as an oboe soloist specializing in contemporary music.

Preface to the Tenth Edition

It is always a challenging task to revise a book that has already enjoyed many years of success. It is an honor to be asked to undertake this latest revision of what has now been many editions. I have had a deep belief in these books ever since I first used them as a young theory teacher in 1967 when they were first available. With a great deal of history behind me, and the highest respect and regard for all of Paul Harder's diligent efforts, I again offer various revisions and enhancements that I believe keep to the original spirit of Dr. Harder's programed concept, and that I hope all users will find helpful as they work through these pages.

In making the revisions, I have responded to comments and suggestions from reviewers and current users of the book. Earlier revisions have contained additions made to the supplementary exercises and to the Appendix material. In selected places throughout the book, I have continued to clarify definitions or to demonstrate to the reader that there are always alternatives to the ideas presented and that the reader should explore those alternatives either independently or in class with the instructor. Therefore, this edition sees a number of changes throughout the book. I hope that the differences in theoretical and analytical approaches (which, I know, will always be there) work comfortably with previous editions and also provide many interesting points of discussion in class. I'm quite sure that Dr. Harder never intended this volume to be the final, definitive answer but, rather, to provide an informed point of departure for exploring the many anomalies that are always to be found in musics everywhere.

The exposition of the material is accomplished through a step-by-step process. To some, this approach may seem mechanical, but it does ensure, in general, a good understanding of the basic tenets of the materials of the so-called common practice period in music. I emphasize that this approach does not preclude the presentation of alternatives or the exploration of other ways in which composers may work with various cause-and-effect relationships, rather than following any set of "rules." A rich learning experience can be created for instructors and students alike as they explore together the many exceptions to the so-called rules or principles. This allows them to ultimately link all that they study to actual musical literature or to create many varieties of assignments to solidify the understanding of the basic framework presented in these pages.

The reviser continues to be grateful to both The Paul Harder Estate and Pearson Education for providing helpful comments and support throughout the revision process. I am also indebted to the late Mildred Harder for having provided me access to all notes and support materials Dr. Harder used in the original creation of his book and for her past comments and moral support. I also thank colleagues Dr. David Stech, Dr. Larry Solomon, Dr. J. Timothy Kolosick, Dr. Timothy Kloth, Dr. Kenneth Rummery, Dr. Margaret Mayer, Dr. Deborah Kavasch, Dr. David Sills, Prof. David Foley, Dr. Tim Smith, and Dr. Lewis Strouse for their comments, encouragement and assistance on revision ideas over the past several editions. While a number of reviewers provided very helpful suggestions for this edition, I specifically thank Shaun Naidoo, Chapman University, Orange, CA; Joel Knudsen, Butler Community College, El Dorado, KS; Craig E. Ferrin, Salt Lake Community College, Salt Lake City, UT; Katherine Domingo, Indiana University, Bloomington, IN; Jeanette Winsor, Tidewater Community College, Virginia Beach, VA; Jerry Skelley, Cape Cod Community College, West Barnstable, MA. I also thank Debra Nichols, who copyedited this edition and provided many helpful changes and suggestions. I am grateful to all concerned and am most appreciative of the help they have provided. I hope users of this volume will find many hours of rich, musical learning to enhance their developing musicianship.

GAS

Preface to the Fifth Edition

The refinements incorporated into the fifth edition are designed to make this book an even more useful aid for learning the materials and practices of tonal harmony. One change concerns the summaries that follow the expository section of each chapter: many have been expanded for a more complete overview of the main points covered. The summaries, plus all new mastery frames, help the learner assess or comprehend the material in each chapter before proceeding to the next. Another change involves the supplementary assignments, which are also all new. In addition, they are now organized so each may be removed from the book as a separate entity, facilitating their submission to the instructor for evaluation.

The chief emphasis in this two-part study of tonal harmony is on the basic elements of harmony that have retained their validity throughout the period from about 1600 to 1900. Music from this period is still very much a part of our musical life. Not only does a large part of the current repertoire consist of eighteenth- and nineteenth-century music, but tonal harmony is the basis of practically all commercial music. All composers, no matter what style they generally may employ, turn to tonal harmony when such material is appropriate to their expressive purpose. This book is not devoted to the study of any one composer's works, nor is it limited to four-part writing; various applications of harmonic principles are shown in musical examples drawn from a variety of periods and compositional types.

Since most of the music we hear and perform is based on tonal harmony, it is essential that serious students become familiar with this system. For the composer, competence in writing requires thorough understanding of techniques practiced by composers of previous generations. For the performer, the ability to convey delicate nuances and subtleties of phrasing often stems from a cultivated sensitivity to harmonic processes.

Experience has shown that the type of programed instruction used in this book can lead to rapid, yet thorough mastery of musical concepts and techniques. Also, it has proved versatile in that it can be used not only by a single student working independently, but also by students in large classes. Still more important is the flexibility that programed material brings to the instructor. The core of knowledge contained in this book may be expanded by emphasis upon creative writing, analysis, or the study of music literature. Because students evaluate their own exercises, the instructor is free to prepare more vital and creative supplementary learning experiences.

The development of this course was supported by the Educational Development Program at Michigan State University. The author is grateful to Dr. John Dietrich, Assistant Provost, and Dr. Robert Davis, Director of the Educational Development Program, for their assistance; also to Drs. Jere Hutcheson, Clifford Pfeil, and Gary White, who helped develop practical classroom methods. Particular tribute, though, must be paid to the many students who, over a period of several years, assisted in proving out the approaches incorporated in this book. Thanks also go to Rita Fuszek, Professor of Music at California State University, Fullerton, the diligent pianist who recorded the examples contained in the cassettes that accompany this book. And finally, special thanks go to my wife, Mildred, who has not only typed countless pages over the years, but provided helpful comment and moral support.

Paul O. Harder
(1923–1986)

How to Use This Text

Do not begin this study of tonal harmony without thorough knowledge and/or review of the fundamentals of music including scales, key signatures, intervals, and triads. You are strongly urged to review the author's *Basic Materials in Music Theory,* also published by Prentice Hall if you need to "brush up" on these skills.

This book features the use of programed instruction to convey conceptual information and provide drills to develop techniques for handling harmonic materials. In programed instruction, information is presented in small, carefully sequenced parcels that combine in cumulative fashion to help you master the subject. The parcels into which the material is divided are called *frames.* Most frames require a written response, which may be a word or two, or perhaps the solution to a musical problem.

The principal part of each frame is located on the right-hand side of the page. The answers, which appear on the left-hand side, should be covered with the answer cover, a slip of paper, a ruler, or with the hand. After you write your response, uncover the answer and check your work immediately. There are many cases in which your answer need not be exactly the same as that supplied by the text. You should consider your response correct if it conveys the same meaning as the one given. Use common sense to decide whether or not you comprehend a particular item. Because each step is small, you should make few mistakes.

Each chapter ends with a series of "mastery" frames. These frames allow you to evaluate your mastery of key points—concepts and skills essential to coping with matters that lie ahead. *Do not proceed unless your handling of the mastery frames assures you that you are ready to continue.*

Mastery frames are identified with double numbers to prevent confusion with the frames that constitute the body of the text. *References to the frames that cover the subject of each question are provided along with the correct answers.* Avail yourself to these references in order to focus remedial study precisely on the points missed. Because the mastery frames are concerned with the essential matters covered in each chapter, you will find that they are useful for later review. There are also Supplementary Assignments, which are intended primarily for use in a classroom setting. The answers to these assignments are contained in the *Instructor's Manual for Steinke Harmonic Materials in Tonal Music, Parts I and II,* which is available on request from the publisher. In all chapters Supplementary Activities are also given. These can be carried out in class, alone, or with a colleague.

Many musical examples are given in the text to acquaint you with the way various composers use harmonic devices. You should play these at a piano or keyboard, play the compact disc, or program them in a computer for playback, so that they are actually *heard.* It is not sufficient to approach this study on an intellectual level alone; you must have command of the harmonic vocabulary as an aural phenomenon as well as bring to bear your musical experiences as both a performer and a listener. The purpose of conceptualizing musical processes is to render more understandable the responses elicited by the auditory stimuli of music. Remember, music is an *aural* art; it is apprehended better by the ear than by the eye. So try to sing or play each example as it is presented. In this way the relation of symbols to sound will become real and functional.

It is assumed that the study of the materials in this book are, or will be, supplemented with appropriate ear-training experiences. Some suggestions for ear training are given in the Supplementary Activities sections of the text, but they are offered in the context of being activities that are supplementing other, more comprehensive ear training. (For in-depth study of ear training, the Ear Training section of the *Bibliography for Further Study*, p. 380, may be referenced.)

A beside a frame indicates that the music in that frame or example is reproduced on the compact disc.

An Important Perspective for the Study of Harmony

One would suppose that, by now, the study of tonal harmony would be passé. After all, Western art music, with its wide, attendant vocabulary of chords, has become more diffused and of a broader scope through the compositions of the impressionists of the late nineteenth century and the atonalists of the early twentieth century. The impressionists—Debussy in particular—created an expression of the conception of tonality through the use of nontertian chords (chords not built by thirds) and nonfunctional streams of chords, as well as by the expansion of tonal frontiers. By the end of the first decade of the twentieth century, Arnold Schönberg had shown in works such as *Pierrot Lunaire* that expressive music could indeed be created without resorting to either traditional Western tonality or tertian harmony. The dodecaphonic, or twelve-tone, system was designed to effectively negate any lingering influences of Western harmonic practices. This system, as employed by members of the second Viennese School (Webern and Berg, in addition to Schönberg), as well as by countless others during the succeeding decades of the twentieth century, led to a larger body of music, including many highly expressive works.

Harmonic art music, however, is still with us, perhaps due, in part, to the minimalist and neo-romantic movements of the late twentieth century. So, far from being dead, the several streams of harmonically oriented music are alive and well. Indeed, most of the music heard through Western mass media (and a great deal elsewhere) is based on Western harmonic practices. This is true, also, of music performed in churches and studied in schools. Even concert and recital programs reveal a strong adherence to the so-called standard repertoire, with the inclusion of only an occasional nontonal work. There is, of course, the somewhat rare program devoted exclusively to contemporary music. Unfortunately such programs tend to have little impact, considering the overwhelming amount of earlier, Western-style art music heard.

What accounts for the persistence of earlier music? Reasons can only be stated as speculation. A few follow:

1. There are those who would point to the "natural" basis of harmonic music. Because the harmonic series is a phenomenon of nature, the generation of chords by thirds (tertian harmony) and the relation of roots to the tonic according to precepts derived from the series can be seen not only as being ordained by nature, but also as possessing special moral sanction.

2. Perhaps because many people in the world's societies, from birth, have heard little other than harmonic music, preference is given to the familiar; choice is made on the basis of conditioning, which produces an inertia of values.

3. Music in which tones bear relatively simple acoustical relations to one another is easier both to sing and to apprehend. Much folk music of the world, for example, tends to display preference for limited range and relatively small intervals, as well as emphasis on the perfect fourth and fifth—intervals that may have special tonal significance for some listeners.

4. It is apparent that the expressive resources of tonal music in general have not been exhausted. The rapidly changing styles of much commercial music demonstrate that fresh drafts of musical expression still remain to be drawn from the well of harmonic resources, both Western and non-Western.

Rationale aside, harmonic music clearly constitutes the bulk of what is heard by Western and other societies at large. It also dominates the music studied and performed by students in Western and non-Western schools of music. These realities justify the continued study of tonal harmony, and the time is not in sight when this study will be without meaning and thus disappear from the standard music curriculum.

(Please note that the discussion from this point focuses entirely on Western art music ideals. No less important is the evolution of music styles and principles in other parts of the world. Those ideals are outside this discussion, but *they are certainly no less important to study and understand to be an informed musician.*)

The two basic parameters of music are *temporal* (time) and *sonic* (sound). With respect to the sonic parameter, two principal methods of organization have evolved in Western music: *counterpoint* (linear) and *harmony* (chordal). The technique of counterpoint developed much earlier than the concept of harmony as an independent musical principle. From about the beginning of the tenth century to nearly 1600, the chief organizing principles were related to counterpoint. But from the beginning, the effect of voices sounding together was recognized as an important factor. This is evidenced by the changing preferences for intervals during the course of musical evolution.

Early in the development of counterpoint, the chief consonances were perfect unisons, octaves, fourths, and fifths. Open sonorities such as 1–5–8 were the main consonant sonorities, with complete triads (1–3–5) appearing as passing occurrences. The frequency of triads gradually increased after 1300, occurring even at cadence points, except for the final cadence where perfect consonances (1–5–8) were still preferred. From about the middle of the fifteenth century, complete triads in both root position and first inversion predominated, but music from this period displays no systematic approach to harmonic progression, except at the cadences, where plagal, authentic, and Phrygian cadences are used.

After 1600 the preeminence of the first, fourth, and fifth scale degrees began to be established, and greater consistency of root movement developed. This led to the establishment of major/minor tonality, which supplanted the modal system of the medieval and Renaissance periods. During the Baroque period, the vocabulary of chords was enlarged to include various altered chords such as the Neapolitan sixth and secondary dominants. Chromaticism and systematic modulation also developed at this time. In response to the classical ideals of clarity, lightness, and balance, harmonic action tended to be simpler and more formula driven. The form-defining function of contrasting tonalities, however, became even more important; also, there was more frequent modulation to distant keys.

Harmony received its fullest development during the Romantic period (1825–1900), during which time the tonal horizon was pushed back to the very limits of equal temperament, and the repertoire of chords was expanded by the use of the complete chromatic scale. Frequent use of altered chords, coupled with modulations to distant keys, led to the eventual disintegration of tonality, and the fall of tonality brought down the whole structure of tonal relations and chord structures associated with tertian harmony. But, as we have seen, harmonic music refuses to die; its emotive power is still strong. And, although it appears that the evolution of harmony was complete by 1900, harmonic materials may still be explored for new ends.

The evolution of harmony also may be traced through the writings of various theorists. For this purpose, some of the major contributions to the field of harmonic theory will be briefly reviewed. It is surprising that recognition of harmony as an independent musical parameter occurred so late. After all, several contrapuntal lines produce simultaneous sounds, and for several centuries prior to 1600, many of these sounds resulted in chords. But pre-Baroque technique exploited the interval as the basic constructive unit—the concept of the chord did not exist. What we recognize as chords today were viewed then as conglomerations of intervals. The first recognition of the chord as an entity occurred in Gioseffo Zarlino's *Istituzioni armoniche* of 1558. In this work Zarlino refers to the *harmonia perfetta,* which results from the first six tones of the natural harmonic series. It is, in effect, the major triad. Being the first to recognize the triad as a harmonic entity, Zarlino is the father of modern harmonic theory.

A still greater contribution to harmonic theory was made by Jean-Philippe Rameau, whose treatise *Traité de l'Harmonie* was published in 1722. Many of the principles set forth by Rameau are still employed today to explain harmonic processes. Rameau's writings are extensive and involved. His primary contributions, however, are threefold:

1. He postulated that the lowest note of the triad in 1–3–5 position is the root and is the generator of the third and fifth. Also, this note (1) remains the root when the chord is inverted to either 3–5–8 (first inversion) or 5–8–10 (second inversion).

2. The roots of chords, as opposed to the actual bass line, constitute the "fundamental," and the fundamental bass is the true motivator of the harmony. The result of this principle is to reduce the number of harmonic entities and provide a simple method for relating chords to one another and to the tonal center.

3. The symmetrical structure of harmonic tonality was identified by Rameau, who, recognizing the fundamental acoustical nature of the perfect fifth, also saw the subdominant and dominant as straddling the tonic (IV–I–V), the dominant a fifth higher, the subdominant a fifth lower. It was Rameau who first used the term *sous-dominante* to designate the "lower" dominant.

Rameau, like Zarlino, based his theories on the natural harmonic series and mathematics. Most later harmonic theorists did likewise. Some, however, chose other bases for their speculations. For example, in 1754 Giuseppe Tartini published his treatise *Trattato di musica,* in which reference is made not only to the natural harmonic series and mathematics but also to geometry. In 1853, Moritz Hauptmann published his *Die Natur der Harmonik und Metrik,* in which a philosophical approach based on Hegel's dialectical metaphysics is employed.

The theorists reviewed here, plus many others,* felt that they were dealing with harmony as a science, that basic principles that would explain music phenomena and more, lay hidden, waiting only to be discovered and proved. But this has proved to be a chimera (fantasy); for no harmonic theory, including Rameau's, is free of inner contradictions. There have been many near misses; but nature has not cooperated by providing a closed system to tone relations, at least in terms of the kind of music with which people have to date been concerned.

In returning to the opening statement, we now realize that: the study of tonal music is not passé nor is the study of Western art music principles passé. Even with the passage of centuries, basic concepts still "rule" to a great extent and provide an important underpinning to many musics throughout the world with modifications, blendings, and adjustments to suit a particular milieu—yet, these "concepts" provide a kind of basic "operating system," to borrow from today's technology. In that sense they are still relevant and important to understand.

*Please see the *Bibliography for Further Study,* p. 379, for sources on other theorists.

Chapter 1.0
Some Definitions

The elements of music include rhythm, melody, timbre, texture, and harmony. Some of these are virtually universal; they are exploited in music of all ages and cultures. Music without rhythm, for example, can hardly be imagined. Harmony, on the other hand, is missing from music that is outside the Western art music tradition. Even in Western music harmony was established as an independent element in the relatively recent past. From only about 1600 did consistent usage gradually establish patterns of harmonic and tonal relations, which eventually were codified by theorists to form a "science of harmony." But harmony quickly became a central concern, and ultimately superceded even counterpoint, which had provided the technical basis for musical composition since about the ninth century.

During the eighteenth and nineteenth centuries composers were so preoccupied with the expanding harmonic system that other musical elements—particularly rhythm—were neglected. But harmony served these composers well. It provided the fountainhead of style and expression—from harmony stemmed not only melody, but form. Most of the music heard today (this includes nearly all Western commercial music) is from the eighteenth to mid-twentieth centuries, or is based on similar harmonic principles. For this reason the study of harmony is essential for those who wish to be knowledgeable listeners or competent performers.

Harmony has two dimensions. One is "vertical"—several tones sounding simultaneously (chords); the other is "horizontal"—successions of chords within a tonal system. Thus the study of harmony involves two things: types of chords; and how chords relate to one another. The discussion will begin by explaining what is meant by tonal music. Next, several terms that relate to tonality and chords will be defined and some basic analytical symbols will also be introduced.

tonal	1.1 Most of the music composed between 1600 and 1900 is based upon major and minor scales. Music of this type is generally called TONAL music. In tonal music one tone (a tonic or keynote) predominates over the other tones of the scale. This tonic is the same as the first note of the scale. Music in which one tone generally predominates over the other tones of the scale is called ____________ music.
B♭	1.2 What is the tonic of the B♭ major scale? ____________
e	1.3 What is the tonic of the e minor scale? ____________
	1.4 Music that is based on the C major scale is said to be in the key of C Major. The KEY of a composition corresponds to the tonic (or keynote) of the scale that is used.

(Continued on the next page)

f♯	A composition in the key of f♯ minor is based primarily on the ____________ minor scale.
F♯ 2 G 6 A 4 B 3 C 1	1.5 But being "in a key" involves more than merely using the notes of a particular scale. The melody below, for example, uses some of the notes of the G major scale, and the prominence of the tonic (G) is heightened because the melody begins and ends on G. Carey, *America*  Only five notes of the G major scale are used. Count the number of times each note occurs and list them below: F♯ ______ G ______ A ______ B ______ C ______
tonic (or keynote)	1.6 Iteration (repetition) is an important means of causing one tone to predominate over other tones. In simple tonal music the tone that receives the greatest stress through iteration is often the ____________.
tonality	1.7 It is common to speak of music as being in a particular key. This is a way of identifying the scale that serves as the basis for the music. The term TONALITY means practically the same thing as *key.* This term is often used in a broader sense, however, to refer to any music that centers on a single tone regardless of the tonal system employed. Within the context of this study the terms *key* and *tonality* will be used synonymously. A composition in the key of C major may also be said to be in the ____________ of C Major.
A major	1.8 What is the tonality of a composition that is based primarily upon the A major scale? ____________

key	1.9 Music in which a single tone tends to predominate over the others may be said to be TONAL. In tonal music one tone takes precedence over all the others; this tone is called the TONAL CENTER. What is another name for the tonal center? The _____________ center.
first	1.10 The keynote is which note of the scale? The _____________.
Yes	1.11 Do the terms tonal center, tonic, key center, and keynote have approximately the same meaning? _____________
(No response required.)	*Expository Frame* 1.12 The points made thus far are these: The *key* of a composition may be established by using the notes of a particular scale; by beginning and ending on the keynote; and by iteration of the keynote. The *tonal center* is the tone that predominates over all the others. This tone is also called the *tonic* or *keynote.* Any music that tends to be oriented to a tonal center is said to be *tonal.* The *tonality* of a composition corresponds to the tonal center.
tonal	1.13 Harmony that is associated with tonal music is called TONAL HARMONY. Within the limits of this study tonal harmony will mean harmony based upon major and minor scales. Harmony based upon the major-minor scale system is called _____________ harmony.
tones	1.14 Before continuing with the study of tonal harmony some important distinctions must be made. In the next few frames please note the differences between *intervals, chords,* and *triads.* The basic component of harmony is the chord. These, in turn, are the result of several tones sounding simultaneously. Chords are vertical structures consisting of several _____________
	1.15 The simultaneous sounding of two tones produces a *harmonic interval,* but do not confuse an interval with a chord. Although a single interval may occasionally imply a chord, *at least three tones are required to* produce a complete chord.*

*In impressionistic music as well as some later twentieth-century styles, two tones do occasionally function as a chord. In such cases the term *dyad* may be used.

(Continued on the next page)

Vertical structures form either intervals or ____________.

chords

1.16 Two tones sounding together produce an interval. A chord, however, consists of at least ____________ tones.

three

1.17 Are all of the structures below chords? ____________

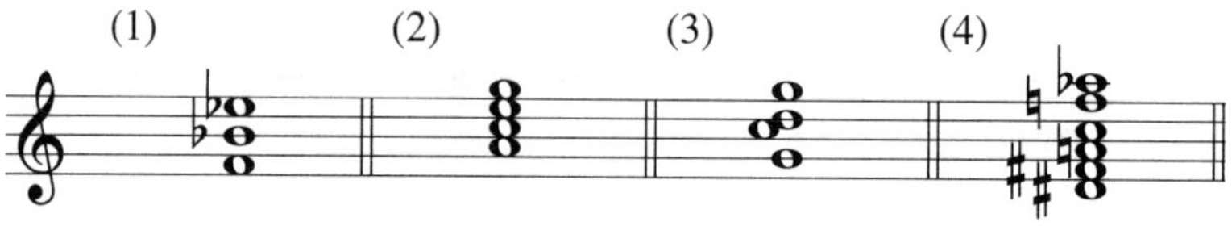

Yes

1.18 Are all of the structures below chords? ____________

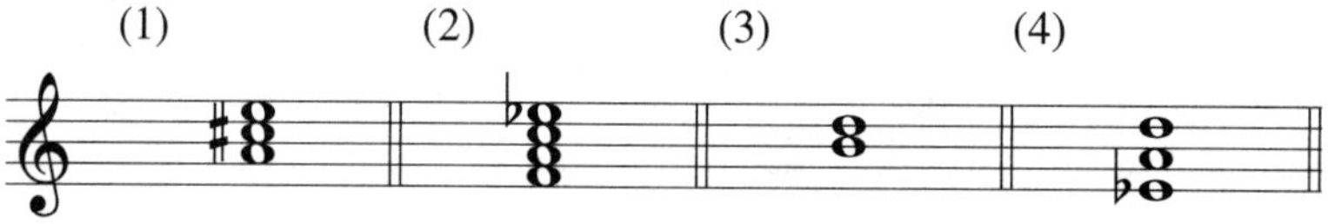

No
(Item [3] contains only two notes. This is called an interval.)

1.19 A chord of three tones is also called a TRIAD. Are all of the chords below triads? ____________

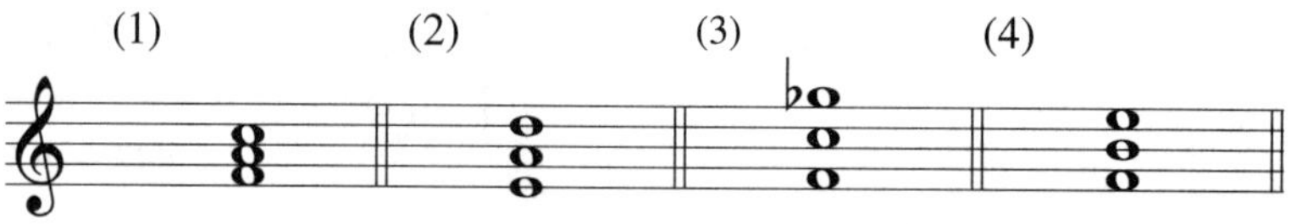

Yes

1.20 Although any three tones sounding simultaneously produce a triad, within the system of tonal harmony triads are constructed of superimposed thirds.

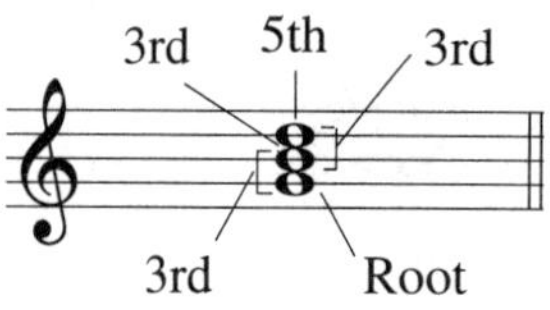

The note on which a triad is built is called the ROOT. Triads consisting of superimposed thirds are part of the

system of _____________ harmony.

tonal

1.21 Consider each note of the C major scale below to be the root of a triad. Write a triad on each note. *(Use no accidentals.)*

KEY OF C MAJOR

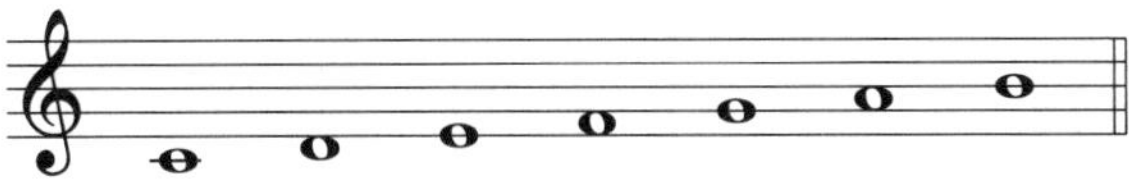

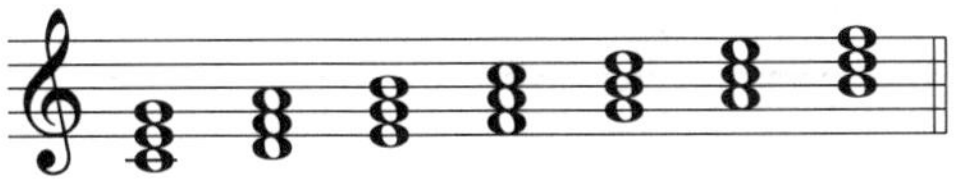

1.22 The triads just written use only the notes of the C major scale. These are called DIATONIC triads. Diatonic triads are constructed only of notes contained in the scale being used.

Triads that utilize only the notes of the scale are

called _____________ triads.

diatonic

1.23 Which of the triads below is NOT a diatonic triad?

_____________.

(1) (2) (3) (4)

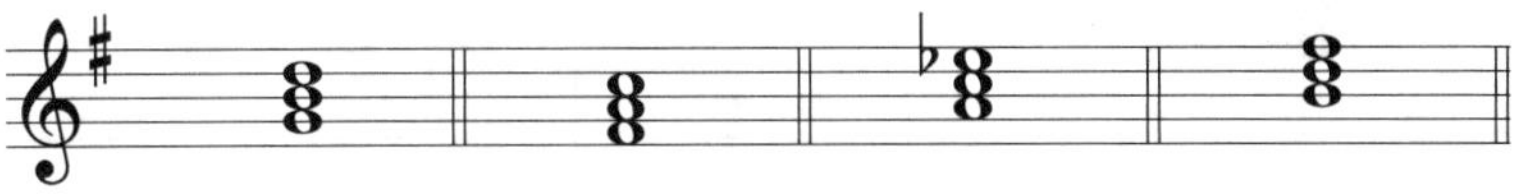

(Key of G Major)

(3)
(E♭ is not a diatonic tone in the key of G Major.)

1.24 Which of the triads below is NOT a diatonic triad?

_____________.

(1) (2) (3) (4)

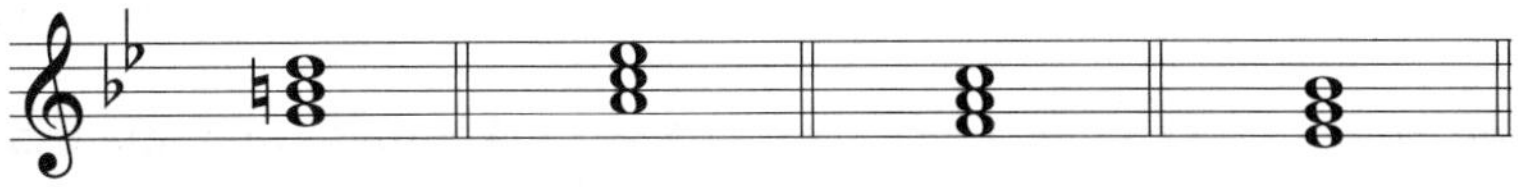

(Key of B♭ Major)

(1).
(B♮ is not a diatonic tone in the key of B♭ Major.)

1.25 If a triad contains a tone that is foreign to the key,

can it be called diatonic? _____________

No

1.26 A triad may be constructed on each of the seven degrees of the major scale.

KEY OF D MAJOR

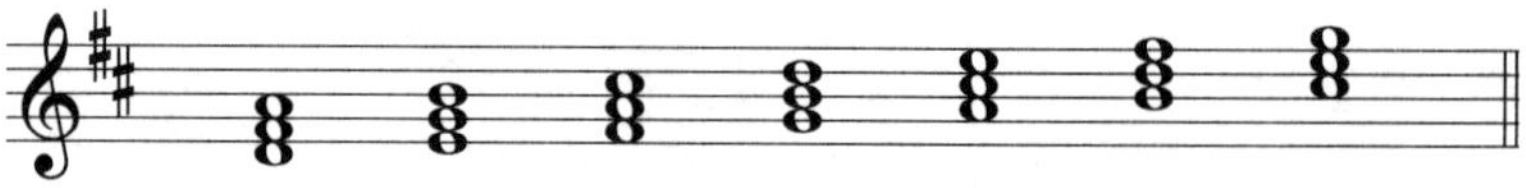

Is each of these triads a diatonic triad? ____________

Yes

1.27 How many diatonic triads are contained in a major key? ____________

Seven

1.28 Construct a diatonic triad on each degree of the E♭ major scale.

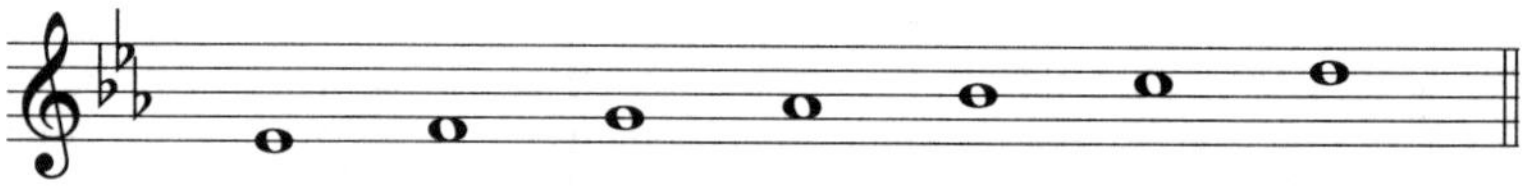

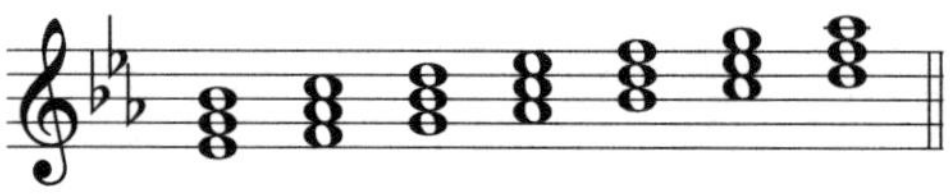

1.29 Construct a diatonic triad on each degree of the B major scale.

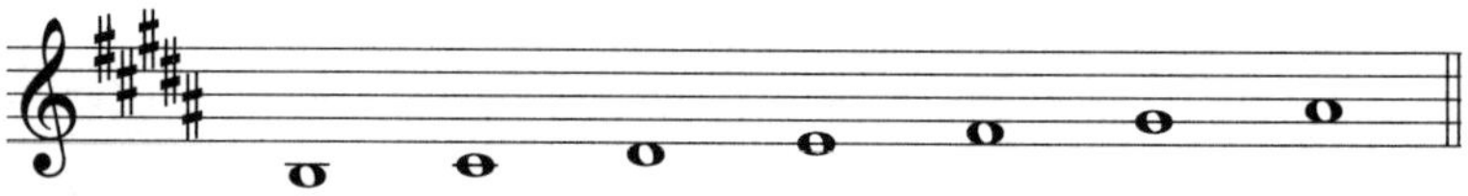

1.30 Diatonic triads utilize only the notes that are included in the scale being used. In the *harmonic* minor scale the raised seventh degree is considered diatonic since it is part of the scale. The seven diatonic triads in the key of d minor, using the harmonic minor scale, are shown below.

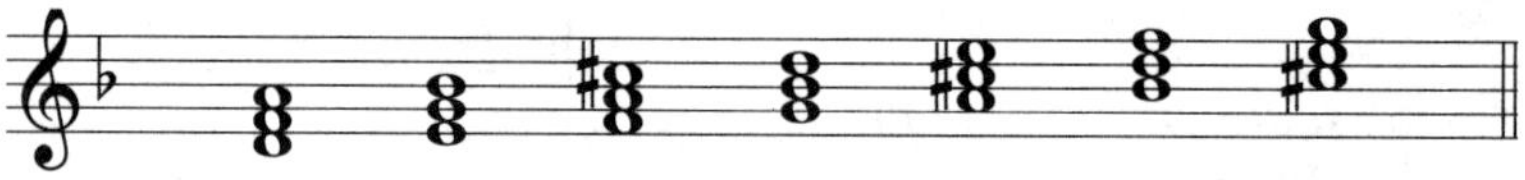

Some of the triads above contain an accidental (c♯).

Are these diatonic triads? ____________

Yes
(c♯ is a diatonic note in the d harmonic minor scale.)

1.31 Construct a diatonic triad on each degree of the e harmonic minor scale. *(Apply accidentals where necessary.)*

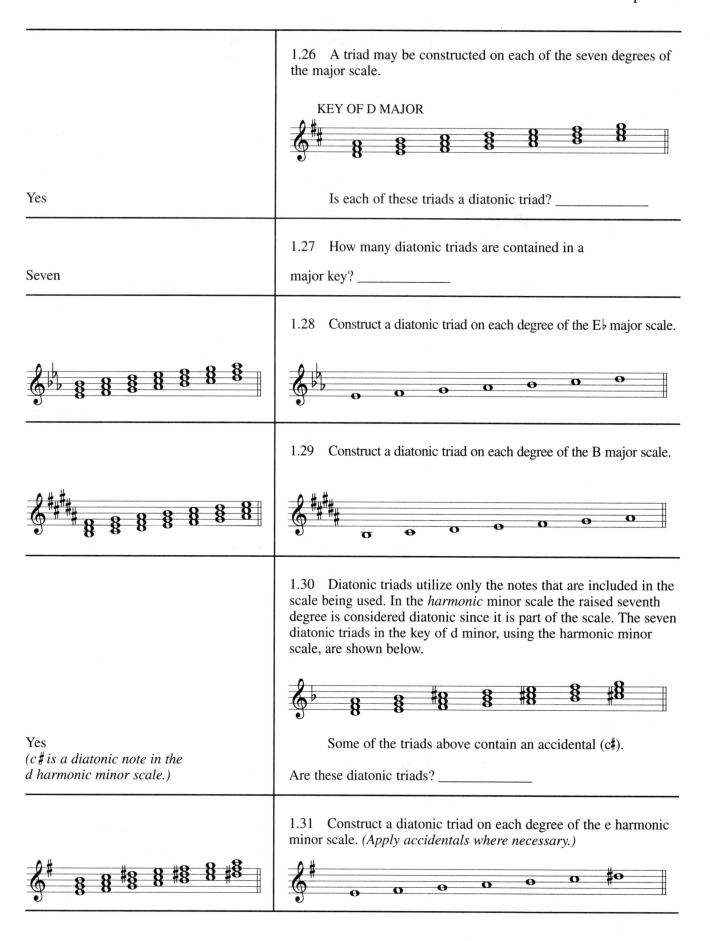

1.32 Construct a diatonic triad on each degree of the f harmonic minor scale. *(Apply accidentals where necessary.)*

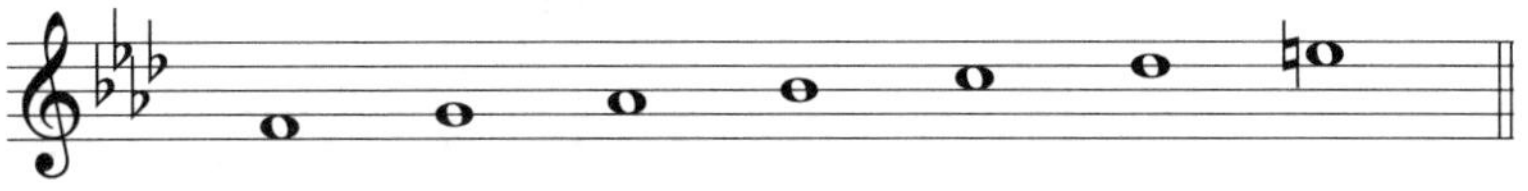

(No response required.)

Expository Frame

1.33 *Intervals* combine to produce the basic component of harmony—chords. *Triads* are chords of three tones. In the system of tonal harmony triad tones are related by thirds. *Diatonic* triads use only scale tones.

1.34 Chord symbols* consisting of roman numerals are used to identify triads built on the various degrees of the scale. (An alternative analysis is also shown as one of several that might be used. Unfortunately, there is not a standardized symbol set that has been adopted. Also this alternative does not address the scale degree or relationship to the tonic.)

KEY OF D MAJOR

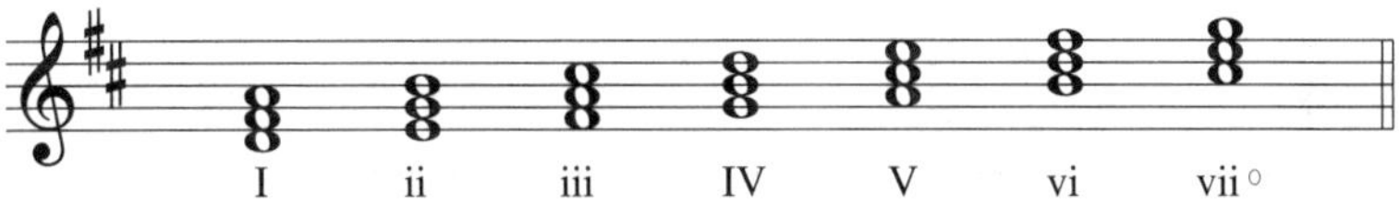

	I	ii	iii	IV	V	vi	vii°
Alternative:	D	Emi	F♯mi	G	A	Bmi	C♯dim (°)

KEY OF D MINOR (harmonic)

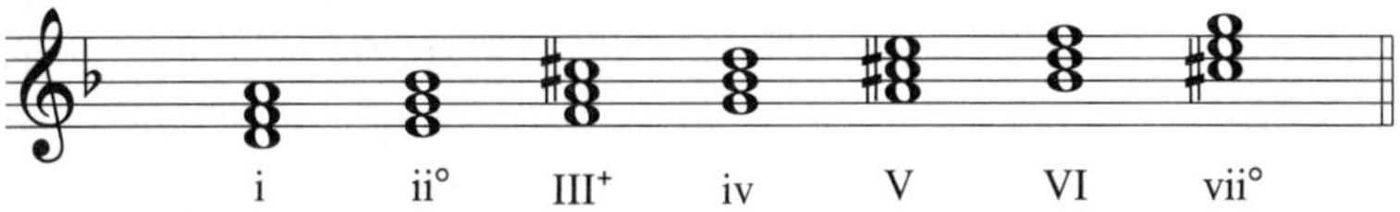

	i	ii°	III⁺	iv	V	VI	vii°
Alternative:	Dmi	Edim(°)	Faug(+)	Gmi	A	B♭	C♯dim(°)

Composers in the common-practice period do not necessarily confine their selection of diatonic triads in minor to the harmonic form of the minor scale. In the minor mode some prefer the major quality mediant triad (III) rather than the augmented form (III^+) derived from the harmonic minor. In analysis, one should be alert for these varying occurrences.

*Chord symbols of the common-practice period (roman numerals and figured bass) have evolved over the twentieth century to the present, in the West, in a number of ways to meet the needs of the composers, arrangers, and analysts of music. While this text primarily addresses music of the common-practice period, it attempts to point out some crossovers of chord symbols between differing styles of Western music by offering alternative ways to analyze or represent chords. See p. 353, *Appendix A* to assist in making comparisons.

(Continued on the next page)

scale	The roman numerals used to identify the various triads of a key correspond to the degrees of the ____________.
major	1.35 Notice in the preceding frame that the roman numerals have different forms depending upon the quality of the triads. *Study the chart below:* TYPE OF TRIAD — SYMBOL Major = I, IV, V, (III) Minor = ii, iii, vi Diminished = ii°, vii° Augmented = III+ A Roman numeral consisting of capital letters denotes a ____________ triad.
plus *(or cross)*	1.36 An augmented triad is indicated by a *capital* roman numeral followed by a ____________ sign.
circle	1.37 A diminished triad is indicated by a *lowercase* roman numeral followed by a ____________.
True	1.38 A minor triad is indicated by a *lowercase* roman numeral. (True/False) ____________
Major Diminished Augmented Minor	1.39 Name the triad *quality* (major, minor, diminished, or augmented) indicated by each chord symbol. (1) IV ____________ (2) ii° ____________ (3) III+ ____________ (4) vi ____________
No *(Item [3] represents a diminished triad.)*	1.40 Do all of the roman numerals below represent triads of identical quality? ____________. (1) vi (2) iii (3) ii° (4) iv
Yes	1.41 Do all of the roman numerals below represent triads of identical quality? ____________. (1) I (2) VI (3) IV (4) V

Major

1.42 What type of triad is indicated by the roman numerals in the preceding frame? _____________

---

(3)

1.43 Which roman numeral represents a *minor* triad? _____________

(1) V (2) III+ (3) ii (4) vii°

---

(4)

1.44 Which roman numeral represents an *augmented* triad? _____________

(1) ii° (2) III (3) vi (4) III+

---

(2)

1.45 Which roman numeral represents a *diminished* triad? _____________

(1) ii (2) vii° (3) III (4) V

---

(3)

1.46 Which roman numeral represents a *major* triad?

____

(1) III+ (2) ii (3) IV (4) iv

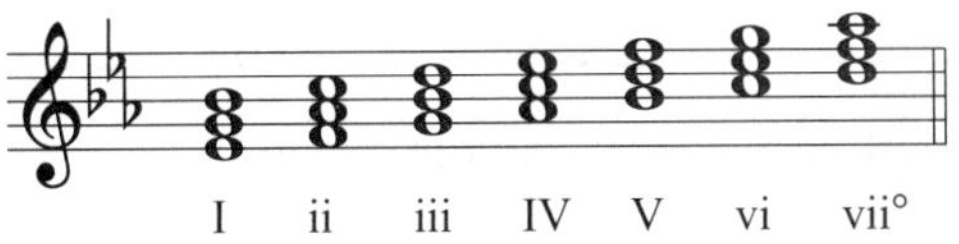

1.47 Write the remaining roman numerals to represent the triads built on the seven degrees of the E♭ major scale. *(Be sure the quality of each triad is reflected by the form of the roman numeral.)*

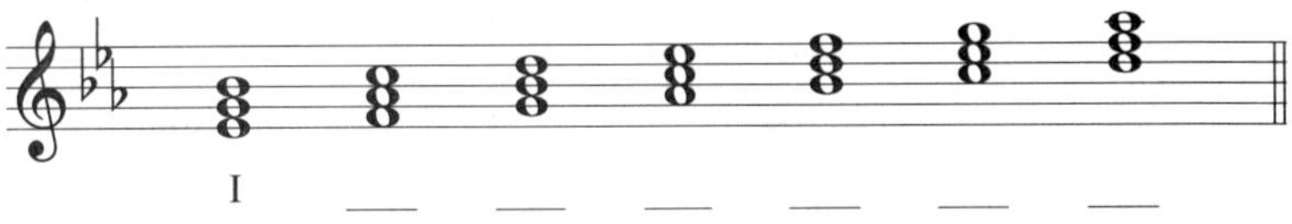

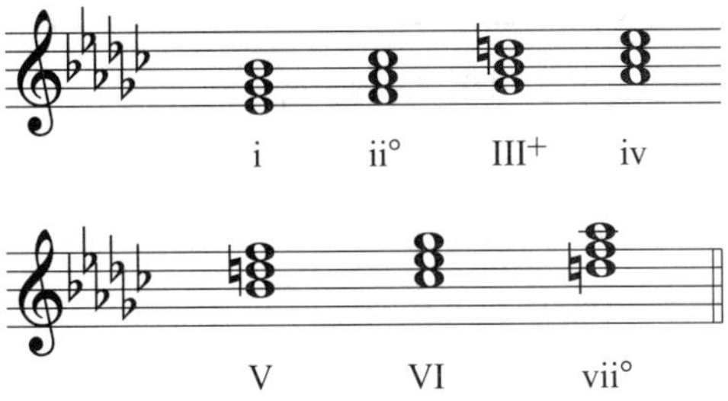

1.48 Write the roman numeral to represent the triad built on the seven degrees of the e♭ harmonic minor scale. *(Be sure the quality of each triad is reflected by the form of the roman numeral.)*

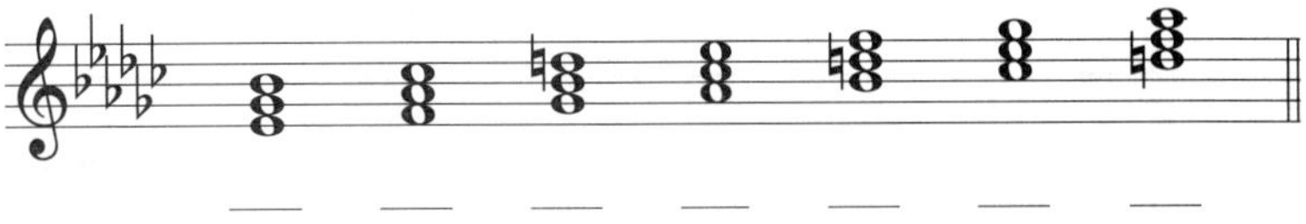

1st: major 2nd: minor 3rd: minor 4th: major 5th: major 6th: minor 7th: diminished	1.49 Complete the list below: THE QUALITY OF TRIADS USING THE MAJOR SCALE The triad on the 1st degree is ____________. The triad on the 2nd degree is ____________. The triad on the 3rd degree is ____________. The triad on the 4th degree is ____________. The triad on the 5th degree is ____________. The triad on the 6th degree is ____________. The triad on the 7th degree is ____________.
1st: minor 2nd: diminished 3rd: augmented 4th: minor 5th: major 6th: major 7th: diminished	1.50 Complete the list below: THE QUALITY OF TRIADS USING THE HARMONIC MINOR SCALE The triad on the 1st degree is ____________. The triad on the 2nd degree is ____________. The triad on the 3rd degree is ____________. The triad on the 4th degree is ____________. The triad on the 5th degree is ____________. The triad on the 6th degree is ____________. The triad on the 7th degree is ____________.
minor	1.51 The quality of the triad on the fourth degree of the harmonic minor scale is ____________.
major	1.52 The quality of the triad on the sixth degree of the harmonic minor scale is ____________.
minor	1.53 The quality of the triad on the first degree of the harmonic minor scale is ____________.
major	1.54 The quality of the triad on the fifth degree of the harmonic minor scale is ____________.
False *(This triad is minor.)*	1.55 The triad on the sixth degree of the major scale is major. (True/False) ____________.

True

1.56 The triad on the second degree of the harmonic minor scale is diminished. (True/False) ____________

False

(This triad is augmented.)

1.57 The triad on the third degree of the harmonic minor scale is major. (True/False) ____________.

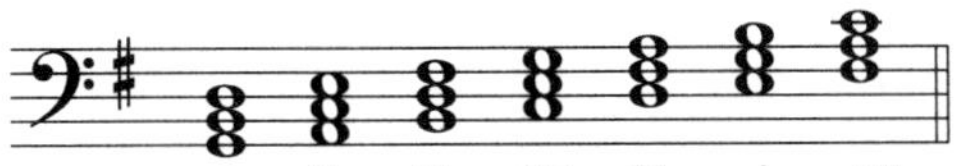

I ii iii IV V vi vii°

Alter.: G Ami Bmi C D Emi F♯dim

1.58 Analyze with roman numerals the triads built on the seven degrees of the G major scale. Use second line for an alternative analysis.

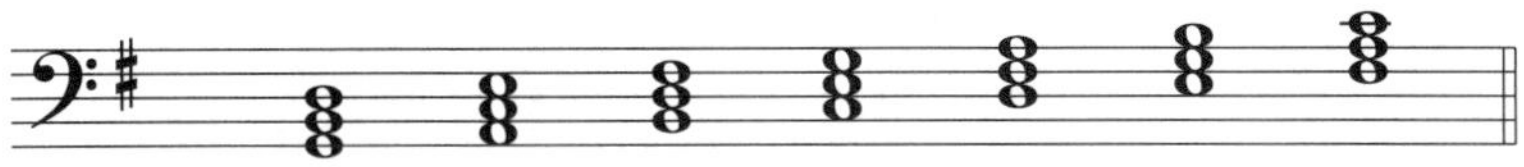

___ ___ ___ ___ ___ ___ ___

Alternative: ___ ___ ___ ___ ___ ___ ___

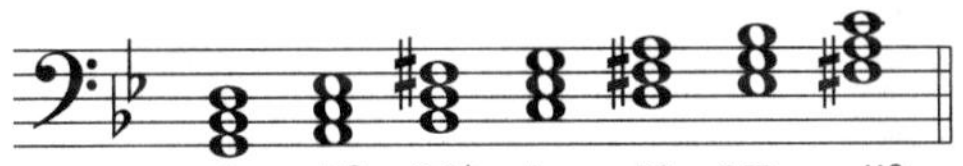

i ii° III⁺ iv V VI vii°

Alter.: Gmi Adim B♭aug Cmi D E♭ F♯dim

1.59 Analyze with roman numerals the triads built on the seven degrees of the g harmonic minor scale. Use second line for an alternative analysis.

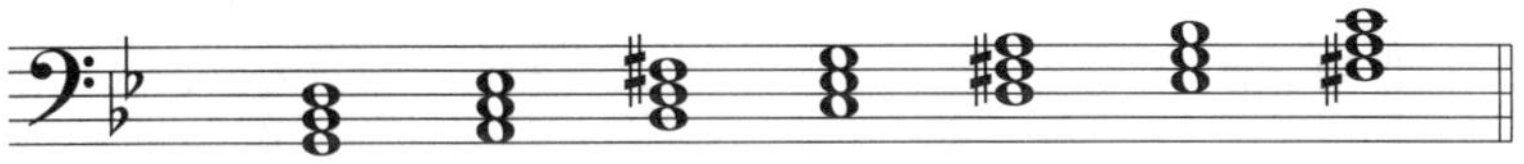

___ ___ ___ ___ ___ ___ ___

Alternative: ___ ___ ___ ___ ___ ___ ___

(No response required.)

Expository Frame

1.60 The benefit gained from using various forms of roman numerals is being made aware of the *specific quality* of each chord. This, in turn, increases one's sensitivity to the actual sounds represented by the notes.

Major

1.61 When analyzing with roman numerals the key is identified by an abbreviation of its name followed by a colon (:).

Compare the designations below:

E♭ Major = E♭:
e♭ minor = e♭:

Notice that a *capital* letter is used to indicate a major key, whereas a *lowercase* letter is used for a minor key.

The symbol (B:) represents the key of B ____________.

---

(1) F:

(2) a♭:

(3) E:

1.62 Write the proper designation for each key.

(1) F Major ____________

(2) a♭ minor ____________

(3) E Major ____________

1.63 Write the proper designation for each key.

(1) g♯ minor ______________

(2) D Major ______________

(3) b♭ minor ______________

(1) g♯:
(2) D:
(3) b♭:

1.64 What key is indicated by each symbol?

(1) A: The key of ______________.

(2) c♯: The key of ______________.

(3) d: The key of ______________.

(1) A Major
(2) c♯ minor
(3) d minor

1.65 What key is indicated by each symbol?

(1) b: The key of ______________.

(2) G♭: The key of ______________.

(3) C♯: The key of ______________.

(1) b minor
(2) G♭ Major
(3) C♯ Major

1.66 Write the proper chord symbol in each case. *(Be sure to check the quality of each triad.)*

(1) (2) (3)

B♭: ___ e: ___ D: ___

(1) (2) (3)
I III+ ii

1.67 Continue as in the preceding frame.

(1) (2) (3)

d: ___ E♭: ___ f♯: ___

(1) (2) (3)
iv iii V

1.68 Continue as in the preceding frame. *(Note use of bass clef.)*

(1) (2) (3)

A♭: ___ c♯: ___ B♭: ___

(1) (2) (3)
IV VI V

(1) (2) (3)

vii° vi i

1.69 Continue as in the preceding frame.

(1) (2) (3)

g: ___ B: ___ b♭: ___

(1) (2) (3)

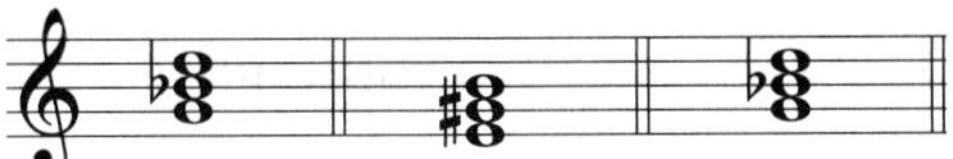

d: iv A: V E♭: iii

1.70 Write the triads indicated by the roman numerals. *(No key signature is supplied, so you must apply accidentals to those notes which need them.)*

(1) (2) (3)

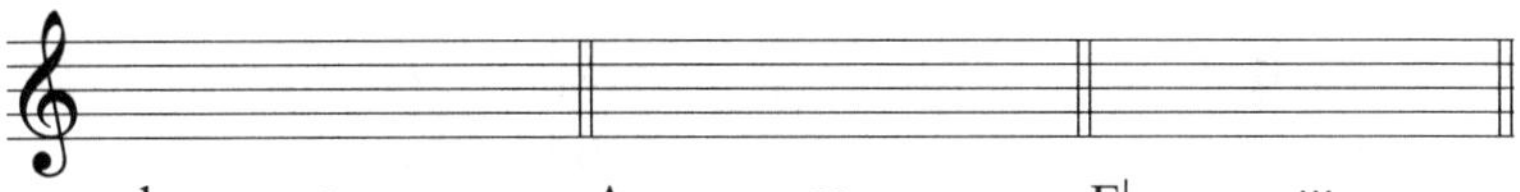

d: iv A: V E♭: iii

(1) (2) (3)

g: vii° c: VI F♯: ii

1.71 Continue as in the preceding frame.

(1) (2) (3)

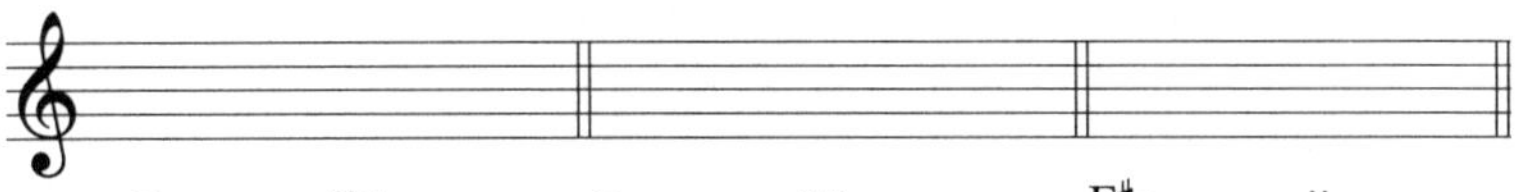

g: vii° c: VI F♯: ii

(1) (2) (3)

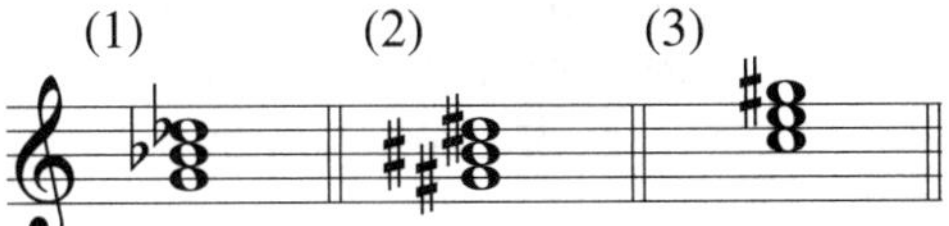

A♭: vii° c♯: V a: III+

1.72 Continue as in the preceding frame.

(1) (2) (3)

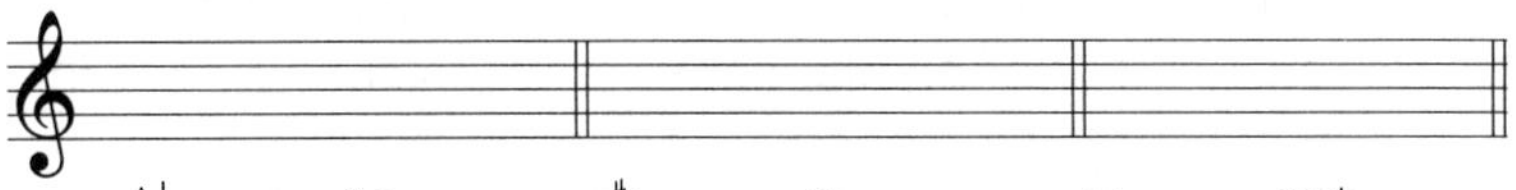

A♭: vii° c♯: V a: III+

(1) (2) (3)

D: vi E♭: IV a: ii°

1.73 Continue as in the preceding frame.

(1) (2) (3)

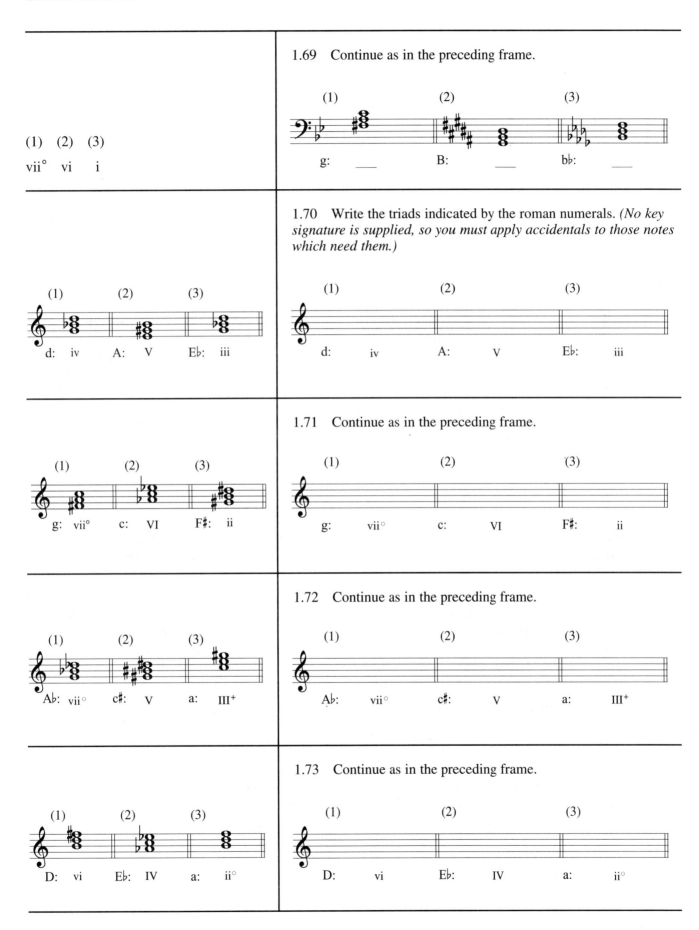

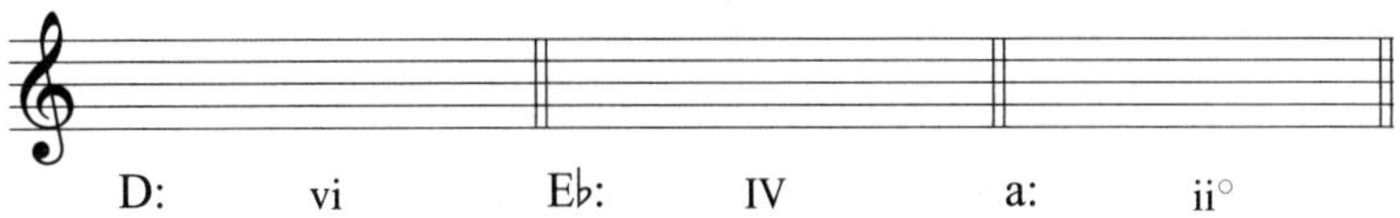

D: vi E♭: IV a: ii°

(No response required.)	*Expository Frame* 1.74 The first step in harmonic analysis is to identify the key. This involves not only locating the tonal center, but also identifying the mode (major or minor). A capital letter represents a major key (A: = A Major); a lower case letter represents a minor key (a: = a minor). Active awareness of key and mode is absolutely essential to a knowledgeable approach to both performance and theoretical study. The symbols that have been introduced are designed to sharpen perception and awareness.

Summary

In tonal music a single tone is caused to predominate over the others. This tone is called the *tonal center* and is the same as the *tonic* of the scale being used.

Two superimposed intervals of a third produce a chord of three tones called a *triad.* There are four types of triads in the major-minor scale system (major, minor, diminished, and augmented). These four types of triads provide the basic harmonic material of tonal music.

For the purpose of analysis triads are identified by chord symbols consisting of roman numerals. These correspond to the scale degrees on which the triads are built. Various forms of chord symbols are used to show the quality of each triad as below:

TRIAD QUALITY	SYMBOLS	
Major	I, IV, V, (III)	(capital letters)
Minor	ii, iii, vi	(lowercase letters)
Diminished	ii°, vii°	(circle added to lowercase letters)
Augmented	III+	(plus sign added to capital letters)

Chord symbols of the common-practice period (roman numerals and figured bass) have evolved over the twentieth century to the present, in the West, in a number of ways to meet the needs of the composers, arrangers, and analysts of music. While this text primarily addresses music of the common-practice period, it attempts to point out some crossovers of chord symbols between differing styles of Western music by offering alternative ways to analyze or represent chords. See p. 353, *Appendix A* to assist in making comparisons.

The terms that are explained in this chapter are listed below in the order presented:

tonal	tonal center	harmonic interval
tonic (keynote)	tonal harmony	root
key	intervals	diatonic (triads)
iteration	chords	chord symbols
tonality	triads	roman numerals

Mastery Frames

3. Tonal center (1.1–.12)	1–1 Indicate the term on the right that conveys practically the same meaning as the one on the left. Tonic ____________ 1. Tonality 2. Root 3. Tonal center
2. Key (1.4–.13)	1–2 Indicate the term on the right that conveys practically the same meaning as the one on the left. Tonality ____________ 1. Chord 2. Key 3. Tonal harmony
(1) Interval (3) Chord (2) Chord (4) Interval (1.14–.19)	1–3 Identify each example as either an interval or a chord. (1) ____________ (3) ____________ (2) ____________ (4) ____________ (1) (2) (3) (4) 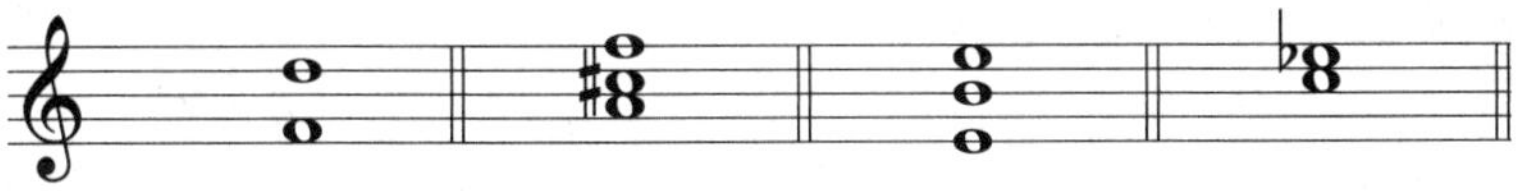
3 (1.19)	1–4 How many tones are required to produce a triad? ____________.
thirds (1.20)	1–5 Triads within the system of tonal harmony are based on a note called the *root,* and they are constructed of superimposed ____________.

1–6 Triads that employ only the notes of the prevailing key are called ______________ triads.

diatonic (1.22–.33)

1–7 Which are diatonic triads in the key of B♭ major? ______________

(1) (2) (3) (4)

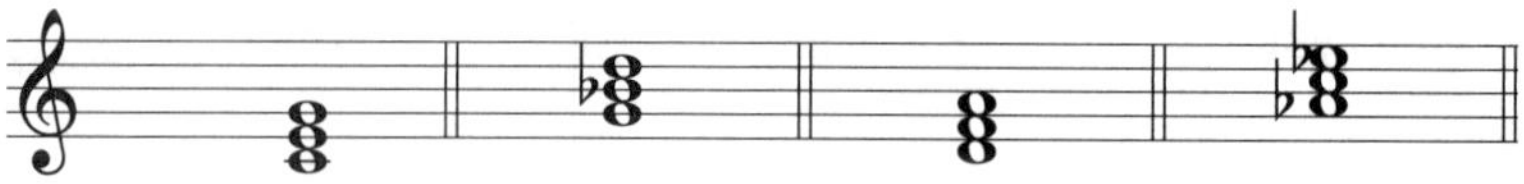

(2), (3). (1.22–.33)

1–8 Identify the triad *quality* indicated by each of the chord symbols.

(1) IV ______________ (3) ii° ______________

(2) vi ______________ (4) III+ ______________

(1) Major (3) Diminished

(2) Minor (4) Augmented (1.35–.46)

1–9 Identify the key indicated by each of the symbols below.

(1) B♭: ______________

(2) E: ______________

(3) f♯: ______________

(4) g: ______________

(1) B♭ Major

(2) E Major

(3) f♯ minor

(4) g minor (1.61–.65)

1–10 Write chord symbols for each of the triads below.

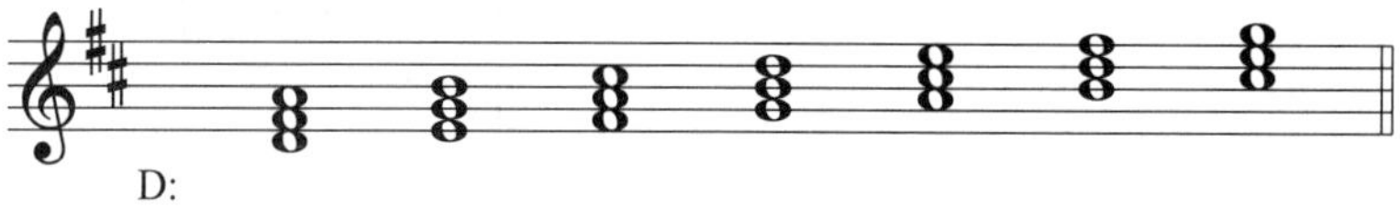

D: ___ ___ ___ ___ ___ ___ ___

Alternative: ___ ___ ___ ___ ___ ___ ___

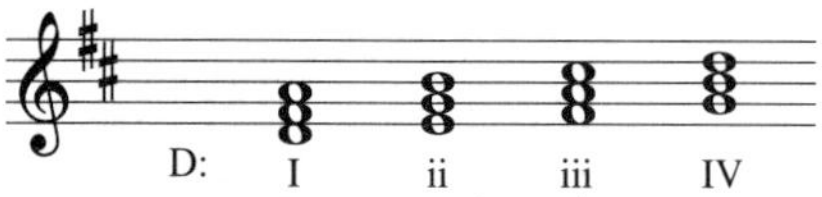

D: I ii iii IV

Alter.: D Emi F♯mi G

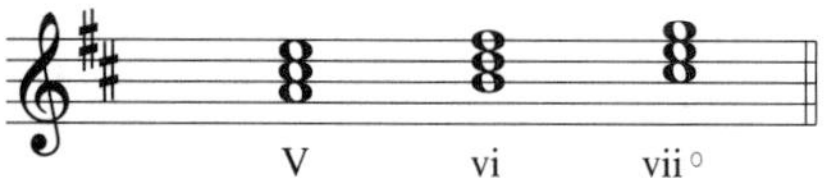

V vi vii°

A Bmi C♯dim

(1.58)

1–11 Write chord symbols for each of the triads below.

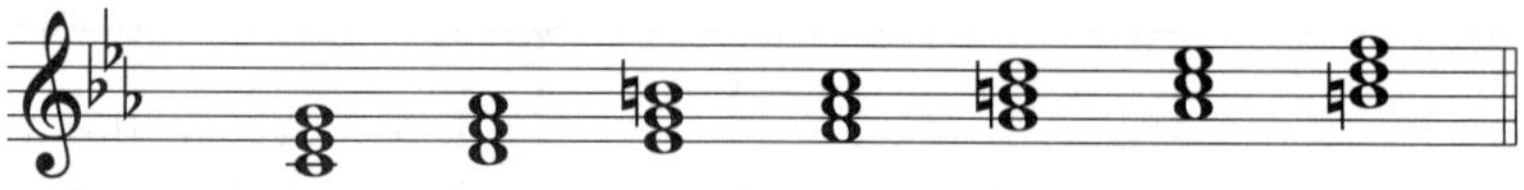

c: ___ ___ ___ ___ ___ ___ ___

Alternative: ___ ___ ___ ___ ___ ___ ___

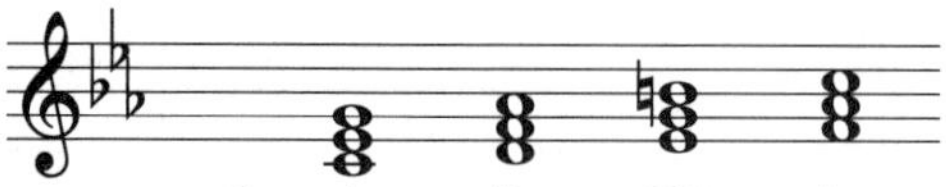

c: i ii° III+ iv

Alter.: Cmin Ddim E♭aug Fmi

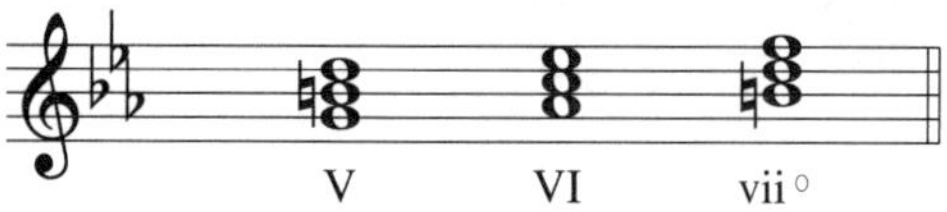

V VI vii°

(1.59)

1–12 Indicate the type of triad that occurs on each degree of the *major* scale.

Scale Degrees	Triad Types
(1)	_____
(2)	_____
(3)	_____
(4)	_____
(5)	_____
(6)	_____
(7)	_____

(1) Major

(2) Minor

(3) Minor

(4) Major

(5) Major

(6) Minor

(7) Diminished

(1.49)

1–13 Indicate the type of triad that occurs on each degree of the *harmonic minor* scale.

Scale Degrees	Triad Types
(1)	_____
(2)	_____
(3)	_____
(4)	_____
(5)	_____
(6)	_____
(7)	_____

(1) Minor

(2) Diminished

(3) Augmented

(4) Minor

(5) Major

(6) Major

(7) Diminished

Supplementary Activities

(For Chapters 1.0–3.0)

1. Consult a music dictionary such as *The New Harvard Dictionary of Music* (Cambridge, Mass.: The Belknap Press of Harvard University Press, 1986) or *The New Grove Dictionary of Music and Musicians* (New York: Oxford University Press, 2004) for articles on the new terms being learned in these chapters, such as tonal center, key, triads, chords, diatonic, and so forth. Continue to do this to discover new musical terms both here in the text and elsewhere in your musical studies. *(Note that these dictionaries as well as others are generally available online via university/school libraries or otherwise.)*

2. Utilizing other melodies or "tunes" that are known to you, try to determine what note is the tonal center of the melody or tune. Try to do this either through examination of the notation or by ear. This kind of exercise can complement and strengthen work already being done in ear training exercises with melodic and harmonic dictation. As an adjunct to these exercises, work on creating short, original melodies that clearly convey a tonal center. What factors help convey a tonal center in a given melody or short phrase? How does the melody relate to the harmony—whether actual or implied?

3. Practice examining simple musical excerpts for their chord qualities, that is, major, minor, augmented, or diminished. Determine which degree of the scale upon which they are built? What roman numeral or chord symbol would represent the chord? Do you think the chords create "progressive" or "forward" movement? Do chords sound "open" or "close" to you? What relationships can be observed between the "voices"?

4. Consider developing in-depth essays on the importance of tonality or harmony in either Western or non-Western musics, or both, by exploring books listed in this book's bibliography, in a library, or through a search on the Internet. Another essay could be developed on the use and evolution of figured-bass symbols. Are the musical, shorthand symbols used today in jazz and popular music just a further evolution of the figured bass of earlier times?

5. The importance of continuing ear training activities, which have hopefully already started in previous studies of music fundamentals, cannot be stressed too much. To quote from the author's statement about this from *Basic Materials in Music Theory:*

> "Full musical comprehension requires both the ear and the mind: Sounds and their related symbols must be sensed as well as understood. An extensive ear-training program is usually needed to develop aural discrimination. These ear-training activities, however, [should] have a more modest objective: to reinforce understanding of the material presented in this book. . . . They should, on the other hand, be a useful supplement to class experiences. . . .
>
> Musicians must become acutely sensitive to sounds and time relations. To develop sensitivity, one must do more than passively listen. Both the sounds and the way those sounds affect a person must be analyzed. By being aware of responses to musical stimuli, a mastery of musical expression will be gained.
>
> BMT, p. 15

Therefore, it is most important that a full range of ear training activities, centered around rhythmic, melodic and harmonic dictation exercises, be continued during one's study of these harmonic materials. The value of excellent ear training work ultimately becomes a "priceless" commodity for a well-prepared and well-trained musician.

Supplementary Assignments

The material supplied here is intended to be both useful in itself and suggestive of other supplementary work designed by instructors to serve their students' particular needs.

ASSIGNMENT 1–1 Name ______________________

1. Write a brief definition of each term.

   a. Tonic ______________________

   b. Tonality ______________________

   c. Tonal harmony ______________________

2. What note is the tonal center of the melody below? ______________________

3. Write a brief justification for your answer to question 2. ______________________

4. Compose a single-line melody that clearly establishes the key of B♭ major.

5. Identify the specific features of your melody that contribute to the establishment of the tonality.

____

6. Distinguish between "interval" and "chord." ______________________________

____

____

7. What is a triad? ______________________________

____

____

8. What is meant by the term "diatonic triad"? ______________________________

____

____

9. Identify each example as either an interval or a chord.

(1) ______________ (4) ______________

(2) ______________ (5) ______________

(3) ______________ (6) ______________

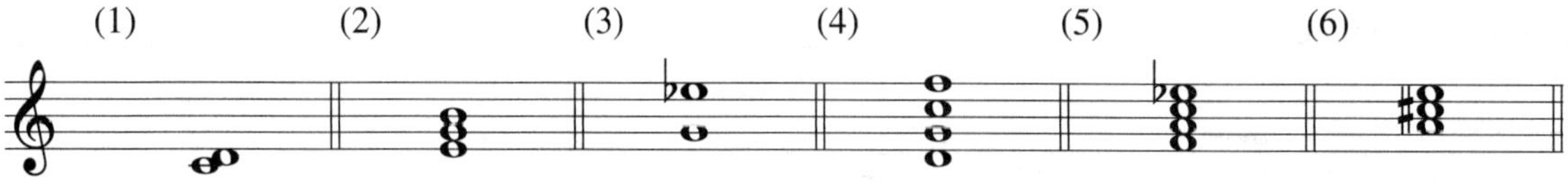

10. List the examples in the preceding question that are triads. ______________________________

11. What interval is the basic building block of triads in the tonal harmonic system? ______________

12. Write all of the diatonic triads in the key of E Major.

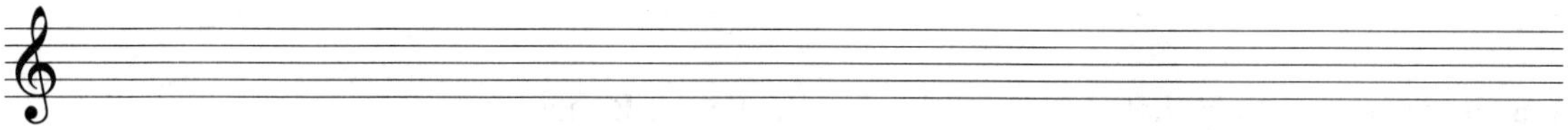

13. Write all of the diatonic triads in the key of g minor (harmonic form).

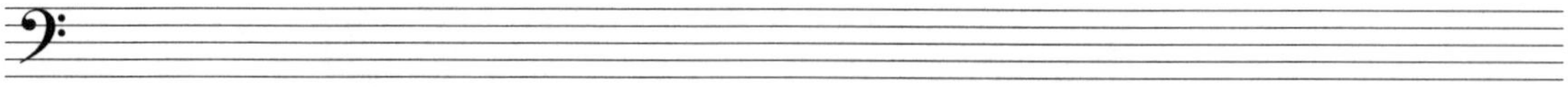

ASSIGNMENT 1–2

Name ______________________________

1. List the *quality* of the diatonic triad on each degree of a major scale.

   Scale degree

   (1) ____________________ (5) ____________________

   (2) ____________________ (6) ____________________

   (3) ____________________ (7) ____________________

   (4) ____________________

2. List the *quality* of the diatonic triad on each degree of a minor scale (harmonic form).

   (1) ____________________ (5) ____________________

   (2) ____________________ (6) ____________________

   (3) ____________________ (7) ____________________

   (4) ____________________

3. Write the chord indicated by each chord symbol. ***(Provide the necessary accidentals.)***

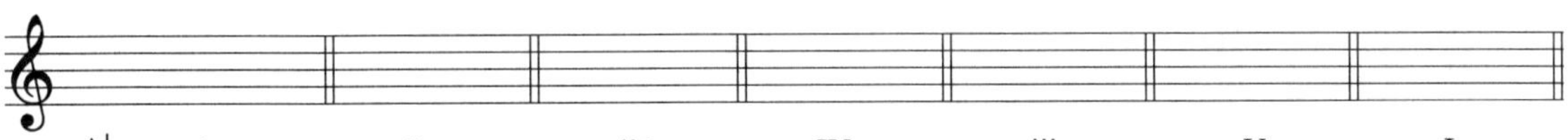

4. Write the chord symbol for each chord.

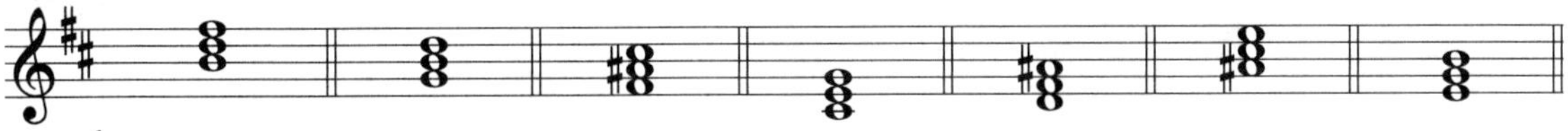

5. Write the chord symbol for each chord.

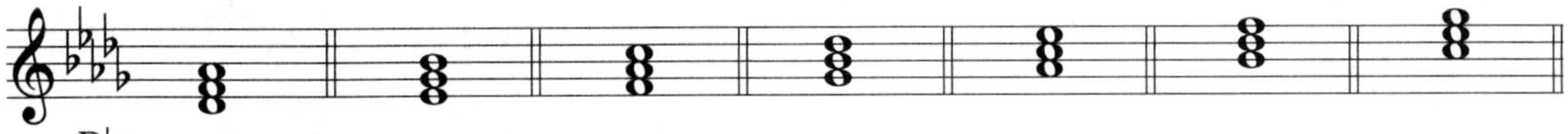

6. Write the chord indicated by each chord symbol.

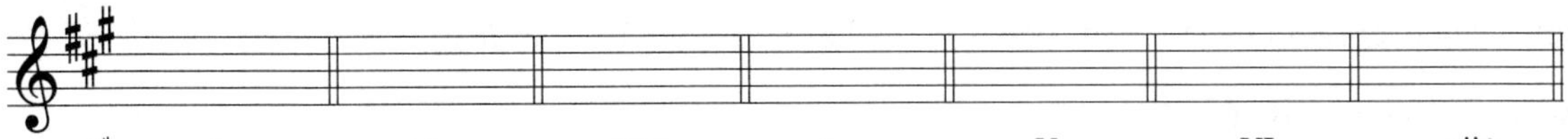

7. Which chord matches the chord symbol?____________________

(1) (2) (3) (4)

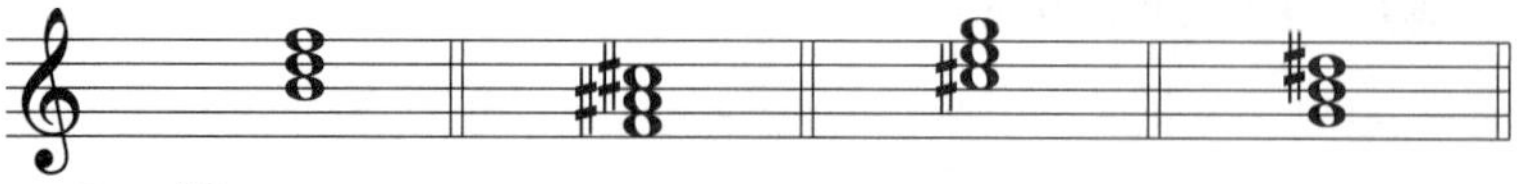

D: vii°

8. Which chord matches the chord symbol?____________________

(1) (2) (3) (4)

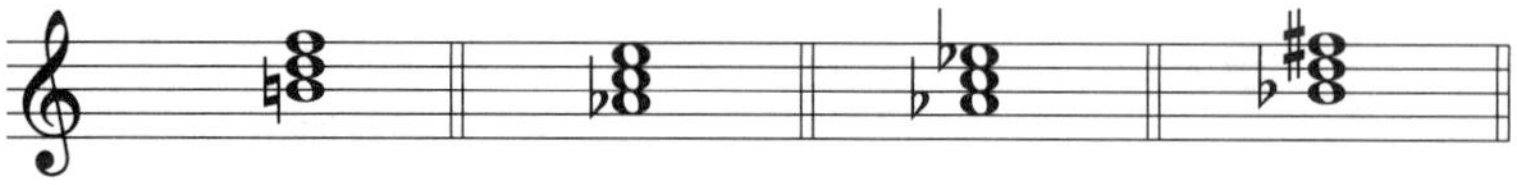

c: VI

9. Which chord matches the chord symbol? ____________

(1) (2) (3) (4)

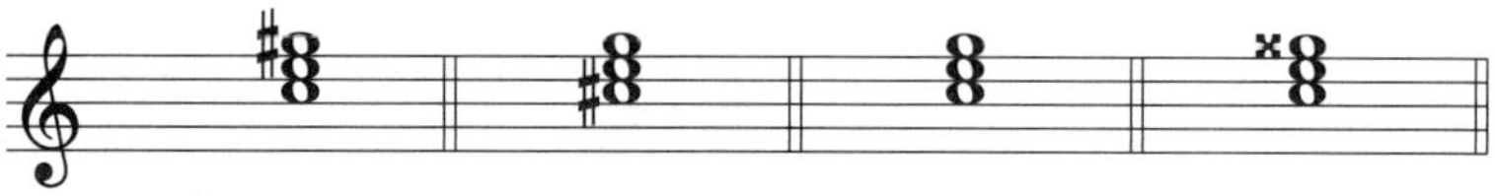

a: III+

10. Which chord matches the chord symbol? ____________

(1) (2) (3) (4)

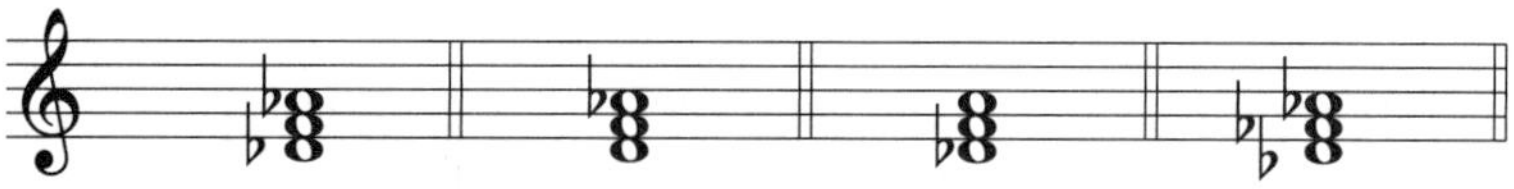

E♭: vii°

11. Which chord matches the chord symbol? ____________

(1) (2) (3) (4)

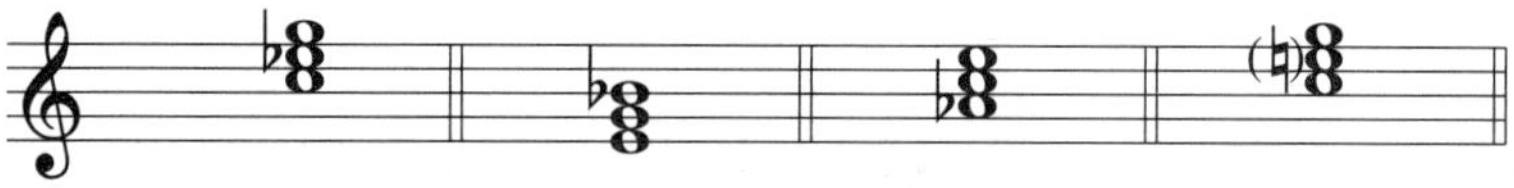

f: V

12. Provide the correct chord symbol for each chord.

(1) (2) (3) (4) (5) (6)

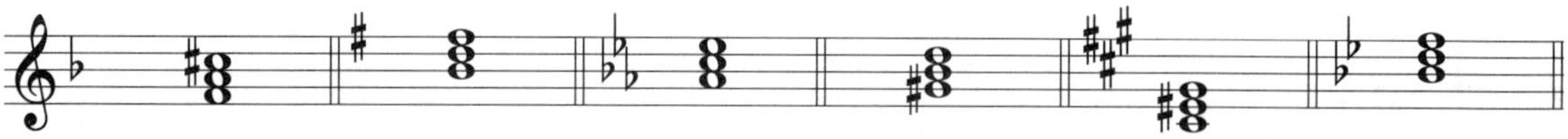

d: ___ G: ___ E♭: ___ a: ___ f♯: ___ B♭: ___

13. How many *major* triads occur in a major key? ________________________________

14. How many *minor* triads occur in a major key? ________________________________

15. On which scale degree do major triads occur in the harmonic minor scale? ________________

16. Does the augmented triad occur in the major scale? ______________________________

17. Does the diminished triad occur in both the major and harmonic minor scales?

Chapter 2.0
The Structure of Tonality

Chords built on the various scale degrees differ not only in quality, but also possess different functions resulting from their position in the scale. Function means two things: the tendency for each chord to relate to the others in a consistent way, and the particular position each chord has in the edifice known as the "structure of tonality." Through chord function, harmony plays a role in the establishment of tonality. It is possible to speak of *harmonic tonality*—the result of consistent patterns of harmonic action—as a reason for a particular tone (or chord) to gain preeminence over the others. By noting the position of the chords in the tonal structure and examining their functions, it becomes possible to develop an understanding of the subtleties of the "language of harmony," often also identified as *functional harmony.*

2.1 Roman numerals are used chiefly for harmonic analysis. In addition to roman numeral terminology, each diatonic triad has a proper name. The name in each case is either derived from the harmonic function of the triad or determined by its position in the scale. The full significance of these names will be understood later in this study, but the diagram below will shed some light upon their meaning and also the structure of tonality.

KEY OF G MAJOR

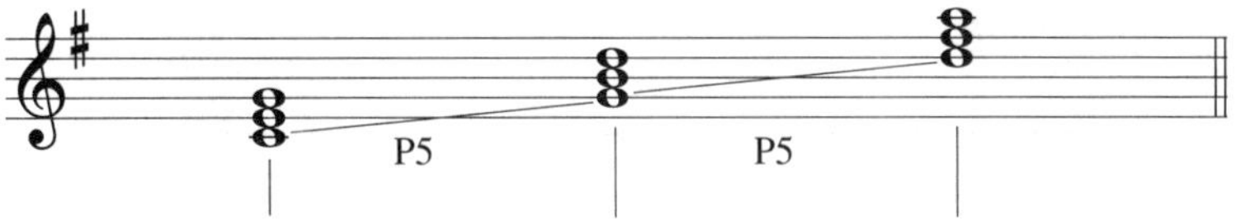

SUBDOMINANT (IV) | TONIC (I) | DOMINANT (V)

The triad that is built on the first degree of the scale (the keynote) is called the _____________.

tonic

2.2 The word TONIC means "tone." This is the proper name given the triad built on the keynote of the scale. Since this tone predominates over the remaining tones, *the tonic triad is the principal triad of the key.*

The tonic triad is built on the _____________ degree of the scale.

first

---

dominant	2.3 Notice in frame 2.1 that the root of the DOMINANT triad is a perfect fifth *above* the keynote (G). Triads whose roots are related by the interval of a perfect fifth have a close relation to one another. This is due to the "fundamental" nature of the perfect fifth.* The triad whose root is a perfect fifth above the keynote is called the ______________. *In acoustics (the scientific study of sound), intervals are expressed by the ratio of frequencies between the two tones. The ratio of the perfect fifth is 3:2. This represents the simplest relationship of all intervals except the unison (1:1) and the octave (2:1). One may read more about this by referring to the Acoustics section of the *Bibliography for Further Study*.
perfect fifth	2.4 The *dominant* triad is so called because of its "dominant" position in the tonality. The root of the dominant triad is the interval of a ____________________________ above the keynote.
above	2.5 Notice in Frame 2.1 that the root of the SUBDOMINANT triad is a perfect fifth *below* the keynote. The subdominant triad is so called because it occupies the same position *below* the tonic that the dominant has ______________ the tonic.
subdominant	2.6 The triad whose root is a perfect fifth *below* the keynote is called the ______________________.
False *(The tonic triad is relatively inactive.)*	2.7 The *tonic, dominant,* and *subdominant* triads are the PRIMARY triads in any key. The importance of this statement will become clear as we progress. Since the tonic triad is built on the keynote (the center of the tonality), it has less harmonic activity than triads built on other degrees of the scale. It is the final chord of most compositions. Because of its position at the center of the tonality the tonic triad may be regarded as a "chord of repose." The three primary triads possess harmonic activity of approximately the same degree. (True/False) ______________.
Perfect fifth	2.8 The *dominant* and *subdominant* triads are both active and tend to progress to the *tonic*. The structure of tonality rests upon the three primary triads. This is due to the fundamental interval by which the roots of the dominant and subdominant chords are related to the tonic. What is this interval? ___________________________.

2.9 The structure of tonality rests upon the foundation of three chords. Name these chords.

(1) ____________________

(2) ____________________

(3) ____________________

(1) Tonic

(2) Dominant

(3) Subdominant
(Any order.)

2.10 Write on the staff the *tonic* triad in the key of e minor. Supply, also, the appropriate roman numeral.

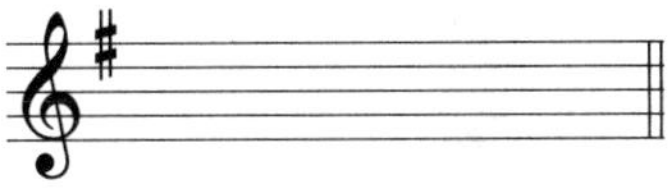

e: ___

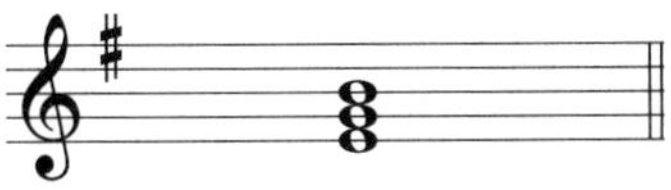

e: i

2.11 Write on the staff the *subdominant* triad in the key of B♭ Major. Supply, also, the appropriate roman numeral.

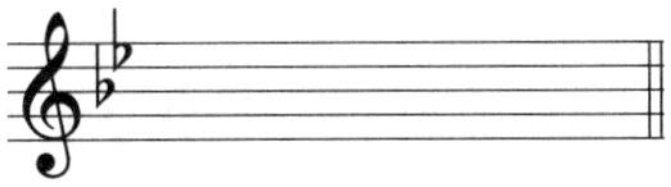

B♭: ___

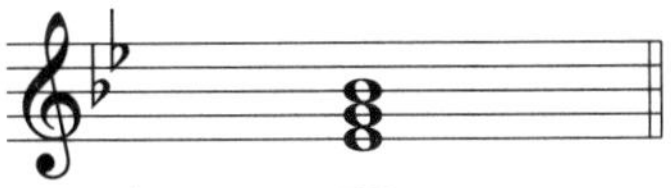

B♭: IV

2.12 Write on the staff the *dominant* triad in the key of g minor *(use the harmonic minor scale).* Supply, also, the appropriate roman numeral.

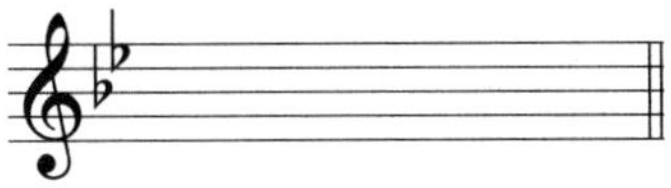

g: ___

g: V

2.13 Write on the staff the *subdominant* triad in the key of b♭ minor *(use the harmonic minor scale).* Supply, also, the appropriate roman numeral.

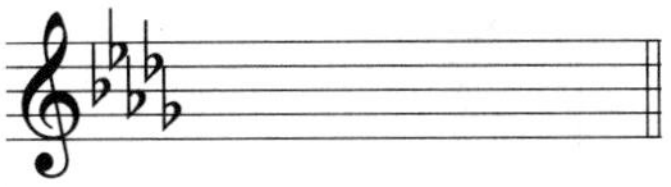

b♭: ___

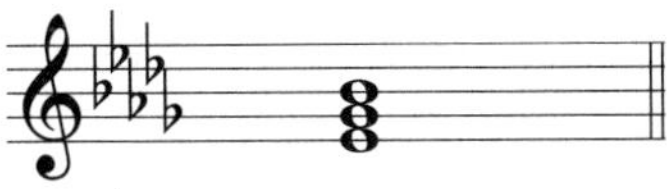

b♭: iv

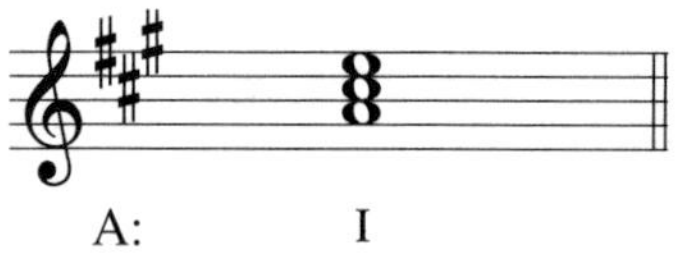

2.14 Write on the staff the *tonic* triad in the key of A Major. Supply, also, the appropriate roman numeral.

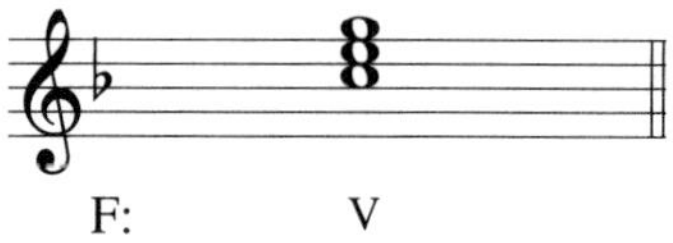

2.15 Write on the staff the *dominant* triad in the key of F Major. Supply, also, the appropriate roman numeral.

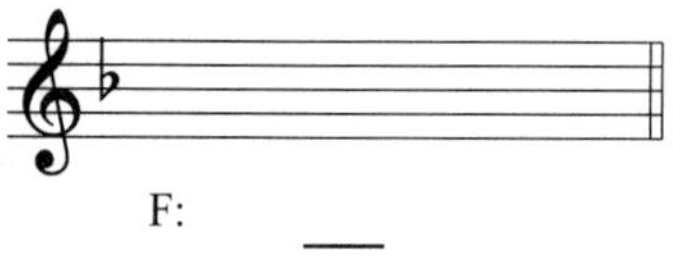

2.16 The triads that are built on tones midway between the tonic and dominant, and the tonic and subdominant, are called the MEDIANT and SUBMEDIANT respectively.

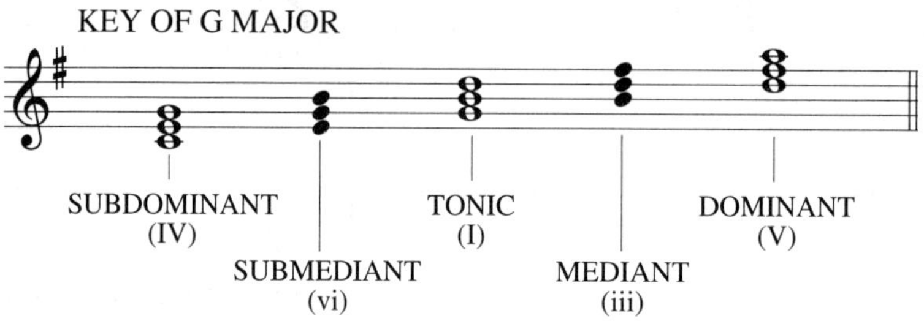

The triad whose root is on the sixth scale degree is called the submediant. The triad whose root is on the third scale degree is called the ________________________.

mediant

2.17 Write the *mediant* and *submediant* triads in the key of A Major.

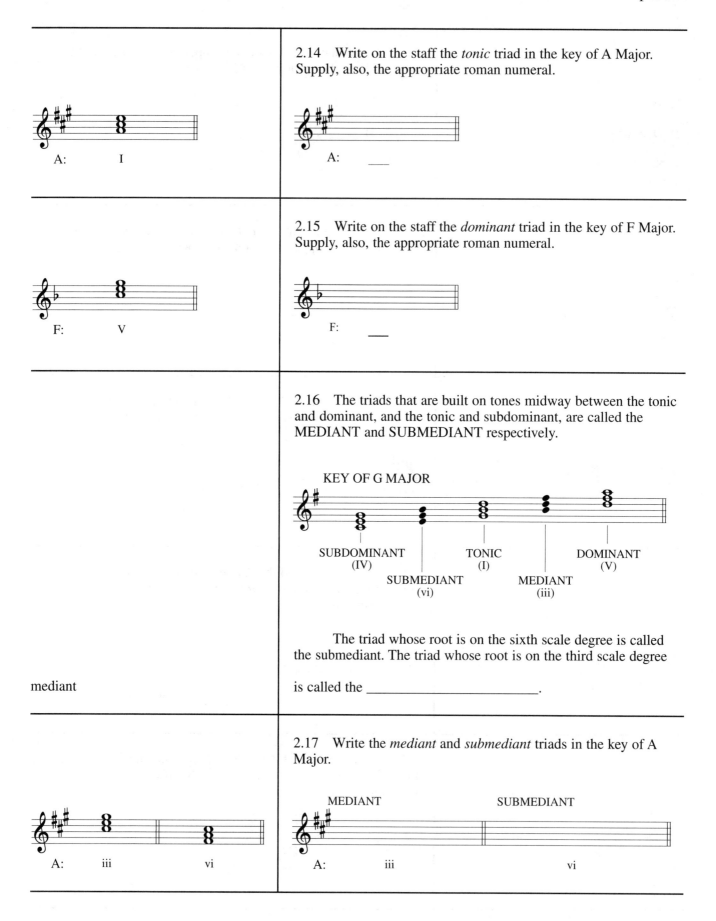

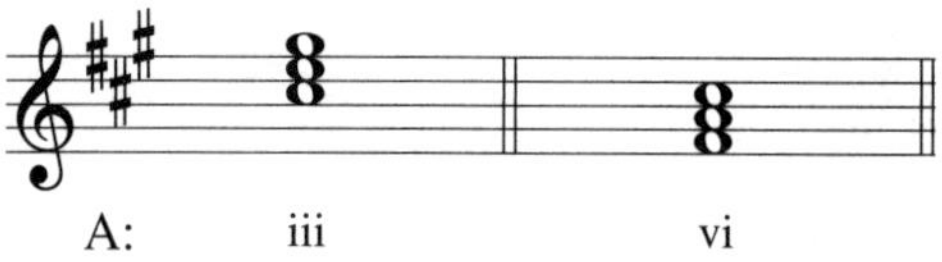

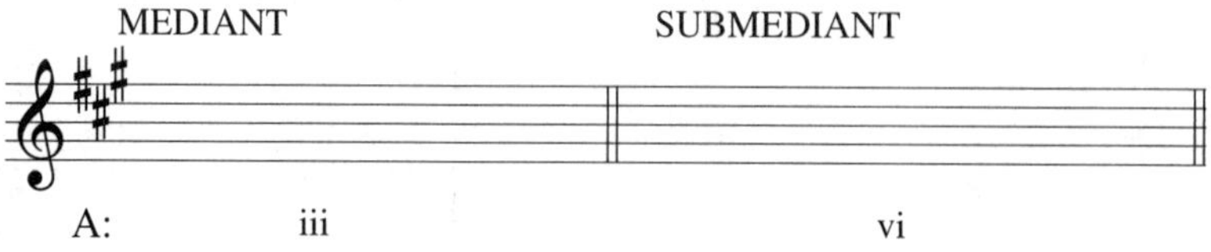

2.18 Write the *mediant* and *submediant* triads in the key of b minor *(use the harmonic minor scale).*

MEDIANT SUBMEDIANT

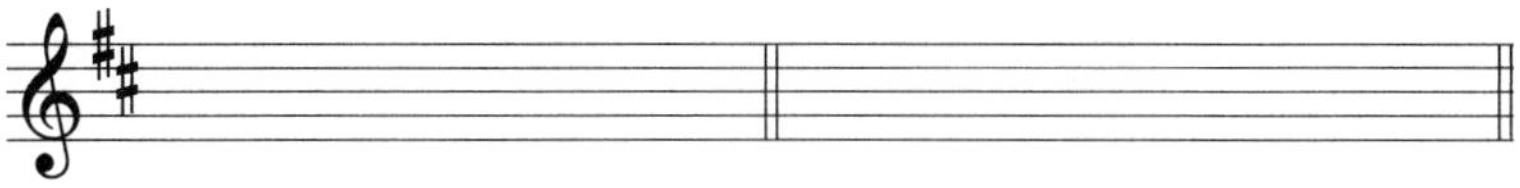

b: III^+ VI

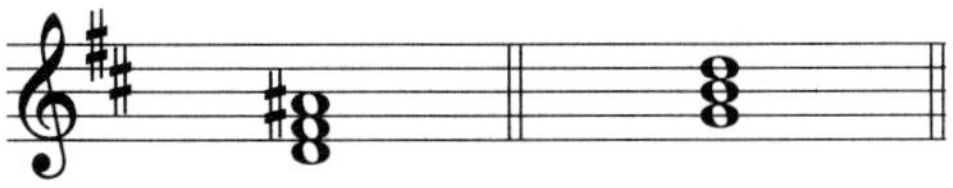

b: III^+ VI

2.19 Write the *mediant* and *submediant* triads in the key of g minor *(use the natural minor scale).*

MEDIANT SUBMEDIANT

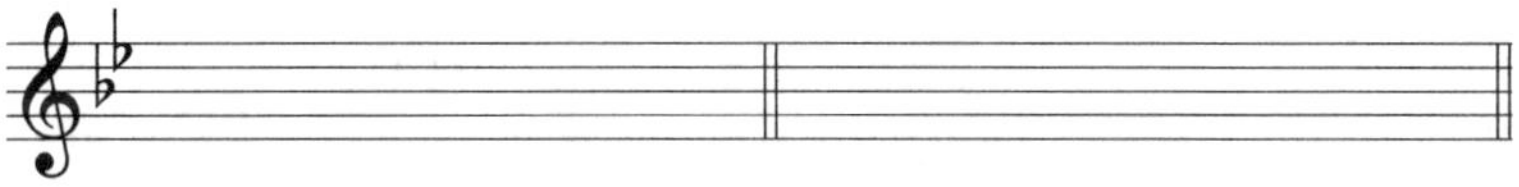

g: III VI

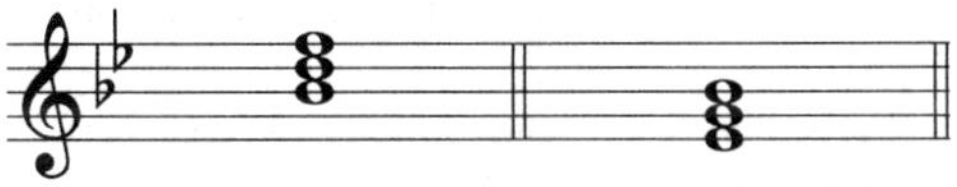

g: III VI

2.20 Write the *mediant* and *submediant* triads in the key of E♭ Major.

MEDIANT SUBMEDIANT

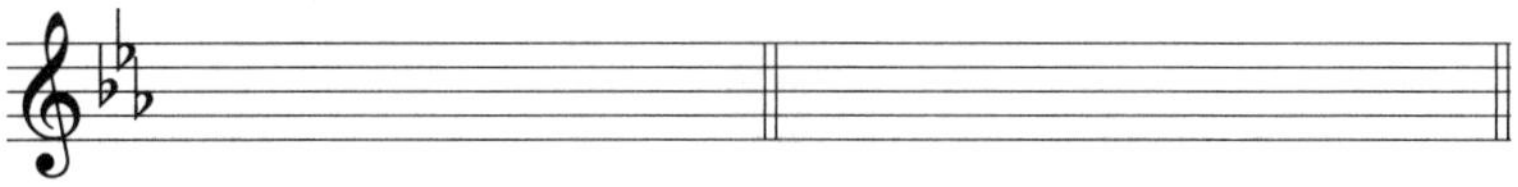

E♭: iii vi

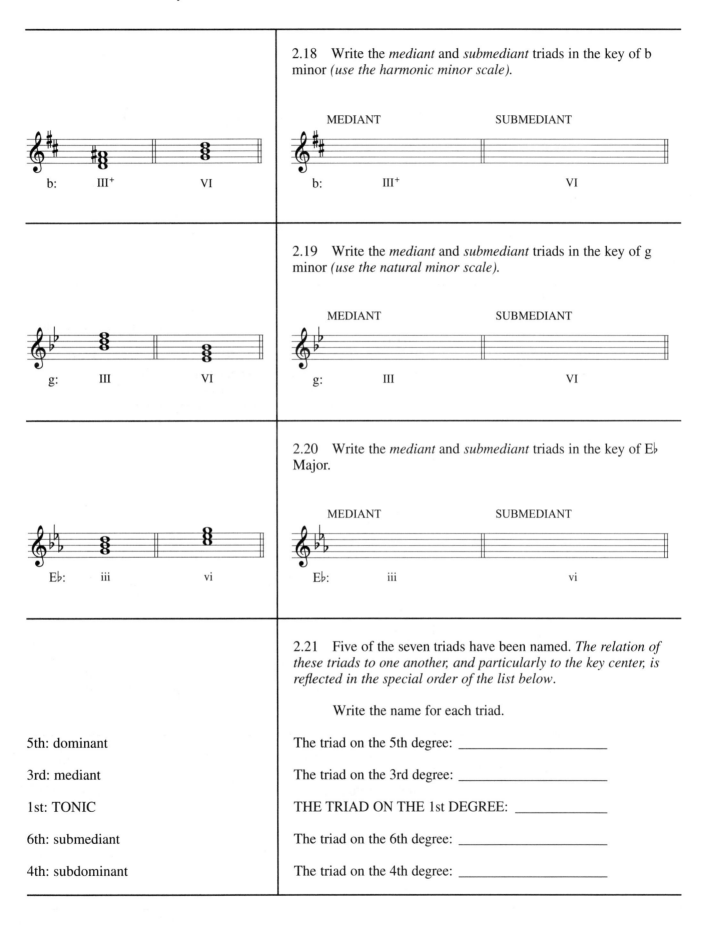

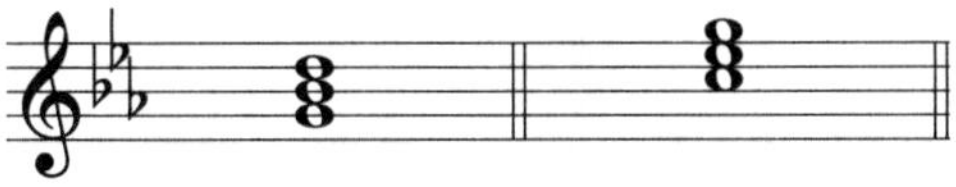

E♭: iii vi

2.21 Five of the seven triads have been named. *The relation of these triads to one another, and particularly to the key center, is reflected in the special order of the list below.*

Write the name for each triad.

The triad on the 5th degree: ____________________

The triad on the 3rd degree: ____________________

THE TRIAD ON THE 1st DEGREE: ____________

The triad on the 6th degree: ____________________

The triad on the 4th degree: ____________________

5th: dominant

3rd: mediant

1st: TONIC

6th: submediant

4th: subdominant

2.22 The two triads yet to be named are shown below:

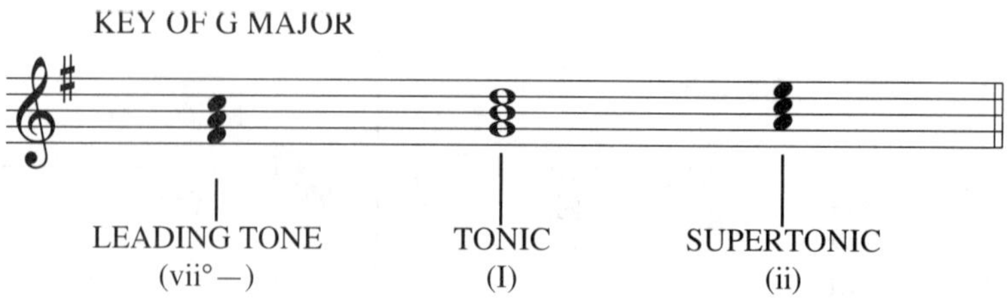

The triad whose root is a half step *below* the tonic is called the LEADING TONE. The triad built on the second degree of the scale is called the ___________________.

supertonic

2.23 The prefix *super* means over, above, or on top of. Thus it is natural that the triad whose root is a second above the tonic should be called the SUPERTONIC.

The LEADING TONE triad derives its name from the fact that its root, being a half step below the tonic, has a very strong tendency to "lead back" to the keynote.

Which of the triads below is the *supertonic* triad in the key of E Major? _____________.

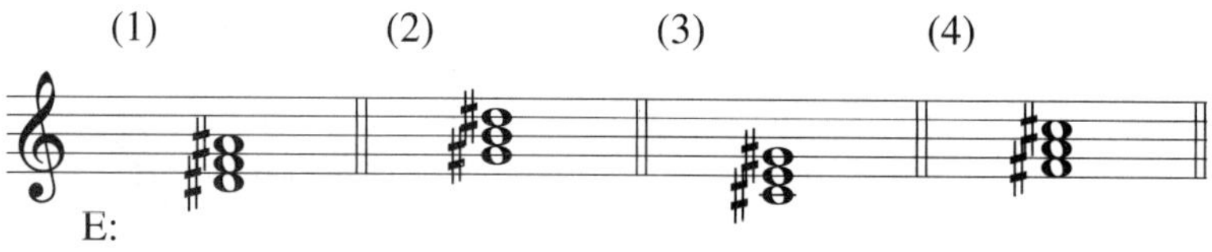

(4)

2.24 Which of the triads below is the *leading tone* triad in the key of F Major? _____________.

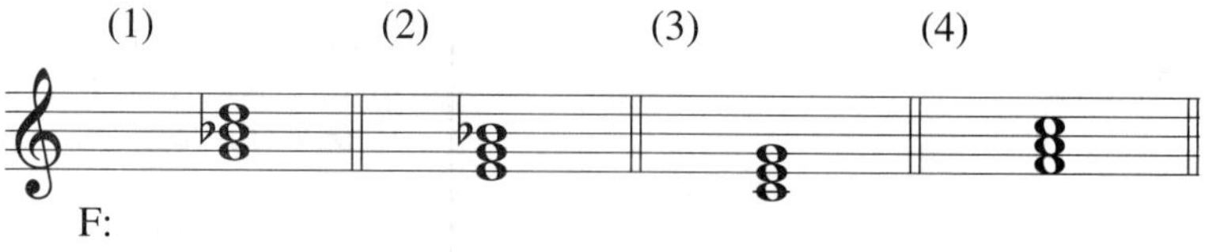

(2)

2.25 Which of the triads below is the *leading tone* triad in the key of b♭ minor? _____________.

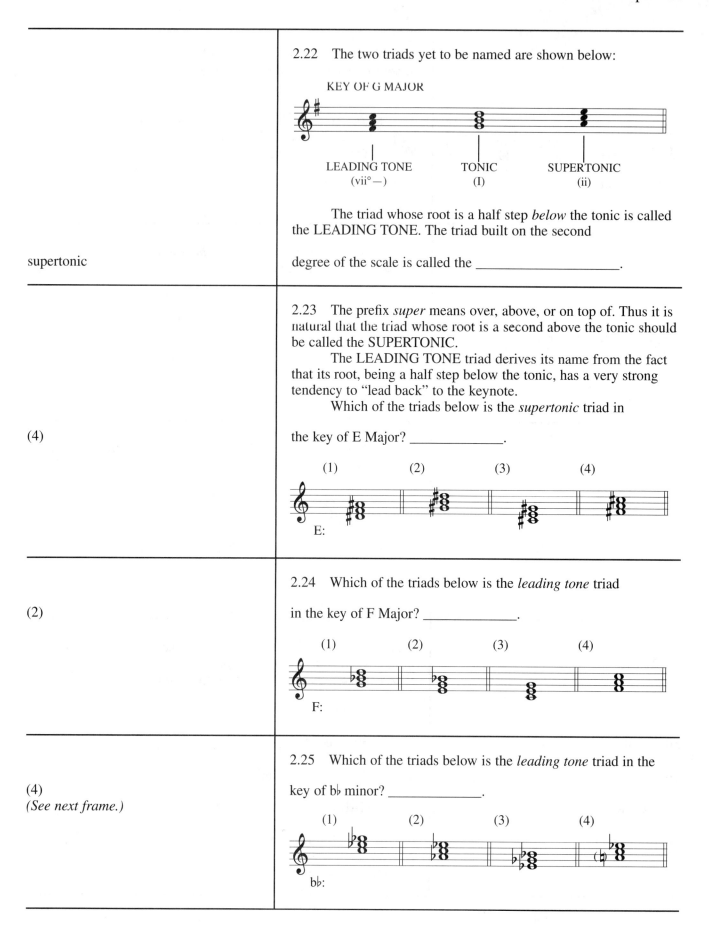

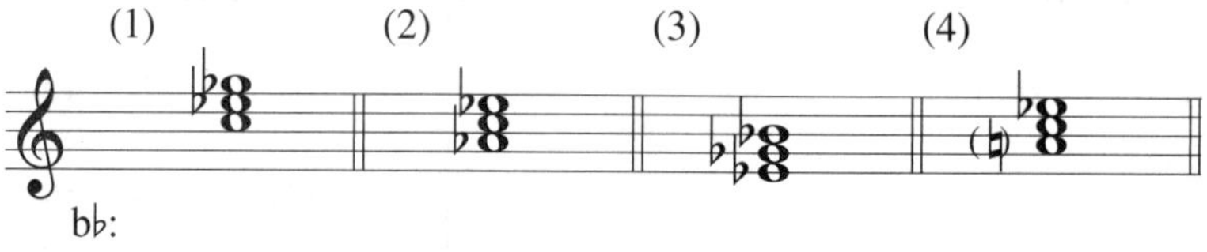

(4)
(See next frame.)

True	2.26 It may be difficult to choose between items (2) and (4) in the preceding frame. The root of the leading tone triad, remember, is a *half step* below the tonic. The triad A♭ C E♭ is a diatonic triad in b♭ natural (or melodic, descending form) minor, but it is NOT a leading tone triad. A triad built on the tone that is a *whole step* below the tonic is called the SUBTONIC. The *subtonic* triad does not occur as a diatonic triad in either the major or harmonic minor scales. (True/False)____________
whole	2.27 The *leading tone* triad is built on a tone that is a half step below the tonic. The *subtonic* triad is built on a tone that is a ____________ step below the tonic. *Remember that the leading tone triad has a much stronger tendency to "lead back" to the tonic, being a half step below, while the subtonic triad, being a whole step below, does not have this tendency.*
Subtonic	2.28 Which term is appropriate for the triad below? (Leading tone/Subtonic) ____________________ KEY OF C MINOR 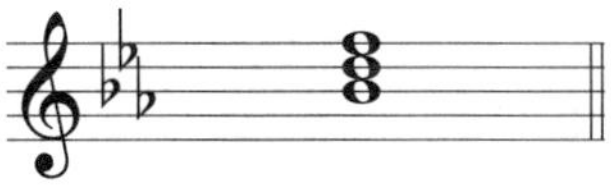
Leading tone	2.29 Which term is specifically for the triad below? (Leading tone/Subtonic) ____________________ KEY OF F MINOR 
(2)	2.30 Which of the triads below is the *leading tone* triad in the key of d minor? ____________ 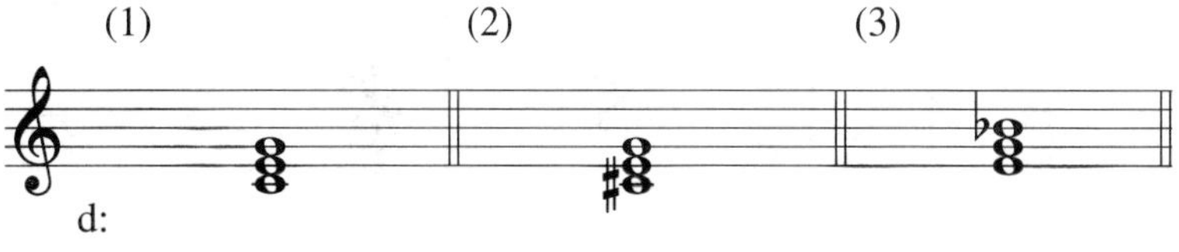

(3)

2.31 Which of the triads below is the *subtonic* triad in the key of f♯ minor? ____________

(1) (2) (3)

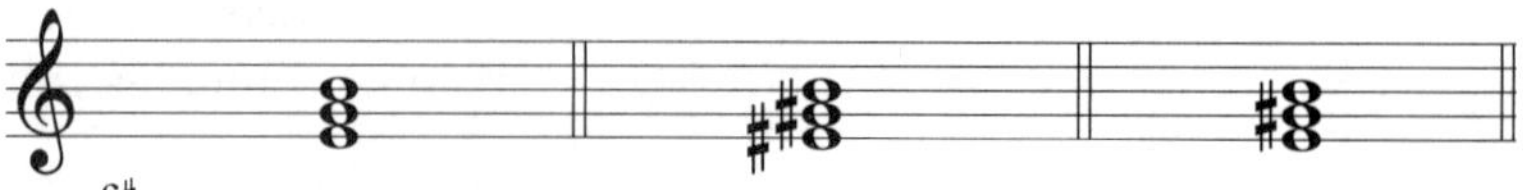

f♯:

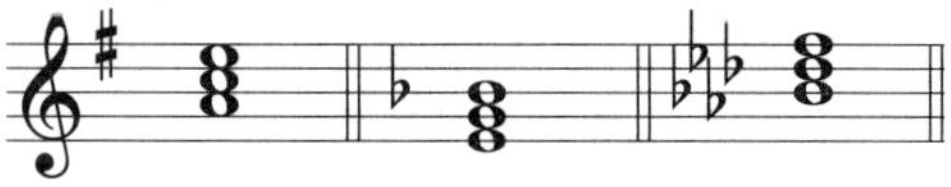

G: ii d: ii° A♭: ii

2.32 The SUPERTONIC triad is located on the second degree of the scale.

Write the *supertonic* triad in each of the keys indicated below:

(1) (2) (3)

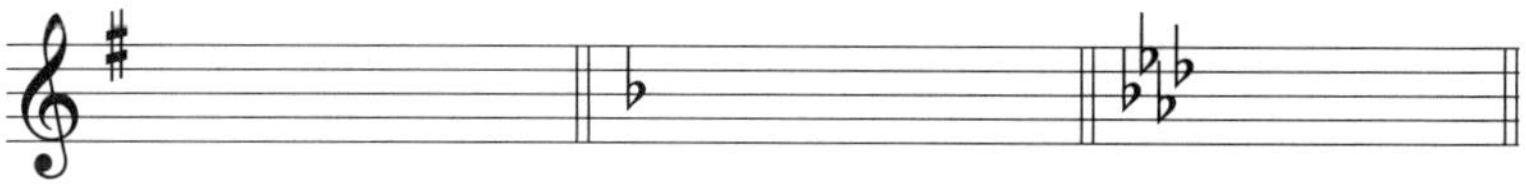

G: ii d: ii° A♭: ii

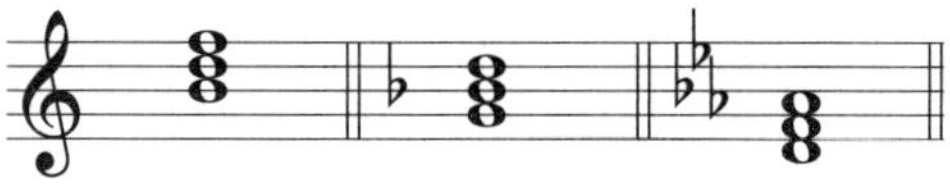

a: ii° F: ii c: ii°

2.33 Write the *supertonic* triad in each of the keys indicated below:

(1) (2) (3)

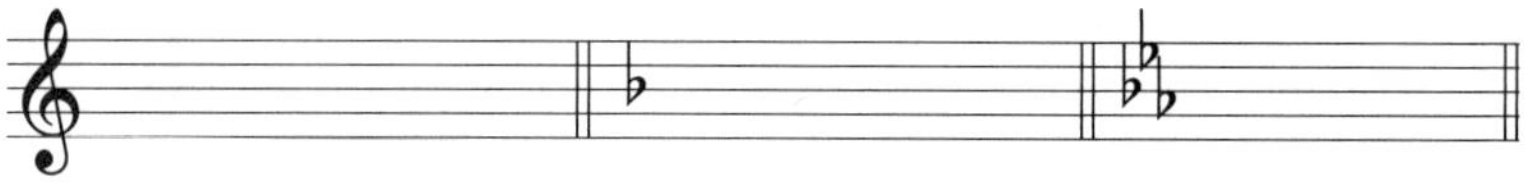

a: ii° F: ii c: ii°

Diminished

2.34 The quality of the *supertonic* triad in a major key is minor. What is the quality of the *supertonic* triad in a minor key

(harmonic minor scale)? __________________

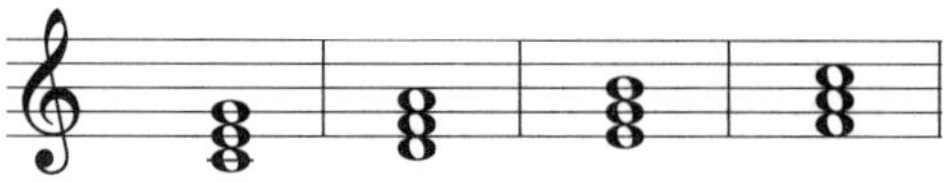

C: I ii iii IV

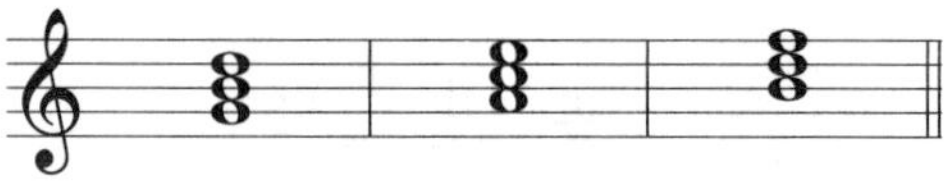

V vi vii°

2.35 Write the roman numeral that is appropriate for each of the triads in the C major scale. *(An abbreviation of the proper name is given for each triad.)*

T ST M SD D SM LT

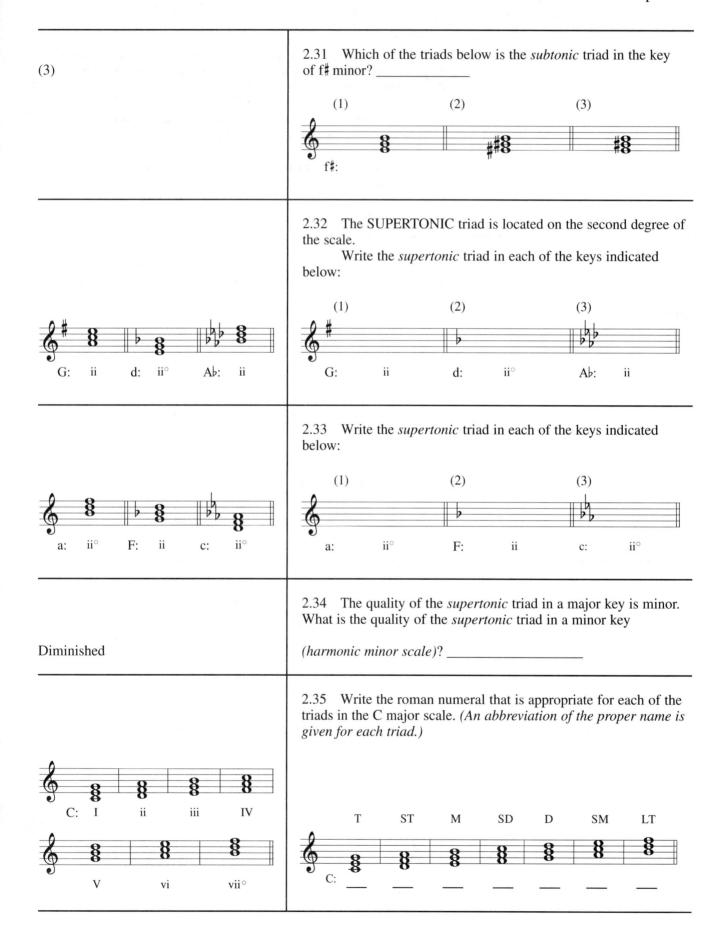

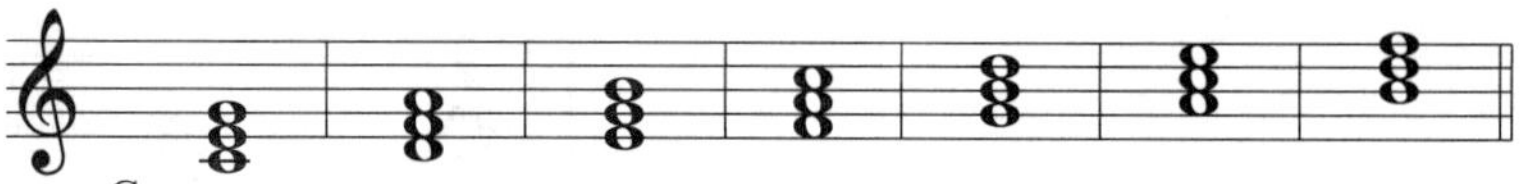

C: ___ ___ ___ ___ ___ ___ ___

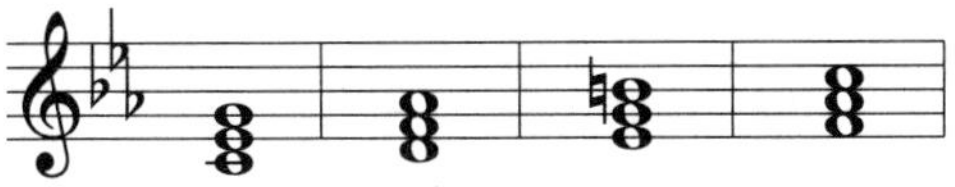

c: i ii° III+ iv

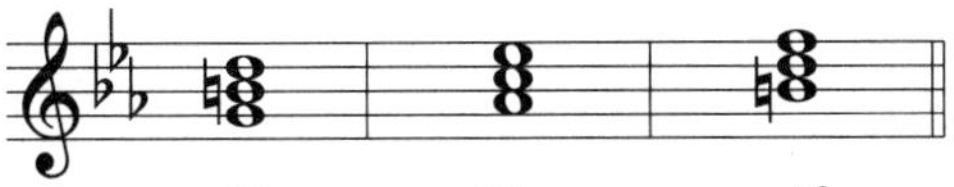

V VI vii°

2.36 Write the roman numeral that is appropriate for each of the triads in the c harmonic minor scale. *(Note the quality of each triad.)*

T ST M SD D SM LT

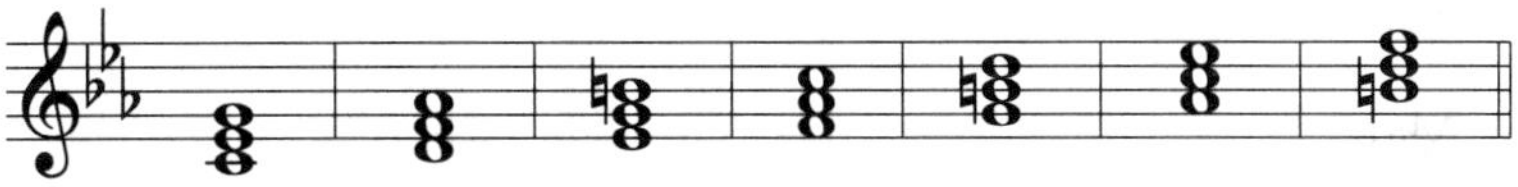

c: ___ ___ ___ ___ ___ ___ ___

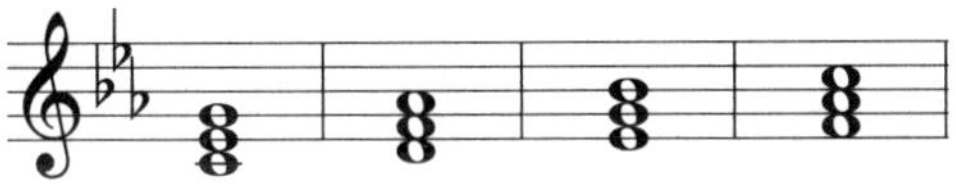

c: i ii° III iv

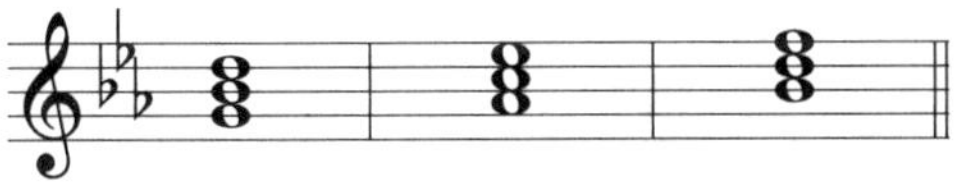

v VI VII

2.37 Write the roman numeral which is appropriate for each of the triads in the c natural minor scale. *(Note the quality of each triad.)*

T ST M SD D SM ST

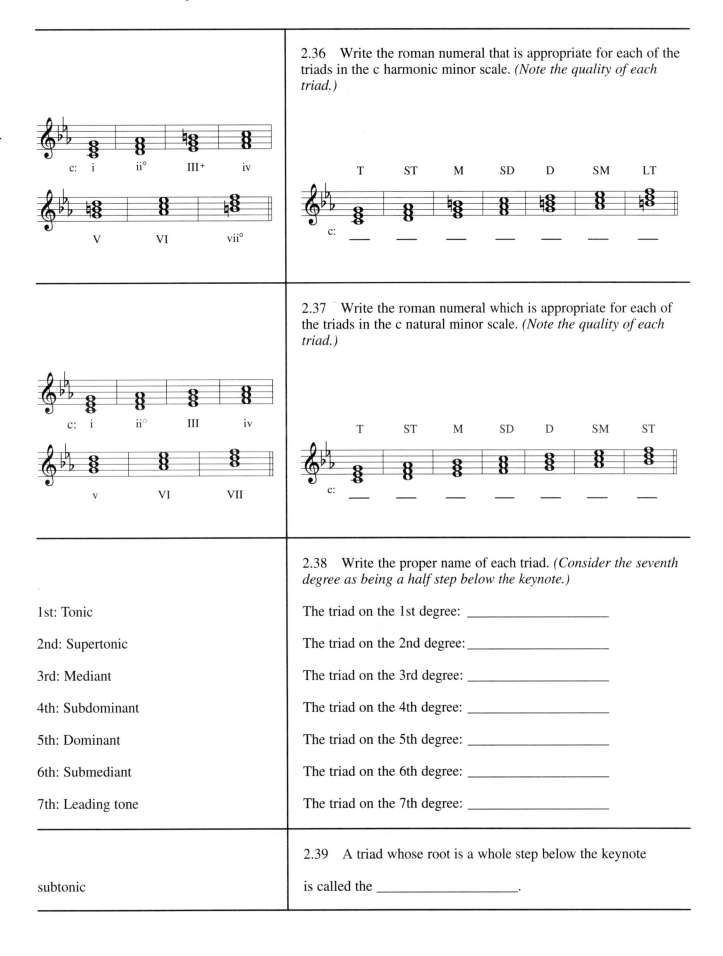

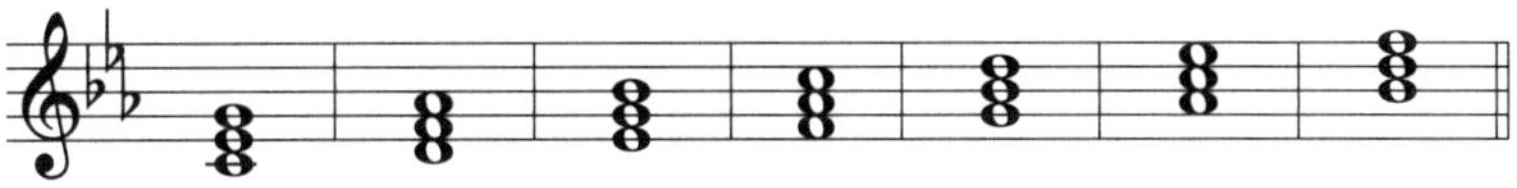

c: ___ ___ ___ ___ ___ ___ ___

1st: Tonic

2nd: Supertonic

3rd: Mediant

4th: Subdominant

5th: Dominant

6th: Submediant

7th: Leading tone

2.38 Write the proper name of each triad. *(Consider the seventh degree as being a half step below the keynote.)*

The triad on the 1st degree: ____________________

The triad on the 2nd degree: ____________________

The triad on the 3rd degree: ____________________

The triad on the 4th degree: ____________________

The triad on the 5th degree: ____________________

The triad on the 6th degree: ____________________

The triad on the 7th degree: ____________________

---

subtonic

2.39 A triad whose root is a whole step below the keynote

is called the ____________________.

1st: Major
2nd: Minor
3rd: Minor
4th: Major
5th: Major
6th: Minor
7th: Diminished

2.40 List the quality (major, minor, diminished, or augmented) of the triads on each degree of a *major* scale.

The triad on the 1st degree: ________________

The triad on the 2nd degree: ________________

The triad on the 3rd degree: ________________

The triad on the 4th degree: ________________

The triad on the 5th degree: ________________

The triad on the 6th degree: ________________

The triad on the 7th degree: ________________

---

	harmonic minor scale	*natural minor scale*
1st:	Minor	Minor
2nd:	Diminished	Diminished
3rd:	Augmented	Major
4th:	Minor	Minor
5th:	Major	Minor
6th:	Major	Major
7th:	Diminished	Major

2.41 List the quality (as above) of the triad on each degree of the:

	harmonic minor scale	*natural minor scale**
The triad on the 1st degree:	________	________
The triad on the 2nd degree:	________	________
The triad on the 3rd degree:	________	________
The triad on the 4th degree:	________	________
The triad on the 5th degree:	________	________
The triad on the 6th degree:	________	________
The triad on the 7th degree:	________	________

*Common-practice composers use this form of the minor scale less often, but one should be alert to its usage.

B♭ D F

2.42 Spell the *tonic* triad in the key of B♭ Major. ____________

A C E♭

2.43 Spell the *supertonic* triad in the key of g minor.

(Use the notes of the harmonic minor scale.) ____________

D♯ F♯ A♯

2.44 Spell the *mediant* triad in the key of B Major. ____________

C♯ E G♯

2.45 Spell the *subdominant* triad in the key of g♯ minor. *(Use the notes of the harmonic minor scale.)* ____________

E♭ G B♭

2.46 Spell the *dominant* triad in the key of A♭ Major.

____

D♭ F A♭	2.47 Spell the *submediant* triad in the key of f minor. *(Use the notes of the harmonic minor scale.)* _____________
C E♭ G♭	2.48 Spell the *leading tone* triad in the key of D♭ Major. _____________
C E G♯	2.49 Spell the *mediant* triad in the key of a minor. *(Use the notes of the harmonic minor scale.)* _____________
E♭ G B♭	2.50 Spell the *mediant* triad in the key of c minor. *(Use the notes of the natural minor scale.)* _____________
A♯ C♯ E	2.51 Spell the *leading tone* triad in the key of b minor. *(Use the notes of the harmonic minor scale.)* _____________
C E G	2.52 Spell the *subtonic* triad in the key of d minor. *(Use the notes of the natural minor scale.)* _____________
(No response required.)	*Expository Frame* 2.53 Do not continue unless the proper names and chord symbols are firmly fixed in your mind. The diagram below for major keys is yet another representation that may help. [4] *Subdominant* (IV) [3] *Mediant* (iii) [2] *Supertonic* (ii) [1] *Tonic* (I) [7] *Leading tone* (vii°) [6] *Submediant* (vi) [5] *Dominant* (V)
tonic	2.54 The tonic triad is built on the center of a tonality—the keynote. Harmonically the tonic triad is relatively static. The other diatonic triads are attracted to it and possess various degrees of activity. The precise relation each triad bears to the tonic (and to the other diatonic triads) is unique and the discovery of these relationships will occupy the discussion for some time. First, some of the basic principles regarding the structure of tonality will be observed. The three primary triads of a tonality are the *tonic, dominant,* and *subdominant.* Which of these triads possesses the least harmonic activity? The _____________.

2.55 Inactive in most cases, the tonic triad is a relatively "neutral" chord. Most compositions begin and end with tonic harmony and a sense of relative repose accompanies the tonic triad whenever it appears within a harmonic phrase.

One of the most active triads is the *dominant.* This triad tends to demand resolution directly to the tonic.

Play the example below:

Beethoven, *Sonata,* Op. 2, No. 3

The harmonic movement is tonic-dominant—a basic progression in tonal music. Because it ends with an active chord (V), it sounds incomplete; refer to such progressions as "opening" progressions.

The tonic and dominant are two of the three primary chords that provide the foundation for the structure of tonality. The root of the dominant triad is the interval of a

perfect _____________ above the tonic.

fifth

2.56 The "opening" progression (I–V) illustrated in the preceding frame is completed when the dominant seventh chord* progresses back to the tonic.

Beethoven, *Sonata,* Op. 2, No. 3

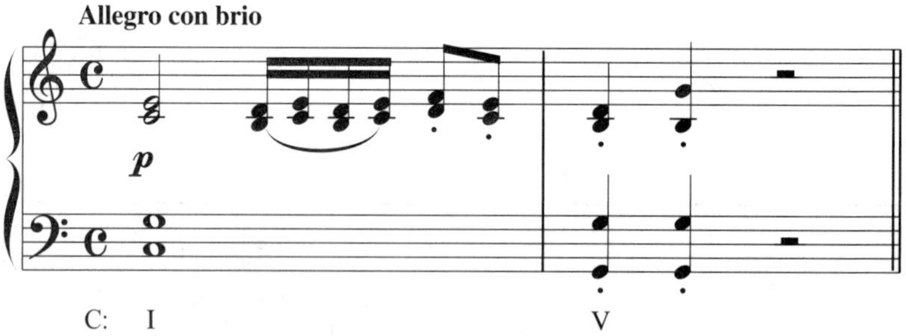

Tonic and dominant harmonies provide the basis for many phrases. Does a series of chords ending on the dominant sound complete?

____

*The dominant seventh chord possesses the same harmonic function as the dominant triad but has greater activity due to the dissonance provided by the seventh. This chord is treated fully in Chapter 6.0.

No
(The opening progression I–V is completed by returning to the tonic.)

2.57 Two of the chords which constitute the three-part foundation of the structure of tonality are the *tonic* and *dominant;* the third is the SUBDOMINANT.

Play the example below:

Mozart, *Sonata,* K. 311

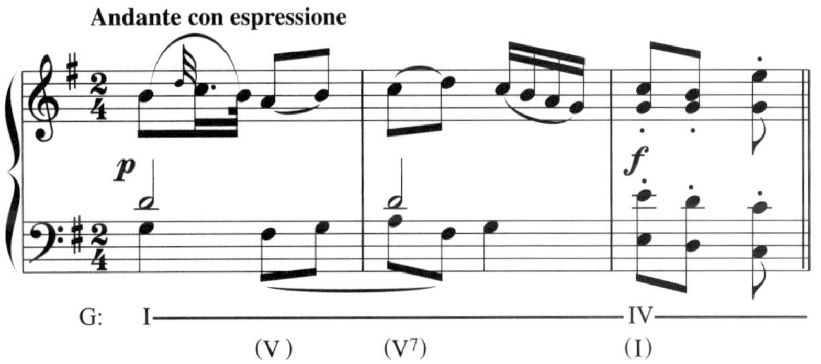

The basic harmonic movement in this example is I–IV. This is another of the common "opening" progressions. The character of the subdominant chord is quite different from that of the dominant. The need for resolution into the tonic is not as strong for the subdominant as for the dominant.

Does the phrase above end with a sense of finality? _______

No
(The tonic chord is required to produce a sense of finality.)

2.58 The "opening" progression I–IV is often completed by IV–I.

Play the example below:

Schumann, *Album for the Young,* Op. 68, No. 10

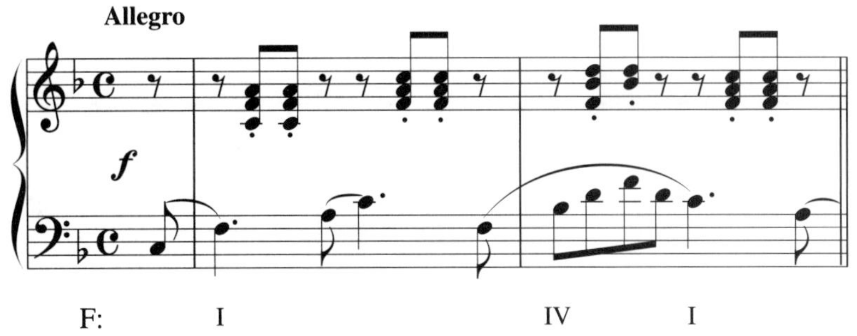

(Continued on the next page)

Both of the "opening" progressions I–V and I–IV are completed by a return to the ______________ triad.

tonic

2.59 The subdominant chord often progresses to the dominant rather than returning at once to the tonic.

Play the example below:

Bach, Chorale: *In allen meinen Taten*

F: I IV V

This example shows another of the basic harmonic progressions (IV–V). The subdominant chord progresses as naturally to the dominant as to the tonic.

The subdominant chord may return immediately to the tonic or it may progress to the ______________.

dominant (V)

2.60 Below is a list of the three *basic* progressions:

OPENING	COMPLETION
(1) I–V	V–I
(2) I–IV	IV–I
(3) (I) IV–V	V–I

Despite their seeming simplicity, these harmonic relations constitute the basic harmonic underpinning of much eighteenth- and nineteenth-century music.

Complete, in terms of the basic progressions, the statement below *(use roman numerals):*

The tonic (I) can progress to ___________ or to ___________.

IV (or to) V
(Any order.)

2.61 Complete, in terms of the basic harmonic progressions, the statement below *(use roman numerals):*

The subdominant (IV) can progress to ______________ or to ______________.

I (or to) V

(Any order.)

tonic (I)	2.62 To what triad is the dominant most likely to progress? The ____________. Note: The dominant moving to the subdominant is not considered a progression but rather a retrogression; see Frames 9.2–.5, 9.17 for further comment.
diminished	2.63 The PRIMARY triads in any key are the tonic, subdominant, and dominant triads. The remaining triads (supertonic, mediant, submediant, and leading tone) are SECONDARY triads. The *primary* triads in any major key are all major triads. The *secondary* triads (in major) are either minor or ____________________.
ii, iii, (and) vi *(Any order.)*	2.64 List with roman numerals the three triads (in major) which are *minor* in quality. ________, ________, and ________.
I, IV, (and) V ii, iii, vi, (and) vii° *(Any order.)*	2.65 Complete the chart below: *Primary triads:* ________, ________, and ________. *Secondary triads:* ________, ________, ________, and ________.
i (and) iv *(Any order.)*	2.66 Two of the primary triads (in harmonic minor) are minor in quality. List these triads: __________ and __________.
ii° (and) vii° *(Any order.)*	2.67 Two of the secondary triads (in harmonic minor) are diminished. List these triads: ____________ and ____________.
perfect fifth	2.68 The primary triads provide the foundation for the structure of tonality. This is due to the fundamental intervallic relationship of the perfect fifth between their roots. (The history of this relationship can be traced back to the eighteenth-century French theorist, Jean-Phillipe Rameau.) 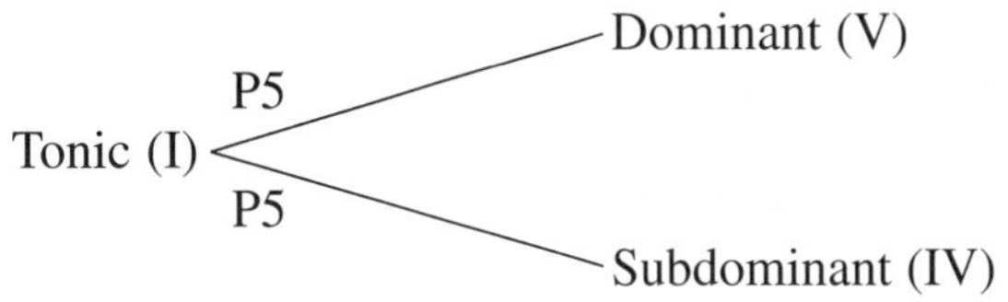 The roots of the dominant and subdominant triads are related to the tonic by the interval of a ____________.

2.69 The relations that the various secondary triads bear to the tonic are shown here:

(Major Tonality)

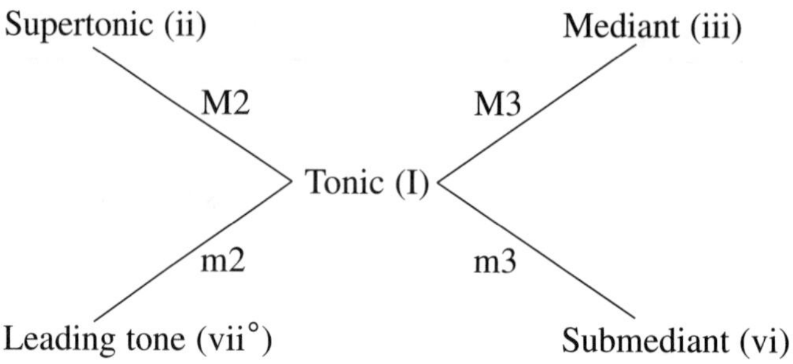

The secondary triads are related to the tonic by

intervals of the second or _____________.

third

2.70 Music in which the primary triads are emphasized tends to sound "positive" and "strong." The overuse of these triads, however, can result in an excessively "stable" or "dull" effect. Secondary triads are used to provide *tonal variety* and to give additional color to the harmony.

Play and compare the two progressions below:

(1)

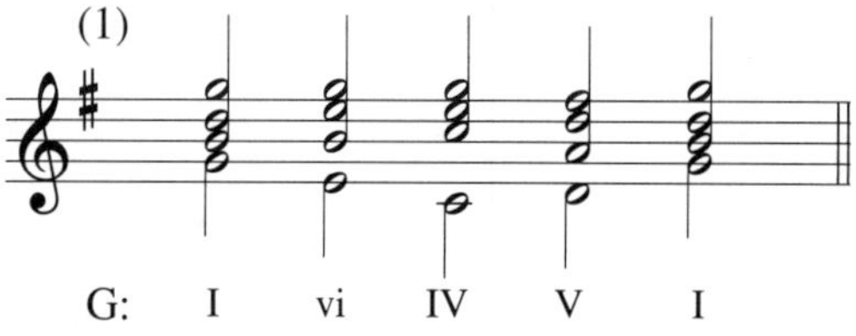

(2)

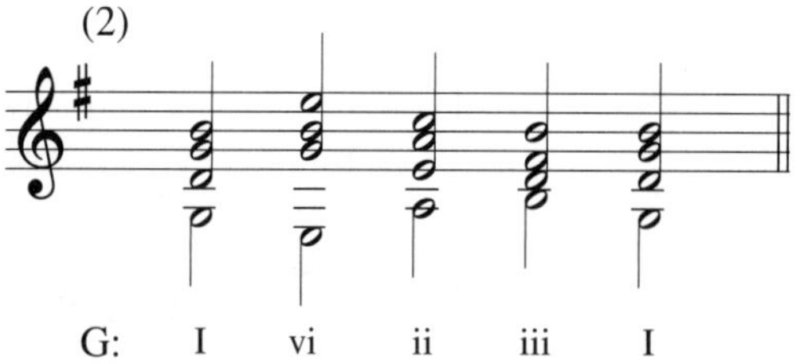

Which of these examples gives the stronger sense of

the key of G Major? (1) or (2) _____________.

(1)
(There is no doubt that [2] is in G major; but, since minor [secondary] triads predominate, the impression of a major key is weakened.)

2.71 Observe the relation of secondary triads to the tonic in *harmonic minor* as follows:

KEY OF G MINOR (Harmonic Minor Scale)

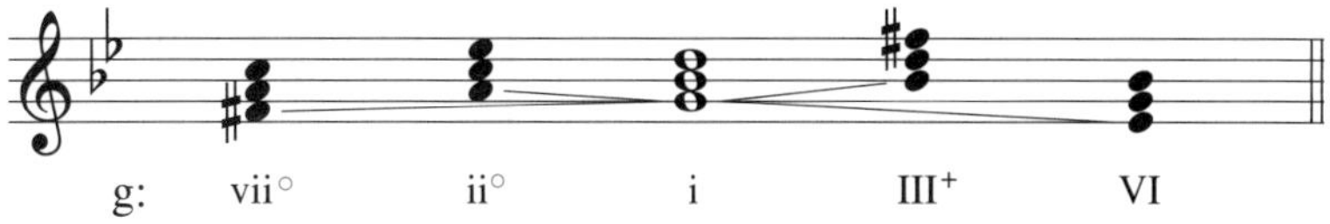

By what interval is the *mediant* triad related to the tonic in harmonic minor? *(Be specific.)* ________________

Minor third

2.72 By what interval (below the tonic) is the submediant triad related to the tonic in harmonic minor? ________________

Major third

2.73 In harmonic minor the root of the *mediant* triad is a minor third above the tonic. In major the root of the *mediant* triad is a ____________ third above the tonic.

major

2.74 In harmonic minor the root of the *submediant* triad is a major third below the tonic. In major the root of the *submediant* triad is a ____________ third below the tonic.

minor

2.75 The root of the *supertonic* triad is related to the tonic by the interval of a major second (above) in both major and minor. Is the quality of this triad the same in major as it is in (harmonic) minor?

____

No
(In major the supertonic triad is minor; but it is diminished in harmonic minor.)

2.76 The root of the *leading tone* triad is related to the tonic by the interval of a minor second (below) in both major and harmonic minor. Is the quality of this triad the same in each case?

____

Yes
(Both are diminished.)

2.77 Each of the secondary triads associates with a specific primary triad.

Study the diagram below:

KEY OF C MAJOR

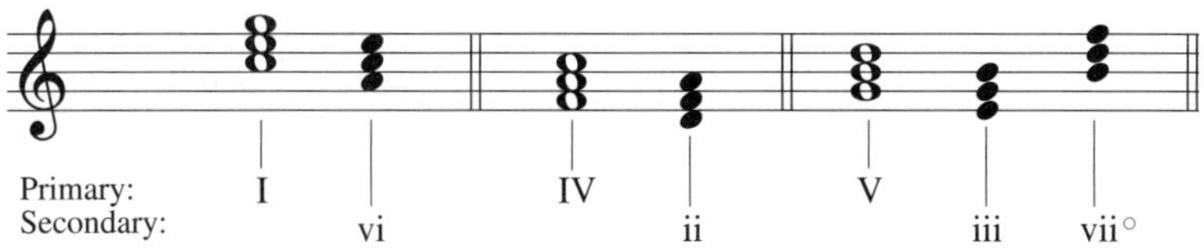

(Continued on the next page)

thirds	Secondary triads are used as substitutes for the primary triads with which they are associated and have similar harmonic functions. What are the intervals between the roots of primary triads and their secondary triads? Major and minor _____________.
I–vi IV–ii V–iii, vii°	2.78 Each secondary triad is located a third *below* its primary triad with the exception of the leading tone (vii°). The harmonic functions of the leading tone and dominant triads are practically identical.* Each tends to progress directly to the tonic. Indicate with roman numerals the secondary triad(s) associated with each primary triad. PRIMARY TRIADS — SECONDARY TRIADS I – _____________ IV – _____________ V – _____________ *The leading tone triad is often considered to be a dominant seventh chord with the root omitted.
subdominant (IV)	2.79 Which primary triad is associated with the supertonic triad? The _______________________ triad.
tonic (I)	2.80 Which primary triad is associated with the submediant triad? The _____________ triad.
dominant (V)	2.81 Which primary triad is associated with the mediant triad? The _______________________ triad.
leading tone (vii°)	2.82 Which secondary triad has practically the same harmonic function as the dominant? The _____________ _____________ triad.

Summary

Roman numerals are used chiefly for harmonic analysis, while proper names *(tonic, supertonic, etc.)* are used when speaking or writing. Since both roman numerals and proper names will be used throughout this study, it is necessary to become fluent in both methods of identifying chords. Whereas proper names do not reveal the quality of triads, roman numerals do. So, be especially careful to choose the form of roman numeral appropriate to the quality of the triad to be represented.

On the other hand, these more exacting descriptions are not as critical in an environment such as pop, commercial, or jazz where chord names (by letter name) and quality (major, minor, augmented, or diminished) become the focus of identification. In these situations the nomenclature (system) previously identified is much more appropriate to use. However, the focus here will be primarily on the exact descriptions to zero in on the harmonic processes needing to be conveyed. Where possible, some crossovers will be made to develop a better understanding of harmonic processes in general.

The three primary triads—I, IV, and V—provide the foundation for the structure of tonality. The roots of the dominant and subdominant triads are related to the tonic by the interval of a perfect fifth. This interval is the "simplest" (see Frame 2.1) by which different chords can be related. This relationship accounts for the fundamental role that these triads play in the establishment of tonality. The tonic (I) is the center of the tonality; the dominant (V) is a perfect fifth *above* the tonic; and the subdominant (IV) is a perfect fifth *below* the tonic.

With respect to primary triads there are three basic harmonic progressions: I–V, I–IV, and IV–V. Each of these is an "opening" progression, which is completed by harmonic movement back to the tonic. Harmonic phrases usually begin on, and ultimately return to the tonic. Thus some typical *basic* harmonic phrases are: I–V–I, I–IV–I, and I–IV–V–I.

Secondary triads are used as substitutes for primary triads for the sake of tonal variety. With only one exception, the roots of secondary triads are the interval of a third *below* the primary triads to which they relate. The exception is the leading tone triad (vii°) whose root is located a third *above* the dominant.

The harmonic function of secondary triads is similar to that of the primary triads with which they are associated. This association is strongest in the case of the dominant and leading tone triads, for each of these triads can progress directly to the tonic. The difference between them is due not to their function, but to their quality (the dominant is major, the leading tone is diminished).

The symmetrical structure of tonality is represented in the diagram below. The tonic (I) is the center of the structure with the other two primary triads (V and IV) spaced a perfect fifth above and below. The entire structure is based on thirds.

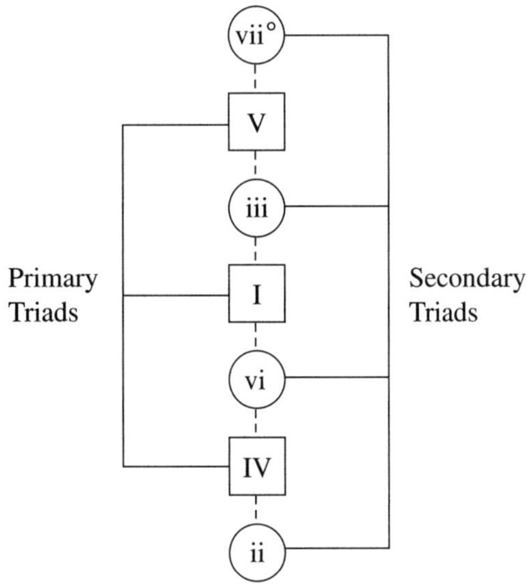

The terms that are explained or used in this chapter are listed below in the order presented:

structure of tonality	mediant	basic progression
harmonic tonality	submediant	opening progression
functional harmony	leading tone	closing progression
tonic	supertonic	basic harmonic phrases (or progressions)
dominant	subtonic	retrogression
subdominant	neutral chord (or triad)	secondary triads
primary triads	active triad (or chord)	tonal variety

Mastery Frames

(5) Dominant (4) Subdominant (1) Tonic (2.1–.6)	2–1 Write the proper name for triads built on the indicated scale degrees. *Scale Degree* — *Proper Name* (5) ________________ (4) ________________ (1) ________________
primary (2.1–.15)	2–2 All of the triads in the preceding frame are (primary/ secondary) ____________ triads.
(Mediant) 3rd (Submediant) 6th (2.16–.21)	2–3 Indicate the scale degree on which each triad is built. Mediant ____________ Submediant ____________
(7) Leading tone (2) Supertonic (2.22–.34)	2–4 Write the proper name for the diatonic triads built on the indicated scale degrees in major or harmonic minor. *Scale Degree* — *Proper Name* (7) ________________ (2) ________________
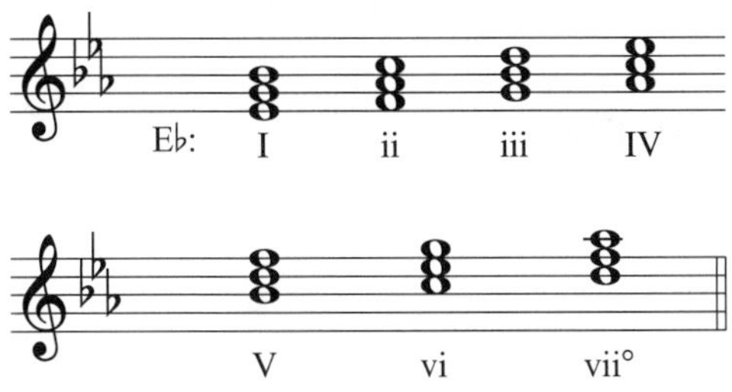 (2.35)	2–5 Write the appropriate roman numeral for each triad. 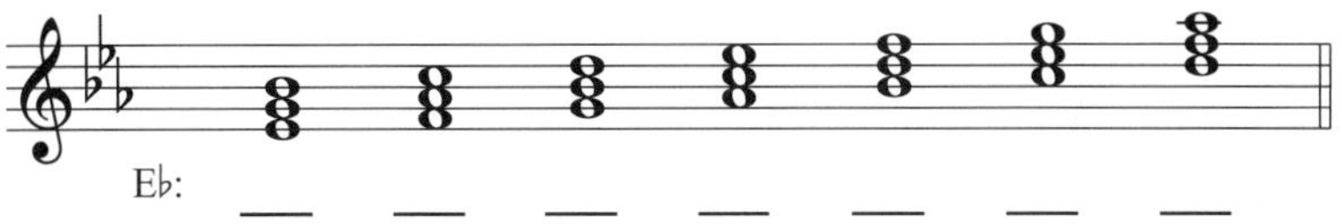

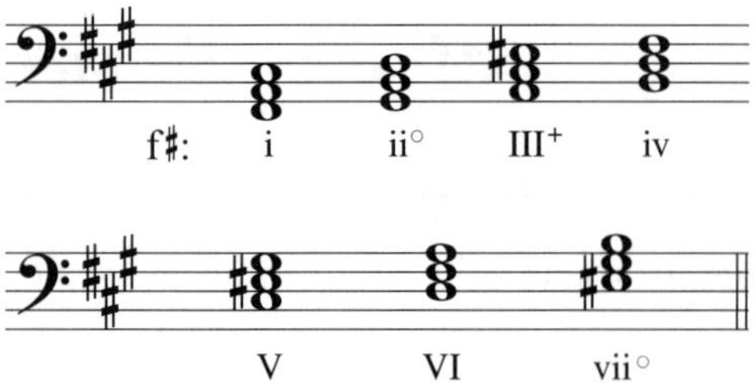

(2.36)

2–6 Write the appropriate roman numeral for each triad.

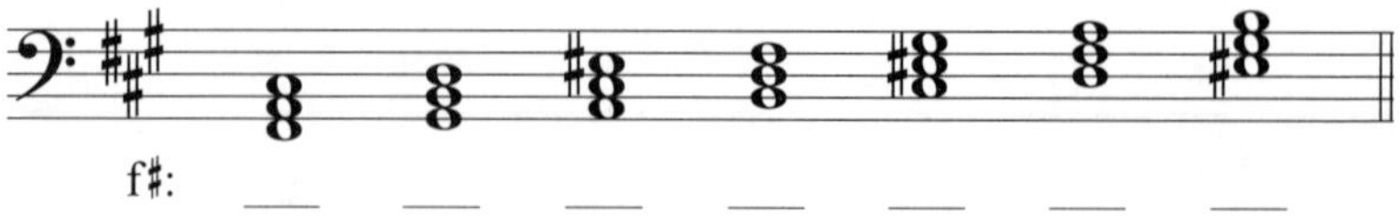

Dominant.

(2.54)

2–7 Which of the two triads below is more active?

____

Tonic Dominant

---

tonic (I)

(2.55–.59)

2–8 "Opening" harmonic progressions such as I–V or I–IV are completed by eventually progressing to the

____________________________.

P
S
S
P
P
S
S

(2.62–.66)

2–9 Identify each triad as either primary (P), or Secondary (S).

Tonic ______
Supertonic ______
Mediant ______
Subdominant ______
Dominant ______
Submediant ______
Leading tone ______

---

vi
ii
iii, vii°

(2.6–.77)

2–10 Indicate with roman numerals the secondary triad(s) associated with each primary triad.

Primary Triad	Secondary Triads
I	______________
IV	______________
V	______________

Supplementary Assignments

ASSIGNMENT 2–1 Name ______________________________

1. Provide the proper names for the three triads represented by the roman numerals below.

   V ____________________

   I ____________________

   IV ____________________

2. Name the secondary triad(s) that relate to each of the primary triads below (use proper names).

   V ____________________

   I ____________________

   IV ____________________

3. Name the triad that rests on the tonal center.______________________________

4. The dominant triad is built on the ____________________ scale degree.

5. Which triad has the same position below the tonal center that the dominant has above?______________

6. Upon which scale degrees are secondary triads built?______________________________

7. Explain the meaning of the terms "mediant" and "submediant." ______________________________

   ____

8. The triad built on the seventh scale degree in major or harmonic minor is called the ______________

   ____

9. Draw a diagram that shows your conception of the structure of tonality.

10. Write the proper roman numeral for each triad.

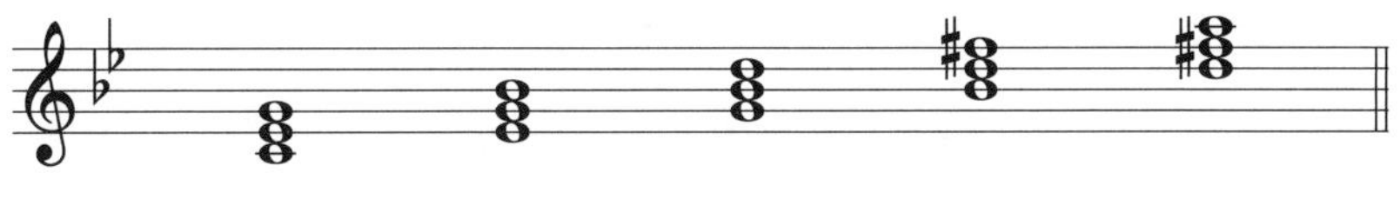

g: ___ ___ ___ ___ ___

11. Write the proper roman numeral for each triad.

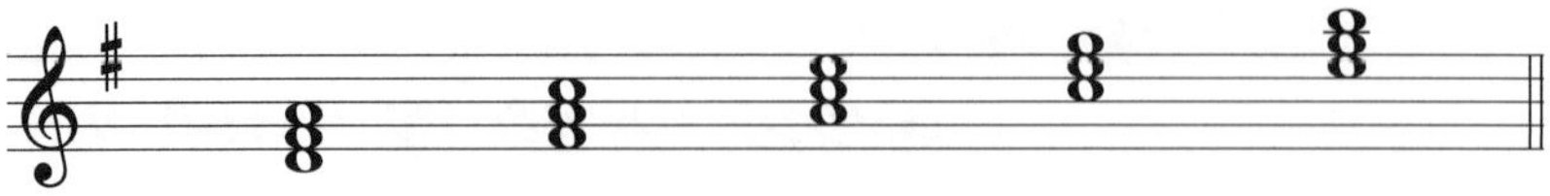

G: ___ ___ ___ ___ ___

12. Write an alternative analysis for each triad.

(a)

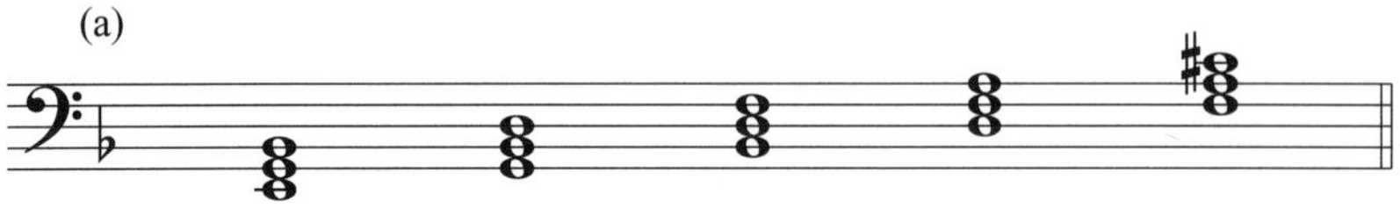

___ ___ ___ ___ ___

(b)

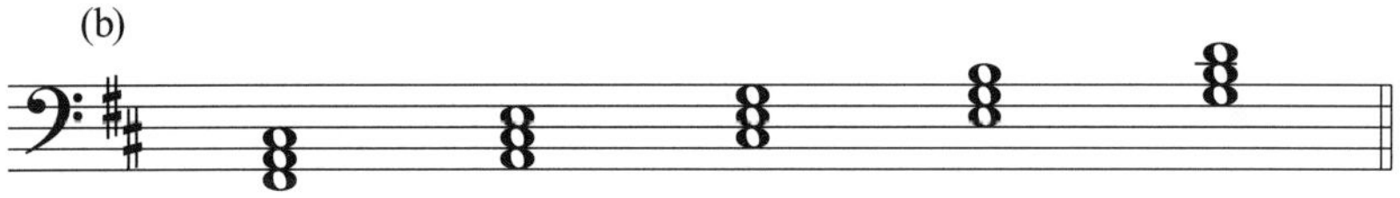

___ ___ ___ ___ ___

13. Indicate the scale degree on which each chord is built.

Subdominant ______________________________

Mediant ______________________________

Supertonic ______________________________

Tonic ______________________________

Leading tone ______________________________

Submediant ______________________________

Dominant ______________________________

14. List the scale degrees where minor triads occur in a major tonality. ______________________________

____

15. Roots of primary and secondary triads are related by the interval of a ______________________________.

16. Show with chord symbols the three primary triads and the secondary triad(s) related to each.

Primary Triads	*Secondary Triads*
______________________	______________________
______________________	______________________
______________________	______________________

ASSIGNMENT 2–2 Name ______________________

1. What is the name of the triad that is built on the tonal center of a key? ______________________

2. Compose a single-line melody based on the indicated harmony.

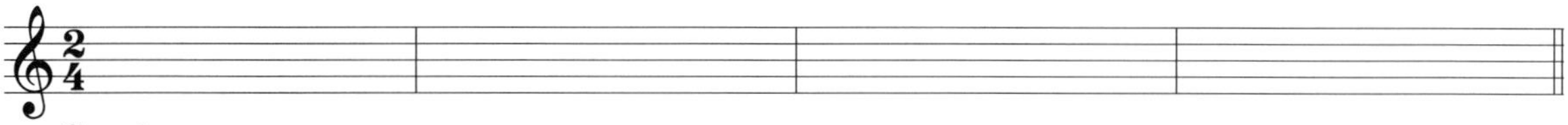

C: I – – – – – – –

3. Describe the effect of the harmony underlying the melody you wrote in question 2.

____

____

4. Use roman numerals to show three "opening" harmonic progressions.

______________ ______________ ______________

5. What is meant by a "closing" progression? ______________________

____

6. Compose a single-line melody based on the indicated chord progression.

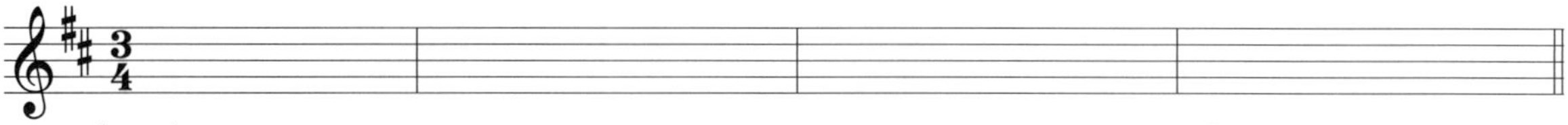

b: i – – V

7. Is the harmonic progression in question 6 an "opening" or a "closing" progression? ______________

8. Compose a single-line melody based on the indicated harmonic progression.

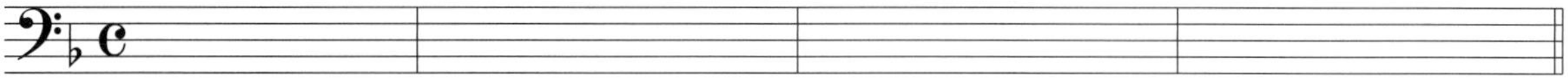

F: IV – V (or vii°—) I

9. Is the harmonic progression in question 8 an "opening" or a "closing" progression? ______________

10. Compose a single-line melody based on the indicated harmonic progression.

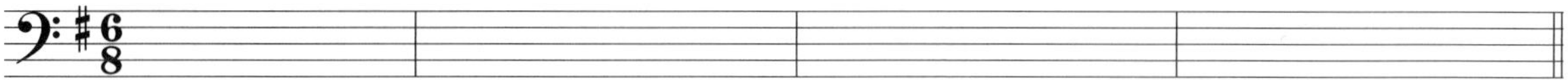

e: i iv V i

11. Compose a single-line melody based on the indicated harmonic progression.

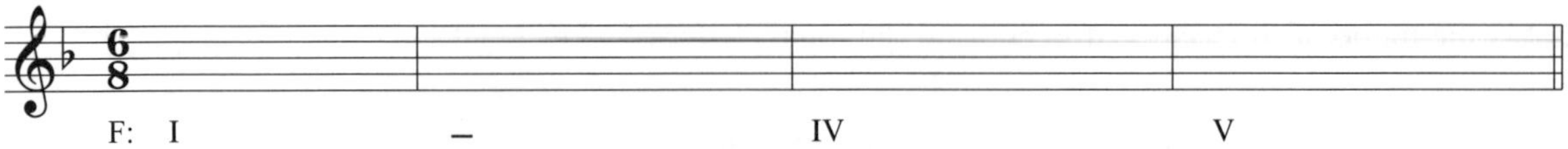

F: I – IV V

12. Compose a single-line melody based on the indicated chord name and quality.

Bmi C♯dim F♯ G

13. What term is used to describe the harmonic progression above? ______________________

14. Which progression is most conclusive? ______________

a. I–IV b. IV–V c. V–iii d. V–I e. V–vi

15. Which progression is most conclusive? ______________

a. I–IV b. vii°–vi c. V–i d. V–iii e. V–vi f. IV–V

16. Write roman numerals to identify the chords that underlie the melody.

d: ___ ___ ___ ___

17. Write roman numerals to identify the chords that underlie the melody.

F: ___ ___ ___ ___

18. Identify the chords by name and quality that underlie the melody.

___ ___ ___ ___ ___ ___ ___ ___ ___

___ ___ ___ ___ ___ ___ ___ ___

Chapter 3.0
Triads in Root Position: Doubling and Spacing

This chapter will begin the mastery of the techniques of writing chords and leading voices smoothly from one chord to another. The first step is to become acquainted with "figured bass" symbols. These symbols constitute a form of shorthand notation and also are used for analysis. Next, the focus will be on principles of doubling and spacing of triads in root position. The basis for this work will be the four-voice chorus. Although this aspect of the study of harmony is rather "mechanical," it nevertheless is vital, both to effective writing and the understanding of factors that affect linear action in harmonic music. The latter, especially, still contributes to musical fluency and effective performance after being around for many, many years.

3.1 A triad is in ROOT POSITION if its root is the lowest tone.

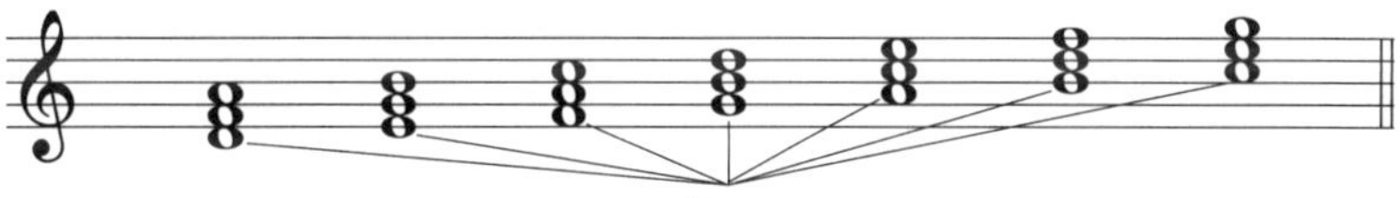

In each of the triads above, the root is the lowest tone.

These triads are in ____________ position.

root

3.2 Write triads in root position as directed. (Capital letter = major; lowercase letter = minor.)

(1) (2) (3)

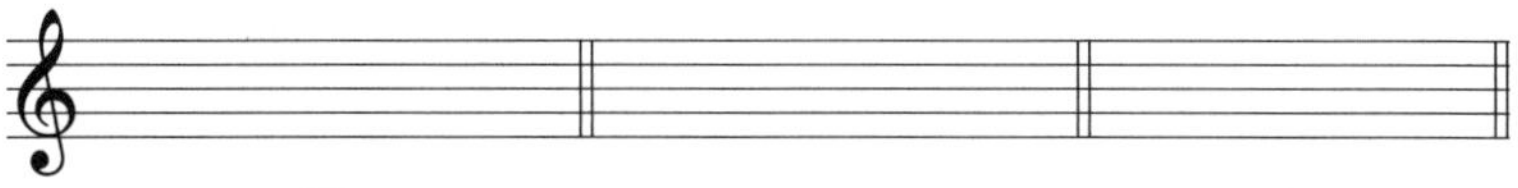

E♭ g B

(1) (2) (3)

3.3 Write triads in root position as directed.

(1) (2) (3)

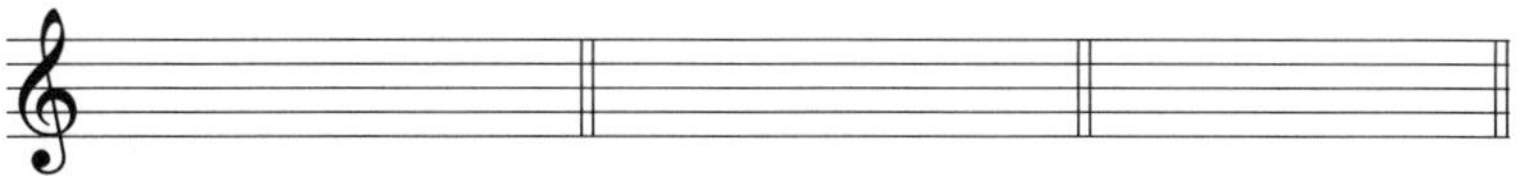

c♯ E g♯

(1) (2) (3)

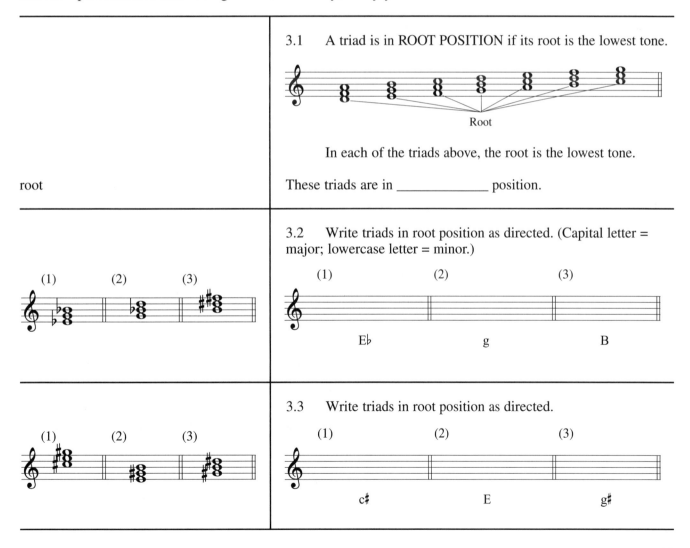

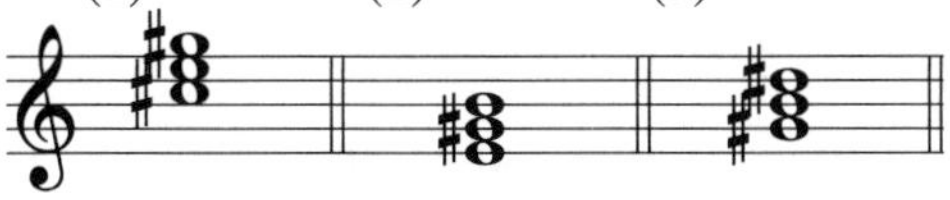

(2)

3.4 Which of the triads below is in root position? __________

(1) (2) (3) (4)

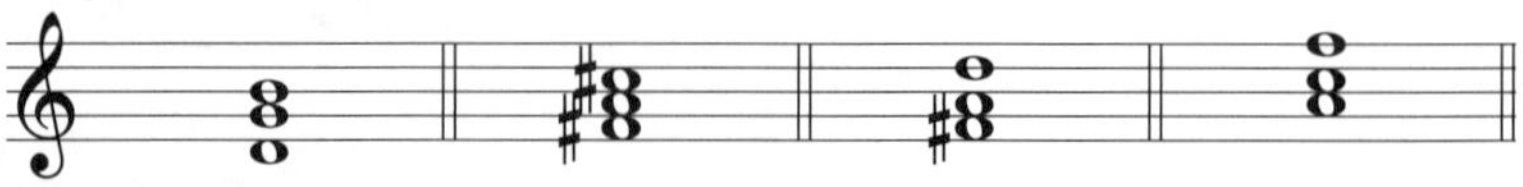

root

3.5 The intervals of a fifth and third occur over the lowest tone of a triad in root position. These intervals sometimes are represented by the numbers 5 and 3. These are called FIGURED BASS SYMBOLS.*

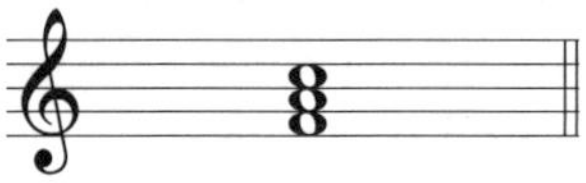

(Note that the greater number is always placed above the smaller.)

Figured bass symbols are merely a listing of the intervals which occur above the lowest note. The numbers 5 and 3 beneath a note indicate a triad in ____________ position.

*Figured bass symbols were widely used during the baroque era as a shorthand notation for players of keyboard instruments. They will be used here for the purpose of analysis and as an aid in teaching the principles of part writing. They may also be useful as an analytical tool in the future as well as to better understand the evolution of pop and jazz chord symbols. Please see p. 355 for information on those chord symbols.

flatted
(or lowered a half step)

3.6 Accidentals applied to the upper notes are shown in the figured bass.*

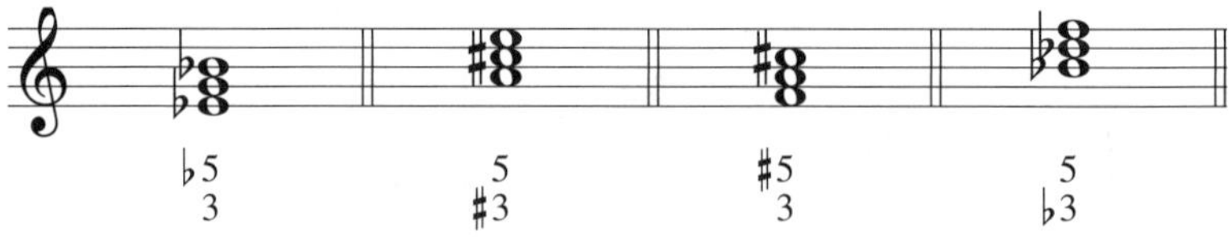

The symbol ♭5 means that the note a fifth above the lowest note is ____________.

*Accidentals applied to the lowest note, or to its duplication one or more octaves higher, are not indicated.

3.7 Figured bass is a shorthand system of indicating notes above the bass (the lowest part). There are several special signs and conventions that must be learned in connection with the use of figured bass symbols.

A slash through a number means that the note represented by the number is RAISED a half step.

Observe the use of this sign below:

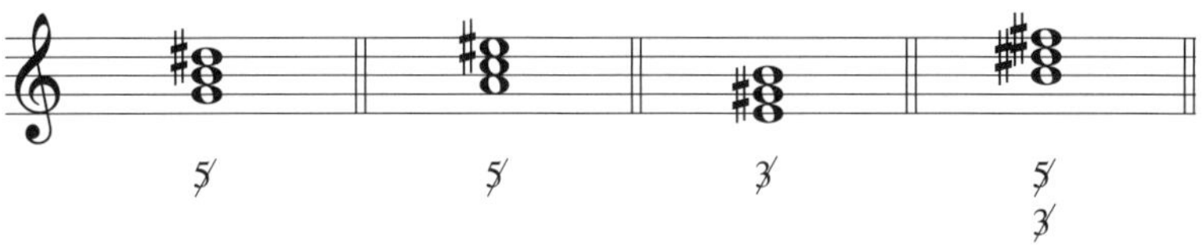

Does the symbol ♯5 mean the same as the symbol 5̸? ________

Yes
(But see the next frame.)

3.8 The figured bass symbols 5̸ and 3̸ do not always refer to the use of sharps (♯). The raising of a tone by a half step is sometimes accomplished by a natural (♮), or a double-sharp (𝄪). The key signature (if any) must be taken into account. Compare the three triads below:

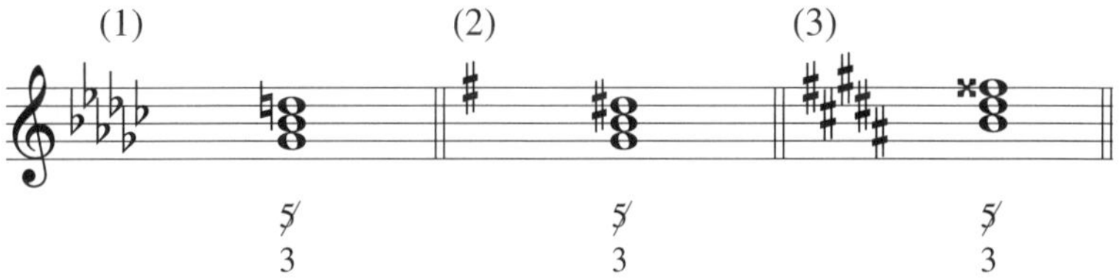

In (1) the fifth of the triad has been raised a half step by the use of a natural (♮); in (2) a sharp (♯) has been used to produce the same result; in (3) a double-sharp (𝄪) has been used.

The symbol 3̸ might be used in place of *any* of the following:

𝄪3, ♯3, or ♮3. (True/False) ____________

True

3.9 Check (✓) the correct option:

1. A slash through a number means that the note represented by the number is raised a half step.
2. A slash through a number calls for a sharp.

True statements:

(1) _______ (2) _______ Both _______ Neither _______

(1) ✓

3.10 Write the triads and apply accidentals as indicated by the figured bass symbols.

(Continued on the next page)

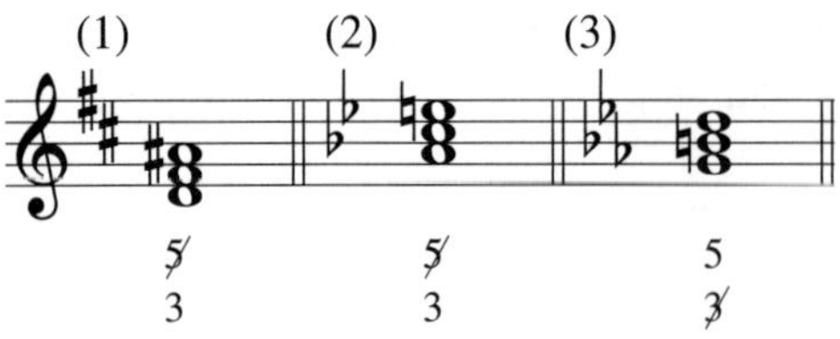

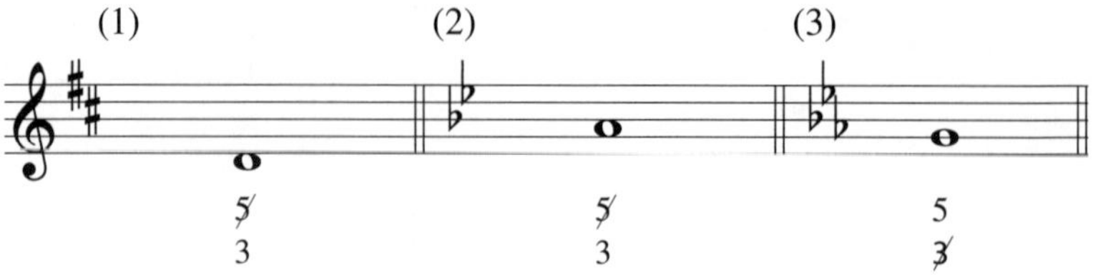

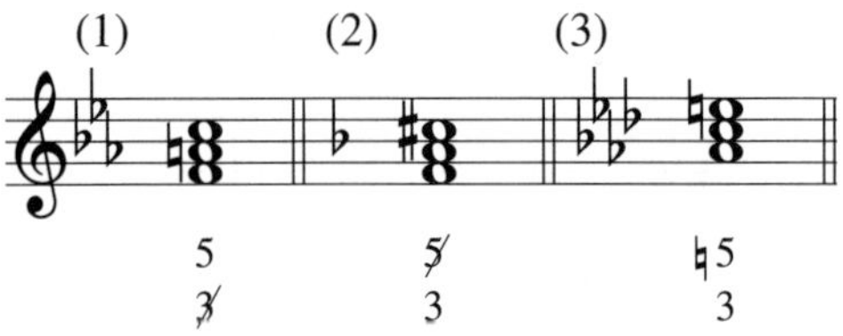

3.11 Write the triads and apply accidentals as indicated by the figured bass symbols.

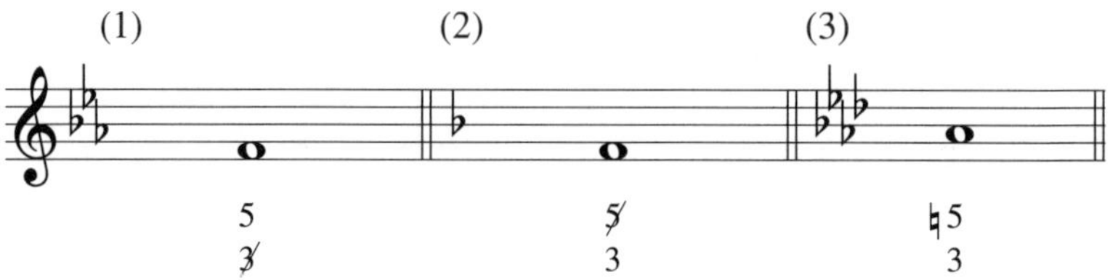

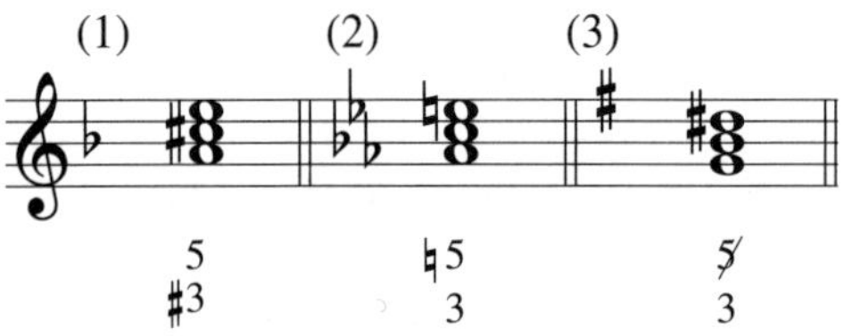

3.12 Notice in (3) of the preceding frame that the raised fifth is indicated by showing the actual accidental used. *Alterations* often are indicated in this manner. No difficulty should be experienced in interpreting such symbols if accidentals are applied exactly as directed by the figured bass.

Write the triads and apply accidentals as directed.

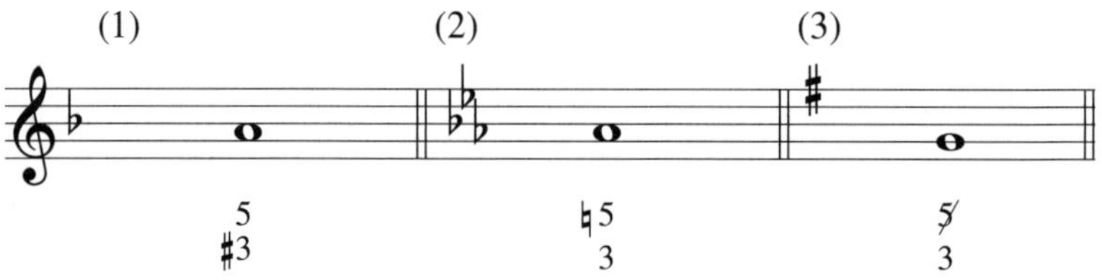

accidental

3.13 An accidental NOT associated with a number refers to the interval of a *third* above the lowest note.

Examine carefully the three examples below:

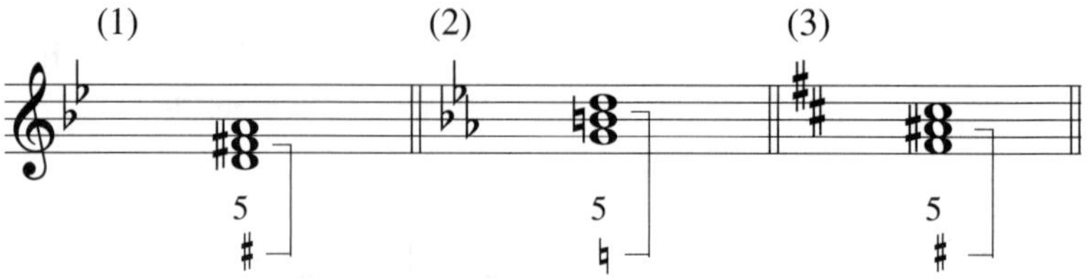

An alteration of the third above the lowest note may be indicated merely by using the appropriate _____________.

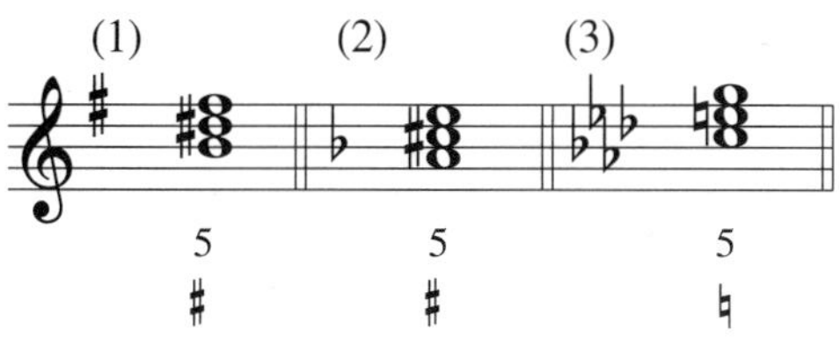

3.14 Write the triads as indicated by the figured bass symbols.

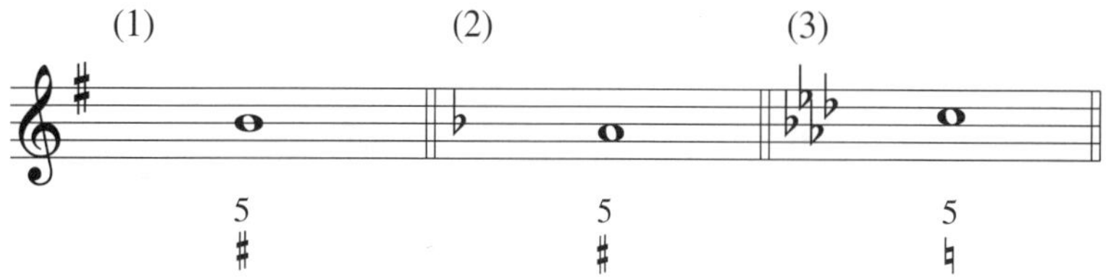

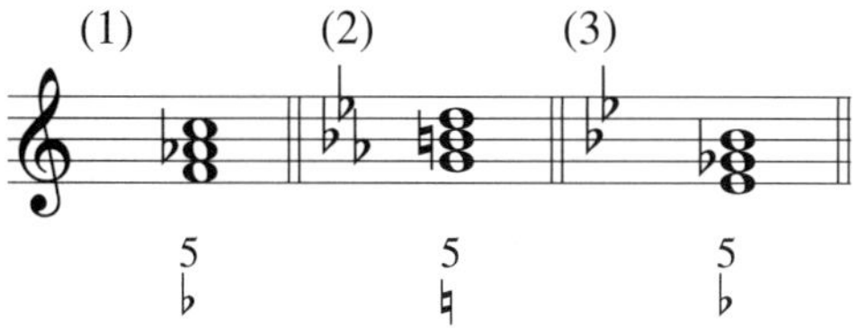

3.15 Write the triads as indicated by the figured bass symbols.

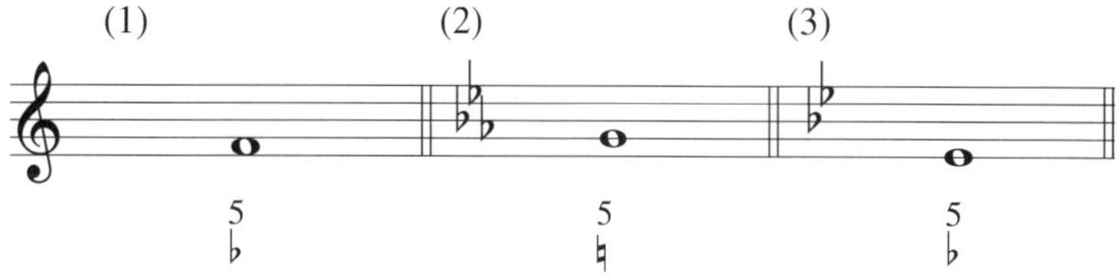

root

3.16 Since figured bass symbols are a shorthand method of indicating chord structures, use only those figures that are necessary. Generally no figuration is given for a triad in root position except to show the alteration (by accidental) of either the third or fifth of the triad.

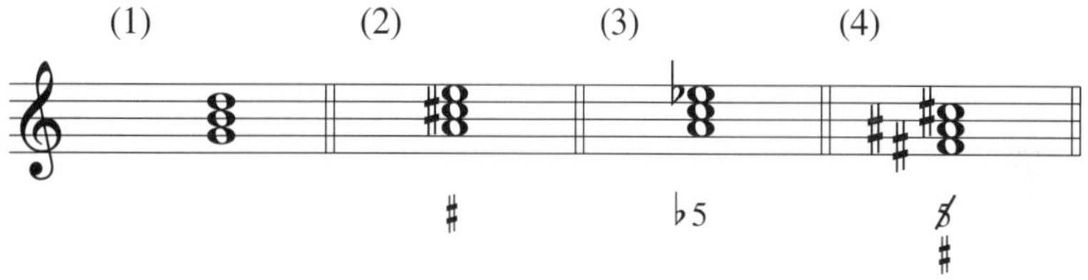

In (1) no figuration is necessary as neither the third nor the fifth is altered; a sharp is used in (2) to show that the third is raised from C to C♯; the symbol ♭5 is used in (3) to show the alteration of E to E♭; the figures 5̸ and ♯ are used in (4) to show that the fifth and third are both raised a half step.

No figuration under a bass note indicates the following:

1. No accidentals appear in the upper parts.

2. The sonority is a triad in ____________ position.

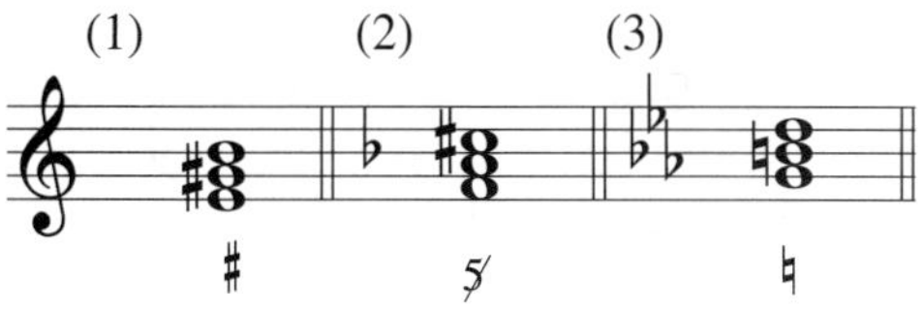

3.17 Write the triads as indicated by the figured bass symbols.

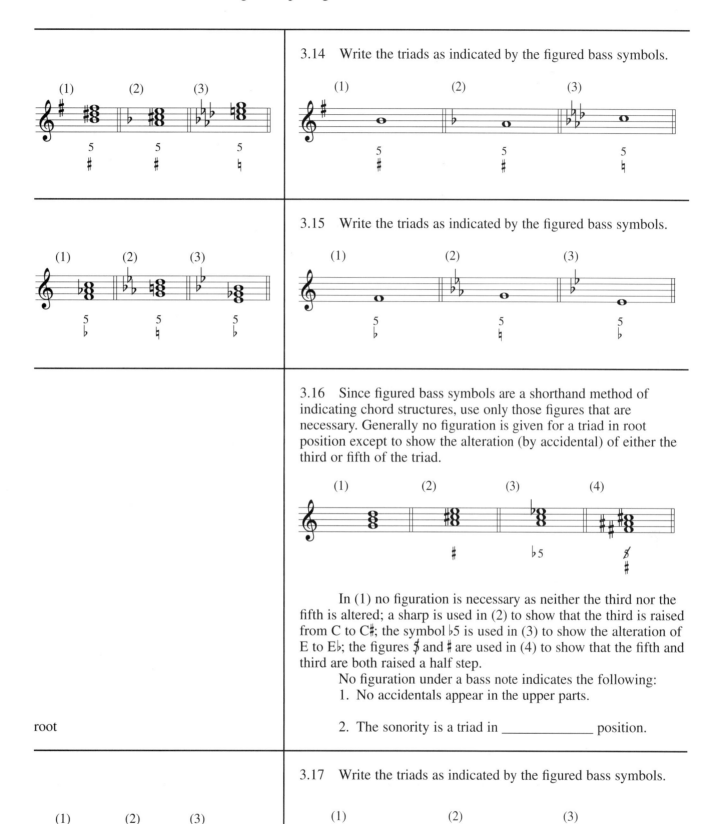

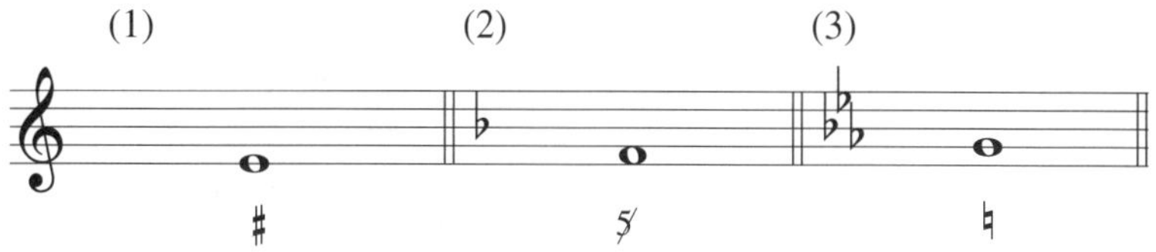

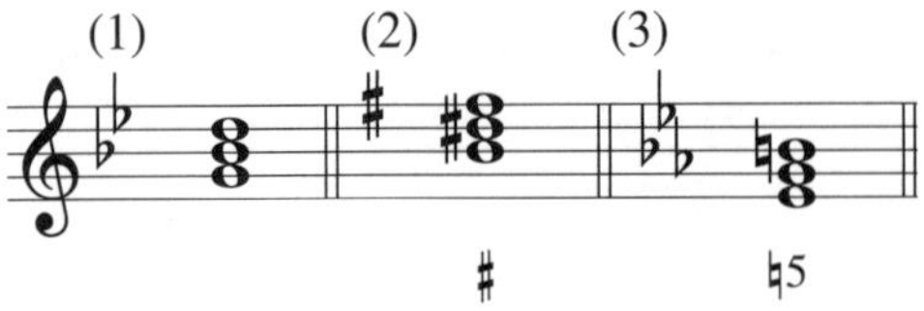

3.18 Write the triads as indicated by the figured bass symbols.

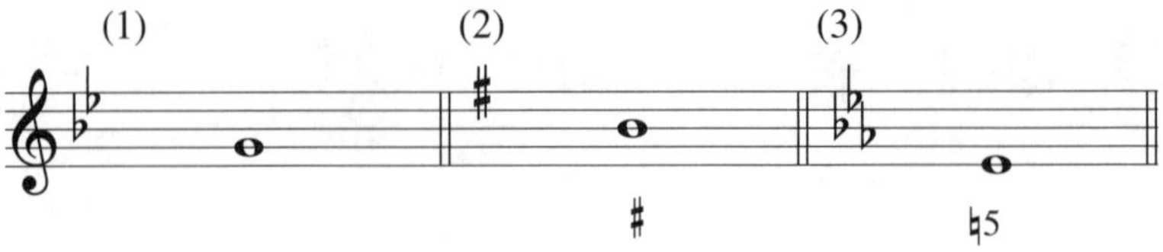

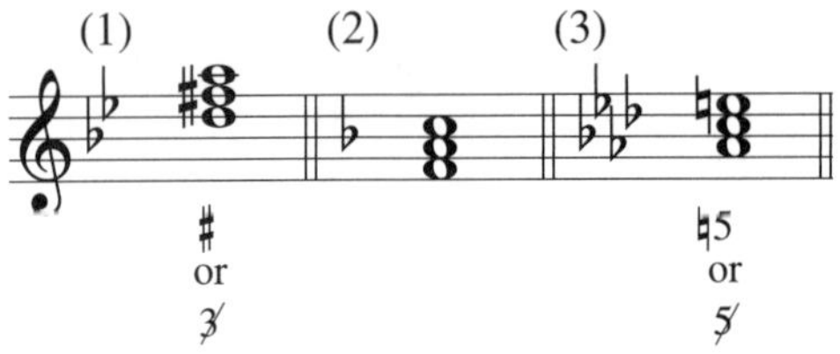

3.19 Write figured bass symbols beneath each triad as needed.

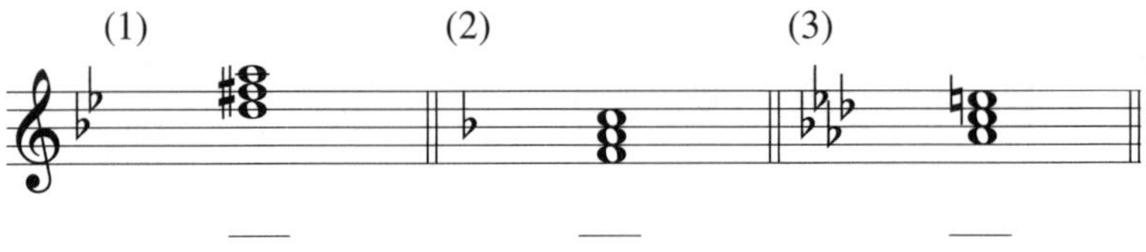

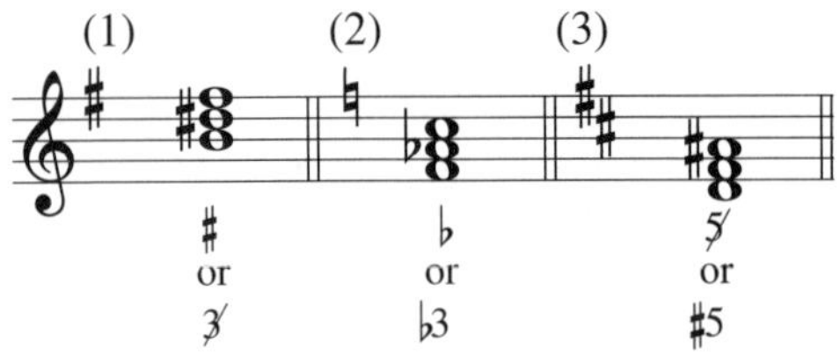

3.20 Write figured bass symbols beneath each triad as needed.

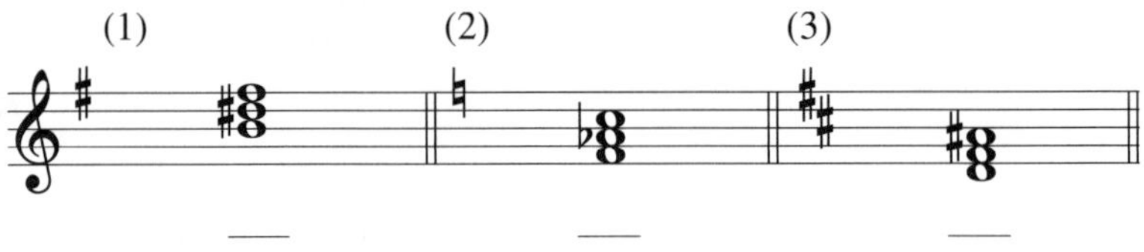

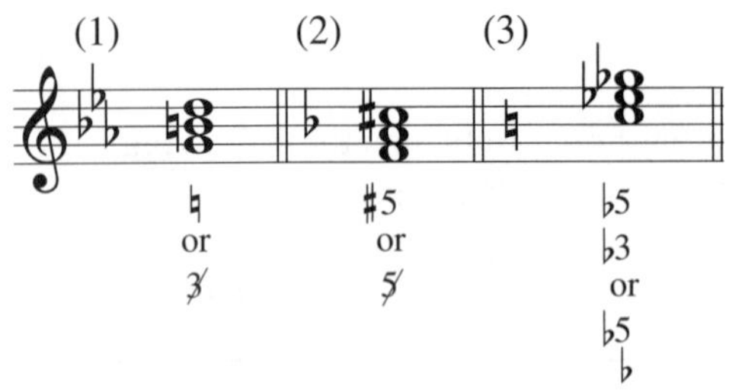

3.21 Write figured bass symbols beneath each triad as needed.

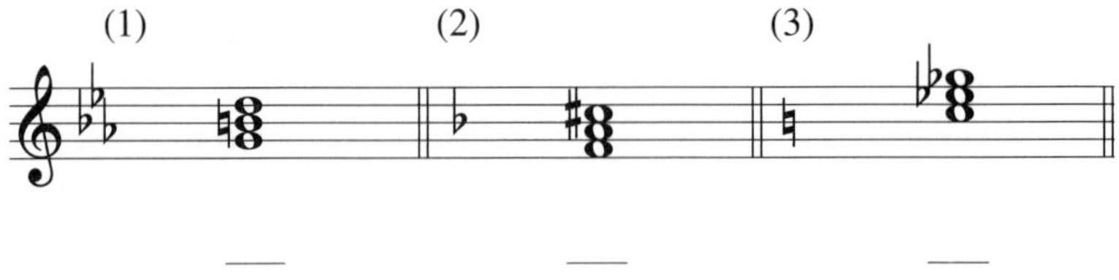

Expository Frame

3.22 Figured bass symbols provide a simple way to indicate chord sonorities and have many other uses, as will be seen later. Interpreting these symbols is easy, if you remember this fact: *Figured bass symbols always indicate intervals above the lowest voice; they are a record of intervals from the bass upward.*

(No response required.)	Other important points to remember are these: 1. A triad in root position usually requires no figuration unless either the third or fifth is altered. 2. A slash through a number means that the note represented by the number is raised a half step. 3. An accidental in the figured bass that is not associated with a number refers to the interval of a third above the bass.
three	3.23 Now, to turn to the specific techniques of *doubling* (assignment of same chord member to two or more voices) and *spacing* (placement of the chord members). *Since triads consist of three tones, no problem of doubling exists if these tones are to be given to three instruments or voices, or if a three-part texture is used in writing for a keyboard instrument. In such cases the triads are complete if the root is given to one part, the third to another, and the fifth to still another.* When working with triads, doubling is generally not a problem unless more than ____________ instruments or voices are used.
four	3.24 Much of the music composed since the middle of the eighteenth century is based on a four-part texture. The utility of this texture has been proved by more than two centuries of use. It provides an agreeable sonority without imposing undue problems of doubling, or of voice leading. The texture that has prevailed as the basis of much of the music for the last 200 years is the ____________-part texture.
(1) Soprano (3) Tenor (2) Alto (4) Bass *(Any order.)*	3.25 Although this study is not devoted exclusively to four-part writing, this texture is so prevalent in music of the baroque, classical, and romantic eras that some time needs to be spent studying it. The more mechanical aspects of part writing will be presented in terms of the four-part chorus, which consists of the soprano, alto, tenor, and bass voices. It is convenient to use this medium as a basis for study since it expresses clearly the four-part texture and the principles upon which attention needs to be focused. Music for the piano or instrumental ensembles may often cloud these principles, yet that music is not irrelevant and will be included later on. Name the voices which constitute the four-part chorus. (1) ____________ (3) ____________ (2) ____________ (4) ____________

3.26 Learn the approximate range for each of the voices.

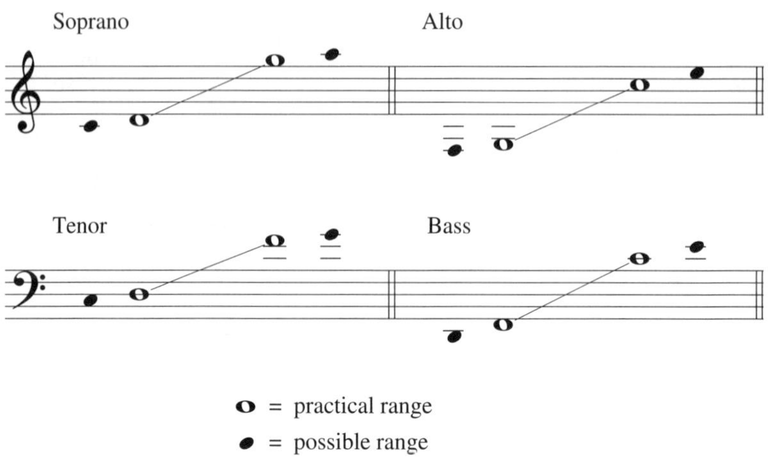

(*No response required.*)

It is impossible to establish absolute limits for voices. Individual singers vary, and such factors as the dynamic level and the color desired in a given passage help determine the appropriateness of particular tones. Generally, though, voices should be kept within the practical ranges given above.

(Study these ranges before continuing with the next frame.)

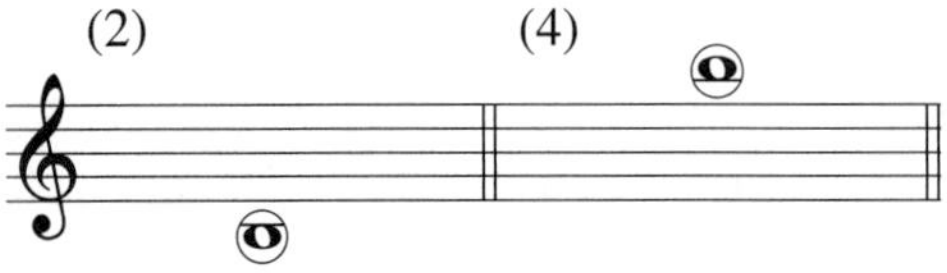

3.27 Circle the notes that are *outside* the possible range of the *soprano* voice.

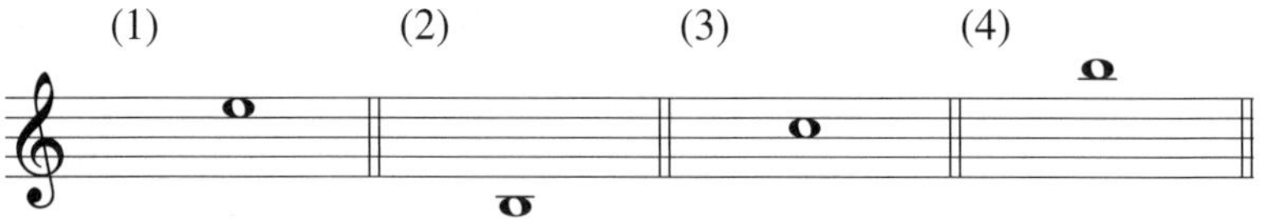

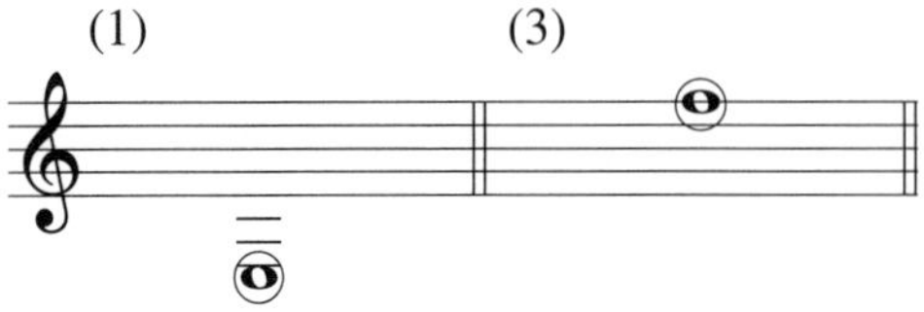

3.28 Circle the notes that are *outside* the possible range of the *alto* voice.

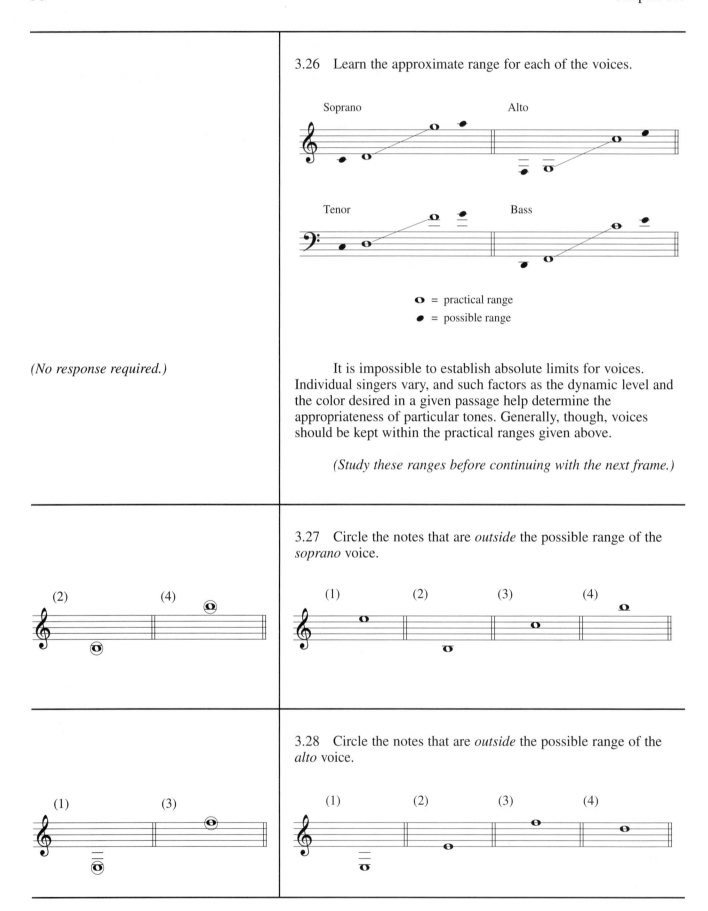

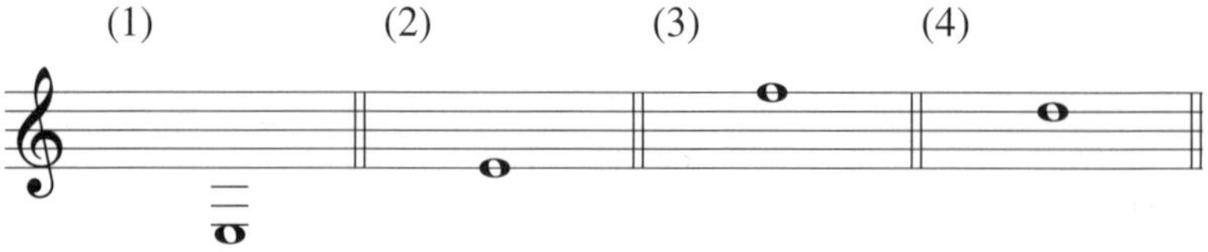

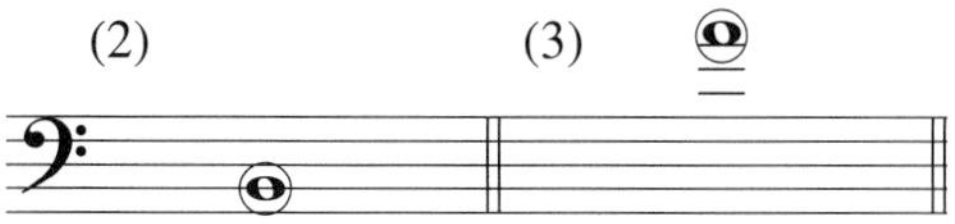

3.29 Circle the notes that are *outside* the possible range of the *tenor* voice.

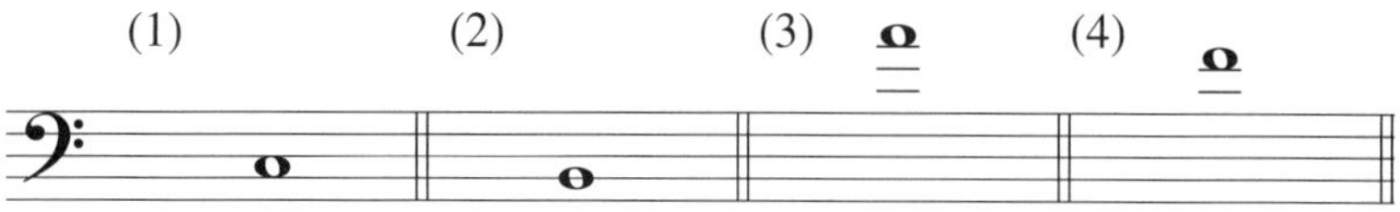

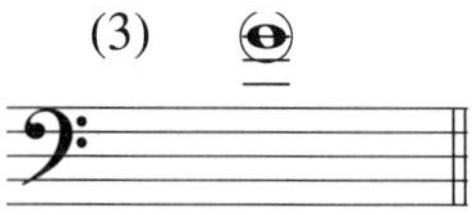

3.30 Circle the note(s) that are *outside* the possible range of the *bass* voice.

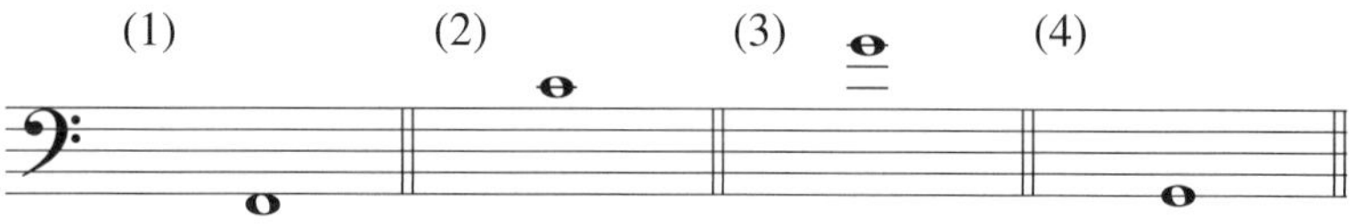

3.31 The voices of the four-part chorus are notated in several configurations on the grand staff as illustrated below:

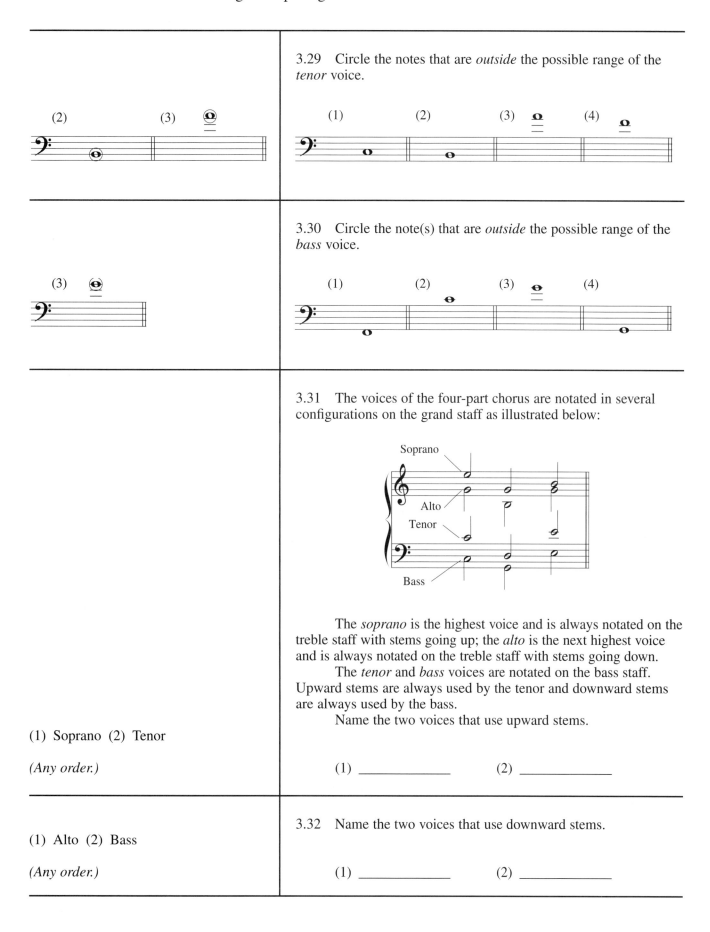

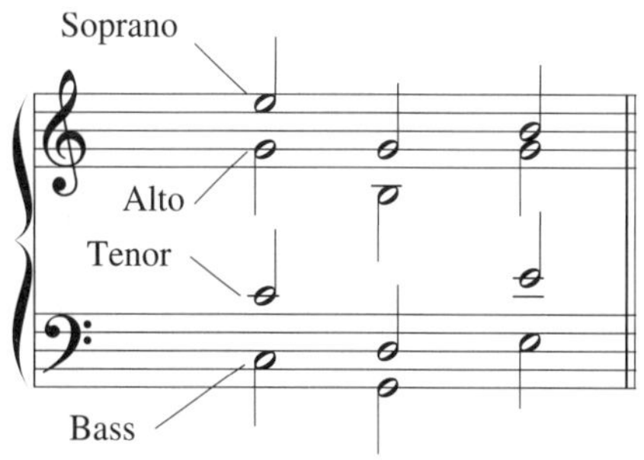

The *soprano* is the highest voice and is always notated on the treble staff with stems going up; the *alto* is the next highest voice and is always notated on the treble staff with stems going down.

The *tenor* and *bass* voices are notated on the bass staff. Upward stems are always used by the tenor and downward stems are always used by the bass.

Name the two voices that use upward stems.

(1) ____________ (2) ____________

(1) Soprano (2) Tenor

(Any order.)

3.32 Name the two voices that use downward stems.

(1) ____________ (2) ____________

(1) Alto (2) Bass

(Any order.)

3.33 Place stems correctly on the notes of each chord by renotating the examples as half notes.

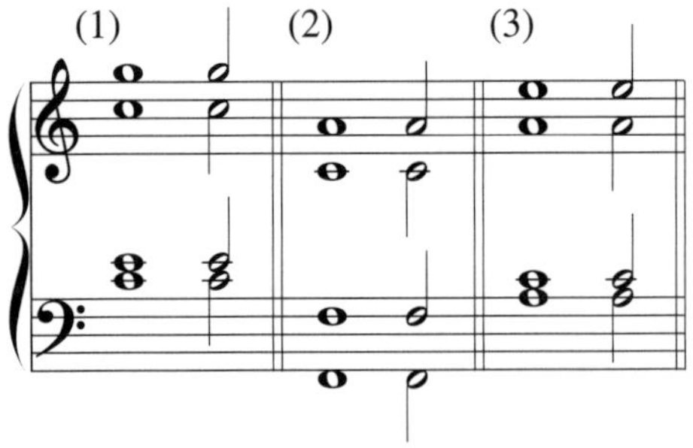

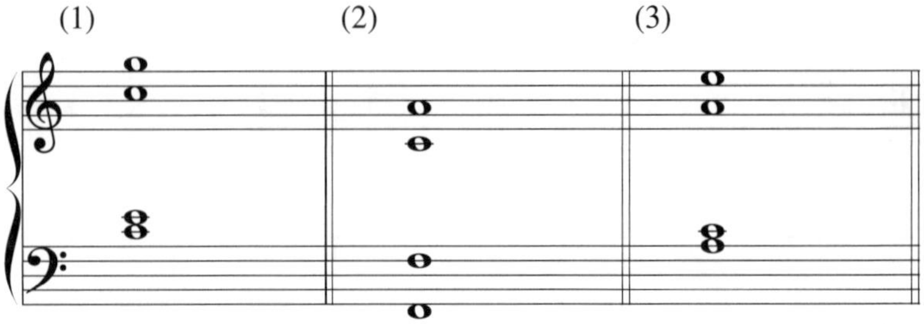

bass

3.34 Sometimes two voices sing the same pitch (doubling); that is, they are said to "double" each other. Notice how this is notated.

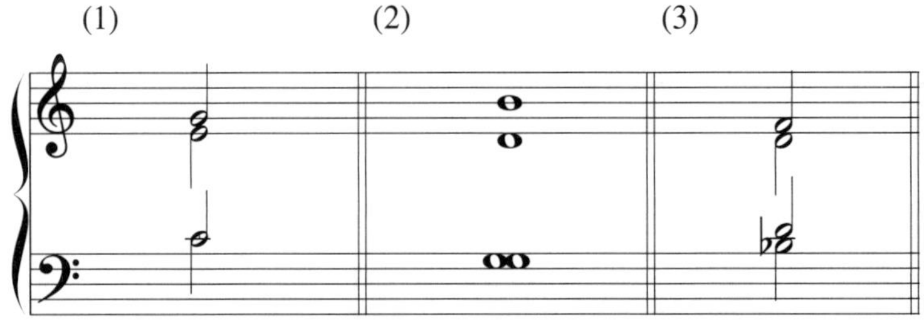

When two voices are to sing the same pitch, two stems are attached to one notehead, or two notes are used when there are whole notes involved. When two voices on different staves sing the same pitch (alto and tenor), it is necessary to write both notes. In two of the above examples the upward stems attached to the notes on the bass staff represent the tenor voice; downward stems

represent the _____________ voice.

alto (and) tenor

3.35 In the normal distribution of voices the soprano takes the highest pitch, the alto the next highest, the tenor the next, and the bass takes the lowest pitch.

When the normal distribution of voices is not observed, the parts are said to be "crossed." Which two voices are "crossed" in the example below?

The _____________ and _____________.

soprano (and) alto

3.36 Which two voices are "crossed" in the example below?

The ____________ and ____________.

(1) Soprano

(2) Alto

(3) Tenor

(4) Bass

3.37 The impetus of melodic writing will cause an occasional crossing of voices in more advanced writing. For the present, however, normal distribution should be observed.

List the voices in their normal distribution *from the highest to the lowest.*

(1) ____________

(2) ____________

(3) ____________

(4) ____________

bass

3.38 The "spacing" of a chord concerns primarily the intervals that separate the three upper voices (soprano, alto, and tenor) from one another. Which of the four voices can *not* be called an upper voice? The ____________.

3.39 The most satisfactory spacing of a chord usually requires that the intervals that separate the soprano and alto, and the alto and tenor, should not exceed an octave.

In (1) and (2) below, no two adjacent upper voices are separated by an interval greater than an octave. In (3), however, the interval between the tenor and alto voices is an eleventh. If carried on for several chords this type of spacing would cause an "empty" effect, so it should be avoided.

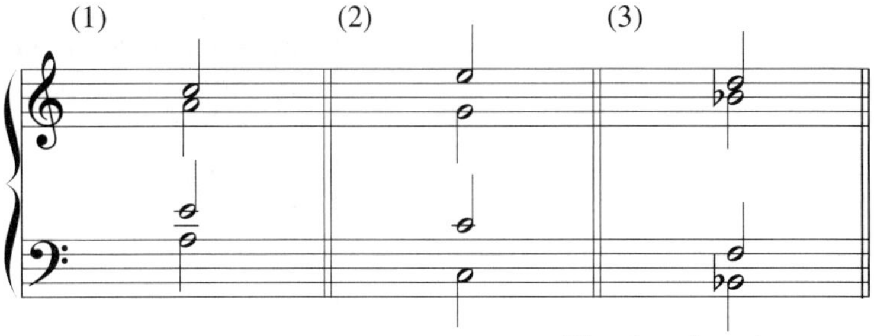

(Continued on the next page)

octave

What is the largest interval by which adjacent upper voices should be separated? The _____________.

---

(2)
(There is a 10th between the soprano and alto.)

3.40 In which case below is there an excessive interval between adjacent upper voices? _____________

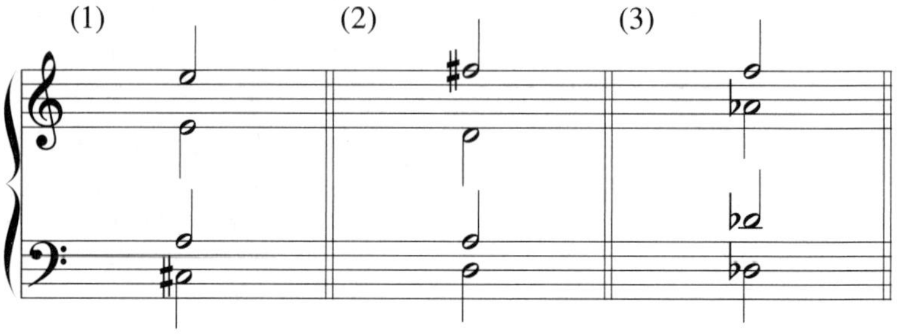

Note: *Not all of the triad tones above are in root position.*

---

(1)
(There is a 10th between the alto and tenor.)

3.41 In which case below is there an excessive interval between adjacent upper voices? _____________

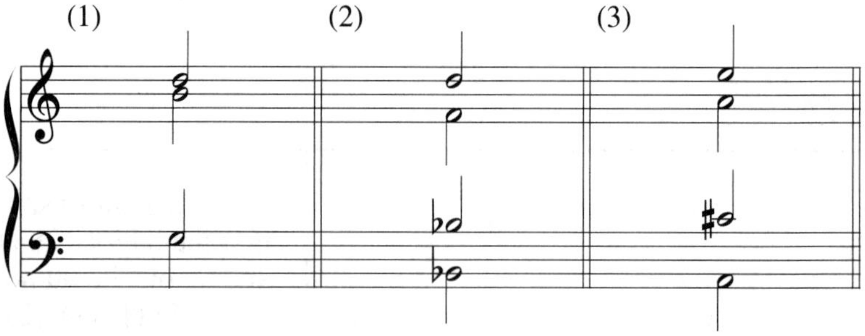

No

3.42 Notice in (3) of the preceding frame that the interval between the tenor and bass is greater than an octave. *This is satisfactory.* An interval as large as a twelfth may separate the tenor from the bass without resulting in an unpleasant sonority. It is the upper voices *(soprano, alto,* and *tenor)* that must observe the octave limitation.

Are there any irregularities in the spacing of the following chords? _____________

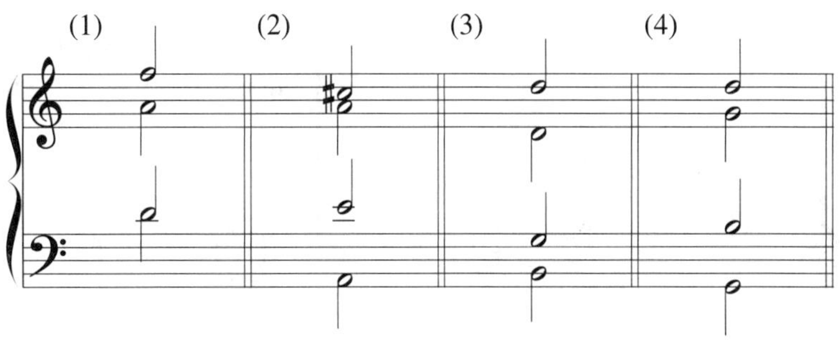

Note: *Not all of the triad tones above are in root position.*

Yes
(In [2] there is more than an octave between the alto and tenor.)

3.43 Are there any irregularities in the spacing of the chords below? _____________

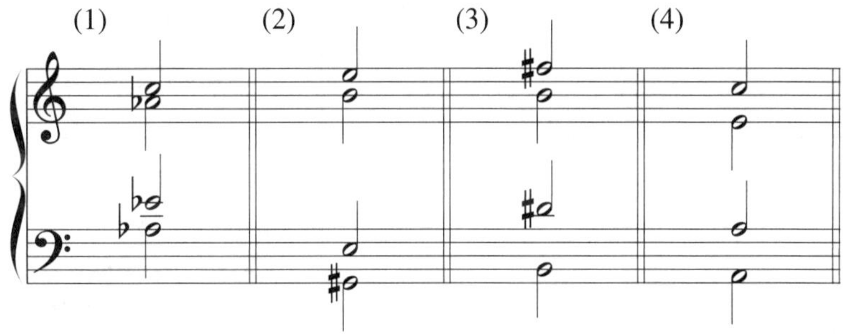

Note: *Not all of the triad tones above are in root position.*

---

root

3.44 If the three tones of a triad are to be given to four voices, it is evident that one of the tones must be doubled. Doubled tones are bracketed in the examples below. In each case the triad tone that is doubled is the (root/third/fifth) _____________.

THE C MAJOR TRIAD

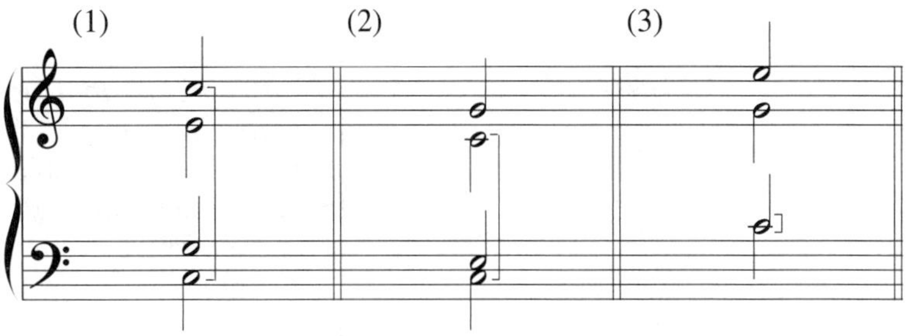

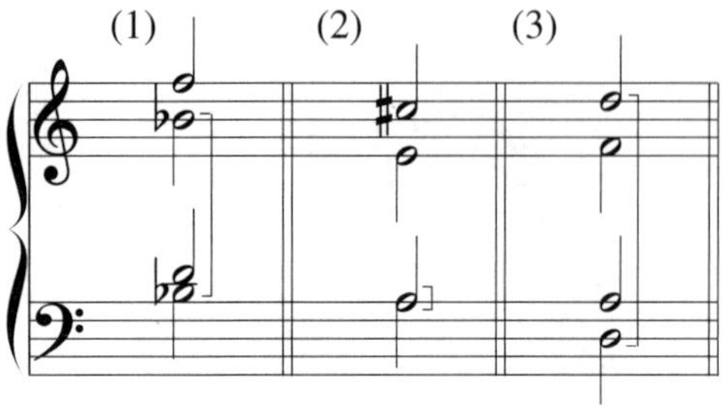

3.45 Draw brackets (as in the preceding frame) to indicate the doubled tones in each triad.

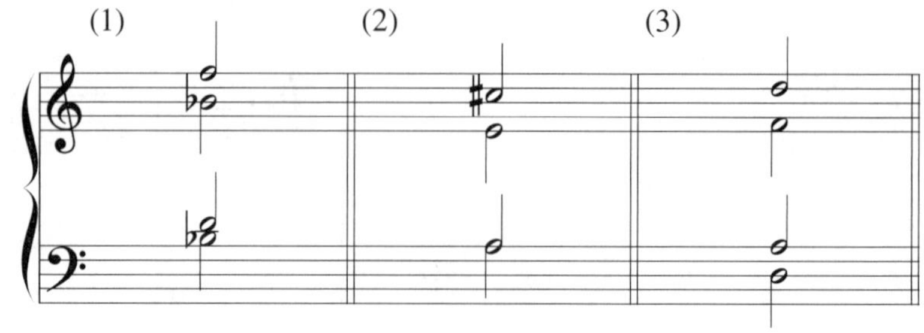

---

root

3.46 The preceding two frames have demonstrated the usual doubling for triads in root position.

Learn this principle:

When a triad is in root position the BASS is usually doubled.

If the bass is doubled in a root position triad, which triad tone is doubled? The (root/third/fifth) _____________.

---

fifth

3.47 When a triad is in root position the BASS is doubled by one of the upper voices. The remaining two voices take the third and fifth of the triad.

A triad in root position will have two roots, one third, and one _____________.

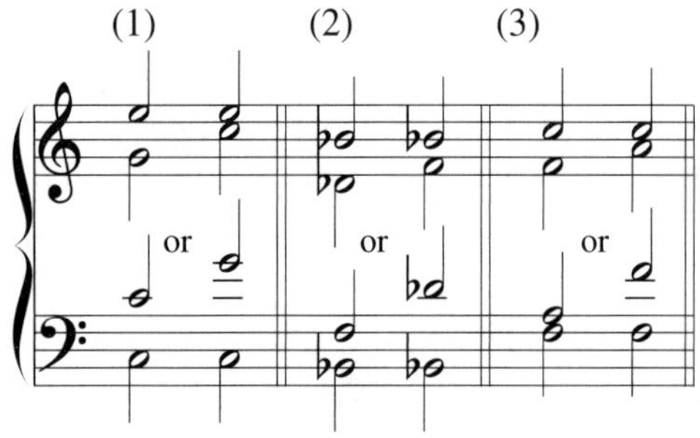

3.48 Add the alto and tenor voices to complete each chord.

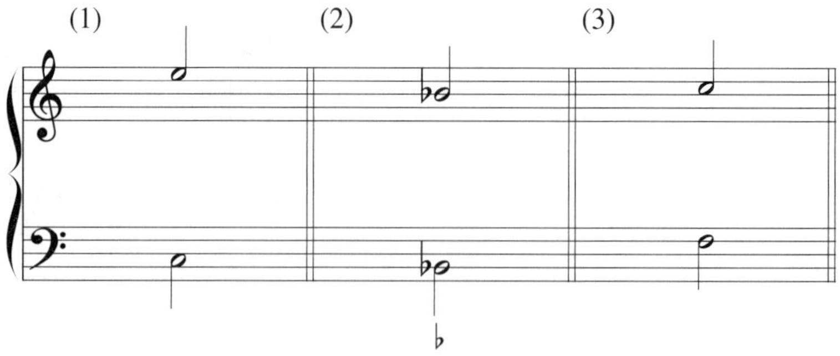

Before looking at the answers check carefully each of the following items:

1. Is the bass doubled?
2. Are the third and fifth present?
3. Are the voices in normal distribution?
4. Is the interval between adjacent upper voices limited to an octave?
5. Are figured bass symbols realized correctly?

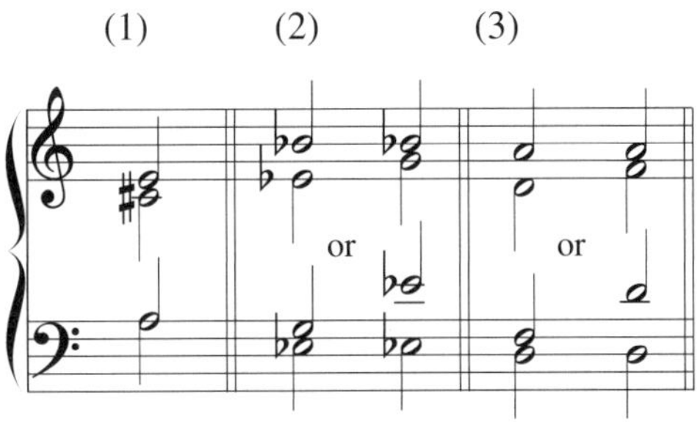

3.49 Add the alto and tenor voices to complete each chord.

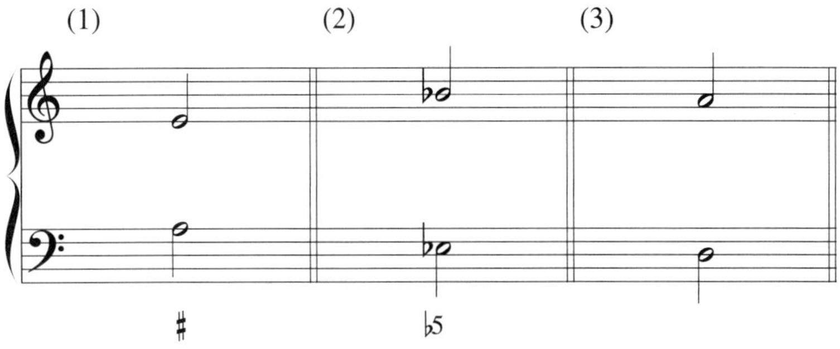

(Before looking at the answers check carefully the five items stated in the preceding frame.)

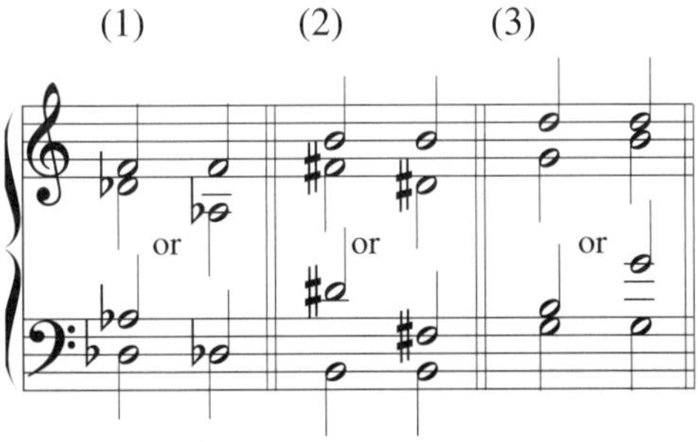

3.50 Add the alto and tenor voices to complete each chord.

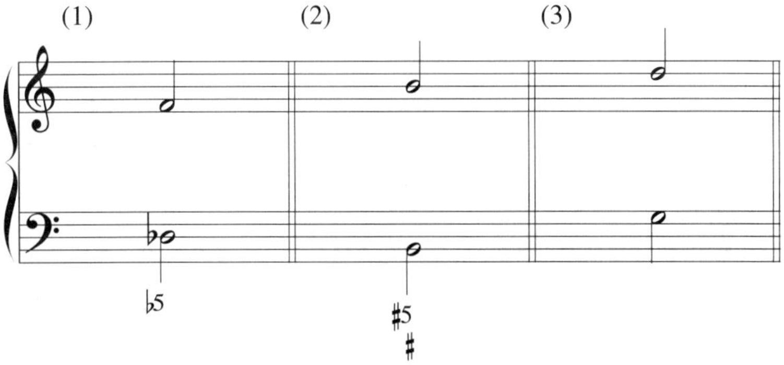

(Before looking at the answers check carefully the five items stated in Frame 3.48.)

Incorrect doubling
(There are two thirds.)

3.51 What is the part writing error in the chord below?

____

The soprano and alto are more than an octave apart.

3.52 What is the part writing error in the chord below?

____

____

Incorrect doubling

(There is no fifth in the chord.)

3.53 What is the part writing error in the chord below?

____

3.54 In the example below, the tones of the C major triad have been spaced two different ways.

(1) (2)

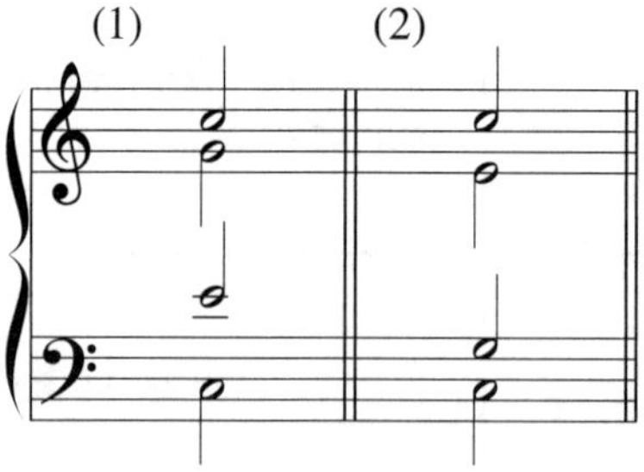

The spacing in (1) is called CLOSE STRUCTURE, and the spacing in (2) is called OPEN STRUCTURE.

Close and *open* structure concern the way the three upper voices are spaced. The spacing of triad tones results in two kinds of structures: these are called ____________ and ____________ structure.

close (and) open

(Any order.)

3.55 Observe in (1) of the preceding frame that the upper voices are as *close* together as they can be. Reading down from the soprano each successive voice takes the next available chord tone.

Soprano – C
Alto – G
Tenor – E

There are no vacant triad tones between the upper voices when a triad is in ____________ structure.

close

3.56 When a triad is in *open* structure there is a vacant triad tone between the soprano and alto, and between the alto and tenor voices. This causes the interval between the soprano and tenor voices to be greater than an octave.

The example below shows a chord in *open* structure. Indicate (with a black notehead) the *unoccupied* triad tone between each of the three upper voices.

THE A MINOR TRIAD

Write Here

3.57 Below is another example of *open* structure. Indicate (with a black notehead) the *unoccupied* triad tone between each of the three upper voices.

THE F MAJOR TRIAD

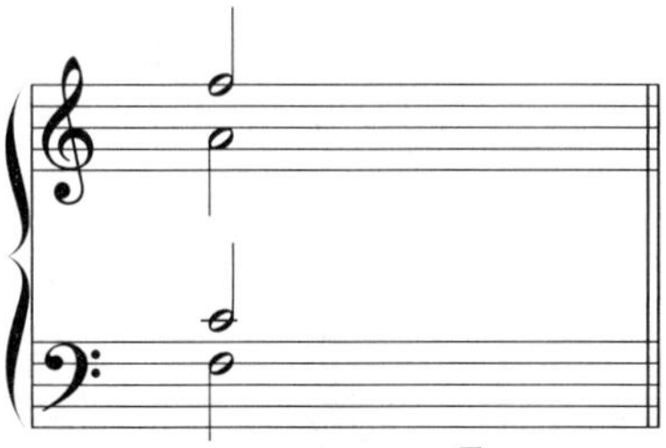

Write Here

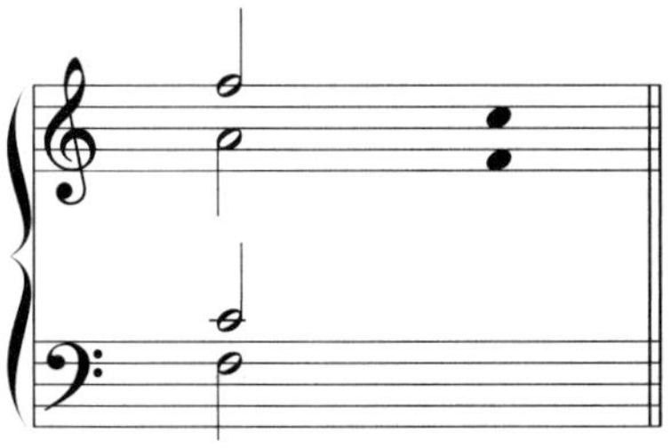

3.58 If, when reading down from the soprano, one finds that each successive voice (soprano, alto, and tenor) takes the next available triad tone, the chord is in ____________ structure.

close

(1) and (4)

3.59 Which of the chords below are in *close* structure?

____

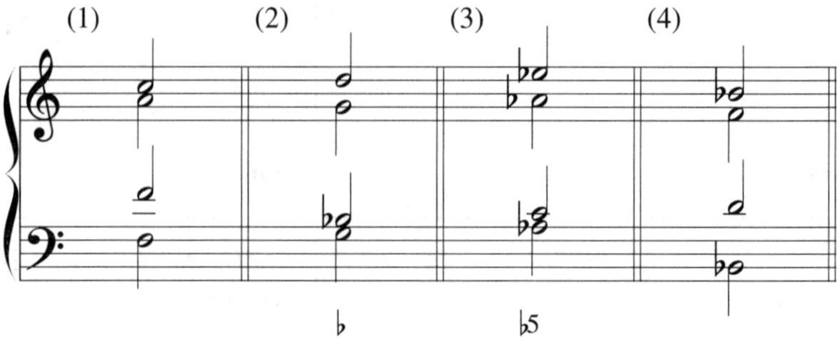

(2) and (4)

3.60 Which of the chords below are in *close* structure?

____

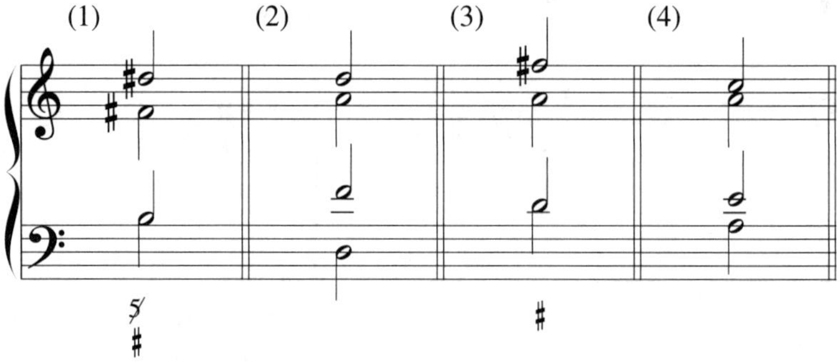

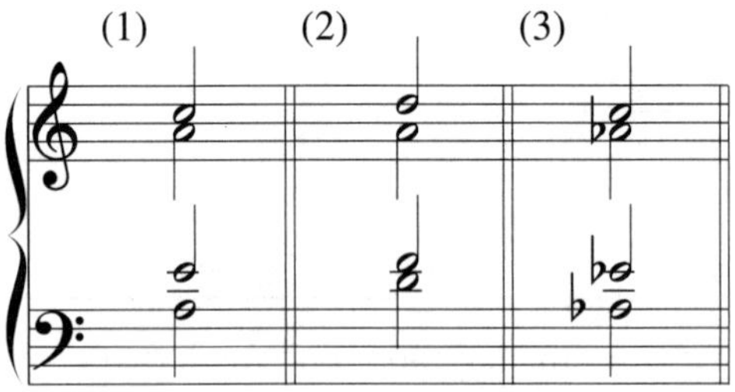

3.61 Write the alto and tenor voices so that each chord is in *close* structure.

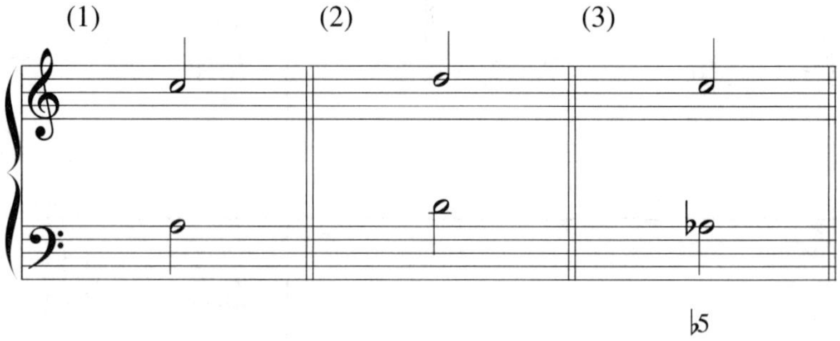

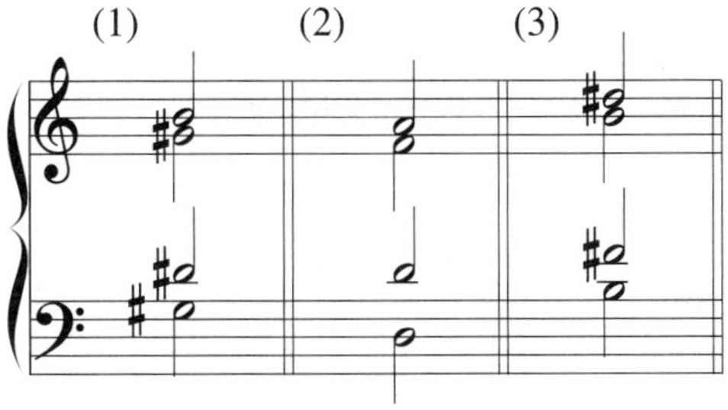

3.62 Write the alto and tenor voices so that each chord is in *close* structure.

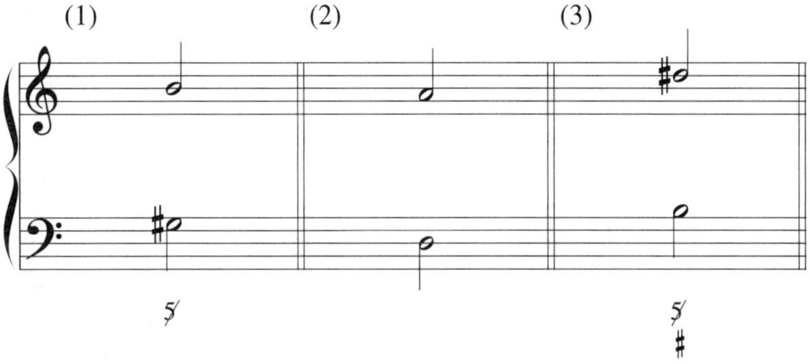

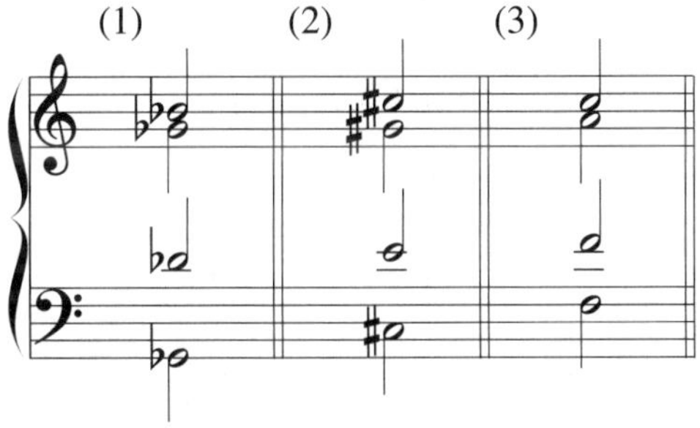

3.63 Write the alto and tenor voices so that each chord is in *close* structure.

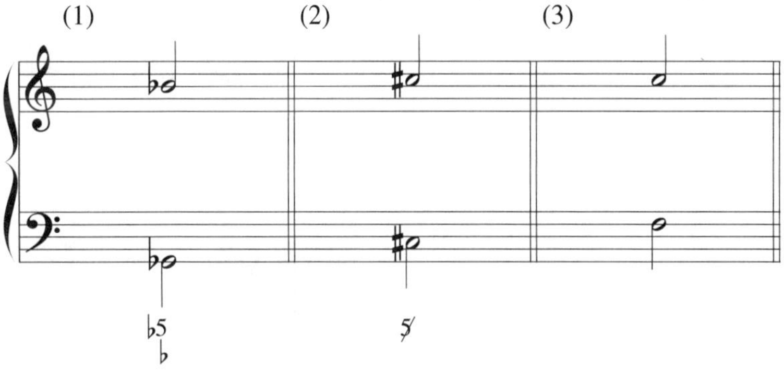

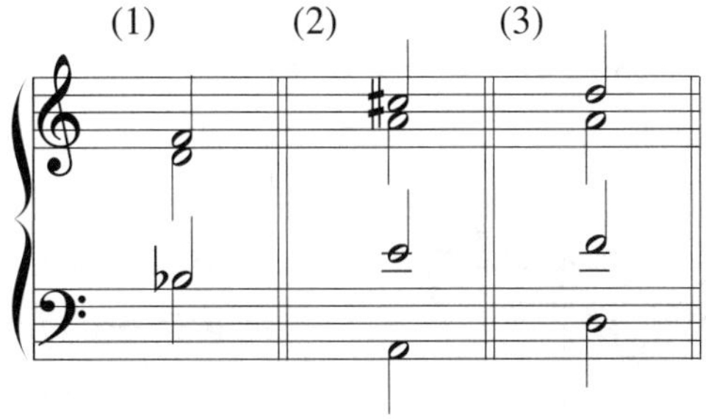

3.64 Write the alto and tenor voices so that each chord is in *close* structure.

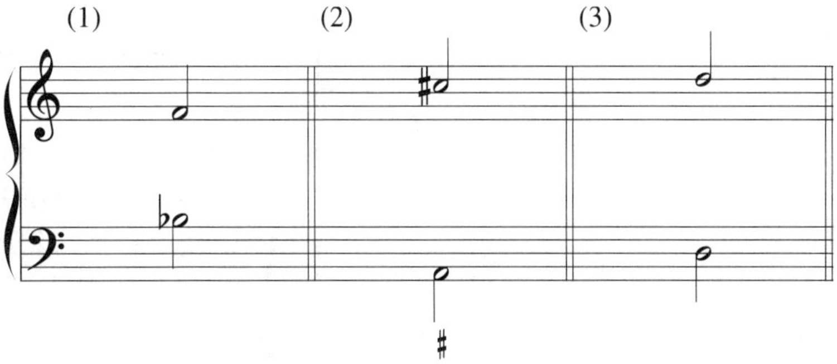

(If no more than four errors in the last six frames have been made, skip to Frame 3.73.)

(No response required.)

Expository Frame

3.65 If mistakes have been made in translating the figured bass symbols, review Frames 3.5–.22.

Review, also, the principles of doubling and spacing stated below:

1. When a triad is in root position double the bass (root).
2. A triad in root position should have two roots, one third, and one fifth.
3. The voices should be distributed normally (the highest tone given to the soprano, the next highest to the alto, the next to the tenor, and the lowest to the bass).
4. There should not be more than an octave between any of the upper voices.
5. *Close* structure means that the three upper voices take successive triad tones. These voices are as close together as the triad permits.

(4)

3.66 Which of the chords is in *close* structure? _____________

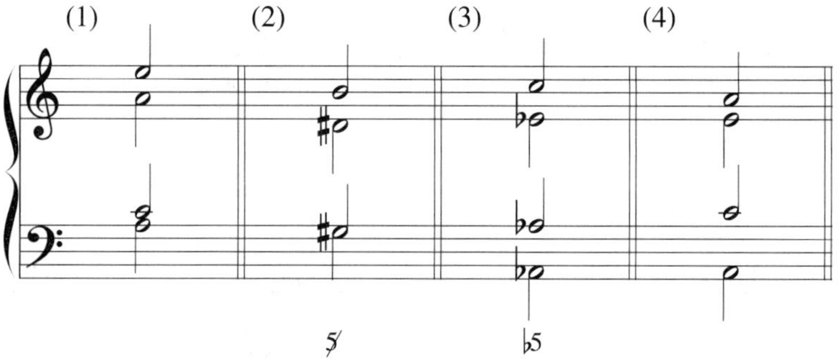

(2)

3.67 Which of the chords is NOT in close structure? __________

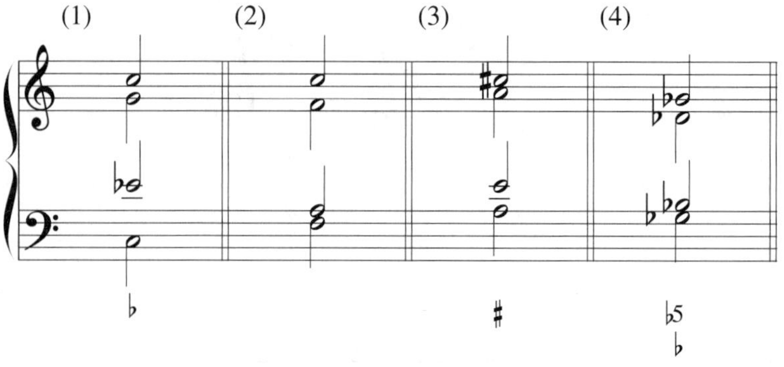

Crossed voices.
(The tenor is higher than the alto.)

3.68 What part writing error is illustrated below? ____________

The interval between the alto and tenor is larger than an octave.

3.69 What part writing error is illustrated below? ____________

____

The figured bass symbol $\not{5}$ has not been realized *(F♯ is needed).*

3.70 What part writing error is illustrated below? ____________

____

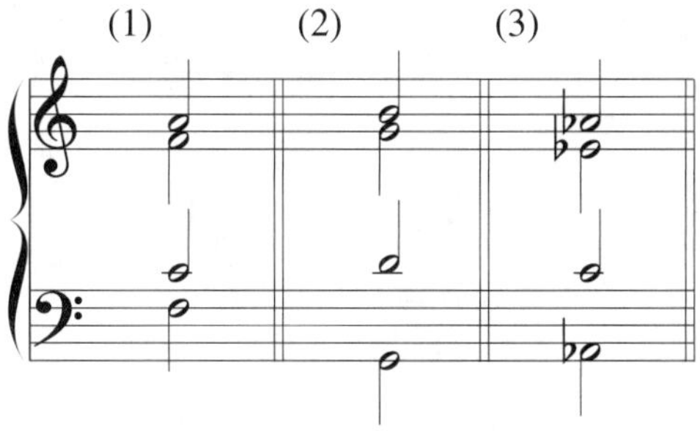

3.71 Write the alto and tenor voices so that each chord is in *close* structure.

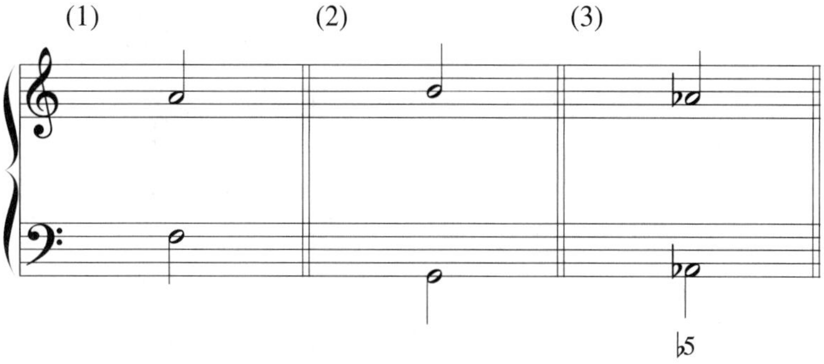

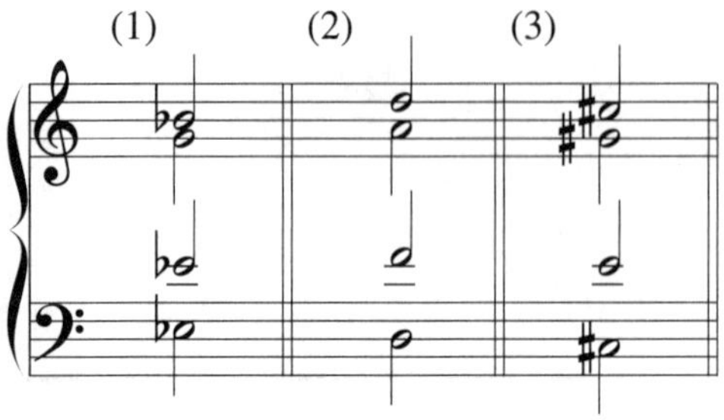

3.72 Write the alto and tenor voices so that each chord is in *close* structure.

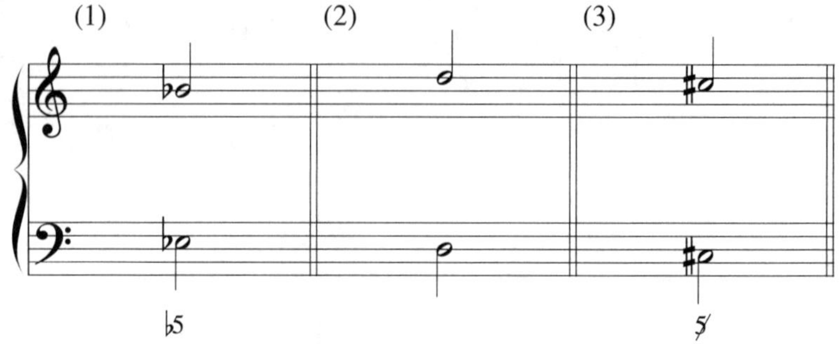

---

open

3.73 If there is a vacant triad tone between each of the three upper voices, the chord is in ____________ structure.

---

(3) and (4)

3.74 Which of the chords below are in *open* structure?

____

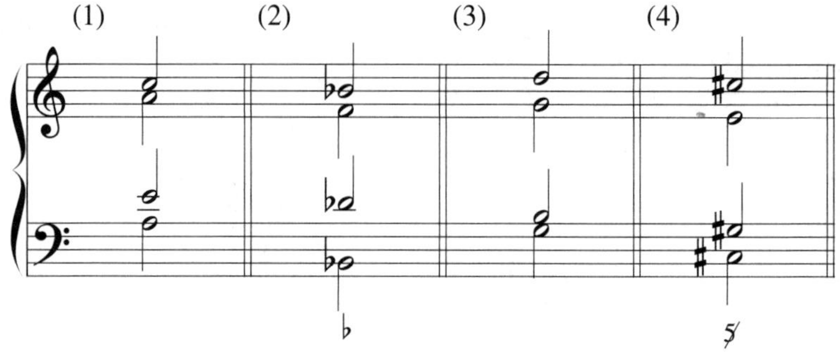

---

(1) and (3)

3.75 Which of the chords below are in *open* structure?

____

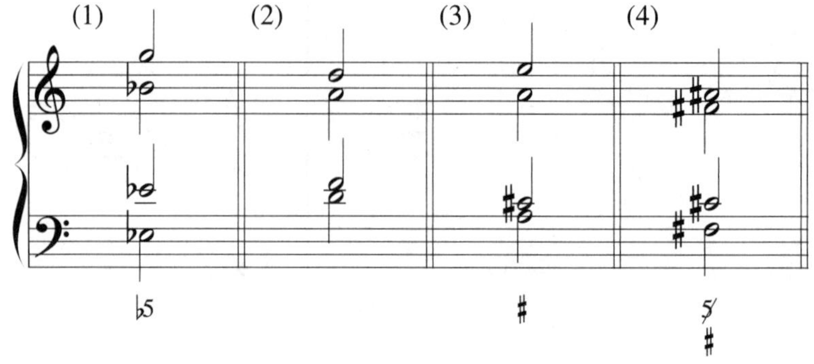

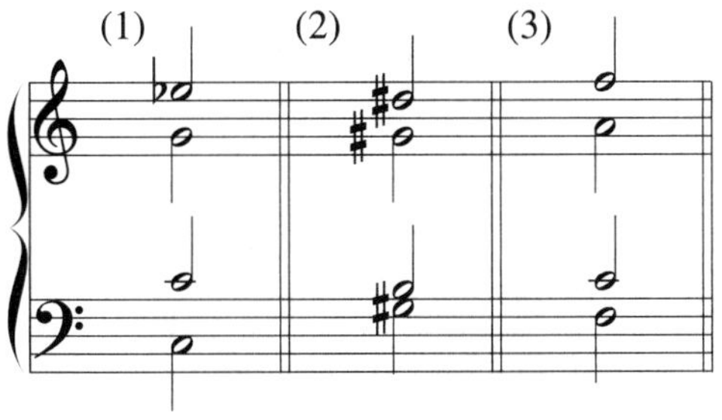

3.76 Write the alto and tenor voices so that each chord is in *open* structure.

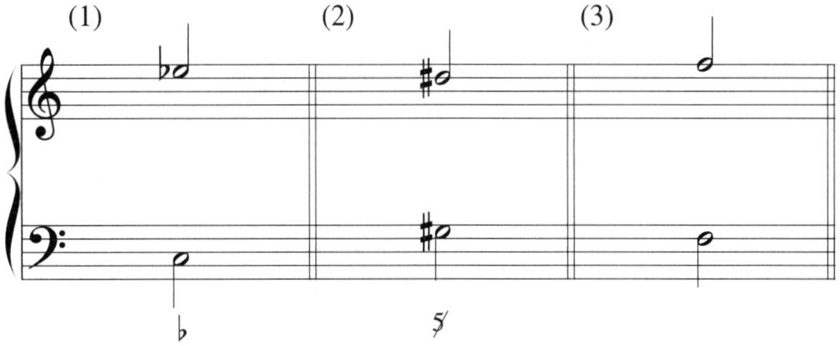

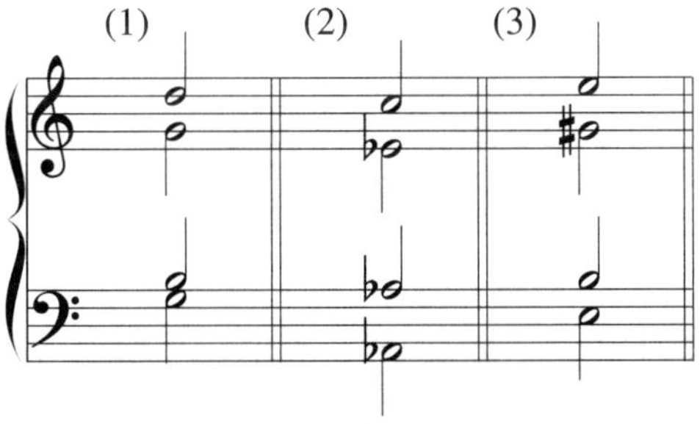

3.77 Write the alto and tenor voices so that each chord is in *open* structure.

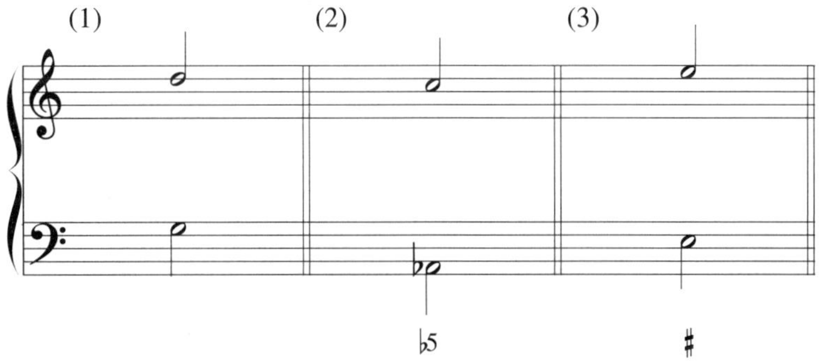

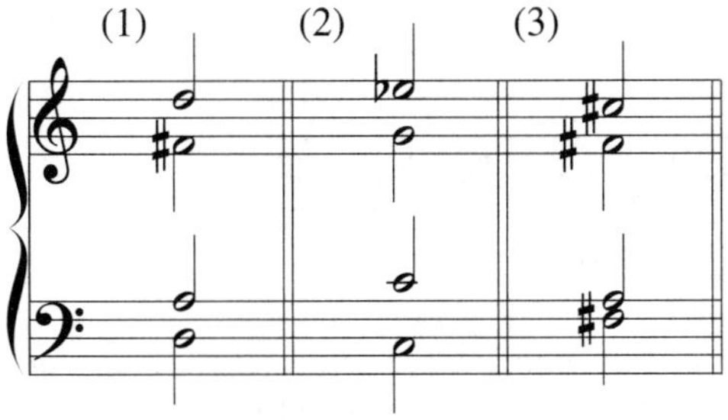

3.78 Write the alto and tenor voices so that each chord is in *open* structure.

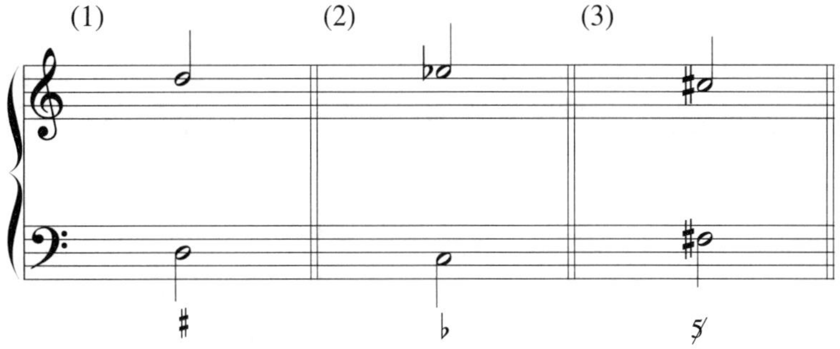

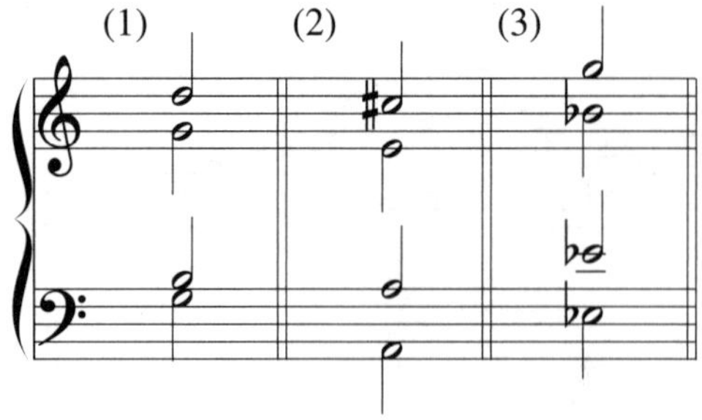

3.79 Write the alto and tenor voices so that each chord is in *open* structure.

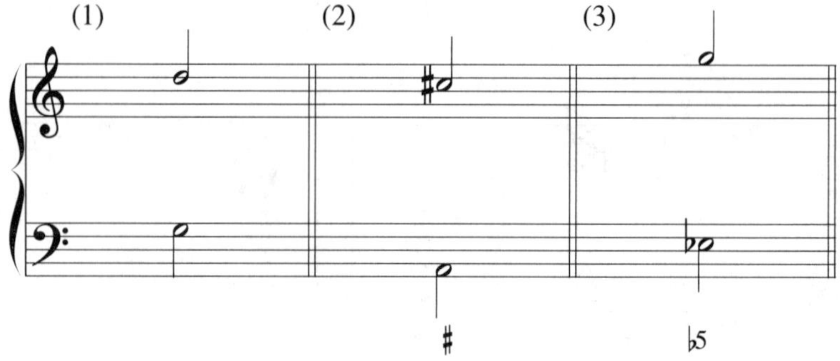

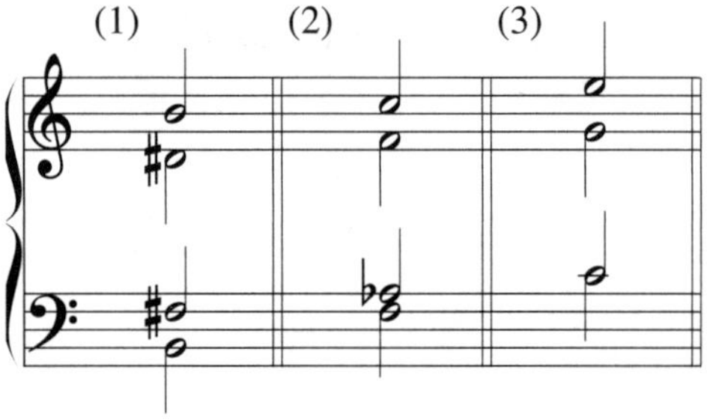

3.80 Write the alto and tenor voices so that each chord is in *open* structure.

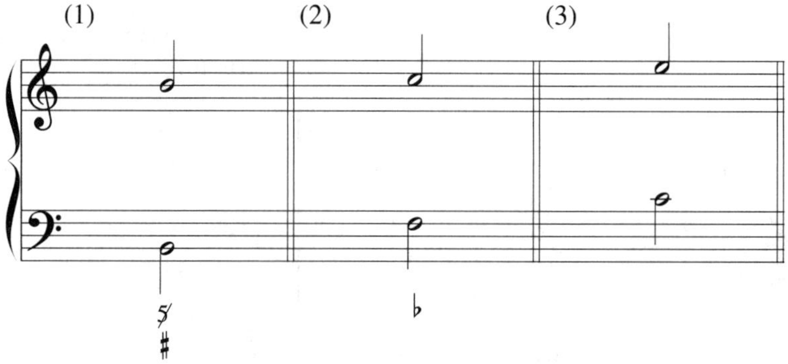

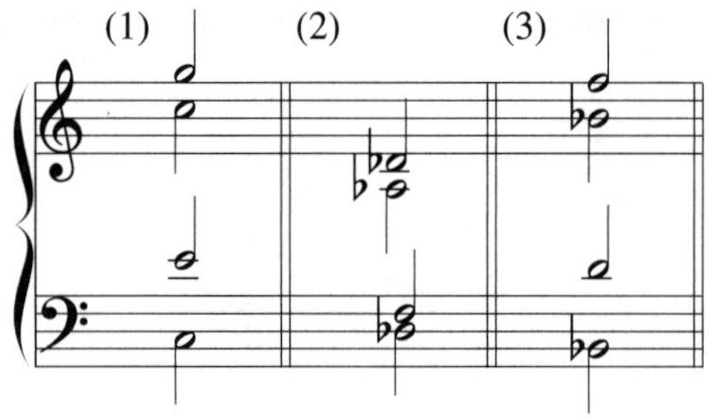

3.81 Due to the location of the given notes, each of the chords below can be written only one way without producing irregularities in part writing.

Write the alto and tenor voices choosing the structure (close or open) which is correct in each case.

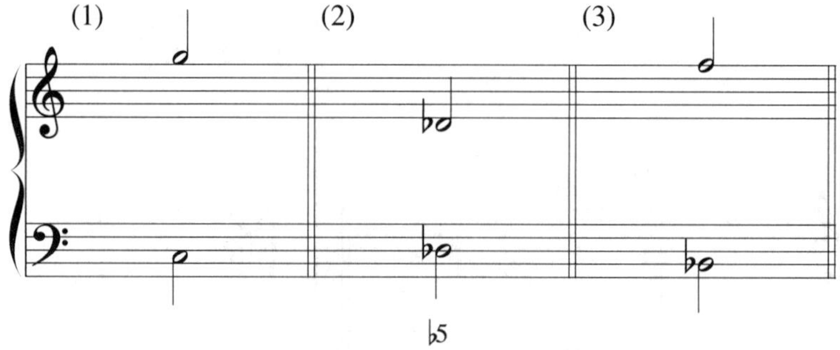

(If your solutions do not agree with the ones given, examine your work to find the errors, and consult an instructor if necessary.)

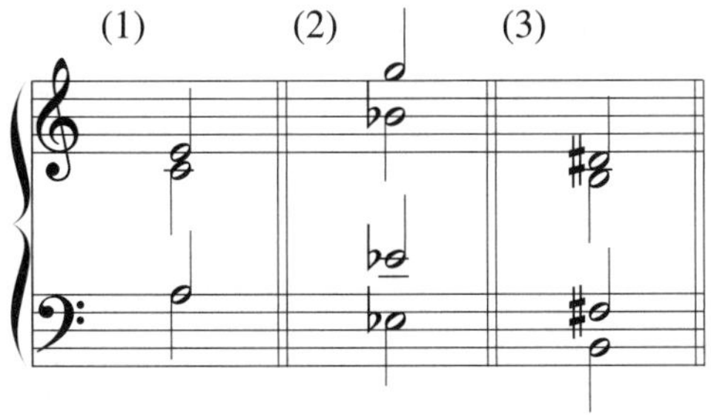

3.82 Continue as in the preceding frame.

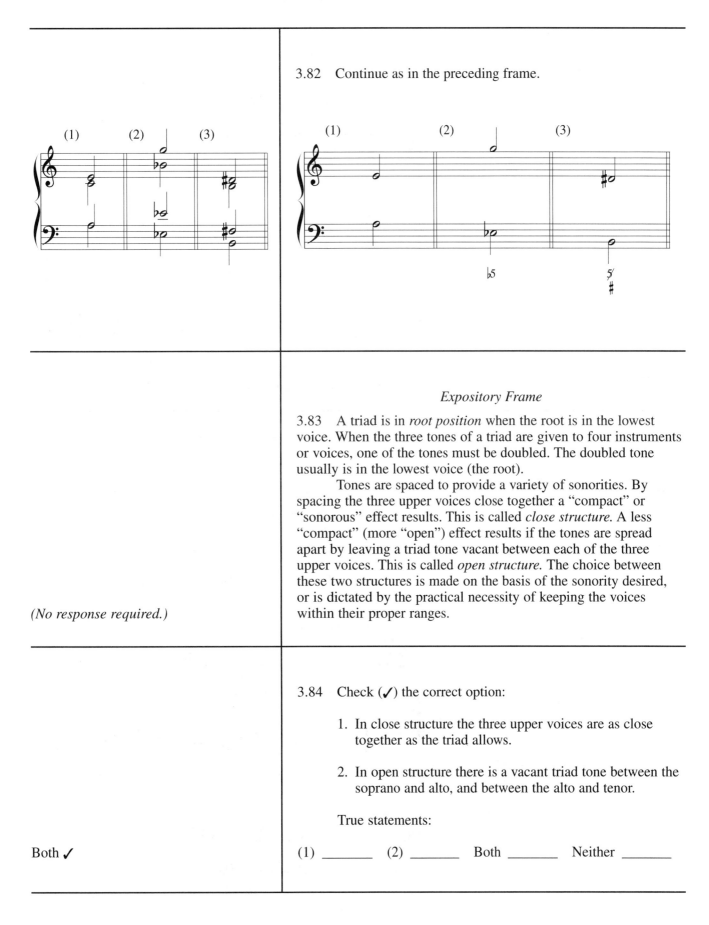

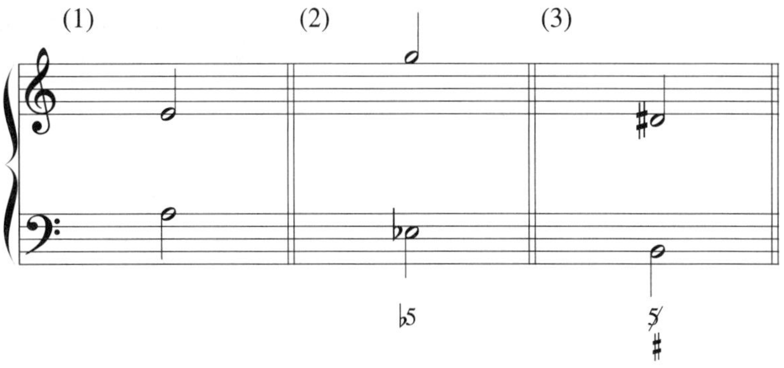

Expository Frame

3.83 A triad is in *root position* when the root is in the lowest voice. When the three tones of a triad are given to four instruments or voices, one of the tones must be doubled. The doubled tone usually is in the lowest voice (the root).

Tones are spaced to provide a variety of sonorities. By spacing the three upper voices close together a "compact" or "sonorous" effect results. This is called *close structure.* A less "compact" (more "open") effect results if the tones are spread apart by leaving a triad tone vacant between each of the three upper voices. This is called *open structure.* The choice between these two structures is made on the basis of the sonority desired, or is dictated by the practical necessity of keeping the voices within their proper ranges.

(No response required.)

3.84 Check (✓) the correct option:

1. In close structure the three upper voices are as close together as the triad allows.

2. In open structure there is a vacant triad tone between the soprano and alto, and between the alto and tenor.

True statements:

(1) _______ (2) _______ Both _______ Neither _______

Both ✓

3.85 The principles of doubling and spacing have been presented in terms of the four-part chorus. Most music based on a four-part texture will display these principles. Music for the piano, instrumental ensembles, and even the orchestra often is based on a four-part texture (sometimes expanded by octave doubling).

Examine the chords marked with asterisks (*) in the following example:

Handel, *Sarabande*

root

Which triad tone is doubled in each instance? The ______________.

Close

3.86 Which of the two structures is demonstrated in the preceding frame? (Open/Close) ______________.

Open

3.87 Which of the two structures is demonstrated by the chords marked with asterisks below? (Open/Close) ______________.

Brahms, *Ein deutsches Requiem,* Op. 45, IV

---

bass

3.88 Which voice (soprano, alto, tenor, or bass) is doubled when a triad is in root position? The ______________.

Summary

If the three upper voices are spaced as close together as possible the chord is in *close* structure. *Open* structure results when there is a vacant chord tone between the soprano and alto, and the alto and tenor voices. In this case the interval between the soprano and tenor voices is greater than an octave. Close structure produces a more "compact" sound than open structure.

The basic principles that govern the doubling and spacing of triads in root position are listed below:

1. The voices should be kept within their practical ranges.
2. The voices should be in normal distribution (avoid crossed voices).
3. The interval between any two adjacent upper voices should not exceed an octave.
4. The bass is usually doubled in four-part writing.

Figured bass symbols are used to quickly convey certain musical facts about chordal structures. They may also be used to indicate melodic movement. The symbols consist mainly of numbers, accidentals, and other signs. Used for whatever purpose, they actually indicate nothing more than intervals above the lowest sounding note.

The figured bass symbols introduced in this chapter are summarized below:

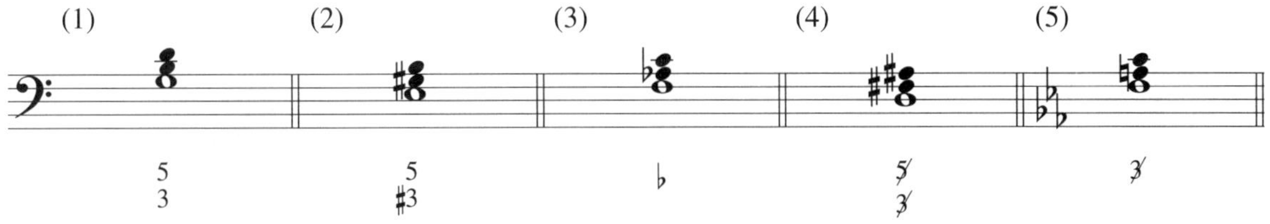

(1) The numbers 5 and 3 indicate a 5th and a 3rd above the note G. The result is a triad in root position.

(2) The figure ♯3 indicates the note G♯. The result is an E major triad.

(3) Used as a figured bass symbol, an accidental that stands alone (and is not associated with a number) affects the note that is a third above the bass, in this case A♭. The result is an f minor triad.

(4) A slash (/) through a number causes the note represented by the number to be raised a half step. In this case both the fifth and third above the bass are raised a half step by the use of sharps.

(5) Here a natural is used to raise the third above the bass. (The natural cancels the A♭ in the key signature.)

Note that the chord symbols used in present day, Western pop, commercial, and jazz music "charts," "lead sheets," and full scores are essentially a modern "kind" of figured bass that builds upon the traditions of the figured bass of older times. In many instances these newer symbols are more effective to use for composition and analysis than the traditional Western, roman numeral and figured bass symbols. (*Please see p. 355 for information on these modern symbols that address the kind and quality of a given chord.*)

The terms that are explained or used in this chapter are listed below in the order presented:

figured bass symbols	three- or four-part texture	crossed (voice crossing)
root position	four-part chorus	adjacent
flatted (lowered)	soprano	close structure
slash	alto	open structure
raised	tenor	vacant tone (unoccupied triad tone)
alteration	doubling (double)	sonority
spacing	bass	

Mastery Frames

root (3.1–.4)

3–1 When the root of a triad is in the lowest voice, the triad is in ____________ position.

(1) (2) (3)

(3.1–.4)

3–2 Write triads in root position as directed.

(1) (2) (3)

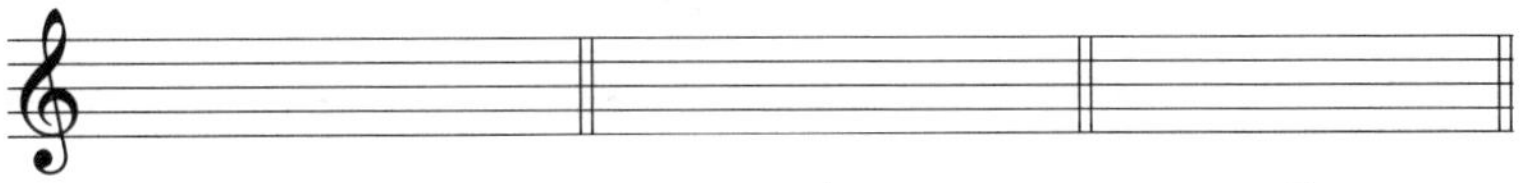

D a♭ F♯

(1) (2) (3)

(3.5–.22)

3–3 Write the triad as indicated by the figured bass symbols.

(1) (2) (3)

(1) 5̸ ♯ (2) ♭ (3) 5 3

(1) (2) (3)

(1) ♯ or 3̸ (2) ♭5 ♭3 or ♭5 ♭ (3) 5̸

(3.5–.22)

3–4 Write the figured bass symbols beneath each triad as needed.

(1) (2) (3)

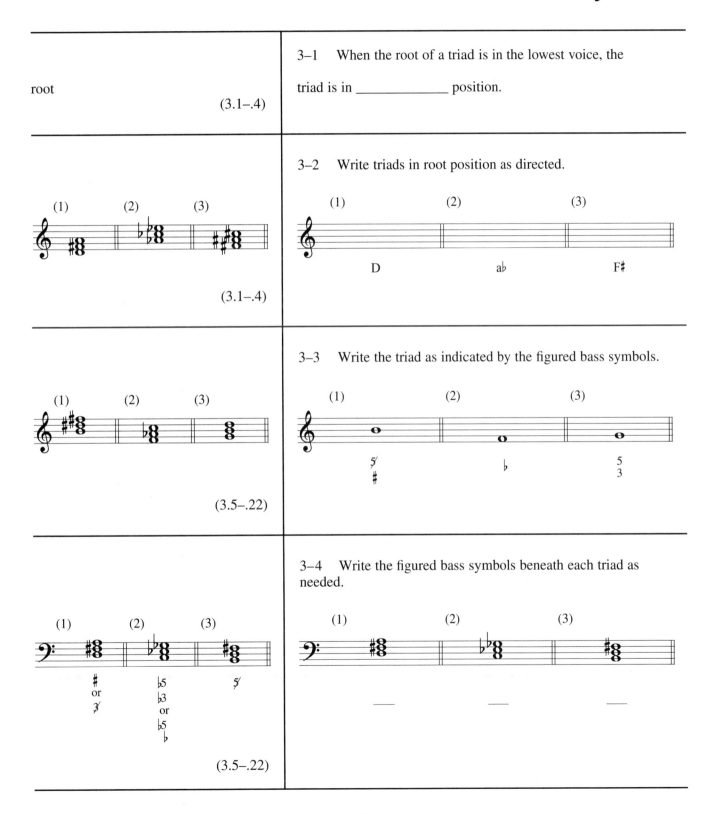

___ ___ ___

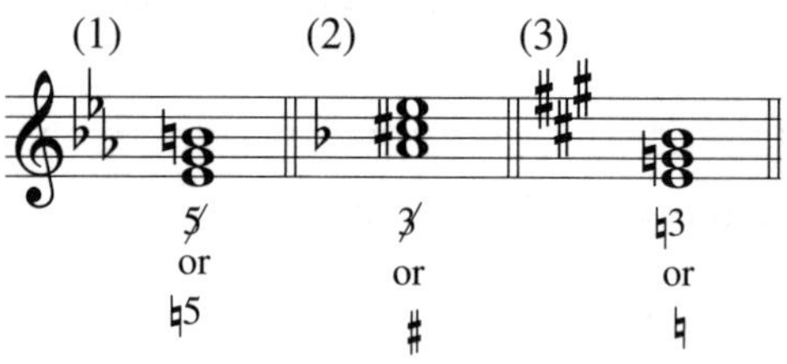

(3.5–.22)

3–5 Write the figured bass symbols beneath each triad as needed.

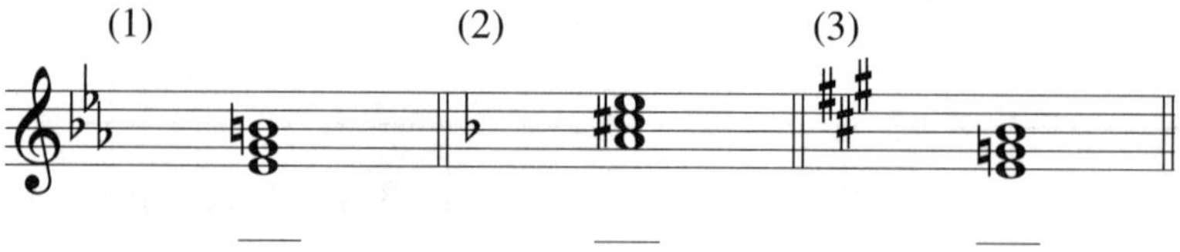

---

root (bass)

(3.44–.45)

3–6 In four-part writing, a triad in root position will usually have the ____________ doubled.

---

(1) and (3)

(3.44–.47)

3–7 Which chords have *incorrect* doubling? ____________

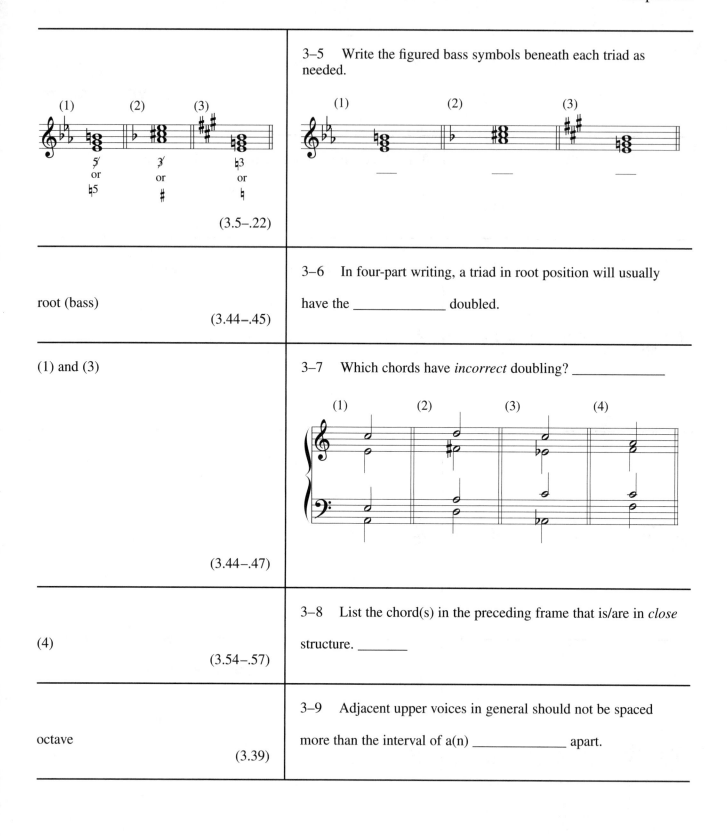

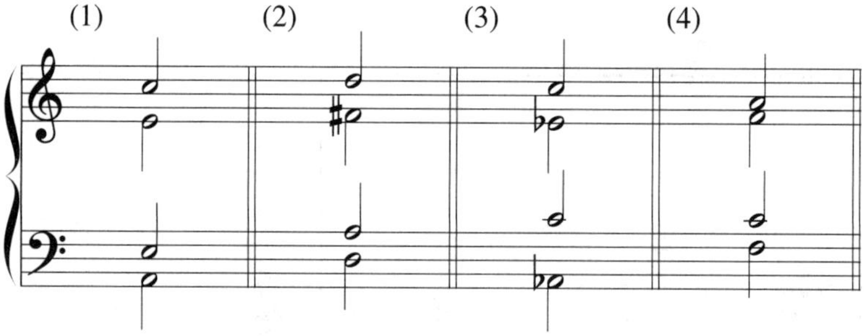

---

(4)

(3.54–.57)

3–8 List the chord(s) in the preceding frame that is/are in *close* structure. _______

---

octave

(3.39)

3–9 Adjacent upper voices in general should not be spaced more than the interval of a(n) ____________ apart.

Supplementary Assignments

ASSIGNMENT 3–1 Name ______________________________

1. Which of the triads are in root position?____________

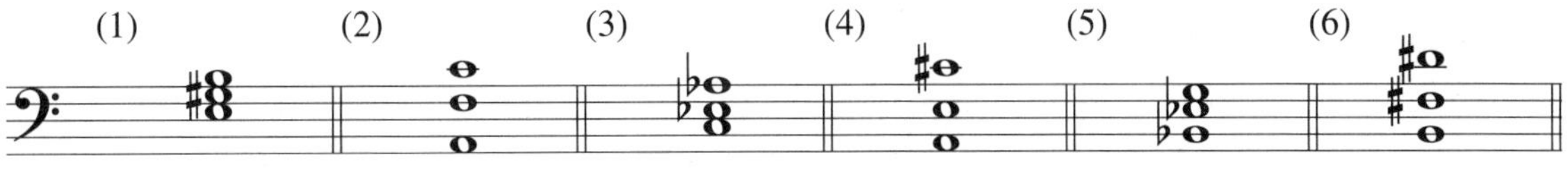

2. Write triads in root position as directed. (Capital letter = major; lowercase letter = minor.)

3. Write the triads indicated by the figured bass symbols.

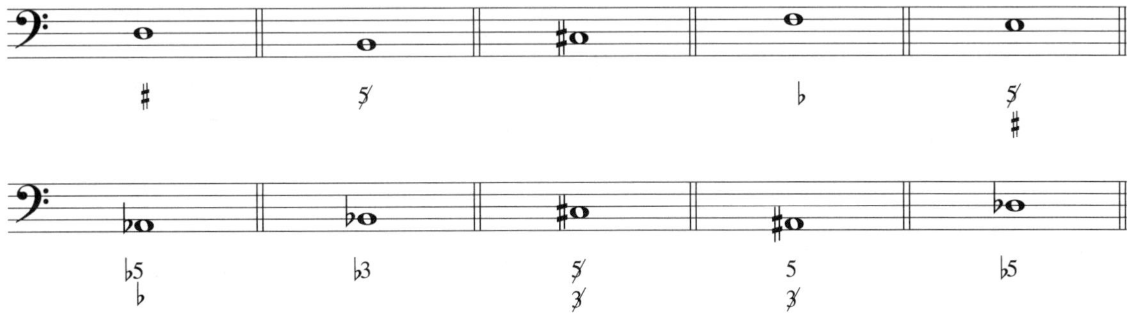

4. Supply the figured bass symbols where needed.

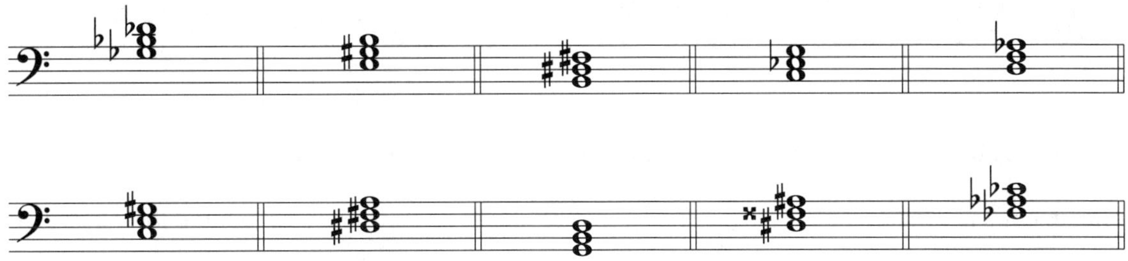

5. Identify each triad by name and quality using the alternative method covered previously.

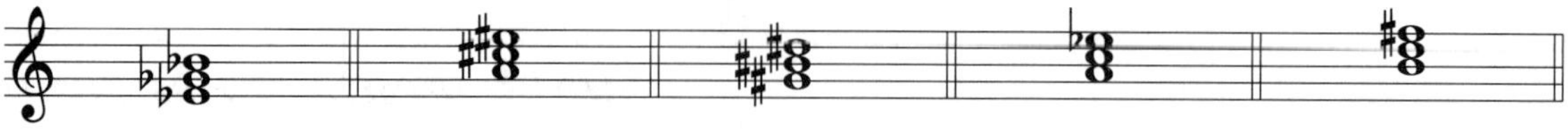

___ ___ ___ ___ ___

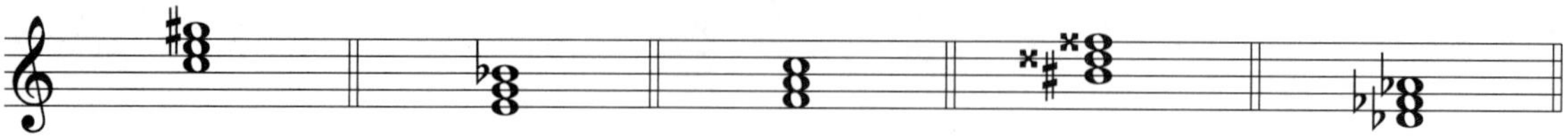

___ ___ ___ ___ ___

6. Write triads (chords) as indicated.

E Gmi F♯dim Cmi E♭aug

G♯mi D♭mi A♯ Edim B

7. Indicate the approximate range for each voice of the four-part chorus.

Soprano Alto

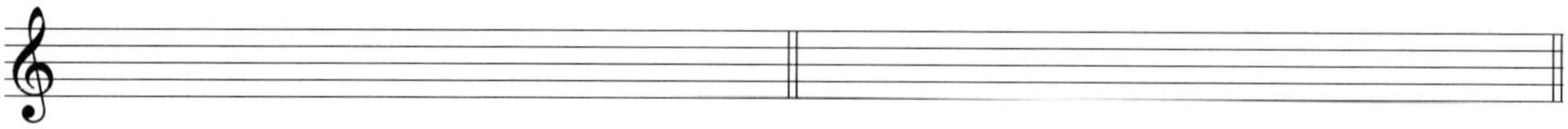

Tenor Bass

8. Which chords are in *close* structure? ________________________

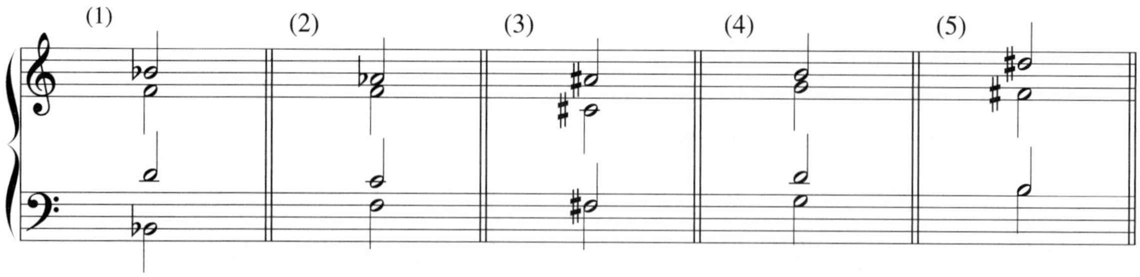

9. What interval should not be exceeded when spacing adjacent upper voices?________________________

10. An interval as large as a(n)__________________________________may separate the lowest two voices.

ASSIGNMENT 3–2 Name ______________________________

1. Write the missing two voices for each chord. *(Use close structure.)*

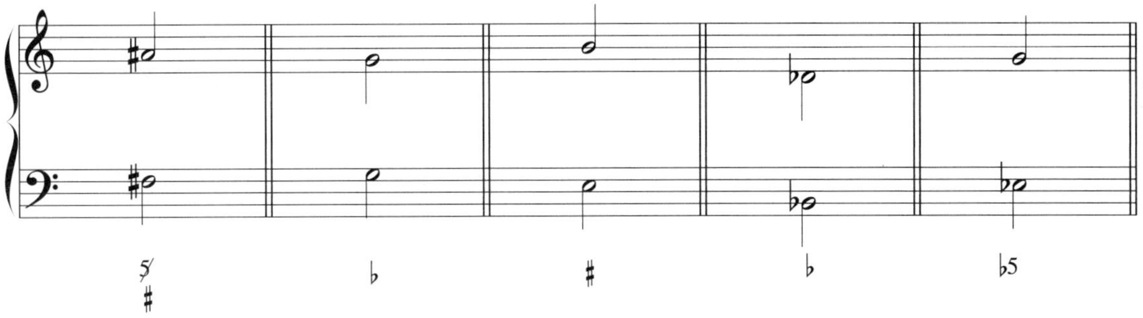

2. Write the missing two voices for each chord. *(Use open structure.)*

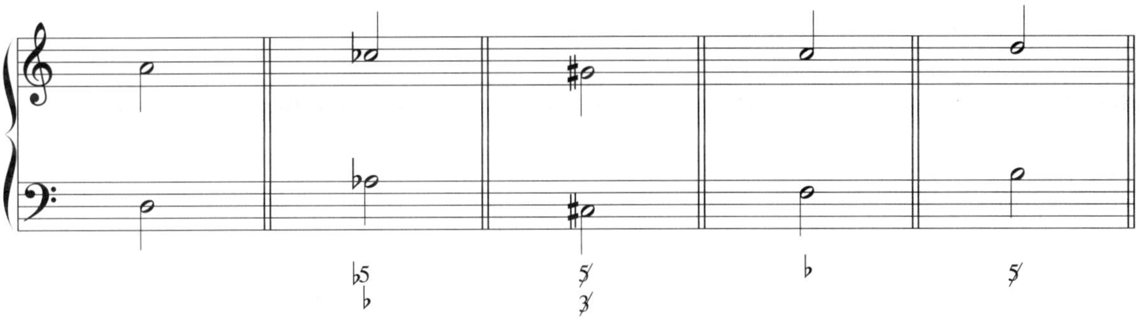

3. Choose one or more of the options for each example.

(A) ____________ (B) ____________ (C) ____________ (D) ____________ (E) ____________

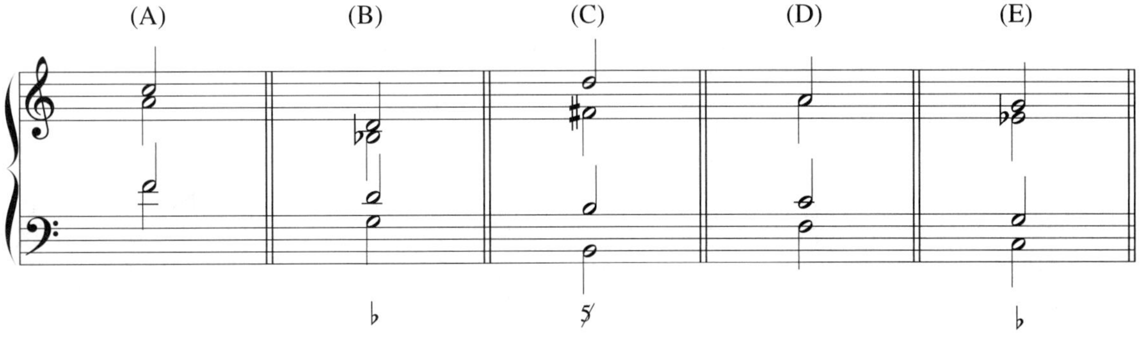

(1) Crossed voices

(2) Incorrect spacing

(3) Incorrect doubling

(4) Voice out of normal range

(5) No error

4. Supply the figured bass symbols for each chord.

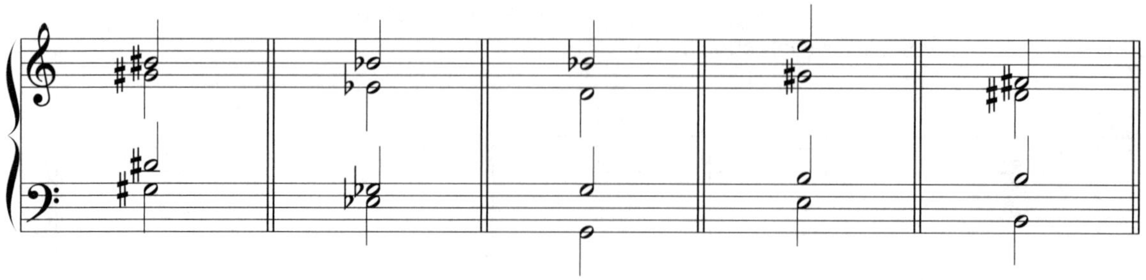

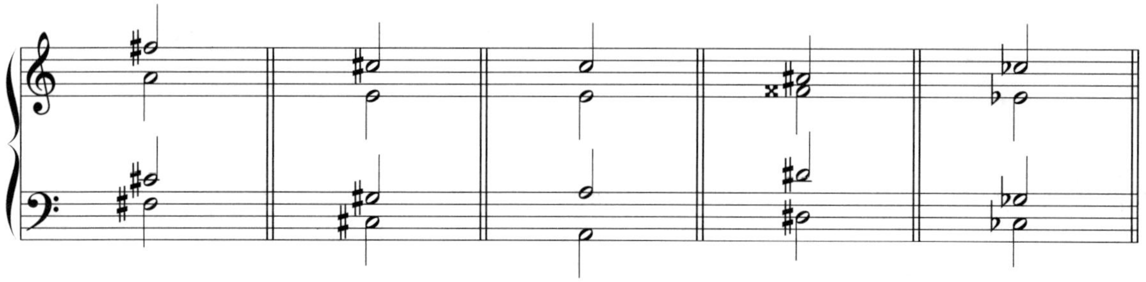

5. Write the three upper voices using either open or close structure. Observe all rules of doubling and spacing.

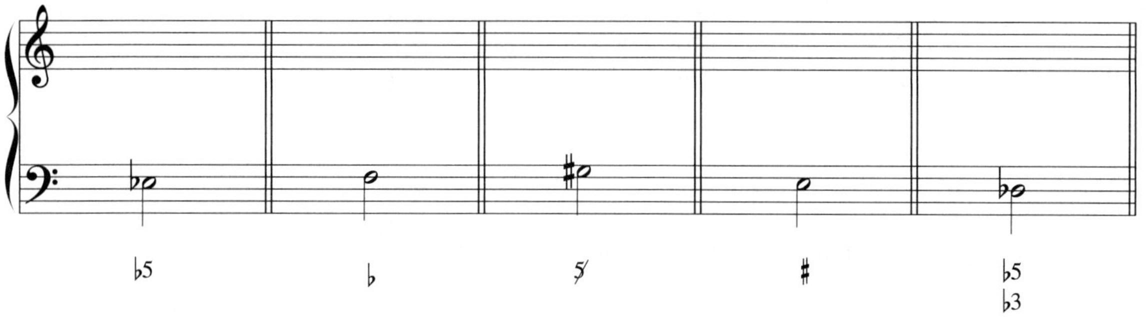

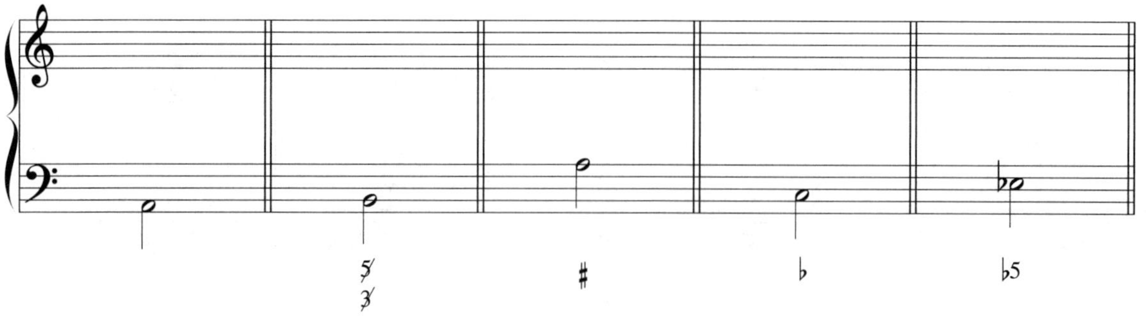

Chapter 4.0
Triads in Root Position: Voice Leading

Chords are the result of several voices sounding simultaneously. When several chords occur in succession it is desirable that each voice produce an agreeable melodic line. With reference to tonal harmony in the traditional (Western) styles of the eighteenth and nineteenth centuries this means that the voices should lead smoothly (with few leaps) from one chord to the next. The principles of voice leading presented in this chapter will serve as guidelines for the effective movement of voices.

These principles, while ancient to us now, still offer a basic approach to the understanding of voice leading that is generally as valid to us today as it was then. New developments have occurred over the years along with many exceptions to the so-called "rules," but the developments and exceptions will always be there. Yet, underlying it all are basic concepts, to be discussed in this chapter, that still serve to guide in achieving a desired, musically effective result, even though a musical choice may ultimately point to an "exception."

4.1 Since harmony consists of several melodic lines sounding together to produce chords, it is important to know how voices relate to one another in terms of relative motion. There are four kinds of relative motion: *similar, parallel, oblique* and *contrary.* We shall examine each of these separately.

Below are three examples of SIMILAR motion:

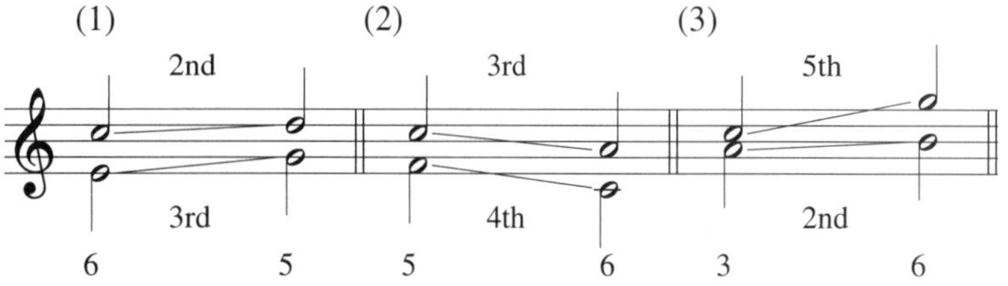

Voices that move in similar motion move in the same direction (up or down), but *not by the same interval.* In (1), for example, the upper voice ascends a second while the lower voice ascends a third. This is reflected by the harmonic intervals produced by the two voices (a sixth followed by a fifth).

In *similar* motion the voices move in the same direction but not by the same ____________.

interval

4.2 Write the notes indicated by the figured bass symbols.

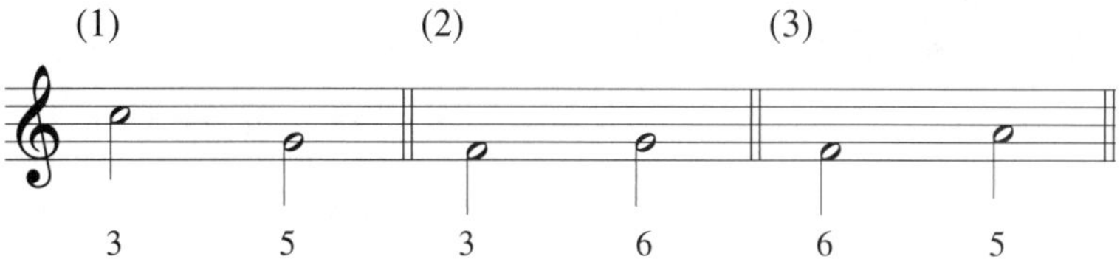

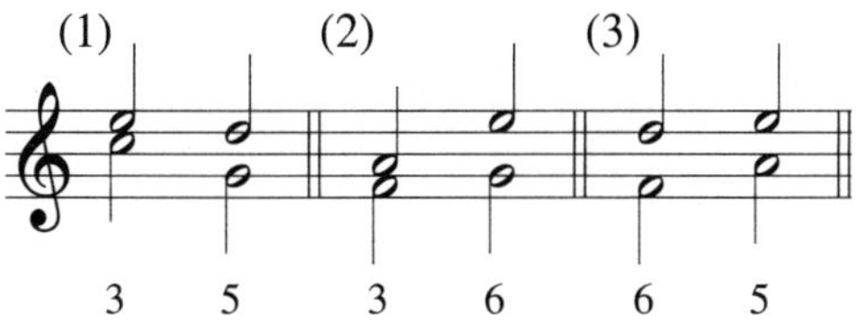

similar

4.3 Each of the examples in the preceding frame demonstrates ______________ motion.

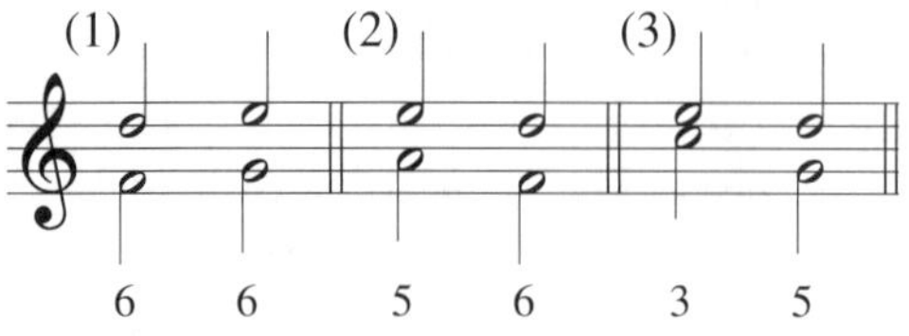

4.4 Write the notes indicated by the figured bass symbols.

False
(See next frame.)

4.5 Each of the examples in the preceding frame demonstrates similar motion. (True/False) ______________

---

(4)

4.6 In the first example of Frame 4.4 the voices move in the same direction *by the same interval.* In similar motion the voices do not move by the same interval.

Which of the examples below demonstrates similar motion? _______

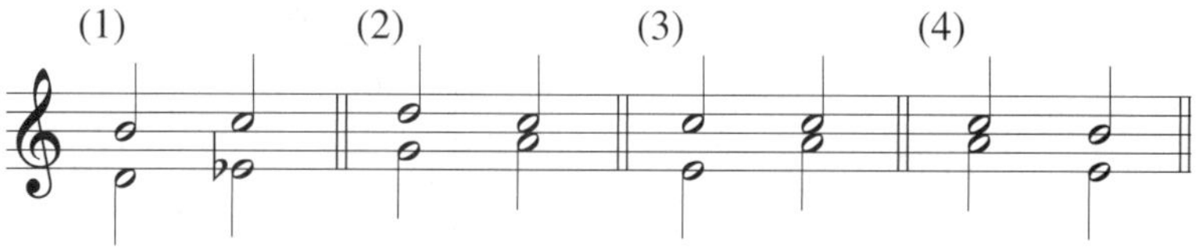

---

interval

4.7 Compare the two examples below:

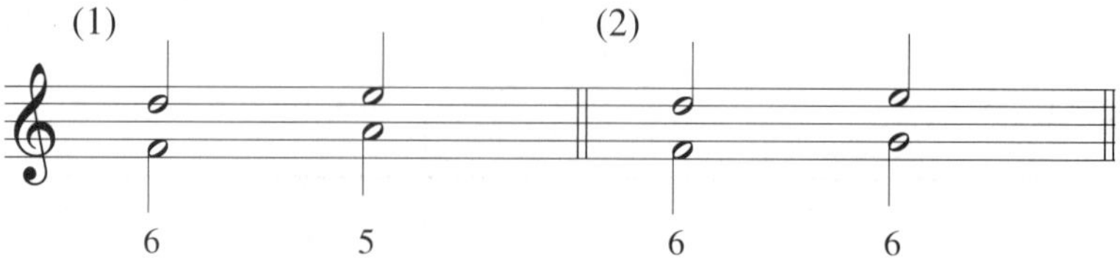

(1) Demonstrates *similar* motion (both voices move in the same direction but not by the same interval). In (2), however, the voices not only move in the same direction, but also by the same interval. This is called PARALLEL motion.

In *parallel* motion the voices not only move in the same direction, but also by the same ______________.

6 6 3 3 5 5

4.8 Write the figured bass symbol for each interval.

(1) (2) (3)

___ ___ ___ ___ ___ ___

---

parallel

4.9 The examples in the preceding frame show that parallel motion is easily detected by referring to the intervals between the two voices. A succession of like intervals such as 3–3, 5–5, or 6–6 produces

_____________ motion.

5 5 3 3 8 8

4.10 Write the notes indicated by the figured bass symbols in each case.

(1) (2) (3)

5 5 3 3 8 8

---

parallel

4.11 Each of the examples in the preceding frame demonstrates

_____________ motion.

---

(2)

4.12 Which of the examples below demonstrates *parallel*

motion? _______

(1) (2) (3) (4)

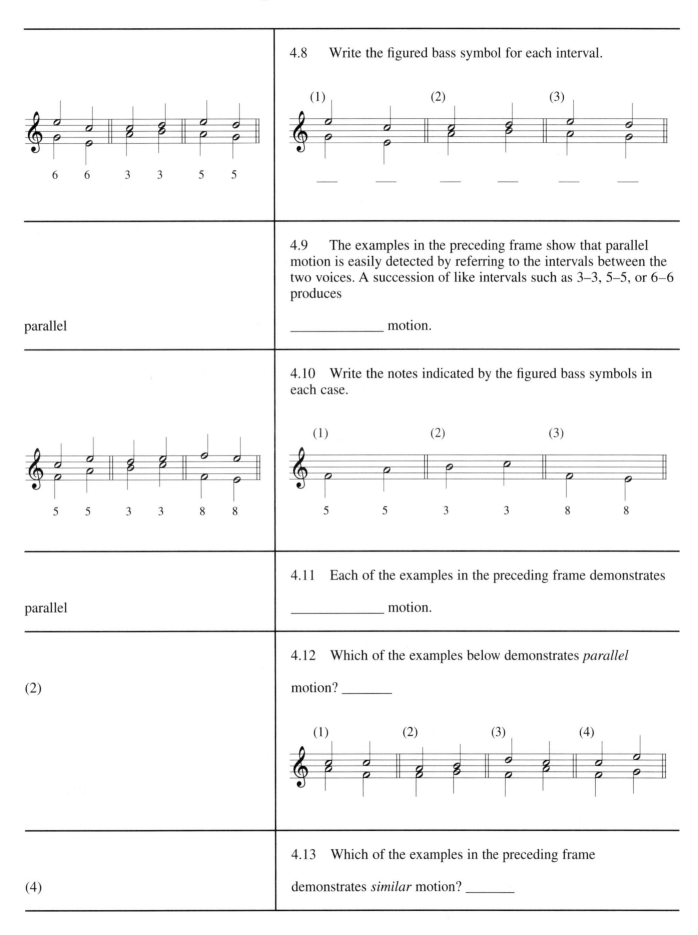

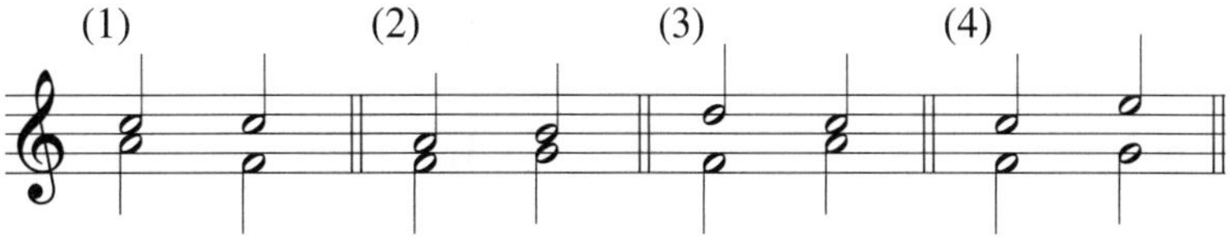

---

(4)

4.13 Which of the examples in the preceding frame

demonstrates *similar* motion? _______

4.14 Compare the two examples below:

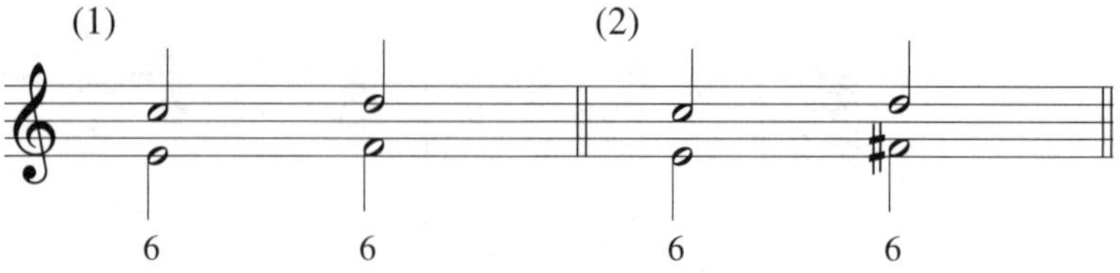

Both (1) and (2) demonstrate parallel motion, yet there *is* a difference: in (1) a minor sixth is followed by a major sixth, whereas both intervals are minor sixths in (2).

From this it can be seen that the term *parallel motion* does not always refer to absolutely parallel voices. Voices move in parallel motion when the basic intervals are the same (third to third or sixth to sixth, etc.) without consideration of the specific quality of each interval.

Both (1) and (2) are examples of parallel motion; but (2), illogically, is "more parallel" than (1).

The term parallel motion does not usually take into account the precise quality of the _____________.

intervals

4.15 When it is necessary to identify absolutely parallel motion, phrases such as "parallel major thirds," "perfect fifths," or "minor sixths" may be used.

Some parallel intervals are forbidden in traditional writing. These are parallel perfect unisons, perfect fifths, and perfect octaves.

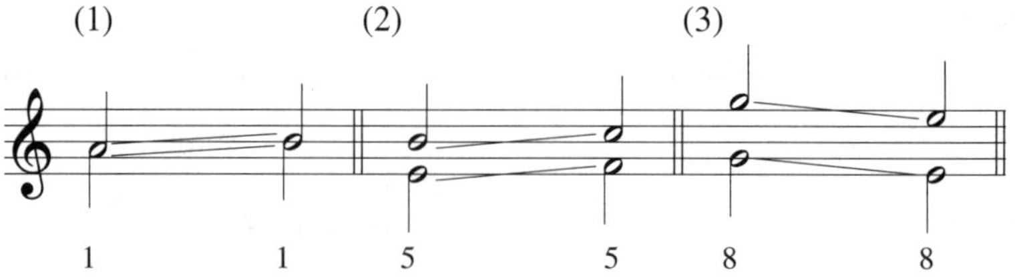

Perfect unisons, perfect fifths, and perfect octaves are such pure consonances that voices moving parallel by these intervals tend to lose their individuality.

List the intervals that should not occur in parallel motion:

(1) _____________

(2) _____________

(3) _____________

(1) Perfect unison

(2) Perfect fifth

(3) Perfect octave *(Any order.)*

(4)

4.16 Which example illustrates incorrect parallel motion? *(Look for consecutive perfect unisons, fifths, or octaves.)* _______

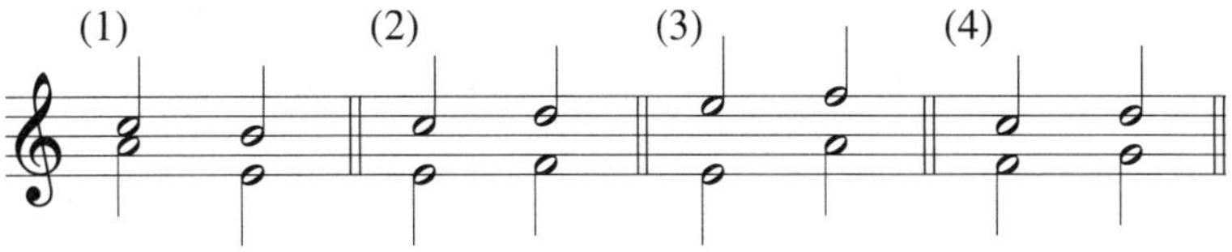

(2)

4.17 Which example illustrates incorrect parallel motion? _______

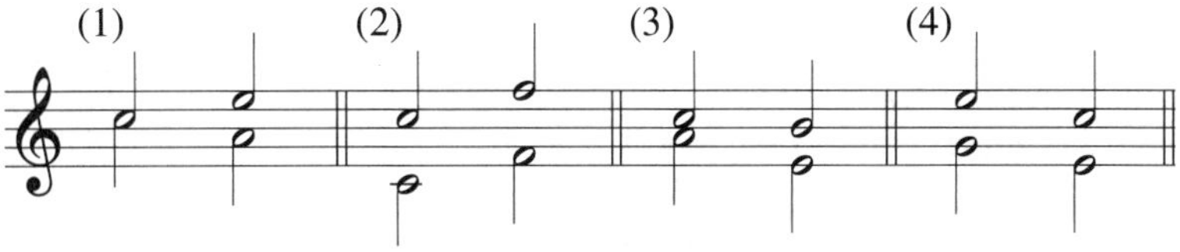

(3)
(Example [5] is NOT incorrect because there is no motion, i.e., no change of pitch in either note.)

4.18 Which example illustrates incorrect parallel motion? _______

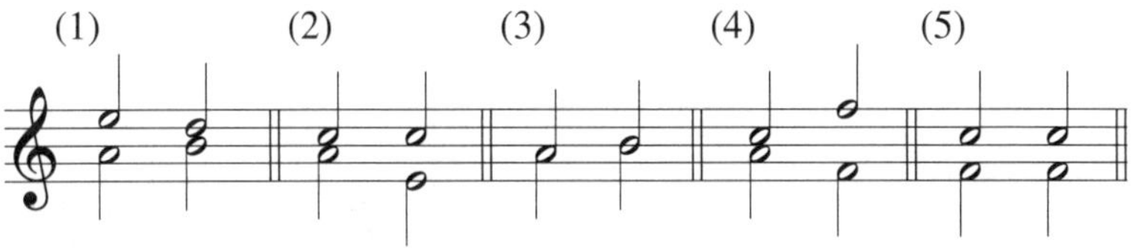

No
(Both [2] and [3] are diminished fifths.)

4.19 Are all of the intervals in the example below perfect fifths?

____

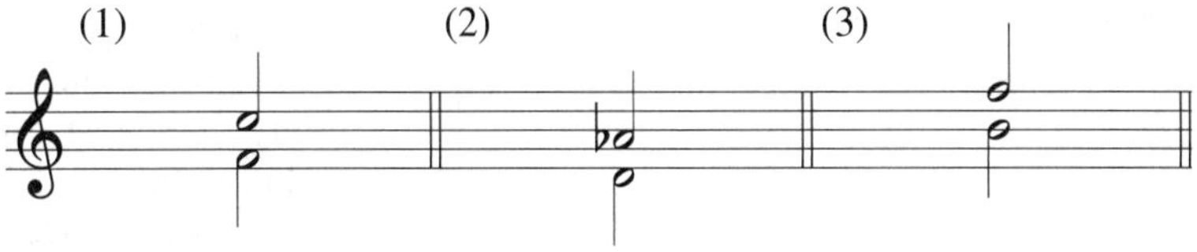

No
(The second interval is a diminished fifth.)

4.20 Parallel fifths are incorrect only if both are *perfect.* Does the example below illustrate incorrect use of parallel motion? _______

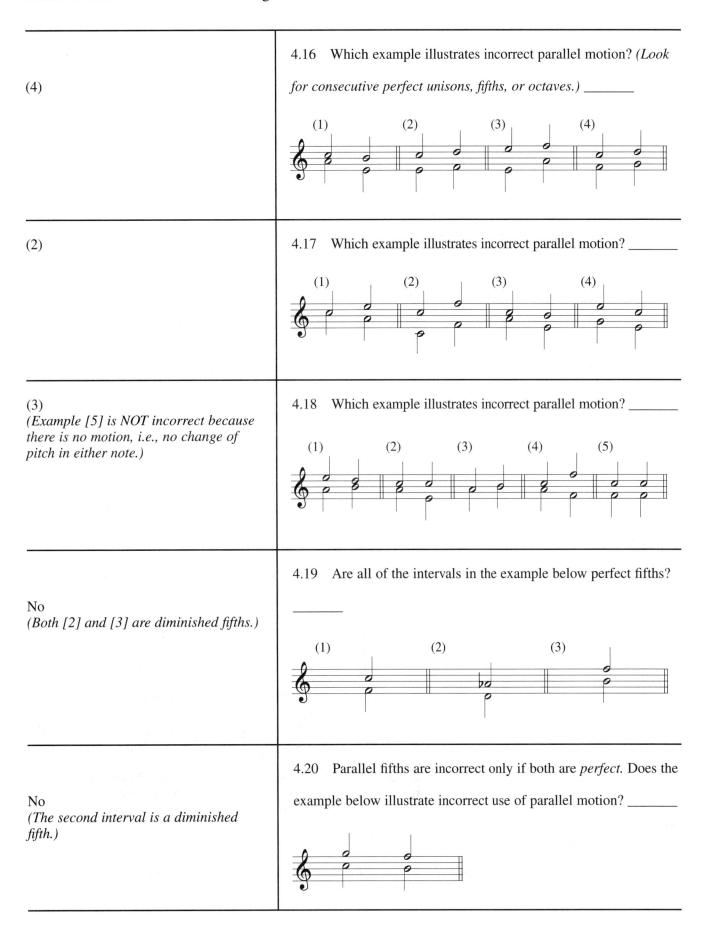

(4)

4.21 The preceding frame demonstrates that parallel fifths are incorrect only if both are *perfect.*

Which of the examples below illustrates *incorrect* parallel motion? _______

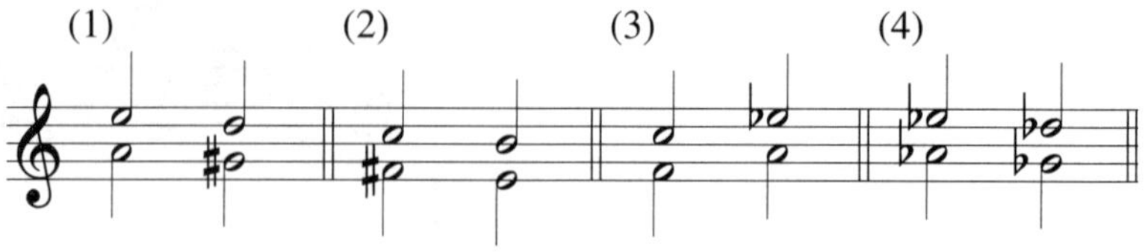

(2) and (5)
(Note in Example [5] that incorrect parallel motion cannot be corrected by a substitution of the same pitch in a different octave, let alone the spacing problem created.)

4.22 Which of the examples below illustrates *incorrect* parallel motion? _____________

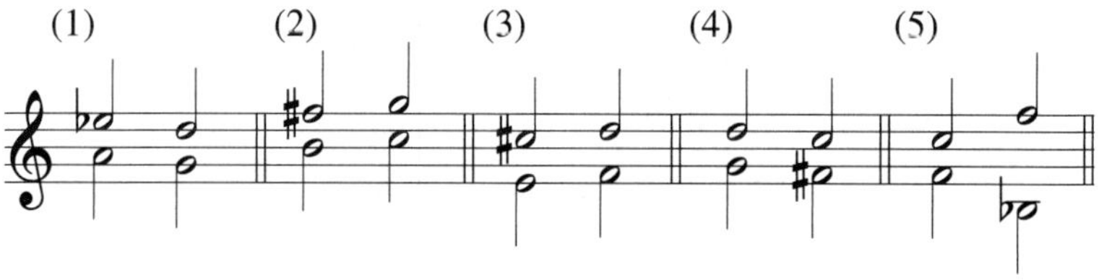

(3)

4.23 In which case is the parallel motion *correct*? _______

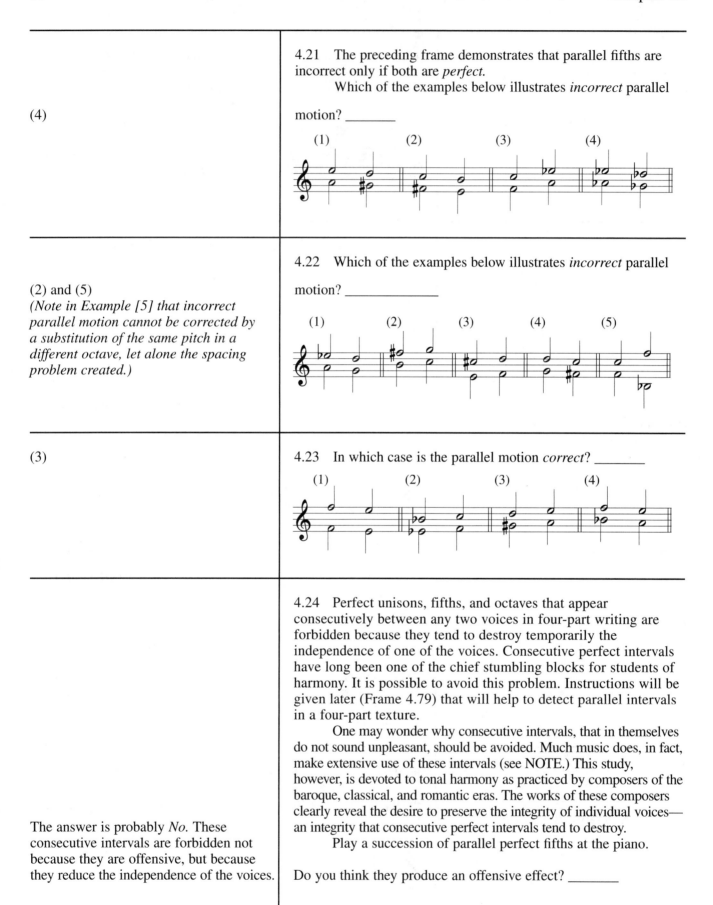

The answer is probably *No.* These consecutive intervals are forbidden not because they are offensive, but because they reduce the independence of the voices.

4.24 Perfect unisons, fifths, and octaves that appear consecutively between any two voices in four-part writing are forbidden because they tend to destroy temporarily the independence of one of the voices. Consecutive perfect intervals have long been one of the chief stumbling blocks for students of harmony. It is possible to avoid this problem. Instructions will be given later (Frame 4.79) that will help to detect parallel intervals in a four-part texture.

One may wonder why consecutive intervals, that in themselves do not sound unpleasant, should be avoided. Much music does, in fact, make extensive use of these intervals (see NOTE.) This study, however, is devoted to tonal harmony as practiced by composers of the baroque, classical, and romantic eras. The works of these composers clearly reveal the desire to preserve the integrity of individual voices—an integrity that consecutive perfect intervals tend to destroy.

Play a succession of parallel perfect fifths at the piano.

Do you think they produce an offensive effect? _______

NOTE: Parallel triads as well as seventh and ninth chords occur frequently in the music of the impressionist composers Debussy and Ravel. Melodic doubling at all intervals is a prominent feature in much twentieth-century music of all styles and genres.

4.25 Check (✓) the correct option:

1. In both similar and parallel motion the voices move in the same direction.

2. In parallel motion the voices move in the same direction and by the same basic interval.

True statements:

(1) _______ (2) _______ Both _______ Neither _______

Both ✓

4.26 OBLIQUE motion is demonstrated in the example below:

(1) (2)

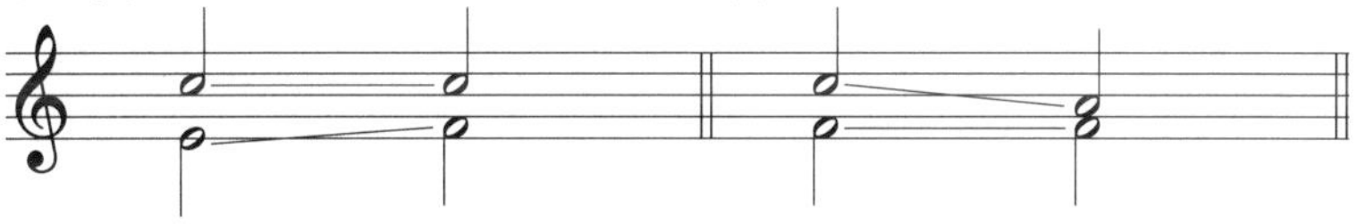

In *oblique* motion one voice is stationary while the second voice moves to another pitch (either upward or downward).

Which of the examples below demonstrates *oblique* motion?

____

(1) (2) (3) (4)

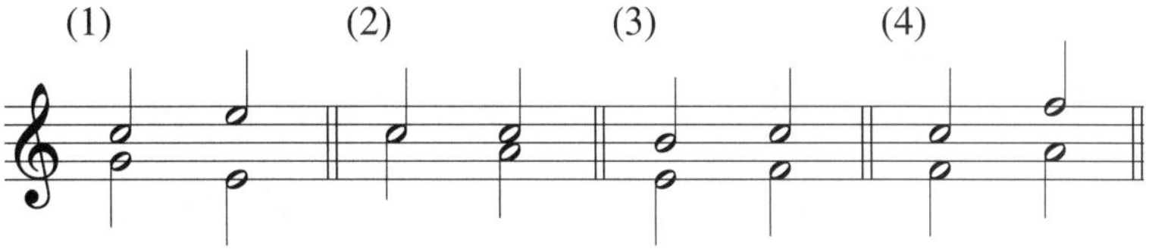

(2)

4.27 Which of the examples below demonstrates *oblique* motion?

____

(1) (2) (3) (4)

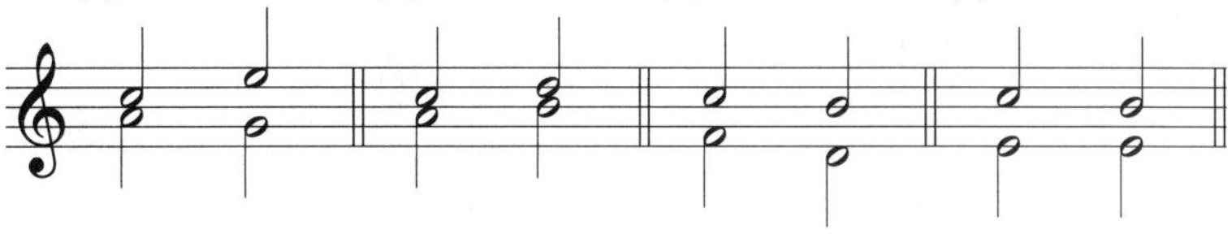

(4)

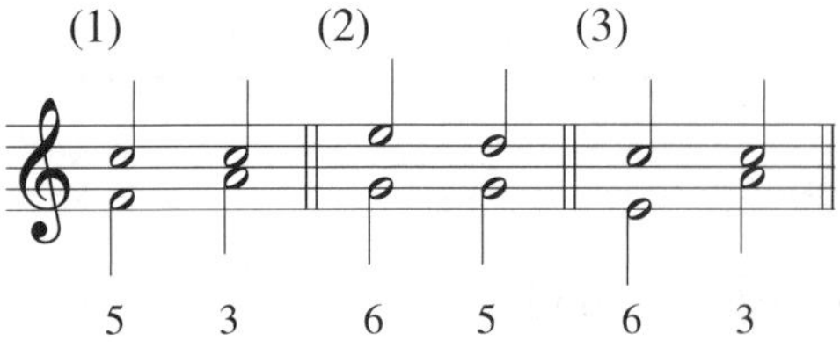

4.28 Write the notes indicated by the figured bass symbols.

oblique

4.29 Each of the examples in the preceding frame demonstrates

____________ motion.

contrary

4.30 CONTRARY motion is demonstrated in the example below:

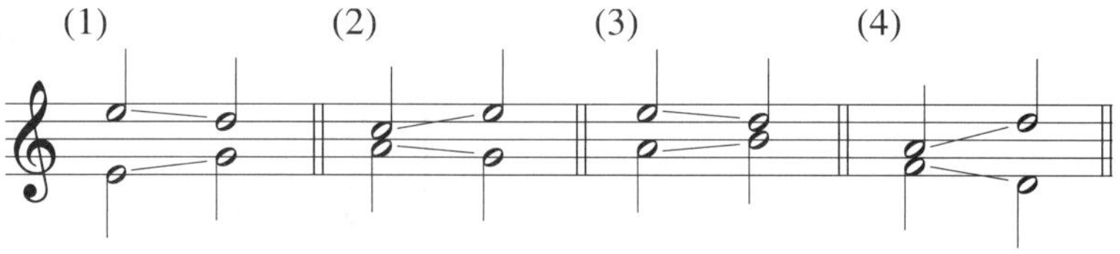

Two voices that move in *opposite directions* produce

____________ motion.

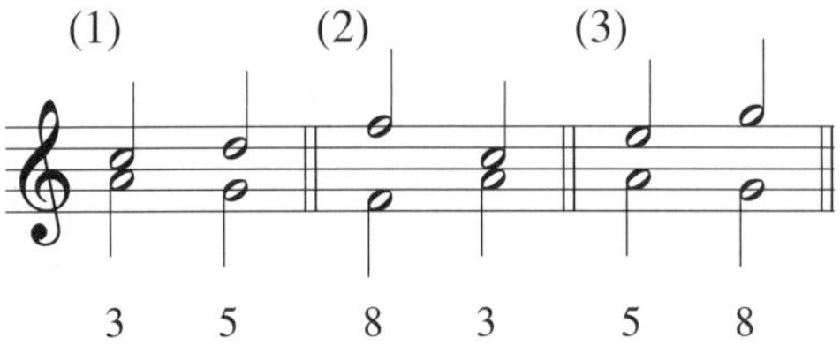

4.31 Write the notes indicated by the figured bass symbols.

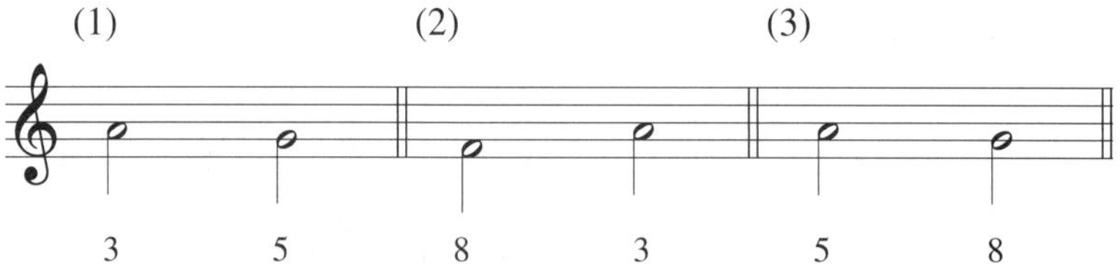

(3)

4.32 Each of the examples in the preceding frame demonstrates contrary motion. In which example below does contrary motion occur? _______

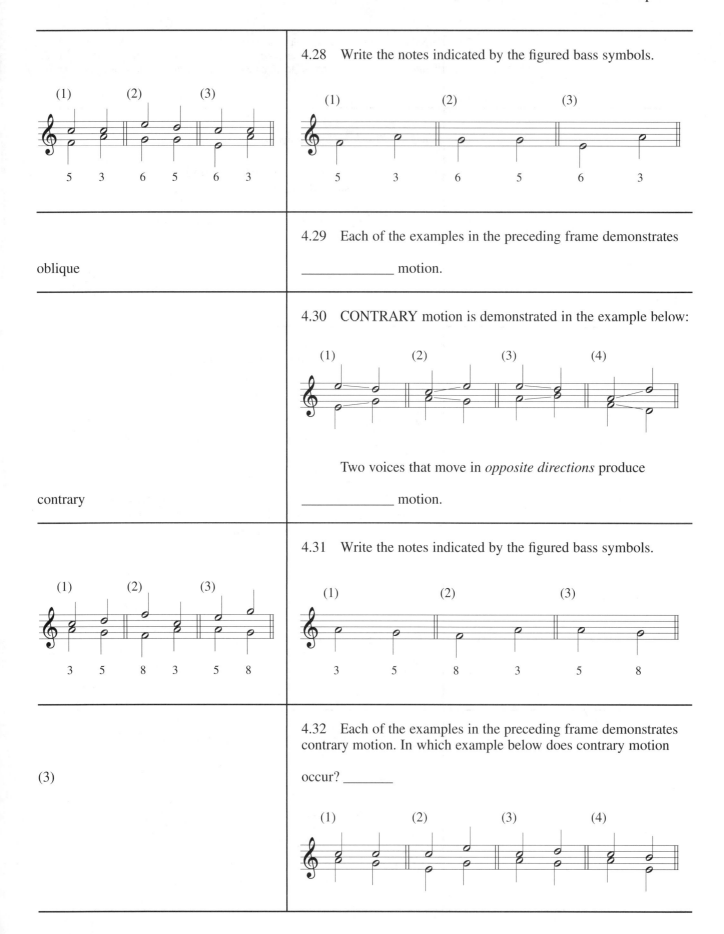

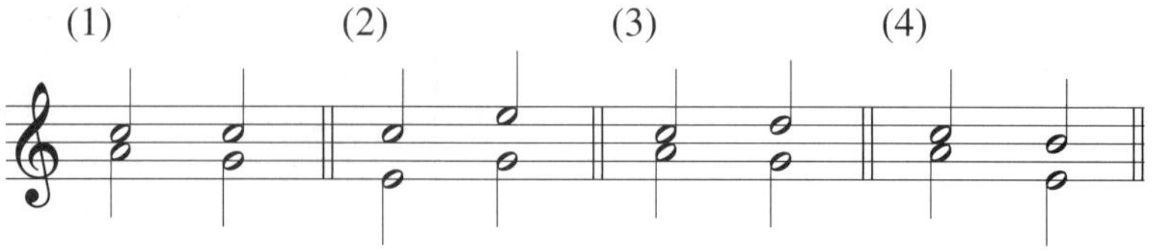

4.33 List the type of motion in each example.

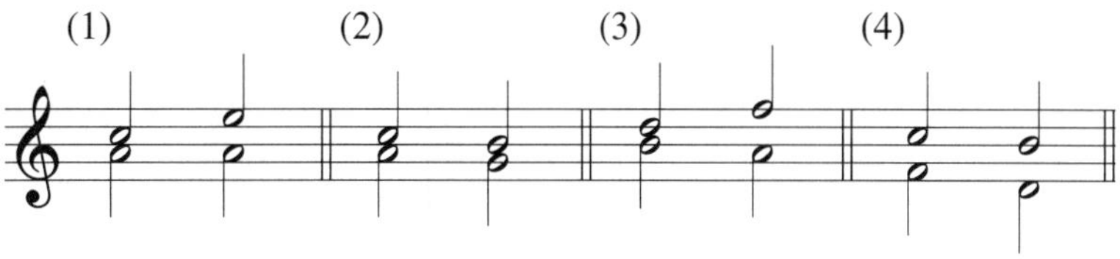

(1) ____________

(2) ____________

(3) ____________

(4) ____________

(1) Oblique
(2) Parallel
(3) Contrary
(4) Similar

4.34 List the type of motion in each example.

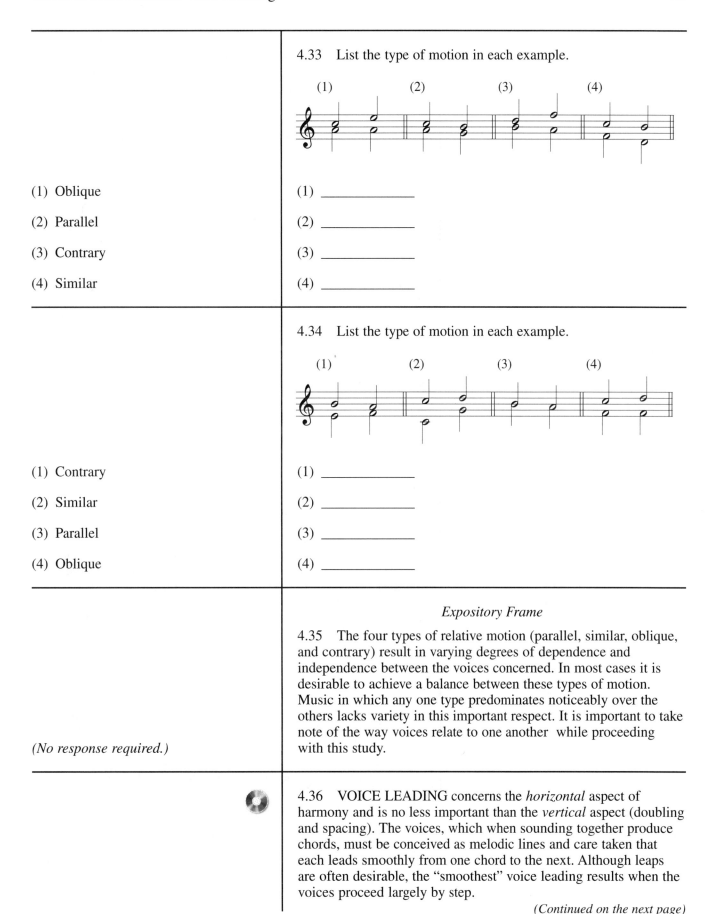

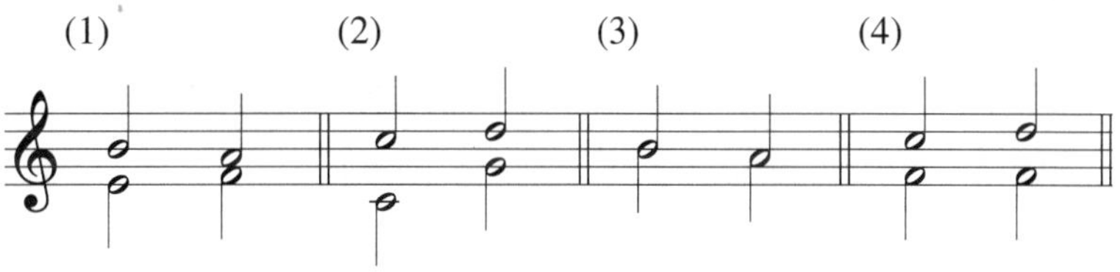

(1) ____________

(2) ____________

(3) ____________

(4) ____________

(1) Contrary
(2) Similar
(3) Parallel
(4) Oblique

Expository Frame

4.35 The four types of relative motion (parallel, similar, oblique, and contrary) result in varying degrees of dependence and independence between the voices concerned. In most cases it is desirable to achieve a balance between these types of motion. Music in which any one type predominates noticeably over the others lacks variety in this important respect. It is important to take note of the way voices relate to one another while proceeding with this study.

(No response required.)

4.36 VOICE LEADING concerns the *horizontal* aspect of harmony and is no less important than the *vertical* aspect (doubling and spacing). The voices, which when sounding together produce chords, must be conceived as melodic lines and care taken that each leads smoothly from one chord to the next. Although leaps are often desirable, the "smoothest" voice leading results when the voices proceed largely by step.

(Continued on the next page)

To demonstrate the characteristics of good voice leading the melodic intervals used in a chorale phrase harmonized by J. S. Bach will be analyzed. Please scan each of the voices separately and count the number of times a tone is followed by the same tone (repetition), the number of times seconds occur, and the number of times leaps of a third occur. Complete the tabulations and indicate the total for each category.

(The soprano has been analyzed as an example.)

Bach, Chorale: *Befiel du deine Wege*

	Rep.	2nd	3rd
S:	0	8	0
A:	2	7	0
T:	2	6	1
B:	2	8	1
T:	6	29	2

	Repetition	2nd	3rd
SOPRANO:	0	8	0
ALTO:	______	______	______
TENOR:	______	______	______
BASS:	______	______	______
TOTAL:	______	______	______

---

stepwise

4.37 Of the total melodic intervals in the preceding example 78 percent are major or minor seconds. Not all music displays such notable smoothness of voice leading. Indeed, melodic leaps of a fourth or more occasionally are used for their expressive value. The example above does serve, however, to demonstrate the smoothness which results when stepwise motion predominates.

Strive for smooth voice leading. This is accomplished by having a predominance of ______________ motion.

---

(4)

4.38 All augmented intervals, but especially the augmented second and the augmented fourth, should be avoided as melodic intervals when writing vocal music. These intervals are awkward to sing and composers of the baroque and classical eras took pains to avoid their use.

Which of the examples below is incorrect (in terms of the above statement)? _______________

augmented second

4.39 What interval is demonstrated in (4) of the preceding frame?

The ____________________ _____________.

---

(3)

4.40 Which example demonstrates awkward melodic movement?

____

(1) (2) (3) (4)

---

augmented second

4.41 What interval is demonstrated in (3) of the preceding frame

The ____________________ _____________.

---

(2)

4.42 Which example demonstrates awkward melodic movement? _______

(1) (2) (3) (4)

---

augmented fourth

4.43 What interval is demonstrated in (2) of the preceding frame?

The ____________________ _____________.

---

(1) M2
(2) A2
(3) P4
(4) A4

4.44 Name the melodic interval of each example (use abbreviations).

(1) (2) (3) (4)

______ ______ ______ ______

---

(2) A2 and (4) A4

4.45 Which of the examples in the preceding frame demonstrate intervals that should be avoided when writing vocal music?

____

Expository Frame

4.46 The augmented second and the augmented fourth sometimes occur as melodic intervals in instrumental music. This is due to the fact that instrumentalists do not have the problem of finding their pitch as do vocalists. Even in instrumental music, however, these intervals often are avoided for the sake of smooth melodic writing. In addition, instrumental music of the eighteenth and early nineteenth centuries was strongly influenced by vocal music. Thus it is natural that vocal melodic concepts should be reflected in instrumental styles.

Melodic intervals of the augmented second and the augmented fourth are not absolutely prohibited, but they should be avoided, particularly in music intended for voices.

(No response required.)

4.47 An augmented second is used as a melodic interval in the example below. Find this interval and indicate it with the sign (└x2┘).

Bach, *Well-Tempered Clavier,* Vol. 1, Prelude XII

(Andante)

4.48 An augmented fourth appears in the example below. Find this interval and indicate it with the sign (└x4┘).

Beethoven, *Sonatina in F Major*

Allegro assai

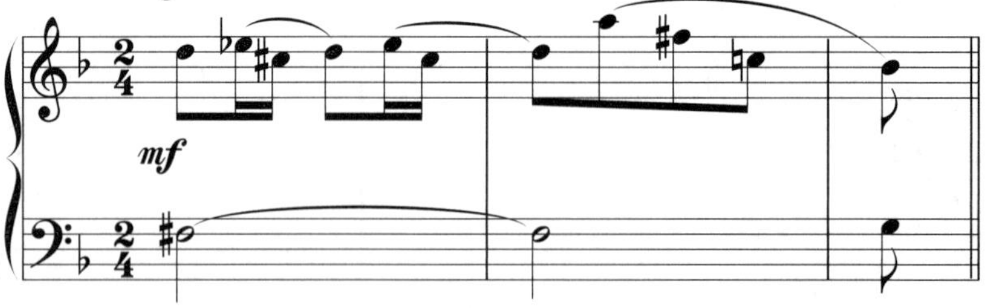

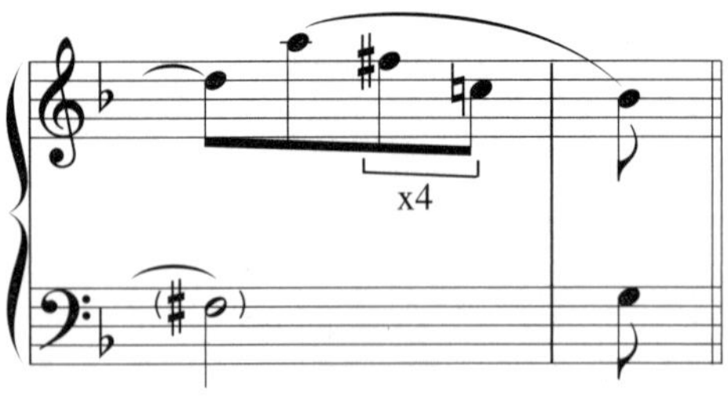

Expository Frame

4.49 The remainder of this chapter is devoted to the mechanics of voice leading. Before proceeding, however, the principles upon which this study will be based are reviewed.

The two chief concerns of part writing are the doubling and spacing of triad tones to produce agreeable sonorities, and leading the voices smoothly from one chord to another so that each voice constitutes an expressive melodic line.

Keep in mind the following principles regarding the part writing of triads in root position:

DOUBLING:

1. When a triad is in root position the bass is generally doubled.
2. Each chord should contain two roots, one third, and one fifth.

SPACING:

3. The voices should be in normal distribution (from upper to lower: soprano, alto, tenor, and bass).
4. The interval between adjacent upper voices should not exceed an octave.

VOICE LEADING:

5. Stepwise motion should predominate in leading voices from one chord to another.
6. Melodic leaps of an augmented interval, but especially the augmented second or augmented fourth, should be avoided.
7. Consecutive perfect unisons, fifths, or octaves are forbidden.

(No response required.)

4.50 When a chord in root position is repeated it is often desirable to change the position of some (or all) of the upper voices. In the example below, the static effect of (1) is avoided in (2) by moving each of the upper voices down one triad tone; in (3) the root and third have been exchanged in the soprano and tenor voices. Thus, for repeated root position chords, try to retain the tones common to each whenever possible and move the remaining tones to the nearest chord tones to achieve correct doubling and spacing.

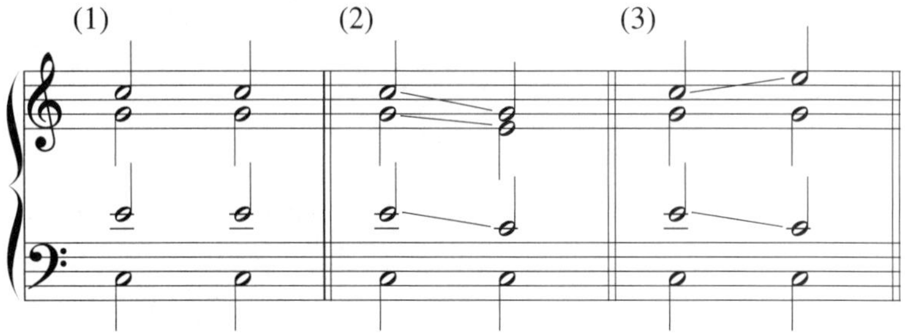

Which triad tone is doubled in each chord above? The

(root/3rd/5th) _______.

root

4.51 Notice that in (3) of the preceding frame there is a change from close to open structure, whereas in (2) both chords are in close structure. Change of structure occurs frequently upon chord repetition.

Write the alto and tenor voices for the second chord in each case *without change of structure.*

(Continued on the next page)

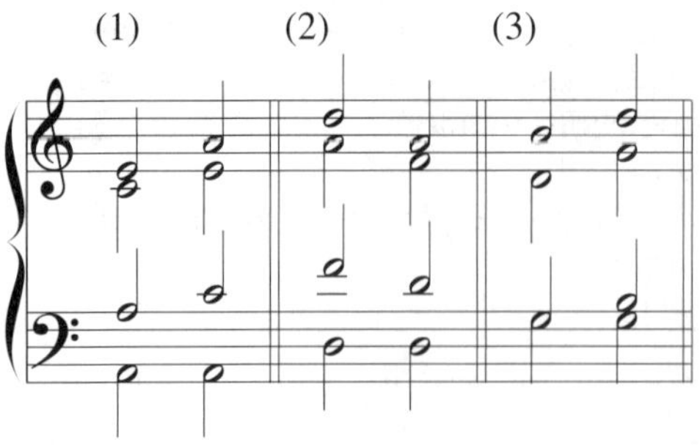

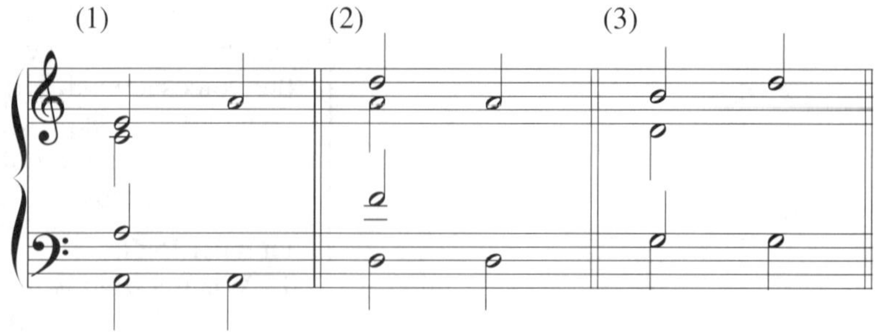

(If solutions do not agree with the answers given, check the doubling and spacing.)

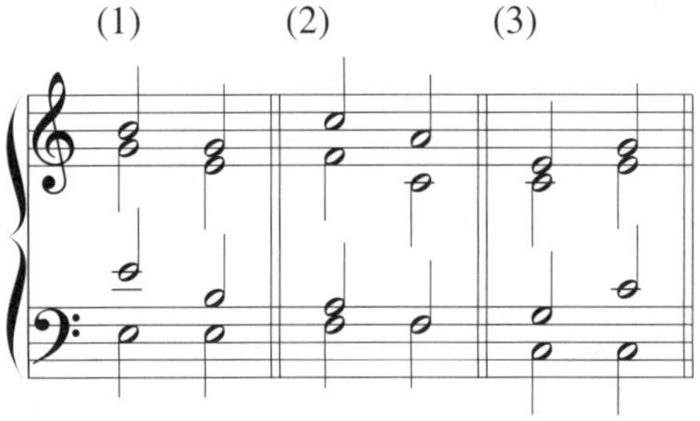

4.52 Write the alto and tenor voices for the second chord in each case *without change of structure.*

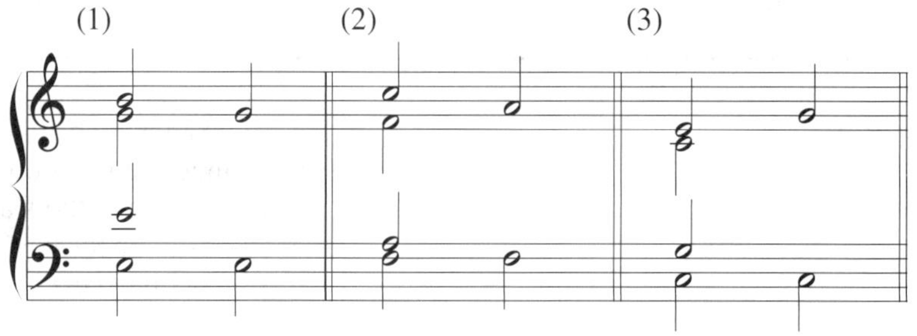

(Continue to check solutions as in the preceding frame.)

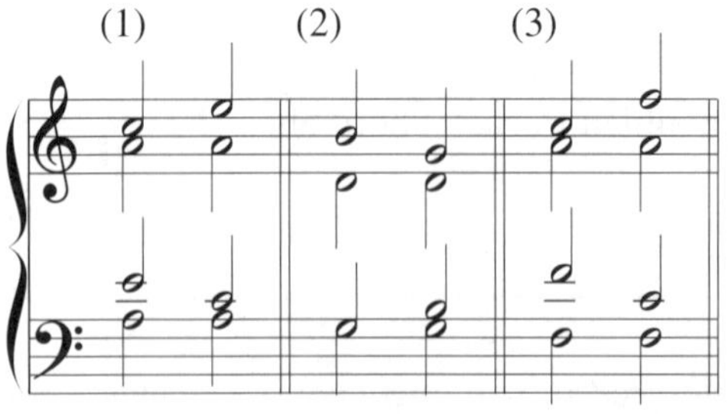

4.53 Write the alto and tenor voices for the second chord in each case. *Change structure on the second chord.*

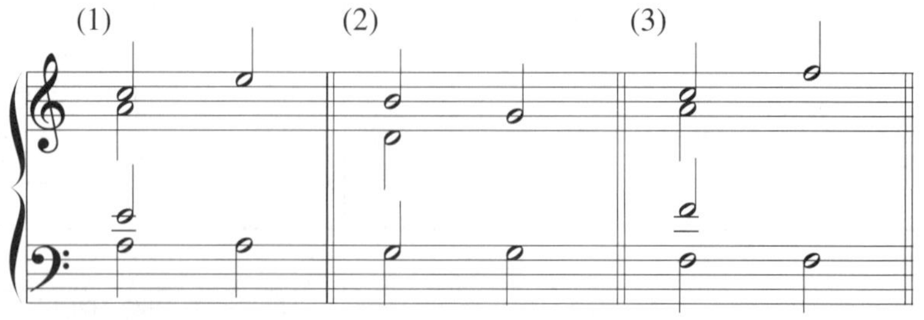

(Before looking at the answers, check: has the structure on the second chord been changed?)

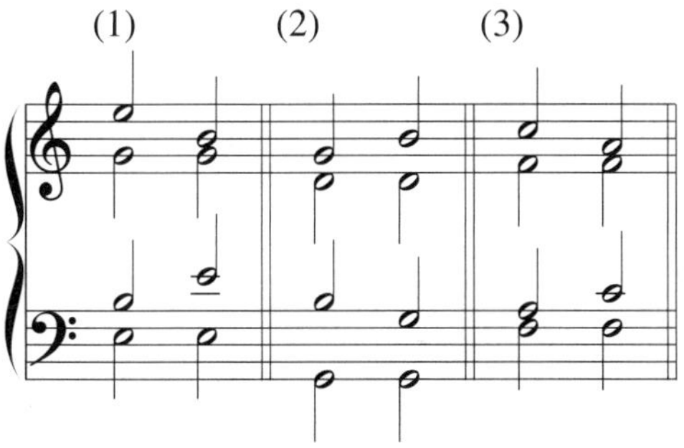

4.54 Write the alto and tenor voices for the second chord in each case. *Change structure on the second chord.*

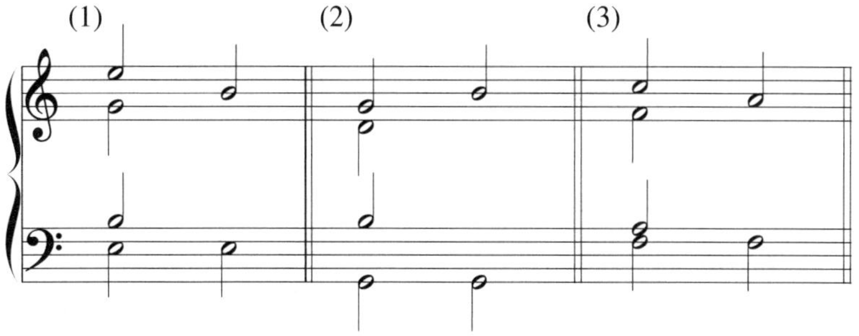

(Has the structure on the second chord been changed?)

Incorrect doubling
(There is no fifth in the second chord.)

4.55 What is the part writing error in the example below?

____

In the second chord the interval between the alto and tenor is greater than an octave. *(Or equivalent statement.)*

4.56 What is the part writing error in the example below?

____

4.57 In a succession of two chords there are often tones that occur in both. These are called COMMON TONES. When a triad is repeated both chords obviously contain the same tones.

(Continued on the next page)

Triad Tones: G - G / E - E / C - C

The two chords above have ____________ common tones.

three

4.58 The part writing of triads that have the same root is relatively simple—the chief concern is with redistributing the tones to produce correct doubling and spacing.

Name the common tones in the chords below: _______

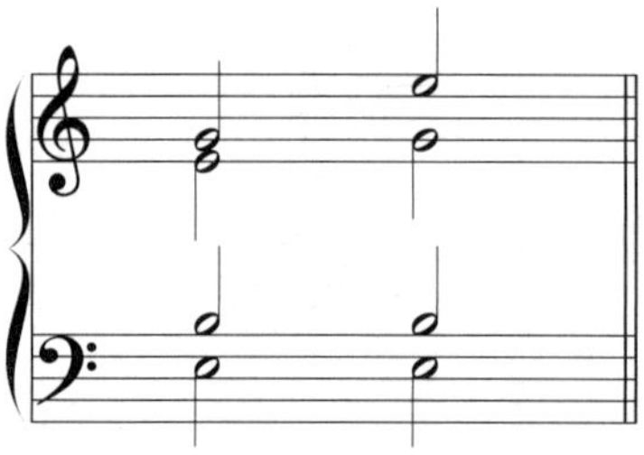

E G B

4.59 Whereas there are *three* common tones when a chord is repeated, there is only one common tone between triads whose roots are a fifth apart.*

(1) (2)

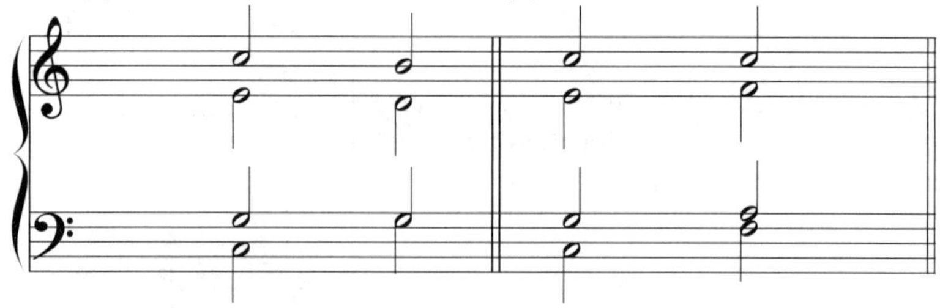

Triad tones:

	(1)		(2)	
	G	D	G	C
	E	B	E	A
	C	G	C	F

In both of these examples the common tone has been retained in the same voice. In (1) the common tone is in the tenor; in (2) it is in the ____________.

*Root movement a fifth upward is the same as a fourth downward and vice versa. Statements regarding root movement by fifths apply equally to root movement by fourths.

soprano

One	4.60 The examples in the preceding frame demonstrate the first method of part writing triads whose roots are a fifth apart. Learn this: PRINCIPLE 1 *When connecting triads whose roots are a fifth (or fourth) apart, retain the common tone in the same voice and move the remaining voices to the NEAREST chord tones to achieve correct doubling and spacing.* How many tones are common to two triads whose roots are a fifth apart? ____________
D	4.61 Name the tone that is common to the triads below: _______ 
Yes *(D has been retained in the tenor.)*	4.62 Has the common tone been retained in the same voice in the preceding frame? _______.
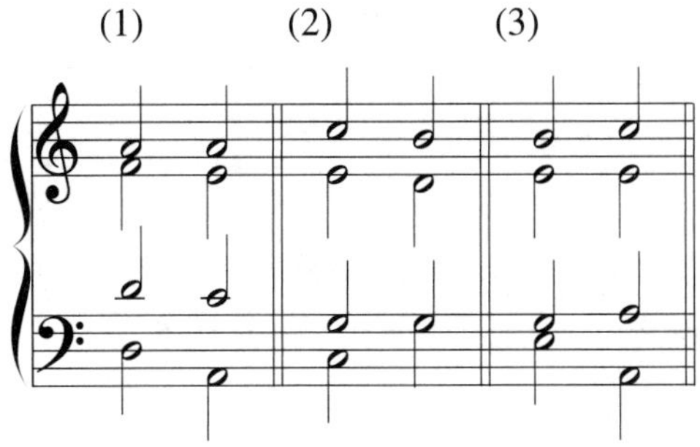	4.63 Write the alto and tenor voices for the second chord in each case. *Retain the common tone in the same voice.* 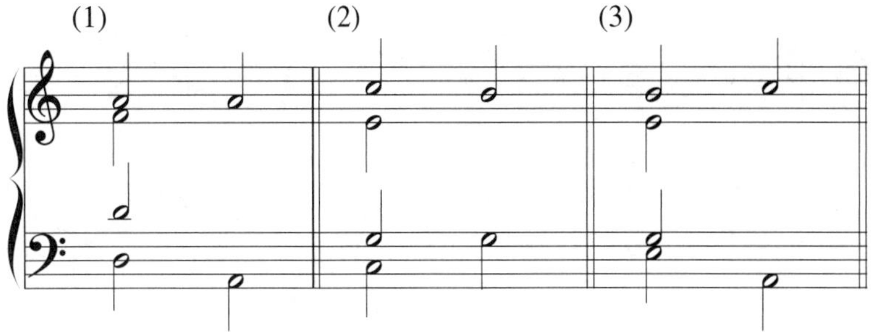

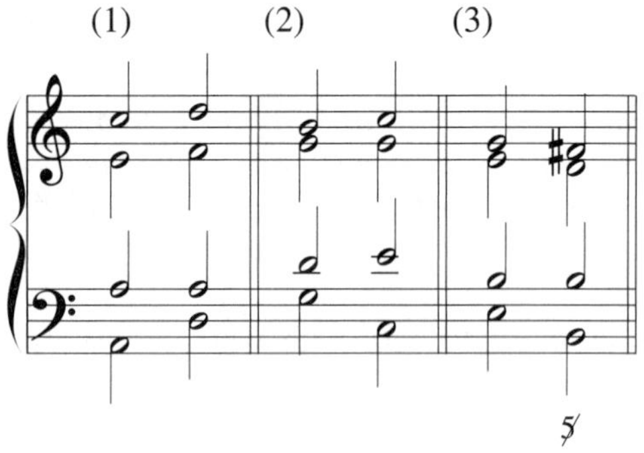

4.64 Write the alto and tenor voices for the second chord in each case. *Retain the common tone in the same voice.*

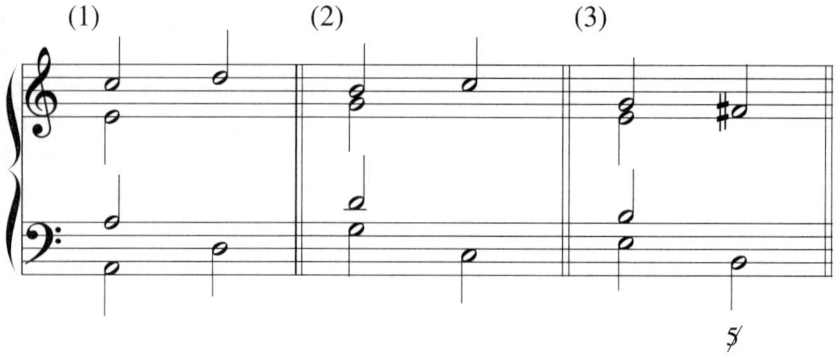

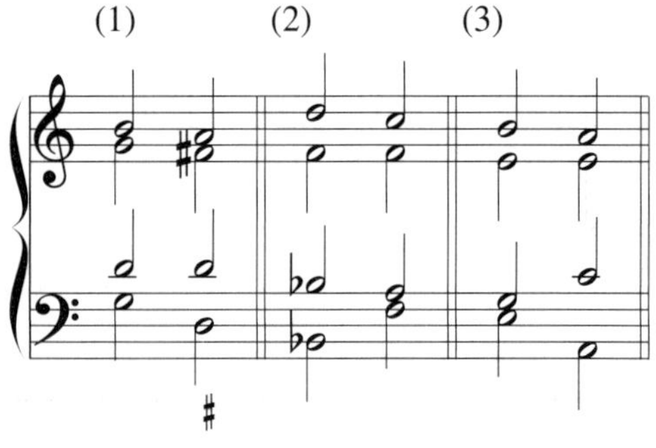

4.65 Write the alto and tenor voices for the second chord in each case. *Retain the common tone in the same voice.*

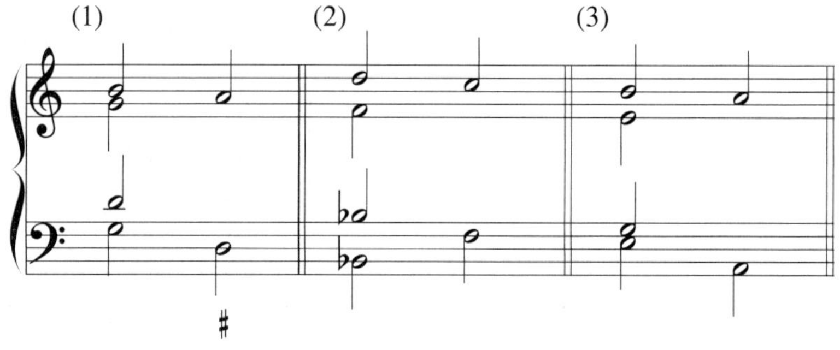

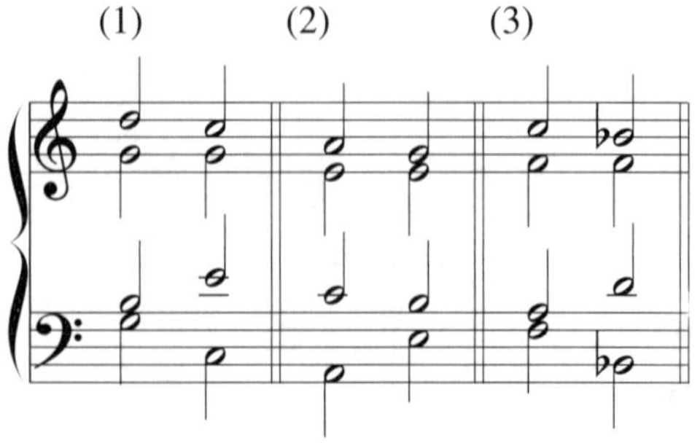

4.66 Notice in (3) of the preceding frame that the tenor was forced to leap a fourth to find a triad tone that resulted in correct doubling and spacing. *This is satisfactory.* Such leaps, however, must not occur too frequently, and should enhance the expressiveness of the melodic lines.

Write the alto and tenor voices for the second chord in each case. *Retain the common tone in the same voice.*

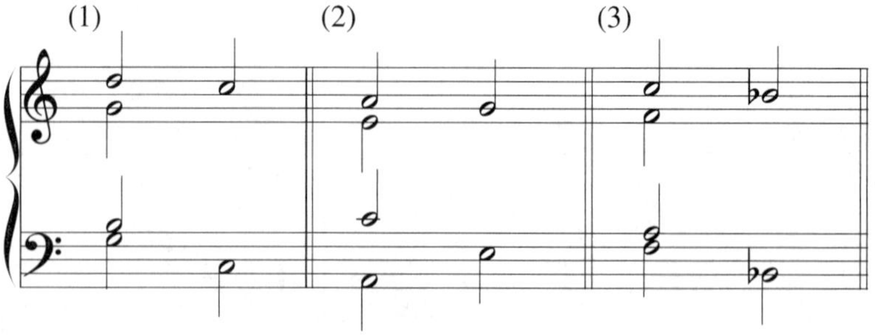

4.67 Examine the example below:

The common tone in this example is G. Has this tone been retained in the same voice? _______

No

4.68 The preceding example demonstrates the second method of part writing triads whose roots are a fifth apart. Learn this:

EXCEPTION 1

If, when connecting triads whose roots are a fifth (or fourth) apart, the common tone is NOT retained in the same voice, move all voices to the NEAREST chord tones that result in correct doubling and spacing.

In the example of the preceding frame the common tone (G) occurs in the alto of the first chord. In the second chord this tone is in the _____________.

tenor

Note that the "Principle List" is one "list" and the "Exception List" another. Each is numbered separately, or, if it is easier, for every principle there is usually an exception, which will be apparent as the discussion progresses.

4.69 The key word in the Exception stated in the preceding frame is "nearest." It is seldom necessary to leap more than a third in any of the upper voices. Any leap larger than a third should be examined carefully; it may be symptomatic of a part writing error.

Write the alto and tenor voices for the second chord in each case. *Do NOT retain the common tone in the same voice.*

(1) (2) (3)

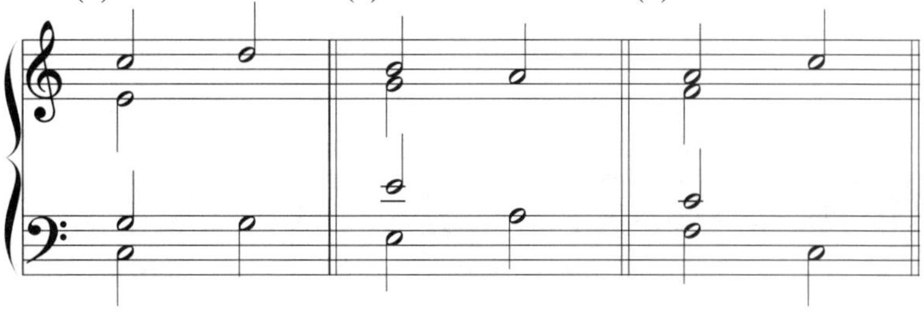

(1) (2) (3)

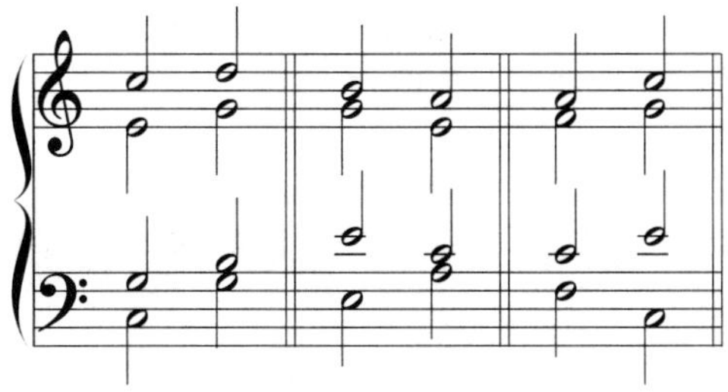

4.70 Write the alto and tenor voices for the second chord in each case. *Do NOT retain the common tone in the same voice.*

(Continued on the next page)

(1) (2) (3)

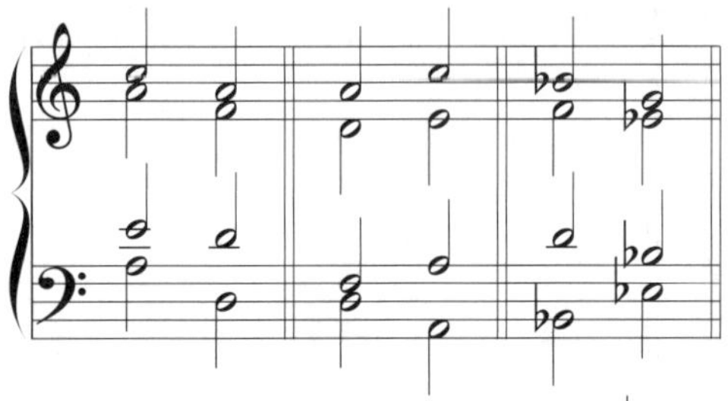

♭5

(1) (2) (3)

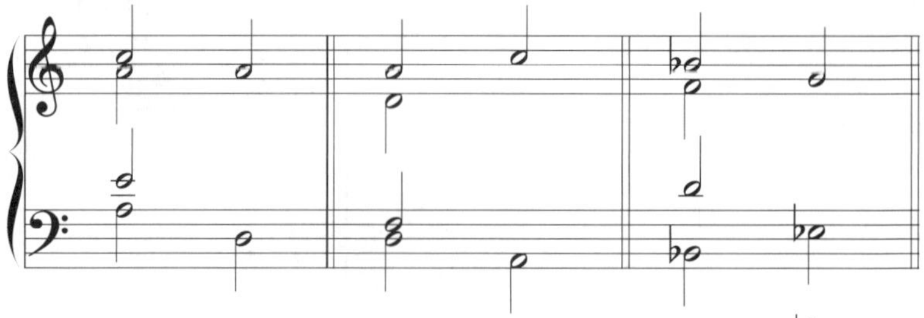

♭5

(1) (2) (3)

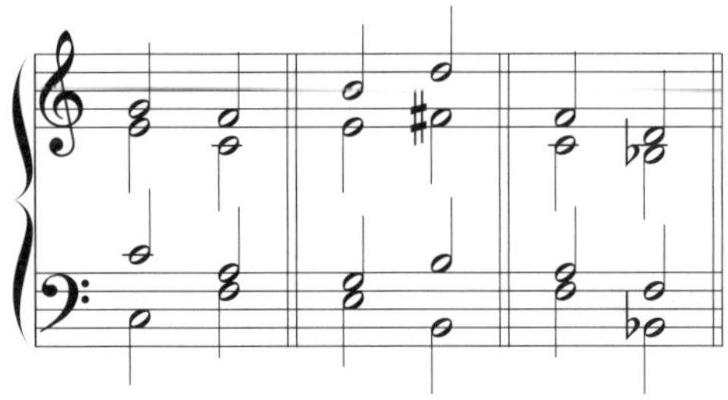

5/

4.71 Write the alto and tenor voices for the second chord in each case. *Do NOT retain the common tone in the same voice.*

(1) (2) (3)

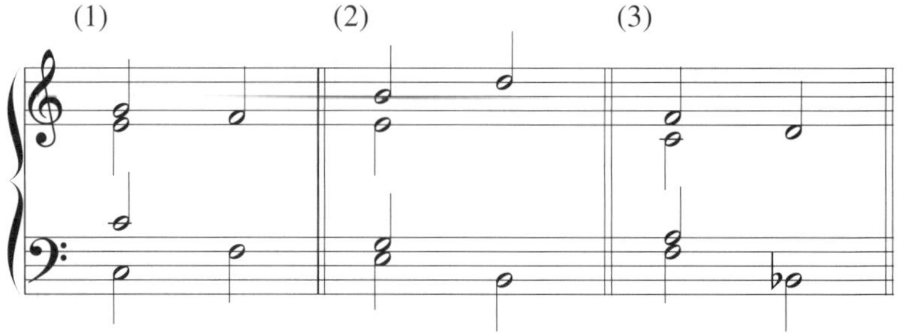

5/

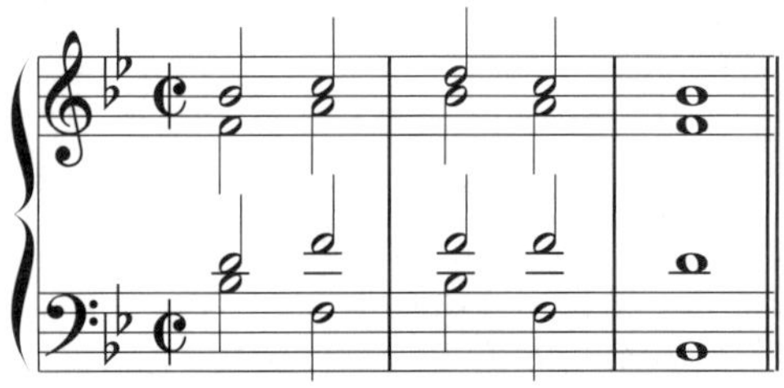

B♭: I V I V I

4.72 Write the alto and tenor voices and supply the roman numeral analysis. *Use CLOSE structure for all chords.*

B♭: ___ ___ ___ ___ ___

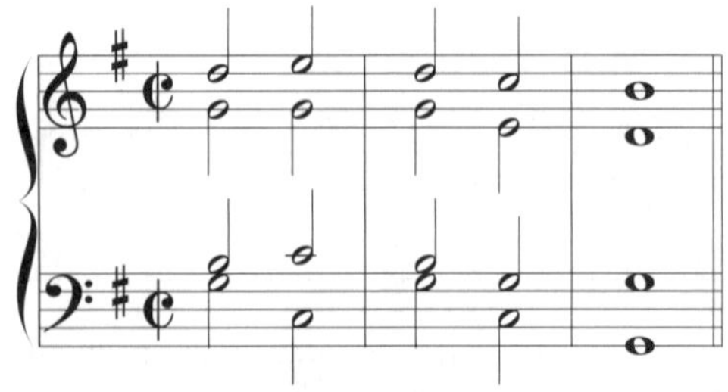

G: I IV I IV I

4.73 Write the alto and tenor voices and supply the roman numeral analysis. *Use OPEN structure for all chords.*

G: ___ ___ ___ ___ ___

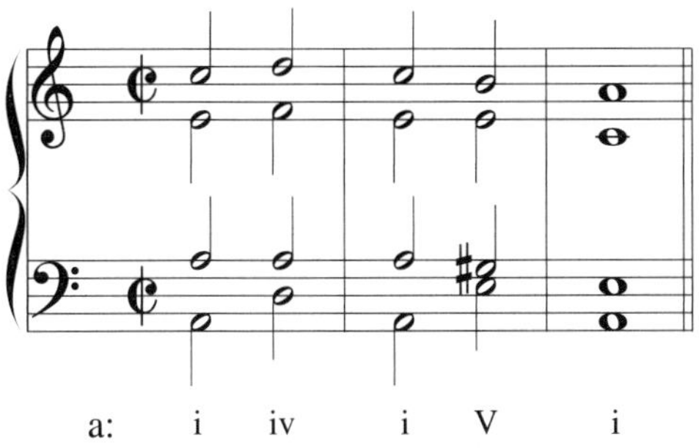

4.74 Write the alto and tenor voices and supply the roman numeral analysis. *Use OPEN structure for all chords.*

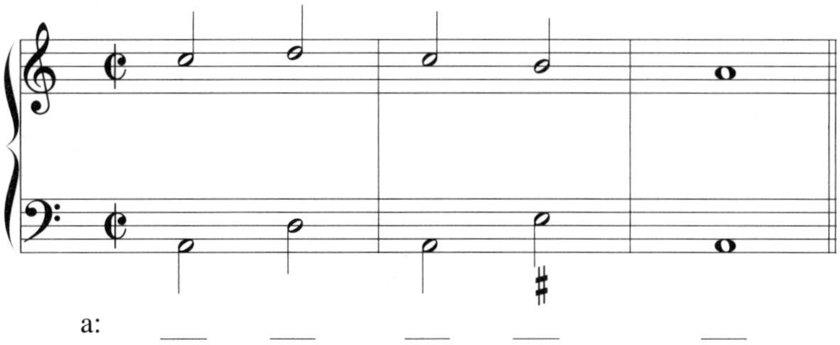

F G
A B
C D

4.75 There are NO common tones between triads whose roots are a second apart. List the triad tone for each of the chords below:

Triad tones: { ___ ___ / ___ ___ / ___ ___ }

No
(There are no common tones.)

4.76 Learn this:

PRINCIPLE 2

When connecting triads whose roots are a second apart, move all the upper voices to the nearest chord tones in CONTRARY MOTION to the bass.

Can a common tone be retained when connecting triads whose roots are a second apart?_______

(1) (2) (3)

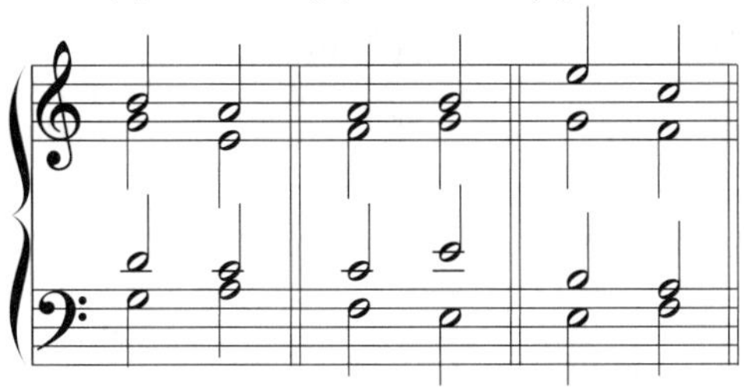

4.77 Write the soprano, alto, and tenor voices for the second chord in each case. Be sure that all of the upper voices move to their nearest chord tone in *contrary motion* to the bass.

(1) (2) (3)

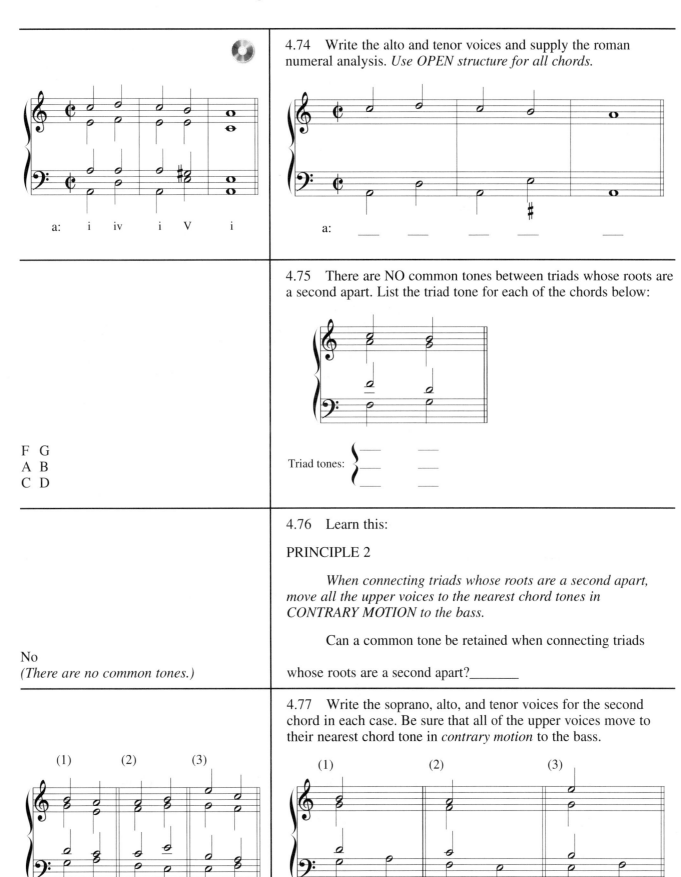

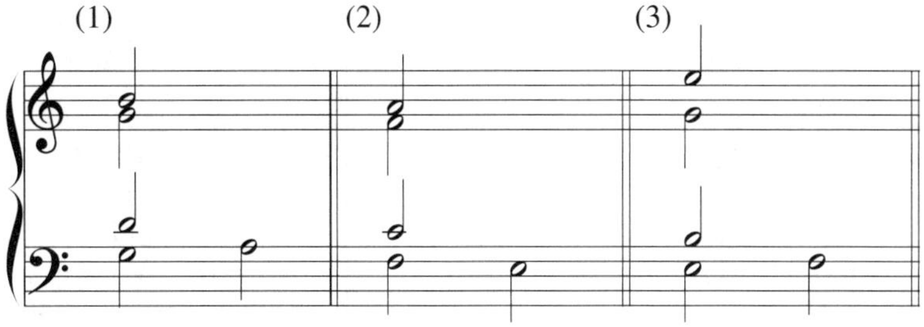

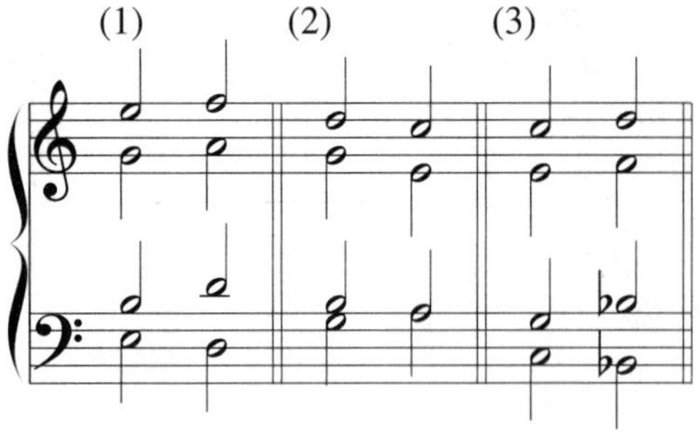

4.78 Write the soprano, alto, and tenor voices for the second chord in each case. Be sure that all of the upper voices move to their nearest chord tone in *contrary motion* to the bass.

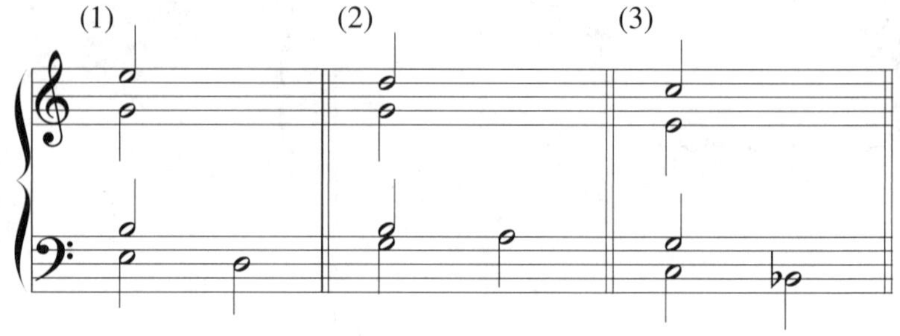

2nd

4.79 If the upper voices fail to move in contrary motion to the bass (when connecting triads whose roots are a second apart), parallel fifths and octaves are likely to occur. In all future work, check for incorrect use of parallel motion each time a chord is part written. *Be especially alert when the bass moves a second.*

To be certain consecutive perfect intervals have not been written, check the motion between each of the voices as follows:

1. From the bass to each of the upper voices.
2. From the tenor to the alto and soprano.
3. From the alto to the soprano.

Incorrect parallel motion is more likely to occur when the bass moves a (5th/2nd) _______.

	1st	2nd
(1)	M3	m3
(2)	P5	P5
(3)	P8	P8
(4)	m3	M3
(5)	m6	M6
(6)	P4	P4

4.80 Apply the method described in the preceding frame by tabulating the intervals between the various voices for each of the chords below (the first has been done as an example):

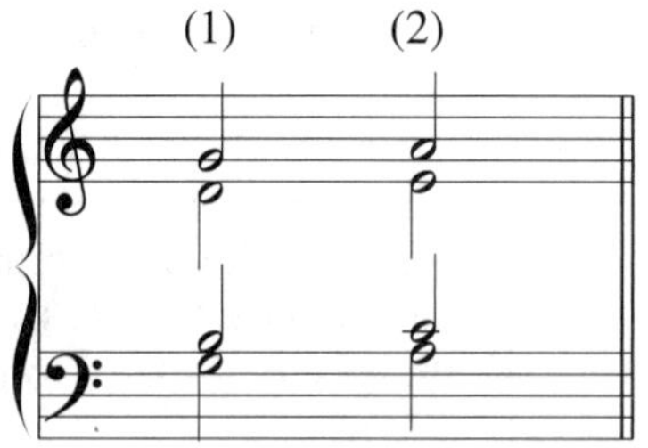

	1st Chord	2nd Chord
(1) Bass and Tenor	M3	m3
(2) Bass and Alto	_______	_______
(3) Bass and Soprano	_______	_______
(4) Tenor and Alto	_______	_______
(5) Tenor and Soprano	_______	_______
(6) Alto and Soprano	_______	_______

bass (and) alto

4.81 In a check, such as that of the preceding frame, incorrect parallel motion shows up as a succession of perfect unisons, fifths, or octaves *between the same two voices.* In this case incorrect parallel motion occurs not only between the bass and soprano, but also between the ____________ and ____________.

	1st	2nd
(1)	m3	M3
(2)	m6	P8
(3)	m3	P5
(4)	P4	m6
(5)	P8	m3
(6)	P5	P5

4.82 For additional practice in detecting incorrect parallel motion tabulate the intervals between the various voices in each of the chords below:

(Note: The first chord is not in root position.)

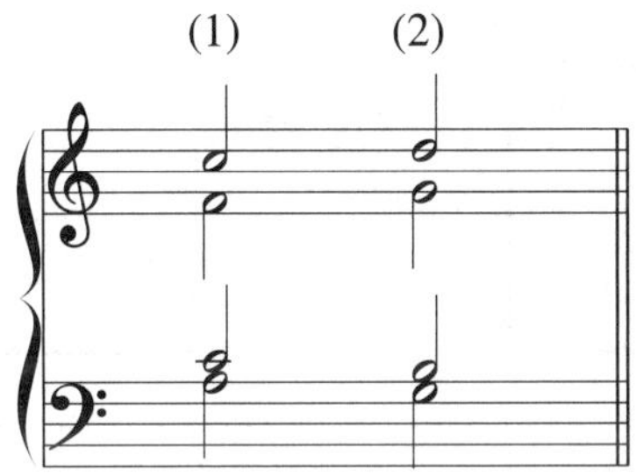

	1st Chord	2nd Chord
(1) Bass and Tenor	_______	_______
(2) Bass and Alto	_______	_______
(3) Bass and Soprano	_______	_______
(4) Tenor and Alto	_______	_______
(5) Tenor and Soprano	_______	_______
(6) Alto and Soprano	_______	_______

---

alto (and) soprano

4.83 Between which voices does incorrect parallel motion occur in the preceding frame? Between the ________ and ________.

---

bass (and) alto

4.84 The method of checking for incorrect parallel motion described in Frame 4.79 seems at first to be laborious. There is no other way, however, to be certain that no mistakes have been made. Ways to speed the process will soon be found. By using this method each time a chord is part written, many careless mistakes will be avoided.

Between which voices does incorrect parallel motion occur in the example on the next page? Between the ____________ and ____________.

(Continued on the next page)

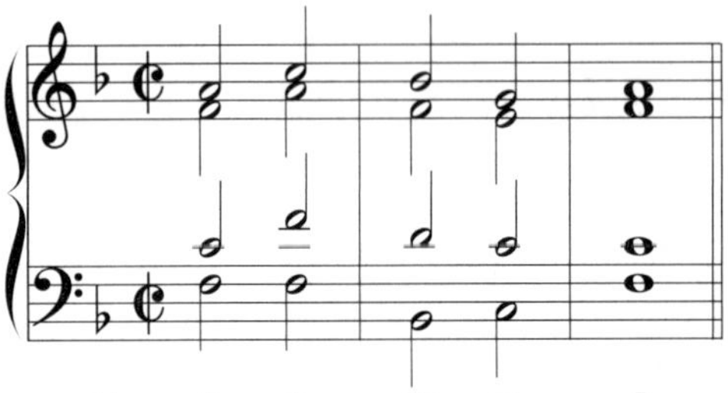

F: I I IV V I

4.85 Write the alto and tenor voices and supply the roman numeral analysis. *Use CLOSE structure for all chords.*

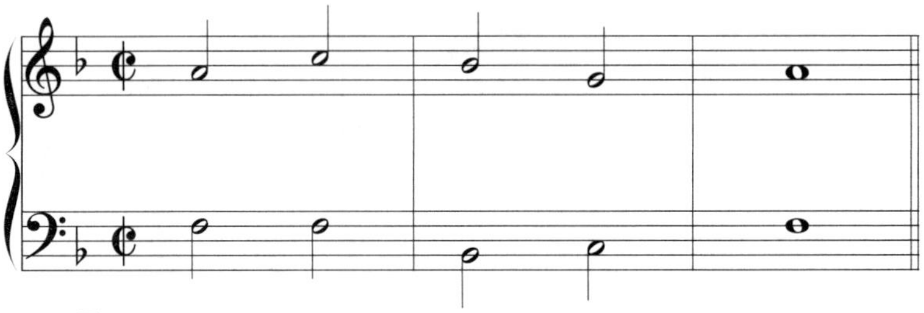

F: ___ ___ ___ ___ ___

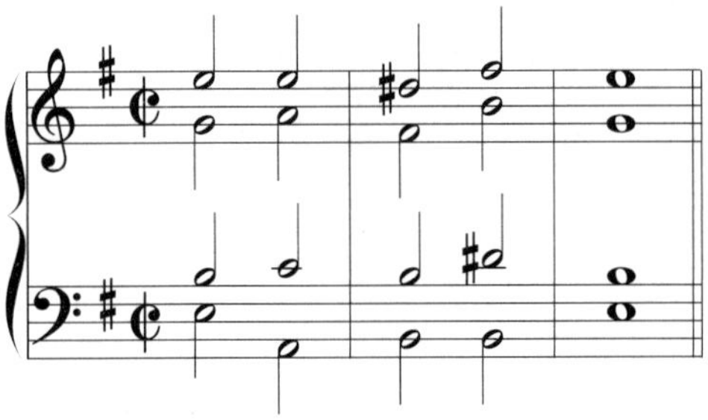

e: i iv V V i

4.86 Write the alto and tenor voices and supply the roman numeral analysis. *Use OPEN structure for all chords.*

e: ___ ___ ___ ___ ___

The bass has not been doubled. *(There are two 3rds instead of two roots.)*

4.87 Examine the progression below:

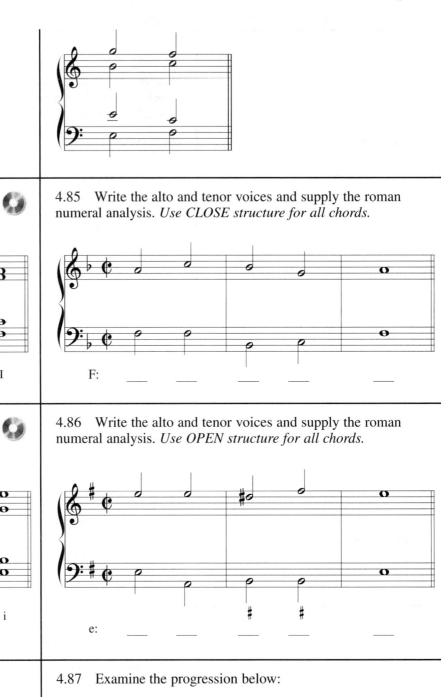

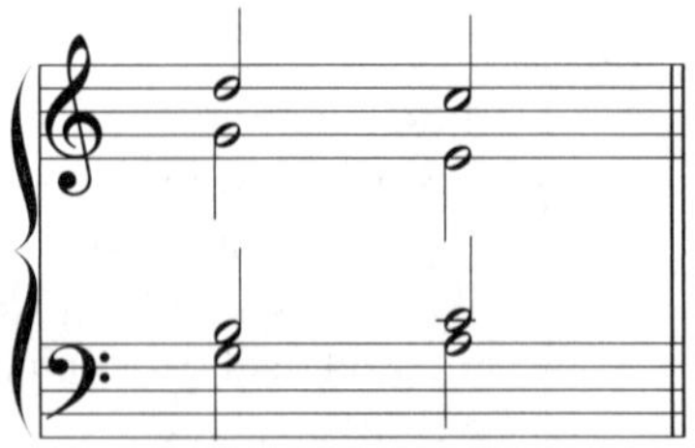

What irregularity occurs in the second chord? ________________

____

4.88 The preceding frame demonstrates an exception to the usual method of part writing triads whose roots are a second apart. Learn this:

EXCEPTION 2

*When the bass moves UP a second, one voice may move in parallel thirds (or tenths) with the bass, resulting in a double third in the second chord.**

Except for the voice that moves in parallel thirds (or tenths) with the bass, all upper voices move normally (down in

_____________ motion to the bass).

*Exception 2 does not apply to the progression IV–V, where it would result in a doubled leading tone. (See Frames 5.91 and 5.98.)

contrary

4.89 Which of the examples below demonstrates the Exception stated in the preceding frame? *(Look for a double third in the second chord.)* _______

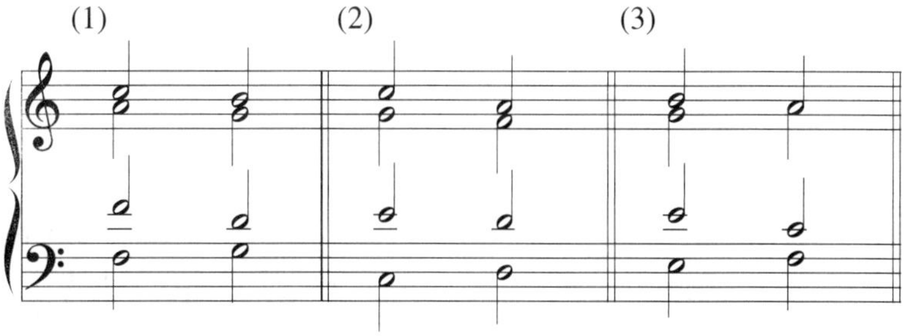

(3)

4.90 Note in (3) of the preceding frame that all of the upper voices move normally (in contrary motion to the bass) except the one that moves up in parallel tenths.

Write the soprano, alto, and tenor voices for the second chord applying the exception stated in Frame 4.88. *(Remember: the third must be doubled in the second chord.)*

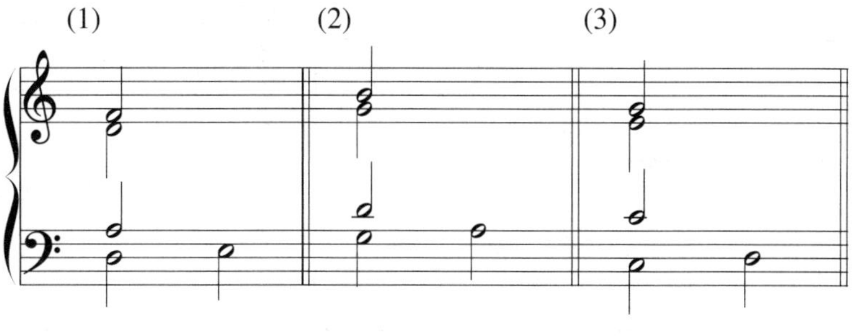

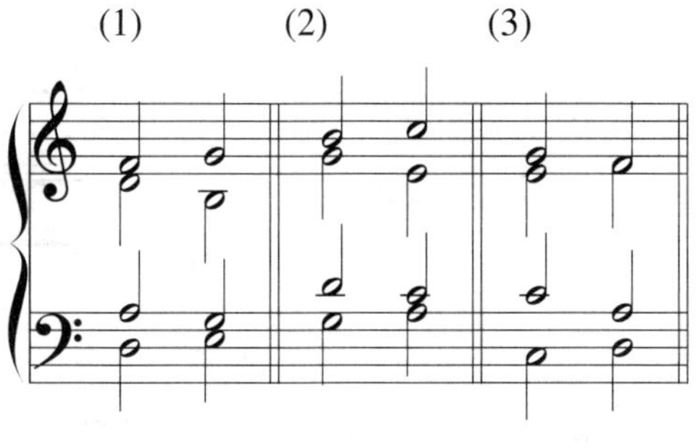

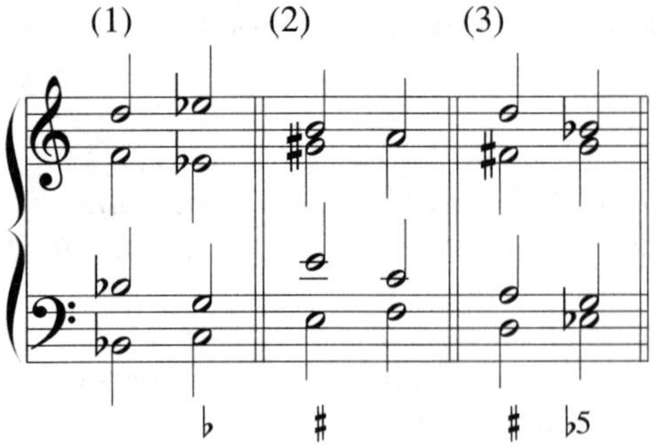

4.91 Continue as in the preceding frame.

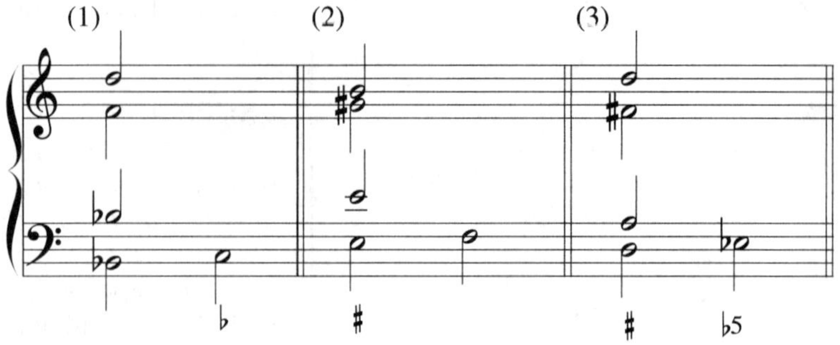

4.92 The irregularity of doubling described in Frame 4.88 is used most often as a means of avoiding the augmented second that otherwise occurs when progressing from V to VI in harmonic minor.

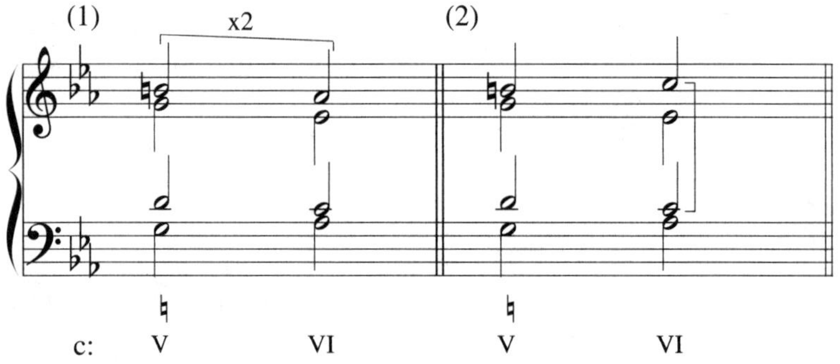

If all voices move in contrary motion to the bass, an augmented second results, as is shown in (1). The usual solution to this problem is shown in (2). The irregular doubling in the second example is less offensive than the augmented second in the first.

When progressing from V to VI in harmonic minor, the second chord will usually contain a doubled _____________.

third

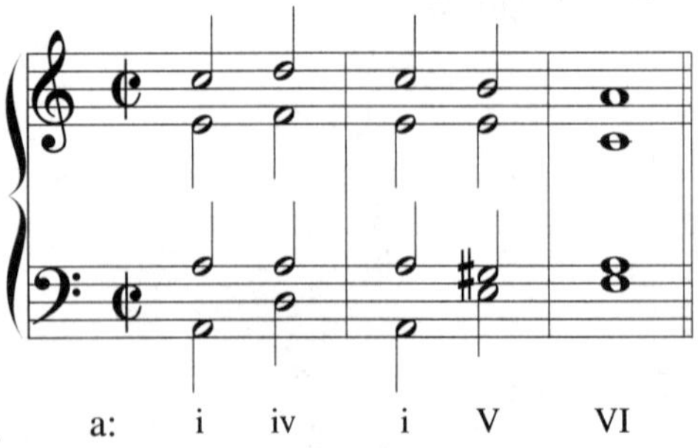

4.93 Write the alto and tenor voices and supply the roman numeral analysis. *(Irregular doubling must occur in the final chord.)*

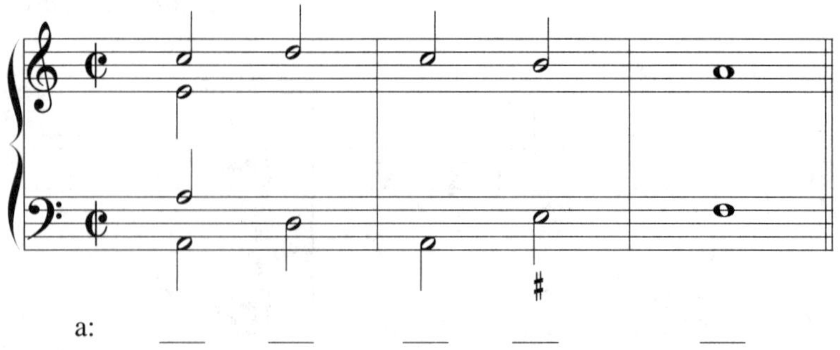

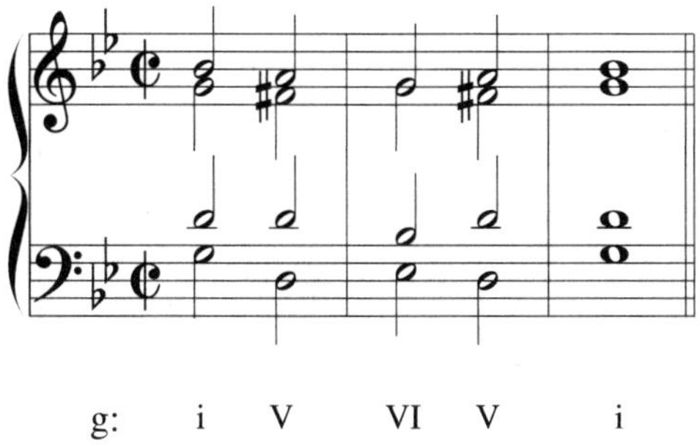

One

4.94 Write the alto and tenor voices and supply the roman numeral analysis.

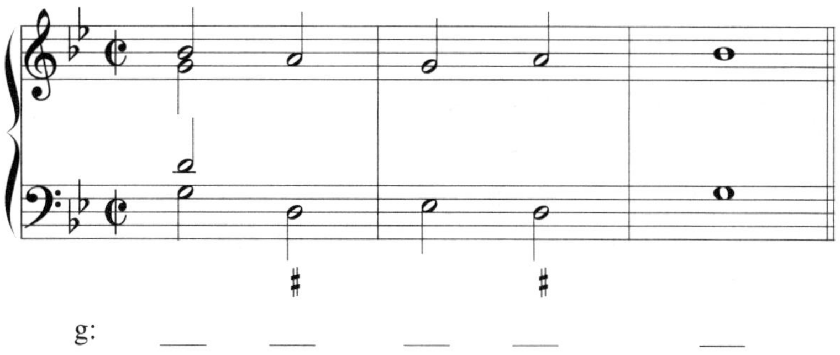

4.95 There are *two* common tones between triads whose roots are a third apart.

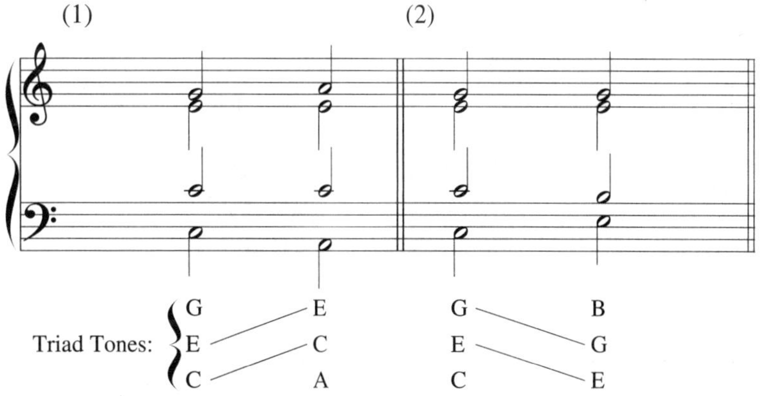

The above example demonstrates the usual method of part writing triads whose roots are a third apart. Learn this:

PRINCIPLE 3

When connecting triads whose roots are a third apart, retain two common tones and move the remaining voice to the nearest chord tone.

In applying the principle stated above, how many of the upper voices will move? _______

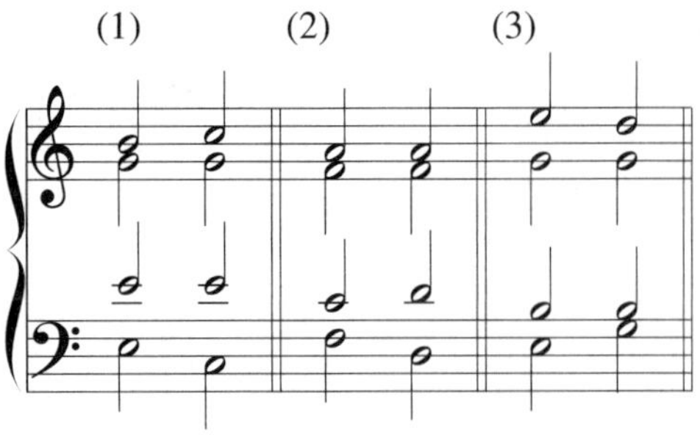

4.96 Write the soprano, alto, and tenor voices for the second chord in each case. *Retain TWO common tones in the same voices.*

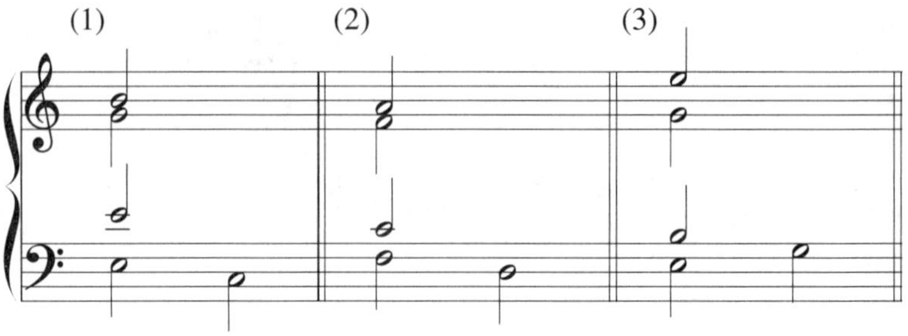

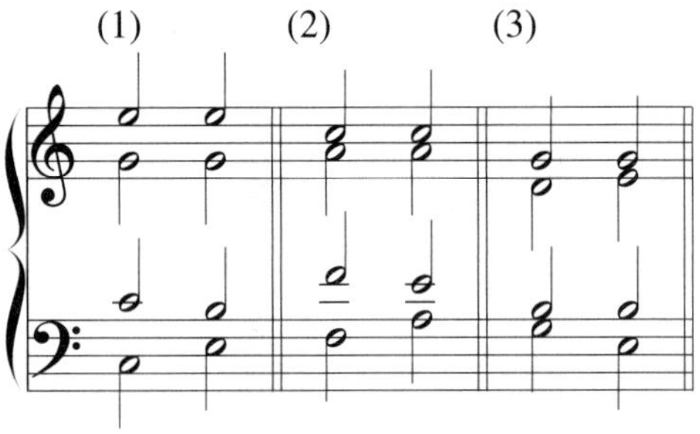

4.97 Write the soprano, alto, and tenor voices for the second chord in each case. *Retain TWO common tones in the same voices.*

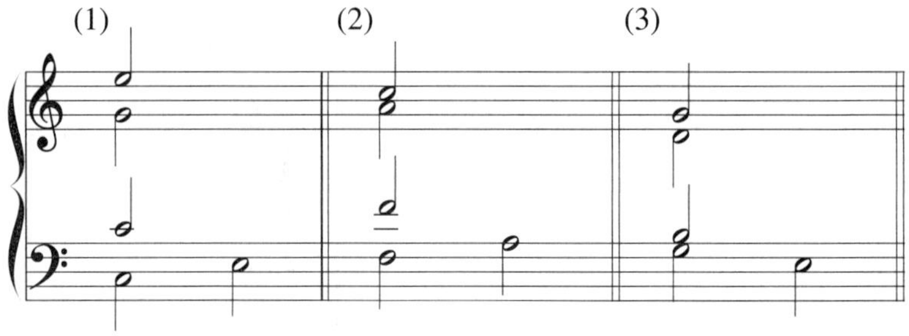

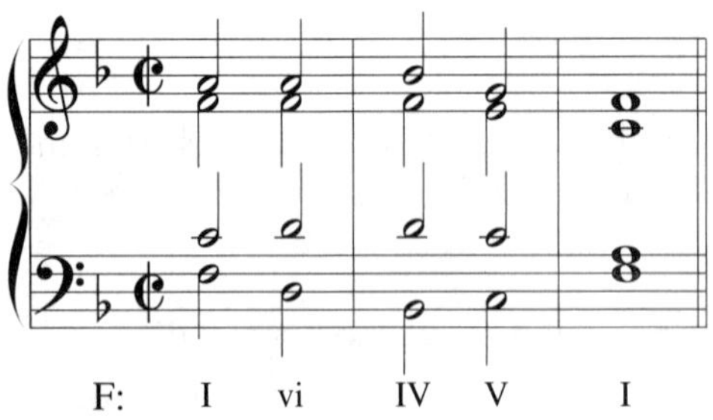

4.98 Write the alto and tenor voices and supply the roman numeral analysis.

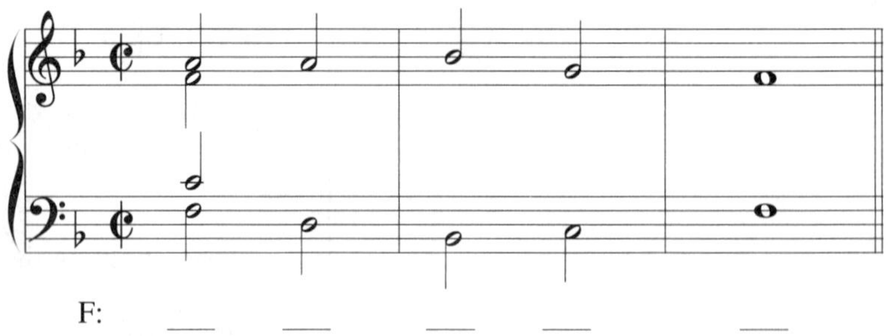

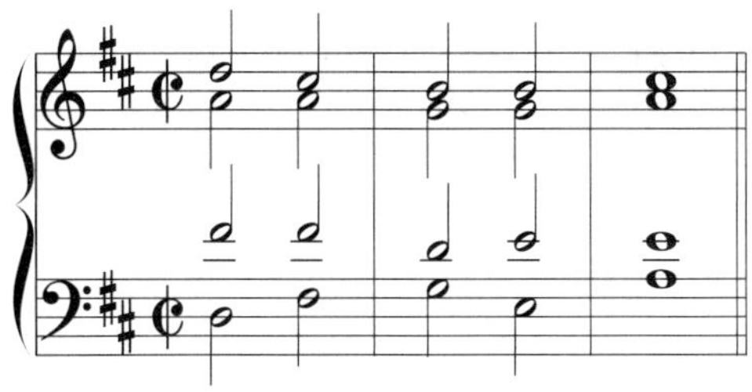

D: I iii IV ii V

4.99 Write the alto and tenor voices and supply the roman numeral analysis.

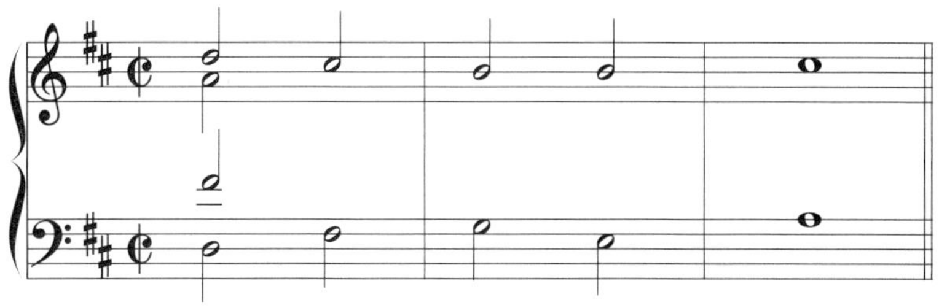

D: ___ ___ ___ ___ ___

a: i VI iv V VI

4.100 Write the alto and tenor voices and supply the roman numeral analysis. *(Take care to avoid having an augmented second in any voice between the last two chords.)*

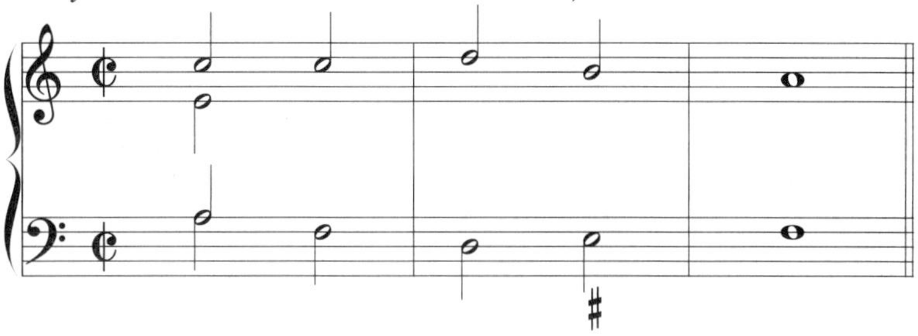

a: ___ ___ ___ ___ ___

4.101 Compare the two examples below:

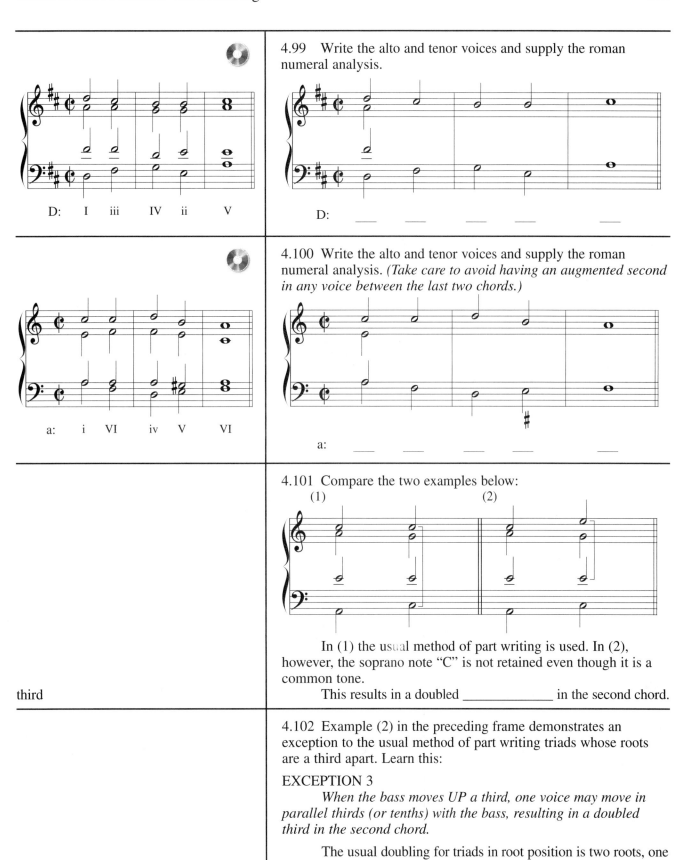

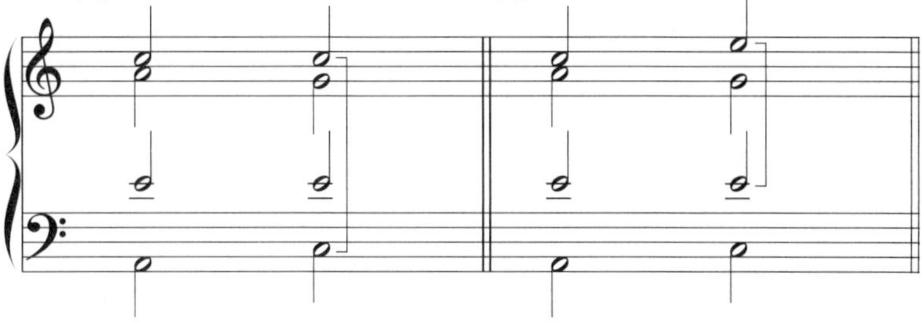

In (1) the usual method of part writing is used. In (2), however, the soprano note "C" is not retained even though it is a common tone.

This results in a doubled ____________ in the second chord.

third

4.102 Example (2) in the preceding frame demonstrates an exception to the usual method of part writing triads whose roots are a third apart. Learn this:

EXCEPTION 3

When the bass moves UP a third, one voice may move in parallel thirds (or tenths) with the bass, resulting in a doubled third in the second chord.

The usual doubling for triads in root position is two roots, one third, and one fifth. In order to avoid more serious errors, sometimes instead of doubling the root, the ____________ may be doubled.

third

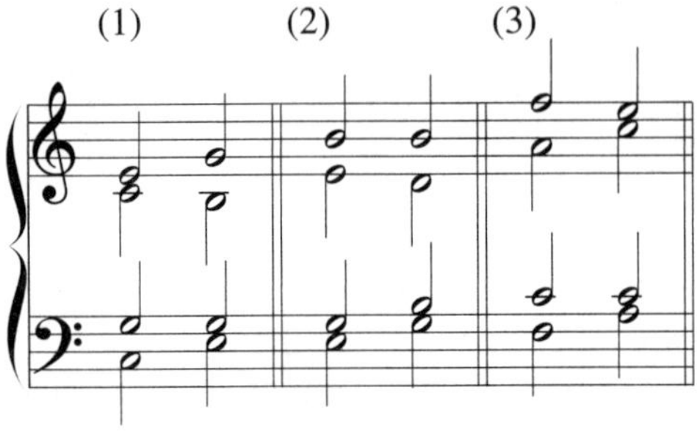

4.103 Write the soprano, alto, and tenor voices for the second chord in each case applying the Exception stated in the preceding frame. *(Remember: the third must be doubled in the second chord.)*

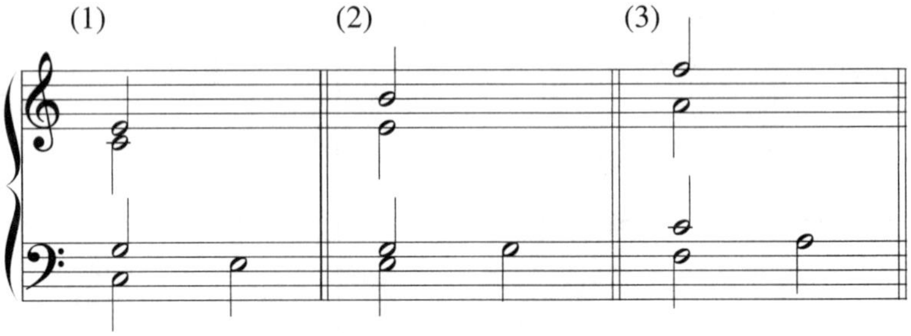

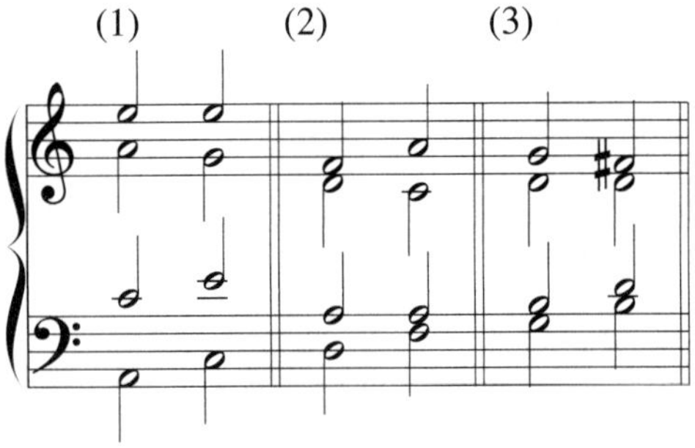

4.104 Continue as in the preceding frame.

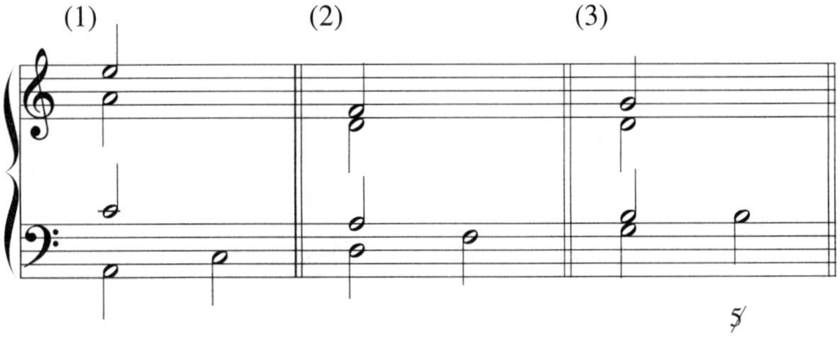

C:	I	I	IV	V	I
Alter.:	C	C	F	G	C

4.105 Write the alto and tenor voices and supply both the roman numeral and alternative analyses*.

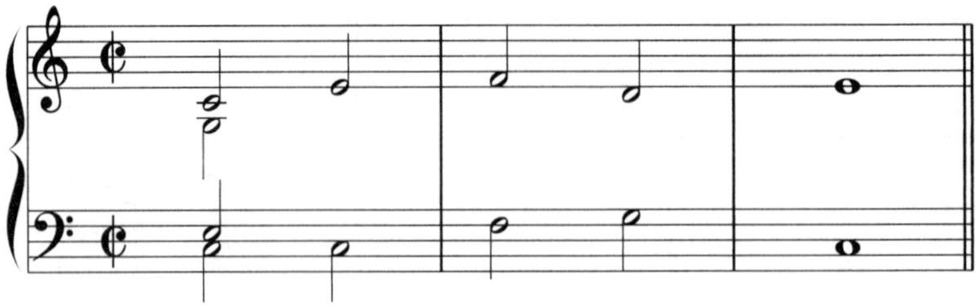

C: ___ ___ ___ ___ ___

Alternative: ___ ___ ___ ___ ___

*Throughout the remaining pages of the text, opportunities will be given to write alternative analyses to have practice in making connections with chord symbols associated with those generally used in pop, commercial, and jazz music scores.

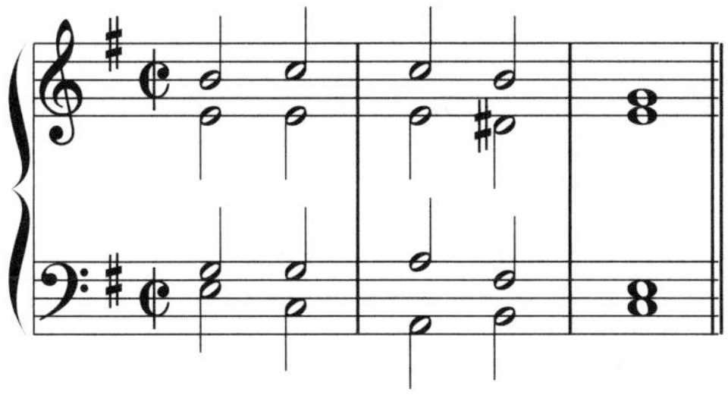

e: i VI iv V VI

Alter.: Emi C Ami B C

4.106 Write the alto and tenor voices and supply both the roman numeral and alternative analyses. *(Be alert when part writing the last two chords.)*

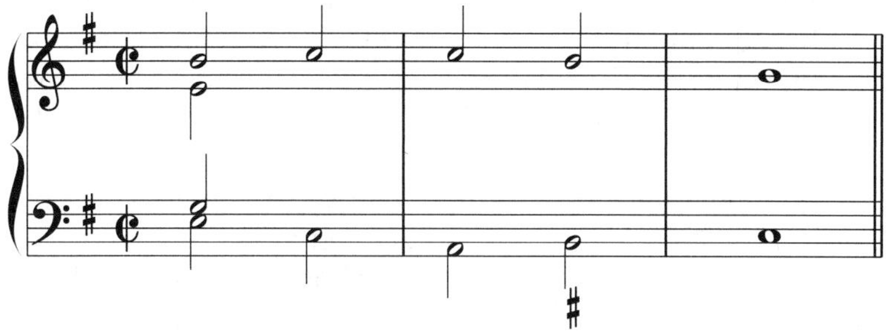

e: ___ ___ ___ ___ ___

Alternative: ___ ___ ___ ___ ___

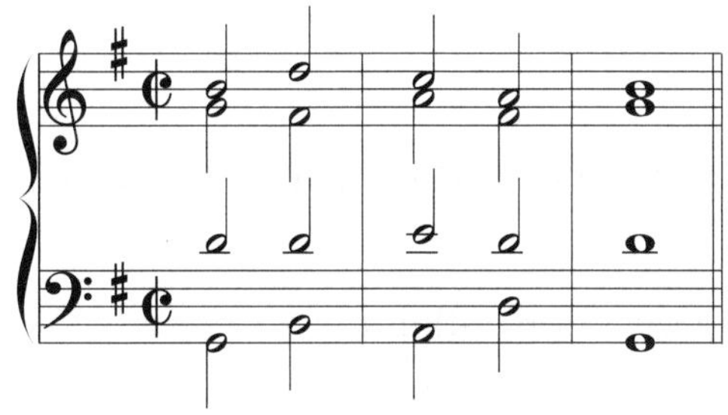

G: I iii ii V I

4.107 Irregular doubling should not occur in several chords in succession. Return immediately to normal doubling after a chord in which irregular doubling occurs.

Write the alto and tenor voices and supply the roman numeral analysis. Irregular doubling will occur at the asterisk. Take care that the doubled tones are left in *contrary* motion.

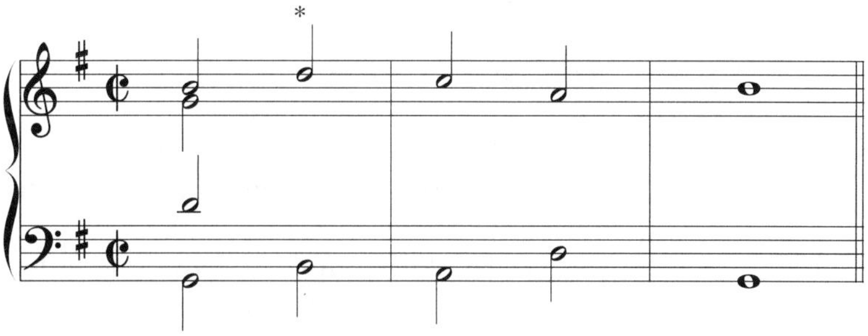

G: ___ ___ ___ ___ ___

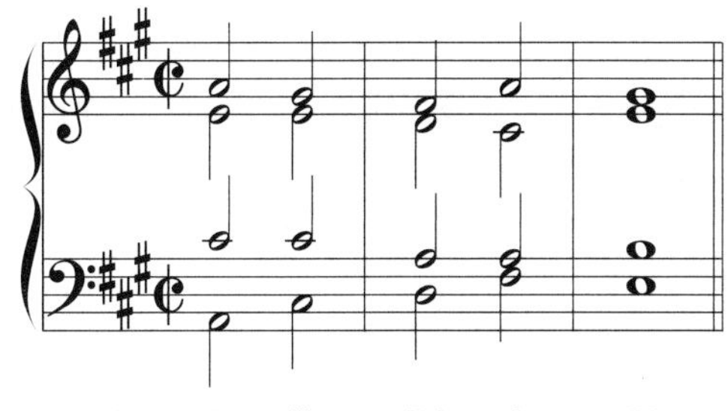

A: I iii IV vi V

4.108 Write the alto and tenor voices and supply the roman numeral analysis. Irregular doubling will occur at the asterisk. Return to normal doubling immediately.

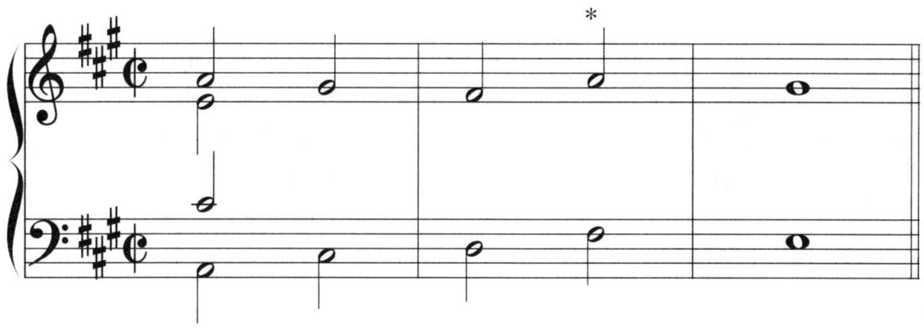

A: ___ ___ ___ ___ ___

Summary

Part writing is not an exact science. No absolute rules can be established to guarantee good musical effects. As this study progresses, it will become increasingly necessary to allow musical instincts to influence decisions. Principles governing doubling, spacing, and voice leading have been established, but all of these are tempered by practical necessities. The nearest thing to a "rule" is the prohibition against parallel perfect unisons, fifths, and octaves. For the present, these should be avoided, even at the expense of normal doubling, spacing, or voice leading.

The most important principle: The smoothest voice leading results if voices always move to the nearest possible chord tones. Retain common tones in the same voice(s) when possible. Leaps in any of the upper voices beyond the nearest chord tones should be carefully scrutinized. Such leaps must be justified as being necessary to avoid more serious flaws such as undesirable melodic intervals (augmented seconds and fourths), or parallel unisons, fifths, or octaves. Of course, leaps sometimes contribute to more effective melodic lines, or are necessary to produce desirable doublings. But for now, use mostly seconds and thirds—and occasionally fourths—as melodic intervals in the soprano, alto, and tenor voices. More frequent use of larger intervals is to be expected in the bass.

These principles should be generally followed for the doubling of triads in root position:

PRINCIPLE 1: When connecting triads whose roots are a fifth (or fourth) apart, retain the common tone in the same voice and move the remaining voices to the nearest chord tones to achieve correct doubling and spacing.

EXCEPTION 1: If, when connecting triads whose roots are a fifth (or fourth) apart, the common tone is *not* retained in the same voice, move all voices to the *nearest* chord tones that result in correct doubling and spacing.

PRINCIPLE 2: When connecting triads whose roots are a second apart, move all the upper voices to the nearest chord tones in *contrary motion* to the bass.

EXCEPTION 2: When the bass moves *up* a second, one voice may move in parallel thirds (or tenths) with the bass, resulting in a doubled third in the second chord.

PRINCIPLE 3: When connecting triads whose roots are a third apart, retain two common tones and move the remaining voice to the nearest chord tone.

EXCEPTION 3: When the bass moves *up* a third, one voice may move in parallel thirds (or tenths) with the bass, resulting in a doubled third in the second chord.

The terms that are explained or used in this chapter are listed below in the order presented:

- voice leading (principles)
- relative motion:
  - similar
  - parallel
  - oblique
  - contrary
- consecutive intervals
- common tones
- redistributing the tones
- augmented intervals
- doubling (principles)
- spacing (principles)

Mastery Frames

4–1 Identify the type of relative motion in each example below.

(1) (2) (3) (4)

(1) Parallel

(2) Similar

(3) Oblique

(4) Contrary

(4.1–.14, 4.26–.34)

4–2 Why is the motion in Example (1) in the previous frame incorrect?

____

____

Parallel perfect fifths normally are forbidden.

(4.15–.24)

4–3 Write the alto and tenor voices and provide the roman numeral analysis. *Use close structure.*

(1) (2) (3)

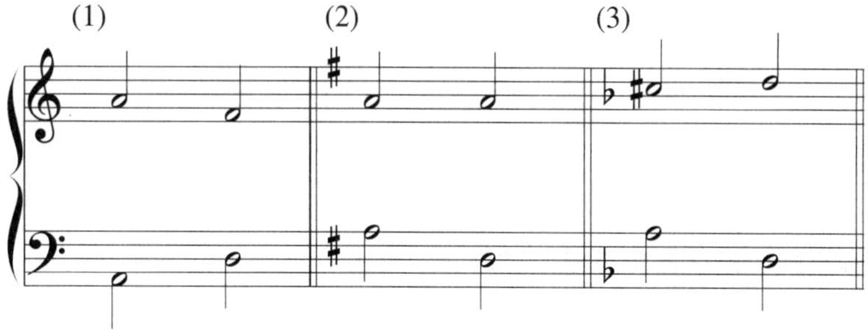

a: ___ ___ G: ___ ___ d: ___ ___

(1) (2) (3)

a: i iv G: ii V d: V i

(4.59–.74)

4–4 In which example in Frame 4–1 has the common tone been retained in the same voice? _______

(3)

(4.59–.62)

(1) (2) (3)

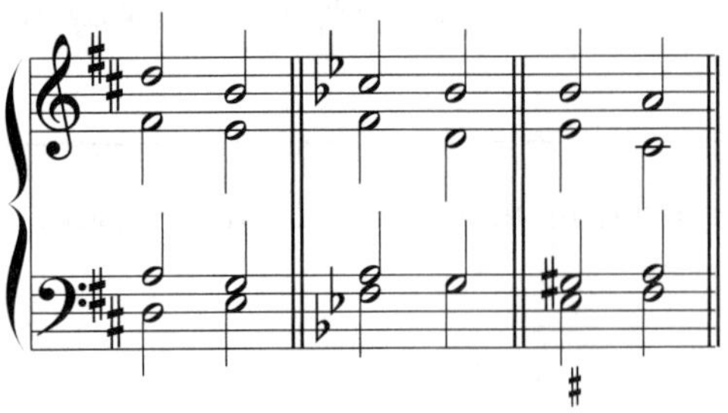

D: I ii B♭: V vi a: V VI

(4.75–.94)

4–5 Write the alto and tenor voices and provide the roman numeral analysis. *Use open structure.*

(1) (2) (3)

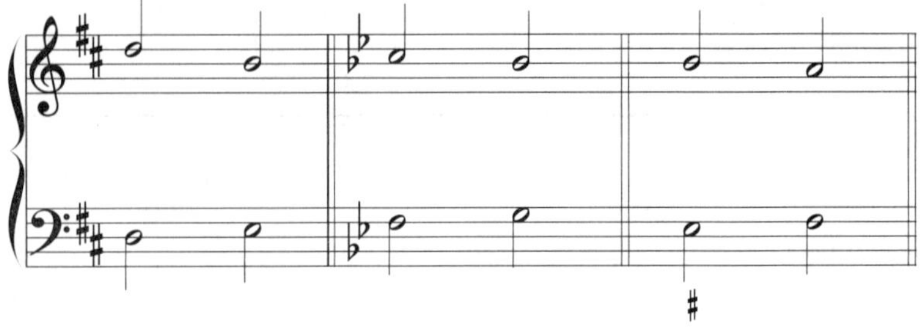

D: ___ ___ B♭: ___ ___ a: ___ ___

To avoid an augmented 2nd in the tenor voice.

(4.92)

4–6 Explain why it was necessary to double the third in the final chord in Example (3) of Frame 4–5.

____

____

____

---

(1) (2) (3)

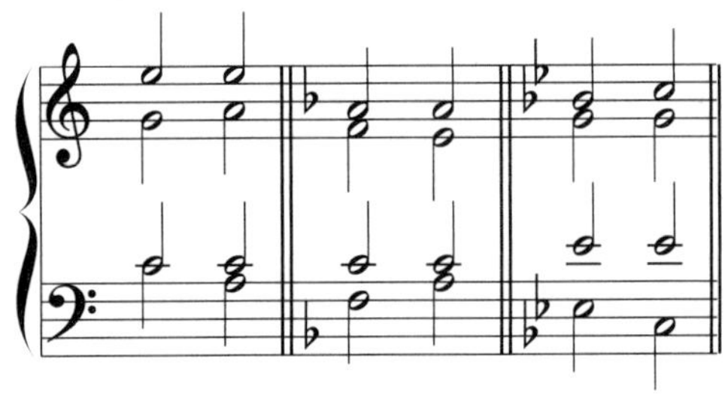

C: I vi F: I iii g: VI iv

(4.95–.108)

4–7 Write the alto and tenor voices and provide the roman numeral analysis. *Use the structure indicated.*

(1) Open (2) Close (3) Close

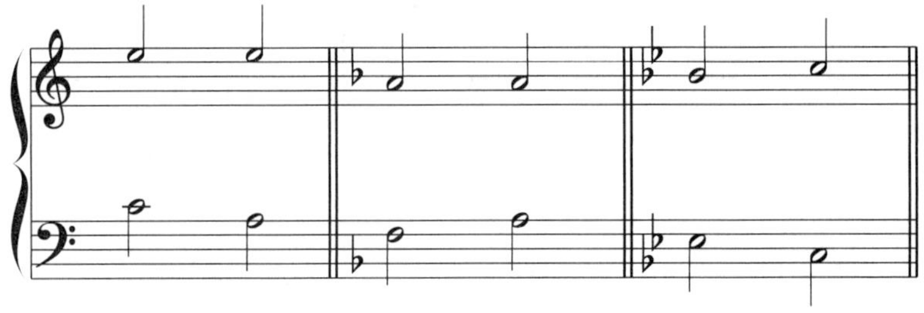

C: ___ ___ F: ___ ___ g: ___ ___

Supplementary Activities

1. Examine short excerpts from different musical styles for the way voices "lead." How are they alike; how are they different? Why are they different? Is the voice leading a significant factor in the definition of the particular musical style?
2. Continue to consult other references for more information about new terms being learned. Work with ear-training exercises that will help to discriminate better how voices move in relation to one another, for example, dictation practice of two musical lines together, then three, then four so that there is clear progression in practice from one line to four or more lines (melodic to harmonic) dictation. This should be ongoing practice throughout the study of this text.
3. Consider developing additional essays on the topics studied thus far, (e.g. voice leading, relative motion, doubling or spacing principles), or develop essays based on musical excerpts being examined, as practice for doing longer essays or analytical papers on whole compositions when a musical vocabulary is fully developed.

Supplementary Assignments

ASSIGNMENT 4–1 Name ________________________________

1. Write an example in two voices of each type of relative motion as indicated.

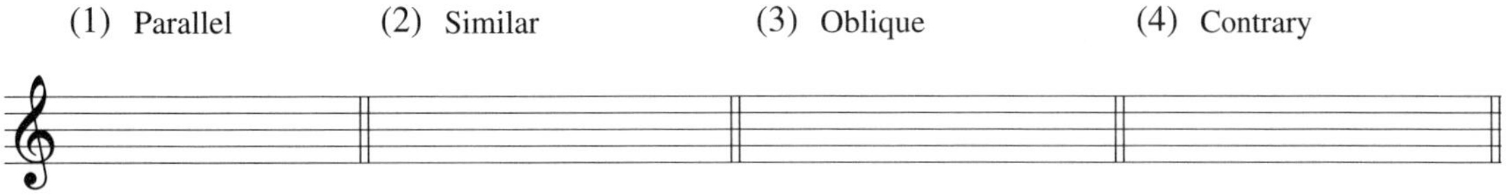

2. Which examples show *incorrect* parallel motion? ____________

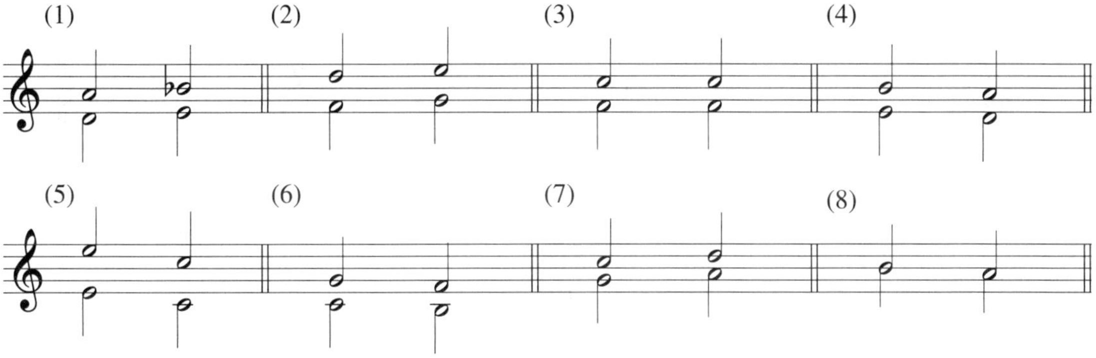

3. Which examples show *incorrect* parallel motion? ____________

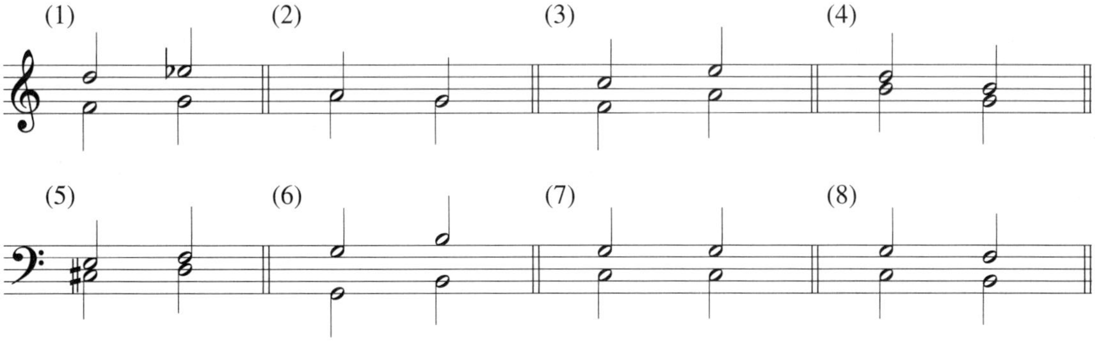

4. Which type of relative motion results in the greatest independence between two voices? ____________

(1) Similar

(2) Parallel

(3) Contrary

(4) Oblique

5. Name the two intervals that should be avoided in melodic writing.

1. ____________________ 2. ____________________

6. Name the undesirable interval that occurs in the example below.

e:

7. Select the preferred version. __________

(1) (2) (3) (4)

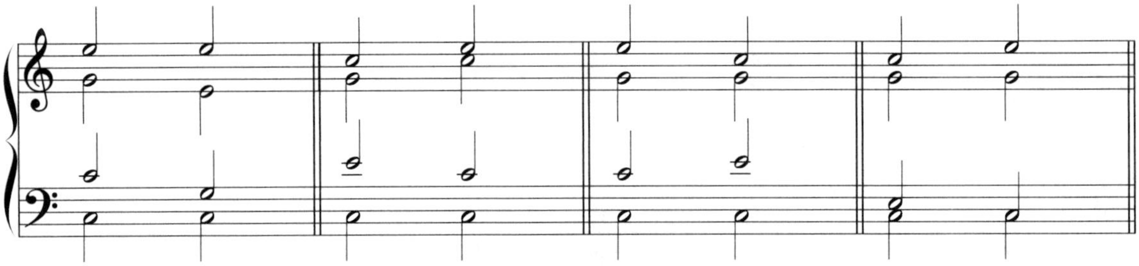

C: I – I – I – I –

8. Select the preferred version. __________

(1) (2) (3) (4)

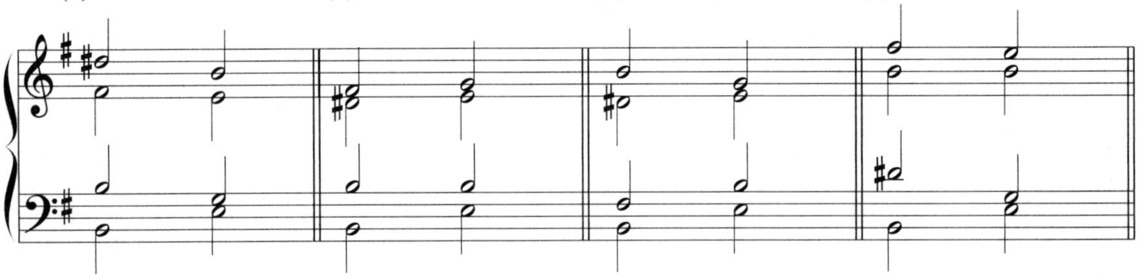

e: V i V i V i V i

9. Select the preferred version. __________

(1) (2) (3) (4)

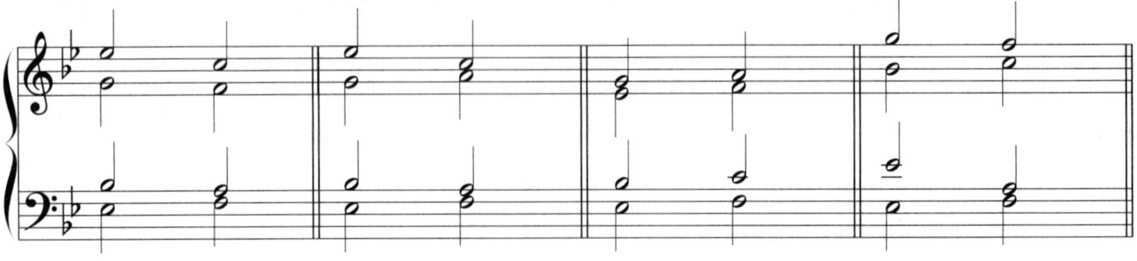

B♭: IV V IV V IV V IV V

ASSIGNMENT 4–2 Name ______________________________

1. Write the alto and tenor voices. *(Observe the rules of doubling and spacing.)*

(1) (2) (3) (4)

b: V VI Eb: I iii G: I I d: iv i

2. Write the alto and tenor voices. *(Observe the rules of doubling and spacing.)*

(1) (2) (3) (4)

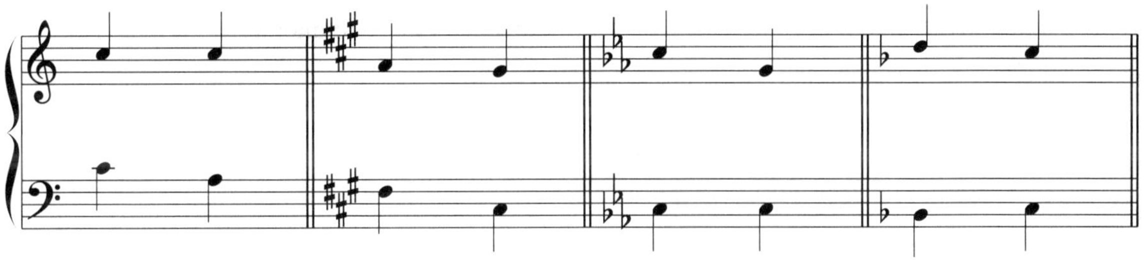

C: I vi f♯: i V c: i i F: IV V

3. Choose one or more of the options below for each example.

(A) ______________________ (B) ______________________ (C) ______________________

(A) (B) (C)

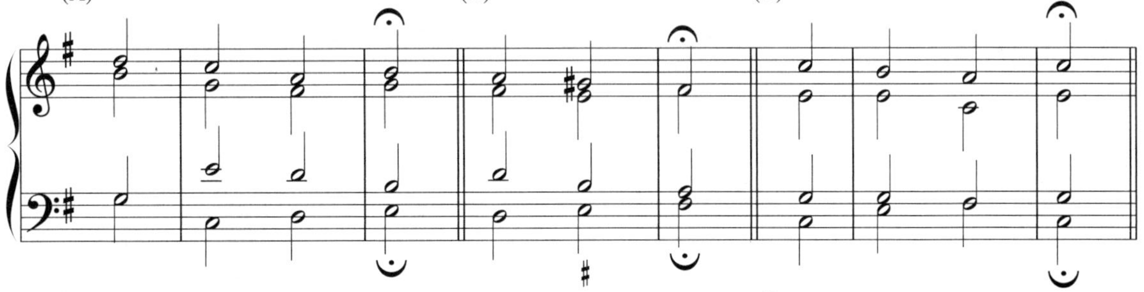

G: a: C:

(1) Incorrect doubling

(2) Incorrect spacing

(3) Incorrect melodic interval

(4) Incorrect parallel motion

(5) No error

4. Choose one or more of the options below for each example.

(A) ______________ (B) ______________ (C) ______________

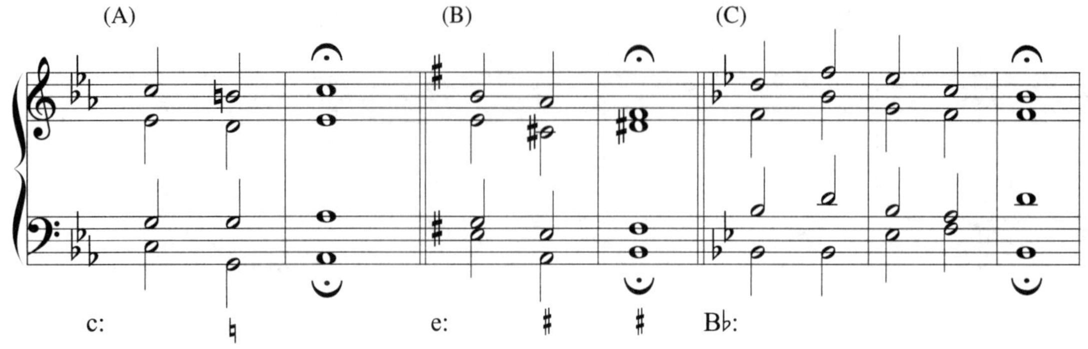

(1) Incorrect doubling
(2) Incorrect spacing
(3) Incorrect parallel motion
(4) Figured bass not realized
(5) No error under the circumstances

5. Write the alto and tenor voices and analyze with both roman numerals and alternative figures. For example (C) write the alto, tenor, and <u>bass</u> voices as well as analyze.

(A)

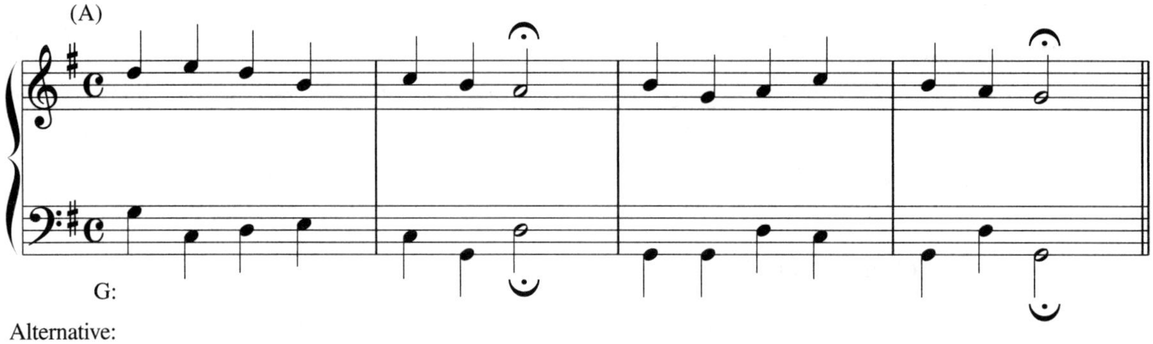

Alternative:

(B)

Alternative:

(C)

D:

Alternative:

Chapter 5.0
Triads in First and Second Inversion

Depending on whether the root, third, or fifth is in the bass, triads are said to be in: root position, first inversion, or second inversion. Inversions are used to produce a variety of chordal effects and enhance the melodic character of the bass line. The principles that govern the part writing of triads in first and second inversion are presented in this chapter.

lowest *(or bass)*	5.1 A triad is in *root position* when the lowest tone is the root. If the tones of a triad are arranged so that the root is not in the lowest voice, the triad is INVERTED. A triad is inverted by placing the third or fifth in the _____________ voice.
second	5.2 Compare the three chords below: 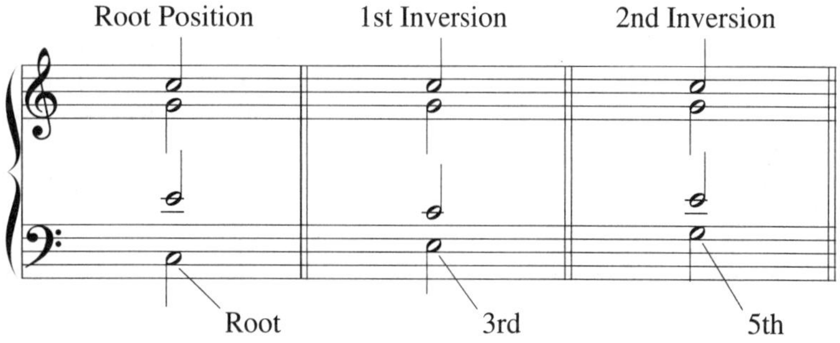 If the third of a triad is in the bass, the triad is in first inversion; if the fifth of a triad is in the bass, the triad is in _____________ inversion.
D	5.3 If the B♭ major triad is in first inversion, what is the lowest note? _______
C♯	5.4 If the f♯ minor triad is in the second inversion, what is the lowest note? _______

G	5.5 If the G major triad is in root position, what is the lowest note? _______
A	5.6 If the d minor triad is in second inversion, what is the lowest note? _______
A♭	5.7 If the f diminished triad is in first inversion, what is the lowest note? _______
bass *(or lowest)*	5.8 It is important to know which tone is the root of each chord. This is no problem when all chords are in root position. But when some of the chords are inverted, the tones must be mentally rearranged in order to locate the root. In progressions that include inversions, the root will not always be in the _____________ voice.
first (or) second	5.9 When analyzing a chord that may or may not be an inversion, it is a good idea to notice first if the notes can be arranged in thirds above the bass. This is because many triads are in root position. If the notes of a triad *cannot* be arranged in thirds above the bass, it means that the triad is in either _____________ or _____________ inversion.
	5.10 To find the root of an inverted triad, mentally rearrange the notes to produce a succession of thirds. The root, of course, will be the lowest note when they are arranged in this manner. Try each successive note until one is found upon which thirds can be built. This demonstrates the process. Notice in the example below that the notes arranged above the bass as in (a) are C E A. The interval E to A is a fourth, so C is not the root. Arranged above the tenor as in (b), however, the notes are A C E. The notes now are arranged in thirds, so the lowest note (A) is the root.

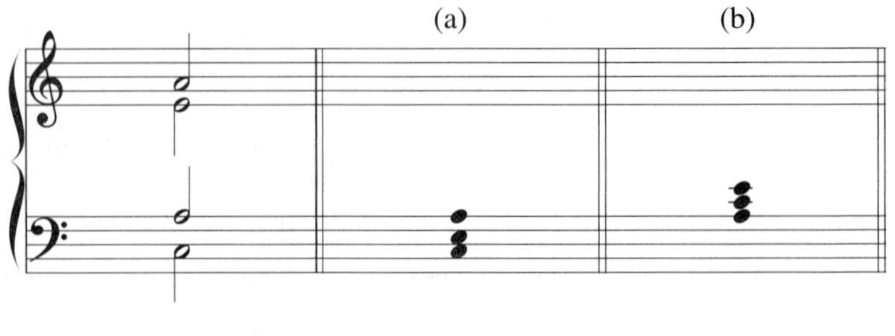

thirds	The root of a triad is always the lowest note when the notes are arranged in ____________.
(1) F (2) G (3) E (4) C♯	5.11 Indicate the *root* of each chord. 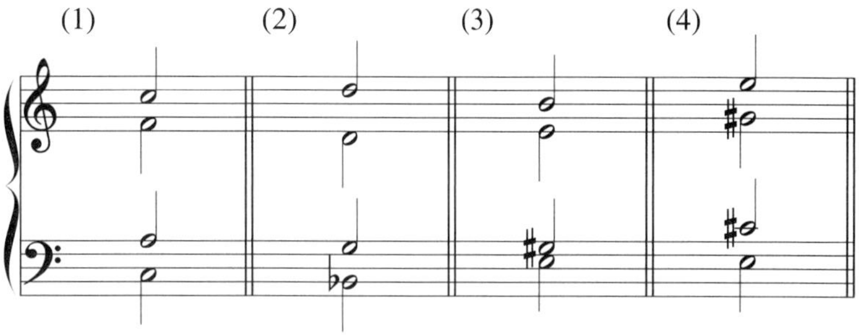 Root: ___ ___ ___ ___
(1) F (2) B (3) A♭ (4) D	5.12 Indicate the *root* of each chord. 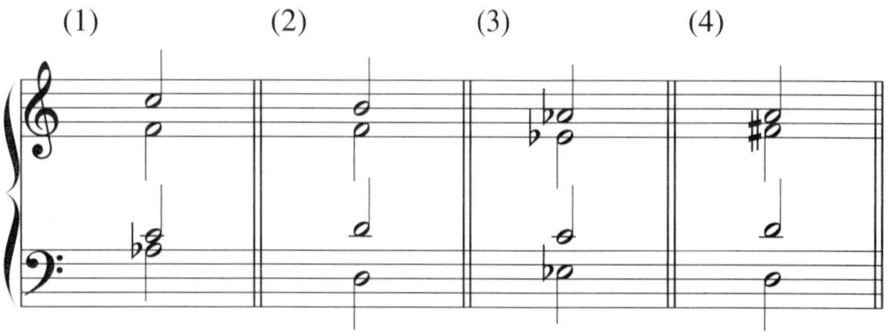 Root: ___ ___ ___ ___
(1) E♭ (2) G♯ (3) F♯ (4) G	5.13 Indicate the *root* of each chord. 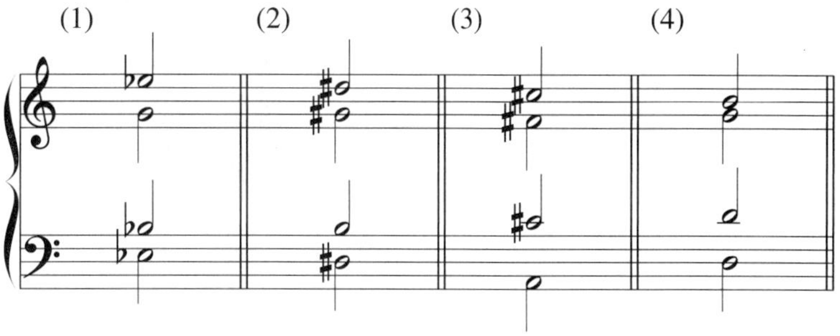 Root: ___ ___ ___ ___

5.14 The root, third, or fifth of a triad may appear in the bass. The same may be said of the soprano. The result is nine possible positions of any triad (with reference to the bass and soprano only).

The G Major Triad (in four voices)

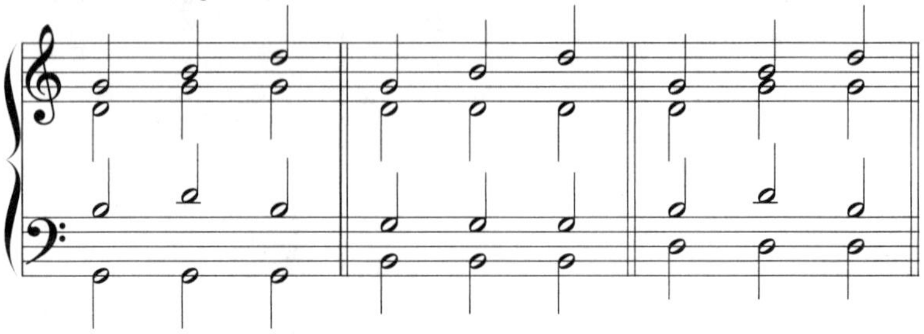

(Play the nine positions of the G major triad as illustrated above. Listen to the different sonority of each position.)

All triads in root position sound alike. (True/False) _______

False
(The note in the soprano and the spacing of the notes affect the sound of a triad.)

5.15 A triad in *first inversion* has the intervals of a sixth and a third above the lowest note.

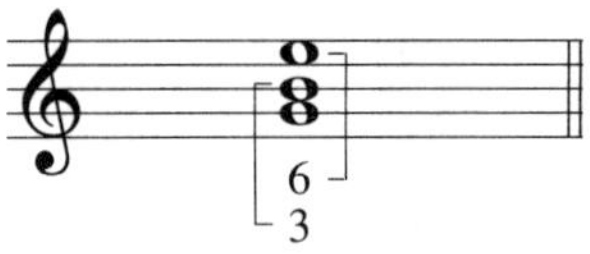

The figured bass symbol $\substack{6\\3}$ indicates a triad in

_____________ inversion.

first

5.16 The number 6 is sufficient to indicate a triad (chord) in first inversion. *The third is understood to be there, but the complete figuration $\substack{6\\3}$ is used only if needed to show alterations.*

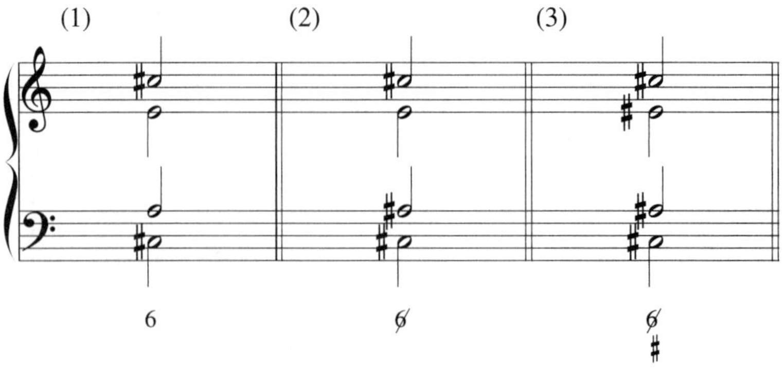

In the example above, the number 6 is adequate in (1) as neither the third nor the sixth is altered; in (2) the A♯ is shown by

the slash through the 6; a sharp is added to the figured bass in (3) to show the alteration of E to E♯.
The number 6 in the figured bass means that the note in the bass is

the (root/3rd/5th) _______ of the chord.

3rd

5.17 Spell the root position **triad** implied by each of the figured bass symbols.

(1) (2) (3)

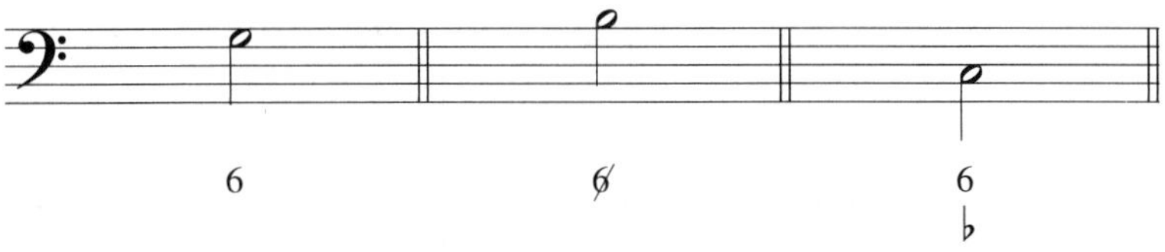

(1) __________ (2) __________ (3) __________

(1) E G B

(2) G♯ B D

(3) A C E♭

5.18 Spell the root position **triad** implied by each of the figured bass symbols.

(1) (2) (3)

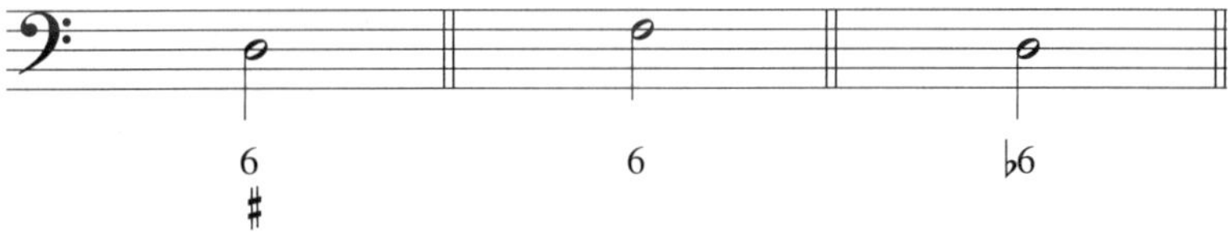

(1) __________ (2) __________ (3) __________

(1) B D F♯

(2) D F A

(3) B♭ D F

5.19 Spell the root position **triad** implied by each of the figured bass symbols.

(1) (2) (3)

(1) __________ (2) __________ (3) __________

(1) E♯ G♯ B♯

(2) D F♯ A♯

(3) A♭ C E♭

5.20 Check (✓) the correct option:

1. The figured bass symbol "6" represents a triad in first inversion.
2. The figured bass symbol "6" means that the bass note is the root of the triad.

True statements:

(1) _______ (2) _______ Both _______ Neither _______

(1) ✓

5.21 A triad in *second inversion* has intervals of a sixth and fourth above the lowest note.

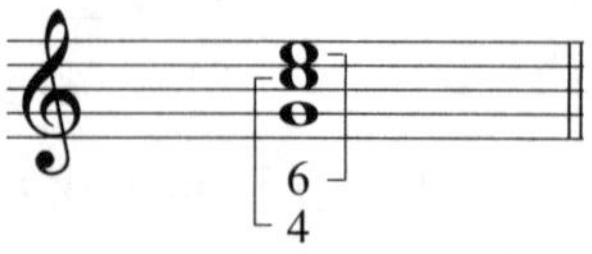

A triad in second inversion is indicated by the figured bass symbol $^6_4$. In second inversion the tone in the bass is the

(root/3rd/5th) _______ of the triad.

5th

5.22 Neither the 6 nor the 4 can be omitted from the figured bass in the case of a triad in second inversion. *Both* ***must*** *be present to have the second inversion chord.*

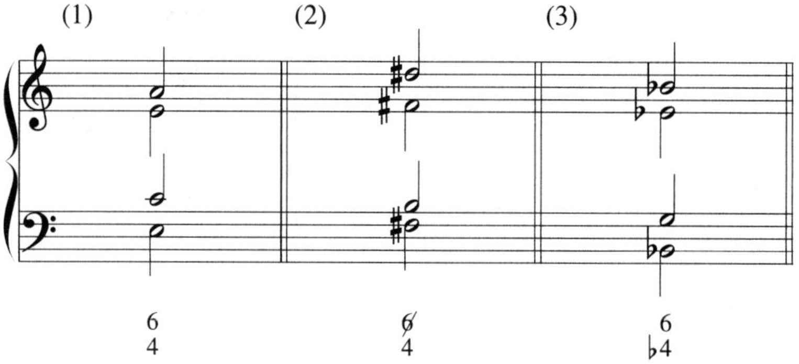

Notice that in (1) both the number 6 and the number 4 are used even though the notes represented by these numbers are not altered.

Write the figured bass symbol which indicates a triad in

second inversion. _______

$^6_4$

5.23 Spell the root position triad implied by each of the figured bass symbols.

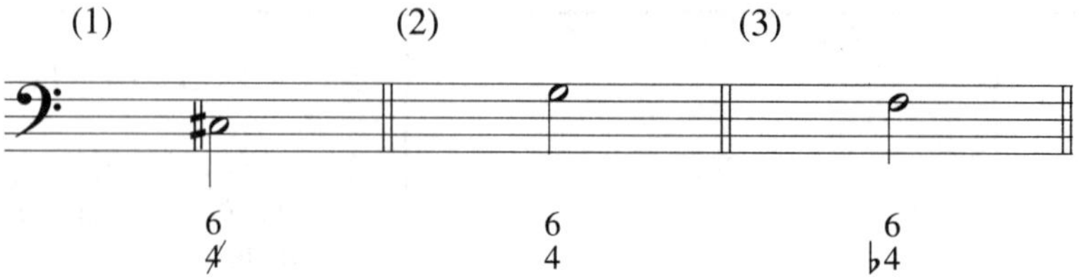

(1) __________ (2) __________ (3) __________

(1) F♯ A C♯

(2) C E G

(3) B♭ D F

(1) E G♯ B

(2) A♭ C♭ E♭

(3) G B D

5.24 Spell the root position triad implied by each of the figured bass symbols.

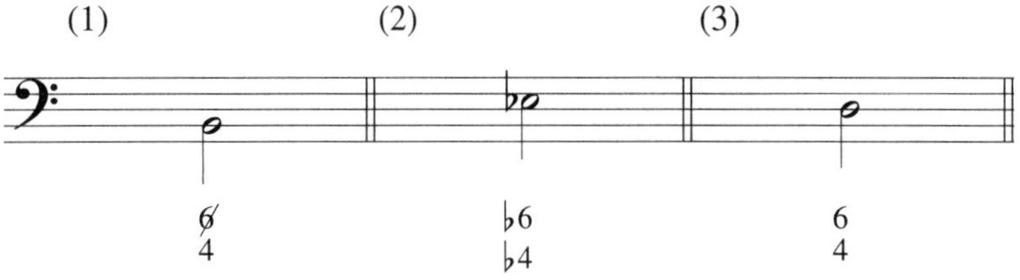

(1) __________ (2) __________ (3) __________

(1) G♯ B♯ D♯

(2) B D♯ F♯

(3) G♭ B♭ D♭

5.25 Spell the root position triad implied by each of the figured bass symbols.

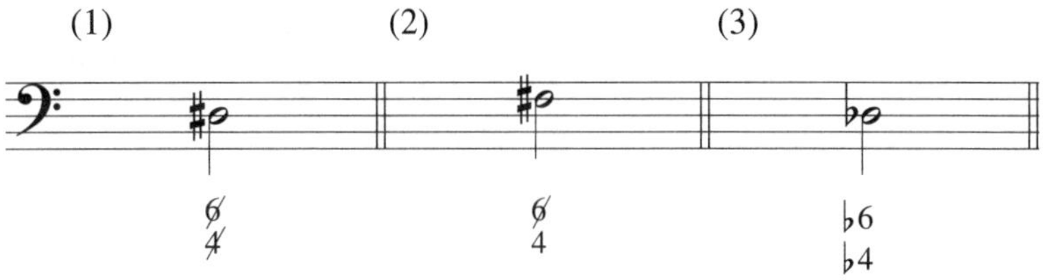

(1) __________ (2) __________ (3) __________

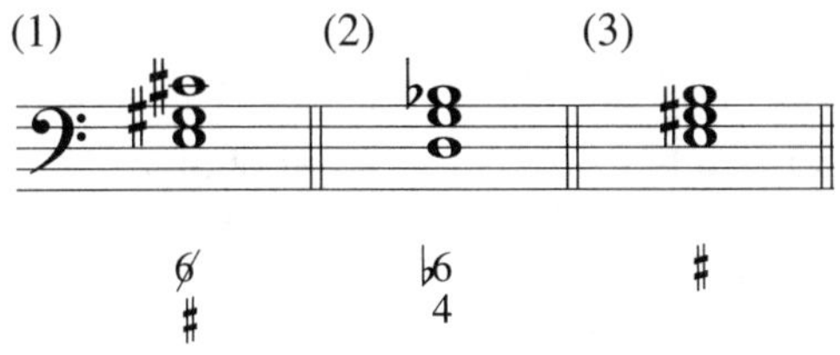

5.26 Write the notes on the staff indicated by the figured bass symbols.

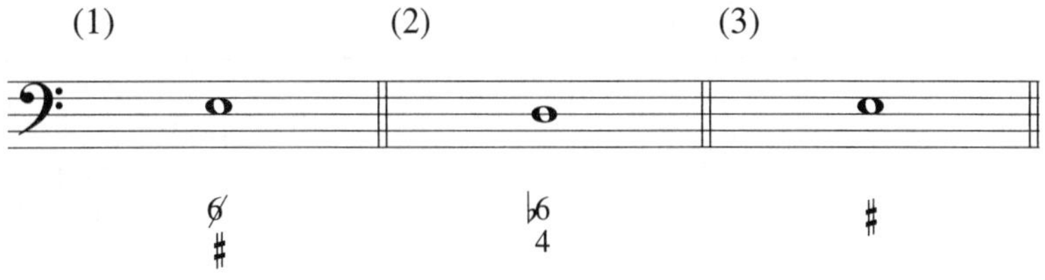

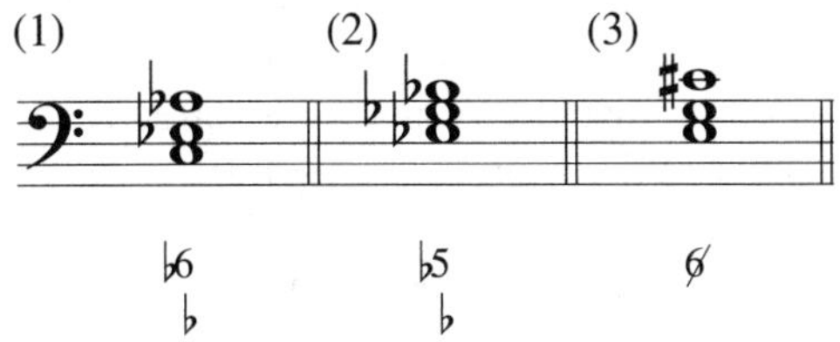

5.27 Continue as in the preceding frame.

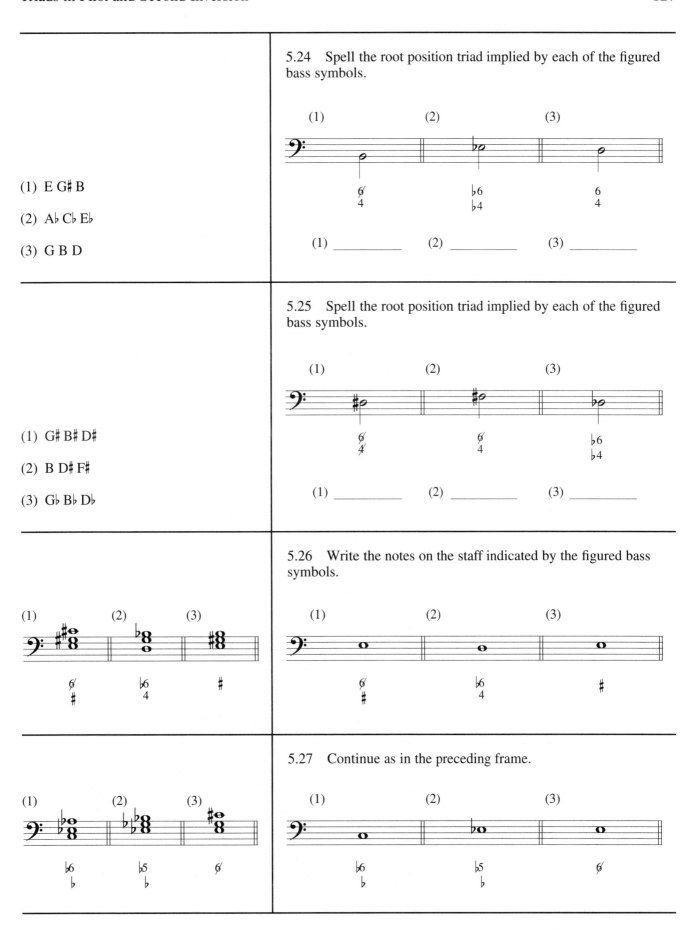

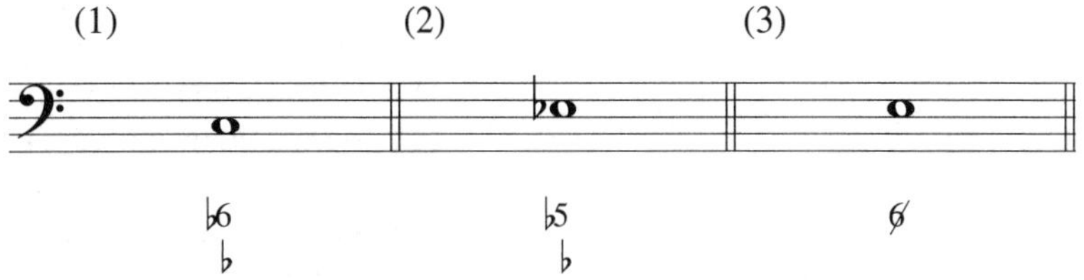

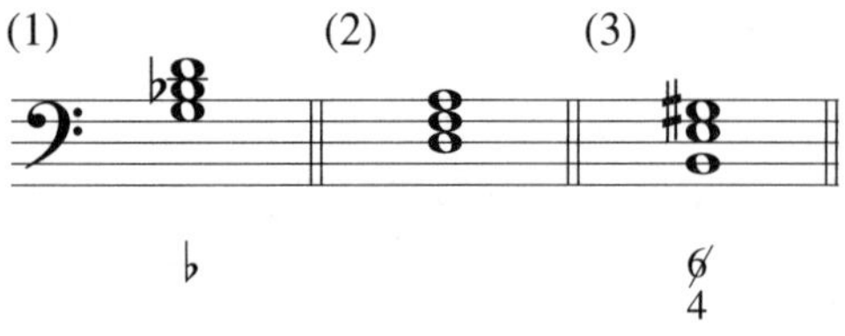

5.28 Continue as in the preceding frame.

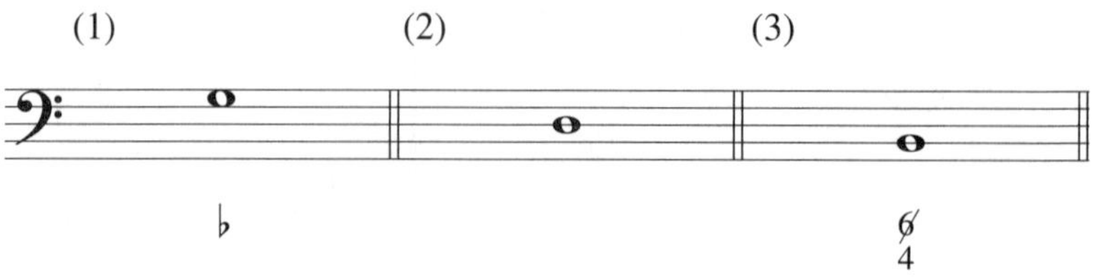

5.29 Play and compare the two examples below.

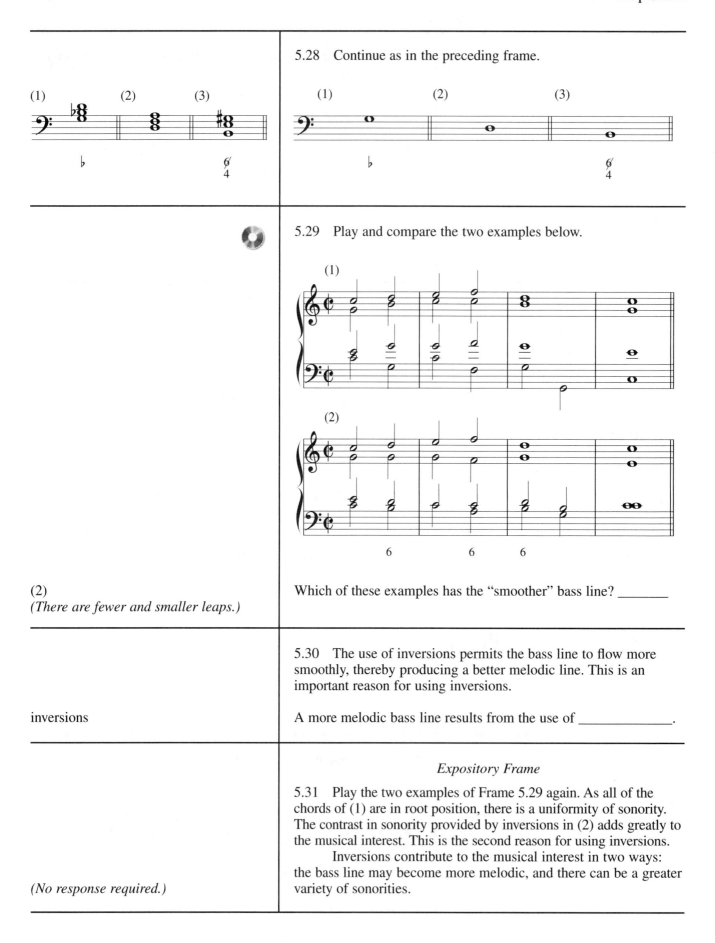

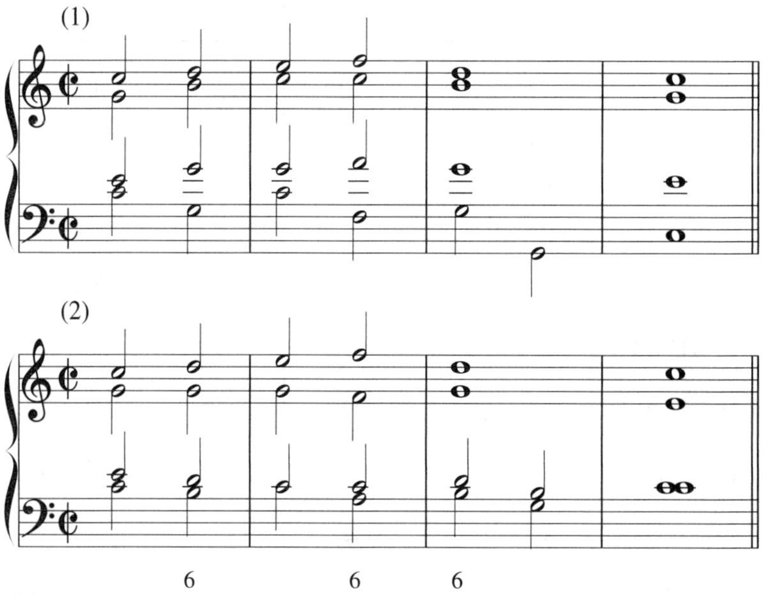

Which of these examples has the "smoother" bass line? _______

(2)
(There are fewer and smaller leaps.)

5.30 The use of inversions permits the bass line to flow more smoothly, thereby producing a better melodic line. This is an important reason for using inversions.

A more melodic bass line results from the use of _____________.

inversions

Expository Frame

5.31 Play the two examples of Frame 5.29 again. As all of the chords of (1) are in root position, there is a uniformity of sonority. The contrast in sonority provided by inversions in (2) adds greatly to the musical interest. This is the second reason for using inversions.

Inversions contribute to the musical interest in two ways: the bass line may become more melodic, and there can be a greater variety of sonorities.

(No response required.)

Expository Frame

5.32 The character of triads varies according to whether they are in root position, first inversion, or second inversion. A person becomes sensitive to these differences through listening experiences. Major and minor triads in root position provide the most stable sonorities. Triads in first inversion, however, are less stable; they help motivate the harmony by demanding resolution into more stable sonorities. A sense of "forward motion" is imparted by the use of first inversions.

Triads in second inversion are still less stable than those in first inversion. Because of the relatively weak sonority of triads in second inversion, they are used sparingly.

(No response required.)

5.33 First and second inversions are shown when analyzing with roman numerals by including the appropriate figured bass symbol as part of the chord symbol. An alternative analysis is also shown. *Note that this kind of analysis* ***does not*** *explain function as well as roman numeral analysis.*

(1) (2) (3)

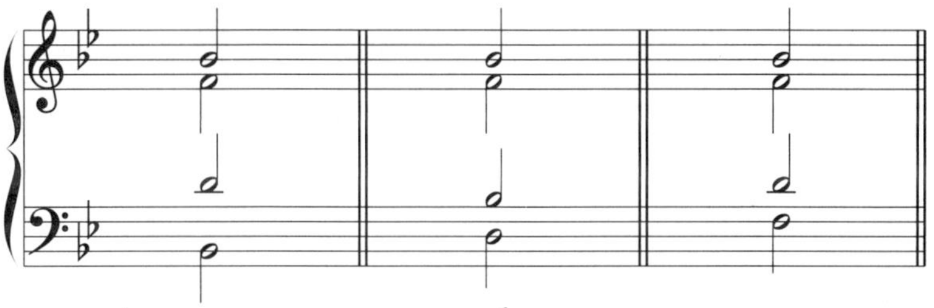

	(1)	(2)	(3)
B♭:	I	I^6	I^6_4
Alternative:	B♭	B♭/D	B♭/F

The number $^6_4$ added to a roman numeral indicates that the chord is in _____________ inversion.

second

5.34 The chord symbol I^6 indicates that the (root/3rd/5th) _______ of the tonic triad is in the bass.

3rd

5.35 Write the appropriate chord symbol in each case. *(Be sure to show the inversion.)*

(1) (2) (3)

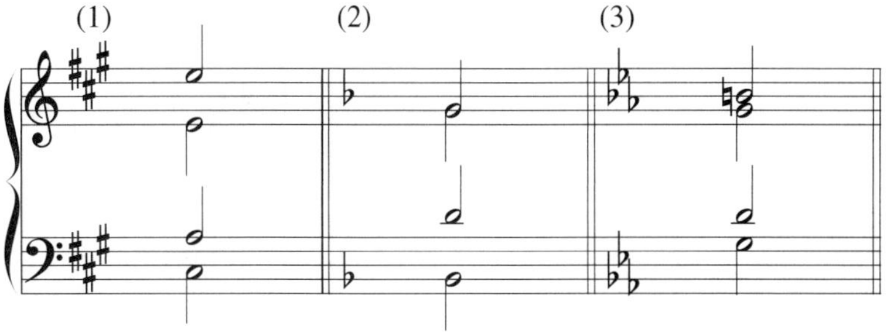

A: ___ d: ___ c: ___

(1) A: I^6

(2) d: iv^6

(3) c: V

(1) e: iv^6_4

(2) D: $vii^{\circ 6}$

(3) B♭: ii^6

5.36 Continue as in the preceding frame.

(1) (2) (3)

e: ___ D: ___ B♭: ___

(1) C: I^6_4 (C/G)

(2) f♯: V^6 (C♯/E♯)

(3) g: i (Gmi)

5.37 Continue as in the preceding frame.

(1) (2) (3)

C: ___ f♯: ___ g: ___

Alternative: ___ ___ ___

soprano

5.38 Now, to turn our attention to part writing triads in first inversion—learn this:

PRINCIPLE 4

When a major or minor triad is in first inversion, the SOPRANO is usually doubled.

(1) (2) (3)

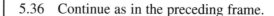

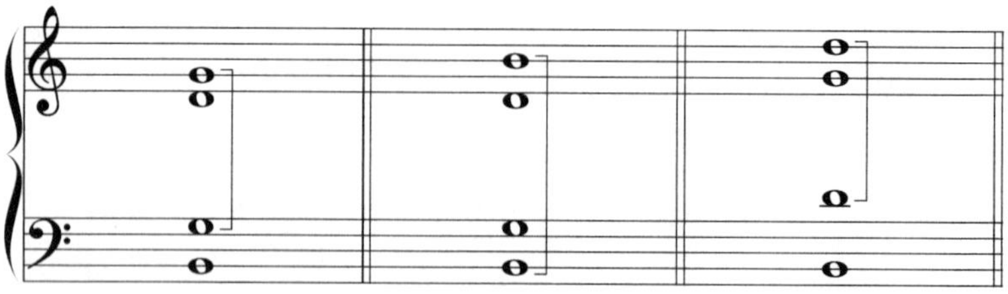

6 6 6

When a triad is in root position, the bass is usually doubled. The voice that is doubled when a triad is in first inversion is usually the _____________.

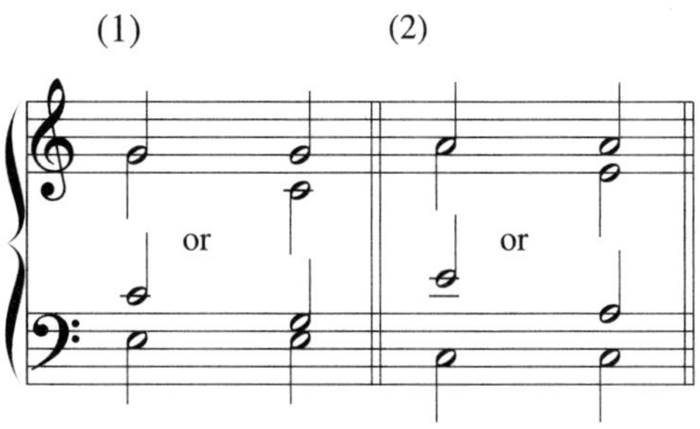

5.39 Write the alto and tenor voices for each chord. *(Be sure the SOPRANO is doubled.)*

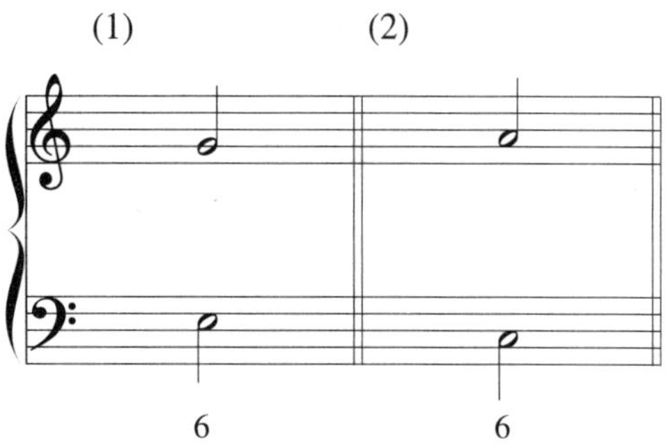

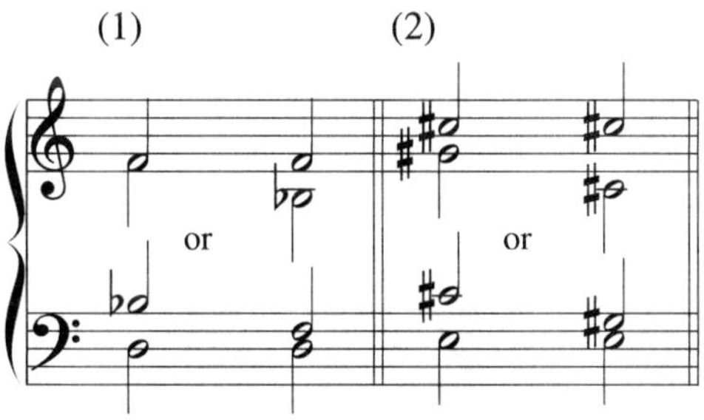

5.40 Continue as in the preceding frame.

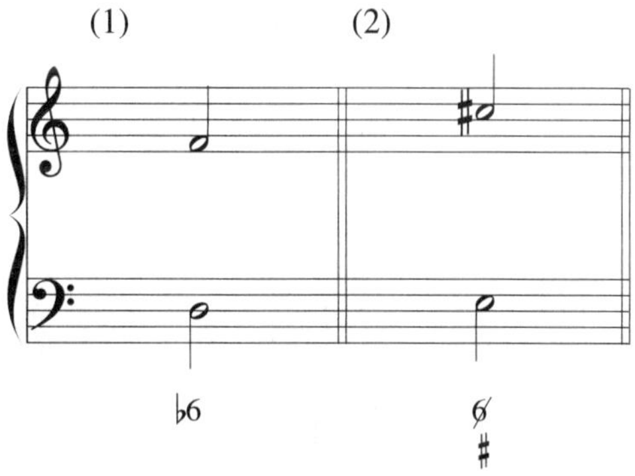

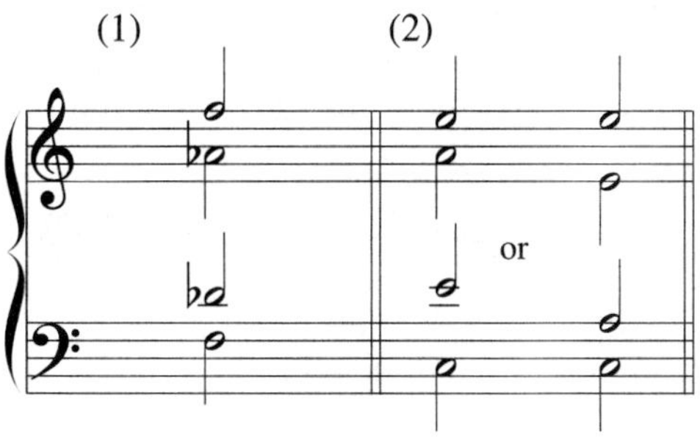

5.41 Continue as in the preceding frame.

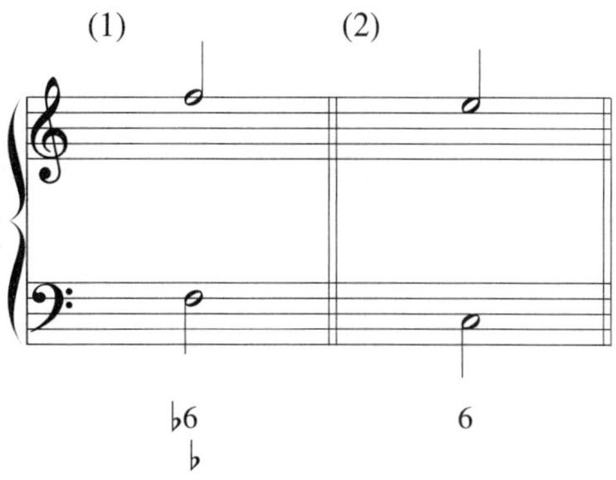

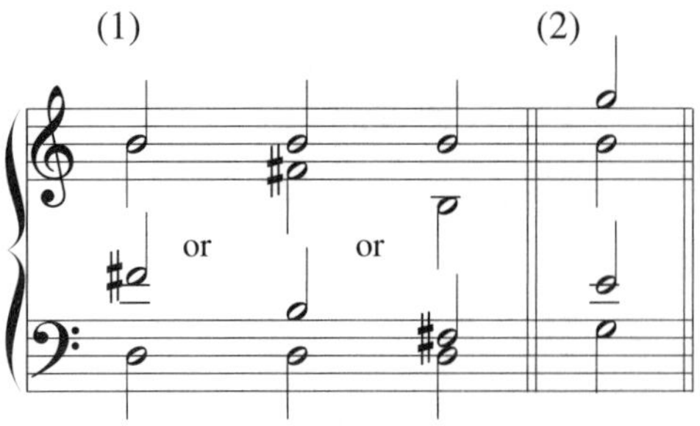

5.42 Continue as in the preceding frame.

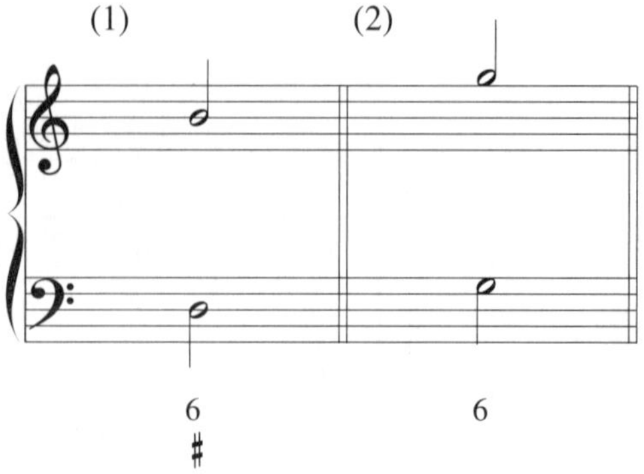

(3)
(There is more than an octave between the alto and tenor voices.)

5.43 The preceding four frames have shown that first inversions often give rise to several possibilities of spacing. Take care that the interval between adjacent upper voices is not larger than an octave, and do not use notes that are outside the normal range of each voice. (See Frame 3.26).

When triads are in first inversion the doubled tone varies. It is the root, third, or fifth depending on which of these is in the soprano.

Which of the triads below contains a part writing error?

____

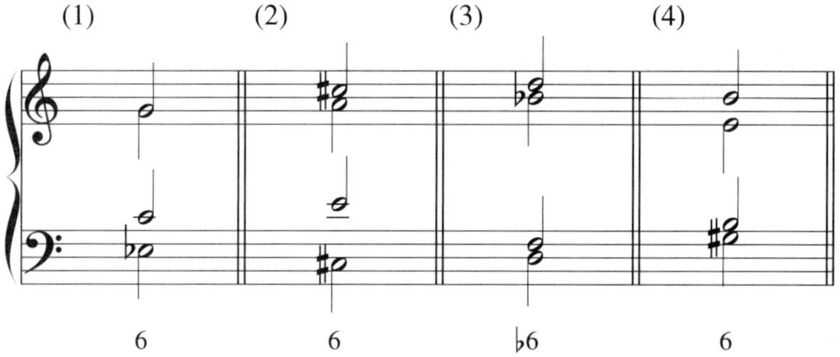

(1) ✓

5.44 Considerable freedom is exercised by composers regarding the doubling of triads in first inversion. Doubling usually is determined by the necessity of avoiding a part writing error, or in order to produce a more desirable melodic line in one or more parts. But in spite of this, it is advisable to try the normal doubling *first,* as this usually provides the most satisfactory solution.

Check (✓) the correct option:

1. Triads in root position usually have a doubled root.
2. Triads in first inversion usually have a doubled 3rd.

True Statements:

(1) _______ (2) _______ Both _______ Neither _______

5.45 When moving from a triad in first inversion to one in root position, follow the steps outlined below:

1. Move the doubled tones in contrary, oblique, or (rarely) similar motion to the nearest chord tones possible.
2. Move the remaining voice* to the tone that will complete the triad or that provides correct doubling.

The example below illustrates step one:

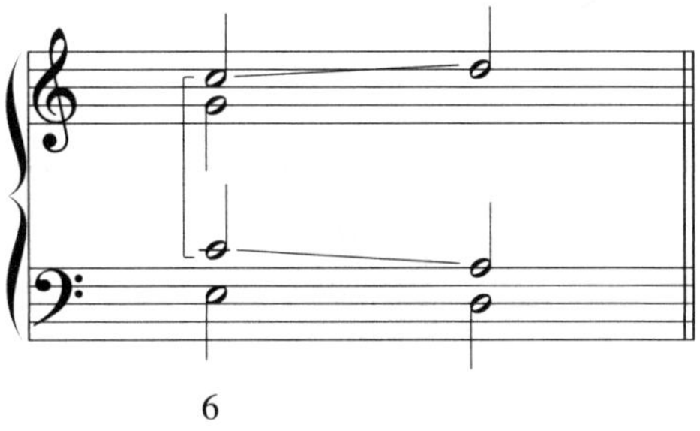

The doubled voices have moved to the nearest chord tones possible in ____________ motion.

contrary

*If the soprano is doubled by the bass, there will be two remaining voices.

5.46 With reference to the example in the preceding frame why is it undesirable to leave the doubled tones as below? ____________

____

Doubled tones must not be left in parallel motion. *(Or equivalent statement.)*

5.47 Step two of the process described in Frame 5.45 is illustrated in (b) below:

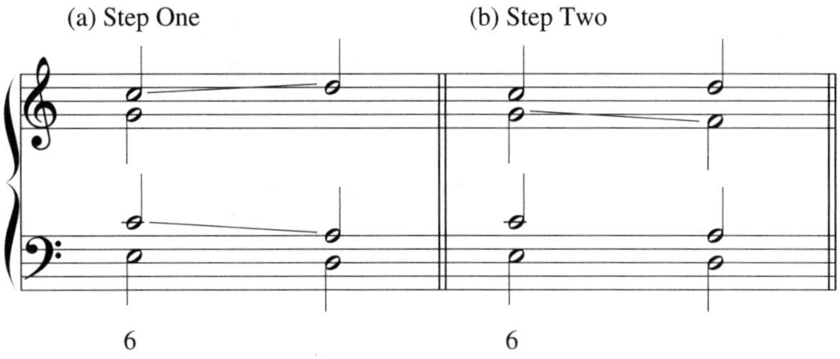

(Continued on the next page)

The triad tone that was needed to complete the chord was the third (F). The voice that moves to complete the triad (as on preceding page) rarely moves more than a second. A larger leap may indicate an error.

Check especially for parallel perfect intervals.

The voice that remains after the doubled voices have found their place in the next chord moves to a tone that completes the triad, or that provides correct _____________.

doubling

5.48 In the example below, perform step one (move the doubled tones in contrary, oblique, or similar motion to the nearest chord tones possible).

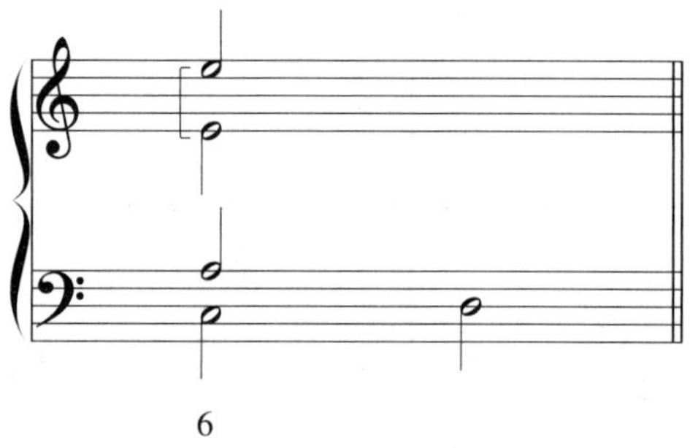

There is only one correct answer. If your solution does not agree with the one given, try to find your mistake. Consult your instructor if necessary.

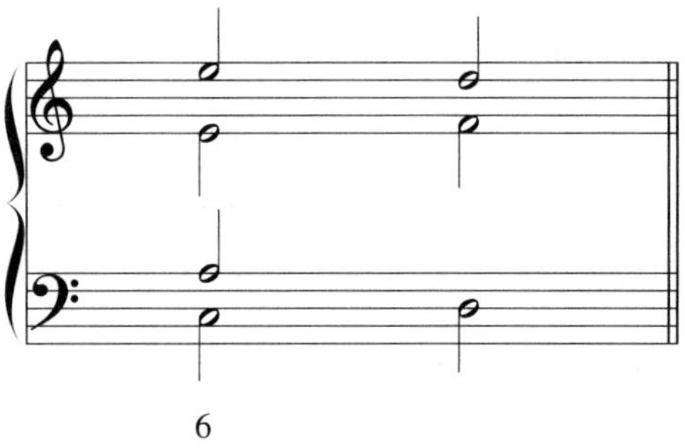

5.49 In the example below, perform step two (move the remaining voice to the tone that will complete the triad or that provides correct doubling).

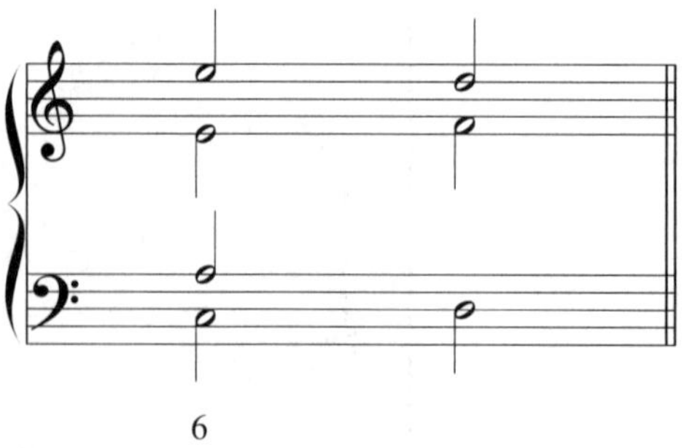

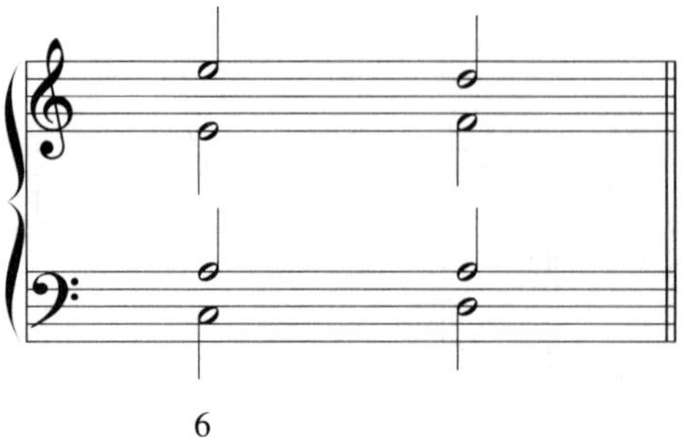

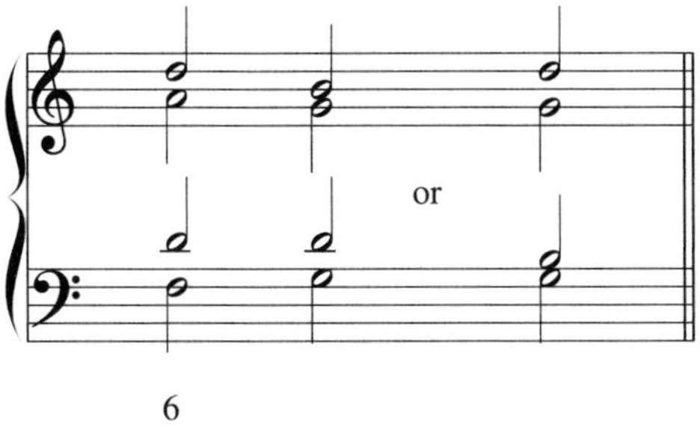

5.50 Partwrite the second chord applying the method presented in Frame 5.45.

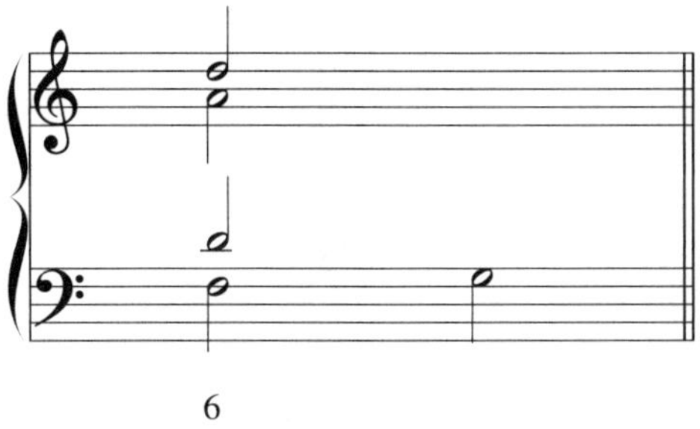

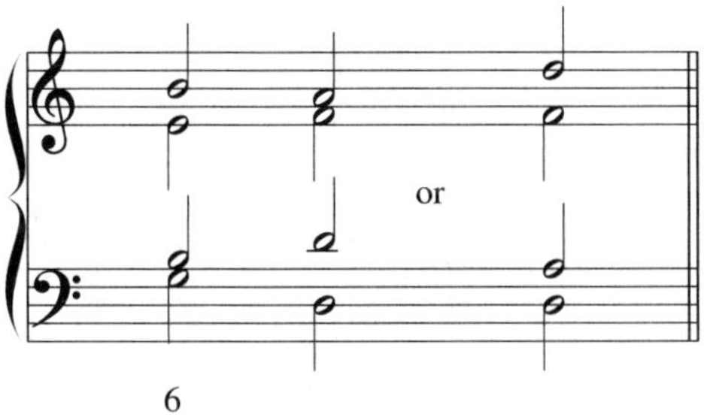

5.51 Partwrite the second chord.

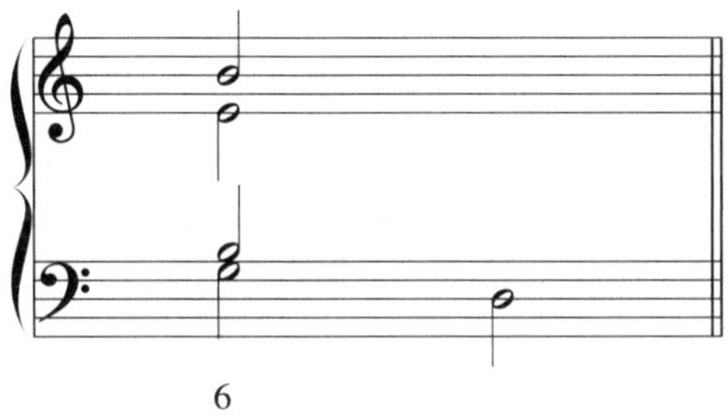

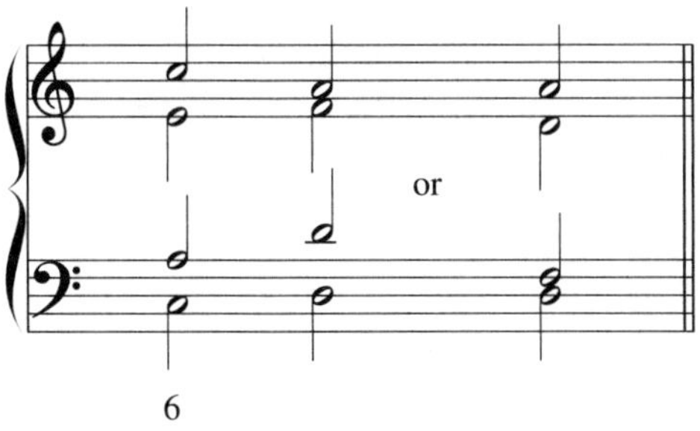

5.52 Partwrite the second chord. Note that, because the soprano is doubled by the bass, *two* voices will remain after the doubled tones have moved. These remaining voices must fit into the chord in order to achieve correct doubling and spacing.

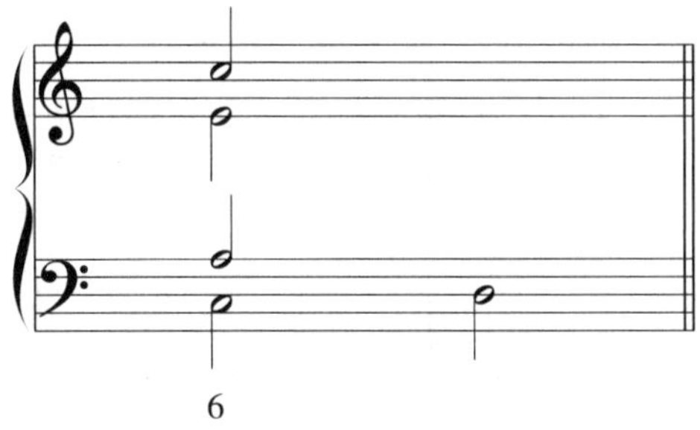

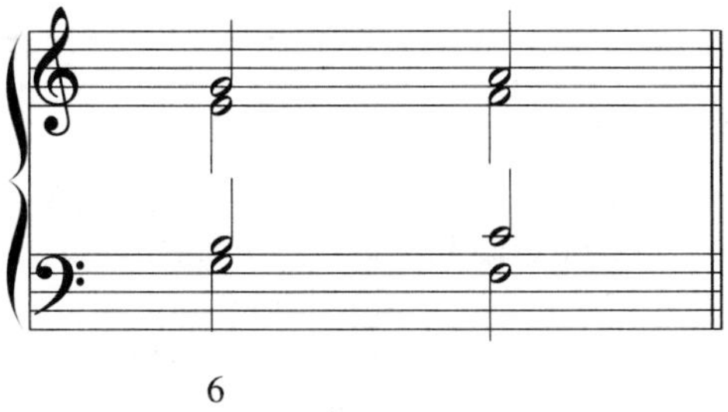

5.53 Partwrite the second chord.

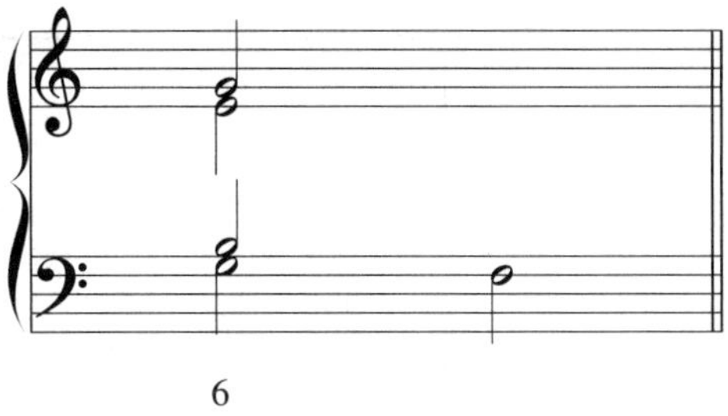

5.54 Continue as in the preceding frame.

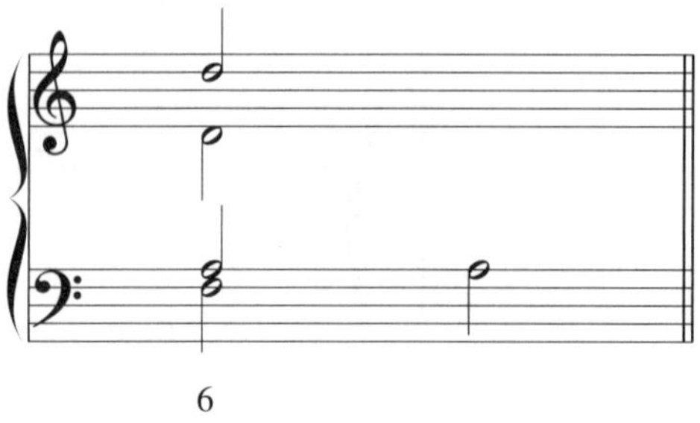

If you chose:

(a) go to Frame 5.56

(b) go to Frame 5.57

(c) go to Frame 5.58

5.55 The first chord below progresses best to (a), (b), or (c) ____________.

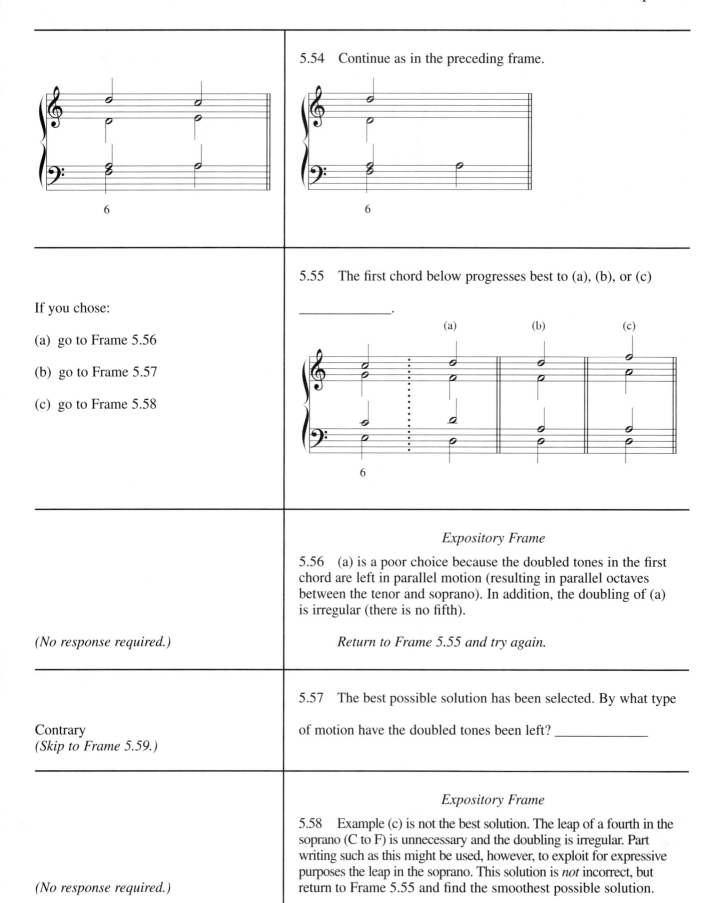

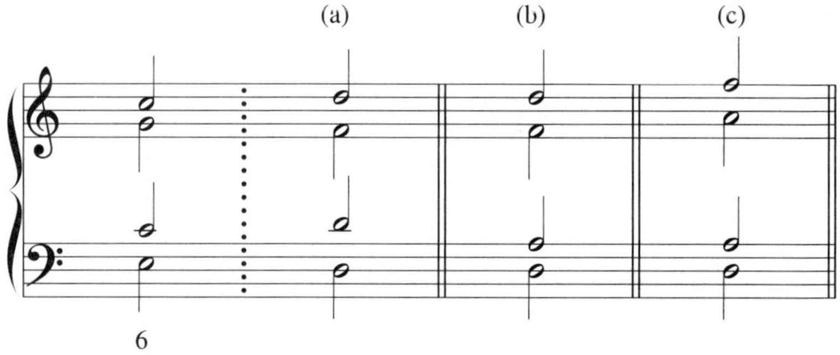

(No response required.)

Expository Frame

5.56 (a) is a poor choice because the doubled tones in the first chord are left in parallel motion (resulting in parallel octaves between the tenor and soprano). In addition, the doubling of (a) is irregular (there is no fifth).

Return to Frame 5.55 and try again.

Contrary
(Skip to Frame 5.59.)

5.57 The best possible solution has been selected. By what type of motion have the doubled tones been left? ____________

(No response required.)

Expository Frame

5.58 Example (c) is not the best solution. The leap of a fourth in the soprano (C to F) is unnecessary and the doubling is irregular. Part writing such as this might be used, however, to exploit for expressive purposes the leap in the soprano. This solution is *not* incorrect, but return to Frame 5.55 and find the smoothest possible solution.

5.59 When moving from a triad in root position to one in first inversion, follow the steps outlined below:

1. Move *into* the doubled tones in contrary, oblique, or (rarely) similar motion. *Move all voices by the smallest possible intervals.*
2. Move the remaining voice(s) to the nearest tone(s) that complete(s) the triad or provides correct doubling.

Many errors will be avoided if the doubled tones are written first. The voice that is usually doubled in first inversion triads is

the ____________.

soprano

5.60 The example below illustrates step one of the process described in the preceding frame:

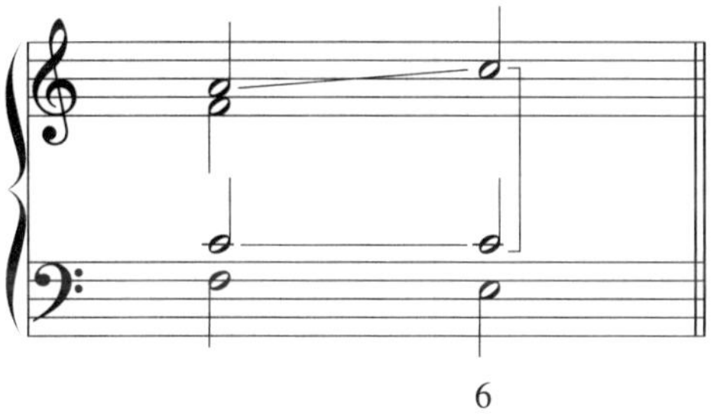

The soprano note is doubled by retaining the common tone in the tenor. Movement into the doubled tones is by

____________ motion.

oblique

5.61 Step two is illustrated in (b) below:

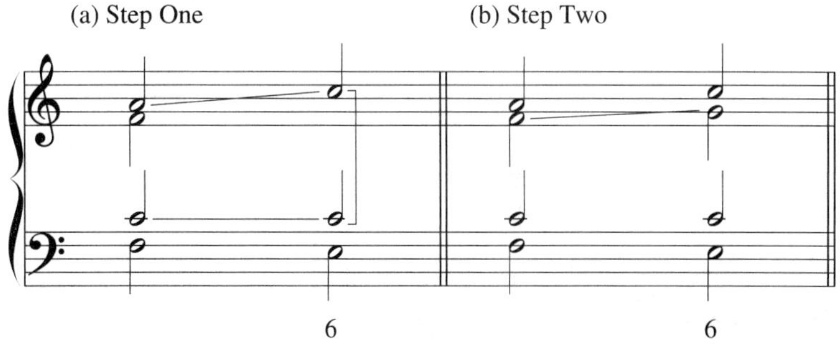

The triad tone needed to complete the chord is the fifth (G). The alto is able to move to this tone without producing incorrect parallel motion.

What type of motion occurs between the bass and alto in (b)?

____

Contrary

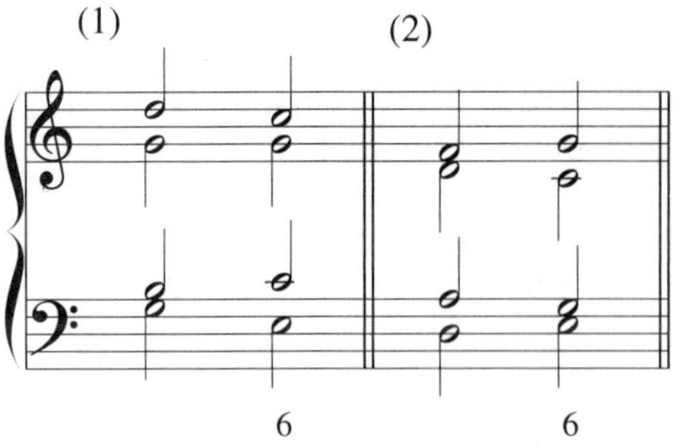

5.62 Write the alto and tenor voices for the second chord in each case, applying the method presented in Frame 5.59.

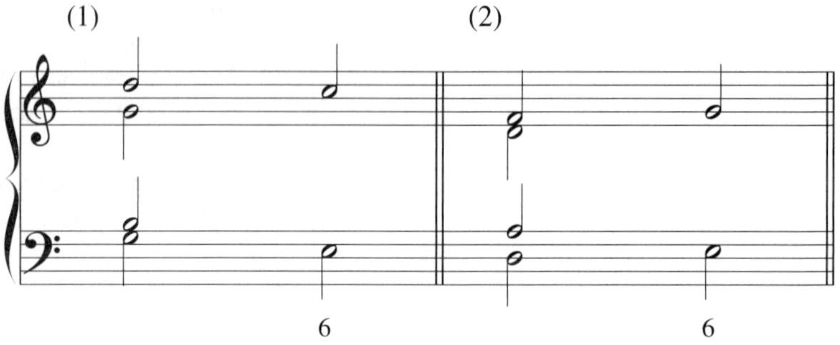

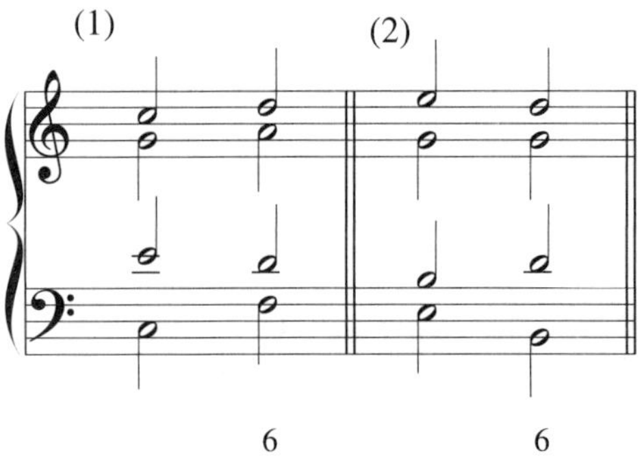

5.63 Continue as in the preceding frame.

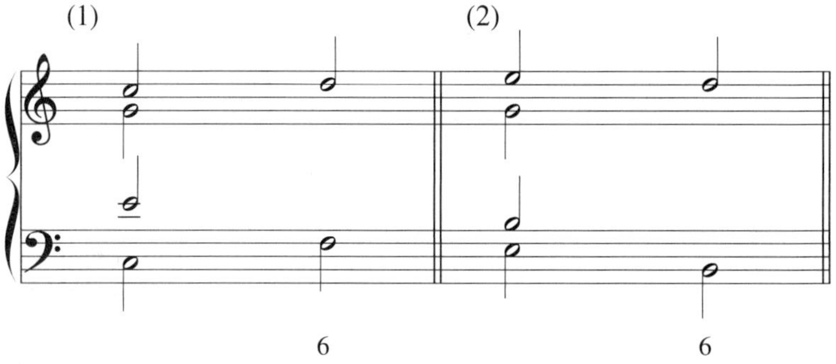

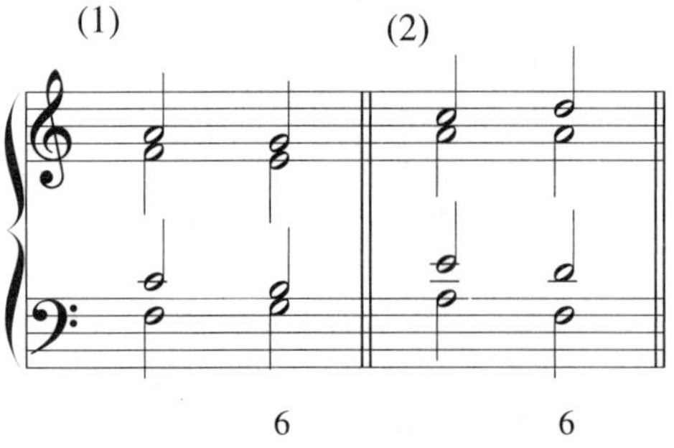

5.64 Continue as in the preceding frame.

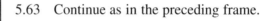

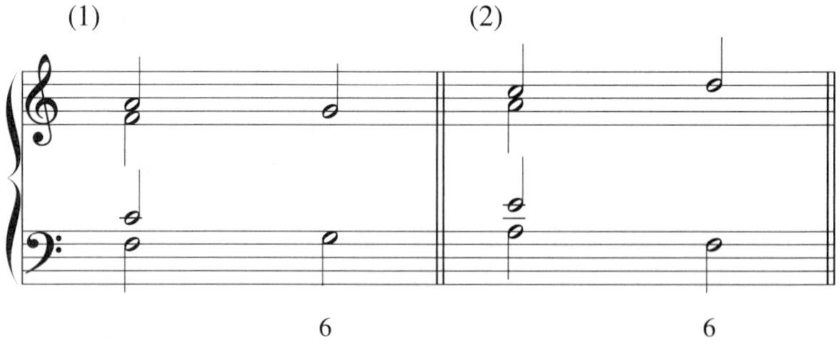

5.65 Write the alto and tenor voices. *(Use normal doubling in all chords; check carefully for incorrect parallel motion.)*

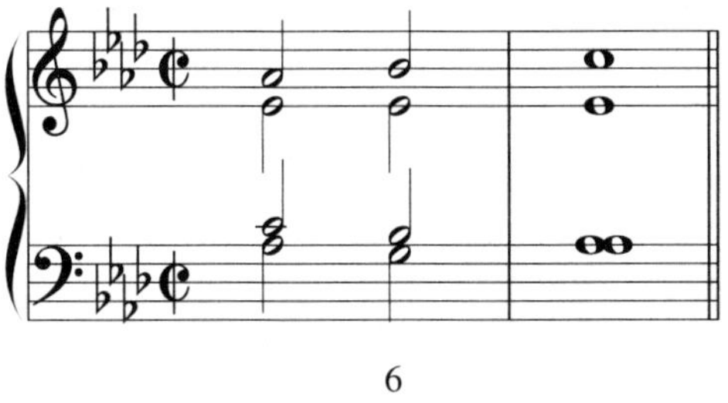

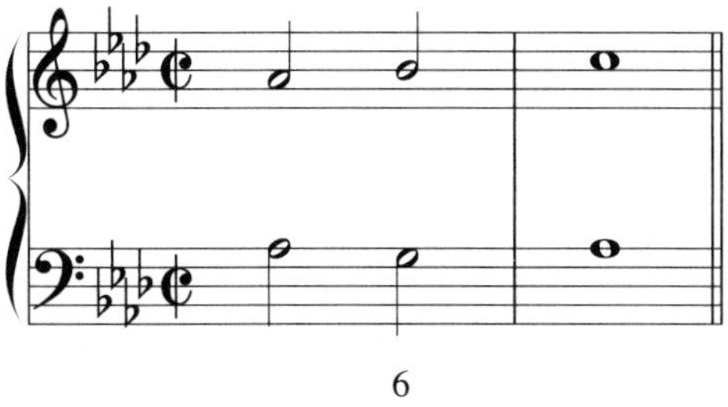

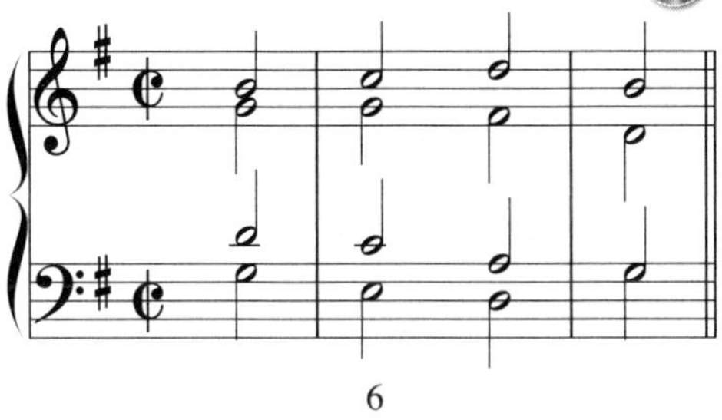

5.66 Continue as in the preceding frame.

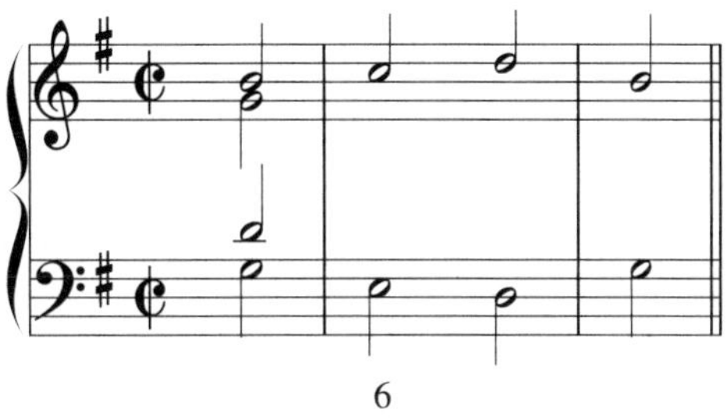

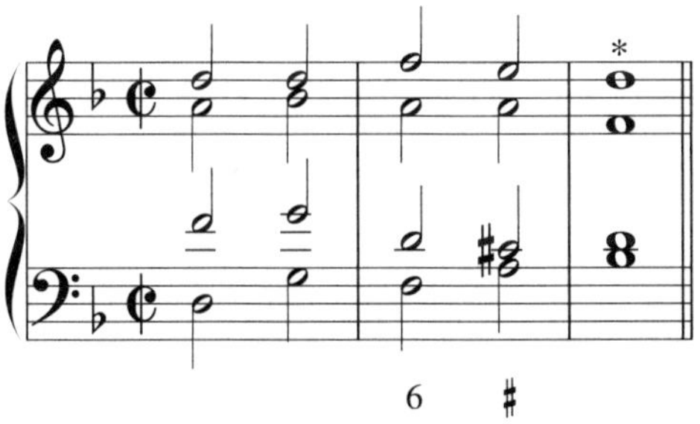

5.67 Continue as in the preceding frame. *(There should be irregular doubling at the asterisk.)*

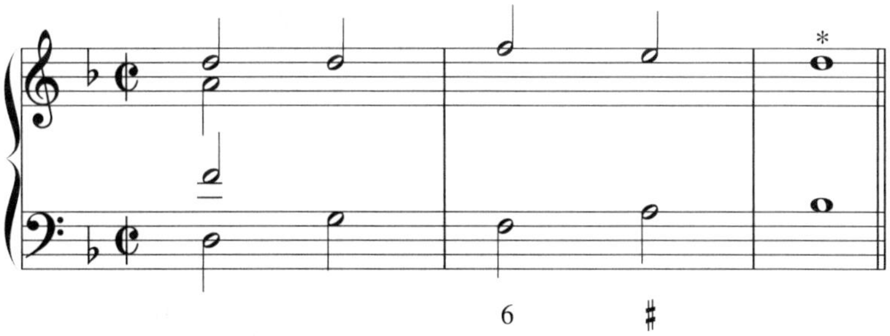

An augmented 2nd used as a melodic interval. *(Or equivalent statement.)*

5.68 What part writing error would have occurred in the preceding frame if the tenor had doubled the bass on B♭ in the final chord?

____

____

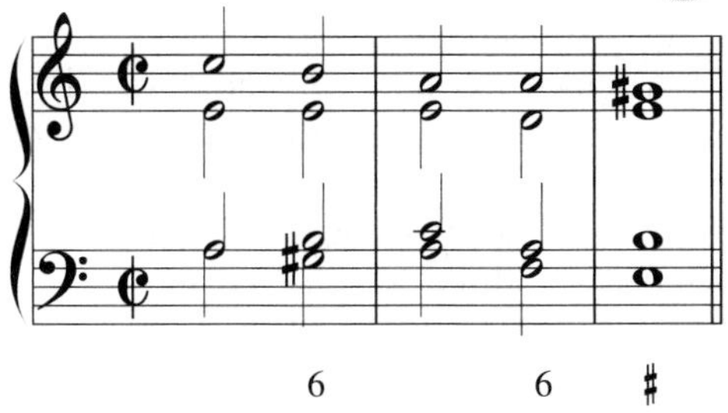

5.69 Write the alto and tenor voices.

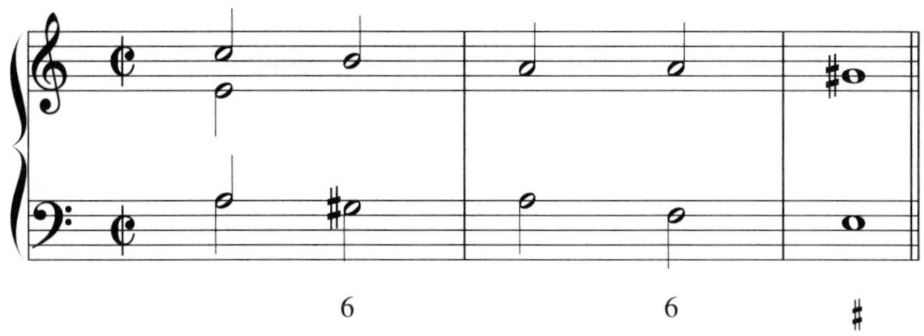

Expository Frame

5.70 The soprano is usually doubled when major or minor triads are in first inversion. But irregular doubling may occur to avoid incorrect parallel motion or undesirable melodic intervals (particularly the augmented second between V and VI in harmonic minor).

The first step when moving into or out of a first inversion should be to write the voices that are doubled.

(No response required.)

5.71 Unlike major and minor triads, the diminished triad is seldom used in either root position or second inversion. This is due to the interval of the diminished fifth that appears between the root and fifth. Compare the three examples below:

(1) Root Position | (2) 1st Inversion | (3) 2nd Inversion

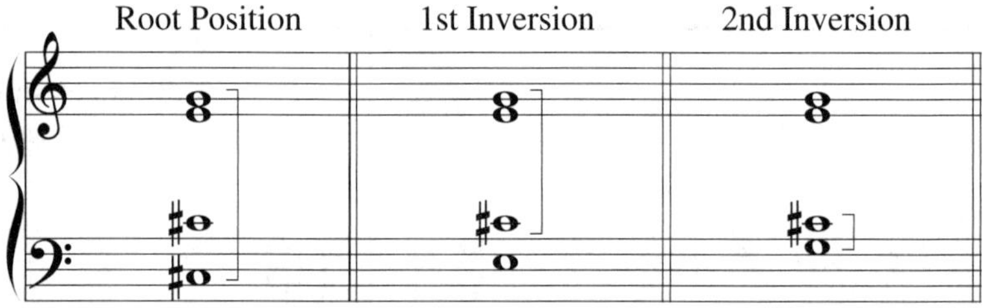

6 | 6/4

In both (1) and (3), the interval of the diminished fifth (or its enharmonic equivalent, the augmented fourth) appears above the *lowest* voice. In (2), however, the diminished fifth appears not above the bass, but above the tenor. In this case the dissonant effect of the diminished fifth is minimized because all the intervals above the bass are consonant (3rd, 6th, and octave).

The diminished triad is rarely used in ____________ position or ____________ inversion.

root (position or)
second (inversion)

5.72 Play diminished triads in various positions to see if you concur that the first inversion provides the most agreeable sonority. At any rate, most of the composers of the eighteenth and nineteenth centuries must have thought so, for they used this inversion more frequently than second inversion and especially more so than root position, which is the least used of the three possible positions.

According to the statements above, which of the following chords provides the most agreeable sonority? _______

(2)

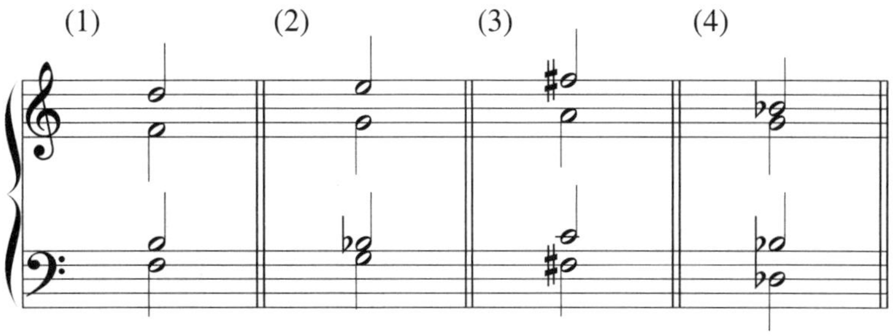

5.73 Which triad tone is doubled in (2) of the preceding frame? (Root/3rd/5th) _______

3rd

5.74 The usual doubling of the diminished triad is illustrated in (2) of Frame 5.72. Learn this:

EXCEPTION 4

Diminished triads usually are in first inversion with the third (the BASS) doubled.

Whereas the soprano is doubled in major and minor triads in first inversion, the diminished triad in first inversion requires that the _____________ be doubled.

bass *(or third)*

5.75 Write the alto and tenor for each of the diminished triads below. *(Be sure to double the BASS.)*

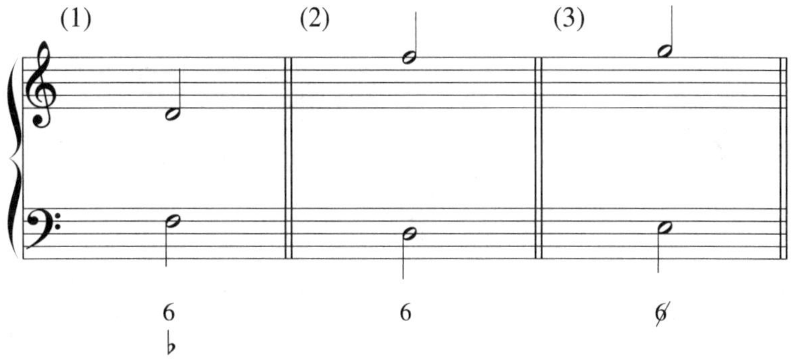

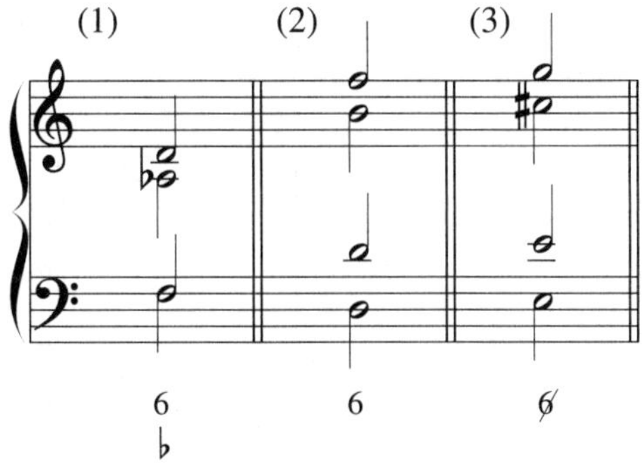

5.76 Continue as in the preceding frame.

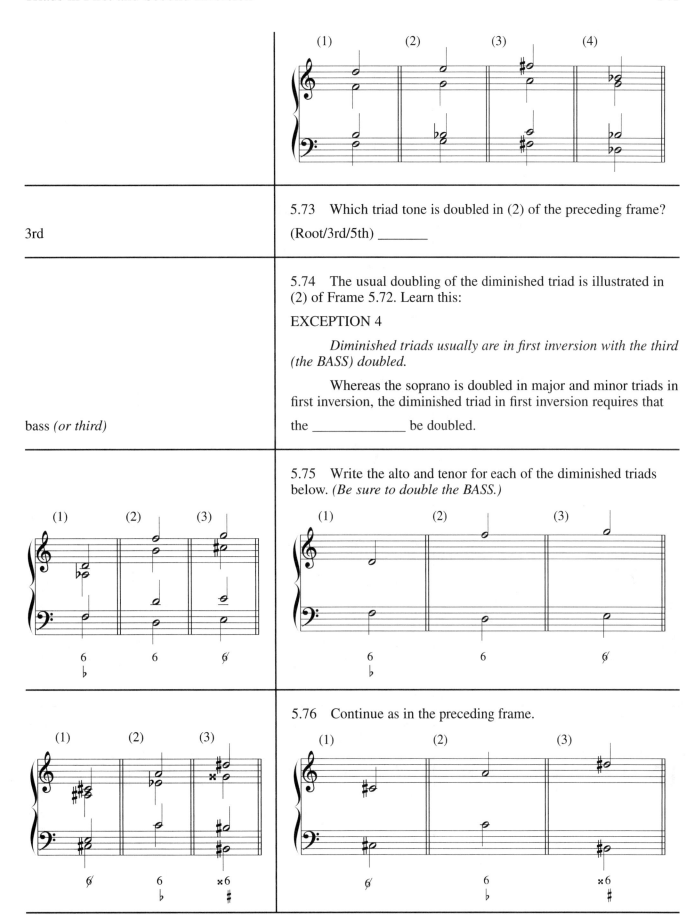

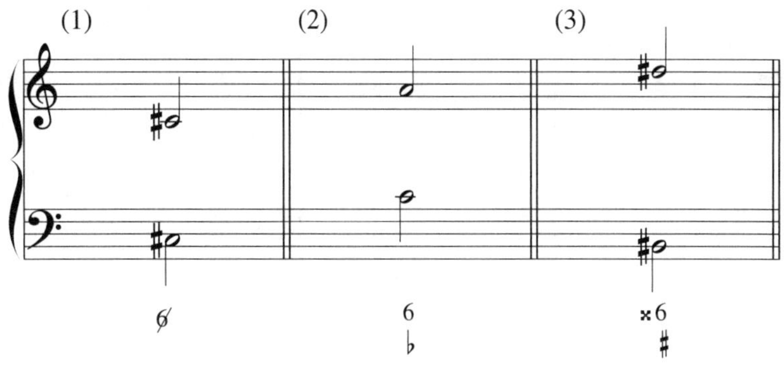

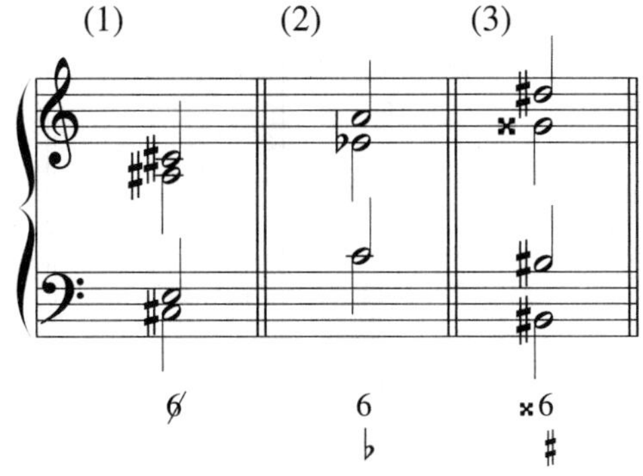

(No response required.)

Expository Frame

5.77 To review briefly the principles of doubling presented to this point:

1. When a major or minor triad is in *root* position, double the BASS.
2. When a major or minor triad is in *first inversion,* double the SOPRANO.
3. Diminished triads should be used in *first inversion* with the BASS (or third) doubled.

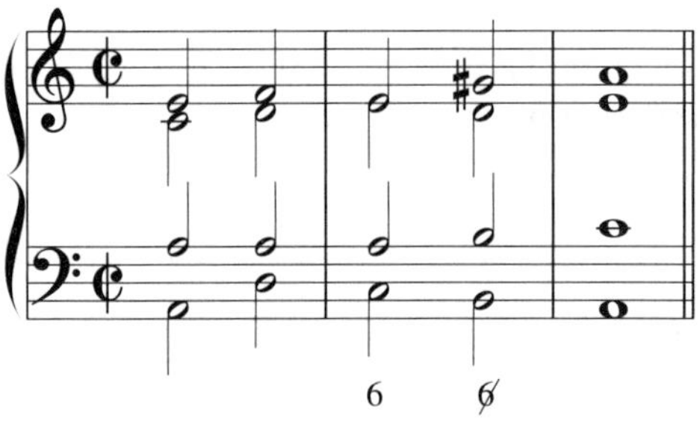

5.78 Since diminished triads are handled differently from major and minor triads, the *quality* of each triad must be determined before writing.

Add the alto and tenor voices. *(Remember: It is best to write first the voice that produces the desired doubling.)*

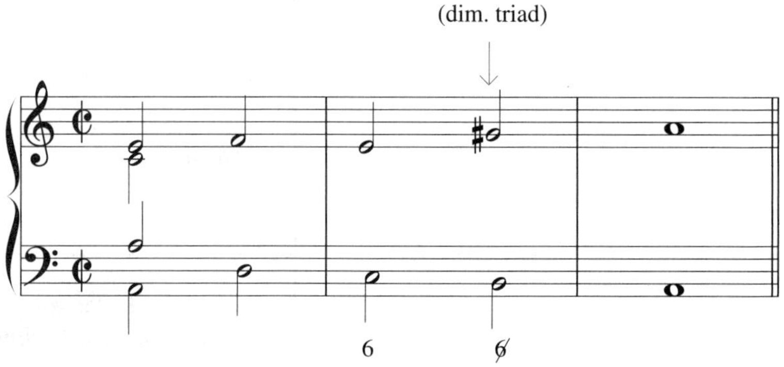

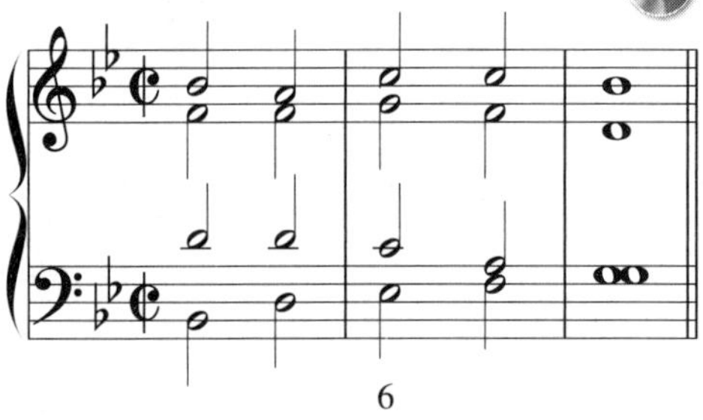

5.79 Continue as in the preceding frame.

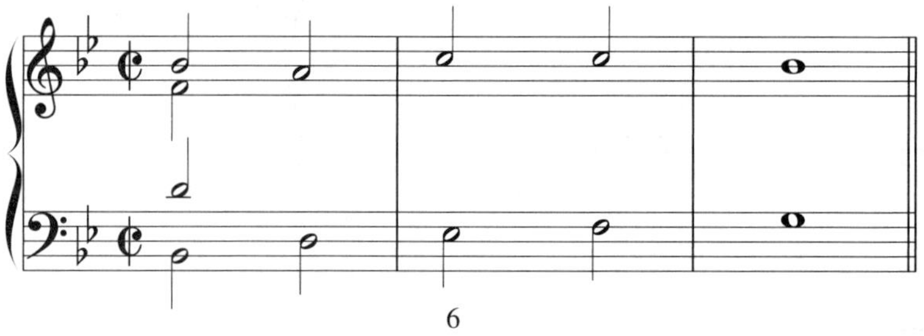

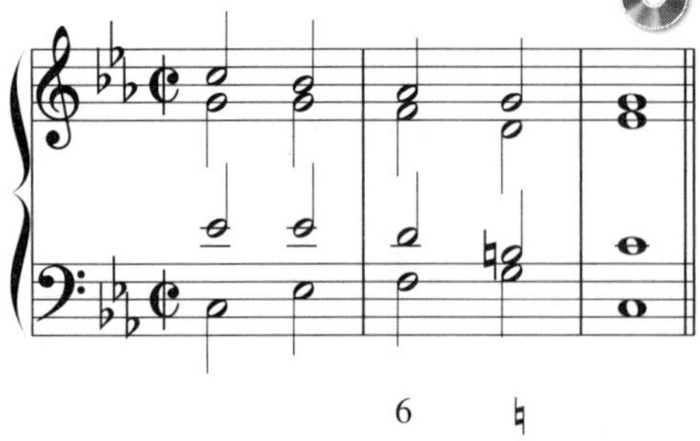

5.80 Continue as in the preceding frame.

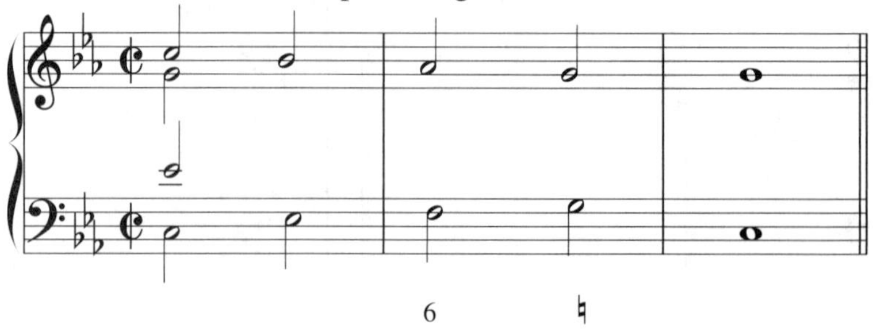

5.81 Refer, again, to the example in the preceding frame. What type of minor scale is used in the soprano voice?

____

____

The descending form of the melodic minor scale *(or natural minor).*

Expository Frame

5.82 The melodic minor scale provides alternate sixth and seventh scale degrees.

THE C MELODIC MINOR SCALE

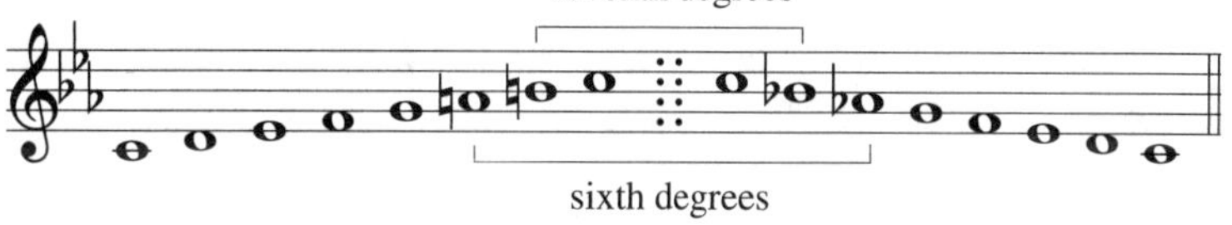

The two forms of the melodic minor scale are used to provide tonal variety, and to avoid the melodic interval of an augmented second that is characteristic of the harmonic minor scale.

(No response required.)

5.83 Note the use of the ascending form of the melodic minor scale below:

Beethoven, *Symphony No. 7,* Op. 92

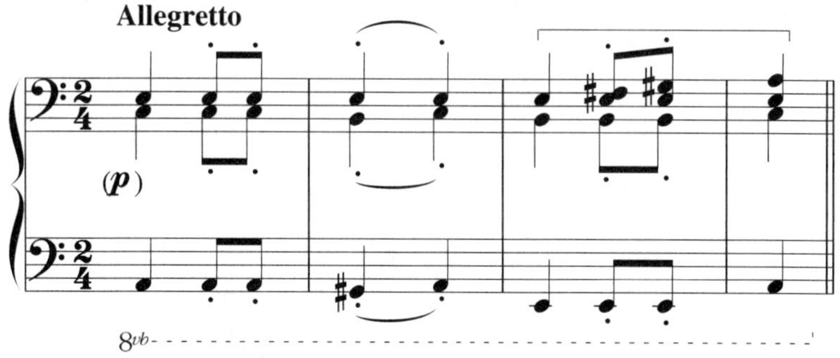

The raised sixth degree of the melodic minor scale is used primarily to avoid the melodic interval of the augmented second that occurs in the _____________ minor scale.

harmonic

5.84 Write the alto and tenor voices. Supply, also, the roman numeral analysis. *(Be sure the quality of each triad is reflected by the type of roman numeral used.)*

(Continued on the next page)

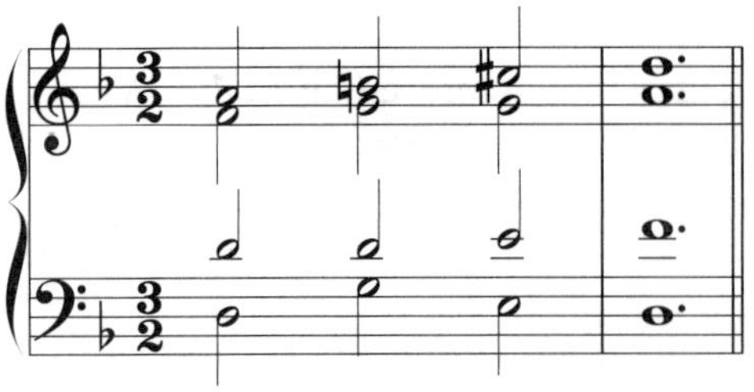

d: i IV vii°6 i

d: ___ ___ ___ ___

g: i III+ VI ii°6 V

5.85 Continue as in the preceding frame.

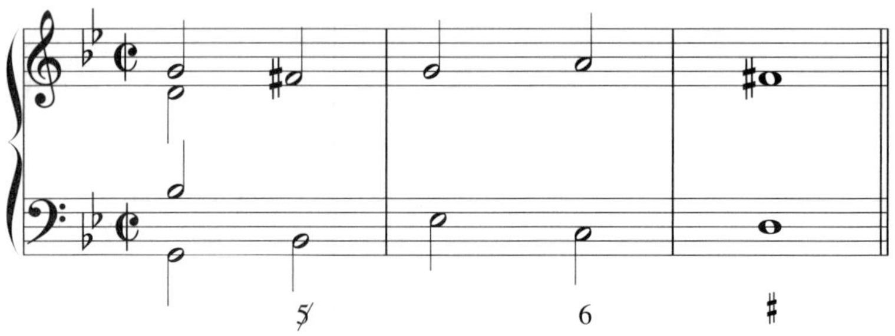

g: ___ ___ ___ ___ ___

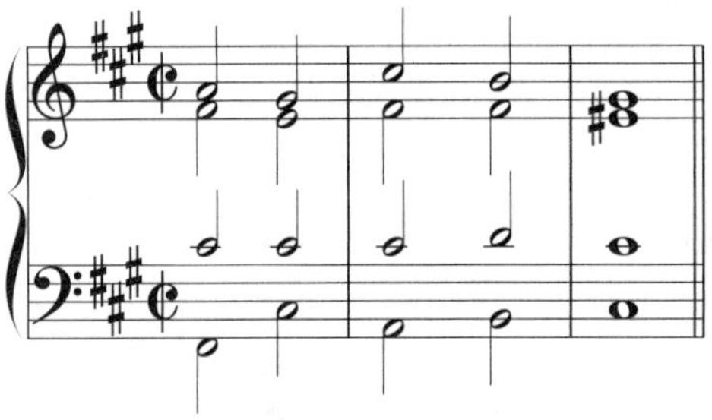

f♯: i v i6 iv V

5.86 Continue as in the preceding frame.

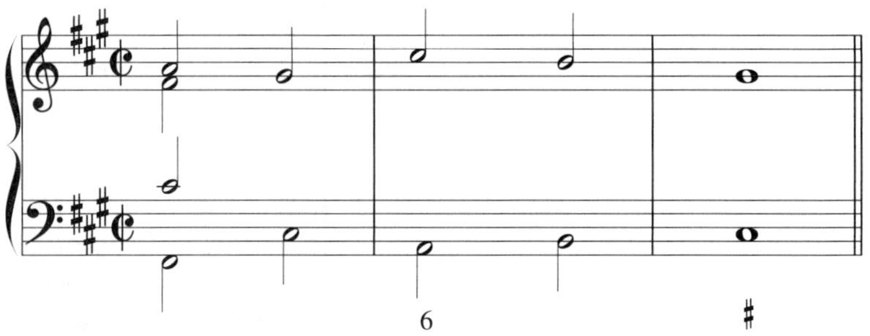

f♯: ___ ___ ___ ___ ___

a: i i6 IV vii°6 I

Alter.: Ami Ami/C D G♯dim/B A

5.87 Continue as in the preceding frame.

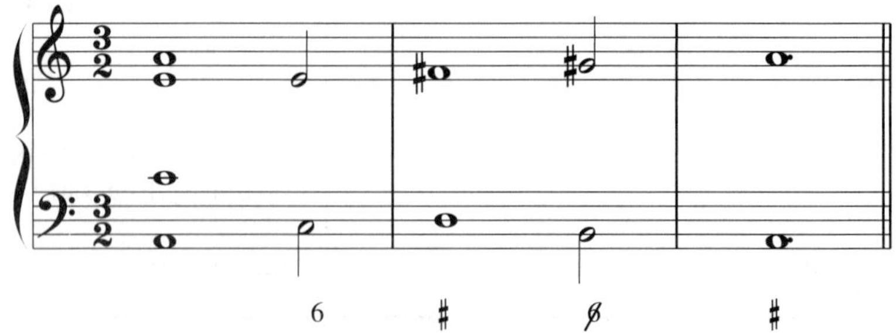

a: ___ ___ ___ ___ ___

Alternative: ___ ___ ___ ___ ___

5.88 When two or more triads in first inversion occur in succession, it often is impossible to use normal doubling in each chord. Notice the parallel fifths and octaves in the example below.

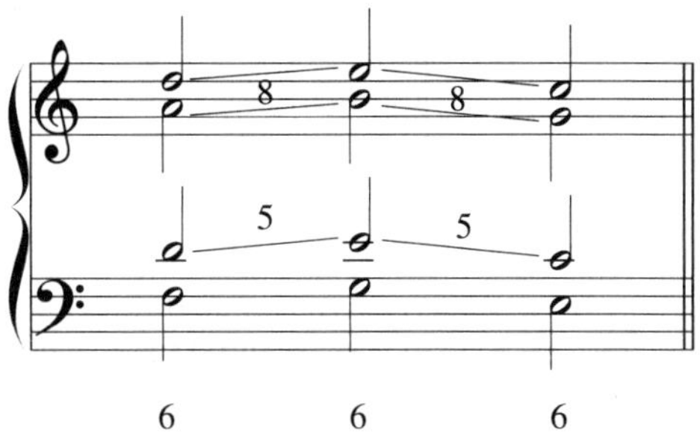

Successive first inversions often lead to the part writing error of ____________.

incorrect parallel motion
(Or equivalent statement.)

5.89 Normal doubling sometimes can be achieved by doubling the soprano in various voices.

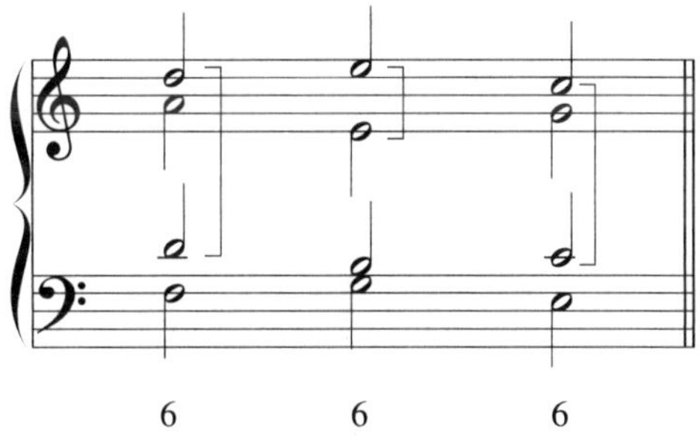

The choice of doubling in such a case is determined by expediency. Alternate doublings are acceptable if they contribute to smooth part writing, or are necessary to avoid incorrect parallel motion. Judged by the above statements, which is the least objectionable, parallel octaves or irregular doubling? __________

Irregular doubling

5.90 Notice in the example below that various pairs of voices are doubled.

Bach, Chorale: *O Herre Gott, dein göttlich Wort*

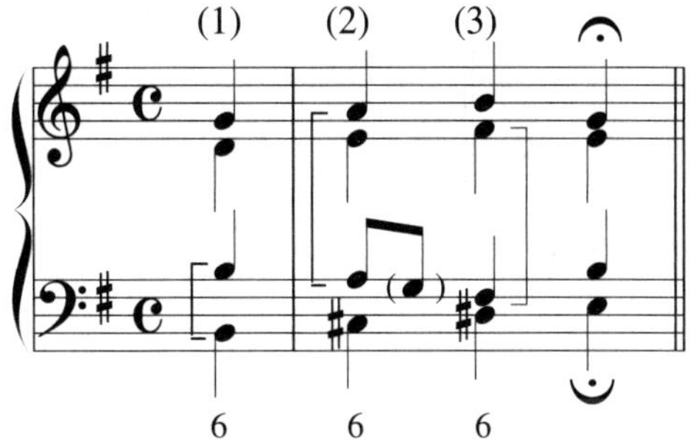

(Continued on the next page)

(1) Third
(2) Root
(3) Fifth

List the triad tone (root, third, fifth) that is doubled in each chord.

Doubled tone

(1) ____________
(2) ____________
(3) ____________

E
(E is the leading tone in the key of F Major.)

5.91 For the sake of effective melodic lines in each voice and to avoid incorrect use of parallel motion, irregular doubling often occurs when several chords in first inversion are used in succession. Active tones, however, should not be doubled. An *active tone* is one that has a strong tendency to resolve in one specific direction. The leading tone, for example, tends to resolve up a half-step to the tonic. Notes that are inflected chromatically are active in the direction of the inflection.

In the key of F Major, which tone is more active, A or E? _______

e: i i6 vii°6 i
Alter.: Emi Emi/G D♯dim/F♯ Emi

5.92 Write the alto and tenor voices. Supply, also, the roman numeral analysis.

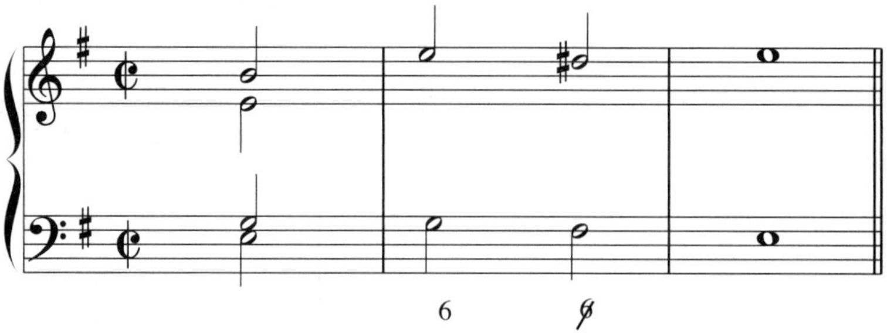

e: ___ ___ ___ ___
Alternative: ___ ___ ___ ___

---

(1)

D: I iii6 ii6 I6 V

5.93 Write the alto and tenor voices. Supply, also, the roman numeral analysis.

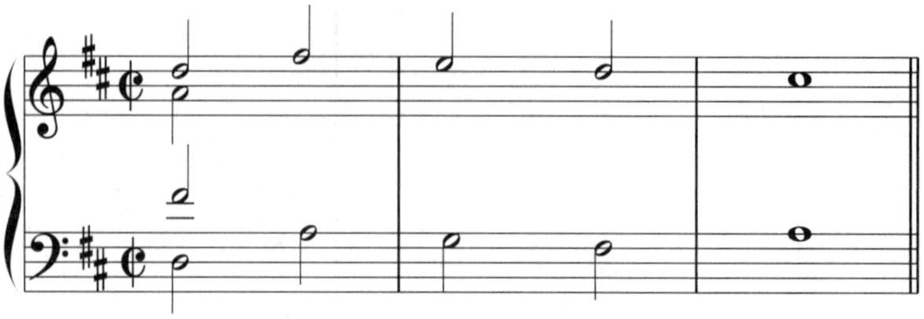

6 6 6

D: ___ ___ ___ ___ ___

or

(2)

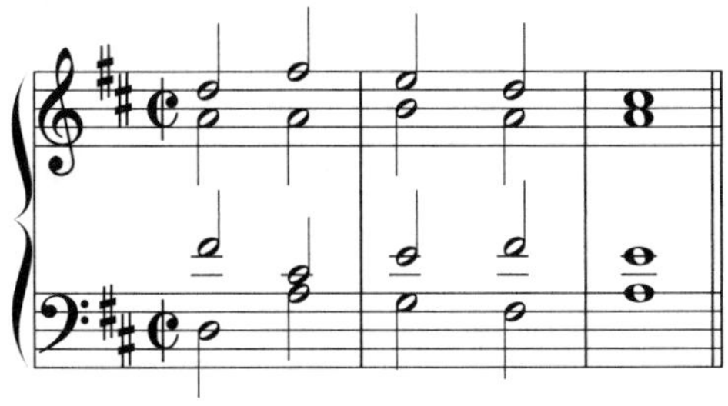

D: I iii6 ii6 I6 V

There are several possible solutions to this exercise. For this reason two answers are given. If your solution does not agree with either of these, check carefully for parallel fifths or octaves and also for awkward leaps. If free from these errors, your answer may be as good as the ones given.

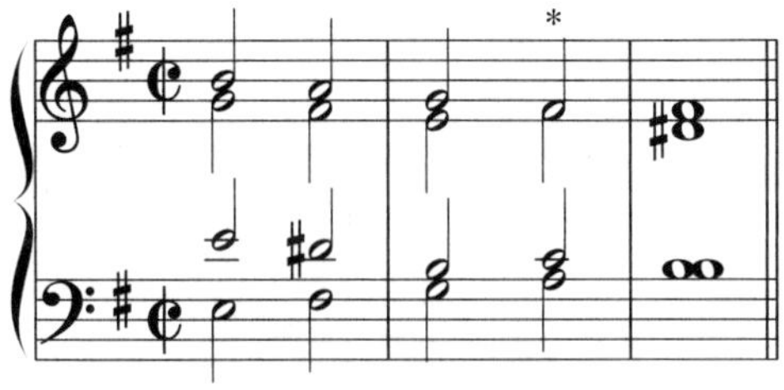

e: i vii°6 i6 ii°6 V

Irregular doubling is necessary to avoid Aug 2nd.

5.94 Write the alto and tenor voices and supply the roman numeral analysis.

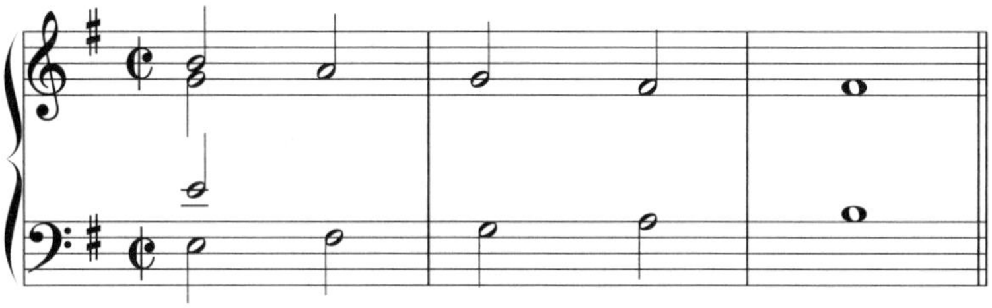

6̸ 6 6 ♯

e: ___ ___ ___ ___ ___

C: I I6 IV6 V6 I

Alter.: C C/E F/A G/B C

5.95 Write the alto and tenor voices and supply the roman numeral and alternative analysis.

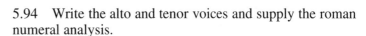

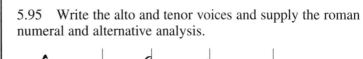

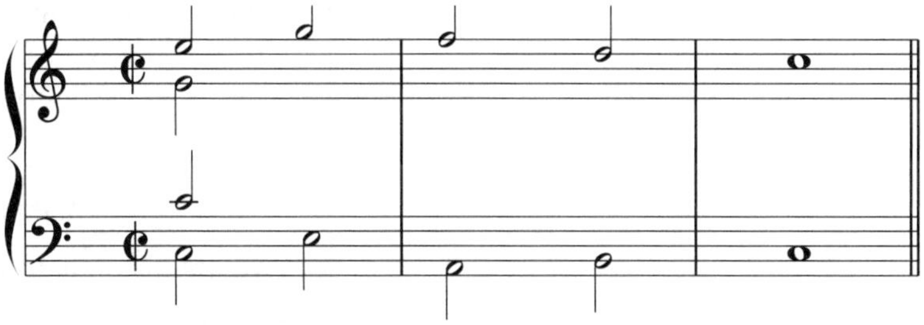

6 6 6

C: ___ ___ ___ ___ ___

Alternative: ___ ___ ___ ___ ___

There are parallel fifths between the alto and tenor, and parallel octaves between the tenor and soprano in the second and third chords. There are also parallel octaves between the soprano and bass in the last two chords.

5.96 What part writing errors can you find in the following example? ________________________________

____

____

____

(Continued on the next page)

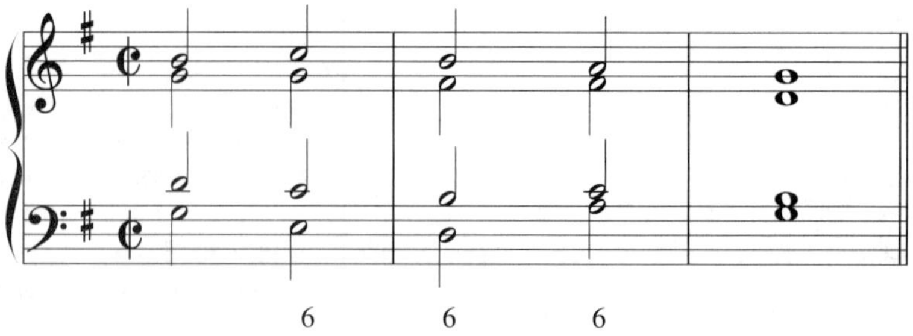

The leading tone (C♯) is doubled in the next-to-the-last chord (or the third of the diminished triad is *not* doubled).

5.97 What part writing error is contained in the example below?

____

____

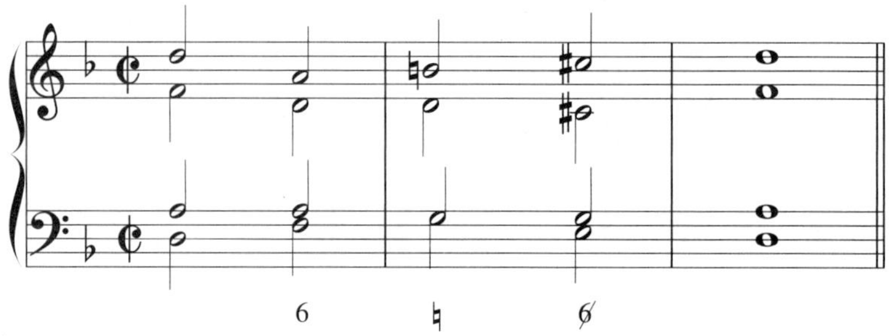

(No response required.)

Expository Frame

5.98 The leading tone is highly active; it is attracted strongly to the tonic, which is only a half step higher. By doubling the leading tone, two voices are motivated in the same direction. Parallel motion results if both voices move to the tonic; if not, the activity of the leading tone is denied in one voice. In either case, undesirable voice leading results. This explains the rule: *"do not double the leading, tone."*

Two other points to bear in mind are these:

1. Parallel fifths, unisons, and octaves are forbidden.
2. Avoid unnecessary leaps. *(Rarely is it necessary for a voice to leap more than a fourth.)*

5.99 The SECOND INVERSION of triads* is not used as frequently as either root position or first inversion. Triads in second inversion are used chiefly as part of a few specific harmonic progressions or musical features. Since their use is relatively limited, it is fairly simple to establish the principles that govern their use. Learn this:

PRINCIPLE 5

When a triad is in second inversion, double the BASS.

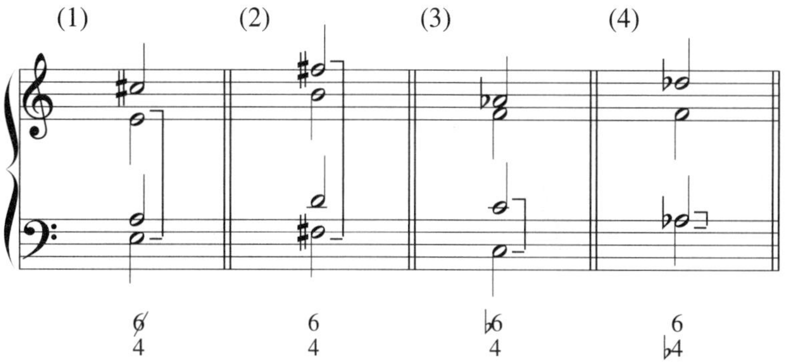

Which triad tone is doubled in each case above? The

5th

(root/3rd/5th) _______.

*Triads in second inversion are often referred to as six-four chords after the figured bass symbol $\frac{6}{4}$, which represents them.

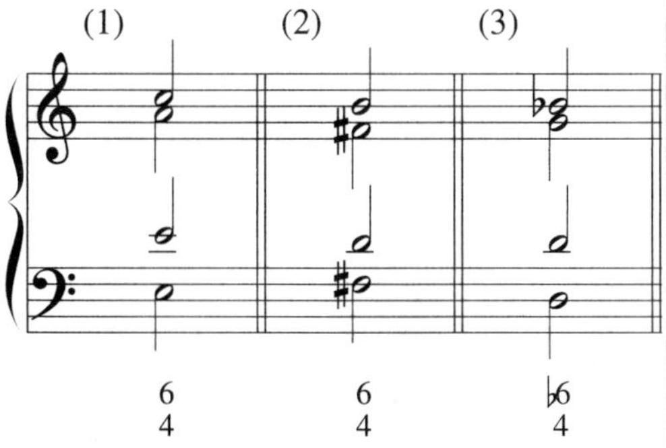

5.100 Write the alto and tenor voices. Use *close structure* for each chord.

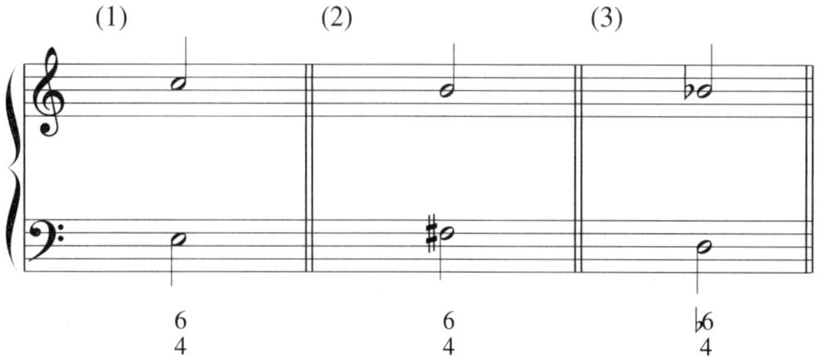

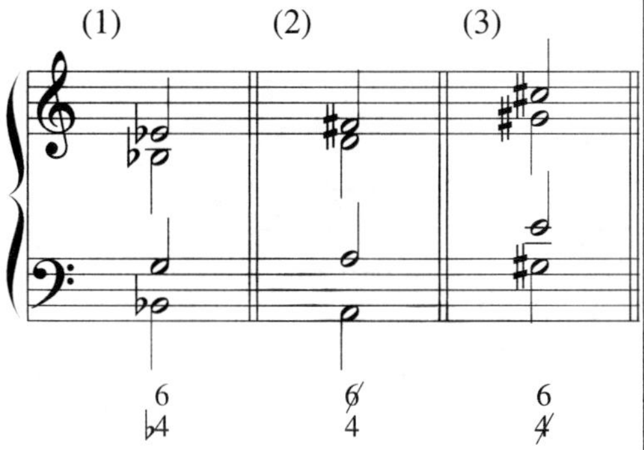

5.101 Write the alto and tenor voices. Use *close structure* for each chord.

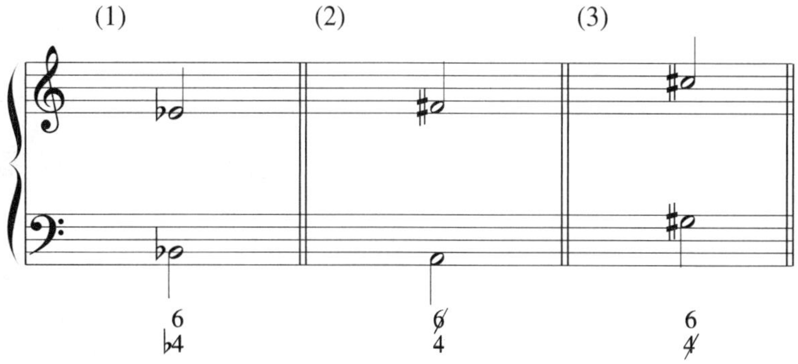

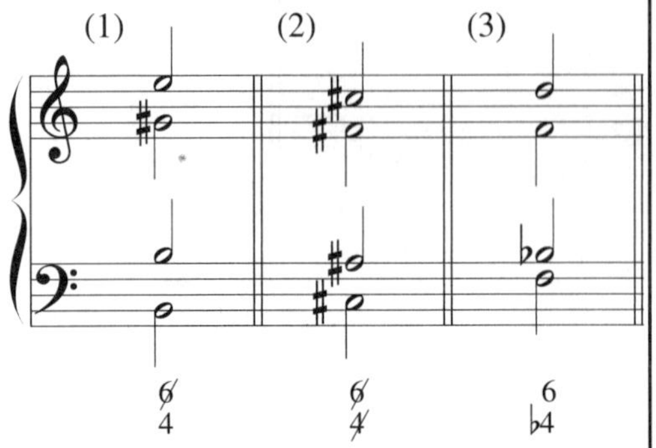

5.102 Write the alto and tenor voices. Use *open structure* for each chord.

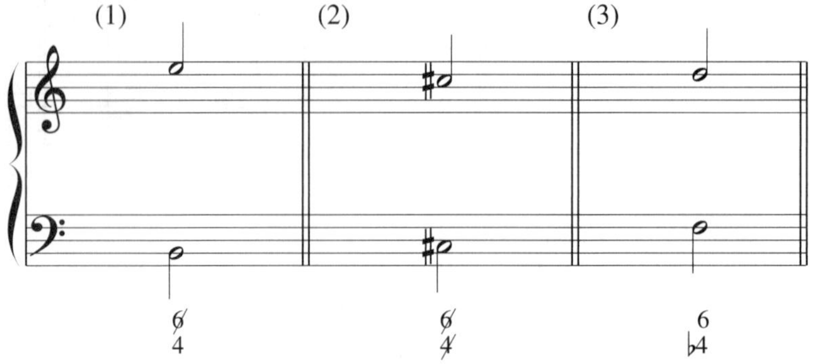

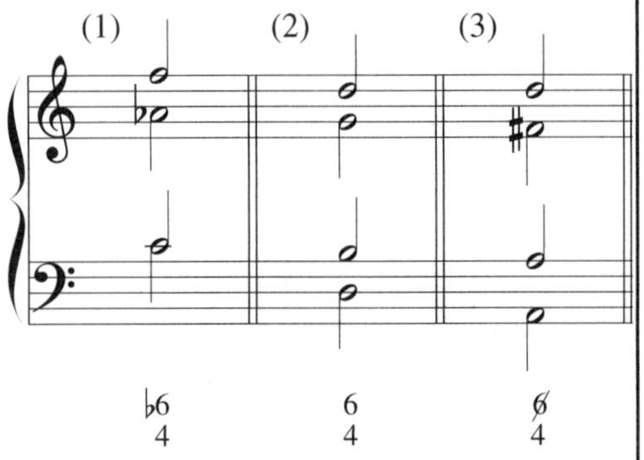

5.103 Write the alto and tenor voices. Use *open structure* for each chord.

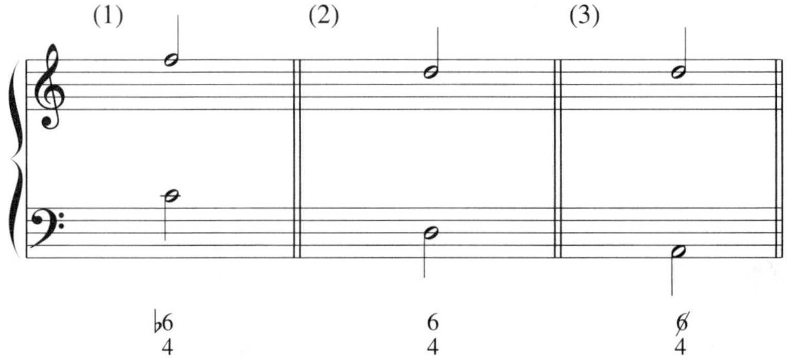

5.104 All second inversions fall into four patterns. From these patterns second inversion triads derive their names: CADENTIAL SIX-FOUR, PASSING SIX-FOUR, PEDAL SIX-FOUR, AND ARPEGGIO SIX-FOUR.

As the name implies, the CADENTIAL SIX-FOUR chord most often occurs at or near a cadence. (See NOTE.)

The example that begins below and continues on the following page includes a cadential six-four chord. Supply the roman numeral analysis for the last two chords.

Mozart, *Sonata,* K. 331

Andante grazioso

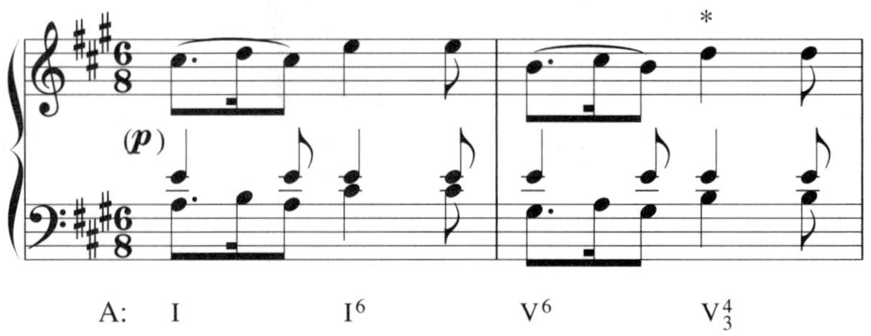

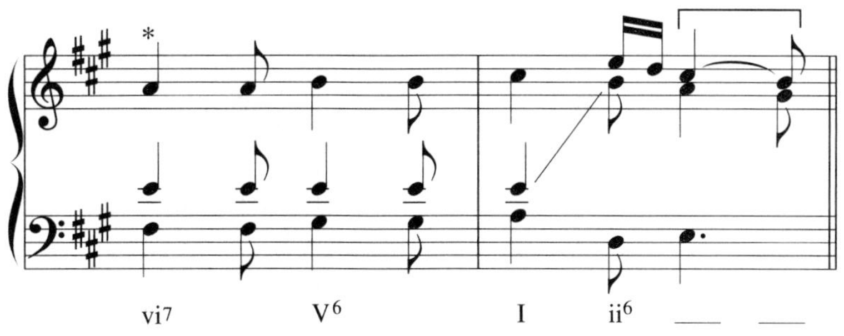

I^6_4 V

Note: A cadence is the close of a harmonic or melodic phrase. Cadences are presented in Chapter 7.0.
* Seventh chords and their inversions are presented in Chapter 6.0.

5.105 Most second inversion triads perform a *nonessential function* due to their relatively unstable sonority.

Play at the piano (or from the recording) the example in the preceding frame. Focus attention upon the effect of the last two chords.

Notice that the tonic six-four chord sounds almost incidental; it could be eliminated altogether by resolving to the dominant on the fourth eighth note of the measure without changing drastically the harmonic effect. Many six-four chords are the result of nonharmonic tones* or are used merely to delay resolution into a stronger chord.

The tonic six-four chord in the preceding frame delays

momentarily resolution into the ________________ chord.

dominant

*Nonharmonic tones are tones that are not part of the harmony. The various types of nonharmonic tones are presented in Chapter 8.0.

5.106 The CADENTIAL SIX-FOUR chord occurs on a strong beat or a strong portion of a beat. The tonic six-four that resolves to the dominant (demonstrated in Frame 5.104) is the most common type. A second type of cadential six-four is shown below:

Bach, Chorale: *Gott sei uns gnädig und barmherzig*

(Continued on the next page)

tonic

In this case the subdominant six-four chord causes the ultimate resolution to the tonic chord to be delayed. With respect to harmonic function, the cadential six-four chord is "unessential." It is used to sustain activity by delaying resolution to either the dominant or the _____________ chord.

False
(Cadential six-four chords occur only on strong beats.)

5.107 Cadential six-four chords may occur on any beat regardless of the meter. (True/False) _______

---

third

5.108 The examples of cadential six-four chords that are shown in Frames 5.104 and 5.106 demonstrate the voice leading that is normally used.

Two of the upper voices move DOWN BY STEP.

THE CADENTIAL SIX-FOUR

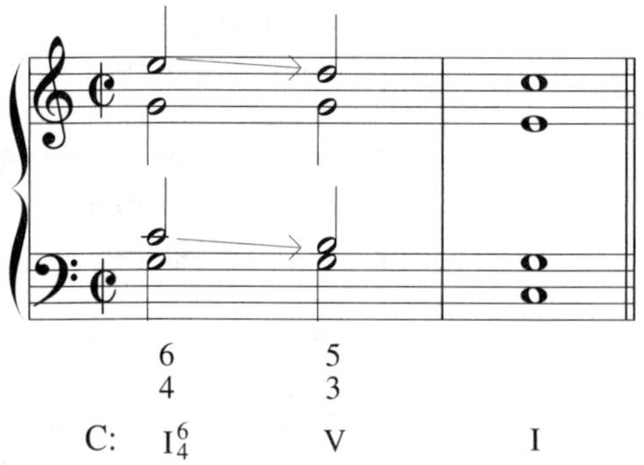

In the example above, the usual resolution of the cadential six-four chord is reflected by the figured bass symbol: the sixth above the bass moves to the fifth, and the fourth above the bass moves to the _____________.

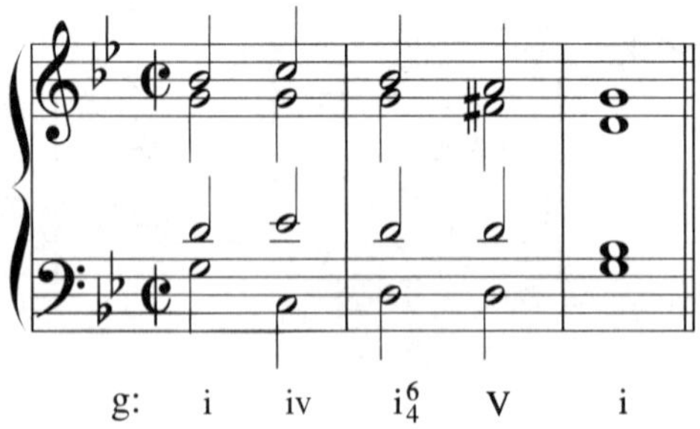

5.109 Write the alto and tenor voices. Supply the roman numeral analysis.

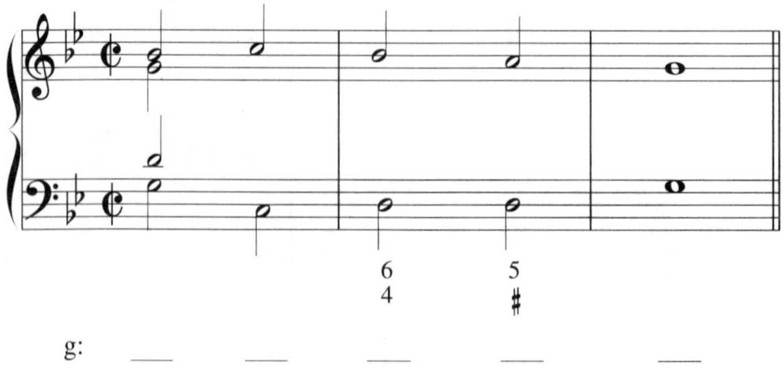

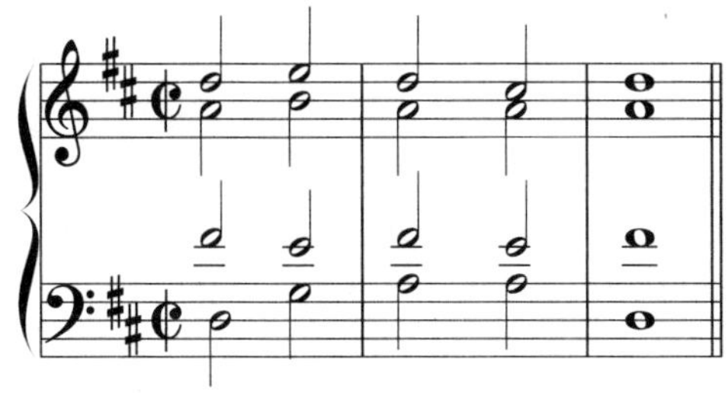

D: I ii6 I$^6_4$ V I

5.110 Write the alto and tenor voices. Supply the roman numeral analysis.

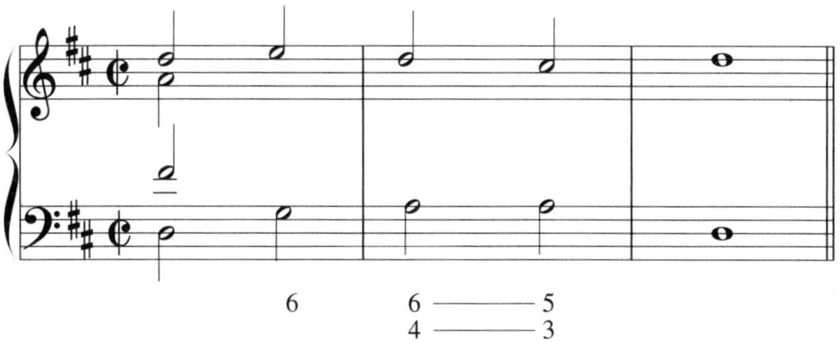

D: ___ ___ ___ ___ ___

A♭: I ii6 I$^6_4$ V

Alter.: A♭ B♭mi/D A♭/E♭ E♭

5.111 Write the alto and tenor voices. Supply the roman numeral and alternative analysis.

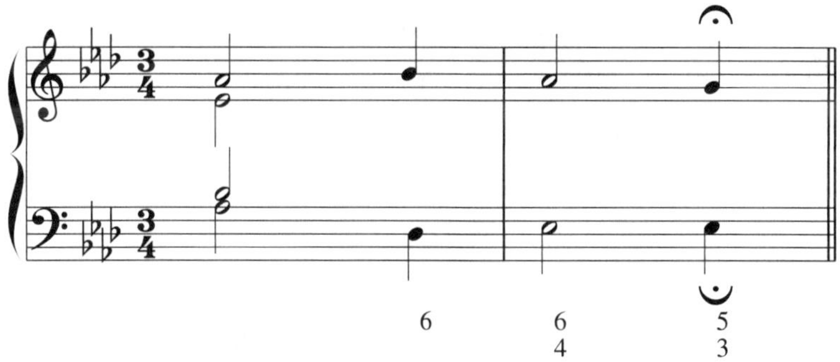

A♭: ___ ___ ___ ___

Alternative: ___ ___ ___ ___

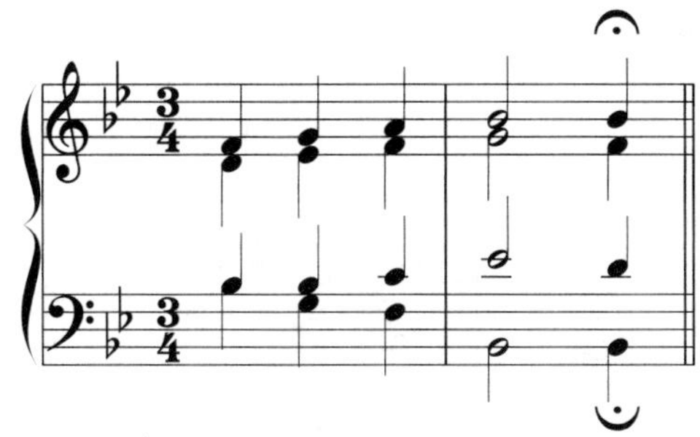

B♭: I IV^6 V IV$^6_4$ I

5.112 Write the alto and tenor voices. Supply the roman numeral analysis. *(Write all chords in close structure.)*

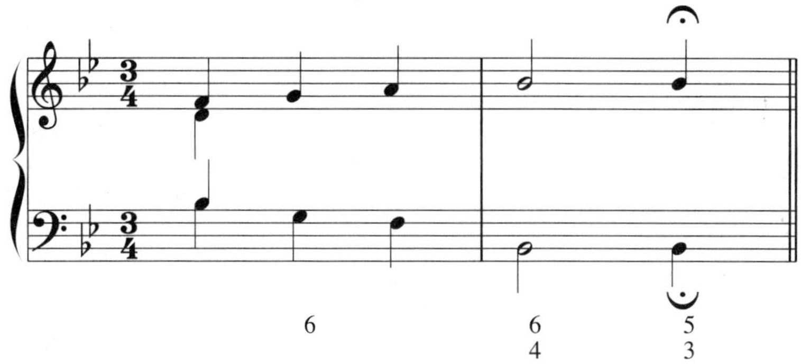

B♭: ___ ___ ___ ___ ___

5.113 *Summary of principles governing the use of cadential six-four chords:*

1. The cadential six-four chord occurs in a pattern of two chords over the same bass note. There are two patterns:

(a) over the dominant (I^6_4–V)

(b) over the tonic (IV^6_4–I)

2. The cadential six-four occurs on a *strong beat* of the measure or on a *strong portion of a beat.* The resolution occupies a relatively weak position.
3. The upper voices that move upon the resolution of a cadential six-four usually move *down by step.*

In a typical cadential six-four pattern, is the six-four chord as stable a sonority as the chord that follows it? _______

No

5.114 In terms of principles stated in the preceding frame, the cadential six-four chord in the example below is used incorrectly for two reasons. What are these errors?

(1) ____

____

(2) ____

____

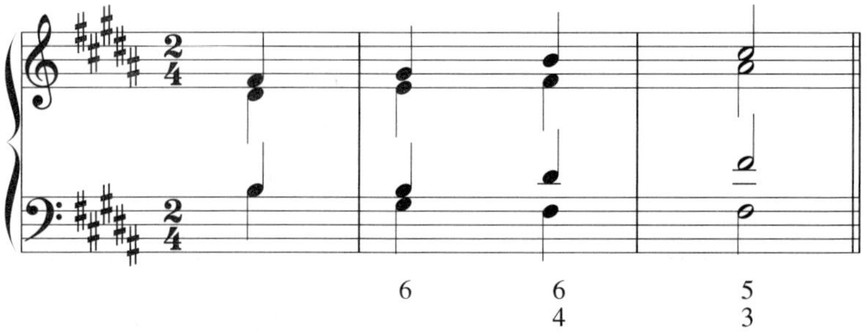

(1) The upper voices resolve upward rather than downward;

(2) The six-four chord should occur on a strong beat.

(In your own words.)

5.115 Irregularities in the resolution of cadential six-four chords sometimes are caused by melodic considerations.

Mozart, *Quartet,* K. 387

Molto Allegro

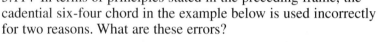

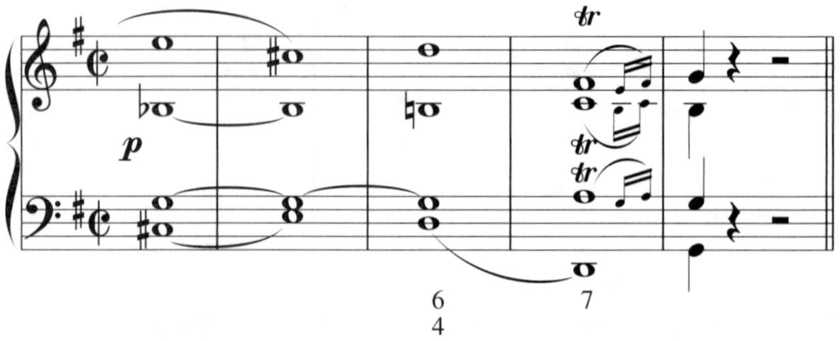

In the preceding example, do any of the upper voices resolve "normally" (down by step)? _______

No

5.116 The "irregularities" in the resolution of the cadential six-four shown in the preceding frame are justified by the more emphatic effect that results.

Demonstrated here (as often is the case) is that melodic requirements take precedence over such considerations as doubling, spacing, and normal resolution. Principles have been established as a guide in such matters, but they are not absolute rules and practical necessity of the desire to produce more effective melodic lines occasionally will cause one to ignore them.

In the "normal" resolution of the cadential six-four chord, the upper voices that move usually move (up/down) _____________ by step.

down

5.117 Below is an example of a PASSING SIX-FOUR chord.

Brahms, *Ein deutsches Requiem,* Op. 45, IV

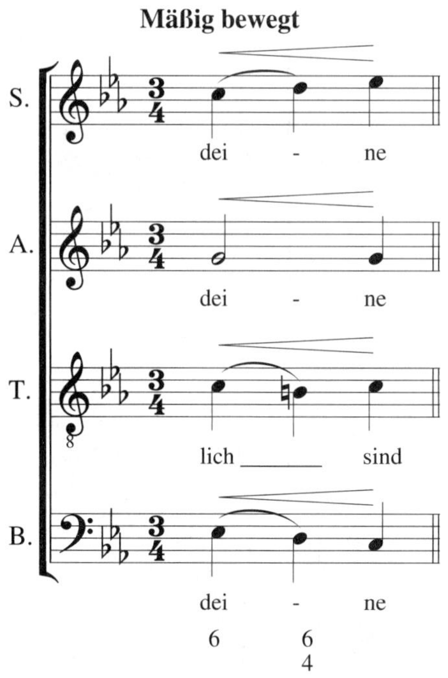

In this example the passing six-four chord is used to connect a triad in first inversion with the same triad in _____________ position.

root

5.118 Most passing six-four chords occur on a weak beat and connect either a triad in first inversion with the same triad in root position (as in the preceding frame), or the reverse. Both of these patterns are shown below:

(1)

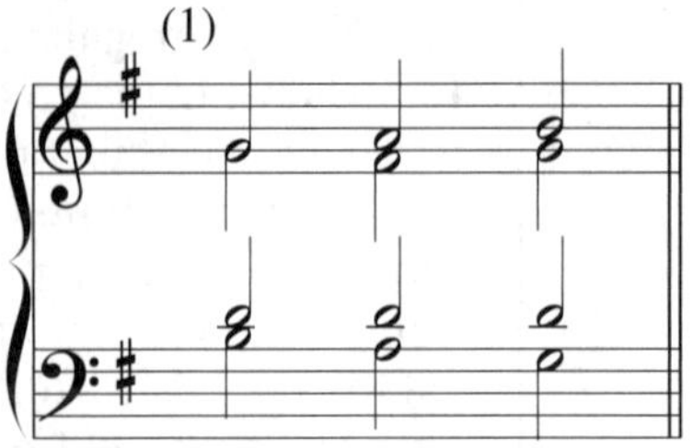

G: I^6 V^6_4 I

(2)

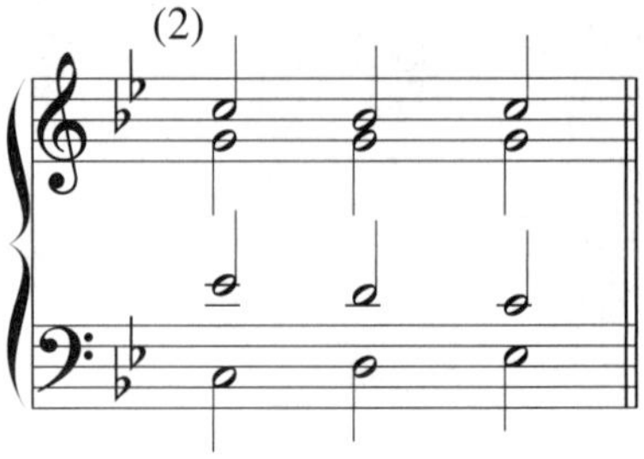

g: iv i^6_4 iv^6

Does irregular doubling occur in any of the chords? ______

No

5.119 The passing six-four may appear between the root position and first inversion of any chord, but it is most often associated with either the tonic or subdominant chords.

Write the alto and tenor voices and supply the roman numeral analysis.

$\overset{6}{4}$ (6 slashed) 6 ♯

d: ___ ___ ___ ___ ___

d: iv i V^6_4 i^6 V

5.120 Write the alto and tenor voices and supply the roman numeral analysis.

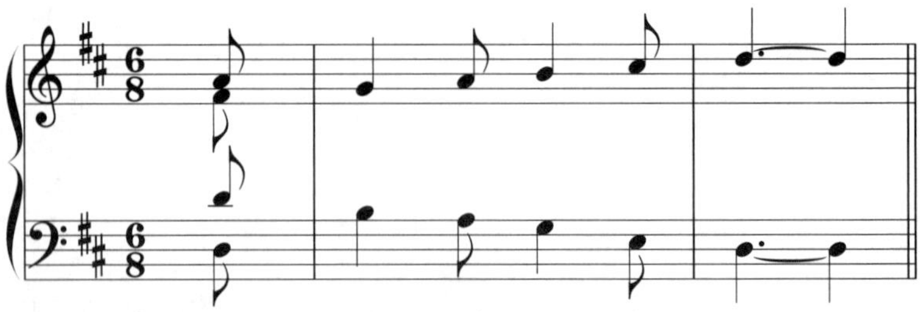

6 $\overset{6}{4}$ 6

D: ___ ___ ___ ___ ___ ___

D: I IV^6 I^6_4 IV $vii^{\circ 6}$ I

Bb: I IV I^6_4 IV^6 V^6 V vi

Alter.: B# Eb Bb/F Eb/G F Gmi

F/A

5.121 Write the alto and tenor voices and supply the roman numeral and alternative analysis.

6 6 6
4

Bb: ___ ___ ___ ___ ___ ___ ___

Alternative: ___ ___ ___ ___ ___ ___ ___

e: i V^6_4 i^6 $ii^{\circ 6}$ V i

5.122 Write the alto and tenor voices and supply the roman numeral analysis.

(Note that the chord at the asterisk is a diminished triad. Double appropriately.)

6̸ 6 6
4

e: ___ ___ ___ ___ ___ ___

(No response required.)

Expository Frame

5.123 Most passing six-four chords occur in the chord patterns below *(the reverse order is equally good):*

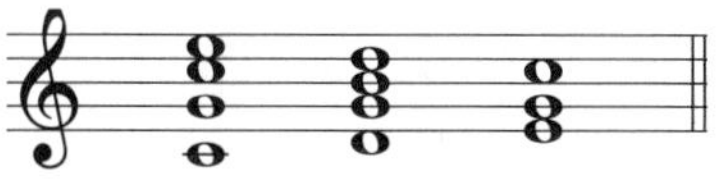

C: I V^6_4 I^6

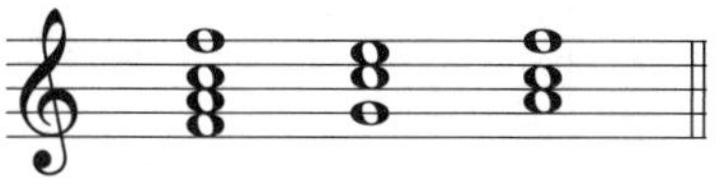

C: IV I^6_4 IV^6

Notice that, except for inversion, the first and last chords are the same.

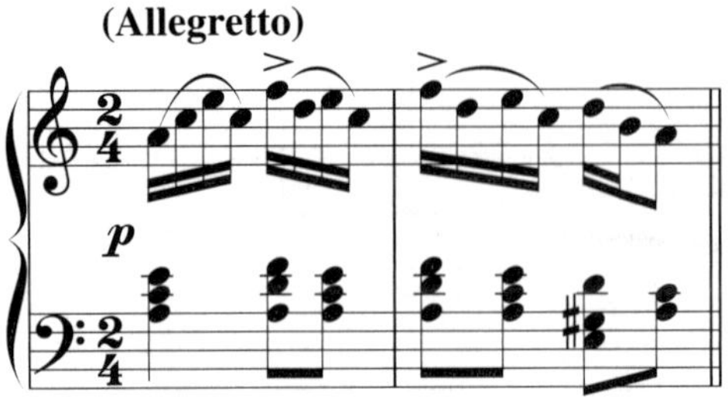

a: i iv^6_4 i iv^6_4 i V^7 i

5.124 The PEDAL SIX-FOUR chord* is demonstrated twice in the example below. Supply the roman numeral analysis of the first five chords.

Schumann, *Album for the Young,* Op. 68, No. 11

6 6
4 4

a: ___ ___ ___ ___ ___ V^7 i

*The pedal six-four chord is related to a nonharmonic tone device called *pedal* or *pedal point.* This is presented in Chapter 8.0 (Frame 8.105–.110). Other terms for the pedal six-four chord used by some writers are *embellishing* six-four, *auxilliary* six-four, and *stationary* six-four.

5.125 Another example of the pedal six-four chord is shown at the asterisk below:

Mozart, *Sonata,* K. 545

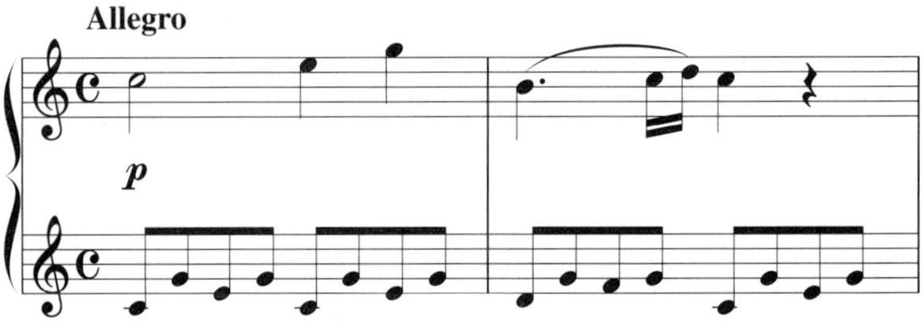

C: I V^4_3 I

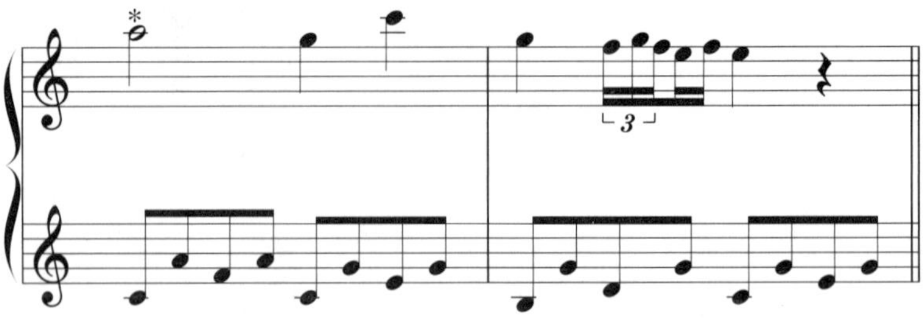

IV^6_4 I V^6 V^4_3 I

subdominant

The pedal six-four chord occurs over the same (or repeated) bass note. It rarely is used except over the tonic, so the chords usually involved are the tonic-______________-tonic.

1 2

a: i iv$^6_4$ i ii°^{6} i$^6_4$ V VI

1. *a diminished triad.*
2. *3rd is doubled void parallel 5ths and octaves.*

5.126 Write the alto and tenor voices and supply the roman numerals.

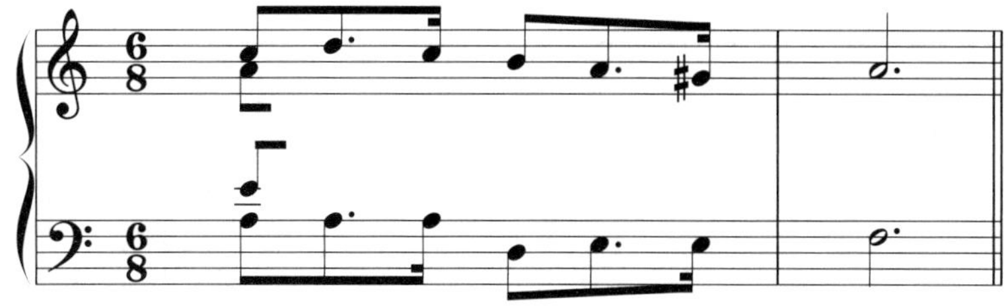

6/4 5/3 6 6/4 ♯

a: ___ ___ ___ ___ ___ ___ ___

G: I IV$^6_4$ I IV^6 I^6 V

Alter.: G C/G G C/E G/B D

5.127 Write the alto and tenor voices and supply the roman numeral and alternative analysis.

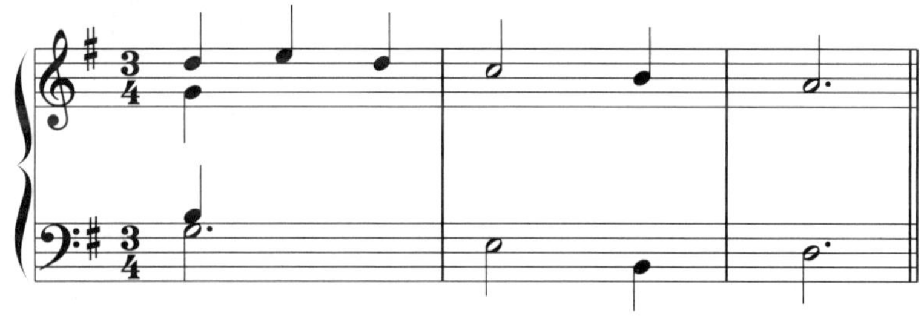

6/4 5/3 6 6

G: ___ ___ ___ ___ ___ ___

Alternative: ___ ___ ___ ___ ___ ___

Expository Frame

5.128 If the tones of a chord are sounded successively rather than simultaneously, the result is an *arpeggio.* The ARPEGGIO SIX-FOUR is produced by arpeggiation in the bass. The chord at the asterisk is an arpeggio six-four.

Beethoven, *Quartet,* Op. 18, No. 2

Adagio cantabile

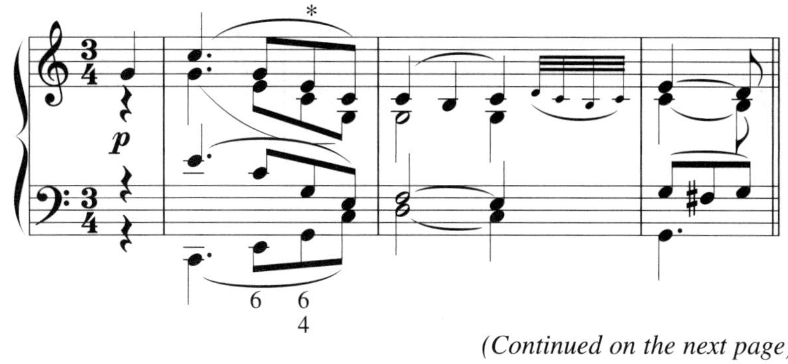

(Continued on the next page)

(No response required.)

The arpeggio six-four usually falls on a weak beat or weak portion of a beat and is preceded by the same chord in either root position or first inversion.

---

piano

5.129 Arpeggiation is a prominent feature in piano music of the nineteenth century. It results in rich sonorous effects due to the large number of strings that can be caused to vibrate and the rhythmic animation. The arpeggio six-four, particularly in piano music, is often merely illusion. When the damper pedal is depressed, all the strings are permitted to vibrate; thus the lowest tone continues to supply the foundation for the chord. Such a case is illustrated below:

Chopin, *Prelude,* Op. 28, No. 6

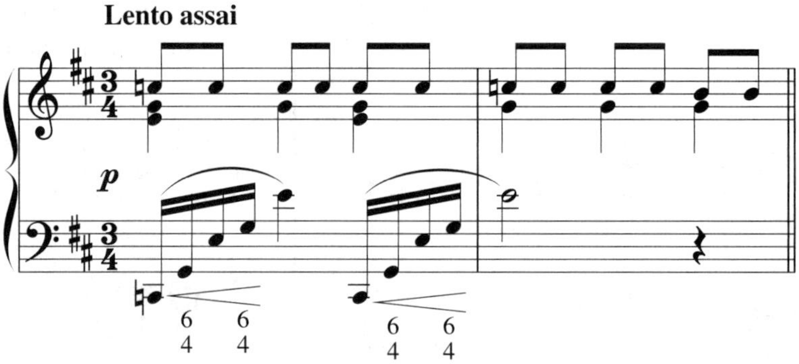

The arpeggio six-four occurs frequently in music for the _________.

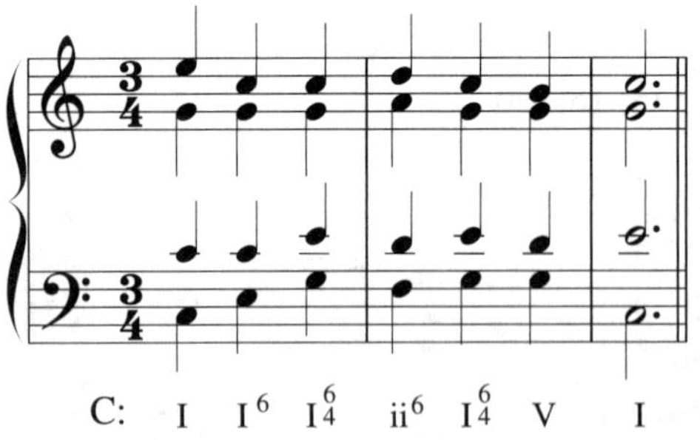

5.130 Write the alto and tenor voices and supply the roman numeral analysis.

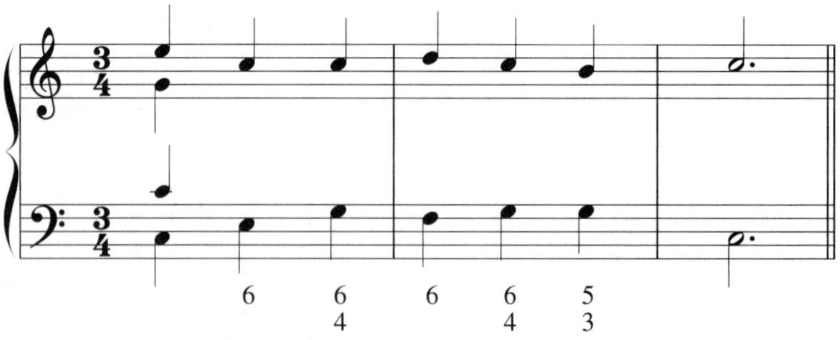

C: ___ ___ ___ ___ ___ ___ ___

d: i i^{6_4} V^{6_4} V i^6 i^{6_4} ii$^{\circ 6}$ V

Alter.: Dmi Dmi/A A Dmi/F Dmi/A A
A/E Edim/G

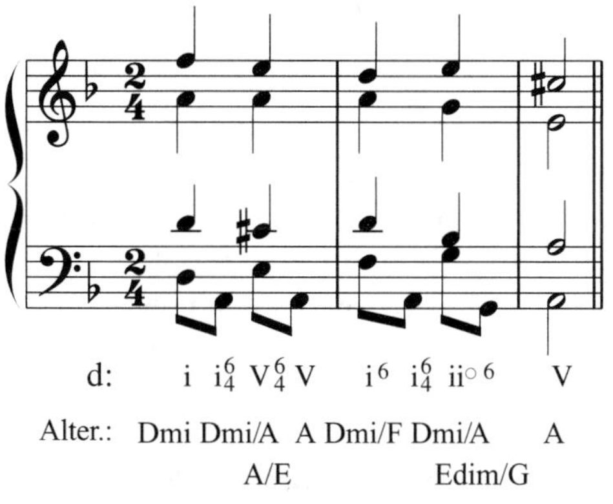

 5.131 Write the alto and tenor voices and supply the roman numeral and alternative analysis.
(*Use the same quarter-note rhythm as in the soprano voice.*)

$\begin{matrix}5\\3\end{matrix}$ — $\emptyset$ $\begin{matrix}\\4\end{matrix}$ $\begin{matrix}6\\6\end{matrix}$ — $\begin{matrix}6\\3\end{matrix}$ —

d: __ __ __ __ __ __ __ __

Alternative: __ __ __ __ __

A: I I^6 I^{6_4} V^6 V^{6_4} V I

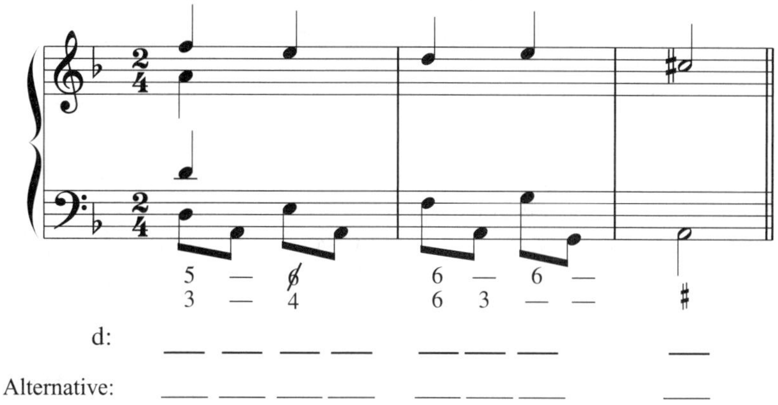

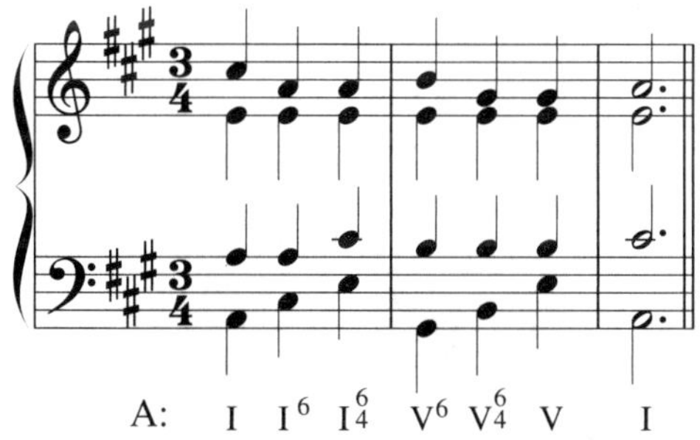

5.132 Write the alto and tenor voices and supply the roman numeral analysis.
(*Use regular doubling for each chord.*)

6 6 6 6
4 4

A: __ __ __ __ __ __

e: i i^6 i^{6_4} iv iv^{6_4} iv^6 V

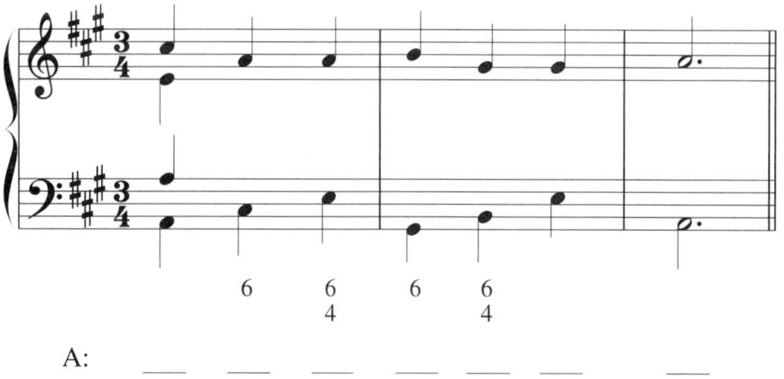

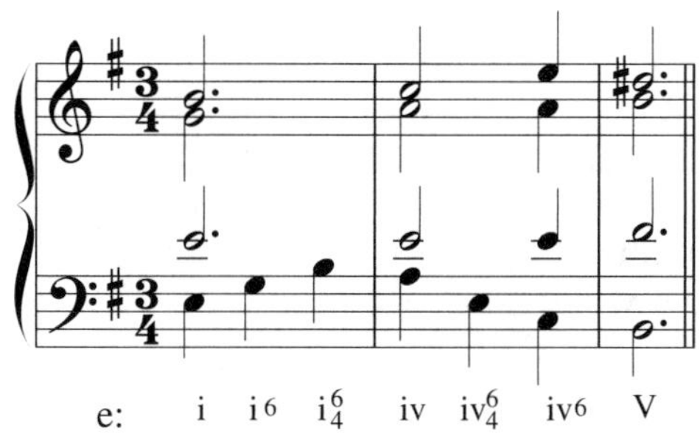

5.133 Write the alto and tenor voices and supply the roman numeral analysis.

6 6 6 6
4 4 #

e: __ __ __ __ __ __ __

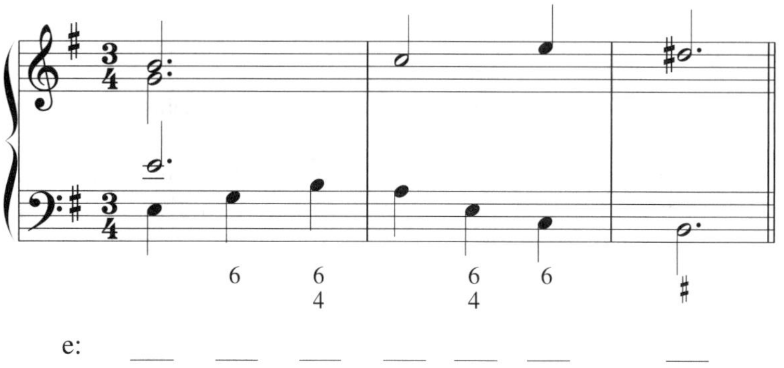

Summary

When all or most of the chords are in root position, the bass line tends to be angular. Inversions help smooth out the bass and enhance its melodic character. Inversions also provide variety with respect to chordal sonority. The interplay of sonorities that results from chords in various positions and inversions contributes significantly to the musical effect.

Care should be taken not to use chords in second inversion too frequently. Because they have relatively weak sonority, their use is limited mainly to the four standard types presented in this chapter (cadential, passing, pedal, and arpeggio). Six-four chords were used more frequently and with greater freedom as the nineteenth century progressed; they nevertheless constitute only a small percentage of the total. First inversions, however, occur frequently. Their slightly unstable effect gives a sense of forward motion to the harmony. This is especially true when the chord is approached from a chord with a different bass note.

These additional principles should generally be followed for the doubling of triads in first and second inversion:

PRINCIPLE 4: When a major or minor triad is in first inversion, the *soprano* is usually doubled.

EXCEPTION 4: When a diminished triad is in first inversion, the *bass* is doubled.

PRINCIPLE 5: When a triad is in second inversion, the *bass* is doubled.

Note: *Principle 5 does not have an exception.*

THE FOUR TYPES OF SIX-FOUR CHORDS.

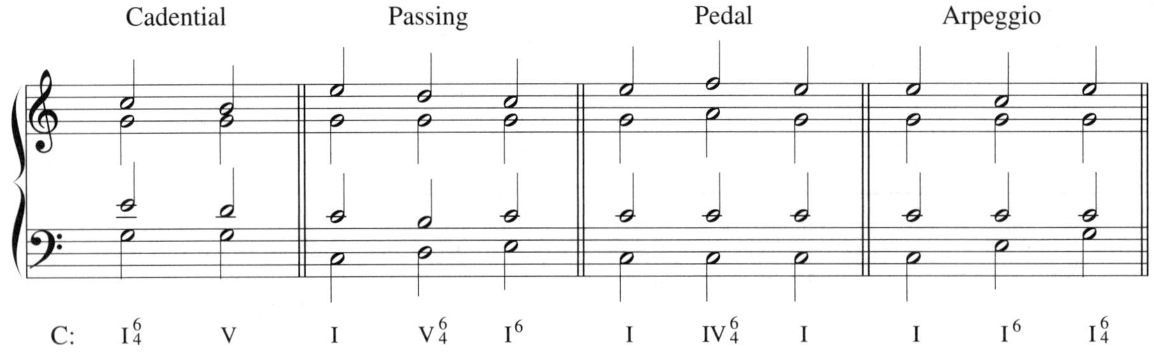

The terms that are explained or used in this chapter are listed below in chronological order:

- root position
- first inversion
- second inversion
- inverted (triad)
- sonority
- incorrect parallel motion
- irregular doubling
- active tone
- cadential six-four
- passing six-four
- pedal six-four
- arpeggio six-four
- irregular resolution
- nonessential function

Mastery Frames

5–1 Identify the triad position indicated by each of the following figured bass symbols.

(1) 6____________

(2) $^6_4$____________

(3) $^5_3$____________

(1) First inversion

(2) Second inversion

(3) Root position

(5.1–.28)

5–2 Complete the triads as indicated by the figured bass symbols.

(1) (2) (3) (4)

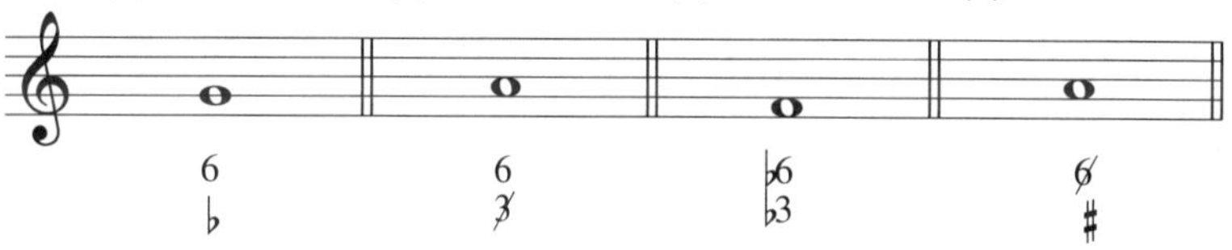

(1) (2) (3) (4)

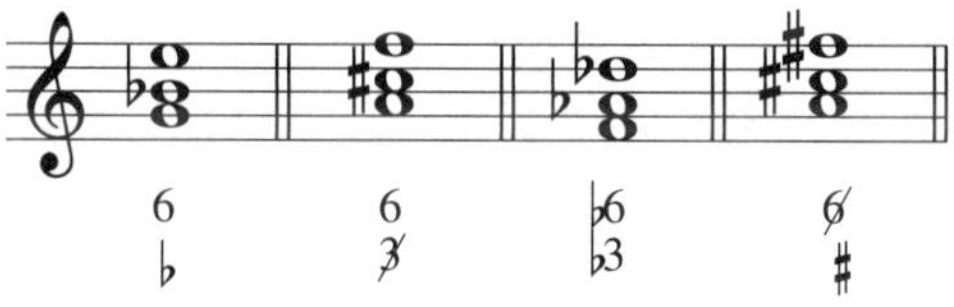

(5.15–.20)

5–3 Complete the triads as indicated by the figured bass symbols.

(1) (2) (3) (4)

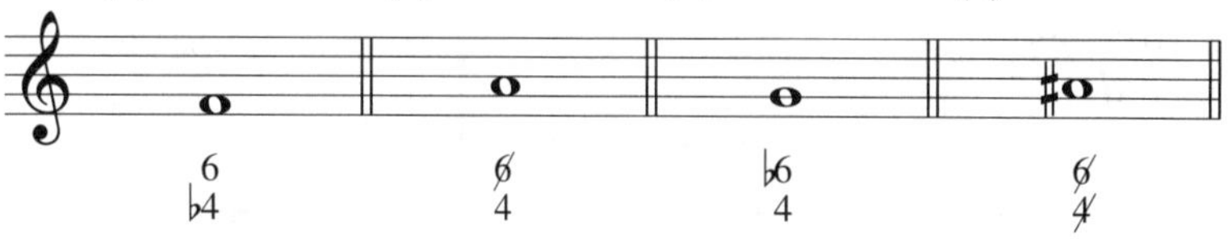

(1) (2) (3) (4)

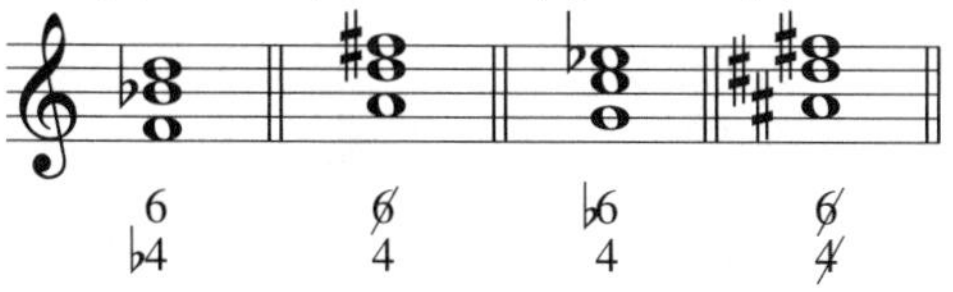

(5.21–.25)

5–4 Write the appropriate roman numeral for each triad. *Indicate inversions.*

(1) (2) (3)

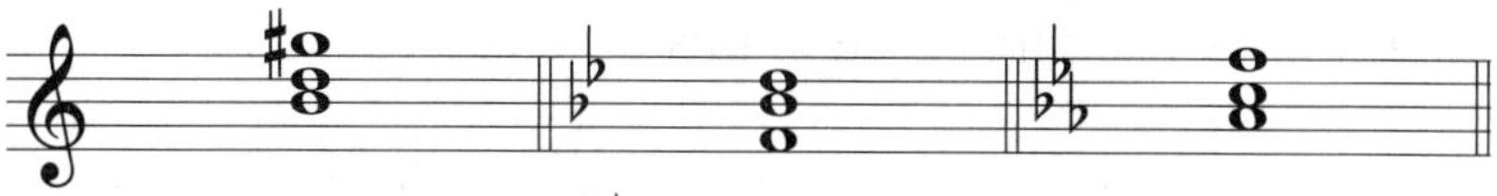

a: _____ B♭: _____ c: _____

(1) a: vii°^{6}

(2) B♭: I$^6_4$

(3) c: iv^6

(5.33–.37)

(1) D: IV$^6_4$ (G/D)

(2) f♯: V^6 (C♯/E♯)

(3) d: III$^{+6}_4$ (Faug/C♯)

(5.33–.37)

5–5 Write the appropriate roman numeral for each triad. *Indicate inversions.* Also write an alternative analysis.

(1) (2) (3)

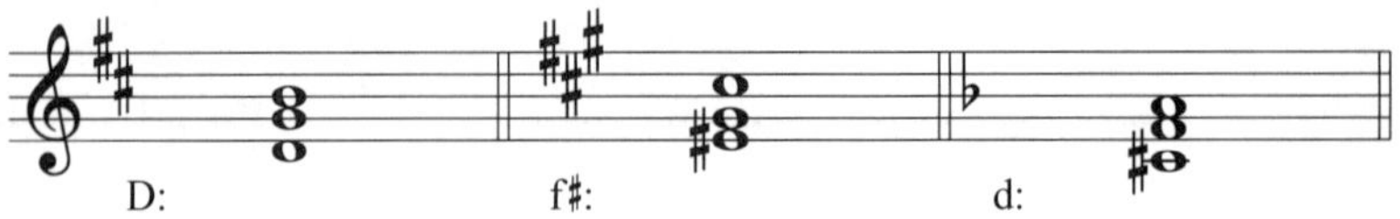

D: ______ f♯: ______ d: ______

Alternative: ______ ______ ______

(5.38–.116)

5–6 Write the alto and tenor voices. *Use open structure.*

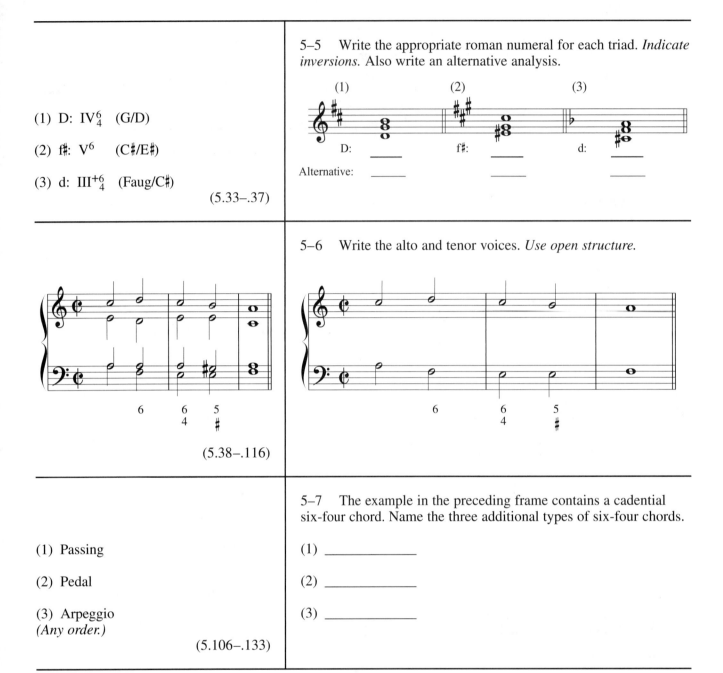

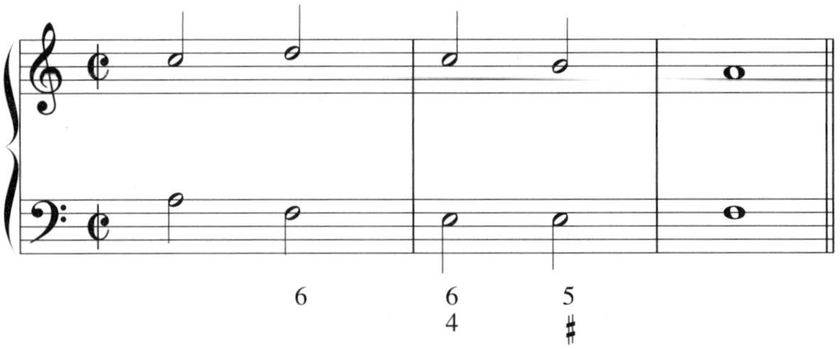

(1) Passing

(2) Pedal

(3) Arpeggio
(Any order.)

(5.106–.133)

5–7 The example in the preceding frame contains a cadential six-four chord. Name the three additional types of six-four chords.

(1) ____________

(2) ____________

(3) ____________

Supplementary Activities

1. Continue activities of examining musical excerpts, as suggested in previous chapters, by incorporating identification of chord inversions and developing short essays around these excerpts or new terms introduced in this chapter.

2. Focus ear training exercises on the identification of inversions in harmonic dictation and in general musical listening.

Supplementary Assignments

ASSIGNMENT 5–1 Name ______________________________

1. Indicate the note that will be in the lowest voice for each of the various positions of the designated triads.

TRIADS	B♭ MAJOR	C♯ MINOR	A♭ MAJOR
Root Position			
First Inversion			
Second Inversion			

2. Place each triad in the proper category by listing numbers.

Root position: ______________________________

First inversion: ______________________________

Second inversion: ______________________________

Bach, Chorale: *Wer weiss, wie nahe mir* (altered)

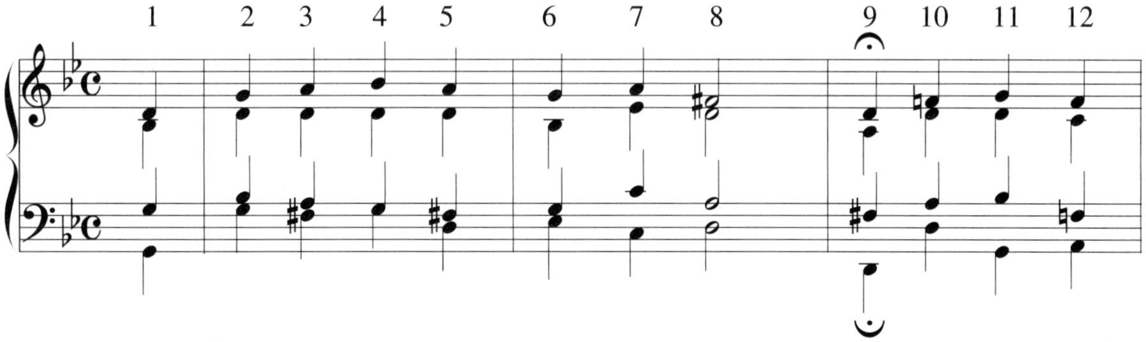

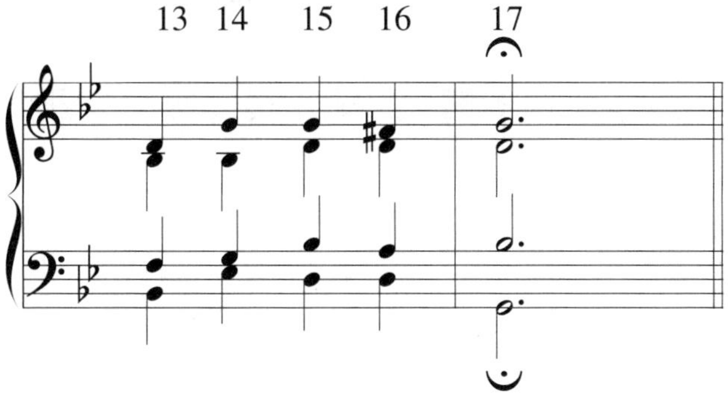

3. When a major or minor triad is in first inversion the doubled voice normally is the ____________________.

4. Diminished triads are usually in first inversion with the ____________________ voice doubled.

5. When triads are in second inversion the doubled voice normally is the ____________________.

6. Write the chords indicated by the figured bass symbols. *(Use correct doubling and spacing.)*

(A)

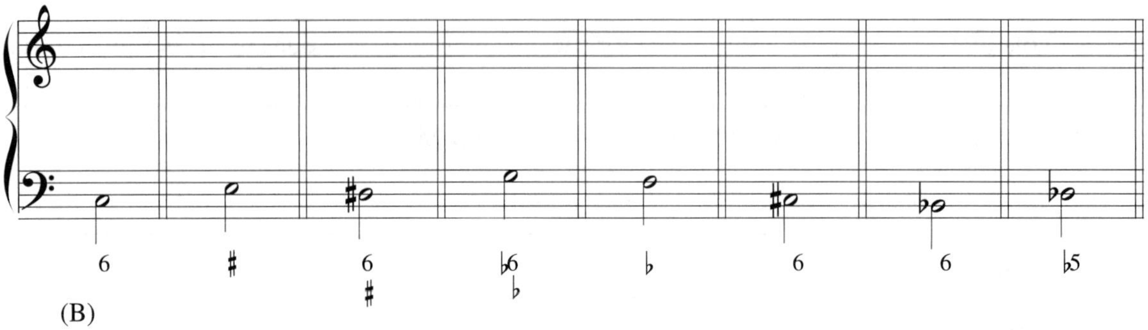

(B)

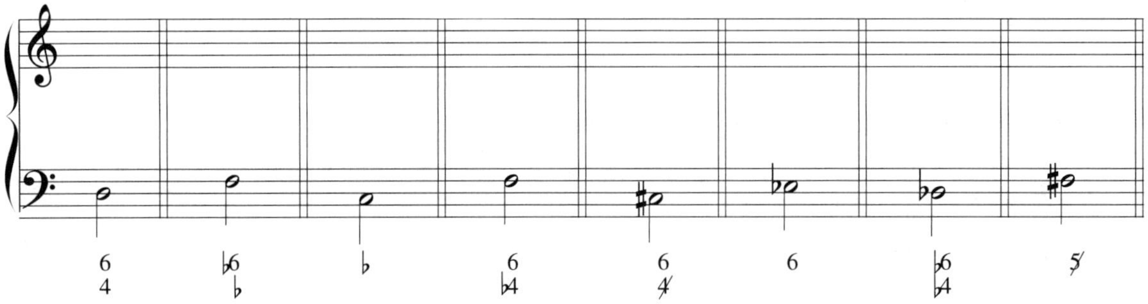

7. Supply the proper chord symbols.

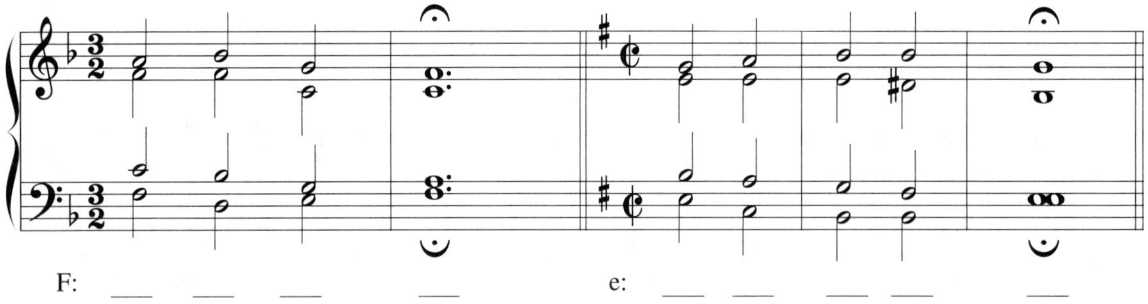

8. Write the alto and tenor voices and provide both the roman numeral and alternative analyses.

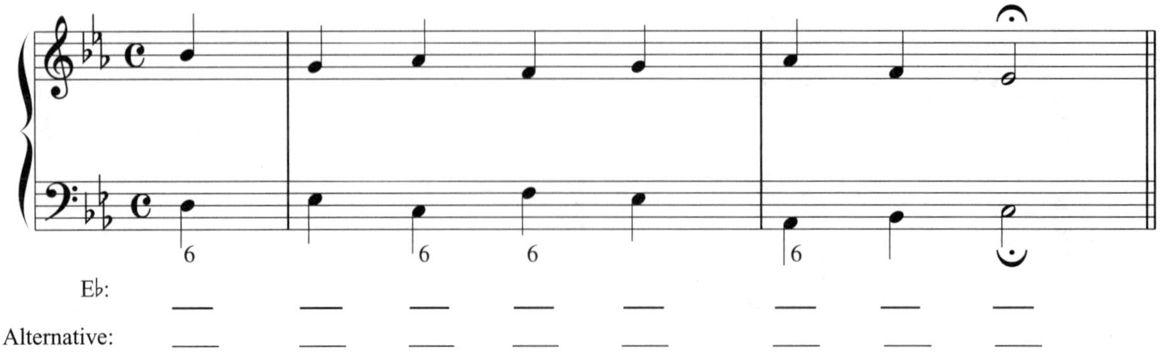

ASSIGNMENT 5–2 Name ______________________

1. Name the type of second inversion illustrated in each example.

(1) ______________________ (3) ______________________

(2) ______________________ (4) ______________________

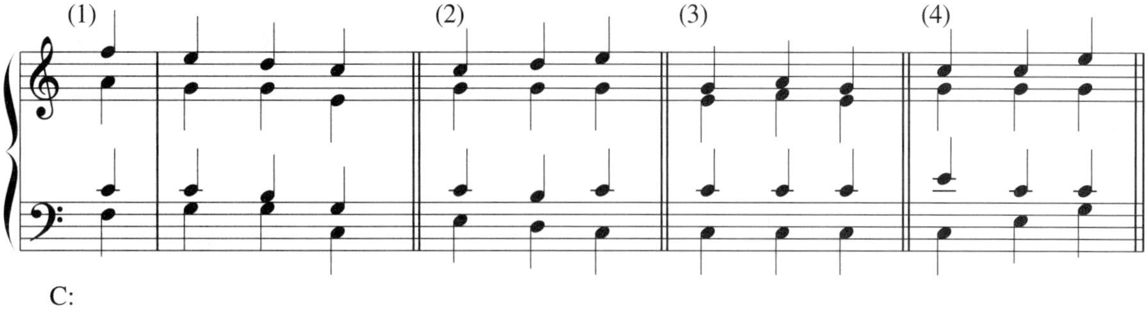

2. Which is the least preferred version? ______________________

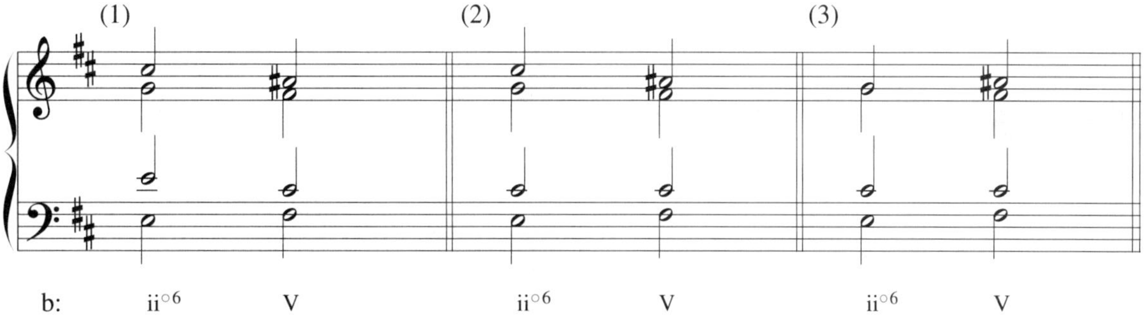

3. Which is the preferred version? ______________________

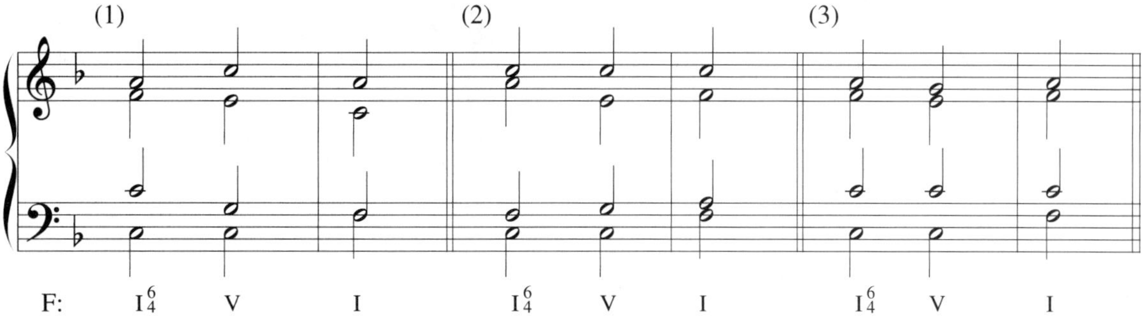

4. Write the alto and tenor voices and provide the roman numeral analysis. For (C) also supply an alternative analysis.

(A)

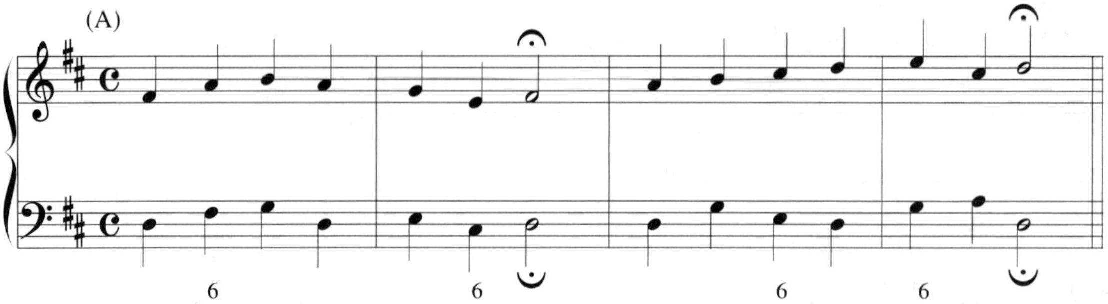

D:

(B)

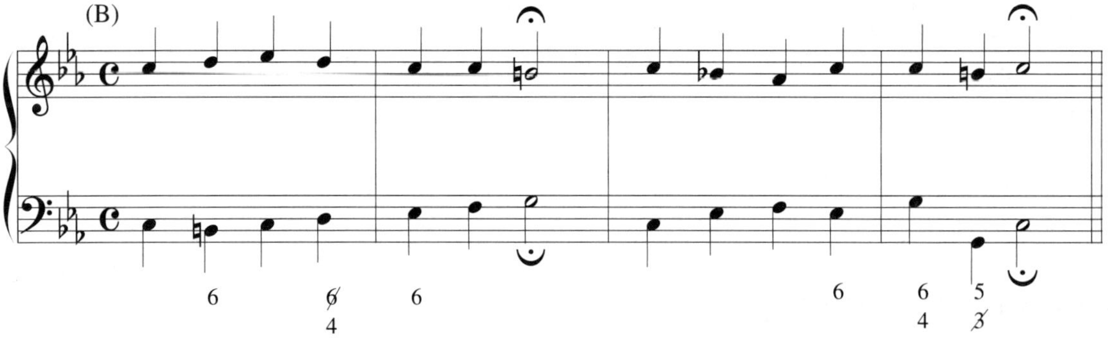

c:

(C)

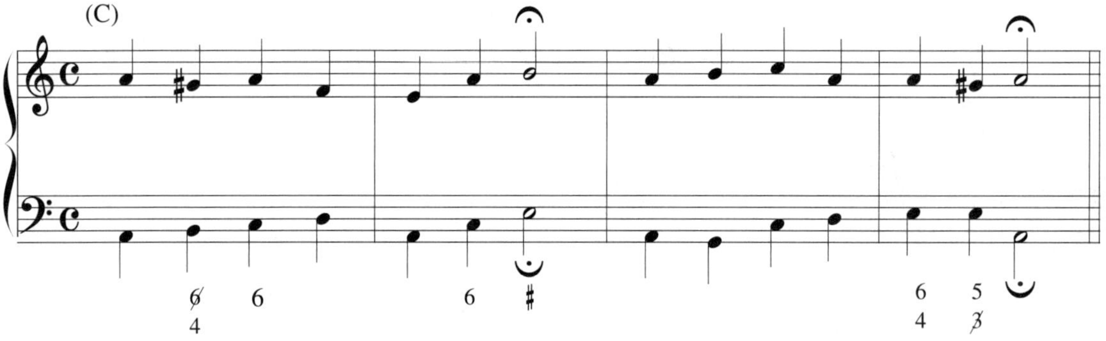

a:

Alter.:

5. Respond appropriately.

A. What is the quality of the first chord?

____

B. Name the 6-4 chord type. ____________________

C. Why is the 6-4 chord incorrectly written?

____

D. Does the V chord resolve as expected? ____________

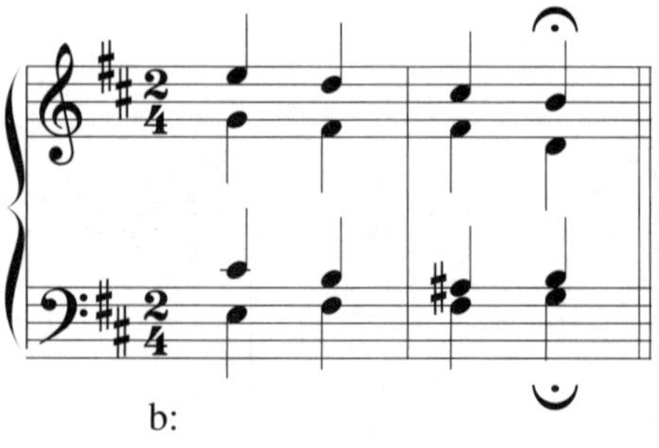

b:

Chapter 6.0
Introduction to Seventh Chords and the Dominant Seventh

The harmonic materials presented in this study thus far have been limited to triads. Most dissonance has been incidental to the harmony—the result of nonharmonic tones. Seventh chords, on the other hand, introduce *dissonance* as an integral part of the harmony. Seventh chords consist of four tones; thus they are more complex than triads. Whereas triads are limited to four types (major, minor, diminished, and augmented), there are seven types of seventh chords. Seventh chords are used not only for their tonal variety, but also for the tension supplied by their dissonance. Urgency of resolution is a feature of seventh chords, and this feature contributes to the sense of harmonic motivation so much a part of more advanced harmonic idioms.

6.1 A SEVENTH CHORD consists of four tones and is written by adding a note the interval of a third above the fifth of a triad.

TRIAD SEVENTH CHORD

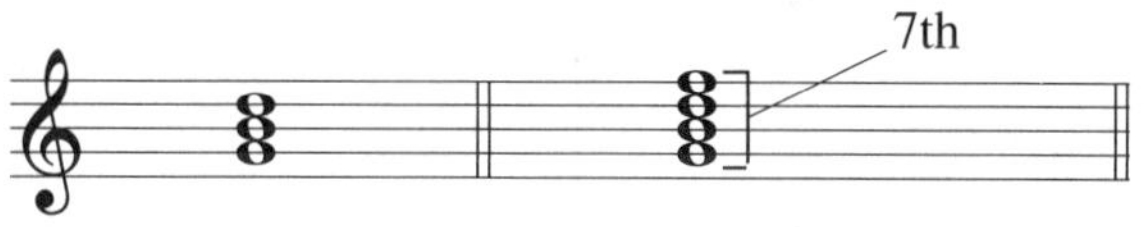

Seventh chords may be regarded as extended triads. Like triads, they consist of superimposed ____________.

thirds

6.2 A chord consisting of a triad plus a fourth note that is the interval of a third above the fifth is called a ____________.

seventh chord

6.3 Write seventh chords by adding a fourth note, an interval of a third above the fifth of each triad.

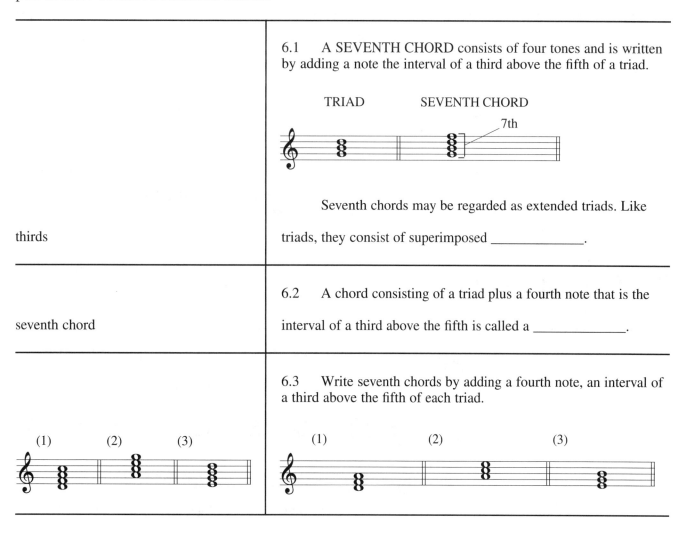

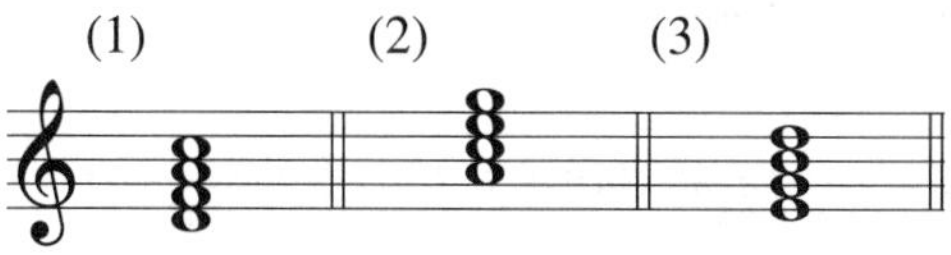

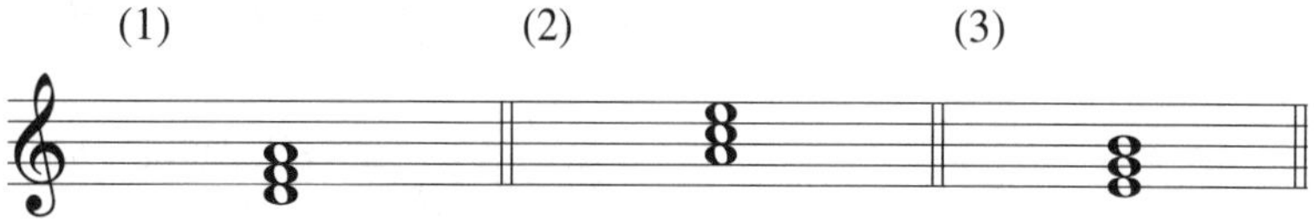

---

(1) (2) (3)

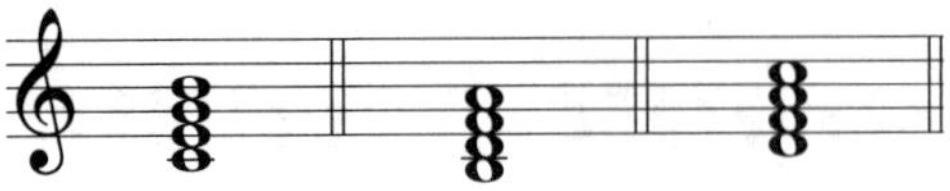

6.4 Write seventh chords as directed. *(Use no accidentals.)* The given note is the *root.*

(1) (2) (3)

(1) (2) (3)

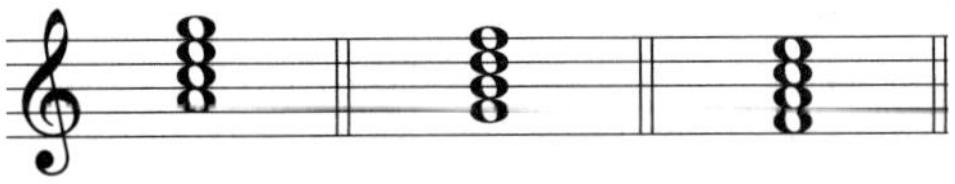

6.5 Write seventh chords as directed. *(Use no accidentals.)* The given note is the *third.*

(1) (2) (3)

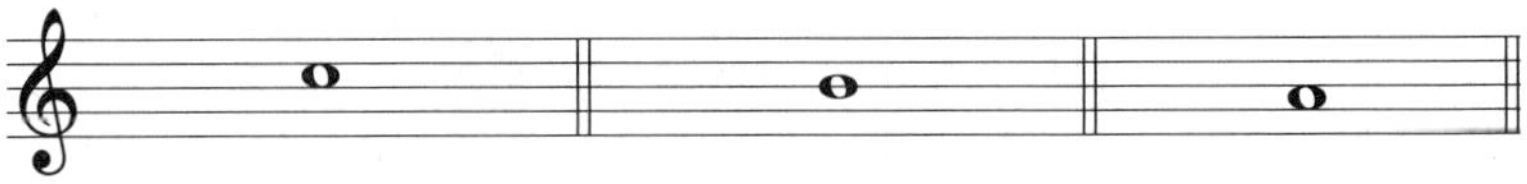

(1) (2) (3)

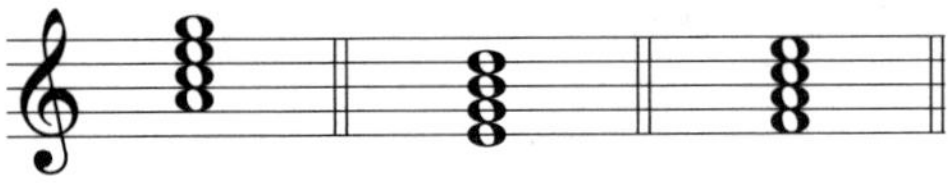

6.6 Write seventh chords as directed. *(Use no accidentals.)* The given note is the *fifth.*

(1) (2) (3)

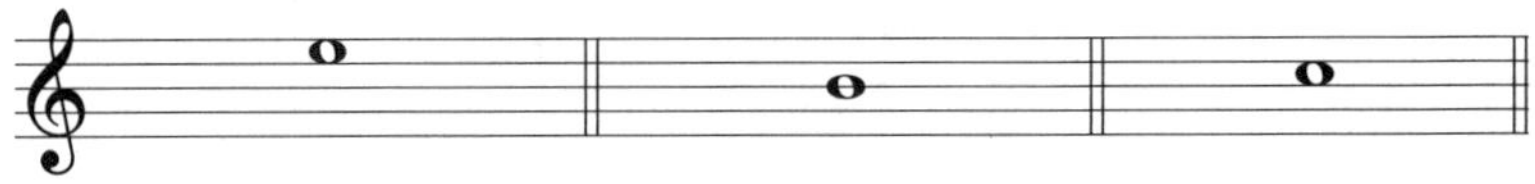

(1) (2) (3)

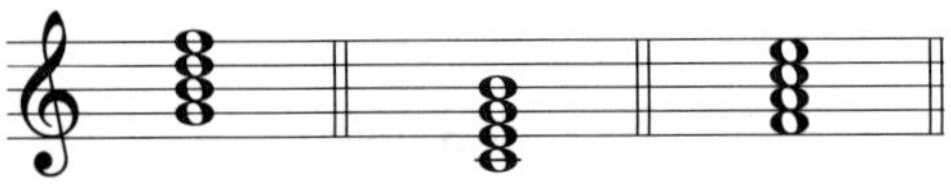

6.7 Write seventh chords as directed. *(Use no accidentals.)* The given note is the *seventh.*

(1) (2) (3)

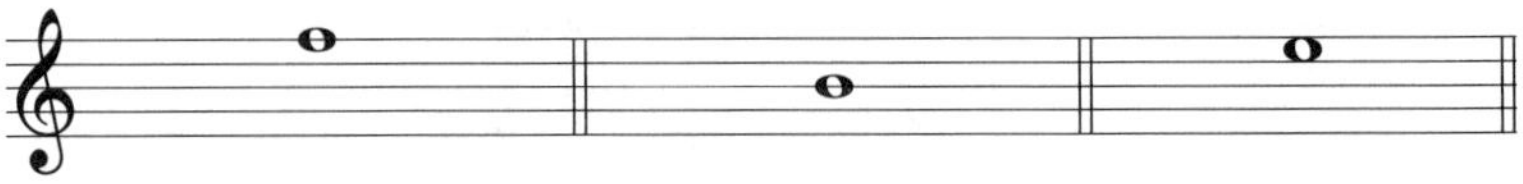

6.8 Seventh chords may be built on any degree of the scale.

KEY OF C MAJOR

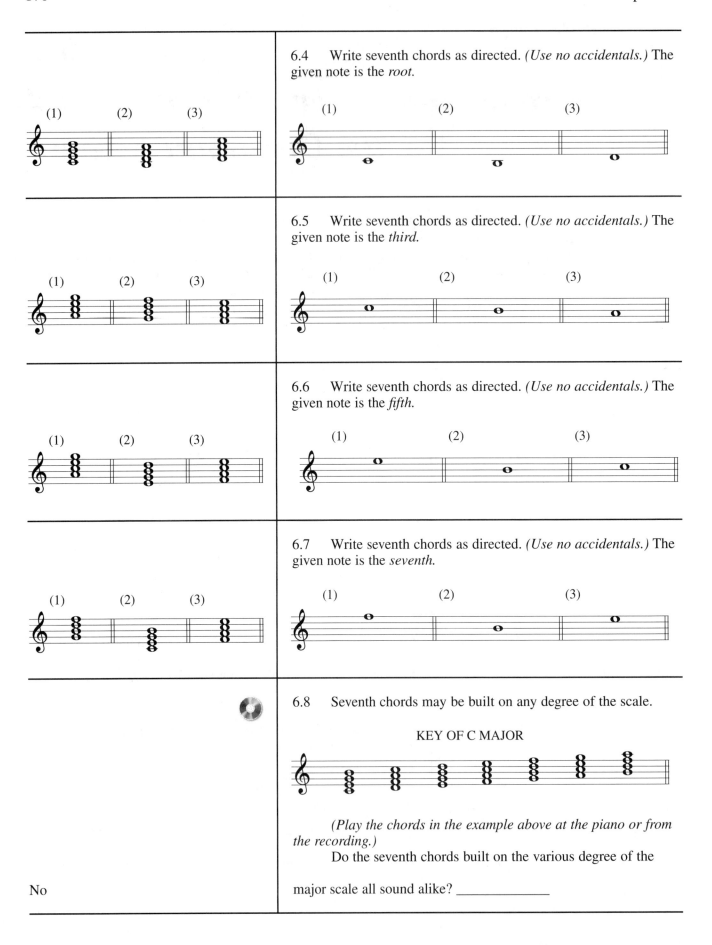

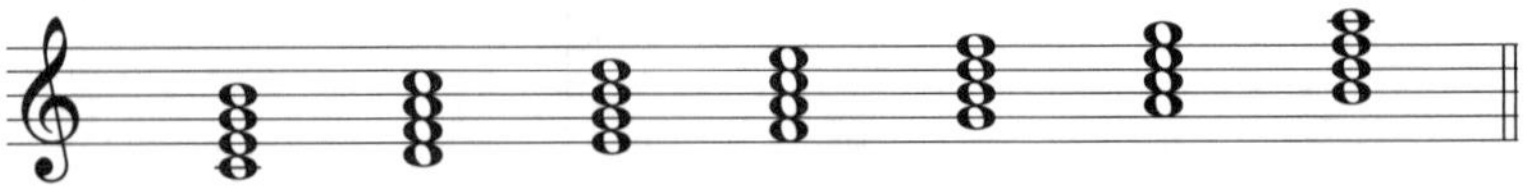

(Play the chords in the example above at the piano or from the recording.)

Do the seventh chords built on the various degree of the major scale all sound alike? _____________

No

6.9 The quality of a seventh chord is identified through two of its features: the type of triad, and the quality of the interval between the root and seventh.

Analyze the seventh chord below as directed.

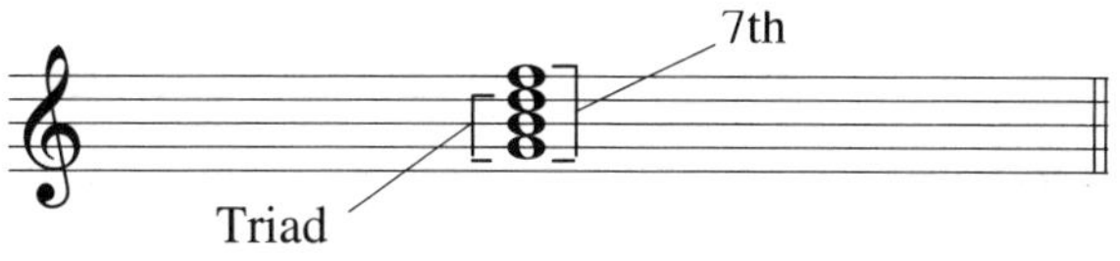

(1) Type of triad: ____________

(2) Quality of 7th: ____________

(1) Major

(2) Minor

6.10 The chord shown in the preceding frame is called a MAJOR-MINOR seventh chord. The first part of this term (major) refers to the type of triad; the second part (minor) refers to the quality of the interval between the root and the ____________.

seventh

6.11 Analyze the seventh chord below as directed.

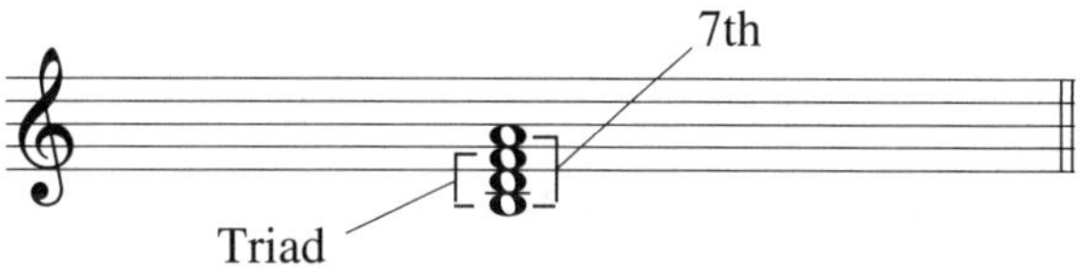

(1) Type of triad: ____________

(2) Quality of 7th: ____________

(1) Diminished

(2) Minor

6.12 The chord shown in the preceding frame is called a ____________-____________ seventh chord.

diminished-minor

6.13 Analyze the seventh chord below as directed.

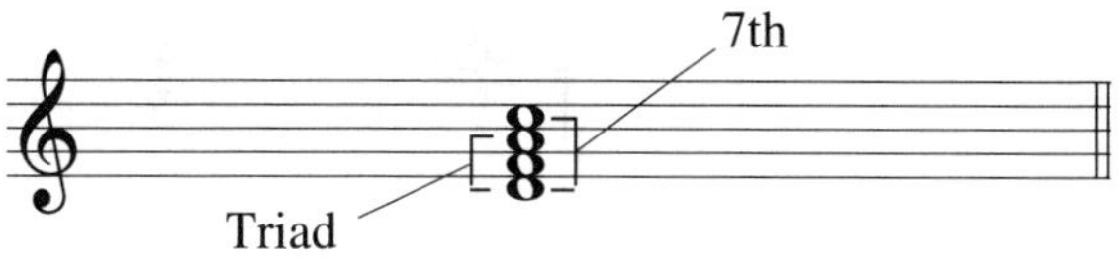

(1) Type of triad: ____________

(2) Quality of 7th: ____________

(1) Minor

(2) Minor

6.14 The chord shown in the preceding frame may be called a MINOR-MINOR seventh chord. It is customary, however, to eliminate one part of the term when the quality of the interval between the root and the seventh is identical to the type of triad. Thus, the term *minor seventh chord* means the same as a

____________ seventh chord.

minor-minor

6.15 A seventh chord that consists of a diminished triad plus the interval of a diminished seventh above the root is called a

____________ seventh chord.

diminished

6.16 Indicate the name of each chord.

(1) (2) (3)

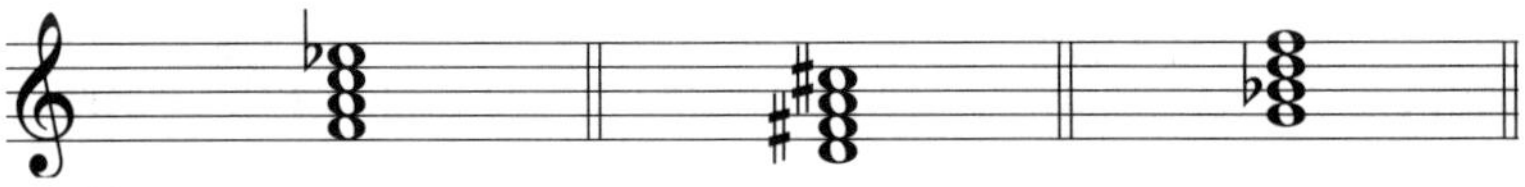

(1) ____________________ seventh chord

(2) ____________________ seventh chord

(3) ____________________ seventh chord

(1) Major-minor

(2) Major

(3) Minor

6.17 If the second chord in the preceding frame is called a major-major seventh chord, or the third chord a minor-minor seventh chord, it is not wrong, as this nomenclature is sometimes used. It is simpler, however, to avoid unnecessary repetition of terms.

The term *diminished seventh chord* indicates a chord consisting of a diminished triad plus the interval of a

____________ seventh above the root.

diminished

6.18 Indicate the name of each chord.

(1) (2) (3)

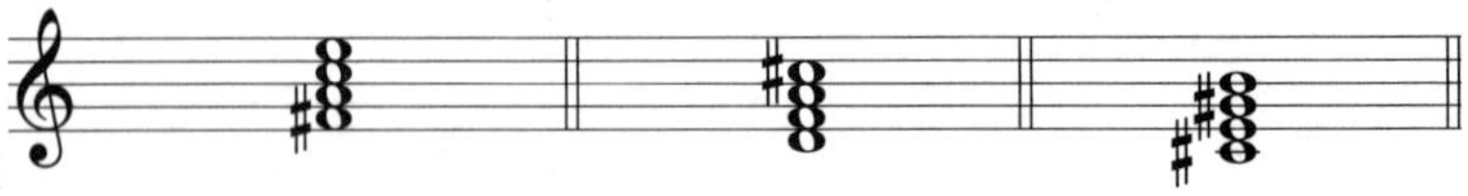

(1) ____________________ seventh chord

(2) ____________________ seventh chord

(3) ____________________ seventh chord

(1) Diminished-minor

(2) Minor-major

(3) Minor

6.19 Indicate the name of each chord.

(1) (2) (3)

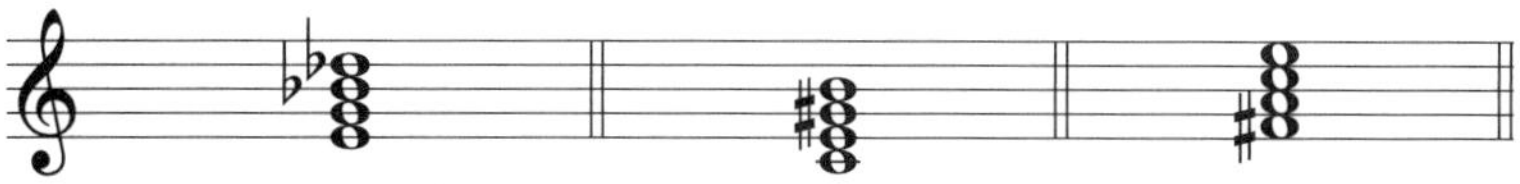

(1) ______________________ seventh chord

(2) ______________________ seventh chord

(3) ______________________ seventh chord

(1) Diminished

(2) Augmented-major

(3) Diminished-minor

6.20 In the major-minor scale system, which is the basis for most of the music of the eighteenth and nineteenth centuries, there are seven types of seventh chords. These are listed below:

(1) Major-minor
(2) Major
(3) Minor
(4) Minor-major
(5) Diminished-minor*
(6) Diminished*
(7) Augmented-major

Because these chords are derived from diatonic scale tones, they are sometimes called DIATONIC SEVENTH CHORDS.

Is the diminished-minor seventh chord *a diatonic* seventh chord? _____________

*Please see Fr. 6.35 for more discussion on these two "diminished" chords.

Yes

6.21 Indicate the quality of each seventh chord built on the various degrees of the *major* scale.

KEY OF D MAJOR

① ② ③ ④ ⑤ ⑥ ⑦

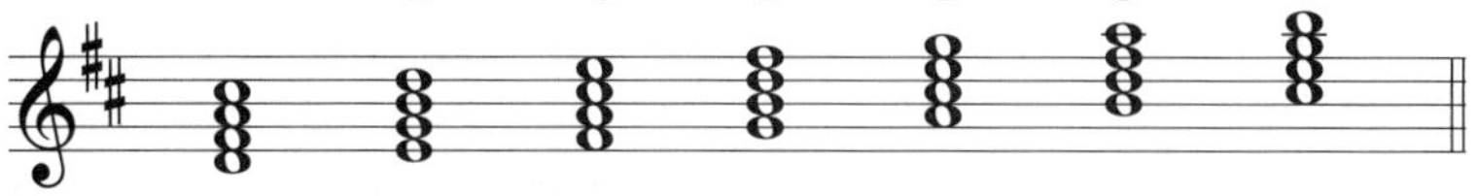

(1) ______________________ seventh chord

(2) ______________________ seventh chord

(3) ______________________ seventh chord

(4) ______________________ seventh chord

(5) ______________________ seventh chord

(6) ______________________ seventh chord

(7) ______________________ seventh chord

(1) Major

(2) Minor

(3) Minor

(4) Major

(5) Major-minor

(6) Minor

(7) Diminished-minor

6.22 Indicate the quality of each seventh chord built on the various degrees of the *harmonic minor* scale.

KEY OF D HARMONIC MINOR

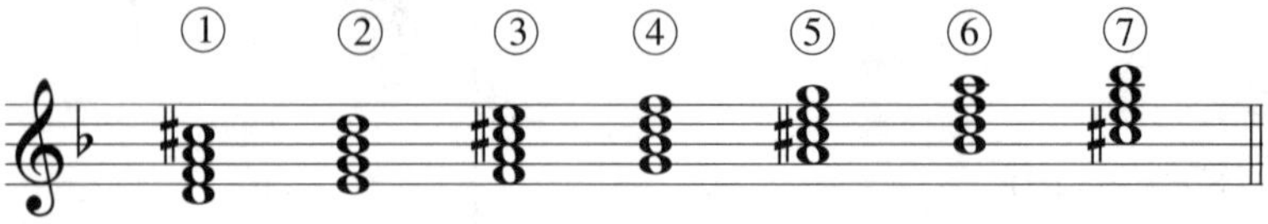

(1) ____________________ seventh chord

(2) ____________________ seventh chord

(3) ____________________ seventh chord*

(4) ____________________ seventh chord

(5) ____________________ seventh chord

(6) ____________________ seventh chord

(7) ____________________ seventh chord

*While an augmented triad (and accompanying seventh) can be formed in the context of the harmonic minor scale, its use in musical literature is quite rare but certainly not unknown.

(1) Minor-major
(2) Diminished-minor
(3) Augmented-major
(4) Minor
(5) Major-minor
(6) Major
(7) Diminished

6.23 Before proceeding, learn the quality of the seventh chord on the various degrees of major and minor scales. It is important to know, for example, that the major-minor seventh chord occurs as a diatonic seventh chord only on the fifth scale degree in either major or (harmonic) minor. Also, play the chords in the preceding two frames at the piano or from the recording to become familiar with their sounds.

The minor-major seventh chord occurs as a diatonic chord only in harmonic minor on the ____________ scale degree.

first

6.24 In the *major* scale, the minor seventh chord appears on the _______, _______, and _______ degrees.

2nd, 3rd, (and) 6th
(Any order.)

6.25 The diminished-minor seventh chord appears on the _______ degree of the *major* scale, and on the _______ degree of the *harmonic minor* scale.

7th, 2nd

6.26 Does the diminished seventh chord occur as a diatonic chord in the *major* scale? _______

No

6.27 Except for the diminished seventh chord (discussed later), the roman numeral used to indicate a seventh chord is the same as for a triad on the same root plus the number seven (7) placed at the upper right-hand corner.

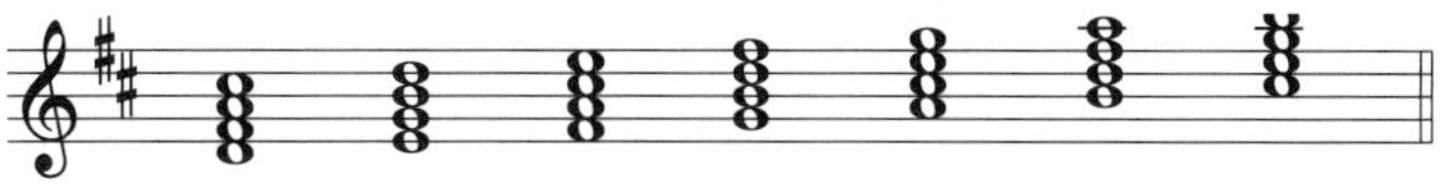

D:	I^7	ii^7	iii^7	IV^7	V^7	vi^7	$vii^{ø7}$
Alternative*:	Dmaj7	Emi7	F♯mi7	Gmaj7	A7	Bmi7	C♯mi7♭5

Notice that the quality of the triad is shown by the form of the roman numeral. The quality of the seventh, however, is not identified. *It is assumed that the seventh is a tone of the diatonic scale unless an alteration is shown.*

Spell the chord indicated by the roman numeral.

A♭: ii^7 ____________

*An alternative analysis is offered here and in Fr. 6.30, but note that there are differing systems in the handling of seventh chords in pop, commercial, and jazz music. See p. 355 for more information on the variety of symbols utilized.

B♭ D♭ F A♭

6.28 Spell the chords indicated by the roman numerals:

(1) D: V^7 ____________

(2) B♭: vi^7 ____________

(3) E: $vii^{ø7}$ ____________

(1) A C♯ E G

(2) G B♭ D F

(3) D♯ F♯ A C♯

6.29 Write the appropriate chord symbol for each chord. *(Indicate quality carefully.)*

(1) (2) (3)

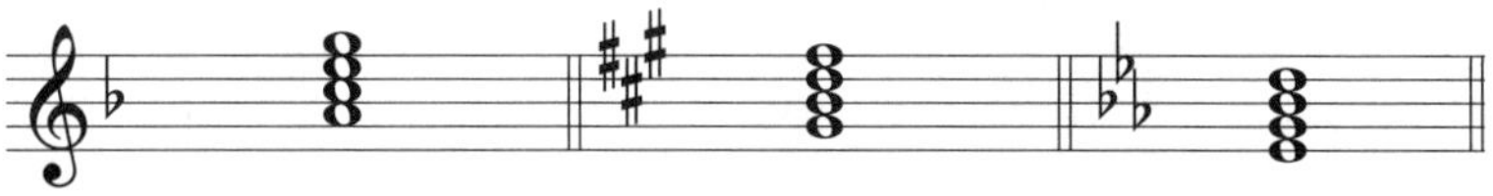

F: ___ A: ___ E♭: ___

(1) iii^7

(2) $vii^{ø7}$*

(3) I^7

*Note: See p. 354 for further explanation of this symbol: ø

6.30 The example below shows the chord symbols used to indicate the diatonic seventh chords in d harmonic minor.

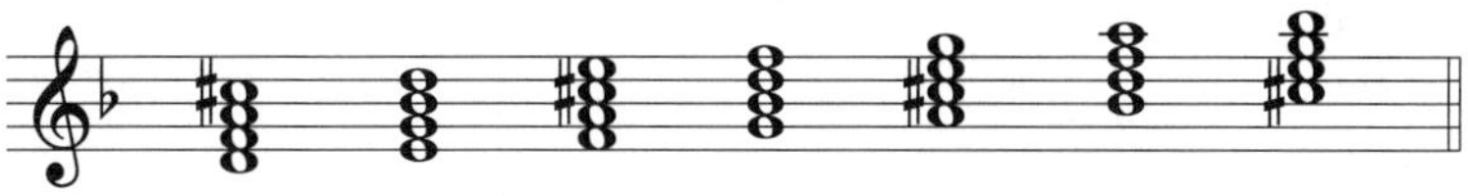

d:	$i^{\not 7}$	$ii^{ø7}$	III^{+7}	iv^7	V^7	VI^7	$vii^{\circ 7}$
Alternative:	Dmi♯7	Emi7♭5	Faug7	Gmi7	A7	B♭maj7	C♯dim7

Three of the chord symbols above need to be explained. These are $i^{\not 7}$, $ii^{ø7}$, and $vii^{\circ 7}$. In the first case the figure $\not 7$ indicates that the seventh of the chord is raised a half step. The slash drawn through the seven distinguishes between this chord (D F A C♯) and the tonic seventh chord in *natural* minor that would consist of the following notes: ______ ______ ______ ______.

D F A C♮

6.31 The quality of the triad is shown by the form of the roman numeral, thus the symbol V^7 is sufficient to indicate the dominant seventh chord in the preceding frame*. But when the seventh is an altered tone it is necessary to show the alteration by the actual accidental used (or by a slash if the note is raised a half step).

(1) (2) (3)

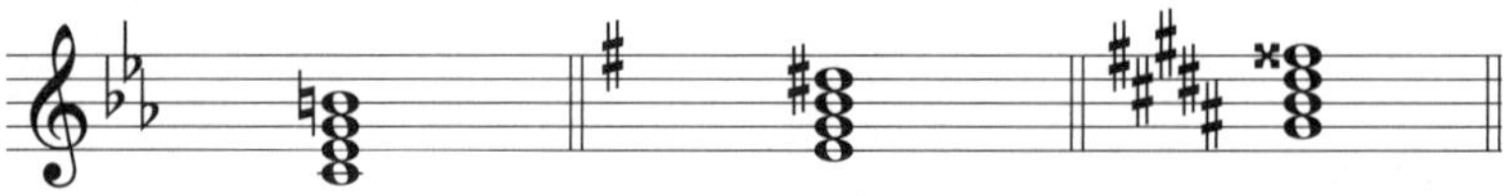

c:	$i^{\natural 7}$	e:	$i^{\sharp 7}$	g♯:	$i^{\times 7}$
	or		or		or
	$i^{\not 7}$		$i^{\not 7}$		$i^{\not 7}$

The chord symbol varies slightly according to the accidental (unless the slash is used).

What is the quality of each chord above?_____________-

_____________ seventh chord.

* The addition of a seventh to the dominant triad *does not* change its function.

Minor-major

6.32 Write the appropriate chord symbol for each chord.

(1) (2) (3)

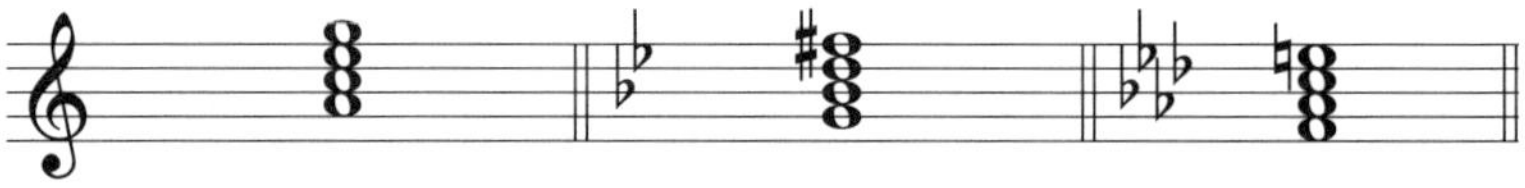

a: ___ g: ___ f: ___

(1) i^7

(2) $i^{\not 7}$ or $i^{\sharp 7}$

(3) $i^{\not 7}$ or $i^{\natural 7}$

6.33 Chord (1) in the preceding frame is a minor seventh chord. The fact that no accidental is used in the chord symbol shows that the _____________ minor scale is used.

natural
(or pure)

6.34 Notes of the natural minor scale are considered "diatonic" and require no special figure in the chord symbol. Alterations (usually the raised sixth or seventh degrees) are shown either by the form of the roman numeral or by a sign indicating the alteration of the seventh.

A note raised in pitch a half step always calls for a sharp in the chord symbol. (True/False) _____________

False.
(If you answered incorrectly review Frames 6.30–.33).

6.35 The second and third chord symbols in Frame 6.30 that need explanation are those used to indicate the supertonic (ii$^{\varnothing 7}$) and leading tone (vii$^{\varnothing 7}$ or vii$^{\circ 7}$) seventh chords. Diminished seventh chords appear frequently and perform a variety of harmonic functions. In this book, for the *diminished-minor* seventh chord (e.g., ii$^{\varnothing 7}$, vii$^{\varnothing 7}$), a circle with a slash denotes a diminished triad with a minor seventh, a so-called *"half-diminished"* seventh chord; for the *fully diminished*, or so-called *"diminished"* seventh chord (vii$^{\circ 7}$), a circle denotes both the quality of the triad and of the seventh.

Spell the chord indicated by the symbol.

g: vii$^{\circ 7}$ ____________

F♯ A C E♭

6.36 Spell the chords indicated by the symbols.

(1) c: vii$^{\circ 7}$ _______

(2) f♯: vii$^{\circ 7}$ _______

(3) b♭: vii$^{\circ 7}$ _______

(1) B(♮) D F A♭

(2) E♯ G♯ B D

(3) A(♮) C E♭ G♭

6.37 Note the difference between the two chords below.

(1) (2)

G: vii$^{\varnothing 7}$ g: vii$^{\circ 7}$

Identify the quality of each chord.

(1) ____________ seventh chord

(2) ____________ seventh chord

(1) Diminished-minor (or half-diminished)

(2) Diminished

6.38 The example in the preceding frame shows that the circle with slash is used in the case of a diminished-minor seventh chord.

The small circle is used only for ____________ seventh chords.

(fully) diminished

6.39 Write the proper symbol for each chord. *(Be sure to check the quality before writing.)*

(1) (2) (3)

d: ___ b: ___ B♭: ___

(1) ii$^{\varnothing 7}$

(2) vii$^{\circ 7}$

(3) vii$^{\varnothing 7}$

(1) $vii^{ø7}$

(2) $ii^{ø7}$

(3) $vii^{°7}$

6.40 Continue as in the preceding frame.

(1) (2) (3)

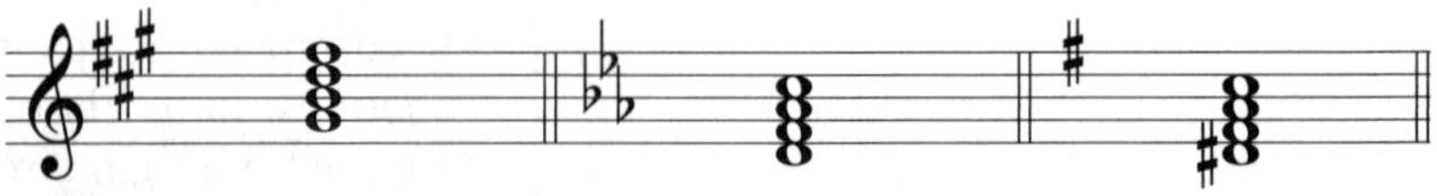

A: ___ c: ___ e: ___

---

(1) B♯ D♯ F♯ A

(2) G B♭ D♭ F

(3) F A C E

6.41 Spell the chords indicated by the symbols. *(Use the notes of the harmonic minor scale.)*

(1) c♯: $vii^{°7}$ ____________

(2) f: $ii^{ø7}$ ____________

(3) a: VI^7 ____________

---

(1) E G♯ B D♯

(2) F♯ A C♯ E♯

(3) D F A♭ C

(4) F A♭ C E♭

(5) G♯ B D F♯

(6) B♭ D(♮) F A♭

6.42 Spell the chords indicated by the symbols. *(Note that some keys are major and some are minor. In the case of minor keys, use the notes of the harmonic minor scale.)*

(1) B: IV^7 ____________

(2) f♯: i^7 ____________

(3) c: $ii^{ø7}$ ____________

(4) D♭: iii^7 ____________

(5) A: $vii^{ø7}$ ____________

(6) e♭: V^7 ____________

---

(1) IV^7

(2) $ii^{ø7}$

(3) $vii^{ø7}$

6.43 Supply the appropriate symbol for each chord.

(1) (2) (3)

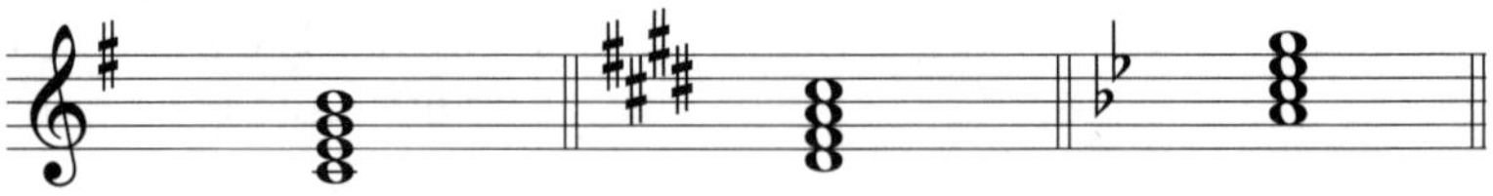

G: ___ c♯: ___ B♭: ___

---

(1) iii^7

(2) V^7

(3) VI^7

6.44 Continue as in the preceding frame.

(1) (2) (3)

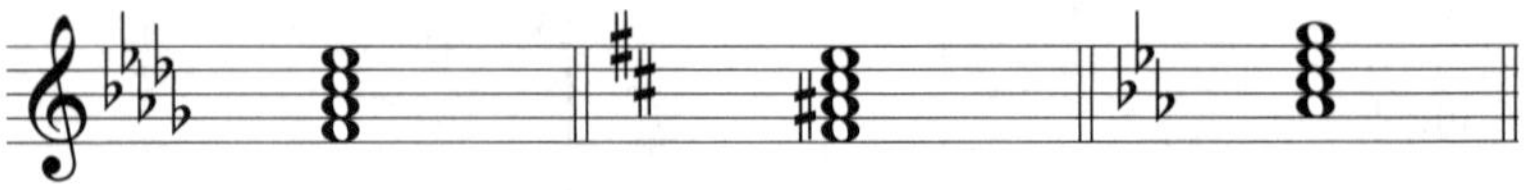

D♭: ___ b: ___ c: ___

(1) III^{+7}

(2) ii^7

(3) i7̸ or i♮7

6.45 Continue as in the preceding frame.

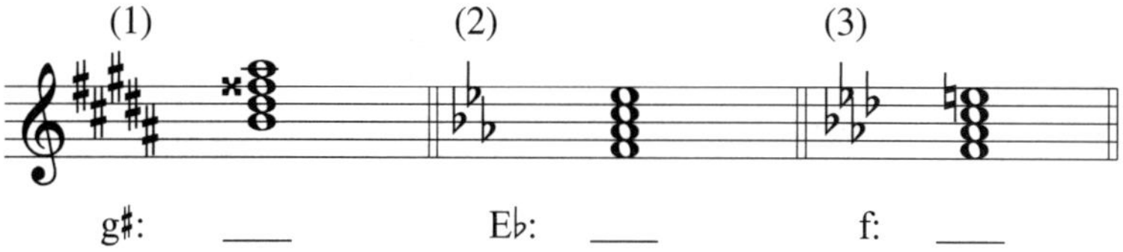

---

(1) $\text{vii}^{ø7}$

(2) $\text{vii}^{\circ 7}$

(3) III^{+7}

6.46 Continue as in the preceding frame.

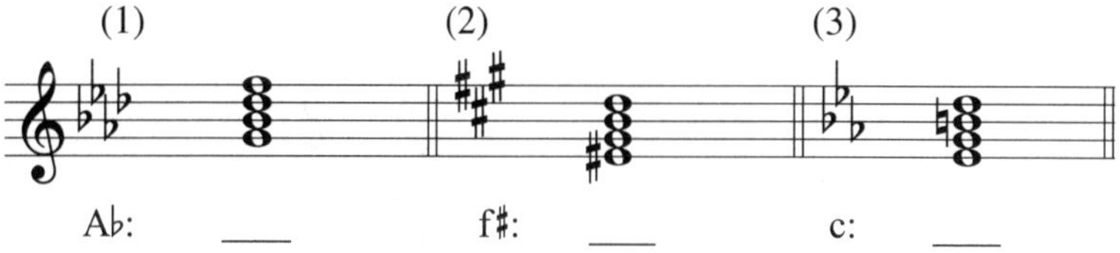

(b) melodic minor

6.47 The alternate sixth and seventh degrees of the melodic minor scale (ascending and descending forms) produce a large number of seventh chords.

KEY OF C MINOR (melodic minor scale)

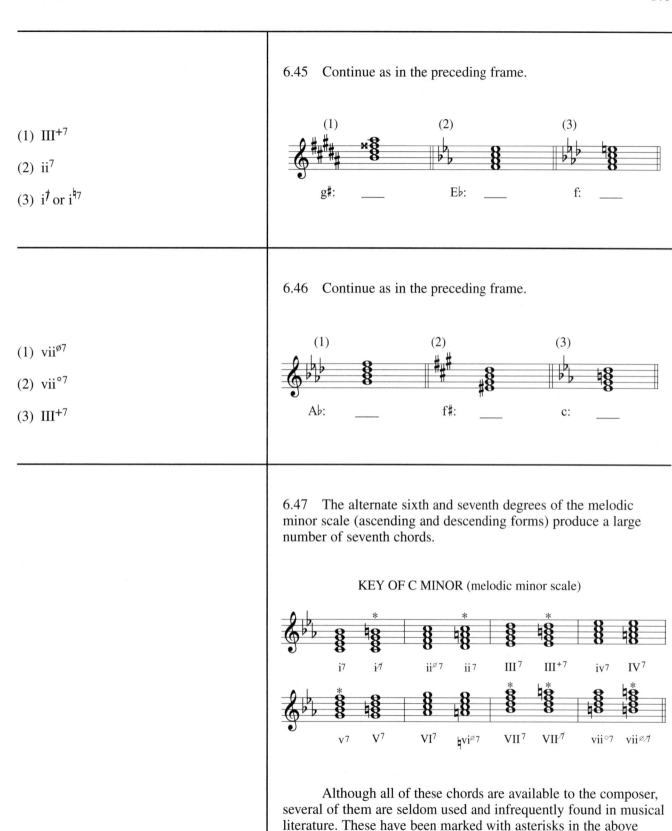

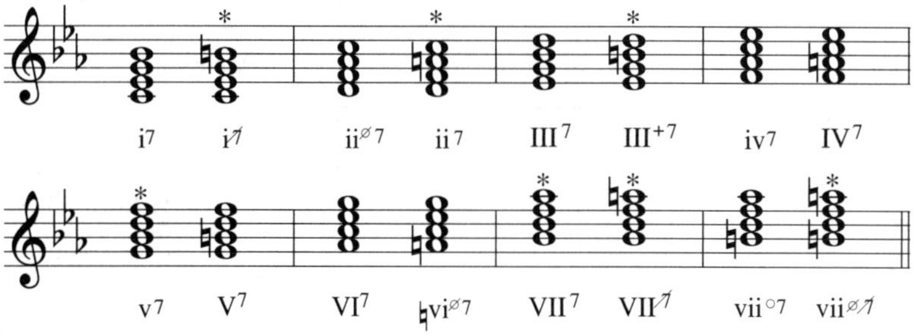

Although all of these chords are available to the composer, several of them are seldom used and infrequently found in musical literature. These have been marked with asterisks in the above example.

Which scale has the most tonal variety (a) harmonic minor, (b) melodic minor, or (c) major? ______________

Expository Frame

6.48 Seventh chord qualities and their corresponding chord symbols in major and minor keys are *partially* summarized below:

Quality	Major	Minor
Mm^7	V^7	V^7
M^7	I^7, IV^7	VI^7
m^7	ii^7, iii^7, vi^7	iv^7
mM^7	—	i^7
dm^7	$vii^{ø7}$	$ii^{ø7}$
d^7	—	$vii^{\circ 7}$
AM^7	—	III^{+7}

(No response required.)

6.49 Seventh chords, like triads, are used in various inversions. The figured bass symbols used to indicate seventh chords in root position are shown below.

(a) Major Key (b) Minor Key

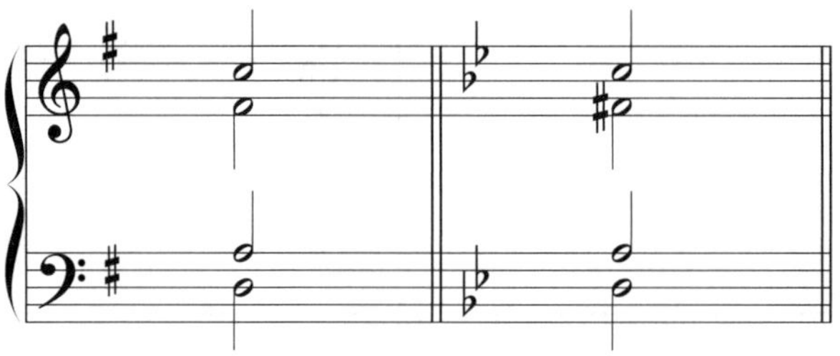

7 7 ♯

G: V^7 g: V^7

The figured bass symbol for a seventh chord in root position is simply the number seven (7) unless either the third or fifth of the chord is altered, in which case the alteration is shown by the appropriate symbol. The figured bass symbol 7 indicates a seventh chord in _____________ position.

root

6.50 The figured bass symbol used to indicate seventh chords in *first inversion* is shown below.

(a) Major Key (b) Minor Key

$\begin{smallmatrix}6\\5\end{smallmatrix}$ $\begin{smallmatrix}6\\5\end{smallmatrix}$

G: V^6_5 g: V^6_5

Notice that the numbers 6 and 5 are incorporated into the chord symbol. Thus the chord symbol itself shows the inversion of the chord.

The figured bass symbol $^6_5$ beneath a bass note indicates a seventh chord in first inversion. Therefore, the note in the bass is the (root/3rd/5th/7th) ____________ of the chord.

3rd

6.51 The chords below are in *second inversion.*

(a) Major Key (b) Minor Key

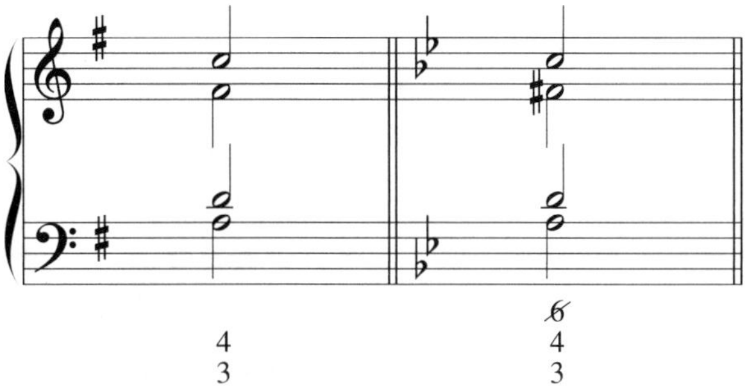

G: V^4_3 g: V^4_3

The symbol $^4_3$ suffices to indicate a seventh chord in second inversion unless the sixth above the bass is altered as in (b) above.* The root of the seventh chord in second inversion is located in this example a (interval) ____________ above the bass note.

4th

*Note both here and in the following third inversion discussion, that figures are used *that are essential to indicate the inversion* ***except if*** *an alteration needs to be shown.*

6.52 The chords below are in *third inversion.*

(a) Major Key (b) Minor Key

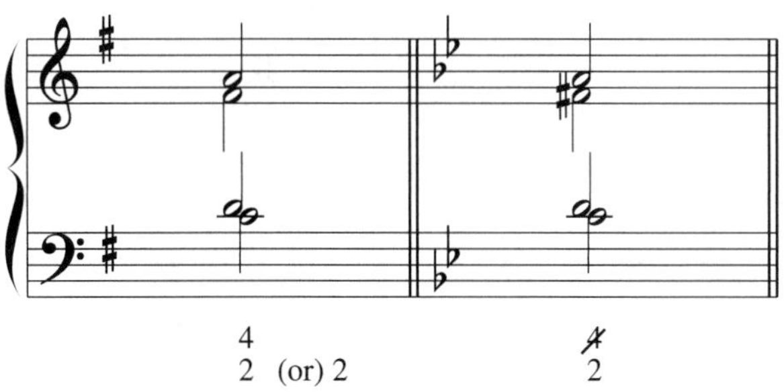

G: V^4_2 g: V^4_2

Usually the symbol $^4_2$ is used to indicate a seventh chord in third inversion, but sometimes this is reduced to merely 2. The figured bass symbol cannot be abbreviated in (b) because the figure ♯4 is needed to show the alteration of F to F♯. When the symbol $^4_2$ (or 2) appears beneath a bass note, that note is the (root/3rd/5th/7th) ____________ of the chord.

7th

6.53 The previous few frames have shown that figured bass symbols are combined with roman numerals to show the various inversions of seventh chords.

Root position:	I^7,	ii^7, etc.
First inversion:	I^6_5,	ii^6_5, etc.
Second inversion:	I^4_3,	ii^4_3, etc.
Third inversion:	I^4_2,	ii^4_2, etc.

These symbols are used consistently throughout this study except when it is of no importance to identify specific inversions.

The figure $^4_3$ signifies that the (root/3rd/5th/7th) _______ of a chord is in the bass.

5th

6.54 Check (✓) the correct option:

1. Chord symbols show not only the scale degree on which chords are built, but also the inversions.
2. The symbol V^6_5 indicates that the third of the dominant seventh chord is in the bass.

True Statements:

(1) _______ (2) _______ Both _______ Neither _______

Both ✓

6.55 Supply the chord symbol for each chord.

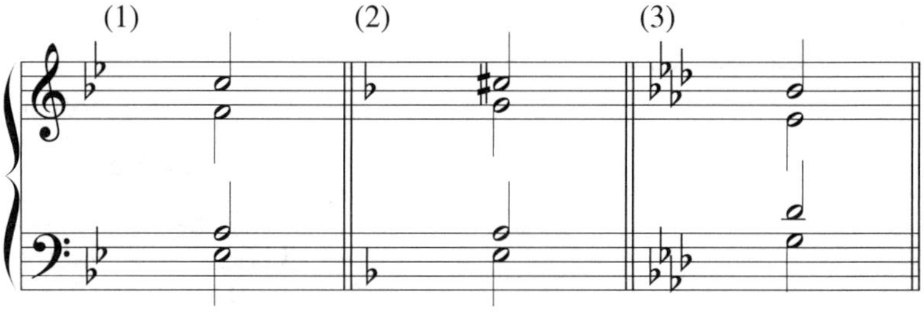

B♭: ___ d: ___ A♭: ___

(1) V^4_2

(2) V^4_3

(3) V^6_5

6.56 Continue as in the preceding frame.

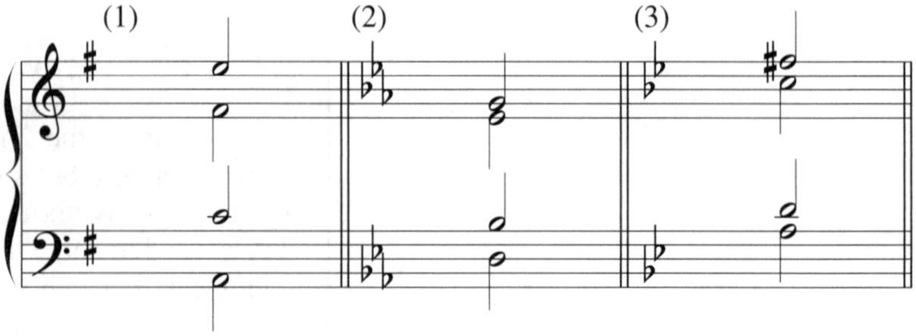

e: ___ E♭: ___ g : ___

(1) $ii^{ø6}_5$

(2) I^4_2

(3) V^4_3

(1) G

(2) F

(3) A

6.57 Indicate the bass note for each chord.

Bass Note

(1) A♭: V^{6}_{5} _______

(2) c: V^{4}_{2} _______

(3) E: $\mathrm{vii}^{\varnothing 4}_{3}$ _______

---

(1) D♭

(2) C♯

(3) F♯

6.58 Slightly more complicated symbols are required to show the inversions of diminished seventh chords.

ROOT POSITION FIRST INVERSION

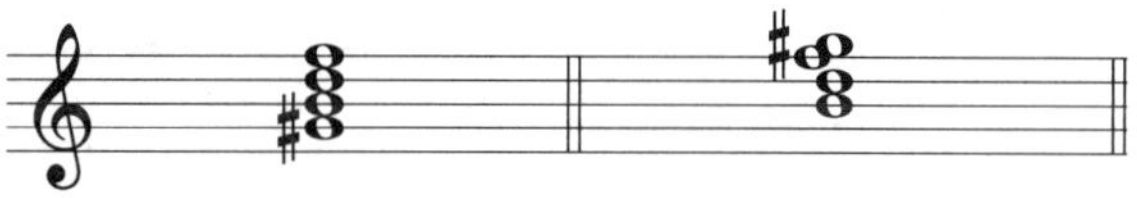

a: $\mathrm{vii}^{\circ 7}$ $\mathrm{vii}^{\circ 6}_{5}$

SECOND INVERSION THIRD INVERSION

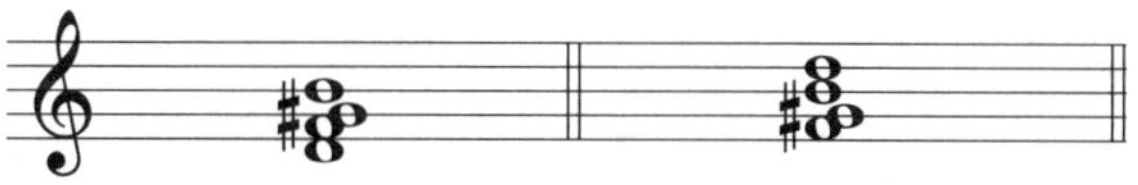

a: $\mathrm{vii}^{\circ 4}_{3}$ $\mathrm{vii}^{\circ 4}_{2}$

Indicate the bass note for each chord.

Bass Note

(1) f: $\mathrm{vii}^{\circ 4}_{2}$ _______

(2) b: $\mathrm{vii}^{\circ 6}_{5}$ _______

(3) c♯: $\mathrm{vii}^{\circ 4}_{3}$ _______

---

(1) $\mathrm{vii}^{\circ 6}_{5}$

(2) $\mathrm{vii}^{\circ 4}_{2}$

(3) $\mathrm{vii}^{\varnothing 4}_{2}$

6.59 Supply the chord symbol for each chord.

(1) (2) (3)

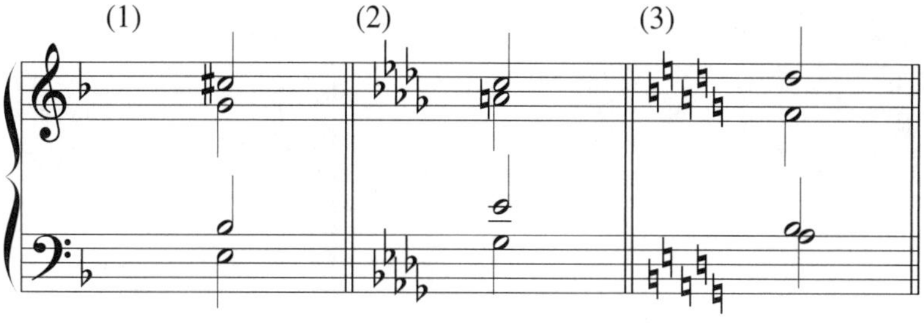

d: ___ b♭: ___ C: ___

(1) $\text{vii}^{ø6}_{5}$

(2) $\text{vii}^{\circ 6}_{5}$

6.60 Chord (3) in the preceding frame is a diminished-minor seventh chord, not a diminished seventh chord. The symbol for the former is $\text{vii}^{ø4}_{2}$; the latter is $\text{vii}^{\circ 4}_{2}$.

Write the appropriate chord symbol for each chord.

(1) (2)

G: ___ g: ___

(1) (2) (3) (4)

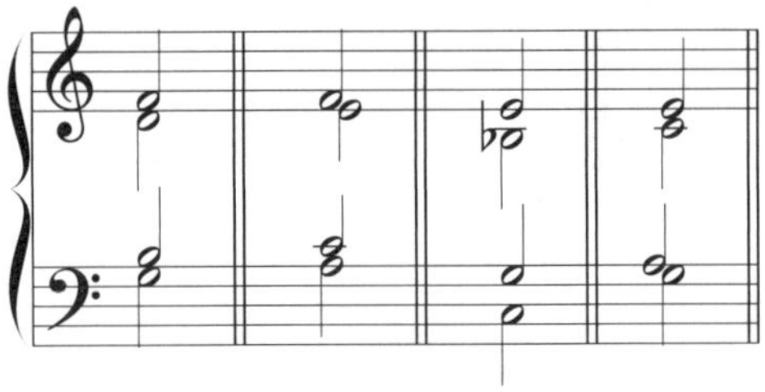

6.61 All four tones of a seventh chord are usually present in simple four-part writing. This means that no doubling is necessary; each of the four voices takes one of the chord tones. Observe this practice in the frames that follow.

Complete the chords as indicated by the figured bass. *(Use close structure.)*

(1) (2) (3) (4)

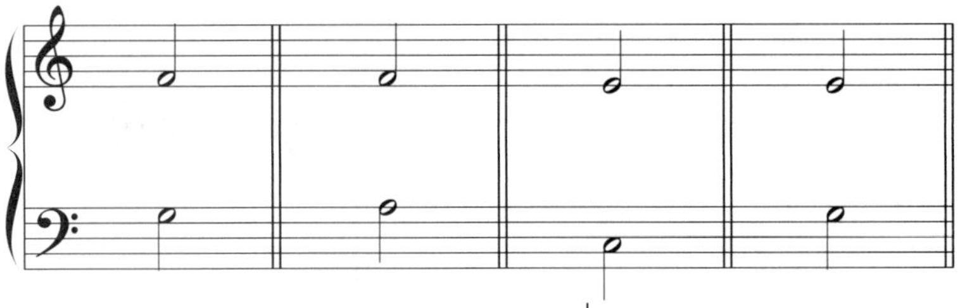

7 $^{6}_{5}$ ♭7 $^{4}_{2}$

(1) (2) (3) (4)

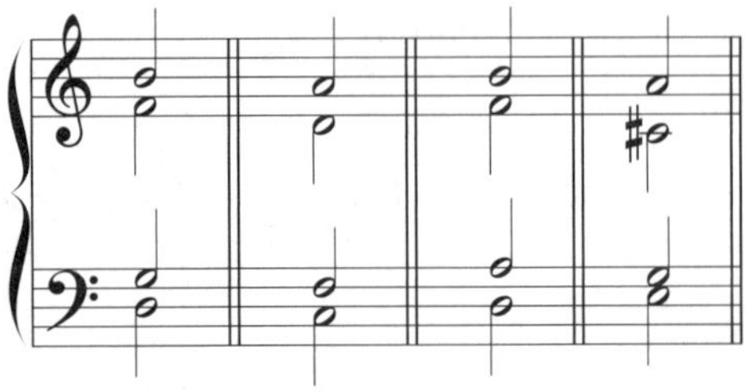

6.62 Complete the chords as indicated by the figured bass. *(Use open structure.)*

(1) (2) (3) (4)

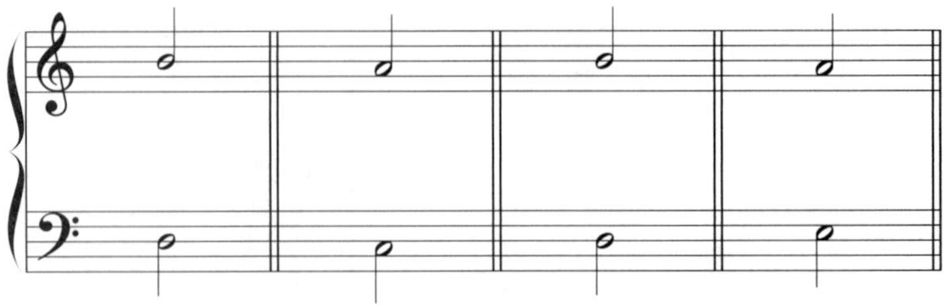

$^{4}_{3}$ 2 $^{6}_{5}$ 6̸ 4 3

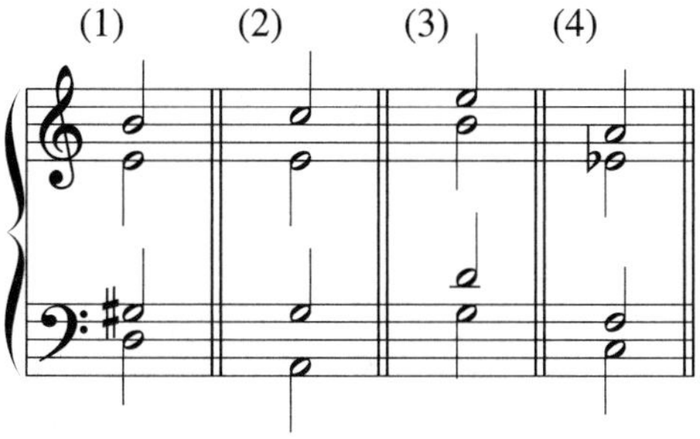

6.63 Complete the chords as indicated by the figured bass. *(Use open structure.)*

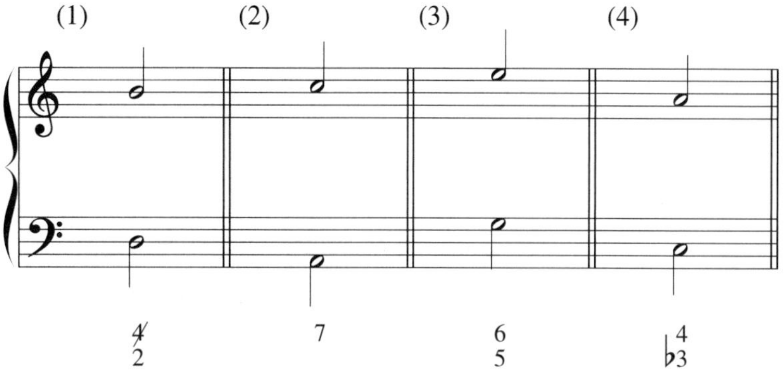

(1) $\substack{6\\ 5}$

(2) 7

(3) $\substack{4\\ 3}$

(4) $\substack{6\\ 5}$

6.64 Write the proper figured bass symbol beneath each chord.

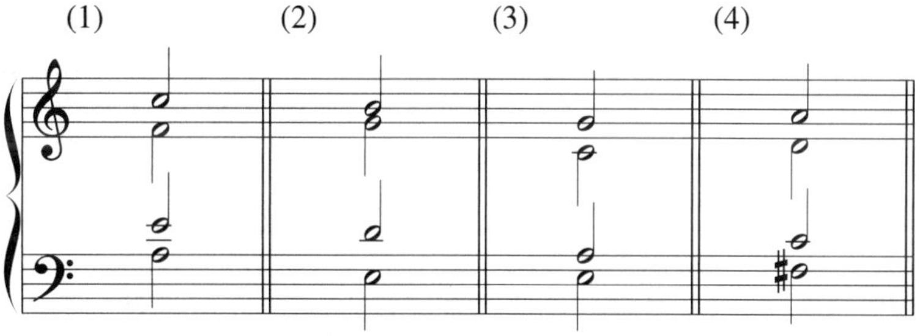

(1) $\substack{4\\ 2}$ or 2

(2) $\substack{7\\ \not 3}$ or $\substack{7\\ \sharp}$

(3) $\substack{\not 6\\ 4\\ 3}$

(4) $\substack{6\\ 5}$

6.65 Continue as in the preceding frame. *(Don't forget to indicate altered notes.)*

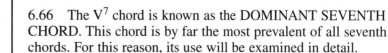

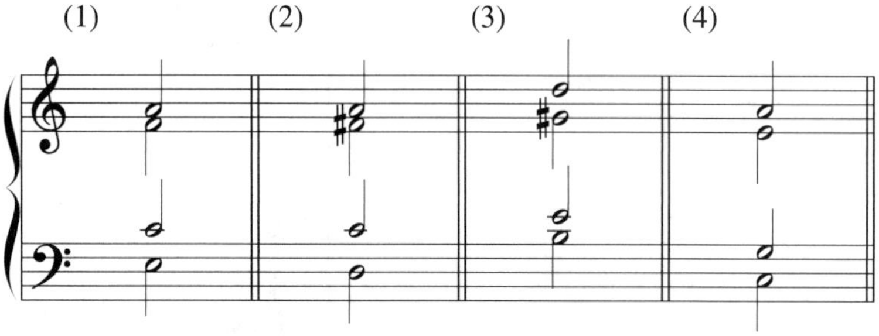

6.66 The V^7 chord is known as the DOMINANT SEVENTH CHORD. This chord is by far the most prevalent of all seventh chords. For this reason, its use will be examined in detail.

Like the dominant triad, the dominant seventh chord usually progresses to the tonic or submediant triads. *The addition of the seventh does not change its function.*

(Continued on the next page)

Supply the roman numeral analysis for the last four chords.

Brahms, *Ein deutsches Requiem,* Op. 45, I

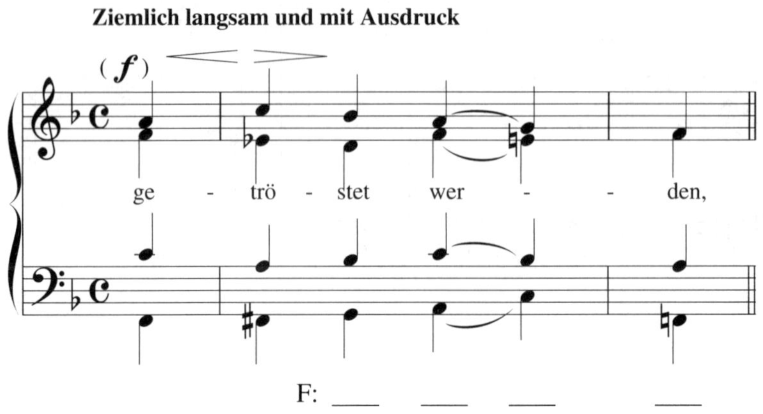

ii – I^6 – V^7 – I

6.67 The dominant seventh chord is a major-minor seventh chord. It consists of a major triad plus a minor seventh above the root. This type of chord has two dissonant elements: the seventh, and the tritone,* which occur between the third and seventh. It is the resolution of these dissonant elements that governs the part writing.

Refer again to the example in the preceding frame. Which two notes comprise the tritone in the dominant seventh chord?

_______ and _______.

*The term tritone means three (whole) tones. It is the same as the augmented fourth or diminished fifth.

B♭ (and) E

6.68 The tritone and its resolution (from the example in Frame 6.66) are shown below:

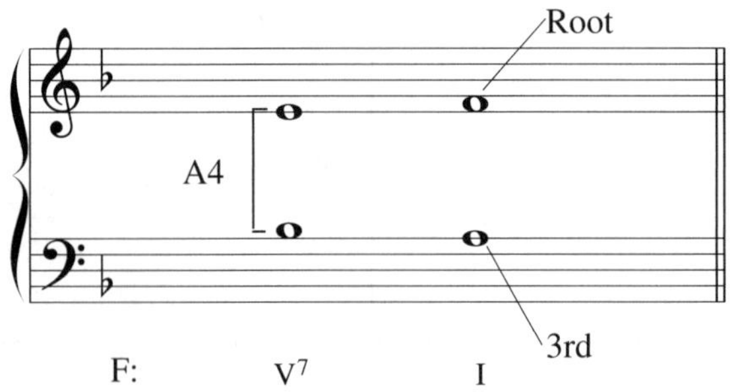

Notice that each of the notes of the tritone (B♭ and E) moves by a half step to the note of resolution. Could the voices find a place in the same chord (F Major) with equal smoothness by moving in the opposite direction? _______

No

6.69 The inversion of the example in Frame 6.68 produces the interval of a diminished fifth.

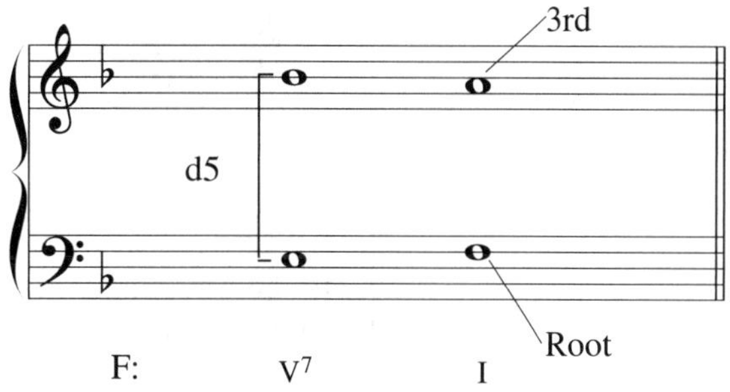

Whereas the tones that constitute the interval of an augmented fourth resolve *outward* to the root and third of the tonic triad, the tones

inward — of a diminished fifth resolve ____________.

6.70 The tendency for the tones of the augmented fourth to resolve outward and those of the diminished fifth to resolve inward is the result of the melodic attraction of active tones to inactive ones.

The inactive tones of the major scale are the tones of the tonic triad. The remaining tones are active, and are attracted to the inactive ones primarily in the direction of the arrows.

KEY OF F MAJOR

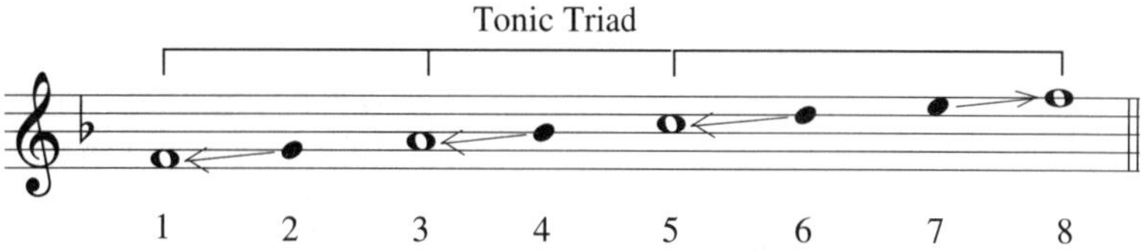

In each case active tones move to the *nearest* member of the tonic triad. The second scale degree is a whole step removed from both the first and third; but, since the attraction of the keynote or tonic (F) is stronger than the third (A), the downward tendency predominates.

Which two of the active scale degrees are only a half step removed from the notes to which they are attracted?

4 (and) 7 — _______ and _______.

6.71 Because of their close proximity to tones of tonic triad, the fourth and seventh are the most active degrees of the major scale. This melodic activity is intensified when they are combined to form a tritone. For this reason, the effective resolution of the dominant seventh chord depends upon resolving the fourth and seventh scale degrees in accordance with their natural tendency.

(Continued on the next page)

(1) (2)

Resolve each tritone to notes of the tonic triad in the smoothest possible manner.

(1) D Major (2) E♭ Major

There are three roots, one third, but no 5th.

6.72 The overriding importance of resolving the tritone according to the melodic activity of its constituent tones often leads to irregular doubling in the chord that follows.

Mozart, *Symphony No. 41,* K.551

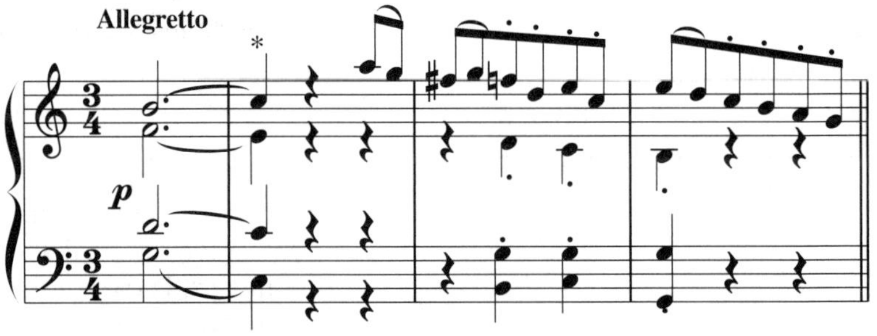

C: V^7 I V^6_5 I V

Describe the irregular doubling in the chord at the asterisk.

____

Yes
(The note D in the soprano is an embellishment.)

6.73 Another dominant seventh chord occurs in the third measure of the example in the preceding frame. In this case the tritone occurs between the soprano and bass voices. Does this tritone resolve normally? ______________

---

(1) (2)

6.74 Write the second chord in each case. *(Be sure to resolve the tritone normally even though irregularities of doubling may occur.)*

(1) (2)

G: V^7 I B♭: V^7 vi

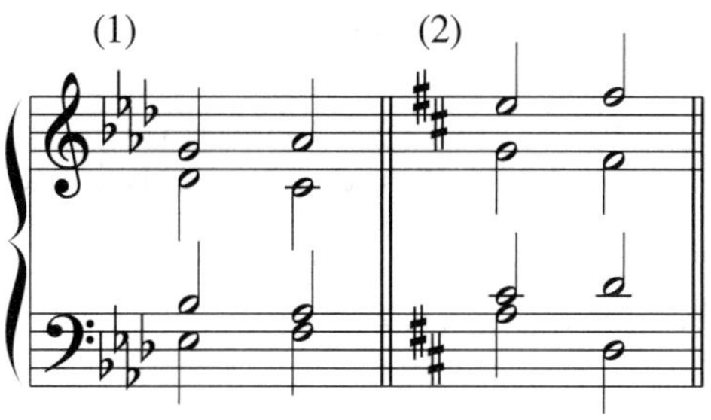

6.75 Continue as in the preceding frame.

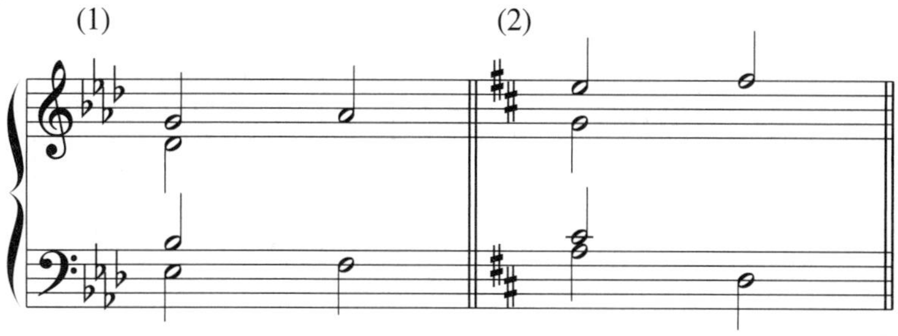

A♭: V7 vi D: V7 I

---

(1)

(But sonority sometimes takes precedence, as will be seen in Frames 6.93–.94)

6.76 Irregularities of doubling that often occur as a result of resolving the tritone normally can be summarized as follows:

The tonic triad may have:

(1) Three roots, one 3rd, but no 5th.

(2) Two roots, two 3rds, but no 5th.

The submediant triad may have:

(1) One root, two 3rds, and one 5th.

Which is more important, to (1) resolve active tones according to their tendency, or (2) produce good sonorities by using normal doubling and spacing? _____________

---

seventh

6.77 Although the fifth, or even the third, of a seventh chord may be omitted, both the root and the seventh must be present.

The other dissonant element, in addition to the tritone, contained in the dominant seventh chord is the _____________ of the chord.

---

(1) Yes

(2) No

6.78 Previous examples have shown that the tendency of the seventh of all seventh chords is to resolve *downward by step.* Very few exceptions to this principle occur.

Answer the following questions about the resolution of the dominant seventh chord in the example below:

(1) Does the seventh resolve downward by step? ______

(2) Does the tritone resolve normally? _______

Bach, Chorale: *Dank sei Gott in der Höhe*

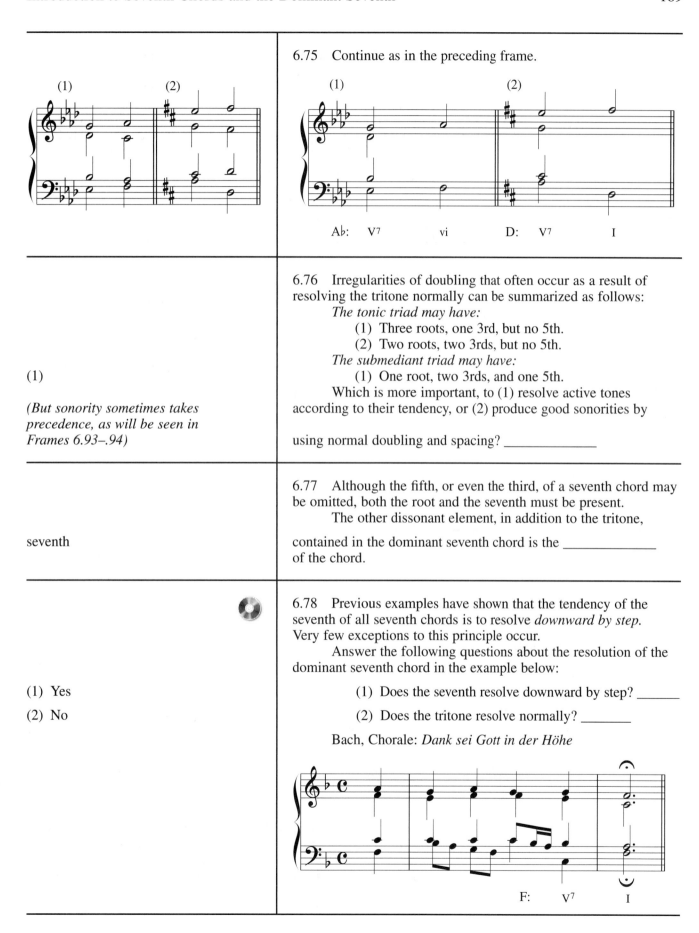

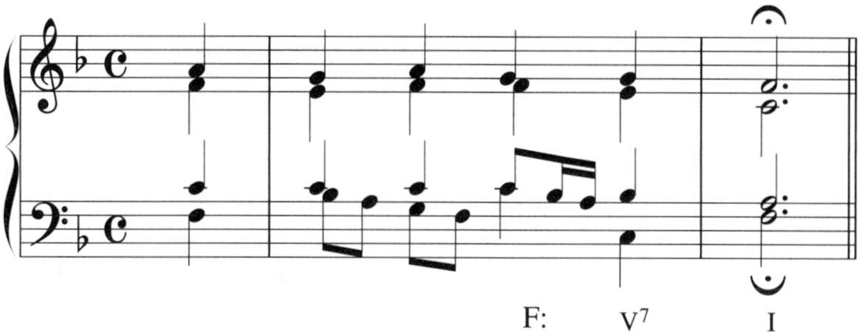

F: V7 I

6.79 The example in the preceding frame shows that, due to the desire to end with the stronger sonority provided by a complete triad, the tritone (B♭–E) is not resolved normally. Specifically, the leading tone (E in the alto voice) drops down to the fifth of the tonic triad instead of obeying its melodic tendency to ascend to the keynote or tonic (F). This occurs frequently in the inner voices, but rarely in the soprano, where the weak melodic effect is more evident.

Although the tritone in this case does not resolve normally, the seventh (B♭ in the tenor voice) moves according to its natural tendency which is _____________ by step.

downward

6.80 Complete the second chord in each case so that a *complete* triad with regular doubling (two roots, one third, and one fifth) results. *(Be sure to resolve the seventh downward by step.)*

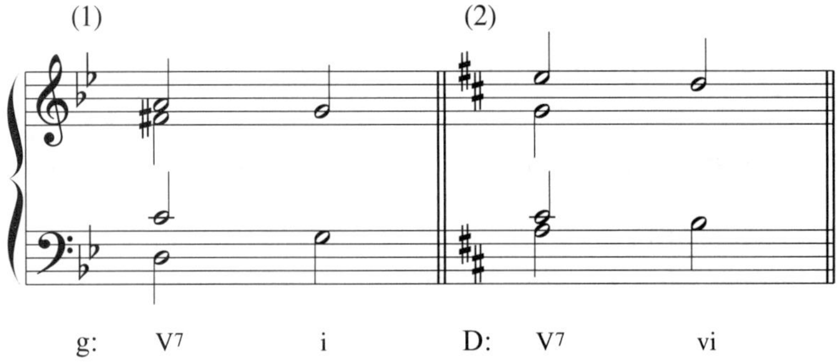

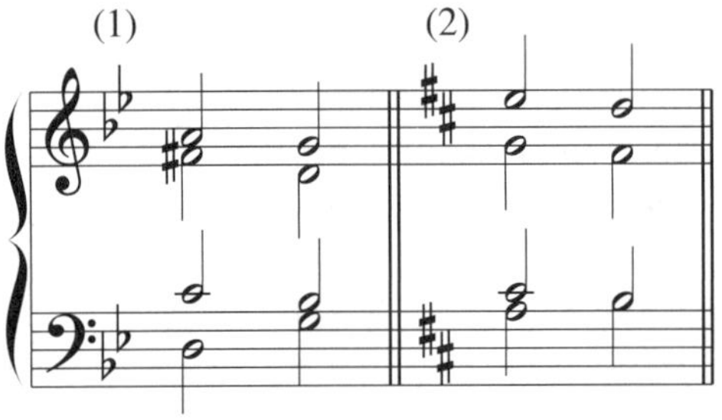

6.81 Continue as in the preceding frame. *(Use no irregular doubling.)*

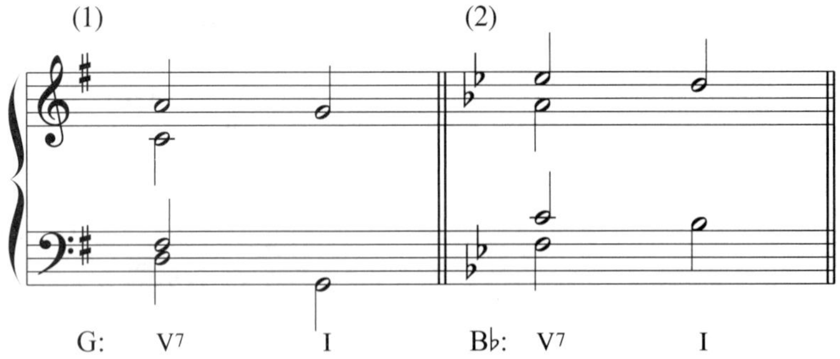

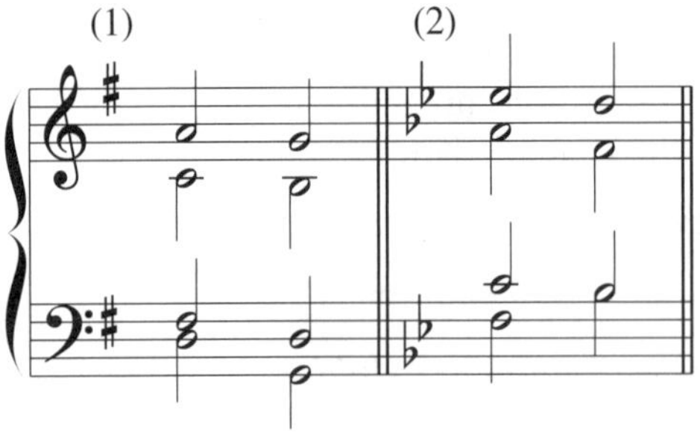

6.82 When the dominant seventh chord is in first inversion, the seventh scale degree is in the bass. Because of its prominent position, the natural tendency of the leading tone to move upward to the keynote (tonic) is intensified. *This tendency should rarely be violated.*

Mozart, *Fantasia in C Minor,* K. 475

D: V^6_5 I V

No

Is there any irregularity in the resolution of the dominant seventh chord in the above example? _______

(1) (2)

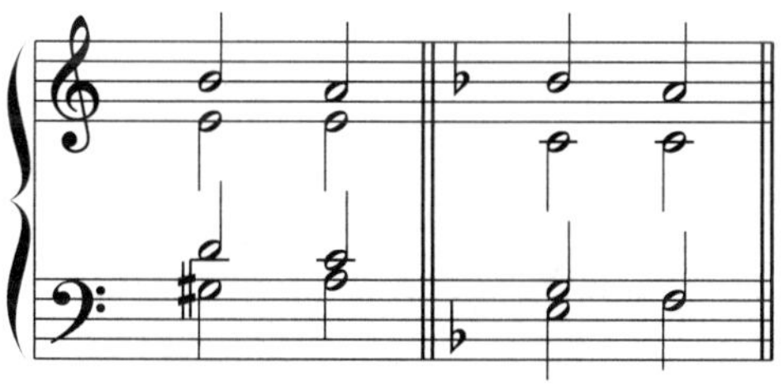

6.83 Write the second chord in each case, in such a way that no irregularity of doubling or resolution of active tones results.

(1) (2)

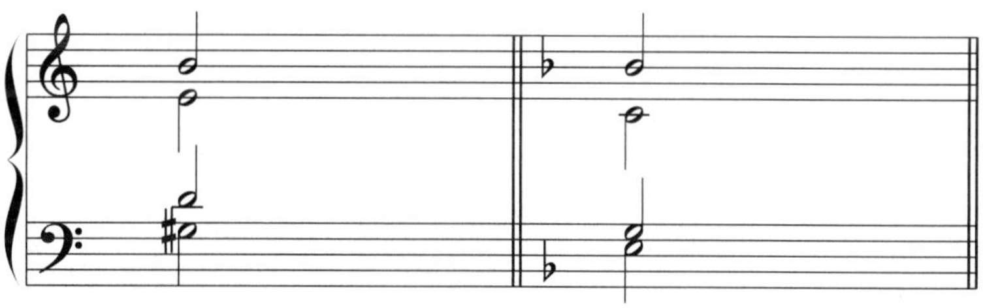

a: V^6_5 i F: V^6_5 I

B♭: vi V I^6 V^6_5 I V I

6.84 Analyze with roman numerals the phrase below. *(Don't be misled by nonharmonic tones [tones extraneous to harmony].)*

Bach, Chorale: *Jesu, Deine tiefen Wunden*

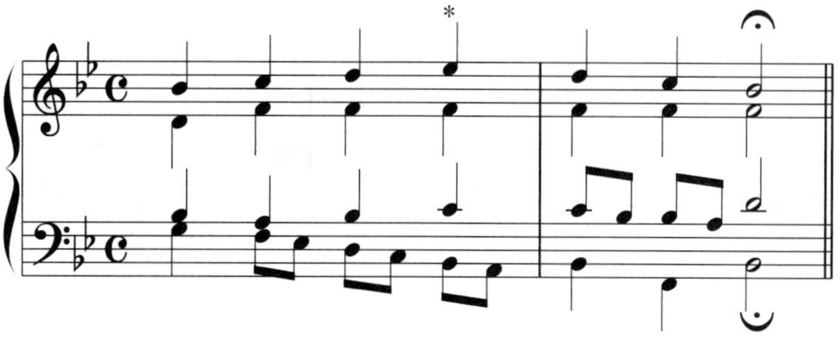

B♭: ___ ___ ___ ___ ___ ___ ___

6.85 The chord at the asterisk in the preceding frame is a dominant seventh chord. Aside from the 9-8 suspension in the tenor (in the following chord), are there any irregularities of doubling or resolution? _______

No

6.86 A dominant seventh chord in second inversion is shown below:

Schumann, *Papillons,* Op. 2

A: I – IV I^6 V^4_3 I

Like triads, seventh chords in second inversion are relatively weak sonorities. The one in the example above is used as a "passing chord" to connect the tonic in first inversion with the same chord in root position.

Which note is in the lowest voice when a seventh chord is in second inversion? (Root/3rd/5th/7th) _______.

5th

6.87 Supply the roman numeral analysis for the phrase below:

Haydn, *Quartet,* Op. 76, No. 4

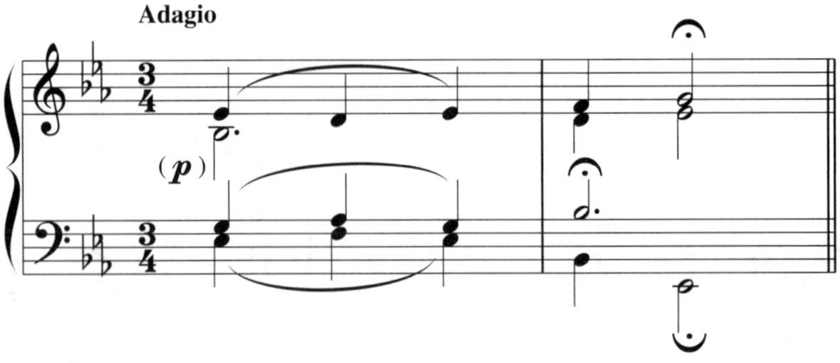

E♭: ___ ___ ___ ___ ___

E♭: I V^4_3 I V I

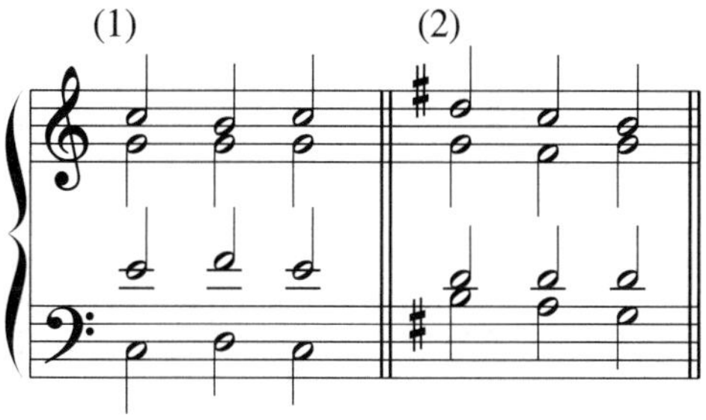

6.88 Complete the part writing in such a way that no irregularities of doubling occur.

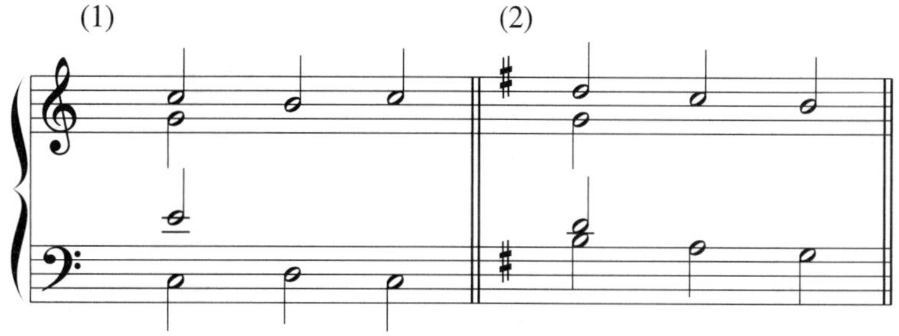

C: I V^4_3 I G: I^6 V^4_3 I

F: vi IV I^6 V^4_3 I V

6.89 Supply the roman numeral analysis for the phrase below.

Bach, Chorale: *Gott lebet noch*

F: ____ ____ ____ ____ ____ ____

6.90 The third inversion has the seventh in the bass.

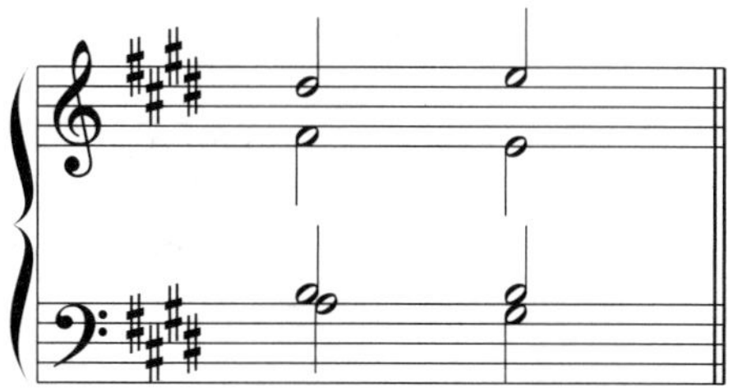

E: V^4_2 I^6

By being in the bass voice, the natural tendency of the seventh to resolve downward (by step) is emphasized. The dominant seventh chord in third inversion almost always resolves (as above)

first

to the tonic triad in ____________ inversion.

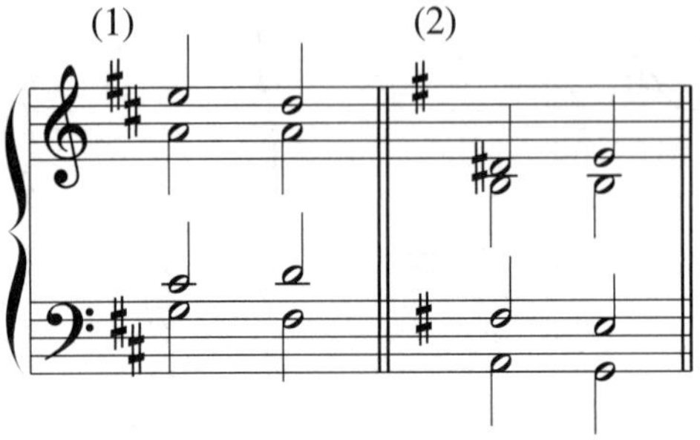

6.91 Write the second chord in such a way that no irregularities of doubling occur.

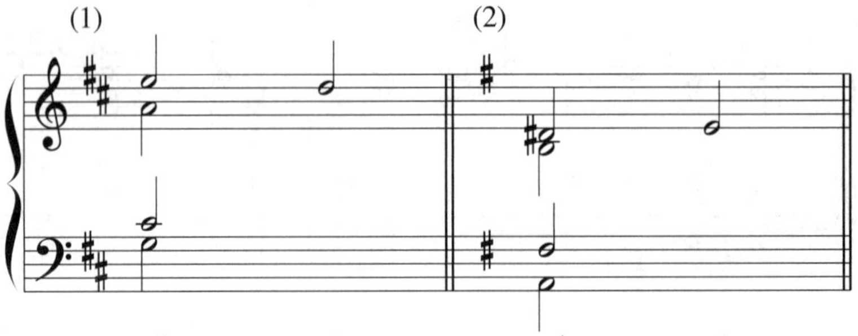

D: V^4_2 I^6 e: V^4_2 i^6

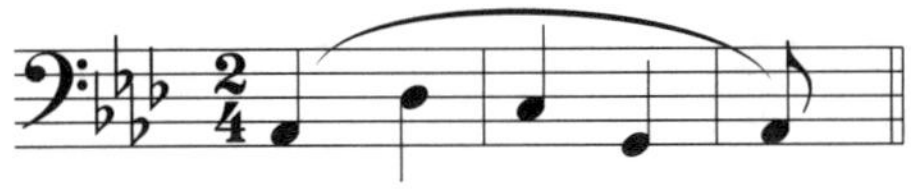

A♭: I V^4_2 I^6 V^6 I

6.92 Supply the roman numeral analysis for the fragment below.

Beethoven, *Sonata,* Op. 13

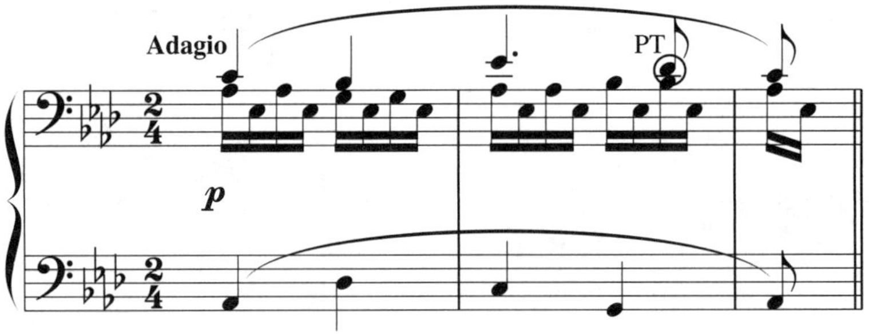

A♭: ___ ___ ___ ___ ___

6.93 In all of the examples shown thus far, the seventh resolves downward by step. Exceptional resolutions of the seventh are extremely rare. Two examples are shown below:

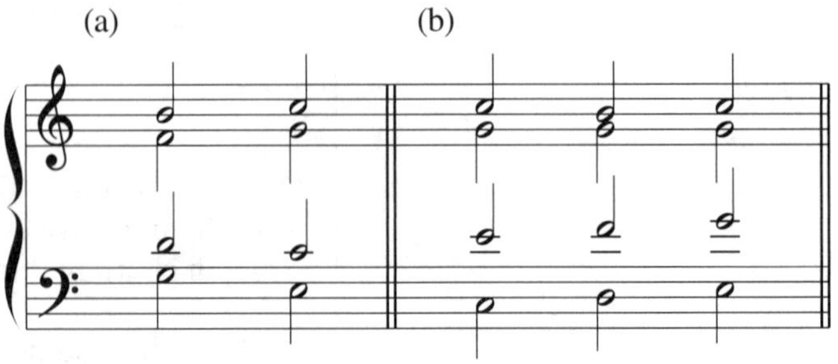

C: V^7 I^6 I V^4_3 I^6

Notice that in both cases the bass voice takes the note to which the seventh would normally have resolved (the third of the tonic triad.)

Learn this principle:

If the bass takes the note of resolution, the seventh may rise to the nearest chord tone.

What is the normal resolution of the seventh?

Downward by step

____

6.94 The tendency for the seventh of a seventh chord to resolve downward by step is seldom ignored. The *approach* to the seventh, on the other hand, is made in a variety of ways. Actually, it may be approached in any way that produces an effective melodic contour, taking into account its tendency to resolve downward.

Greater freedom may be exercised in the approach to the seventh than in its resolution. (True/False) _______

True

Expository Frame

6.95 Whereas the seventh may be approached in any way that results in a good melodic line and satisfactory part writing, several patterns are encountered more frequently than others. These are by preparation, by step, and by leap (from below).

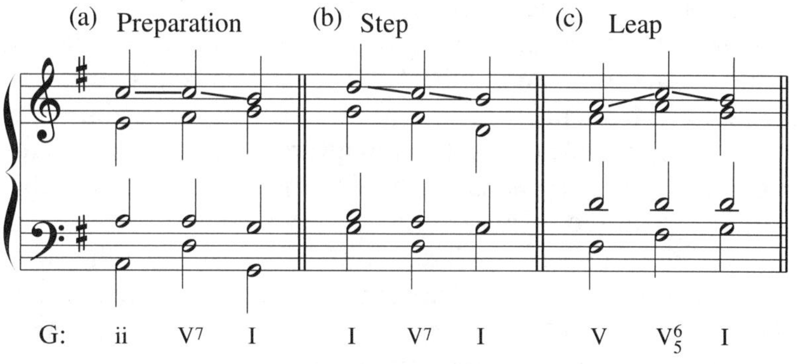

The seventh in each of the above examples may be likened to a nonharmonic tone. In (a), for example, the pattern of approach and resolution suggests a suspension. The pattern in (b) is like that of a passing tone, while the pattern in (c) suggests an appoggiatura.

(No response required.)

Expository Frame

6.96 Like (b) in the preceding frame, the following example shows a seventh approached and left by step. The neighboring tone is suggested by this pattern.

(Continued on the next page)

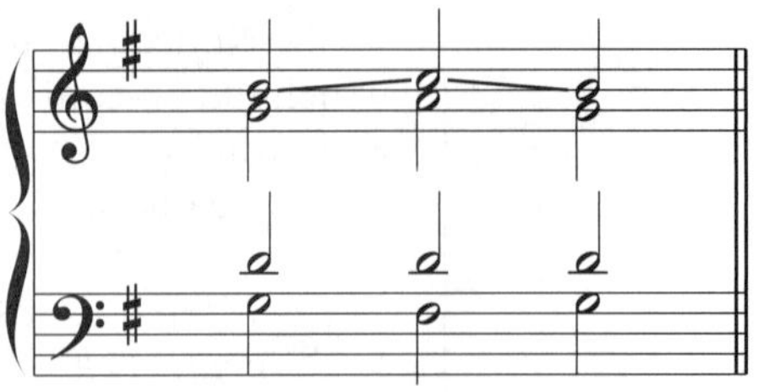

G: I V^6_5 I

(No response required.)

Summary

Seven types of seventh chords are generated by the major-minor system. The various types are named according to two features: (1) the quality of the triad; and (2) the quality of the interval between the root and the seventh. The term "major-minor" seventh chord, for example, means that the chord consists of a major triad with a minor seventh above the root.

The figured bass symbols commonly used to indicate the various positions of seventh chords are shown below:

Root Position	1st Inversion	2nd Inversion	3rd Inversion
7	$^6_5$	$^4_3$	$^4_2$ or 2

(For alternative means of analysis, see chord charts on p. 355.)

The dominant seventh chord is used more frequently than any other. *The addition of the seventh to the dominant triad does not change its function.* In fact, the introduction of a dissonant element (the seventh) serves to increase the activity of the dominant triad and makes more imperative its usual resolution to the tonic or submediant triads.

Two dissonant elements are contained in the dominant seventh chord: the seventh, and the interval of the tritone between the third and seventh. The proper resolution of the tritone, which is dictated by the melodic tendencies of the various scale degrees (the seventh tends to resolve upward while the fourth degree tends to resolve downward), is one of the factors that affects the part writing of passages containing dominant seventh chords. The second factor is the desirability of obeying the tendency of the chord's seventh to resolve downward by step.

Greater freedom is exercised in the approach to the seventh than in its resolution. Nevertheless, the majority of sevenths occur in patterns that suggest nonharmonic tones. The approach by preparation is like the suspension; the approach by step is like the passing tone or the neighboring tone; and the approach by leap is like the appoggiatura.

Dominant seventh chords are used in root position and in all inversions. When the more active tones (the seventh and third) are placed in the bass or soprano, their melodic tendencies are more apparent. Care must be taken in such cases that these tendencies are not violated.

The terms that are explained or used in this chapter are listed below in chronological order:

dissonance
seventh chord
diatonic seventh chords:
- major-minor
- major

minor
minor-major
diminished-minor
diminished
augmented-major

half-diminished
fully diminished
first inversion
second inversion
third inversion

dominant seventh chord
dissonant elements:
- seventh
- tritone

Mastery Frames

Four (6.1–.2)	6–1 How many tones are required to produce a complete seventh chord? _____________.
(1) Quality of triad (2) Quality of 7th (6.9–.22)	6–2 The quality of a seventh chord is represented by a term such as below. Indicate to what feature of the chord each part of the term applies. 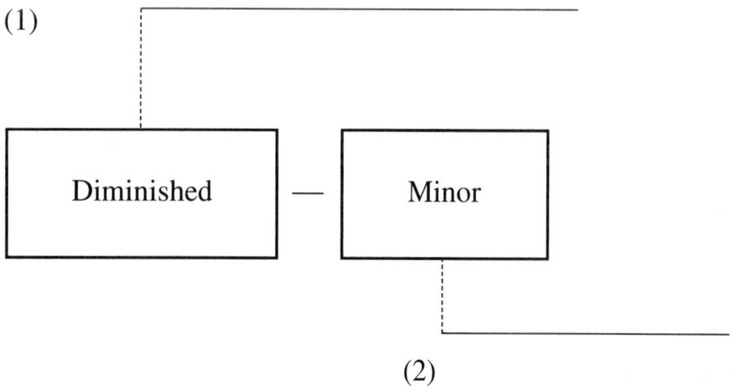
Seven (6.20)	6–3 How many diatonic seventh chords occur in the major-minor scale system? _____________

6–4 Indicate the quality of each of the seventh chords based on the major scale.

① ② ③ ④ ⑤ ⑥ ⑦

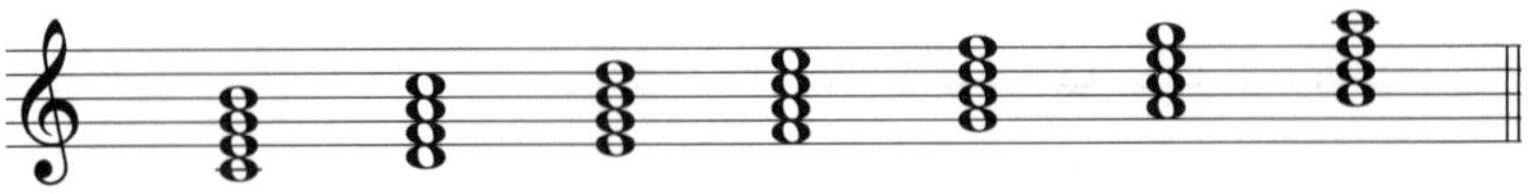

C:

(1) ______________
(2) ______________
(3) ______________
(4) ______________
(5) ______________
(6) ______________
(7) ______________

(1) Major
(2) Minor
(3) Minor
(4) Major
(5) Major-minor
(6) Minor
(7) Diminished-minor

(6.21)

6–5 Indicate the quality of each of the seventh chords based on the harmonic minor scale.

① ② ③ ④ ⑤ ⑥ ⑦

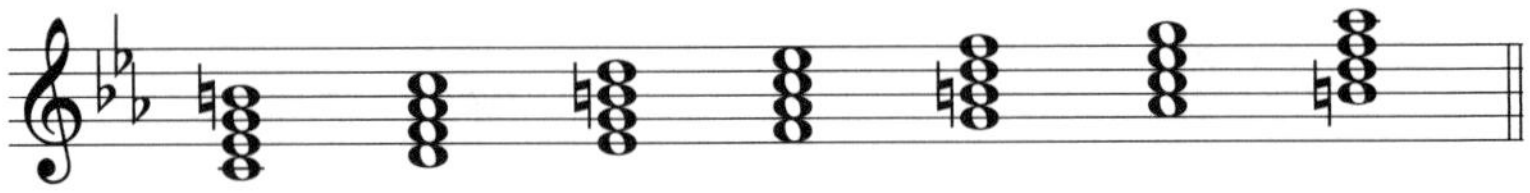

c:

(1) ______________
(2) ______________
(3) ______________
(4) ______________
(5) ______________
(6) ______________
(7) ______________

(1) Minor-major
(2) Diminished-minor
(3) Augmented-major
(4) Minor
(5) Major-minor
(6) Major
(7) Diminished

(6.22)

6–6 Write the appropriate chord symbol for each chord.

(1) (2) (3) (4)

F: ____ b: ____ G: ____ d: ____

(1) $\text{vii}^{ø7}$
(2) V^{7}
(3) ii^{7}
(4) $\text{vii}^{\circ 7}$

(6.27–.35)

(1) (2)

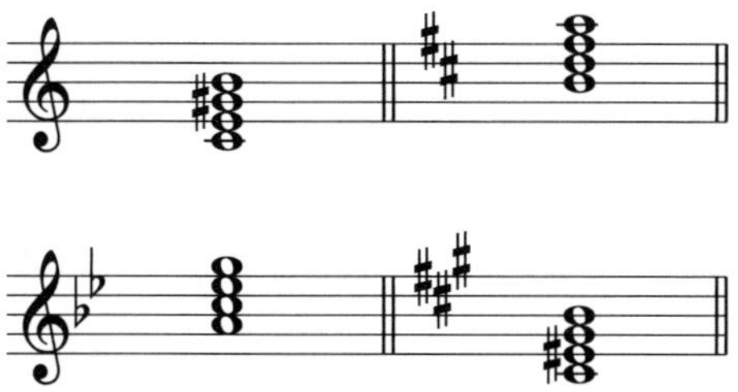

(6.27–.35)

6–7 Write the chord indicated by the chord symbols.

(1) (2) (3) (4)

a: III+7 D: vi7 g: iiø7 f♯: V7

(1) 7

(2) $^6_5$

(3) $^4_3$

(4) $^4_2$ or 2

(6.49–.52)

6–8 Write figured bass symbols that are appropriate for each position of a seventh chord.

(1) Root position _______

(2) First inversion _______

(3) Second inversion _______

(4) Third inversion _______

Third ✓

Seventh ✓

(6.67)

6–9 Check (✓) the two notes of the dominant seventh chord that produce a tritone.

Root _______

Third _______

Fifth _______

Seventh _______

(1) (2)

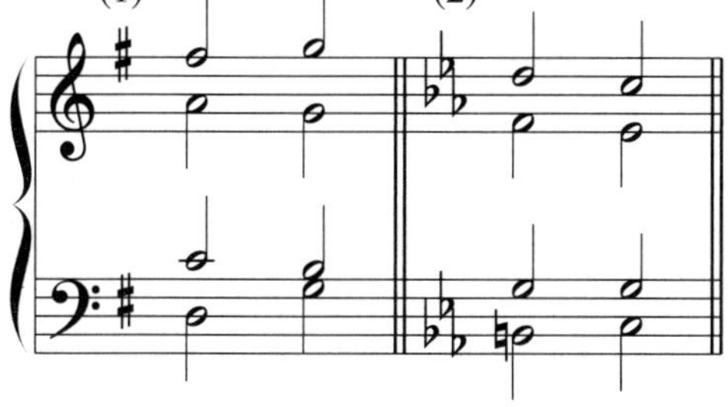

G: V7 I c: V$^6_5$ i

(6.67–.81) (6.82–.84)

6–10 Resolve the dominant seventh chords so that all active tones move according to their normal tendency.

(1) (2)

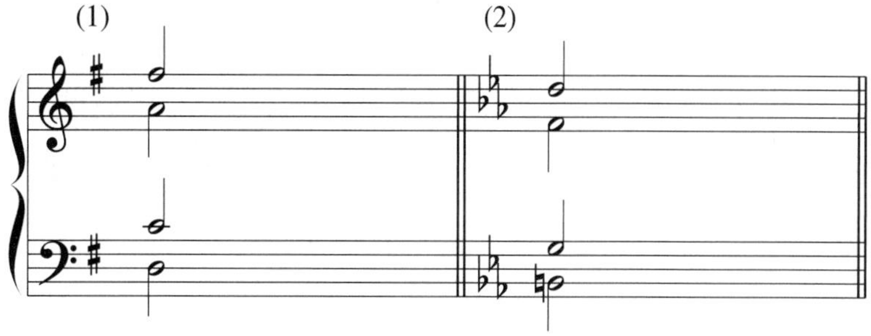

G: V7 I c: V$^6_5$ i

(6.86–.89) (6.90–.92)

6–11 Continue as in the preceding frame.

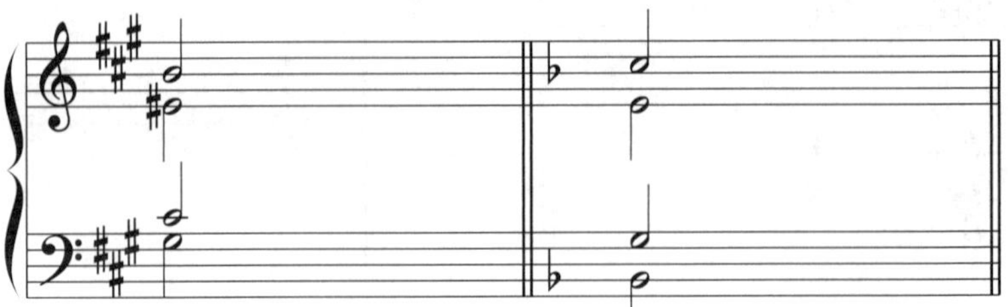

Supplementary Activities

1. Explore the topic of the seventh chord in an essay or short report. Consider how its usage has evolved from the time of Bach to the present in the context of jazz and popular music. Does it still play a role in the art (classical) music of the present day?

2. Incorporate the seventh chords (all types) into any ear training routine. Can seventh chords be readily identified as to quality and even inversion? Try to "spot" these chords in general music listening.

3. Continue to expand analytical abilities by examining longer or more extensive musical excerpts (yet with simple textures) for the identification of chords, their quality and inversion, and the relationship of musical lines to one another; how is the seventh of the chord approached and resolved? Once examined, develop a short essay or report about the findings.

4. Develop short essays about the various composers presented in the chapter: Bach, Mozart, Haydn, Kuhlau, Beethoven, Schumann, and Brahms.

5. If confidence is felt about the musical vocabulary developed up to this point, consider composing a phrase or two, or even a short composition that incorporates this vocabulary. As an additional challenge, try to write a composition in a style similar to one of the composers presented in the chapter.

Supplementary Assignments

ASSIGNMENT 6–1 Name ______________________

1. Write seventh chords as indicated. *(The given note is the root.)*

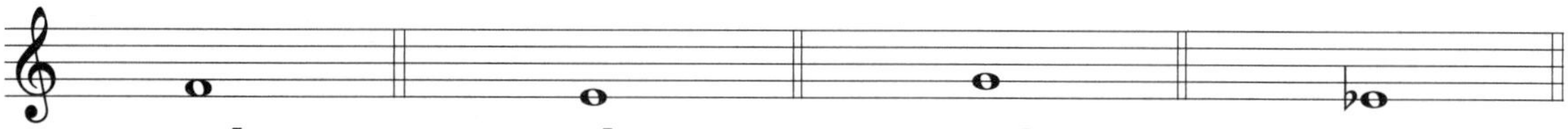

Mm^7 d^7 AM^7 mM^7

2. Write seventh chords as indicated. *(The given note is the third.)*

m^7 M^7 dm^7 M^7

3. Write seventh chords as indicated. *(The given note is the fifth.)*

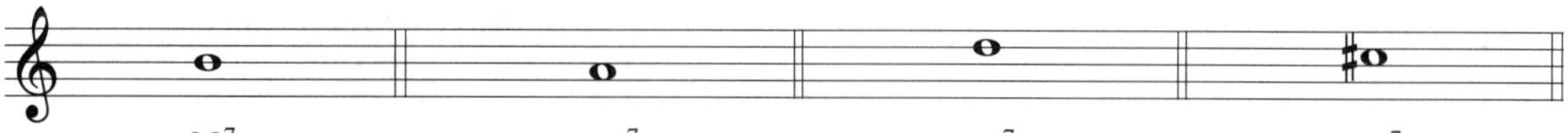

M^7 dm^7 M^7 m^7

4. Write seventh chords as indicated. *(The given note is the seventh.)*

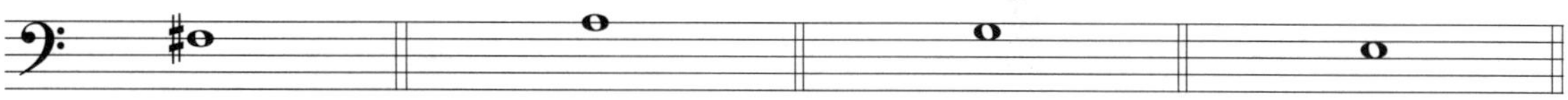

mM^7 AM^7 d^7 Mm^7

5. Write chords as indicated.

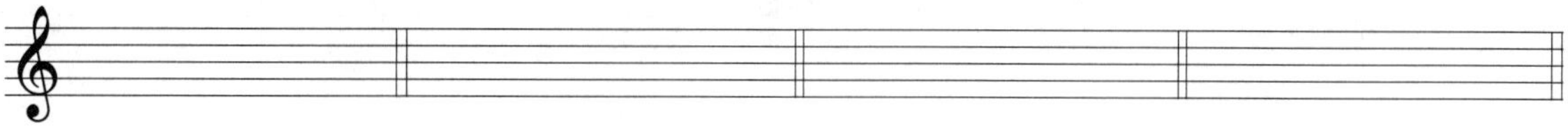

D: V^7 e: vii$^{\circ 7}$ A: IV$^6_5$ d: ii$^{ø 4}_{\ 2}$

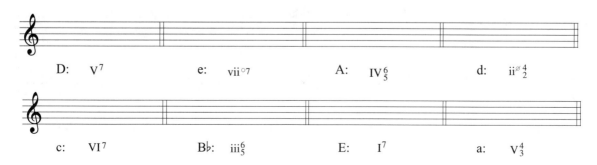

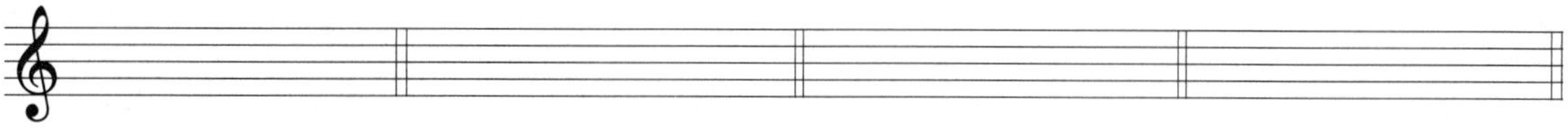

c: VI^7 B♭: iii$^6_5$ E: I^7 a: V$^4_3$

6. In which example is the dominant seventh chord correctly resolved? ______________________

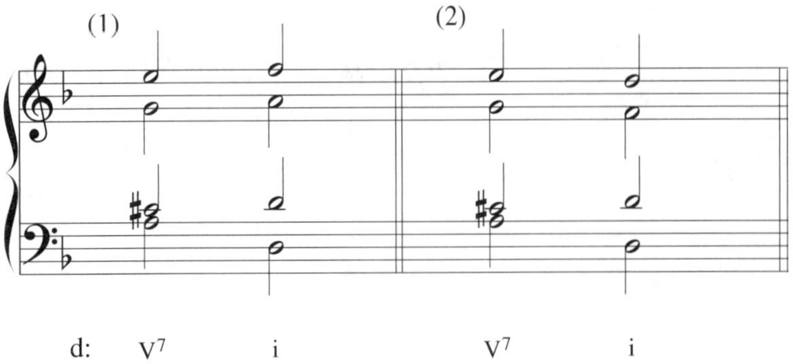

7. In which example is the dominant seventh chord both correctly written and resolved? ____________

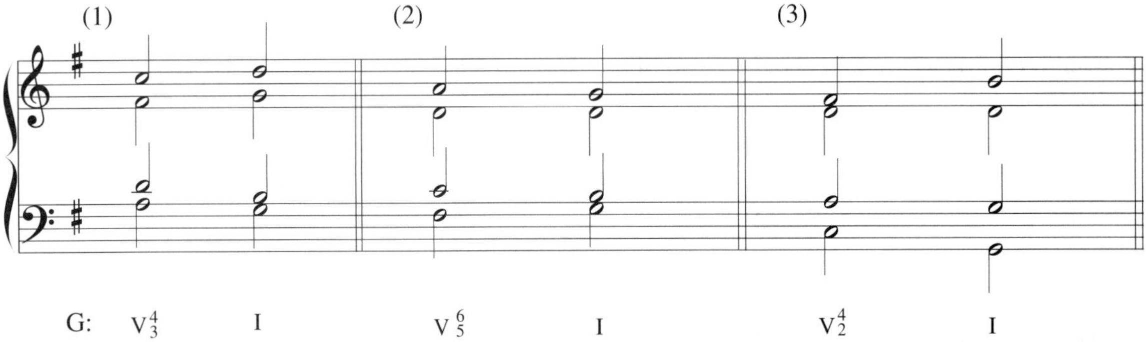

8. Resolve each dominant seventh chord so that all active tones resolve in the direction of their activity.

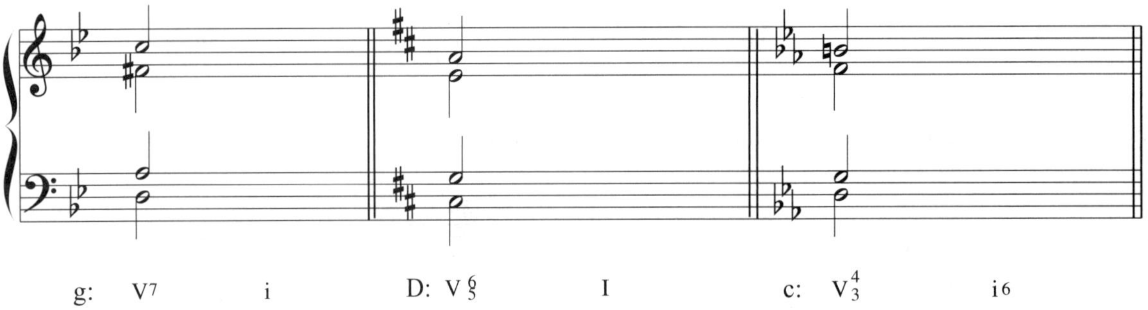

9. Write the indicated seventh chords in four-part harmony.

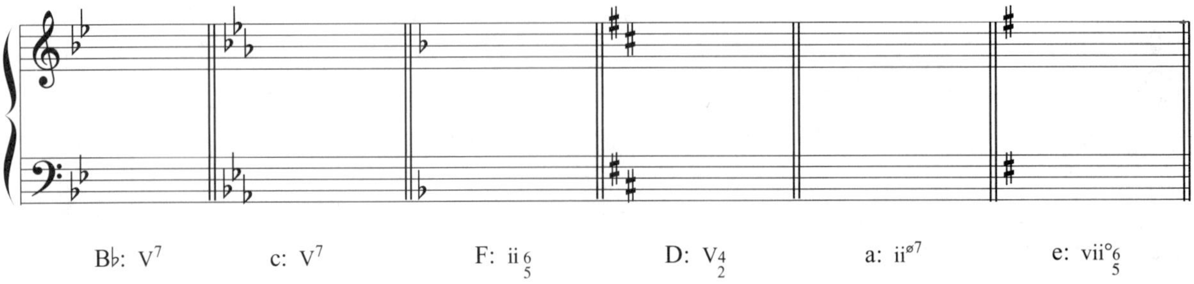

ASSIGNMENT 6–2 Name ______________________________

1. Indicate the quality of each chord. Use symbols such as Mm^7, m^7, etc.

___ ___ ___ ___ ___

2. Write chords as indicated. *(Given note is the root.)*

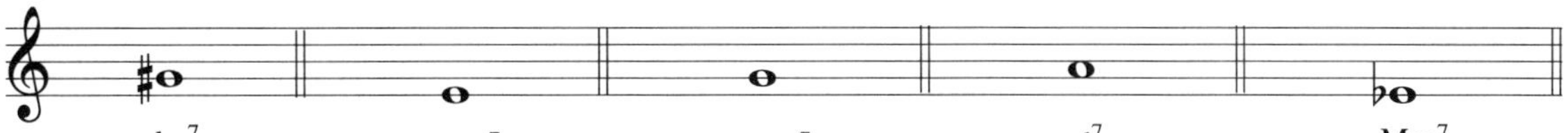

dm^7 AM^7 mM^7 d^7 Mm^7

3. Supply the chord symbol for each chord. *(Indicate inversions.)*

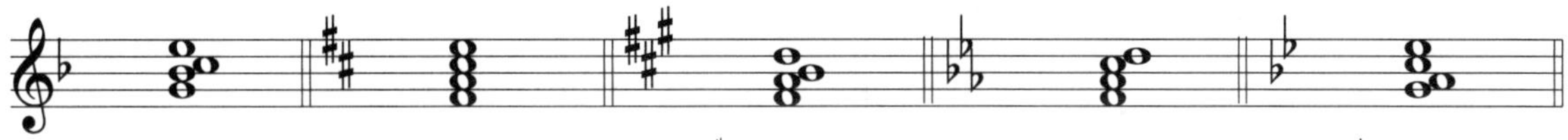

F: ___ D: ___ f♯: ___ c: ___ B♭: ___

g: ___ A: ___ d: ___ E: ___ f: ___

4. Write chords as indicated.

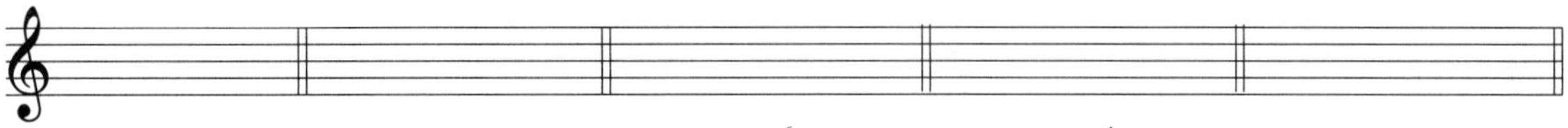

G: $vii^{ø7}$ f: $ii^{ø7}$ B: IV^6_5 D: V^4_3 b♭: VI^7

5. Which chord agrees with the chord symbol? ______________________________

(1) (2) (3) (4) (5)

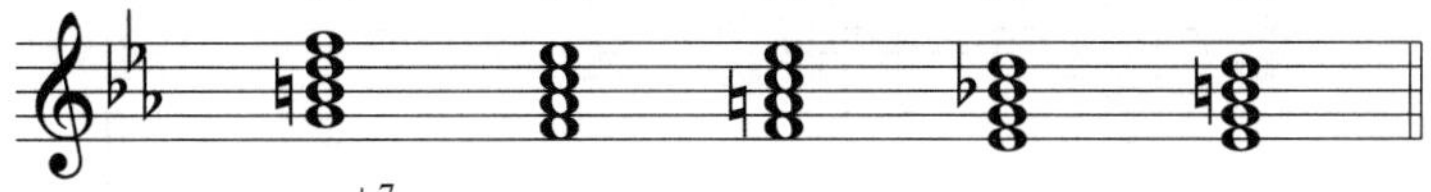

c: III^{+7}

6. Which chord agrees with the chord symbol? ________________

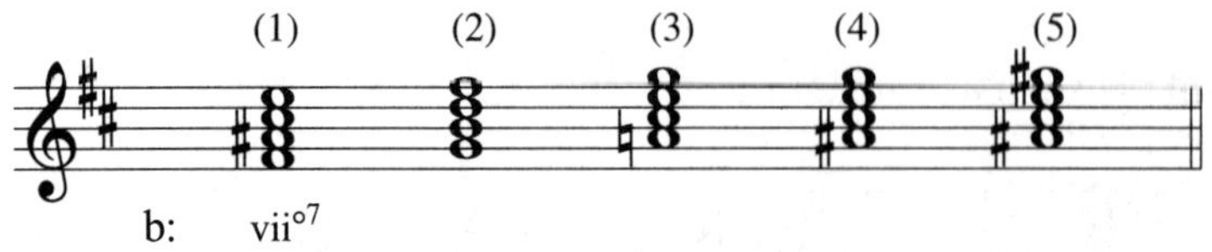

7. Which chord agrees with the chord symbol? ________________

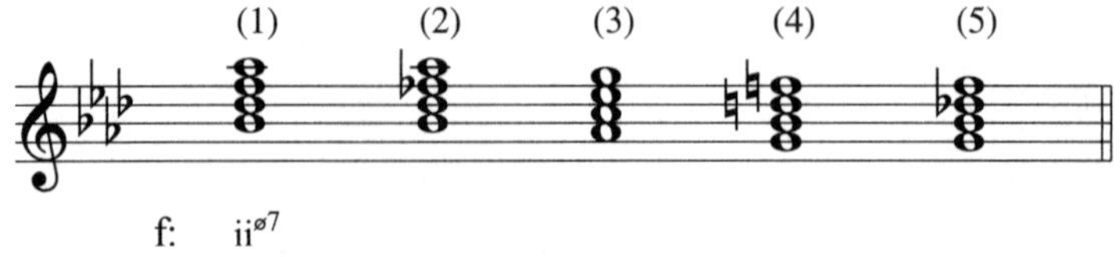

8. In which case is the seventh chord correctly written and resolved? ________________

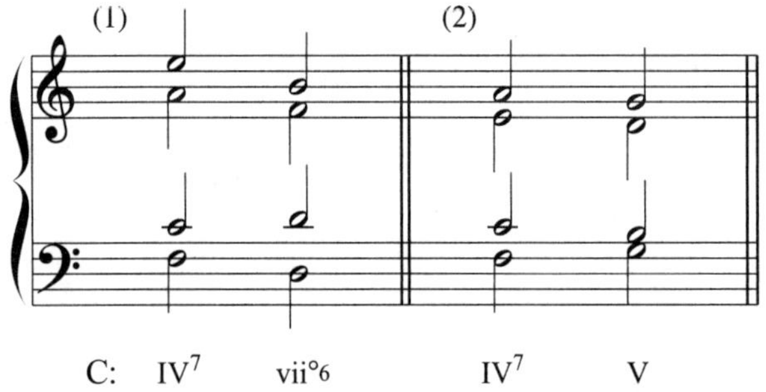

9. In which case is the seventh chord correctly written and resolved? ________________

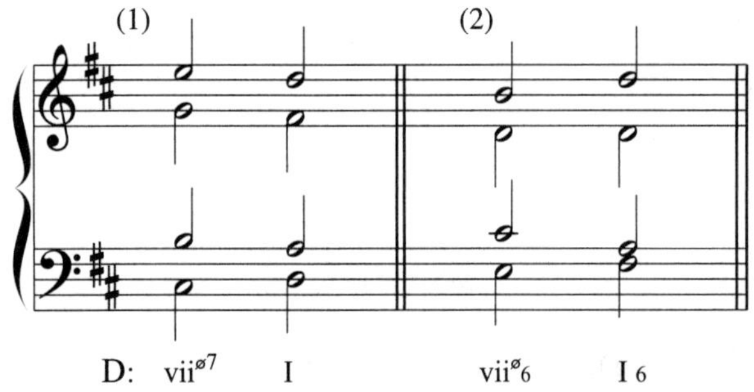

10. Write the second chord in each case so that all active tones are resolved in the direction of their activity.

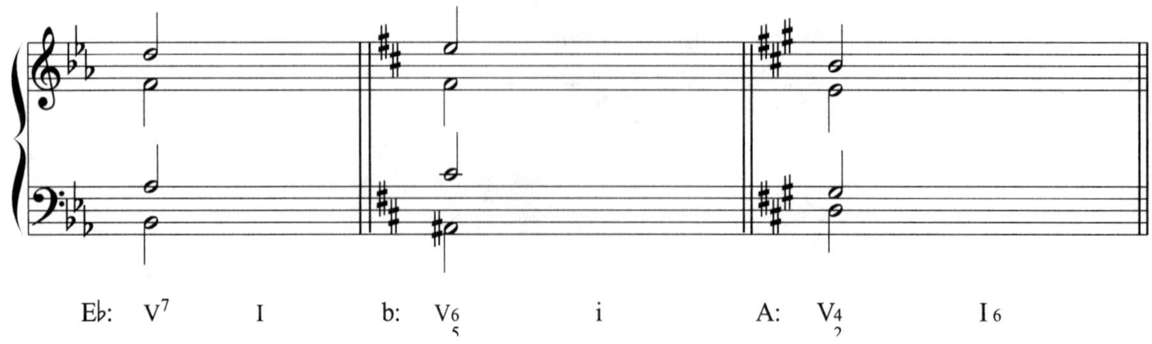

ASSIGNMENT 6–3 Name ______________________

1. Supply chord symbols for the six chords in the example below.

Kuhlau: *Sonatina*

2. Analyze the example below with roman numerals. Also indicate nonharmonic tones.

Mozart: *Fantasia in D minor,* K. 397

3. Use chord symbols to indicate a progression that would permit the seventh to resolve down by step in each case.

Major Key		Minor Key	
ii^7	–_______	ii^{ø7}	–_______
iii^7	–_______	III^{+7}	–_______
IV^7	–_______	iv^7	–_______
vi^7	–_______	VI^7	–_______
vii^{ø7}	–_______	vii$^{°7}$	–_______

4. Add the alto and tenor to the given figured basses. Circle each chord seventh and draw a line from the circle to the note of resolution. Analyze with roman numerals.

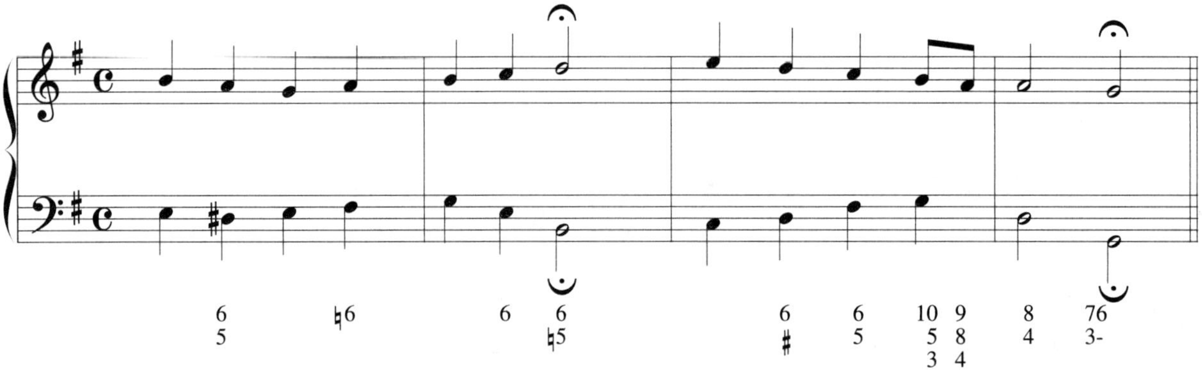

e:

5. Write both a roman numeral and alternative analysis of the following example:

Bach: *Patita II*, Chaconne (Unaccompanied Violin)

d:

Alternative:

Chapter 7.0
Phrase Structure and Cadences

The organized sounds of music elicit a variety of responses—sensual, emotional and intellectual; thus, music may be viewed as a form of communication. Like all communication intended for human consumption, music must take into account the listener's limited attention span. This causes musical ideas to be presented in digestible portions and punctuated in a manner comparable to the chapters, paragraphs, sentences, and phrases of literature. The basic formal unit in music is the *phrase,* and phrases are set off from one another by *cadences.* Cadences provide moments of repose, as well as points of orientation.

Another elemental facet of communication in music is the use of *tension* and *relaxation* to arouse varying types and degrees of emotional response. Tension derives from: harmony, rhythm, timbre, dynamics, texture, and melodic contour. In this chapter the focus is on the contribution of melodic contour to phrase structure. The role of harmonic cadences as terminators of phrases will also be stressed.

phrase	7.1 Music is organized into segments of various lengths and the basic unit of organization is the PHRASE. Most phrases in Western art music are four measures long. The four-measure phrase is so prevalent (especially during the classical period), that it can be regarded as the "normal" phrase length. Nevertheless, phrases both longer and shorter occur. One of the basic units of formal organization is the ____________.
vocal	7.2 Another reason for the organization of music into relatively small units is the fact that, until the rise of pure instrumental music during the seventeenth and eighteenth centuries, music had a predominantly vocal orientation. Even in instrumental music the influence of vocal style continued to be felt until the end of the nineteenth century. Obviously, music that is intended for voices must provide breathing places for the performers. Since instrumental style has long been a reflection of vocal writing, it tends to have the same sort of organization. Breathing places are necessary for the comfort of the listener, too, as there is a tendency to breathe empathetically with the performer. The phrase is a basic unit in the formal organization of music.* While phrases vary in length, their duration is usually about as long as a vocalist comfortably can sustain his or her breath. This is due to the predominantly ____________ orientation of music during the period of tonal harmony. *Rudimentary information regarding phrase structure is presented here as it is vital to the understanding of certain aspects of harmony.

7.3 Shaping elements of the phrase include rhythm, harmony, and melodic contour. The ascending and descending intervals of a melody produce lines, most of which fall into a few simple types. These types will be introduced in the next few frames.

The melody below ascends from a relatively low pitch to a higher level.

Tchaikovsky, *Symphony No. 4,* Op. 36

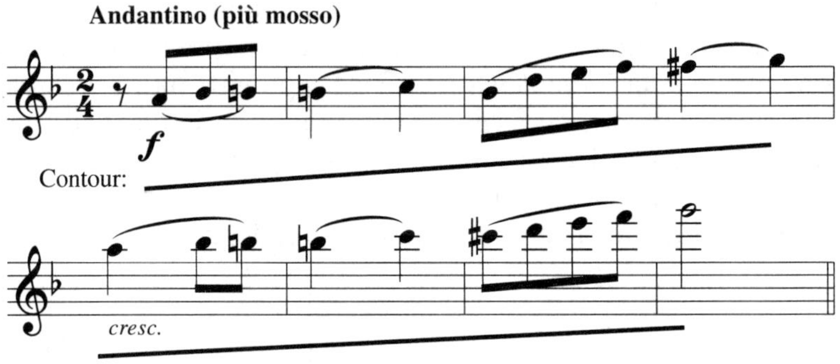

The "shape" of a melody—the line that is traced by its various pitches—is called melodic ______________.

contour

7.4 Another simple melodic contour is shown below:

Franck, *Symphonic Variations* (1885)

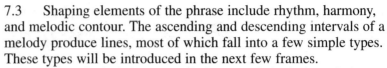

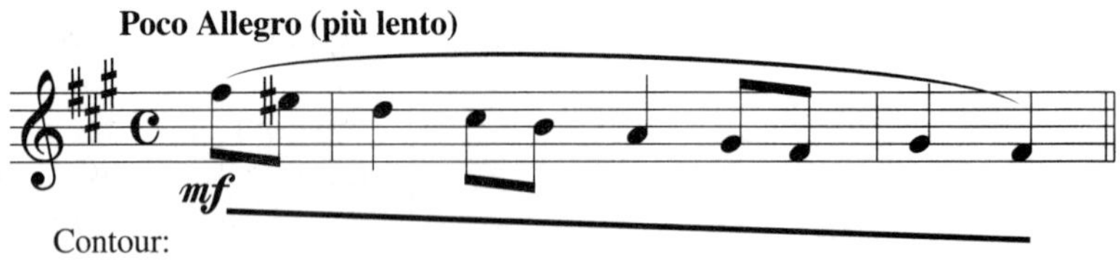

This contour is the reverse of that shown in the preceding frame. Sing or play these two melodies. Which do you feel gives the more pronounced feeling of repose? (Frame 7.3/Frame 7.4)

____

You are entitled to your own opinion, but see next frame.

7.5 Under most circumstances an ascending melodic line generates tension, whereas a descending line provides relaxation. Ebb and flow of tension is an important element of musical expression, and one way tensions and relaxations are produced is through the contour of melodic lines.

Normally tension is produced by an ____________ line, relaxation by a ____________ line.

ascending

descending

Expository Frame

7.6 The melody below illustrates a contour that occurs very frequently. This contour embodies the principle of tension followed by relaxation; the result is a sense of completion—a satisfying musical experience in miniature.

Mendelssohn, *Songs Without Words,* Op. 62, No. 4

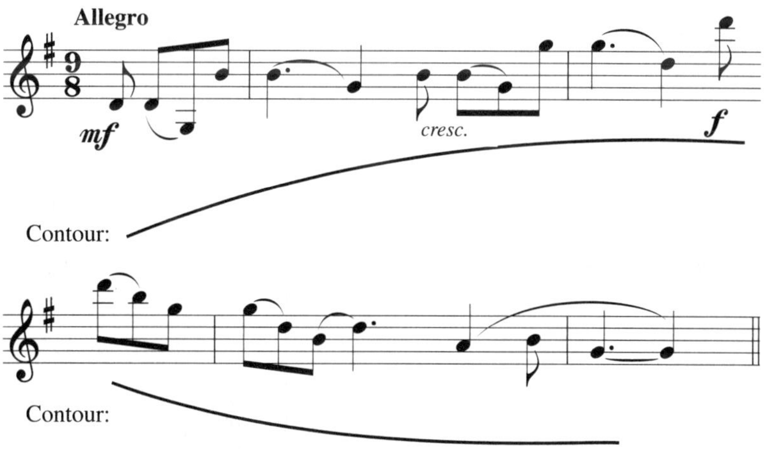

(*No response required.*)

7.7 Draw a profile beneath the melody below that illustrates its contour.

Brahms, *Symphony No. 4,* Op. 98

7.8 The contour illustrated in the preceding frame is the reverse of that in Frame 7.6 and is not as common.

The four basic contours presented thus far are:

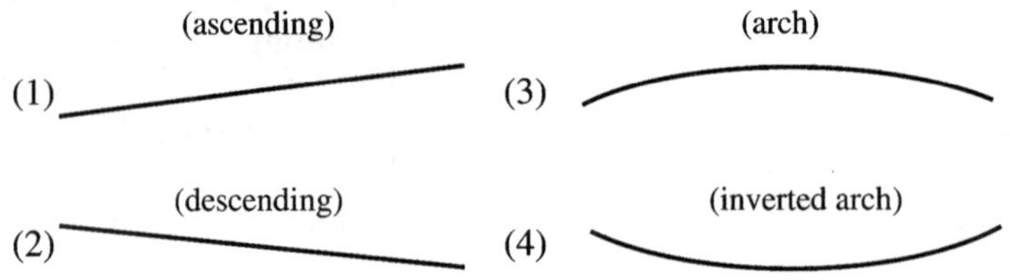

Which of these contours best expresses tension followed by relaxation? _______

(3)

7.9 The combination of (3) and (4) of the preceding frame produces a fifth contour.

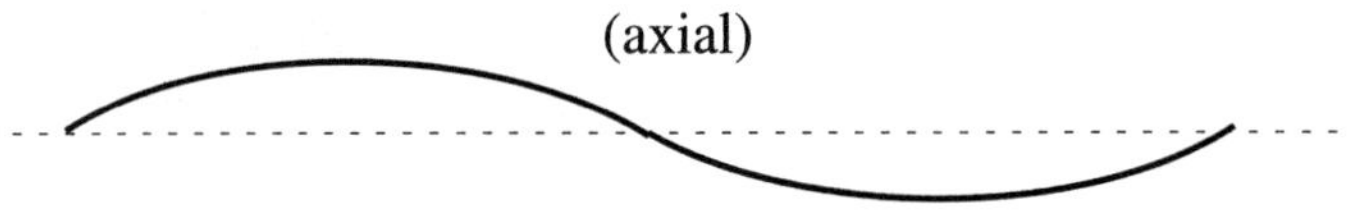

In this case, the melody extends both upward and downward from a central axis. Observe the melody below:

Haydn, *String Quartet,* Op. 3, No. 5

The note C is the axis and both the upper and lower limit is the note _______.

F

7.10 Often rhythmic activity comes momentarily to a halt at the end of a phrase. Longer note values (and sometimes rests) are used at phrase endings to provide the desired degree of repose.

The example consists of two phrases; the asterisks denote the end of each.

Dvorák, *Symphony No. 9,* Op. 95

The desired degree of repose at the ends of phrases results from the contour of the line, but also from a lessening of the

rhythmic | _____________ activity.

7.11 The discussion continues by focusing on how phrases end. As points of repose, cadences are extremely important to the study of harmony. Because they are goals of the phrase itself, cadences have special structural significance. The ear tends to listen for these goals, and relate surrounding material to them. The ends of phrases are called CADENCES.* Learn this:

Cadences are melodic-harmonic formulas that bring phrases to a more or less definite close.

The points of repose that occur at the ends of phrases are

cadences | called _____________.

*The word cadence comes from the Latin root word *cadere,* to fall. The term is descriptive of the most prevalent melodic contour at the ends of phrases (especially in monophonic music such as Gregorian chant).

7.12 There are two types of cadences: final and nonfinal.* Final cadences bring a phrase to a complete close. Nonfinal cadences point forward; they do not conclude a musical idea, but require yet another phrase to resolve their nonfinal effect.

List the two basic types of cadences.

(1) Final | (1) _____________

(2) Nonfinal | (2) _____________

*Final and nonfinal might also be described as terminal and progressive cadences respectively.

7.13 There are two final cadences and two non-final cadences.

FINAL CADENCES	NONFINAL CADENCES
Authentic	Half
Plagal	Deceptive

Authentic and plagal cadences impart a sufficient degree of finality to close an entire composition, or an important section.

(Continued on the next page)

Half and deceptive cadences, on the other hand, lack finality; they can be compared with the colon (:) or the question mark (?), both of which are punctuation marks that imply further elaboration.

Name the two cadences that may close an entire composition.

(1) ____________

(2) ____________

(1) Authentic

(2) Plagal
(Any order.)

Expository Frame

7.14 The chords that produce each of the four cadences are shown below:

Authentic:	V or vii°–I
Plagal:	IV–I
Half:	I, IV, or ii–V
Deceptive:	V–vi

It is surprising that such a limited repertoire of cadences has sufficed for the huge mass of music that is based on tonal harmonic principles. Yet these four cadences have remained valid and have proved their usefulness in the music of several centuries.

Perhaps the continued popularity of tonal music is due, in part, to the orientation provided the listener by only a few cadence types, whose function (final or nonfinal) is so easily perceived. By virtue of their common use over a long period of time, these cadences provide the listener with points of reference regarding the function of a particular phrase in relation to the musical structure as a whole.

(No response required.)

7.15 The AUTHENTIC CADENCE occurs more frequently than any other. It is the strongest and most conclusive cadence. The authentic cadence consists of the chords V–I (V–i in a minor key).

Haydn, *The Creation,* No. 3

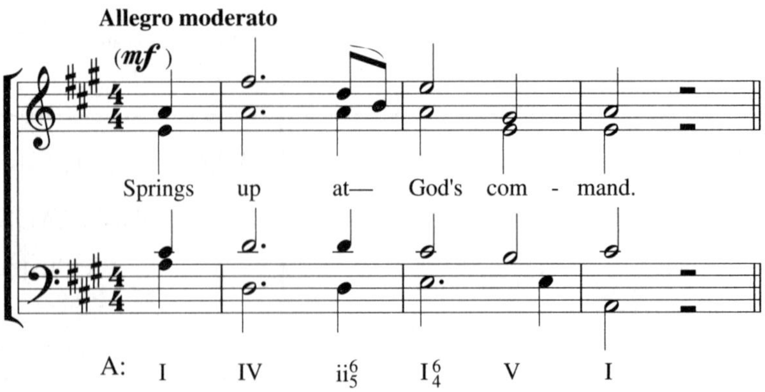

The cadence consists of the final two chords (V–I); but, as is shown in the preceding example, the tonic in second inversion (the cadential six-four) often is included as part of the cadential formula.

What are two chords that produce the authentic cadence?

_______ – _______.

V–I
(or V–i.)

7.16 Another authentic cadence is shown below:

Beethoven, *Symphony No. 8,* Op. 93

Compare the cadence above with the ones shown in the preceding frame. Both are authentic cadences, but they do not have the same degree of finality.

Which produces the stronger sense of conclusion?

(Frame 7.15/7.16) ____________.

Frame 7.15
(There should be no doubt, but consider why.)

7.17 Rhythm contributes to making the cadence of Frame 7.15 sound more conclusive than the cadence of Frame 7.16, but another factor is that the root of the tonic triad is in the soprano in the first case whereas the third is in the soprano in the second.

The cadence in Frame 7.15 is a PERFECT authentic cadence whereas the cadence in Frame 7.16 is an IMPERFECT authentic cadence. The terms *perfect* and *imperfect* refer to the degree of finality imparted by a ____________.

cadence

7.18 To qualify as a PERFECT cadence, the following conditions must be met:

(1) Both chords must be in root position.

(2) The final tonic chord must have the root in the soprano.

Why is the example on the next page *not* a perfect authentic cadence? ______________________________

____

The dominant chord is not in root position.

(Continued on the next page)

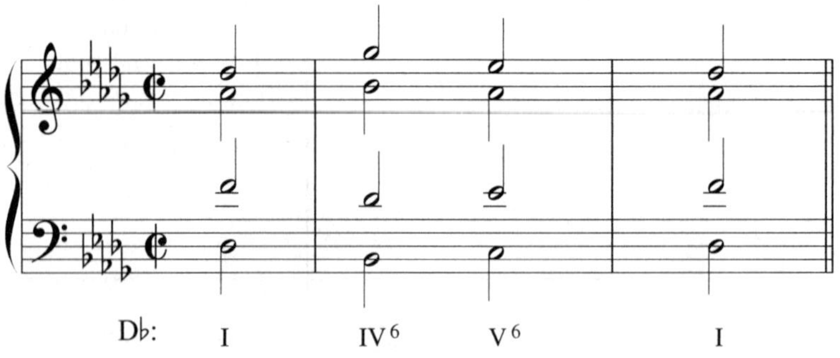

The final chord has the third in the soprano.

7.19 Why is the cadence below *not* a perfect authentic cadence?

____

____

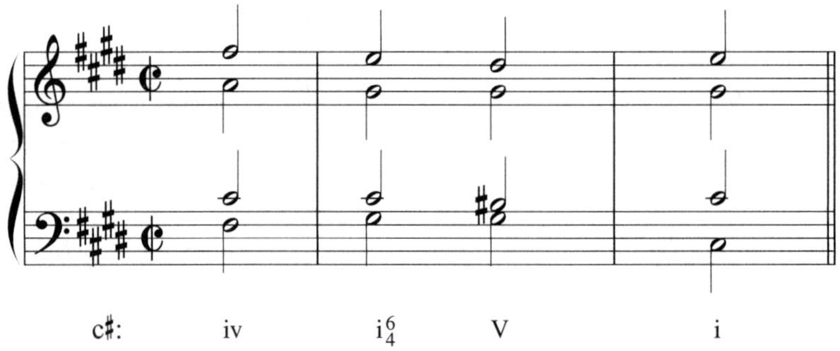

---

(2)

7.20 Which of the cadences below is a perfect authentic cadence? _______

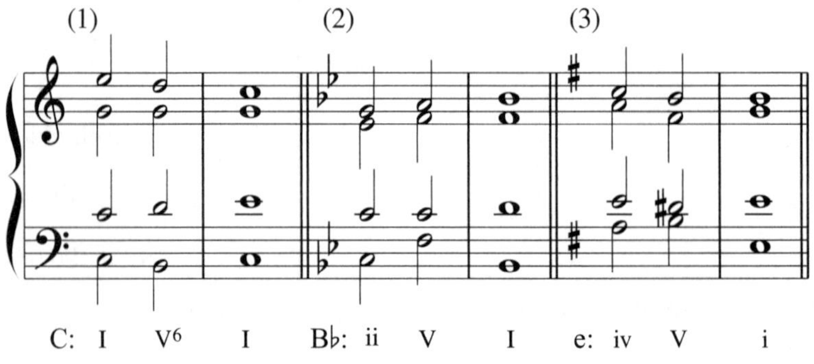

(3)

7.21 Which of the following is a perfect authentic cadence?

____

(1) (2) (3)

g: ii°6 V i6 D: ii V6 I c: i V i

---

(2)

7.22 Which of the cadences below is a perfect authentic cadence? _______

(1) (2) (3)

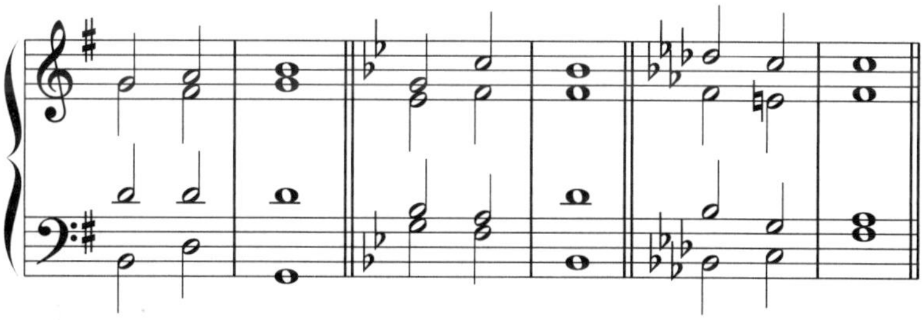

G: I6 V I B♭: IV6 V I f: iv V i

---

major

7.23 The final tonic triad of an authentic cadence in a minor key sometimes is altered to become a major triad. The raised third that produces this effect is called a PICARDY THIRD.

Bach, Chorale: *Das neugeborne Kindlein*

g: i^6_4 V I

The Picardy third causes a minor tonic triad to become a _____________ triad.

7.24 The PICARDY THIRD usually is reserved for the final cadence of a composition or an important section. It generally is felt that a major triad concludes a composition more strongly than a minor triad.

Play the example in the preceding frame substituting B♭ for B♮ in the final chord. Compare the effect of this version with the original. Which do you think is the stronger? (B♭ or B♮)

____

You are entitled to your opinion. Certainly the B♮ produced the "brighter" sound.

d: i iv V I

7.25 Write the alto and tenor voices in accordance with the figured bass symbols. Analyze with roman numerals.

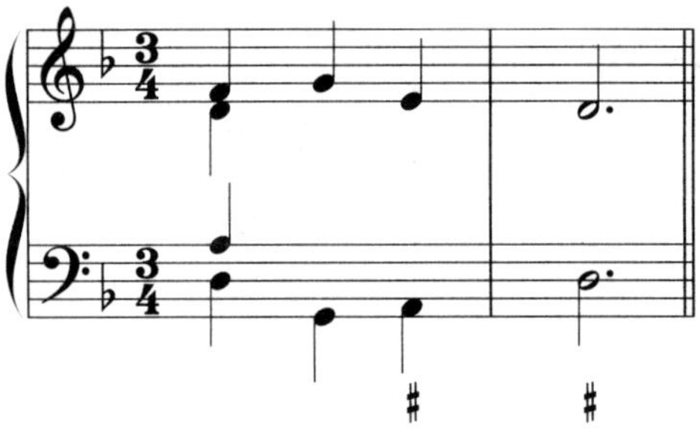

d: ___ ___ ___ ___

True

7.26 The cadence in the preceding frame is a perfect authentic cadence with a PICARDY THIRD. (True/False) ______________

f♯: i iv^6_4 i V^6 I

7.27 Write the alto and tenor voices in accordance with the figured bass symbols. Analyze with roman numerals.

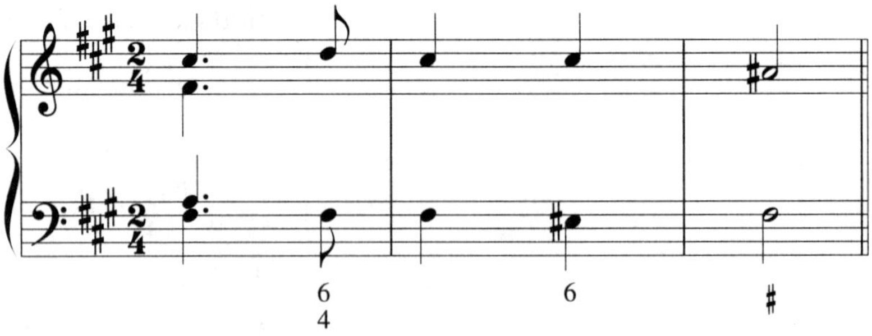

f♯: ___ ___ ___ ___ ___

False
(There is a Picardy third, but the cadence is imperfect.)

7.28 The cadence in the preceding frame is a perfect authentic cadence with a PICARDY THIRD. (True/False) ______________

7.29 Check (✓) the correct option:

1. The PICARDY THIRD generally occurs in the authentic cadence in a minor key.
2. The PICARDY THIRD occurs only in the perfect authentic cadence.

True statements:

(1) _______ (2) _______ Both _______ Neither _______

(1) ✓

7.30 The cadence vii°–I is also an authentic cadence.

Sibelius, *Finlandia,* Op. 26

A♭: vii°6 — I

The vii°–I cadence is classed as an *imperfect* cadence; it does not convey as strong a sense of finality as the perfect authentic cadence (V–I).

The terms perfect and imperfect refer to the degree of finality of a cadence. Since the vii°–I cadence is "weaker" in effect than the V–I cadence, it is called an _____________ authentic cadence.

imperfect

7.31 The vii°–I cadence rarely is used for the final cadence of a composition, but it is useful for the close of phrases within a section. Another example of the vii°–I cadence is shown below:

Handel, Chorale: *Ach Gott und Herr, wie gross und schwer*

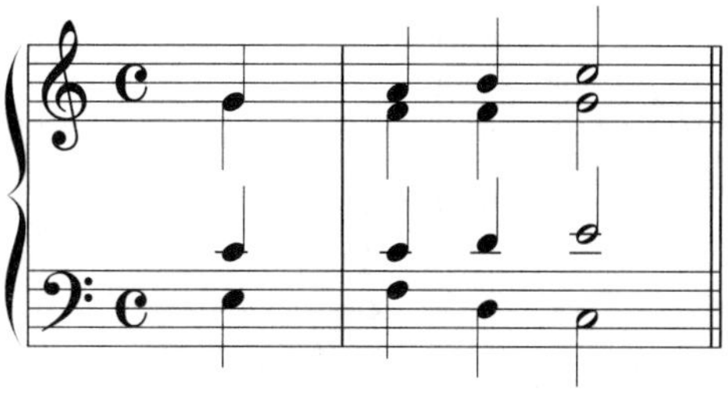

C: ___ ___ ___ ___

Analyze the example above with roman numerals.

C: I^6–IV–vii°6–I

authentic

7.32 The leading tone triad (vii°) has virtually the same harmonic function as the dominant (V), so it may be substituted for V to produce an imperfect ____________ cadence.

d: IV–vii°⁶–i
(Note the use of the ascending form of the melodic minor scale in this example.)

7.33 The leading tone triad may be used to make an imperfect authentic cadence in a minor key.

Bach, Chorale: *Komm, Gott Schöpfer, heiliger Geist*

d: ___ ___ ___

Supply the roman numeral analysis for the last three chords.

g: i V^6 i vii°^{6} i

7.34 Write the alto and tenor voices and analyze with roman numerals.

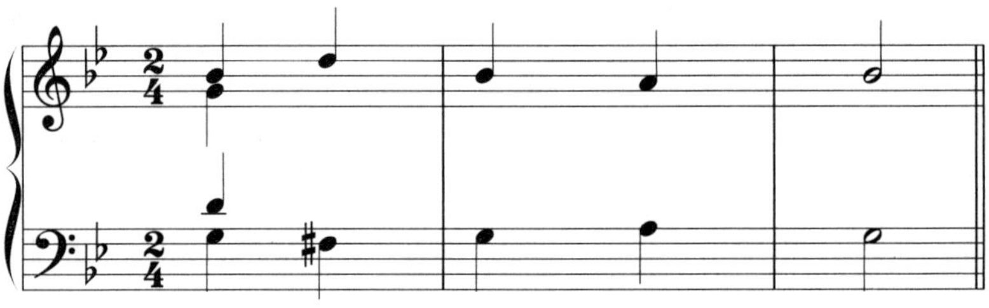

6 6̸

g: ___ ___ ___ ___ ___

f♯: i iv^6 i IV vii°^{6} I

7.35 Write the alto and tenor voices and analyze with roman numerals.

6 ♯ 6̸ ♯

f♯: ___ ___ ___ ___ ___ ___

7.36 Notice in the preceding frame that the ascending form of the melodic minor scale is used in the soprano voice. This is to avoid the augmented second (D to E♯) that would have occurred if harmonic minor had been used.

This example shows that in a minor key, depending on whether or not the sixth scale degree is raised, the quality of the subdominant triad may be either ____________ or ____________.

major (or) minor

7.37 Even though the example in Frame 7.35 is in the key of f♯ minor, the final chord contains an A♯. This device is called a ____________ third.

Picardy

7.38 Write the alto and tenor voices and analyze with roman numerals; also do an alternative analysis.

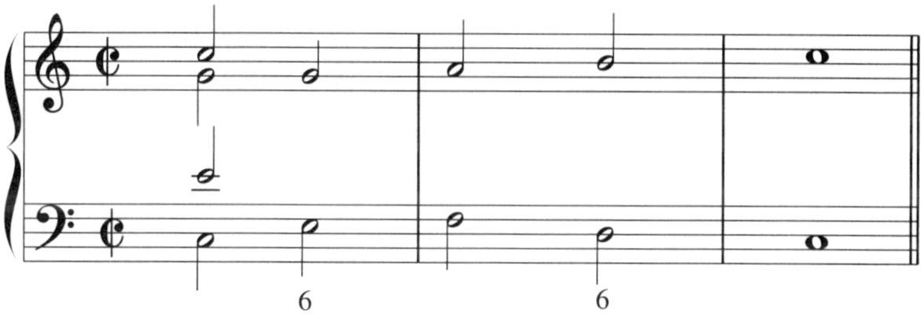

C: ___ ___ ___ ___ ___

Alternative: ___ ___ ___ ___ ___

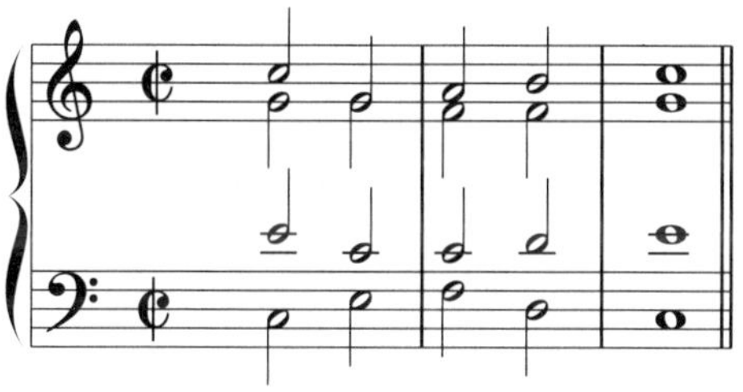

C: I I^6 IV vii°6 I

Alter.: C C/E F Bdim/D C

7.39 Of the two "final" cadences (authentic and plagal) the authentic cadence is used much more frequently. The PLAGAL CADENCE has a "softer," less "positive" effect than the authentic cadence. The plagal cadence consists of the progression IV–I (iv–i in a minor key).

Brahms, *Symphony No. 1,* Op. 68

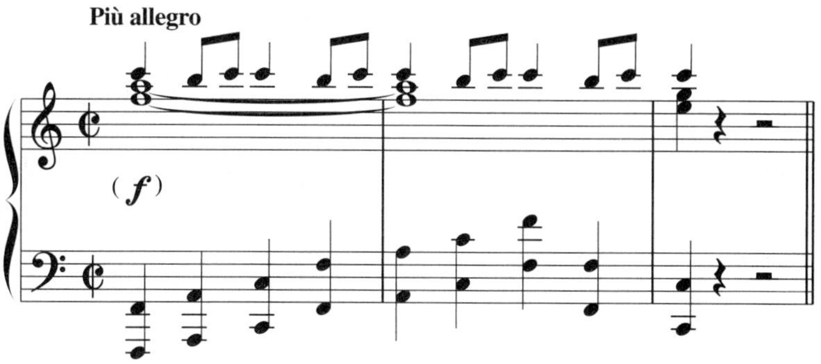

C: IV I

(Continued on the next page)

The plagal cadence is a "final" cadence; it consists of the

progression _______ – _______.

IV–I

7.40 The plagal cadence is the familiar sound of the "Amen" that concludes most religious hymns.

Bourgeois, *"Old Hundredth"*

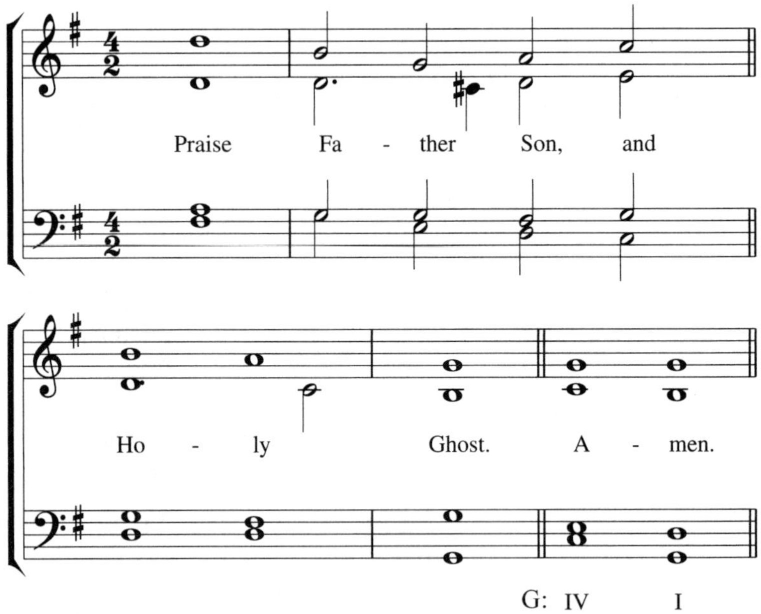

The "Amen" cadence consists of the progression IV–I.

Another name for this cadence is the _____________ cadence.

plagal

7.41 In a manner similar to the "Amen" cadence in the preceding frame, the plagal cadence often appears as an appendage after an authentic cadence. Used in this fashion, the plagal cadence "softens" the effect of the authentic cadence.

I–IV–I

Chopin, *Etude,* Op. 25, No. 8

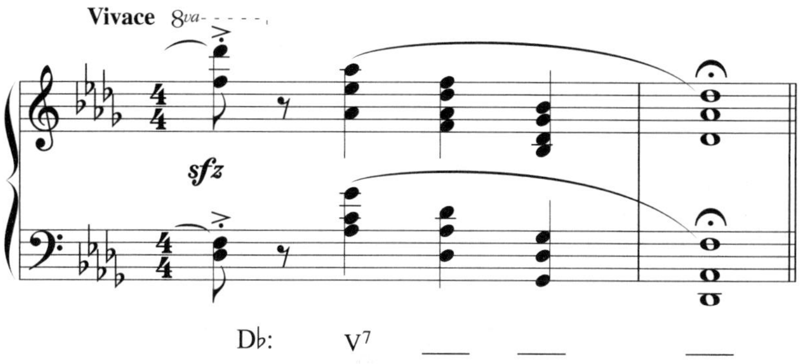

Supply the roman numeral analysis for the final three chords.

---

(3)

7.42 Like authentic cadences, plagal cadences are perfect or imperfect depending upon the degree of finality. A perfect plagal cadence must end with the root of the final tonic chord in the soprano, and both chords (subdominant and tonic) must be in root position.

Which of the cadences below is a *perfect plagal cadence*? _______

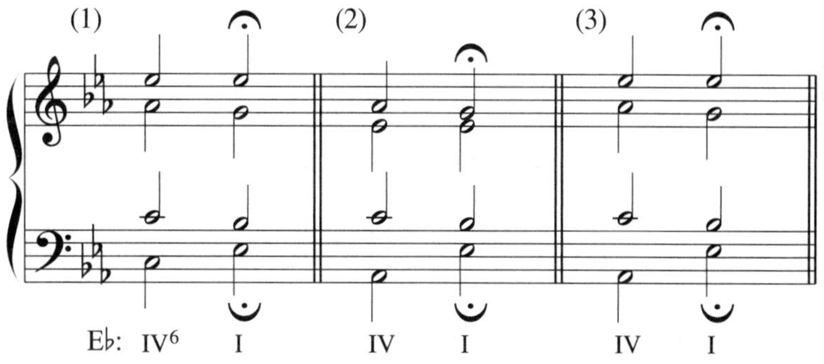

---

(2)

7.43 Which of the cadences below is NOT a *perfect plagal cadence*? _______

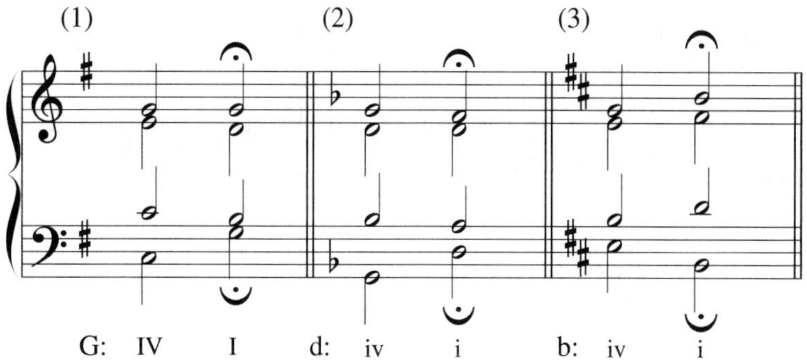

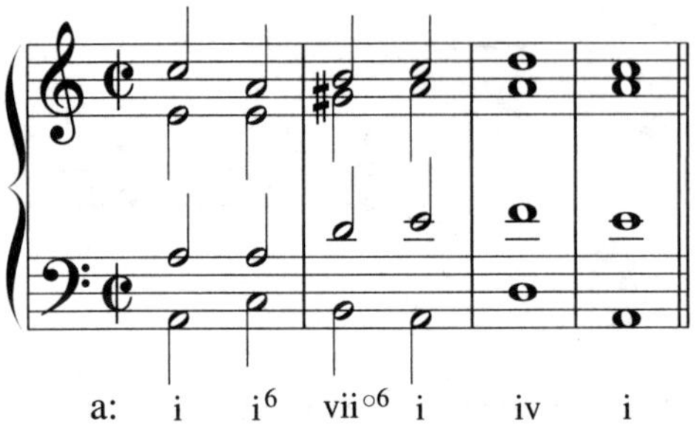

7.44 Write the alto and tenor voices and analyze with roman numerals.

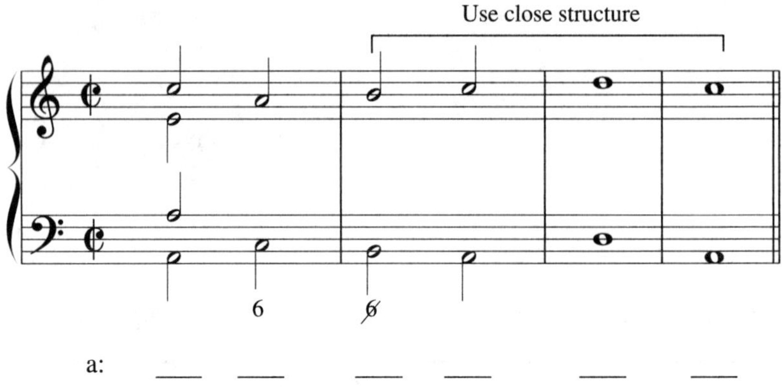

7.45 Write the alto and tenor voices and analyze with roman numerals.

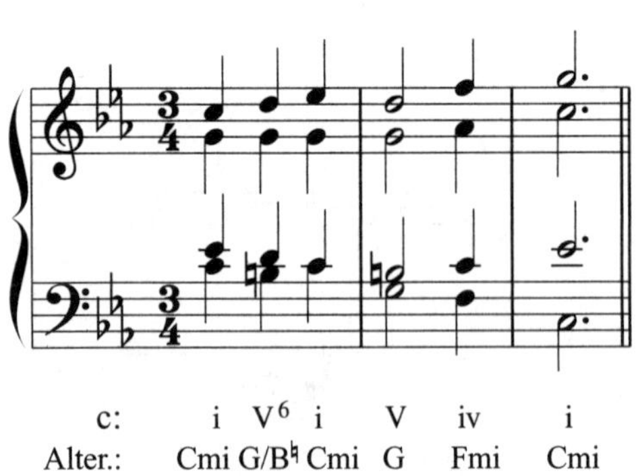

7.46 Write the alto and tenor voices and analyze with roman numerals; also do an alternative analysis.

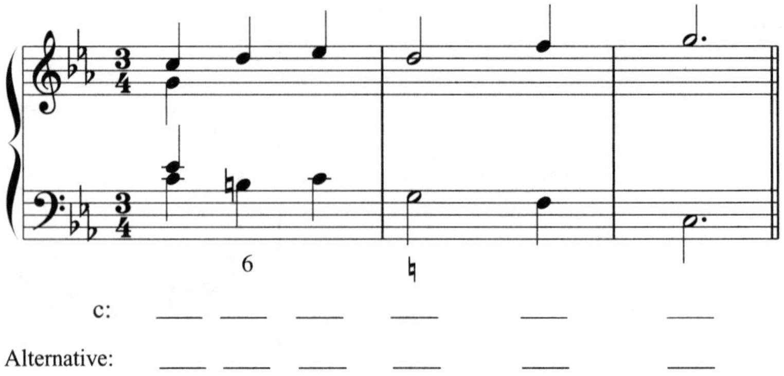

7.47 The cadence in the preceding frame is an imperfect authentic cadence. (True/False) ____________

False
(It is an imperfect plagal cadence.)

7.48 Check (✓) the correct option:

1. Authentic and plagal cadences are final cadences.
2. A composition usually ends with a perfect cadence.

True statements:

(1) _______ (2) _______ Both _______ Neither _______

Both ✓

7.49 Check (✓) the correct option:

1. The progression vii°–I produces an imperfect plagal cadence.
2. Both authentic and plagal cadences may be either perfect or imperfect.

True statements:

(1) _______ (2) _______ Both _______ Neither _______

(2) ✓

Expository Frame

7.50 The two final cadences are *authentic* and *plagal.* These cadences are called *perfect* when the last two chords are in root position and the final tonic chord has the keynote (tonic) in the highest voice. If these two conditions are not met, the effect of finality is weakened and the term *imperfect* is used.

The terms *perfect* and *imperfect* concern final cadences only. In the case of nonfinal cadences (half and deceptive), no terms are used to express the degree of finality.

(No response required.)

7.51 The HALF CADENCE is a nonfinal cadence; it concludes a phrase that is not a complete musical idea in itself and points forward toward yet another phrase.

Schumann, *Album for the Young,* Op. 68, No. 4

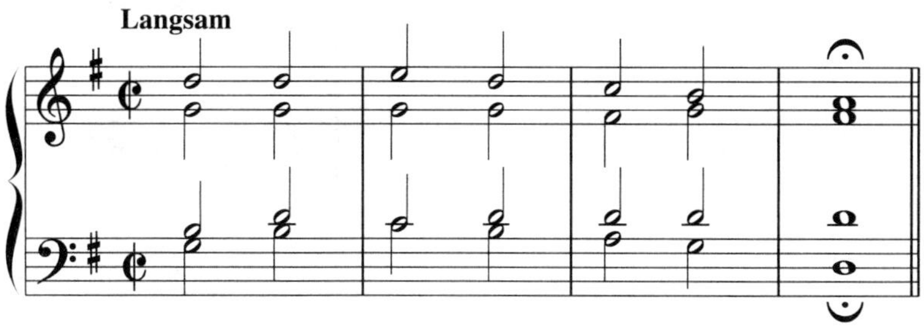

G: I V

(Continued on the next page)

The final chord of a half cadence is usually the dominant.* It may be preceded by the tonic (as shown) or any other chord that provides effective harmonic movement.

The progression ii–V produces a ____________ cadence.

*Half cadences ending on the subdominant triad, while rare, do occur. (See Frame 7.53.)

half

7.52 The cadential six-four often appears as part of a half cadence.

Beethoven, *Sonata,* Op. 49, No. 1

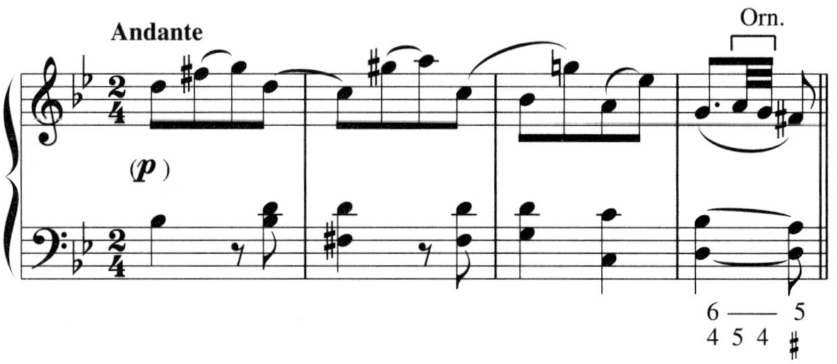

g: i V^6_5 i ___ ___ ___

Supply the roman numeral analysis for the final three chords. *(Be sure the roman numerals accurately reflect the quality of each triad.)*

ii°^{6}–i$^6_4$–V

7.53 The half cadence that ends on the dominant triad is by far the most common type. Half cadences to the subdominant, although rare, provide an interesting effect.

Schumann, *Album for the Young,* Op. 68, No. 4

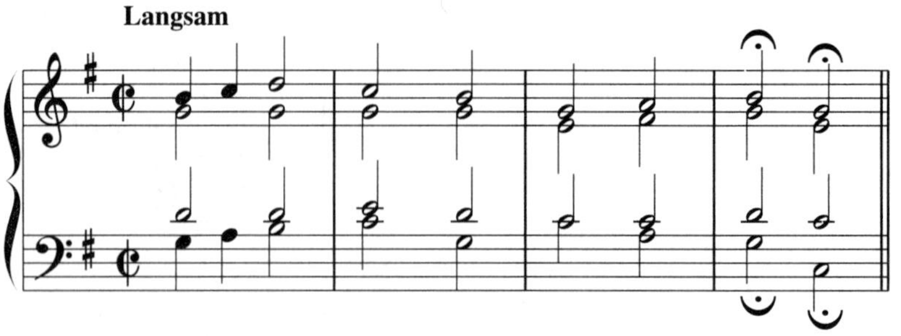

G: I I^6 IV ___ ___ ___ ___ ___

Complete the roman numeral analysis.

I–IV–vii°^{6}–I–IV

Both ✓

7.54 Check (✓) the correct option;

1. The final chord of a half cadence may be IV or V, but V is much more common.
2. The chord preceding the final chord of a half cadence may be any chord that provides effective harmonic movement.

True statements:

(1) _______ (2) _______ Both _______ Neither _______

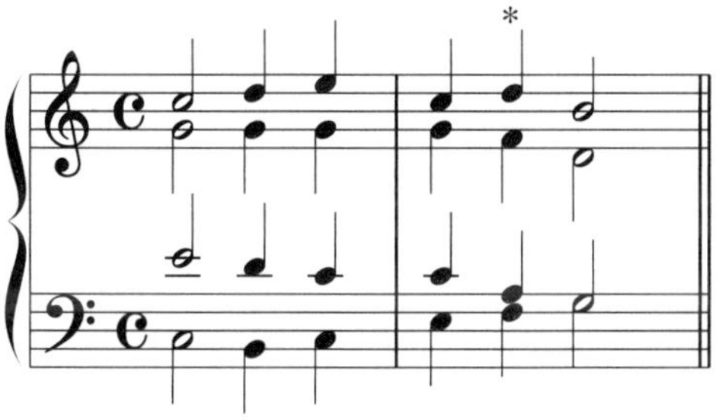

C: I V^6 I I^6 ii^6 V

(The 3rd was doubled at the asterisk to avoid parallel octaves between the soprano and tenor.)

7.55 Write the alto and tenor voices and analyze with roman numerals. *(Irregular doubling is necessary at the asterisk.)*

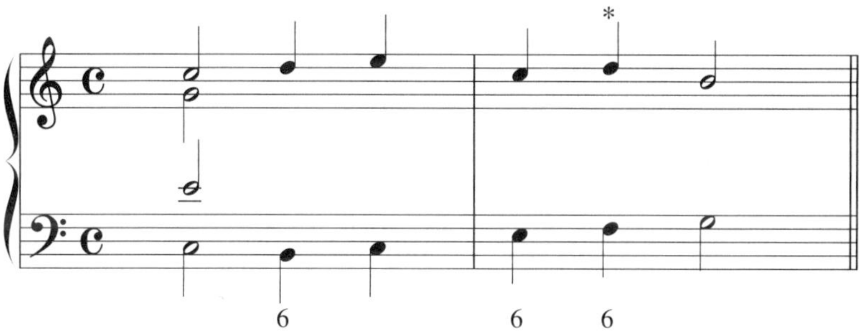

C: ___ ___ ___ ___ ___ ___

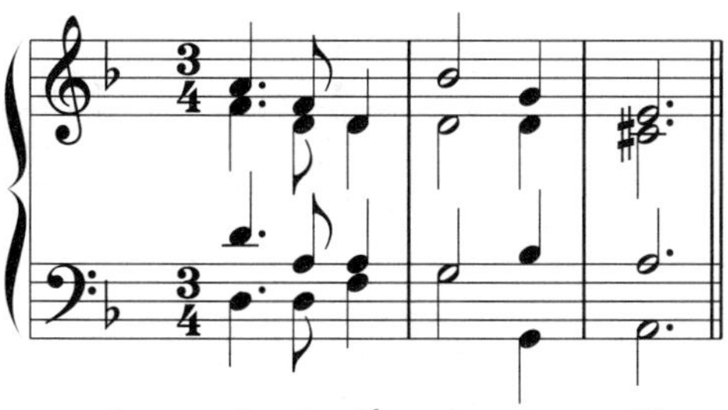

d: i i i^6 iv iv V

7.56 Continue as in the preceding frame. *(The chord at the asterisk should be in open structure. Write all other chords in close structure.)*

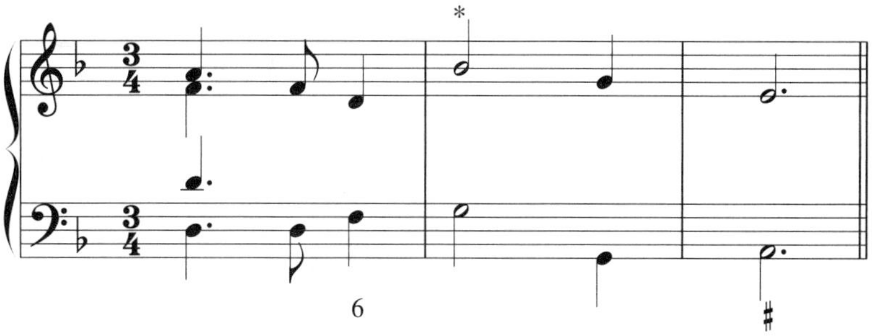

d: ___ ___ ___ ___ ___ ___

G: I vii°6 I6 IV6 I^6_4 V

Alter.: G F♯dim/A G/B C/E G/D D

7.57 Continue as in the preceding frame and also do an alternative analysis.

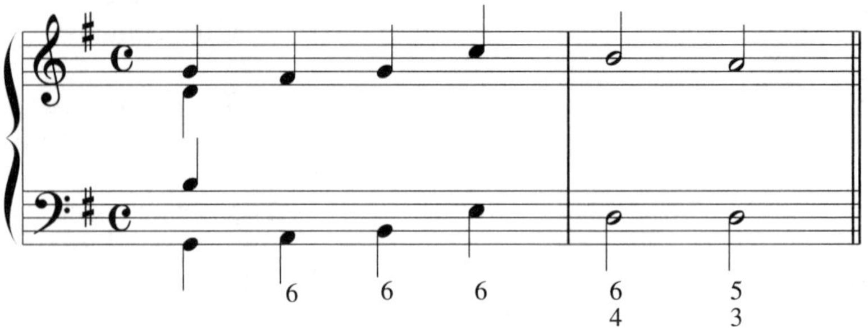

G: ___ ___ ___ ___ ___ ___

Alternative: ___ ___ ___ ___ ___ ___

B♭: I I ii vi IV

7.58 Continue as in the preceding frame.

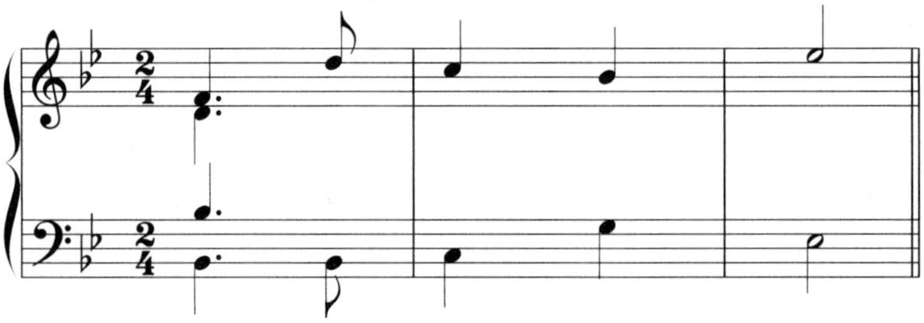

B♭: ___ ___ ___ ___ ___

7.59 A special type of half cadence is shown below; it sometimes is called a PHRYGIAN CADENCE.*

Mendelssohn, Chorale: *Aus tiefer Not schrei' ich zu dir*

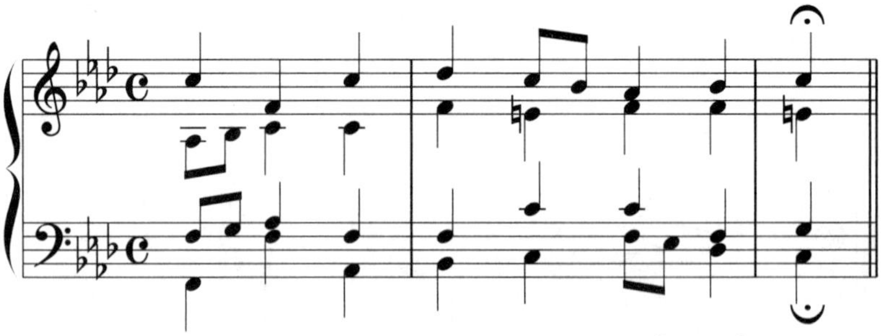

f: iv6 V

*The term Phrygian is applied to the cadence above because it has the same basic structure as the true Phrygian cadence that occurs as vii–I in the Phrygian mode, that is, the half step (between D♭ and C) is similar to the half step found between the first and second scale degrees of this mode. When used in the Phrygian mode, it is a final cadence. Western tonal harmony, however, is devoted so exclusively to major and minor tonalities that it is usually regarded as a type of half cadence.

half

The *Phrygian cadence* is most often a special type of

_____________ cadence.

7.60 The Phrygian cadence consists of the progression iv–V in harmonic minor. There are two ways that it may be written. These are shown below:

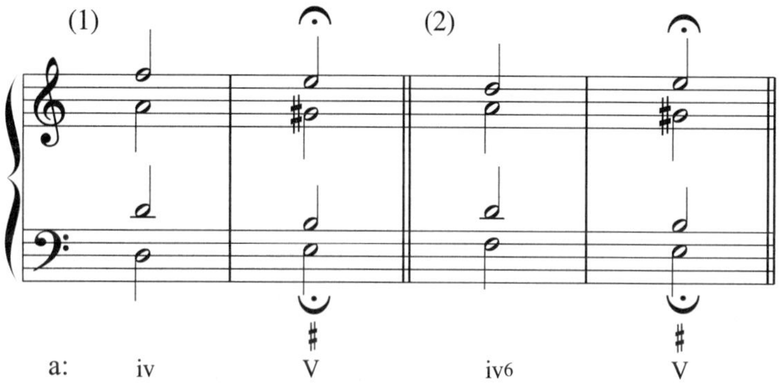

The subdominant chord that precedes the final dominant in a Phrygian cadence may be in either root position or

first

_____________ inversion.

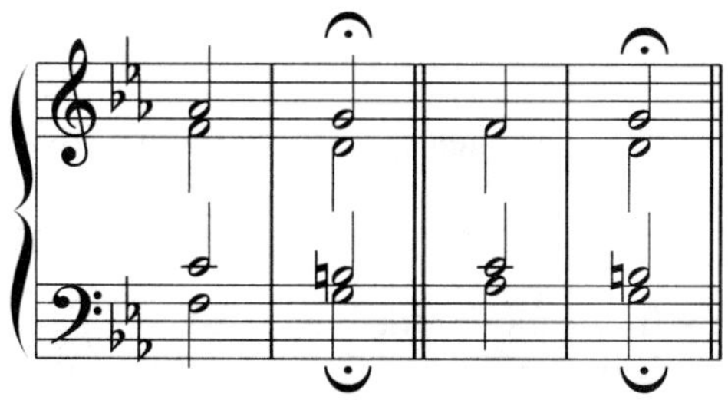

7.61 In the Phrygian cadence the root of the dominant chord is approached by step in contrary motion in the soprano and bass voices.

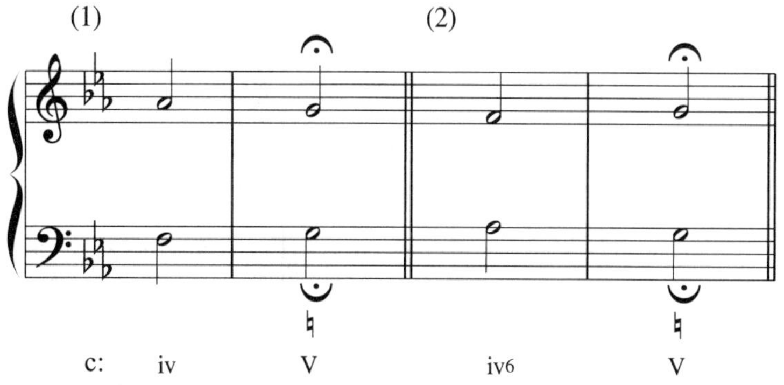

Write the alto and tenor voices for (1) and (2) above.

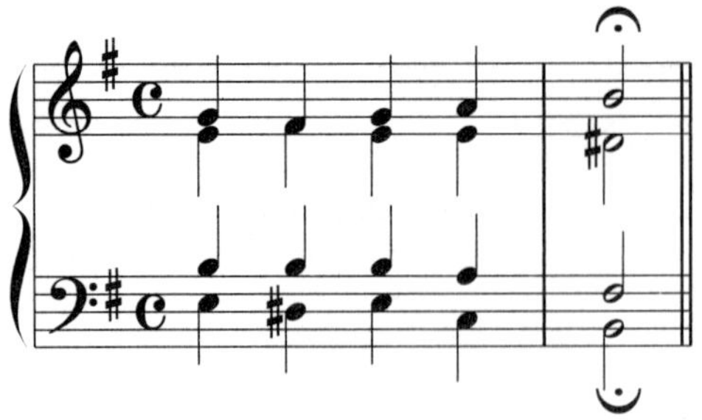

e: i V^6 i iv6 V

7.62 Write the alto and tenor voices and analyze with roman numerals.

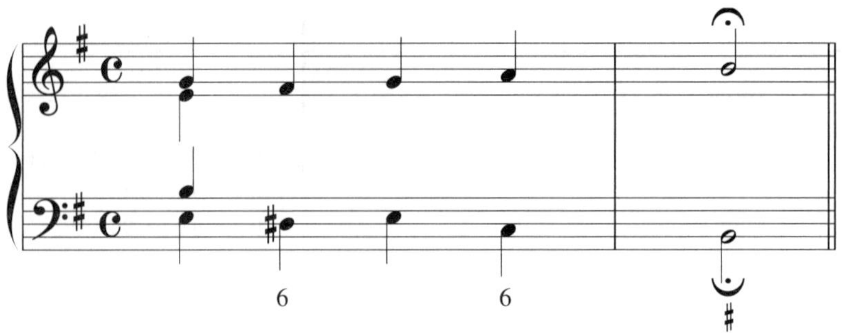

e: ___ ___ ___ ___ ___

Phrygian

7.63 The example in the preceding frame ends with a half cadence, but it is a special type of half cadence. It is a

_____________ cadence.

(1) ii I^6 V I

(2) ii I^6 V vi

7.64 The DECEPTIVE cadence is best understood by referring to the authentic cadence. When another chord is substituted for the final tonic, the expected resolution of the dominant is avoided.

(1) AUTHENTIC

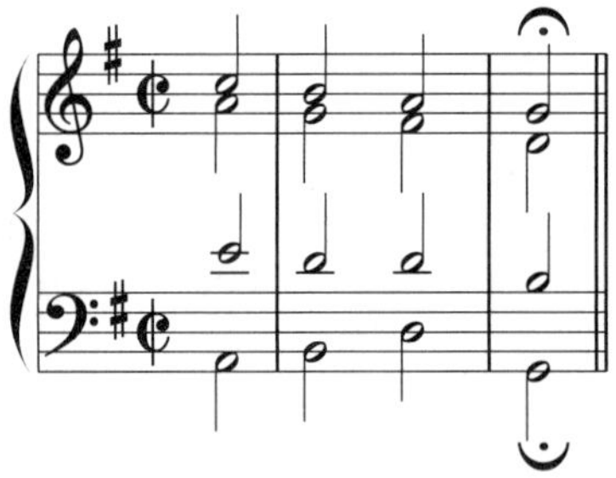

G: ___ ___ ___ ___

(2) DECEPTIVE

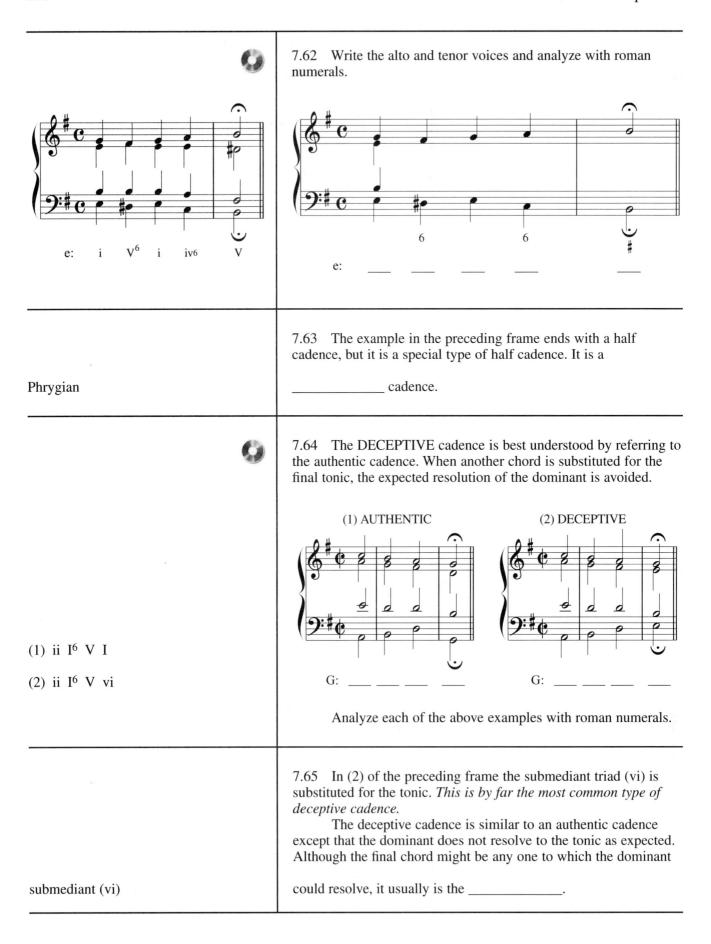

G: ___ ___ ___ ___

Analyze each of the above examples with roman numerals.

submediant (vi)

7.65 In (2) of the preceding frame the submediant triad (vi) is substituted for the tonic. *This is by far the most common type of deceptive cadence.*

The deceptive cadence is similar to an authentic cadence except that the dominant does not resolve to the tonic as expected. Although the final chord might be any one to which the dominant could resolve, it usually is the _____________.

7.66 Composers use the deceptive cadence for variety and to prolong harmonic interest. The deceptive cadence is not a final cadence; several additional chords (or a phrase or two) are required to give a sense of completion following a deceptive cadence.

Play the example below:

Bach, Chorale: *Es ist das Heil uns kommen her*

B♭: ii I^6 V vi

Deceptive

What type of cadence is shown above? _____________

7.67 The deceptive cadence is very effective in a minor key.

Chopin, *Valse Brillante,* Op. 34, No. 2

a: V^7 VI

In a major key the root of the submediant triad is a whole step above the dominant, and the quality of the triad is minor. In a *minor* key the root of the submediant triad is a half step above the

major

dominant, and the quality of the triad is _____________.

7.68 Take care when writing a deceptive cadence in a minor key that an augmented second does not appear in one of the voices.

(Continued on the next page)

Compare the following two examples:

(1) (2)

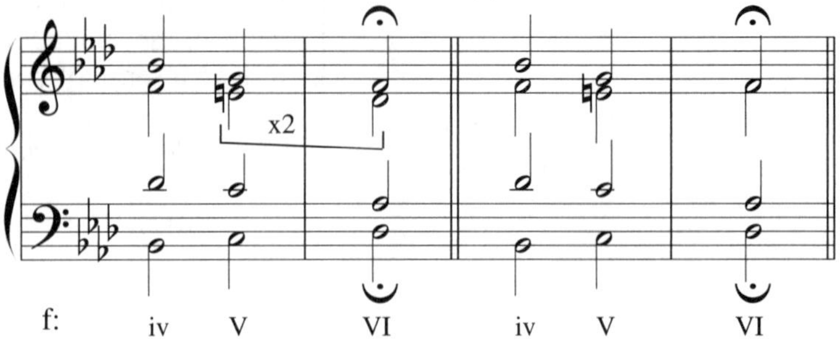

In (1) an undesirable augmented second occurs in the alto. This is corrected in (2) by allowing the alto to double the soprano on the third of the submediant triad. This is the customary way to handle this problem.

In four-part writing the final submediant triad of a deceptive cadence will almost always contain a doubled ______________.

third

7.69 Write the alto and tenor voices and analyze with roman numerals.

(Write all chords in close structure except for the final chord that must contain irregular doubling.)

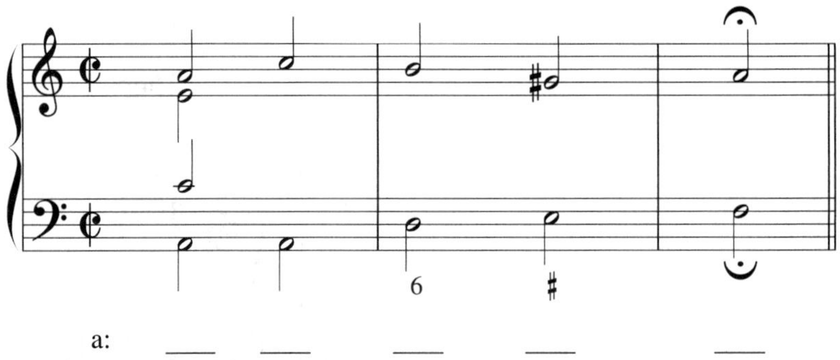

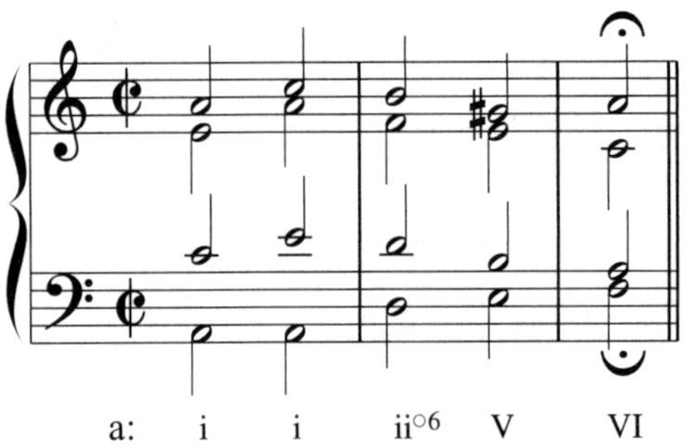

7.70 Write the alto and tenor voices and analyze with roman numerals.

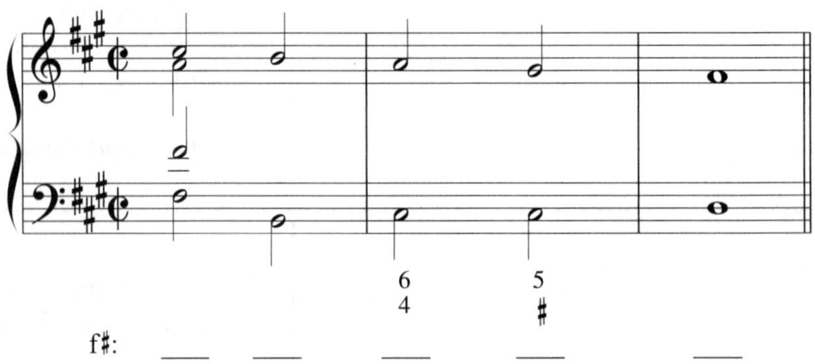

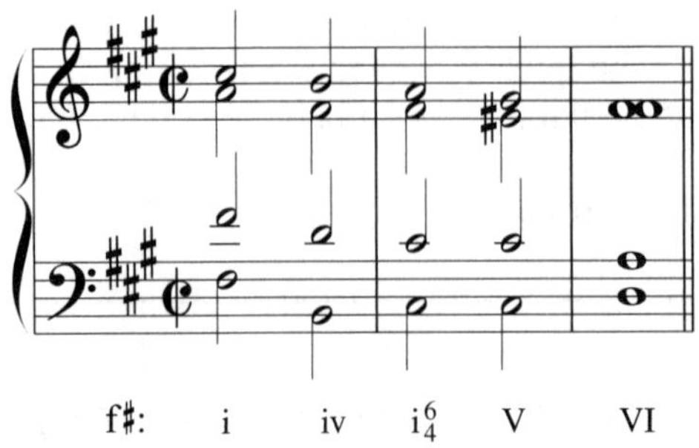

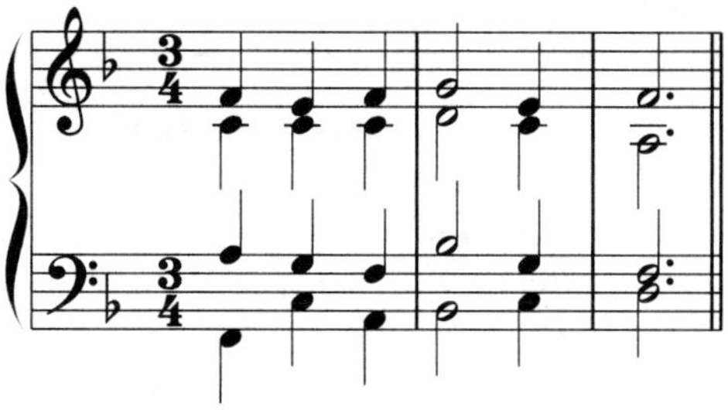

F: I V I^6 ii^6 V vi

7.71 Continue as in the preceding frame.
(The chords at the asterisks should contain doubled thirds.)

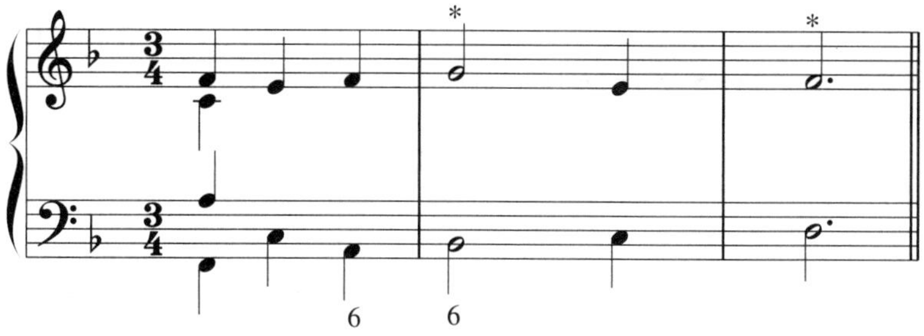

F: ___ ___ ___ ___ ___ ___

D: I I^6 IV I^6_4 V vi
Alter.: D D/F♯ G D/A A Bmi

7.72 Continue as in the preceding frame and also do an alternative analysis.

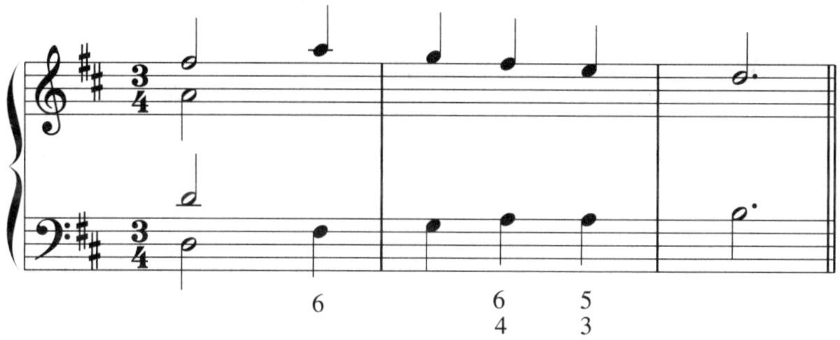

D: ___ ___ ___ ___ ___ ___
Alternative: ___ ___ ___ ___ ___ ___

7.73 To provide an extra element of surprise the submediant chord, which would normally appear in minor, sometimes is used in a major key (See chord at asterisk).

Schubert, *Symphony No. 5 in B♭Major*

Andante con moto

E♭: I^6_4 V^7 VI

The borrowing of a chord from a minor mode for use in its parallel major is discussed in Part II, Chapter 5.0: BORROWED CHORDS. The example above is presented here as it illustrates a common type of deceptive cadence.

(Continued on the next page)

deceptive

The element of surprise is an important feature of the _____________ cadence.

*The terms *modal exchange* or *change of mode* might be used by some writers, rather than *borrowed chord,* to describe this example.

A: I iii ii I^6 V VI

7.74 Write the alto and tenor voices and analyze with roman numerals.

(Watch for parallel fifths between the second and third chords. Remember, also, to double the final chord as if it were in the key of a minor.)

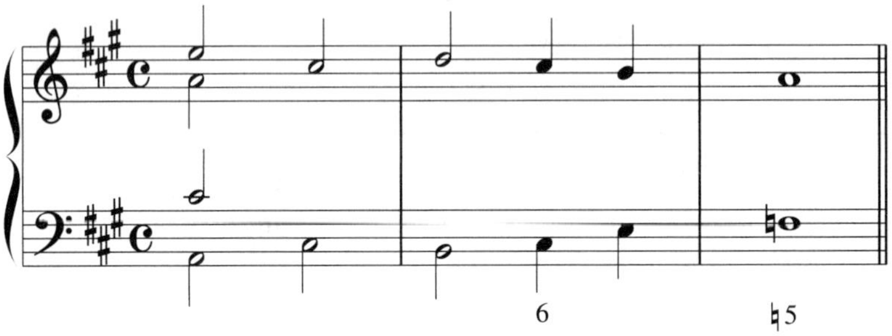

A: ___ ___ ___ ___ ___ ___

If you chose:

(a) go to Frame 7.76

(b) go to Frame 7.77

(c) go to Frame 7.78

7.75 Which of the choices, (a), (b), or (c), produces a correctly written *deceptive* cadence? _____________

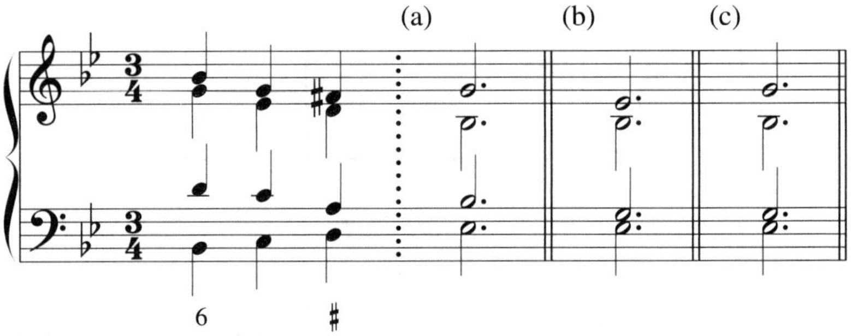

(*No response required.*)

Expository Frame

7.76 Choice (a) results in a chord that has incorrect doubling (there are two fifths). In addition, there are parallel fifths between the bass and tenor voices.

Return to Frame 7.75 and try again.

(*No response required.*)

Expository Frame

7.77 This choice (b) results in normal doubling for a minor triad in root position, but there is an augmented second in the soprano voice (F♯–E♭). This interval should be avoided.

Return to Frame 7.75 and try again.

augmented second

7.78 The correct choice has been made. The third of the submediant triad must be doubled in the deceptive cadence in a minor key. This is to avoid the melodic use of an undesirable interval. What is this interval? The ______________________

If you chose:

(a) go to Frame 7.80

(b) go to Frame 7.81

(c) go to Frame 7.82

7.79 Which of the choices, (a), (b), or (c), produces a correctly written *imperfect authentic* cadence? ____________

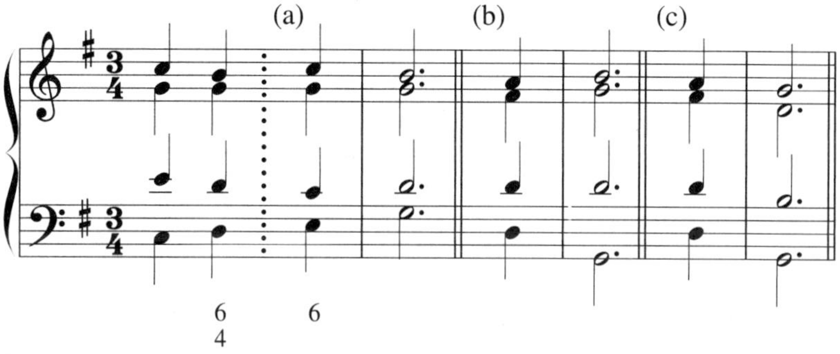

(No response required.)

7.80 Choice (a) results in an imperfect *plagal* cadence.

Return to Frame 7.79 and find the imperfect authentic cadence.

The third of the final chord is in the soprano.
(Or equivalent.)

7.81 The correct choice has been made. What makes this an *imperfect* cadence? ______________________________

____

(Skip to Frame 7.83.)

(No response required.)

7.82 Choice (c) results in a *perfect* authentic cadence.

Review Frame 7.18 then return to Frame 7.79 and try again.

---

(1) Half

(2) Deceptive

7.83 The authentic and plagal cadences are "final" cadences. Name the two "non-final" cadences.

(1) ____________

(2) ____________

Summary

One of the basic formal units of music is the phrase. The phrase is a segment of music that can be assimilated comfortably by the listener. The melodic aspect of a phrase is traced by the successive pitches. Raising pitches tend to create tension; falling pitches tend to relax tension.

Most melodic phrases are based on one of four contours; a fifth contour is a combination of the third and fourth. The basic contours are:

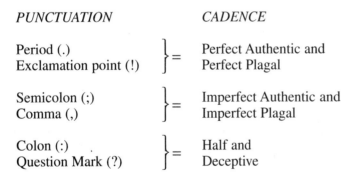

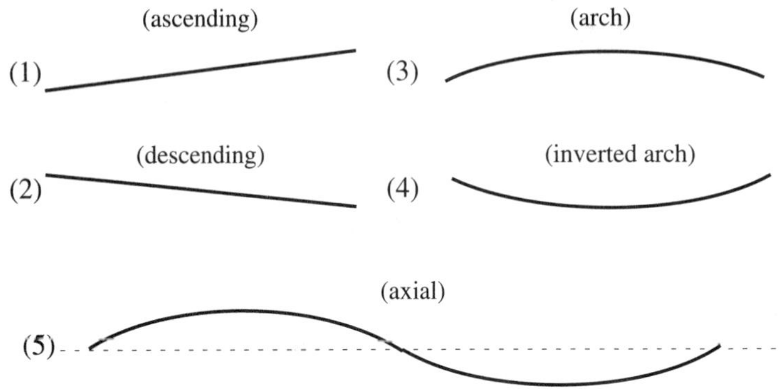

Cadences serve to punctuate the phrases that unite to build larger formal units. The four types of cadences (authentic, plagal, half, and deceptive) provide a very limited repertoire of punctuations. This is one reason why Western art music and really all tonal music in general is easy for the listener to apprehend. Not only is the expressive significance of each cadence type clear, but tonal implications usually are unambiguous. Thus, frequent tonal orientations are provided the listener, and these orientations lend assurance that the path through tonal thickets is not lost.

It is useful to compare cadences with the punctuation marks used in writing.

PUNCTUATION		*CADENCE*
Period (.) Exclamation point (!)	} =	Perfect Authentic and Perfect Plagal
Semicolon (;) Comma (,)	} =	Imperfect Authentic and Imperfect Plagal
Colon (:) Question Mark (?)	} =	Half and Deceptive

Of course, this list must be regarded as being merely suggestive. Musical expression is far too subtle to be neatly pinned down in this fashion, and the analogy between music and language should not be pressed too hard. On the other hand, a sensitivity to the functions of the various types of cadences can be acquired, and personal references—similar to the ones above—might be useful and could be applied to any musical situation.

The terms that are explained in this chapter are listed below in chronological order:

phrase	final cadences:	perfect (cadence)
melodic contour	authentic	imperfect (cadence)
cadence	plagal	Picardy third
ascending line	nonfinal cadences:	cadential six-four
descending line	half	Phrygian cadence
	deceptive	borrowing

Mastery Frames

(1) Deceptive (2) Plagal (3) Authentic (4) Half (7.14)	7–1 Identify the type of cadence represented by the roman numerals. (1) V–vi ______ (2) IV–I ______ (3) V or vii°–I ______ (4) I, IV or ii–V ______
(2) Plagal (and) (3) Authentic (7.13)	7–2 List the cadences in the preceding frame that are final cadences. ______ and ______.
(1) Authentic (2) Plagal (1) e: iv V i (2) B♭: IV I (7.15–.50)	7–3 Name each of the cadences in the example below and analyze: (1) ______ (2) ______ 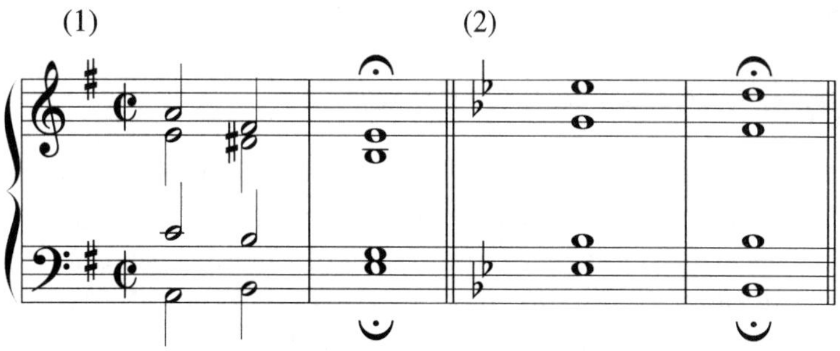 (1) e: ___ ___ ___ (2) B♭: ___ ___
(2) (7.17–.22)	7–4 Which example in the preceding frame shows an imperfect cadence? ______

(1) Deceptive

(2) Half (or Phrygian)

(1) A: ii^6 V vi

(2) d: i iv^6 V

(7.51–.74)

7–5 Name each of the cadences below and analyze:

(1) ________________

(2) ________________

(1) (2)

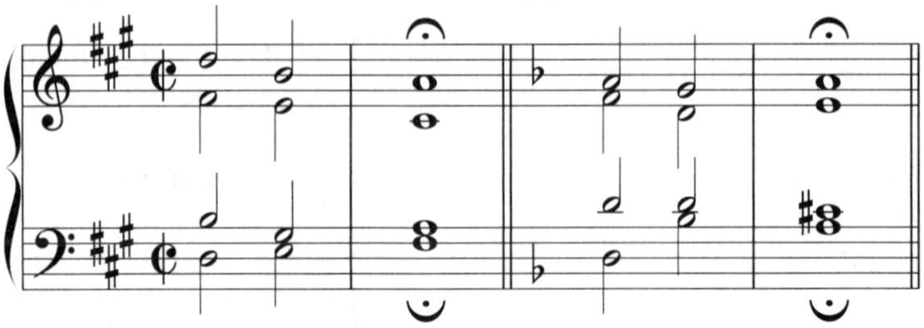

(1) A: ___ ___ ___ (2) d: ___ ___ ___

a: ii°^{6} i$^6_4$ V I

(7.23–.29)

7–6 Change the final chord in the example below to show the use of a Picardy third and analyze:

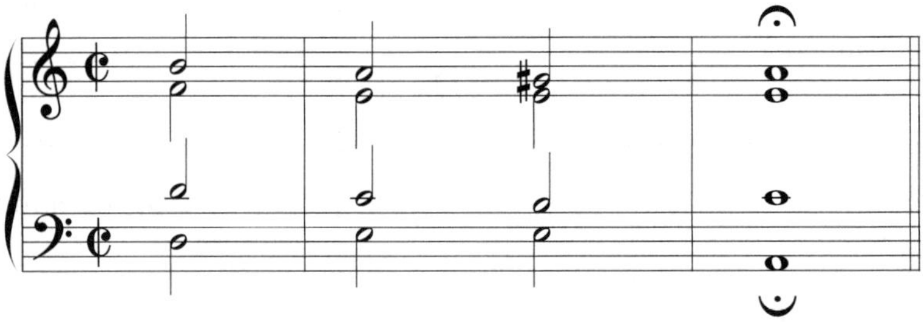

a: ___ ___ ___ ___

Supplementary Activities

1. Explore the topic of the cadence, or particular type of cadence, in an essay or short report. Consider how the cadence has evolved from earlier times (medieval or renaissance) to the present day in the context of as many different types of music wished to be included. Is the cadence a common factor in all musics? Why or why not? A second topic to explore in detail is the phrase and what defines a phrase in different types of music; are there commonalities or differences?
2. Try to expand ear-training practice and general listening to now include perception of the phrase construction and the cadence and the relationships that can be observed between the two. What commonalities and differences can be observed as this is being done? Can different types of cadences be accurately heard?
3. Continue to develop and expand your compositional abilities by creating original phrases and cadences, or expand upon the exercises found in the following Supplementary Assignments.
4. Continue to explore via essay or listening the composers presented in the chapter. Listen to the complete composition from which an excerpt is taken, or to another piece in the same genre, to develop abilities in relating the vocabulary and information of this chapter to actual musical circumstances.

Supplementary Assignments

ASSIGNMENT 7–1 Name ______________________________

1. Compose single line melodies (four to eight measures long) that illustrate the specified melodic contours. Choose your own keys and meters. Indicate tempo, dynamics, and phrasing. Each melody should be analyzed.

(1) Ascending 

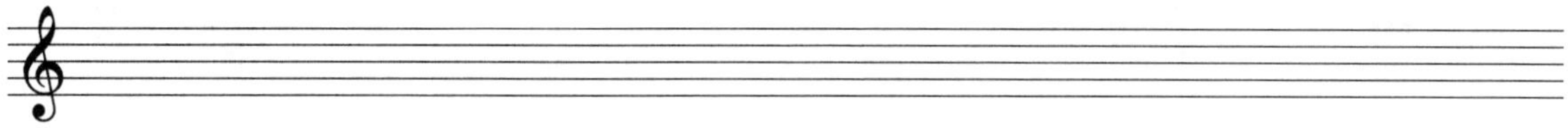

(2) Descending 

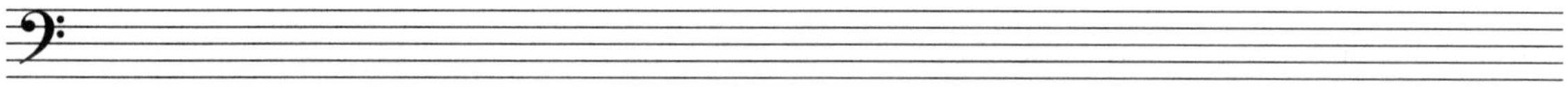

(3) Arch 

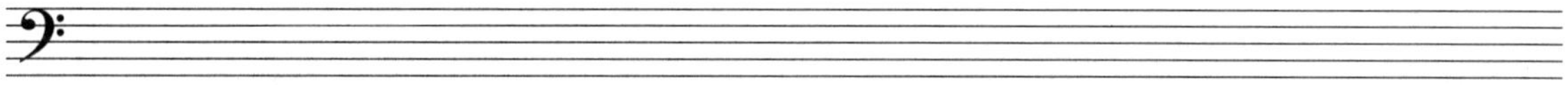

(4) Inverted arch 

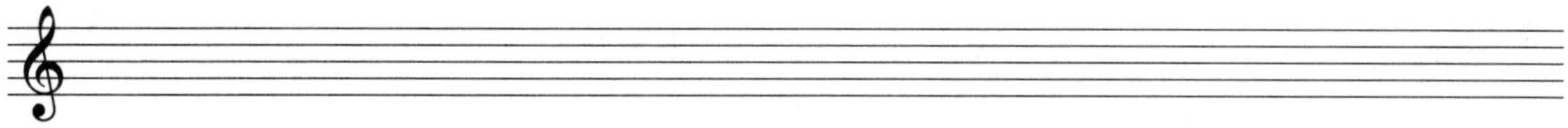

(5) Axial 

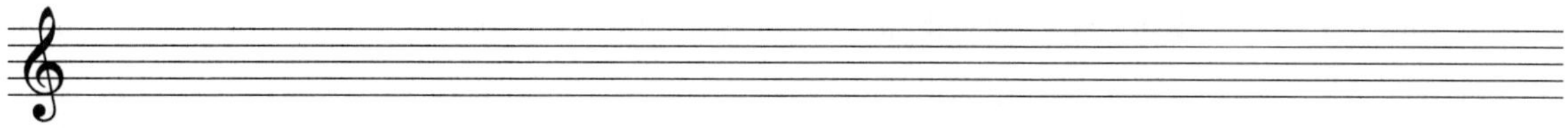

2. Compose other melodies with your own specifications and analyze them.

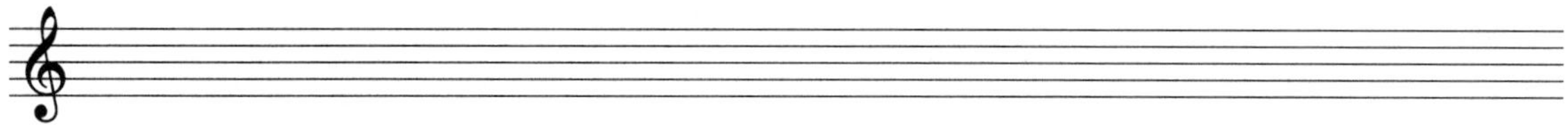

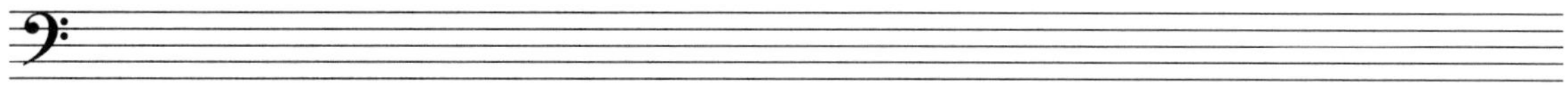

3. Identify these cadences as final or nonfinal:

Half ______________

Authentic ______________

Deceptive ______________

Plagal ______________

4. Identify the cadences below and analyze:

(1) ______________ (2) ______________ (3) ______________ (4) ______________

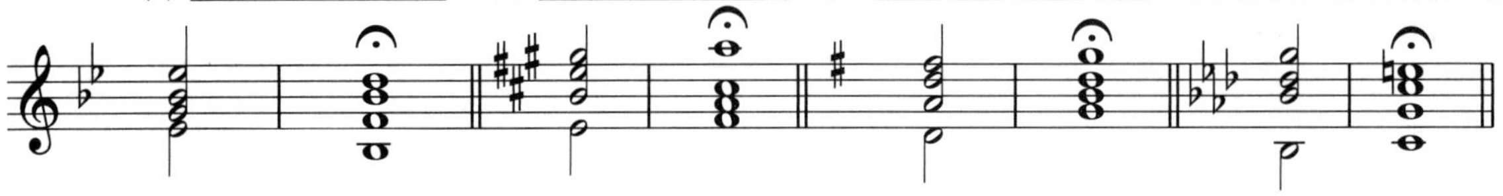

B♭: ___ ___ A: ___ ___ G: ___ ___ f: ___ ___

5. The cadence produced by the chords iv–V (in minor) is called a ______________________________ cadence.

6. Identify the four cadences below and supply roman numerals according to keys specified:

(1) ____________________________ (3) ____________________________

(2) ____________________________ (4) ____________________________

(1) (2) (3) (4)

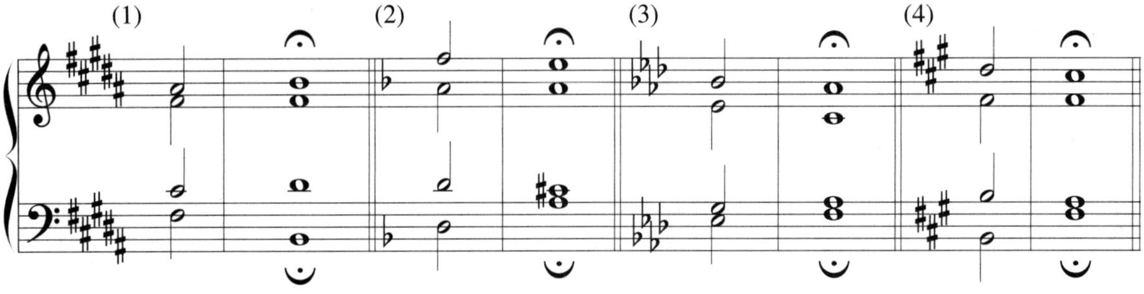

B: ___ ___ d: ___ ___ A♭: ___ ___ f♯: ___ ___

7. Compose and part write other examples of cadences with your own specifications and analyze them.

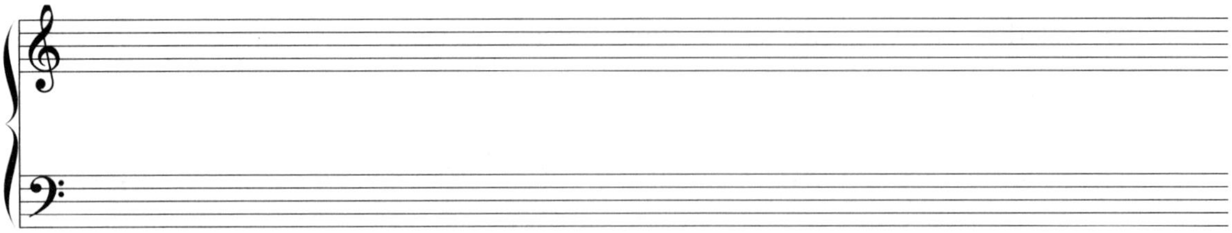

ASSIGNMENT 7–2 Name ______________________________

1. Identify the cadences as either perfect or imperfect.

(1) ______________ (2) ______________

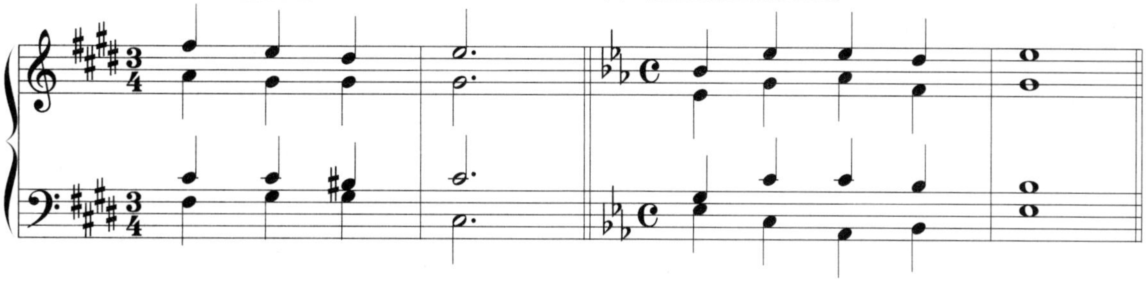

c♯: E♭:

Beethoven, *Symphony No. 8,* Op. 93

(3) ______________________ (4) ______________

D: F:

2. Which example shows a Phrygian cadence? ______________________________

(1) (2) (3)

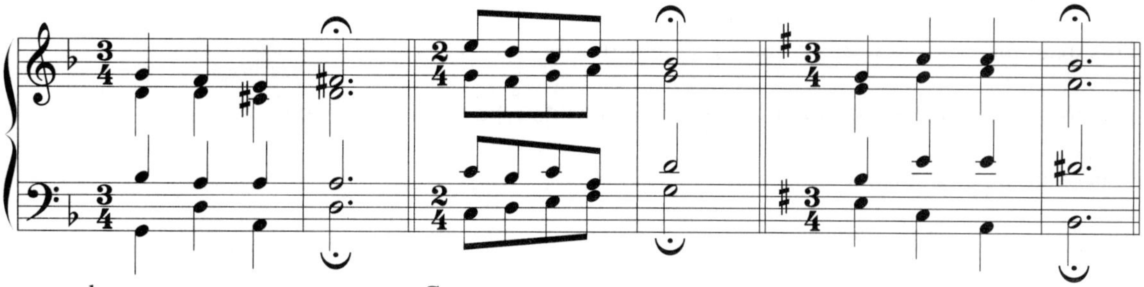

d: C: e:

3. Compose two four-measure phrases based on the harmonic progression below. Write for the piano in homophonic texture. Refer to Appendix B, *Piano Styles.* (For this assignment, style 6 through 9 are recommended; use style 13 if you have more experience with piano.)

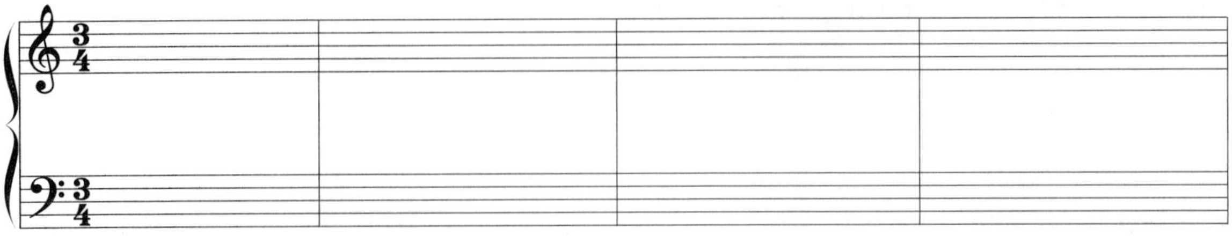

C: I I^6 ii^6 V

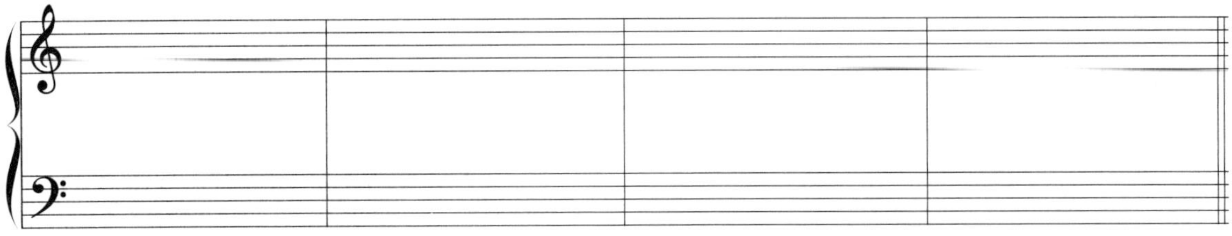

vi IV I^6_4 V I

4. Compose two or more phrases of your own specification on your own staff paper. Write either for the piano or for instruments. Feel free to choose any musical style. Analyze what is composed. Try working from a chord progression you devise, or the reverse—phrase (melody) first, then chords that might be used with it.

5. Answer the questions regarding the example below.

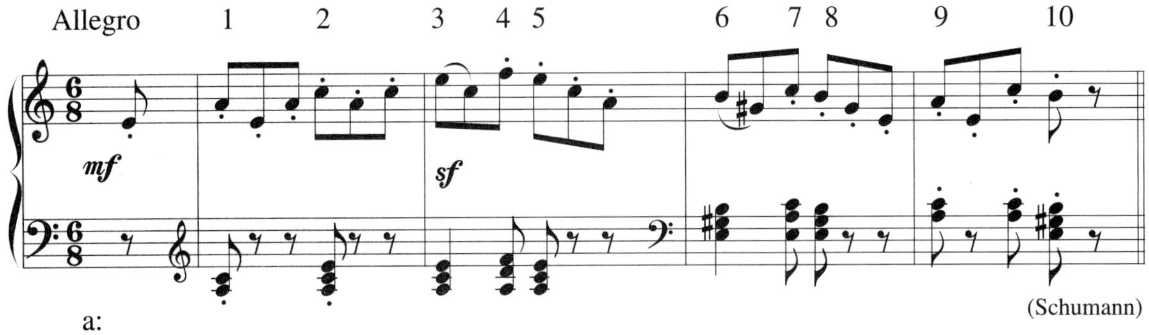

(1) This example consists of only triads in either root position or second inversion. (True/False) ________

(2) The chords that are in second inversion are all of one type. Identify this type. ________________

(3) This example ends with a ____ cadence.

(4) Which form of the minor scale is used in the example? ______________________________

Chapter 8.0
Nonharmonic Tones

The tones of a musical composition belong to one of two groups: *harmonic tones*—those that constitute chords; and *nonharmonic tones*—those that are extraneous to the harmony. If all tones were harmonic, music would be excessively consonant. Although not all nonharmonic tones are dissonant, most are, and their usage or reason stems from the dissonant tensions they produce. Nonharmonic tones also contribute to smoother melodic lines and greater rhythmic animation.

8.1 Most music contains many tones that are not included in the harmony. These are called NONHARMONIC TONES.

Since the note C is not part of the chord that is sounding at the moment it appears, it is called a ____________ tone.

nonharmonic

8.2 Whether or not a note is called a nonharmonic tone sometimes depends upon the analysis. *Not all nonharmonic tones are dissonant.*

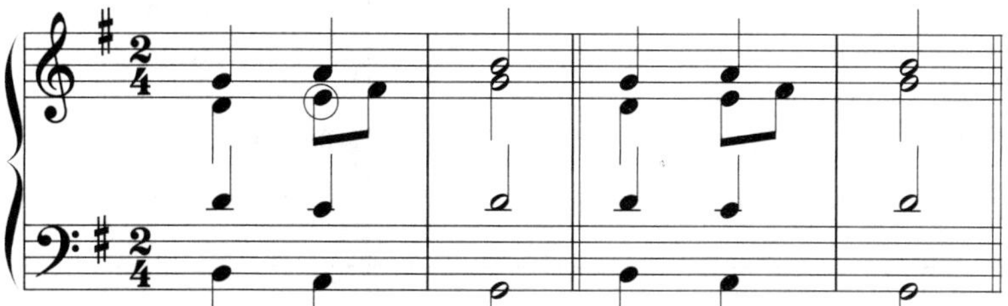

(Continued on the next page)

In (1) the note E is called a nonharmonic tone because it is not part of the harmony as it is analyzed. In (2), however, two chords (ii and vii$^{\circ 6}$) are analyzed on the second beat; this causes both the E and F♯ to be included in the harmony.

Any tone that is not part of the harmony as it is analyzed is called a nonharmonic tone. (True/False) _____________

True

8.3 Nonharmonic tones originate in the melodic and rhythmic aspects of music. Melodies often contain a greater number of notes than can be accommodated by the harmony. Occasionally very rapid harmonic rhythm is used to harmonize each note of a melody, but such practice becomes tiresome if carried on too long.

Schumann, *Symphonic Studies,* Op. 13

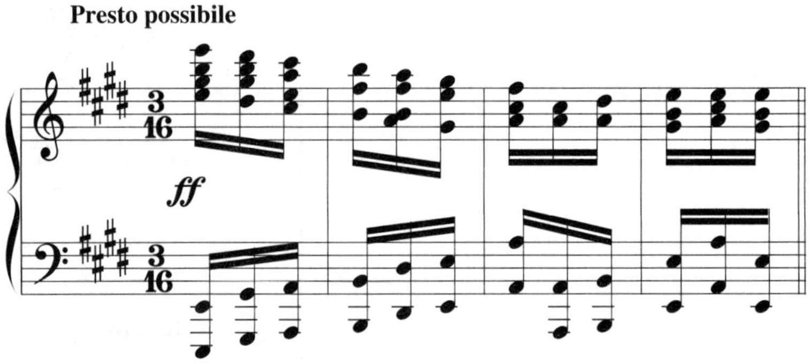

All of the notes in the above example are included in the harmony; thus, in spite of very rapid melodic movement, there are no nonharmonic tones.

Rapid harmonic rhythm tends to reduce the number of nonharmonic tones. (True/False) _____________

True

8.4 The harmonic rhythm of the following example is much slower than that shown in the preceding frame. The circled notes are not included in the harmony.

Beethoven, *Sonata for Violin and Piano*

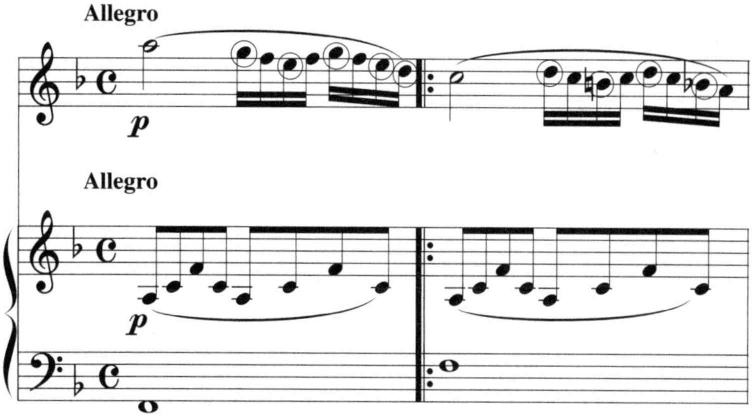

F: I

vi ii

Music that has slow harmonic rhythm tends to contain (few/many) ____________ nonharmonic tones; however, musical examples can also be found with slow harmonic rhythm and many harmonic-only tones.

many

8.5 Nonharmonic tones contribute to the smoothness of the melodic lines by reducing the number of leaps. They also increase the rhythmic activity. By staggering rhythmic activity in each of the voices, greater individuality results.

Each voice has little individuality in the example below as the rhythm is the same for each.

Bach, Chorale: *Ach Gott, wie manches Herzeleid* (altered)

(Continued on the next page)

No	Are there any nonharmonic tones in the above example? _______
nonharmonic	8.6 Compare the example below with that in the preceding frame. Bach, Chorale: *Ach Gott, wie manches Herzeleid* 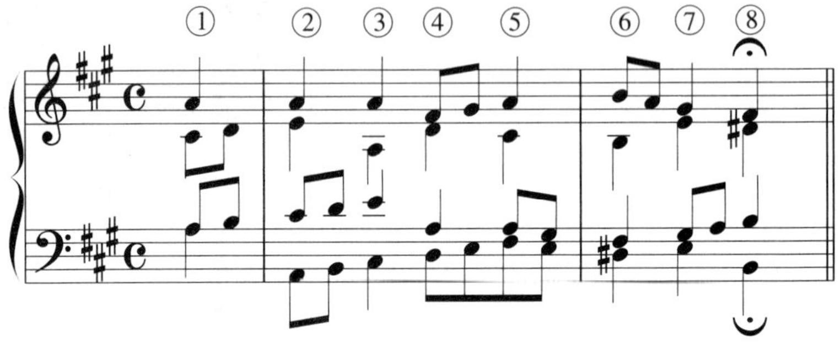 The example above (with nonharmonic tones) suggests that it is much more interesting than the version in the preceding frame. Each voice receives greater individuality through the use of ____________ tones.
No *(Melodies without leaps are monotonous and quite rare.)*	8.7 In addition to greater individuality through rhythmic activity, each voice (Frame 8.6) is a better melodic line. Nonharmonic tones reduce the number of leaps and give the music a more "flowing" quality. Is it desirable for melodic lines to be entirely free of leaps? _______
(No response required.)	*Expository Frame* 8.8 The use of nonharmonic tones often causes irregularities of doubling or in the distribution of the voices. Refer again to Frame 8.5. In the third chord the alto is below the tenor. There would be no reason to cross the voices in this fashion if no nonharmonic tones were employed. Frame 8.6, however, shows why this is desirable. The momentum of the ascending scale line in the tenor carries it up to the note E, and the alto drops down to A to improve the sonority of the chord. Normal distribution of the voices is resumed in the fourth chord. In order to produce expressive melodic lines in each of the voices, irregularities of doubling or an occasional crossing of the voices is tolerated.

1, 5, (and) 7	8.9 In the example of Frame 8.6 there are three chords that contain irregular doubling. Indicate these chords (by number). _______, _______, and _______.
nonharmonic	8.10 In chord 1 (Frame 8.6) there are three roots and one third, but no fifth; chord 5 is in root position, so it would be normal to double the bass rather than the soprano as has been done here; chord 7 has two roots and two thirds, but no fifth. All of these irregularities result from the desire to write more expressive melodic lines through the use of _____________ tones.
(No response required.)	*Expository Frame* 8.11 While the use of nonharmonic tones permits greater freedom of part writing, not all of the "rules" are thrown to the wind. Nonharmonic tones normally do not justify the use of parallel fifths or octaves, nor is it desirable to double active tones (the leading tone, in particular). In fact, it will be found that nonharmonic tones added to part writing that otherwise is correct often produce incorrect parallel motion, so checking more carefully than ever for such error is a "must do."
(2) ✓	8.12 Check (✓) the correct option: 1. Nonharmonic tones must be analyzed as part of the harmony. 2. Nonharmonic tones give rhythmic interest to the voices. True statements. (1) _______ (2) _______ Both _______ Neither _______
Both ✓	8.13 Check (✓) the correct option: 1. Nonharmonic tones often cause irregularities of doubling. 2. A tone that is not part of the harmony as analyzed is a nonharmonic tone. True statements. (1) _______ (2) _______ Both _______ Neither _______

Expository Frame

8.14 There are several kinds of nonharmonic tones and the remainder of this chapter is devoted to naming them and learning to write them correctly. Unfortunately the terminology of nonharmonic tones is not standardized. Writers in the field of music theory often use different terms for the same device, or use the same term in conflicting ways. Even the term "nonharmonic tone" is not universal. Other terms are *accessory tone, bytone, nonchord tone,* and *foreign tone.*

Actually, the name given to a particular nonharmonic tone is of little importance as long as its musical significance and correct interpretation are appreciated. Labels given to musical events are not an end in themselves; they make verbalization possible. Although standardization of terminology would be desirable, and communication greatly facilitated, the fact remains that we must accommodate ourselves to different sets of terms when comparing the writing of various authors. This is not difficult once an understanding of a particular device has been acquired.

Nonharmonic tones are usually classified according to the way they are approached and left. Further classification is made with reference to rhythmic placement.

(No response required.)

8.15 A nonharmonic tone that is approached and left by step in the same direction is called a PASSING TONE (symbol: PT).

Schumann, *Album for the Young,* Op. 68, No. 11

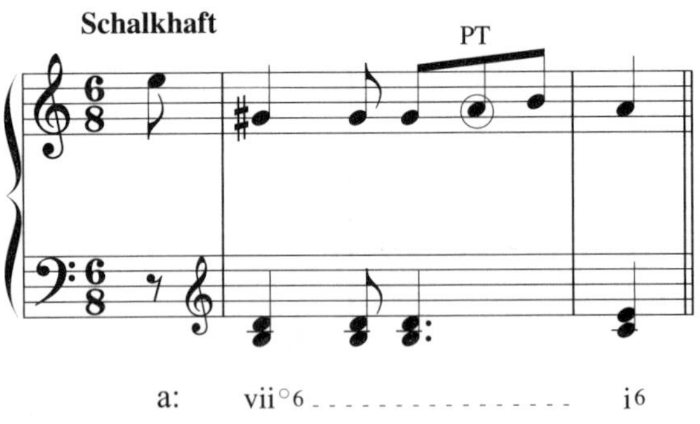

Since the circled note (A) is not part of the harmony, it must be analyzed as a nonharmonic tone. It is called a passing tone

because it is approached and left by ______________ in the same direction.

step

8.16 Passing tones may occur in either ascending or descending direction, and two or more may occur simultaneously.

In the following example there are nine passing tones; draw a circle around each. *(Refer to the roman numeral analysis to identify the notes that are not part of the harmony.)*

Bach, Chorale: *Allein, zu dir, Herr Jesu Christ*

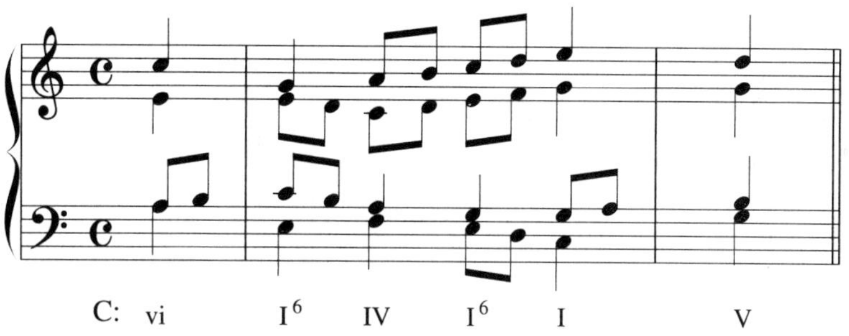

direction

8.17 Notice in the preceding frame that when two or more passing tones occur simultaneously they produce consonant intervals with each other.

Passing tones may occur singly or in groups of two or more. All passing tones are approached and left by step in the same

_____________.

(No response required.)

Expository Frame

8.18 Figured bass symbols are used to indicate melodic movement over a single bass note.

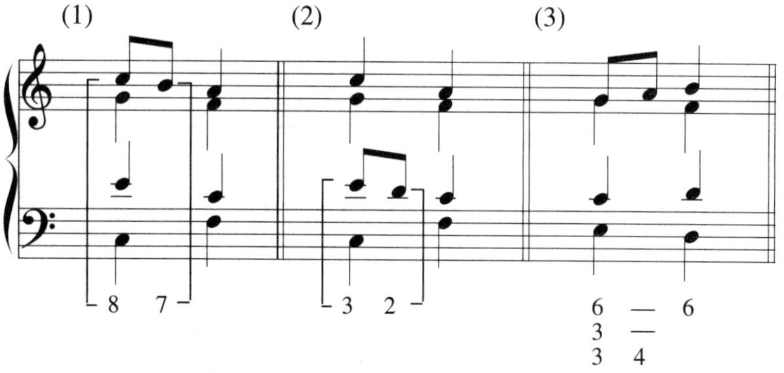

In (1) the numbers 8 7 refer to the notes C and B that occur over the bass note C; in (2) the numbers 3 2 list the intervals between the bass and tenor (the actual intervals of a tenth and ninth are reduced to avoid the use of unnecessarily large numbers); the figuration in (3) is more complete to show the doubled third above the bass and the melodic movement in the soprano.

Numbers in the figured bass that occur *horizontally* beneath a single bass note indicate melodic movement in one of the upper voices.

8.19 Refer again to (3) in the preceding frame. Note that the dashes that follow the numbers 6 and 3 show that the notes indicated by these figures are held while melodic movement occurs in another voice.

Write the alto and tenor voices.

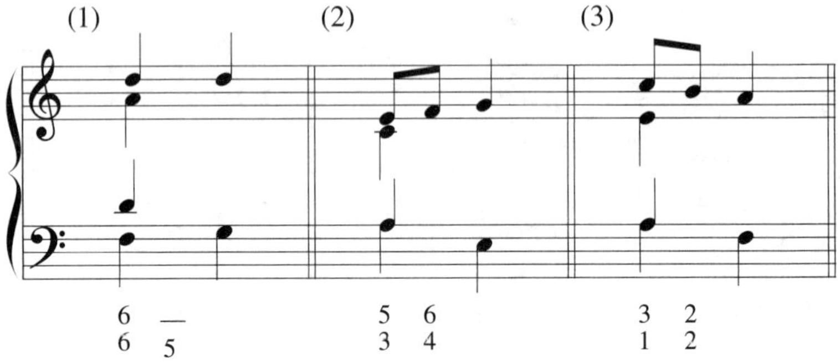

8.20 Write the alto and tenor voices.

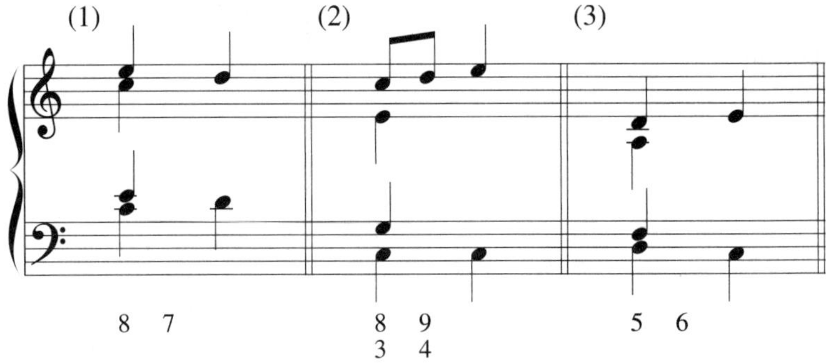

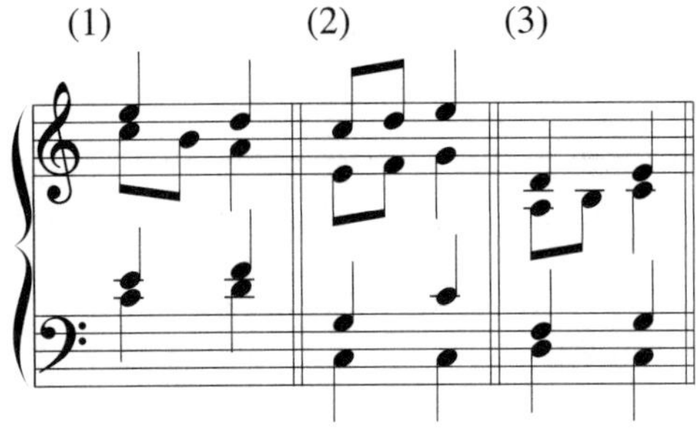

8.21 Write the alto and tenor voices. *(Note that the chord at the asterisk is a diminished triad—double accordingly.)*

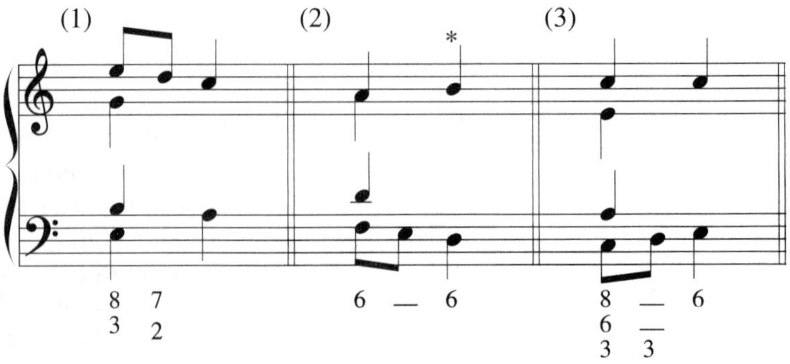

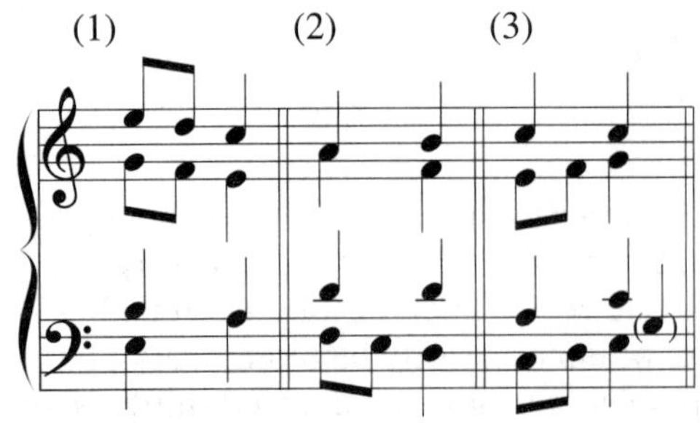

(In [3], the tenor may retain G.)

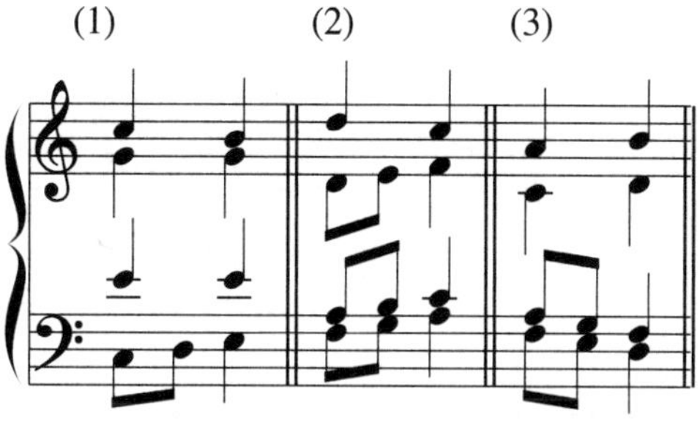

(See next frame.)

8.22 Examples (2) and (3) in the preceding frame show that when melodic movement occurs in the bass, dashes are used to indicate notes that are sustained while the bass moves. Complete the alto and tenor voices. (Remember: numbers in the figured bass represent intervals above the notes *under which the numbers occur.*)

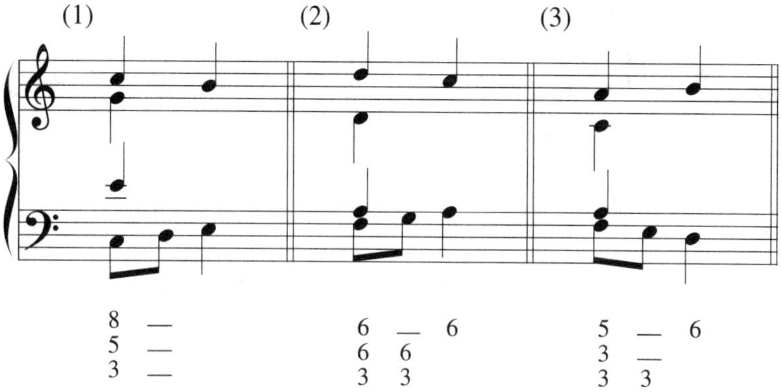

The bass (3rd) should be doubled in a diminished triad in first inversion.

(In your own words.)

8.23 The second chord in (3) of the preceding frame is in first inversion. You may have doubled the soprano (B), but this is incorrect. State the reason why the soprano should *not* be doubled

in this chord. ______________________________

____

8.24 Draw a circle around each passing tone.

Bach, Chorale: *O Ewigheit, du Donnerwort**

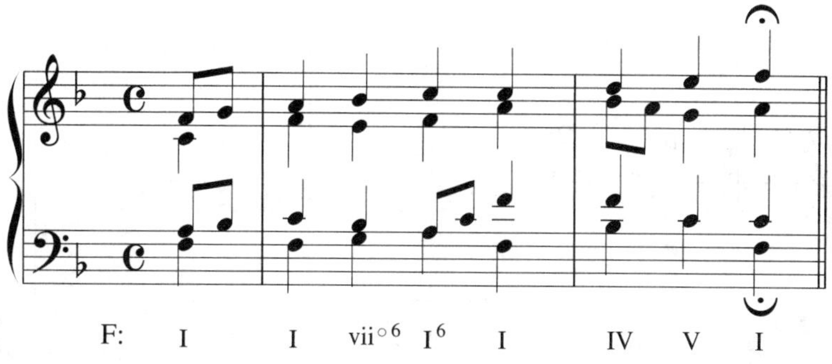

*Because of the wealth of excellent examples of nonharmonic tones in Bach's 371 Chorales, these will serve as the source for many of the exercises in this chapter.

8.25 Complete the alto and tenor voices and draw a circle around each passing tone.

Bach, Chorale: *Was mein Gott will, das g'scheh'*

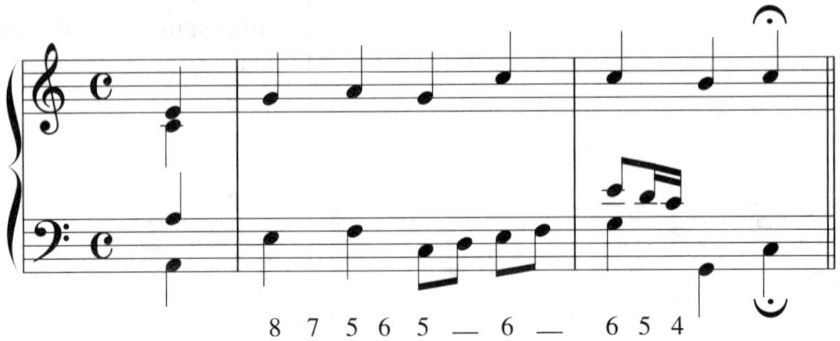

8.26 All of the passing tones to this point have appeared on the weak portion of the beat. These are called UNACCENTED passing tones. Passing tones may also coincide with the strong portion of the beat, in which case they are called ACCENTED passing tones. Which example shows an accented passing tone? _______

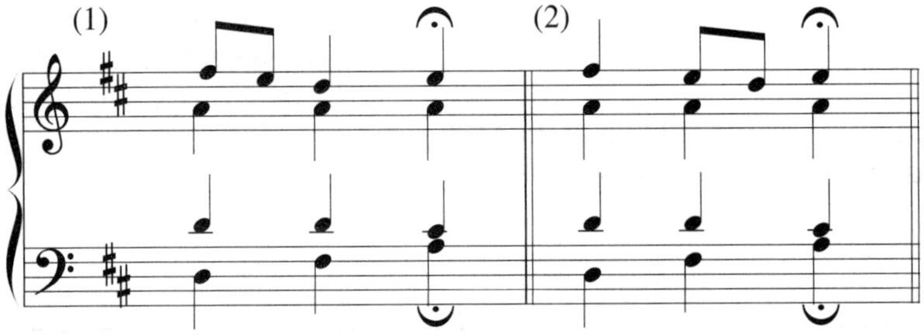

(2)

8.27 Draw a circle around the *accented* passing tones. *(Refer to the roman numeral analysis to find the notes which are not part of the harmony.)*

Bach, Chorale: *Helft mir Gott's Güte preisen*

8.28 Both of the accented passing tones in the preceding frame occur in descending motion. Although used most frequently in this fashion, accented passing tones may also occur in ascending motion.

Bach, Chorale: *Du grosser Schmerzensmann*

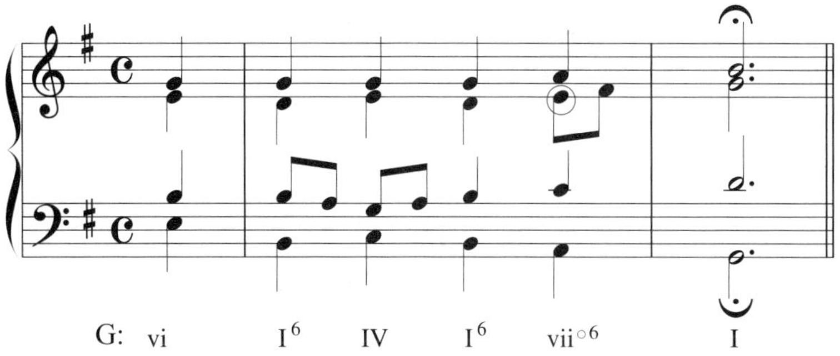

The circled note (E) is nonharmonic with reference to the roman numeral analysis. A different analysis for this beat (ii–vii$^{\circ 6}$) eliminates the nonharmonic tone. The analysis of nonharmonic tones must take into account the ____________ analysis.

harmonic

8.29 Sometimes two passing tones are used in succession. In this case the first is *unaccented* and the second is *accented.*

Bach, Chorale: *Hast du denn, Jesu, dein Angesicht*

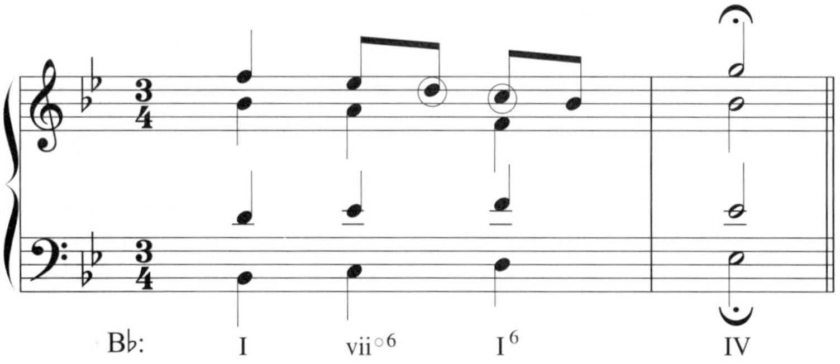

Single passing tones (either accented or unaccented) are used between two harmonic tones a third apart. Two passing tones in succession fill in the interval between two harmonic tones a ____________ apart.

fourth

8.30 Complete the alto and tenor voices in the following example; draw a circle around each passing tone and analyze.

(Continued on the next page)

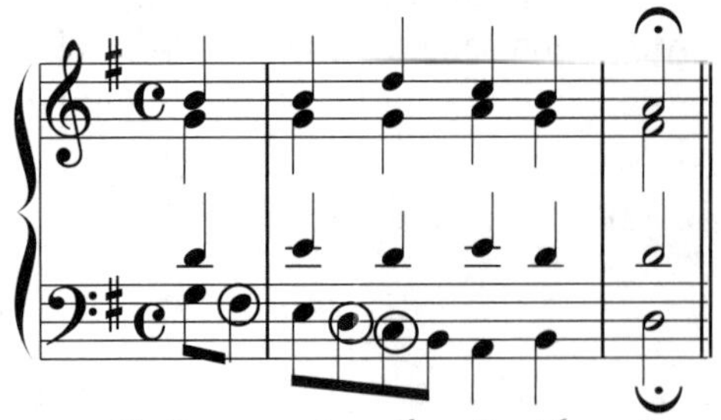

G: I vi I6 ii I6 V

Bach, Chorale: *Du grosser Schmerzensmann* (altered)

5 — 5 — 5 — 6
3 — 2 —
2 —

G: ___ ___ ___ ___ ___ ___

D: I V IV6 V6 I

IV IV6 I

8.31 Complete the alto and tenor voices, draw a circle around each passing tone and analyze.

Bach, Chorale: *Herzlich lieb hab' ich dich, o Herr* (altered)

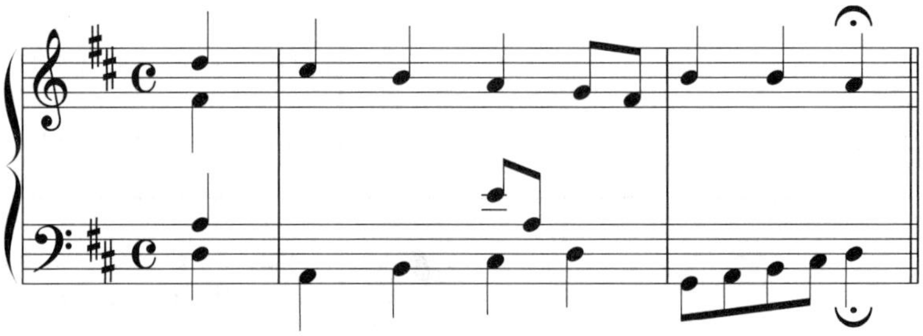

5 6 5 6 6 5 6 — 5 — 5 — 6 —
3 — 3 — 3 — 4 3
3 — 3 6

D: ___ ___ ___ ___ ___ ___ ___ ___

Both ✓

8.32 Check (✓) the correct option:

1. Passing tones are approached and left by step in the same direction.
2. Two or more passing tones may occur simultaneously.

True statements:

(1) _______ (2) _______ Both _______ Neither _______

Neither ✓

8.33 Check (✓) the correct option:

1. Passing tones occur only on weak portions of beats or measures.
2. It is not possible for two passing tones to occur in succession in the same voice.

True statements:

(1) _______ (2) _______ Both _______ Neither _______

8.34 A nonharmonic tone that is approached and left by step with a change of direction is called a NEIGHBORING TONE (symbol: NT).*

Beethoven, *Sonata,* Op. 49, No. 2

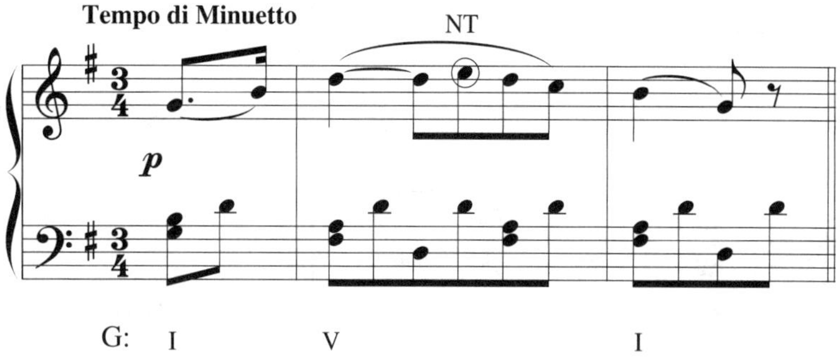

Whereas the passing tone leads by step from one harmonic note to another a third away, the neighboring tone appears between two harmonic notes of the _____________ pitch.

*Other terms for this device are *returning tone, changing tone,* and *auxiliary tone.*

same

8.35 Most neighboring tones occur on weak portions of beats or measures (as in the preceding frame). Accented neighboring tones, although less common, can sometimes be used effectively.

Chopin, *Valse Brillante,* Op. 34, No. 2

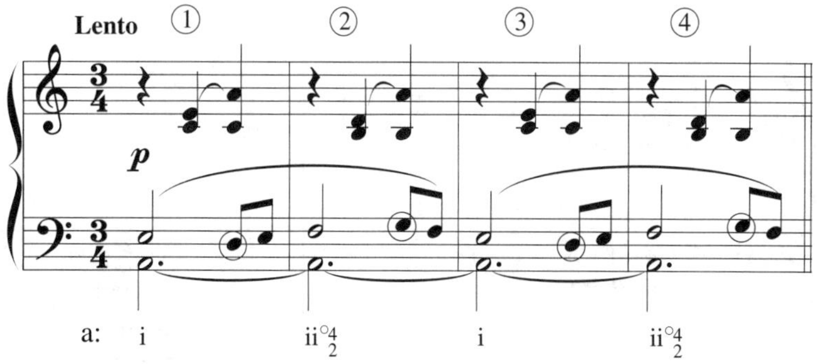

Neighboring tones may be either a step *above* or *below* the harmonic tone. Lower neighboring tones are shown in the first and third measures of the above example. Which measures contain upper neighboring tones? _____________ and _____________.

Two (and) four

8.36 Frame 8.34 and 8.35 show that neighboring tones may be accented or unaccented, and occur (by step) either above or below the harmonic tone to which they relate.

Are most neighboring tones accented or unaccented?

____

Unaccented

8.37 Draw a circle around each neighboring tone. *(Refer to the roman numeral analysis.)*

Kuhlau, *Sonatina,* Op. 20, No. 1

8.38 Two or more neighboring tones may occur simultaneously. Draw a circle around the neighboring tones.

Bach, Chorale: *Herr, nun lass in Friede* (altered)

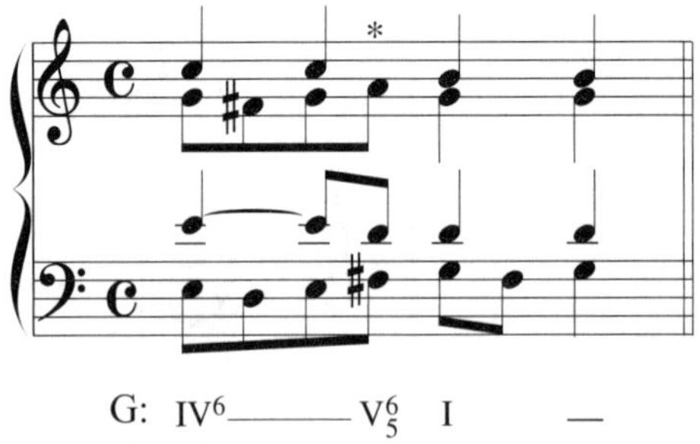

*For this chord, the pitch C is considered a chord tone. Chords with four different pitches (seventh chords) are discussed further in Chapter 6.0, and Chapters 1.0 and 2.0 in *Harmonic Materials in Tonal Music, Part II.*

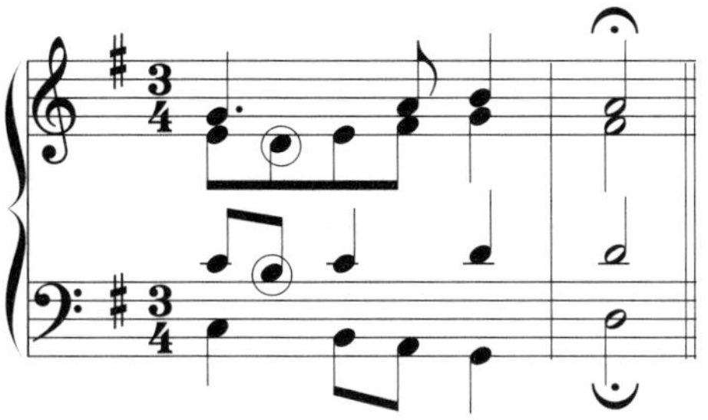

G: IV ii (vii°⁶)I V

8.39 Complete the alto and tenor voices and draw a circle around each neighboring tone; analyze.

Bach, Chorale: *Aus meines Herzens Grunde*

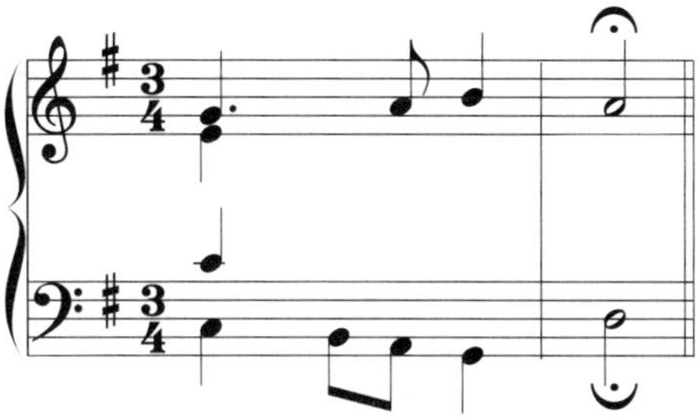

G: ___ ___(___)___ ___

passing tone

8.40 In the preceding frame, the second note in the bass voice (B) is a nonharmonic tone. It is an accented _____________.

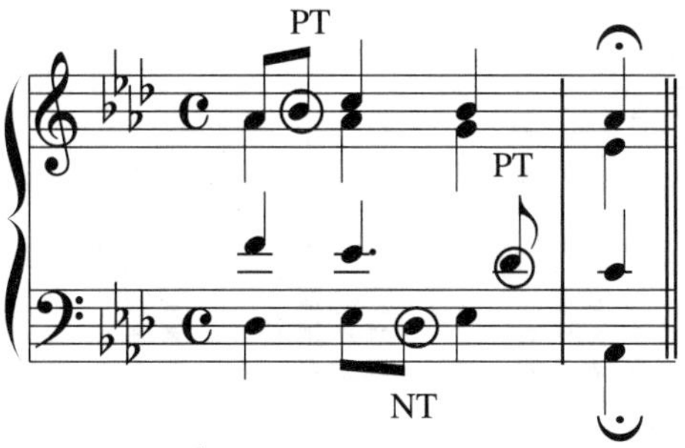

A♭: IV I^6_4 V I

8.41 Complete the alto and tenor voices and label each nonharmonic tone. *(Use the symbols PT and NT.)* Analyze.

Mendelssohn, Chorale: *Aus tiefer Noth schrei' ich zu dir*

A♭: ___ ___ ___ ___

8.42 A nonharmonic tone that is approached by leap and left by step (usually with a change of direction) is called an APPOGGIATURA (symbol: App).*

Beethoven, *Sonata,* Op. 10, No. 1

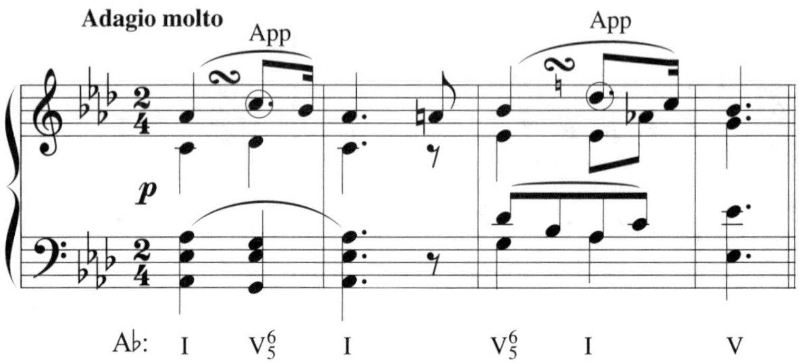

The feature that distinguishes the appoggiatura from both the passing tone and the neighboring tone is that it is approached

leap

by ______________.

*The term appoggiatura comes from the Italian *appoggiare*, "to lean." It describes the effect of this nonharmonic tone, which is that of "leaning" upon the tone to which it resolves. Some writers may also call accented passing and neighboring tones appoggiaturas.

8.43 The appoggiatura occurs most often in a position of rhythmic stress (as in the preceding frame). The example below, however, shows *unaccented* appoggiaturas.*

Tchaikovsky, *Symphony No. 5,* Op. 64

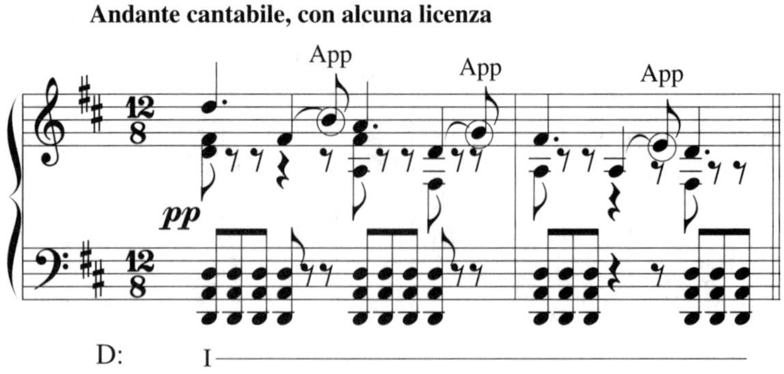

The appoggiatura is a nonharmonic tone that is approached

step

by leap and left by ______________.

*Some writers may not agree that an appoggiatura can be unaccented.

Accented

8.44 Double appoggiaturas are shown in the example below.

Haydn, *Capriccio*

Are the appoggiaturas above accented or unaccented?

____

---

higher

8.45 All of the appoggiaturas shown thus far have been approached by leap from *below.* They also may be approached from *above.*

Brahms, *Piano Concerto,* Op. 83

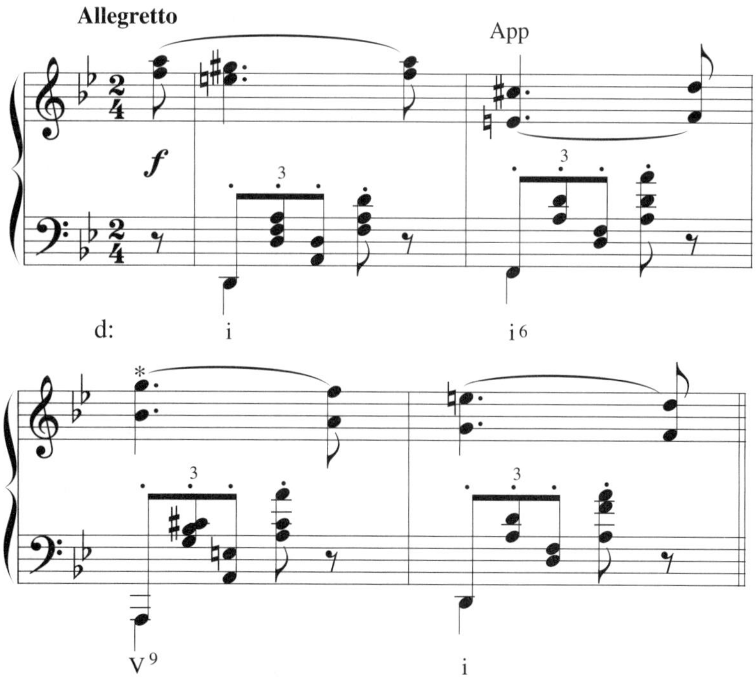

If an appoggiatura is approached from below, the note that follows is a step lower. If an appoggiatura is approached from above, the note that follows is a step ______________.

*For more information on ninth chords, please see *Harmonic Materials in Tonal Music, Part II*, Chapter 11.0, fr. 11.1–48.

8.46 The appoggiatura sometimes appears without preparation.

Bach, *French Suite No. 3*

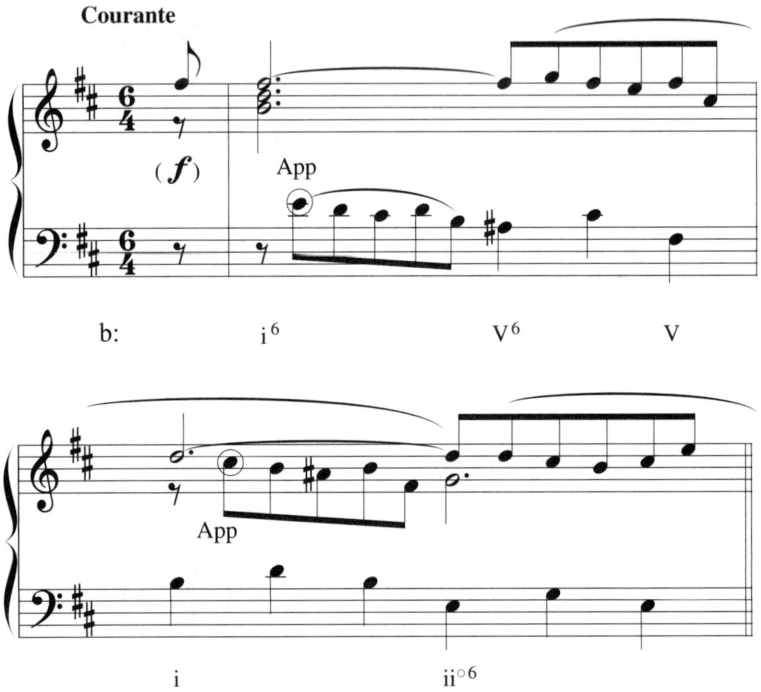

With or without preparation, the appoggiatura is followed by a tone that is a half or whole _____________ away.

step

8.47 Without preparation, the appoggiatura's effect of "leaning" upon the harmonic tone that follows is heightened. The appoggiatura at the asterisk (next page) is an echo of that heard in the preceding measure. This produces a dramatic effect of emotional tension.

Tchaikovsky, *Romeo and Juliet, Overture-Fantasy*

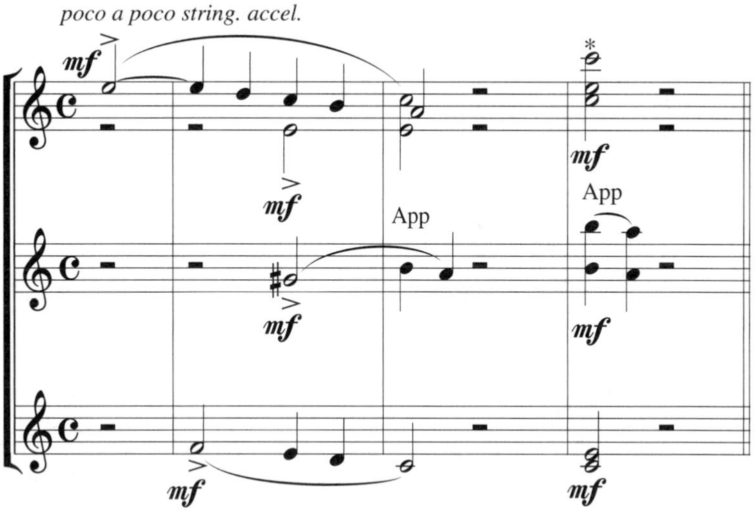

The appoggiaturas above are accented. Are the appoggiaturas in Frame 8.46 accented or unaccented? ____________

Unaccented

8.48 Although the appoggiatura sometimes appears without preparation, it usually is approached by leap. In all cases it is left by step—usually in the direction opposite to its approach (if any). Some of the possible forms of the appoggiatura are shown below:

WITH PREPARATION

(Accented) (Unaccented)

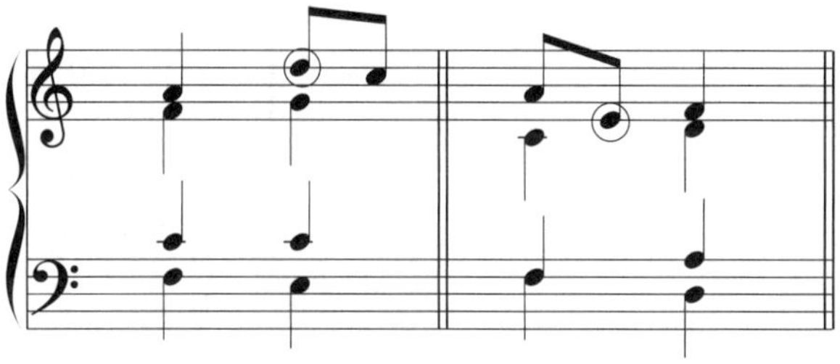

WITHOUT PREPARATION

(Accented) (Unaccented)

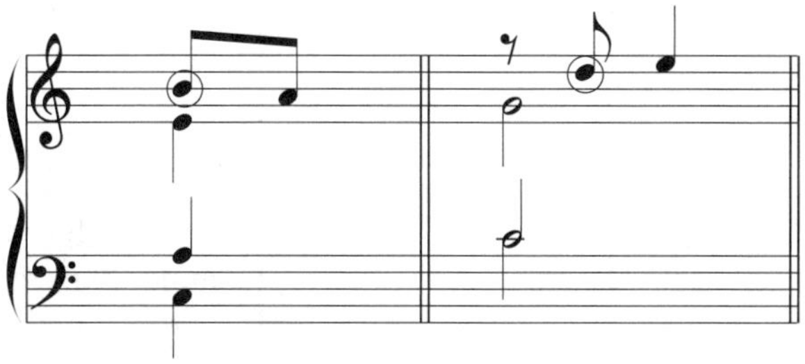

An appoggiatura that is approached from below will usually be left by step in a(n) (upward/downward) ____________ direction.

downward

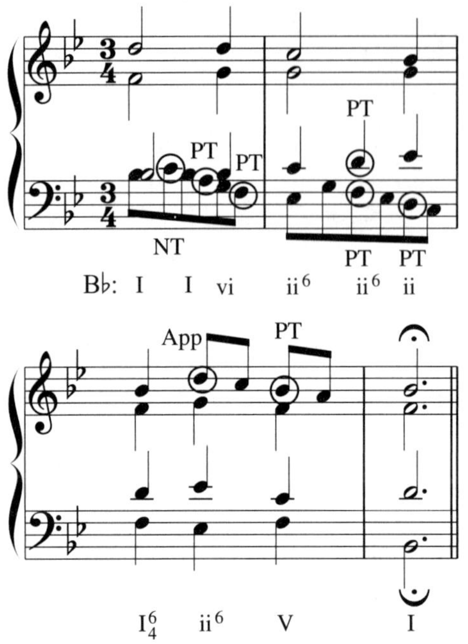

8.49 Complete the alto and tenor voices and label each nonharmonic tone. Analyze *(Use the symbols PT, NT, and App.)*

Bach, Chorale: *Jesu, nun sei gepreist*

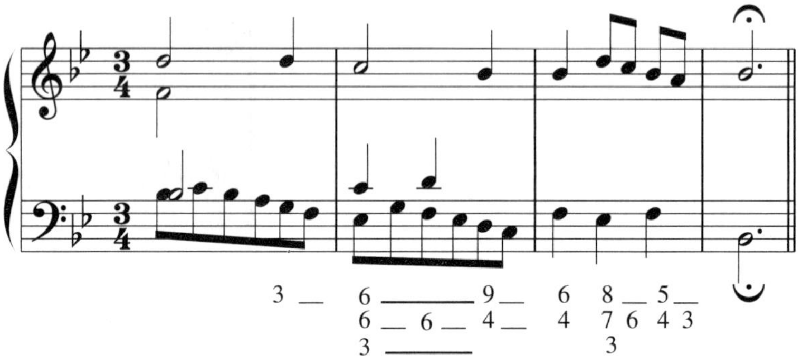

B♭: ___ ___ ___ ___ ___ ___ ___ ___ ___ ___

leap

8.50 A nonharmonic tone which is approached by step and left by leap (usually with a change of direction) is called an ESCAPE TONE (symbol: ET).*

Mozart, *Quartet,* K. 575

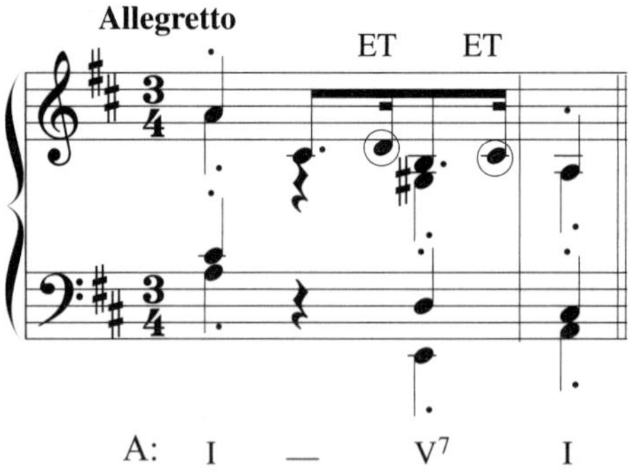

The escape tone's melodic movement is the opposite of the appoggiatura's. Whereas the appoggiatura is approached by leap and left by step, the escape tone is approached by step and left by ______________.

*The escape tone is also known by its French name *échappée.*

8.51 The most common form of the escape tone is shown in the preceding frame (an ascending step followed by a descending leap). The reverse form, however, is also used.

Franck, *Symphony in D Minor*

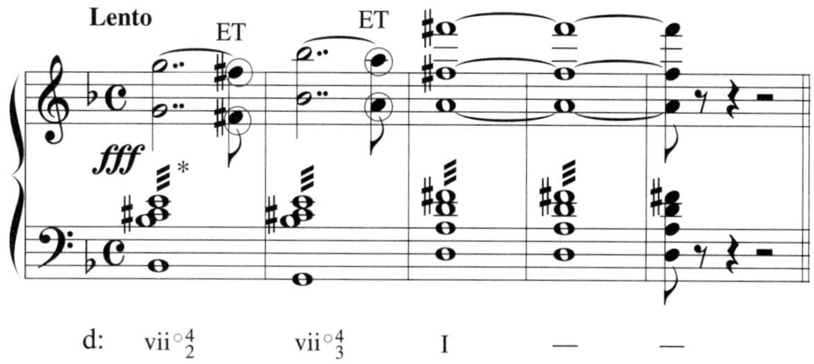

A nonharmonic tone that is approached by step and left by leap is called an ____________.

escape tone

*This marking indicates a *tremolo,* which is the rapid, continuous reiteration of the indicated pitches.

8.52 Double escape tones are shown below:

Bach, Chorale: *Ach Gott, wie manches Herzeleid*

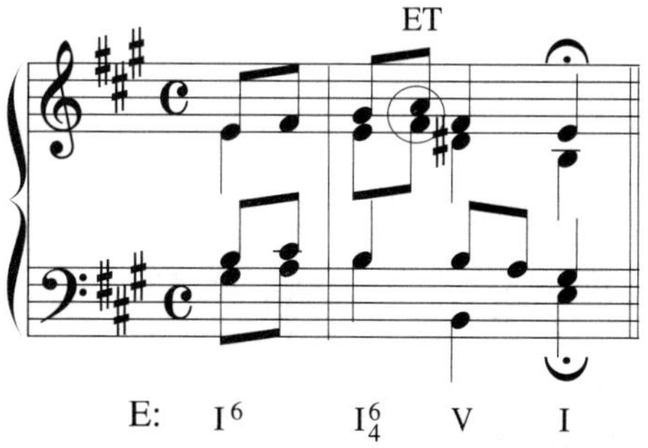

Escape tones which are approached from below are usually left (by leap) in a ____________ direction.

downward

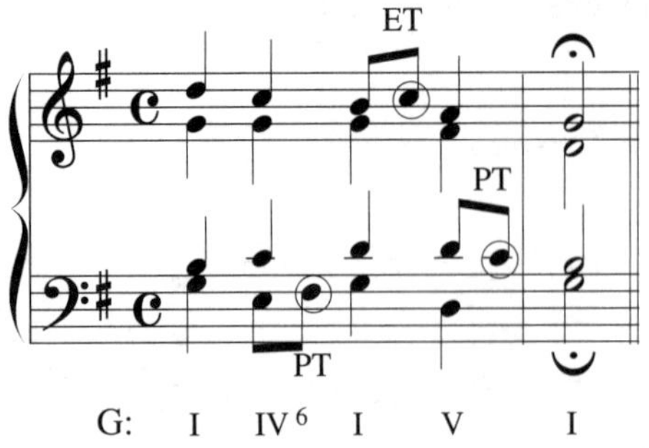

8.53 Complete the alto and tenor voices in the following examples, label each nonharmonic tone and analyze.

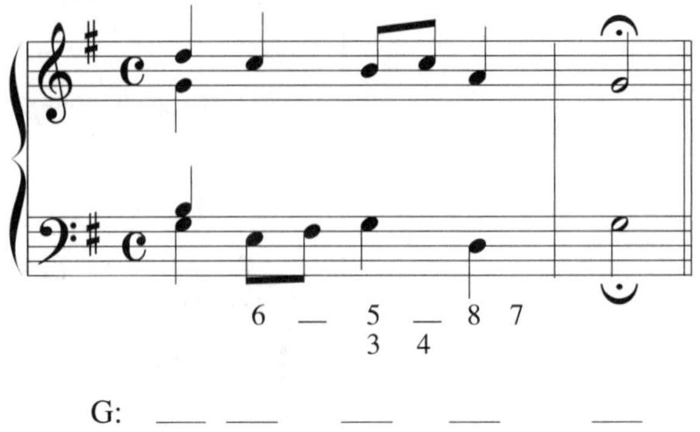

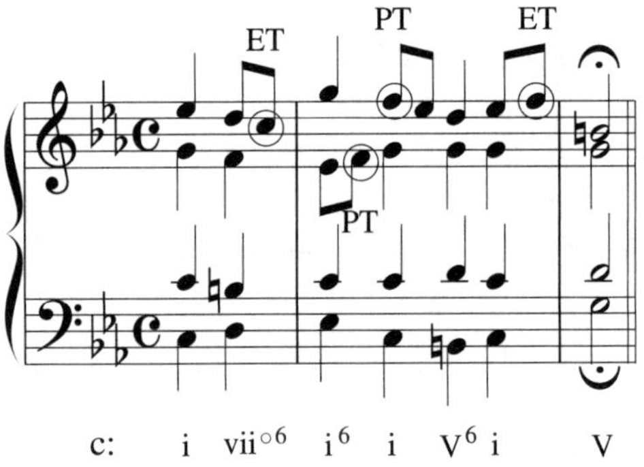

8.54 Complete the alto and tenor voices, label each nonharmonic tone and analyze.

Bach, Chorale: *Nicht so traurig, nicht so sehr* (altered)

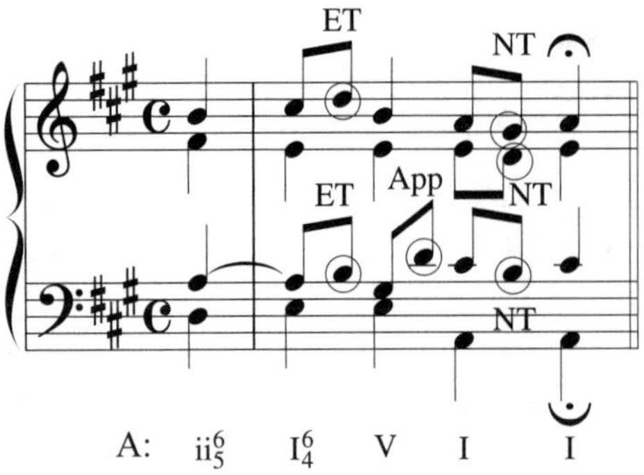

8.55 Complete the alto and tenor voices, label each nonharmonic tone and analyze.

Bach, Chorale: *Gott des Himmels un der Erden* (altered)

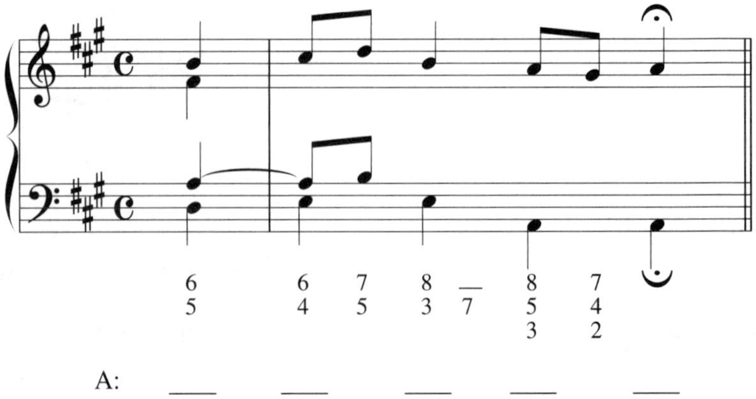

Expository Frame

8.56 The example in the preceding frame shows that several nonharmonic tones may occur simultaneously. Not only are there double escape tones, but also triple neighboring tones.

(No response required.)

8.57 Check (✓) the type of nonharmonic tone shown in the example:

(1) Accented passing tone	_____	(4) Appoggiatura	_____
(2) Unaccented passing tone	_____	(5) Escape tone	_____
(3) Neighboring tone	_____	(6) None of these	_____

(3) ✓

8.58 Check (✓) the type of nonharmonic tone shown in the example:

(1) Accented passing tone	_____	(4) Appoggiatura	_____
(2) Unaccented passing tone	_____	(5) Escape tone	_____
(3) Neighboring tone	_____	(6) None of these	_____

(1) ✓

8.59 Check (✓) the type of nonharmonic tone shown in the example:

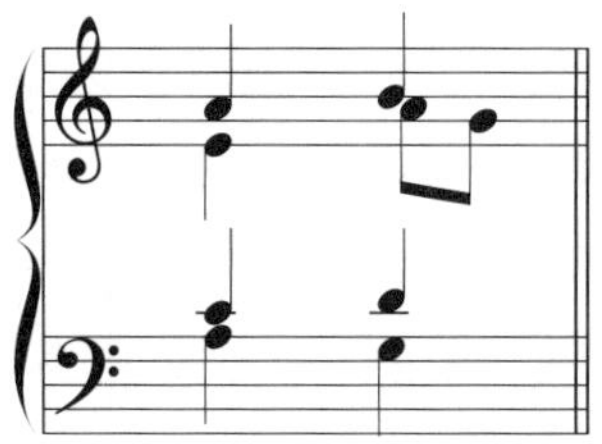

(1) Accented passing tone	_____	(4) Appoggiatura	_____
(2) Unaccented passing tone	_____	(5) Escape tone	_____
(3) Neighboring tone	_____	(6) None of these	_____

(4) ✓

8.60 Check (✓) the type of nonharmonic tone shown in the example:

(1) Accented passing tone _____ (4) Appoggiatura _____

(2) Unaccented passing tone _____ (5) Escape tone _____

(3) Neighboring tone _____ (6) None of these _____

(6) ✓

Expository Frame

8.61 The nonharmonic tone in the preceding frame does not fall into any of the patterns presented thus far. It is approached by step and left by repetition. This type of nonharmonic tone is called an ANTICIPATION (symbol: A).

The name of this nonharmonic tone is an apt description of this musical function. It is a *premature* sounding of a harmonic tone to follow.

The anticipation is always left by repetition of the same note.

(No response required.)

8.62 The approach to the anticipation from *above* by step is shown:

Sibelius, *Finlandia,* Op. 26

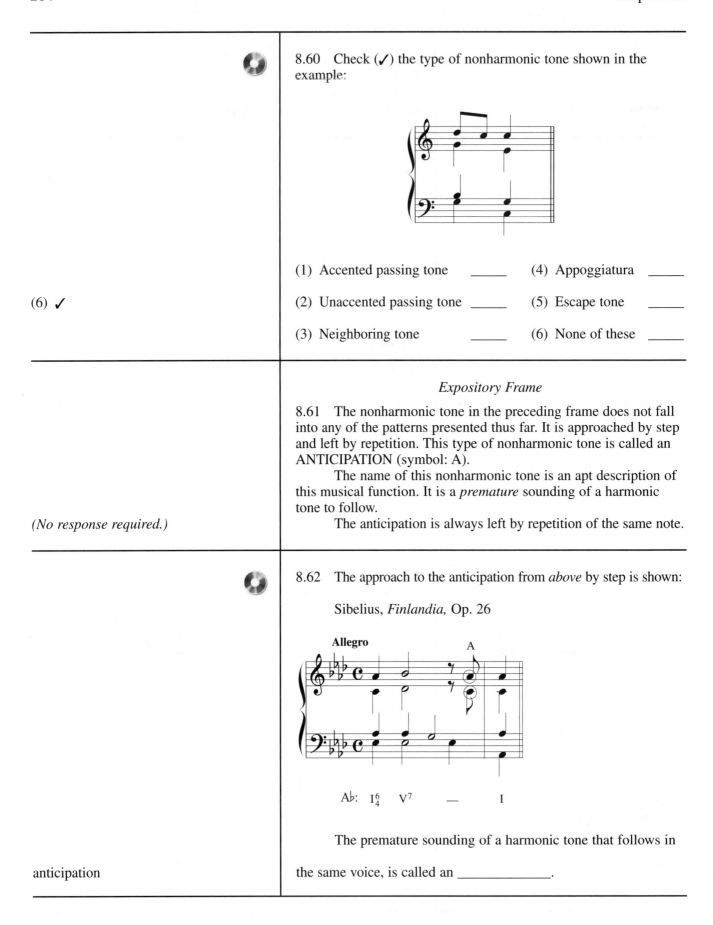

A♭: I^6_4 V^7 — I

The premature sounding of a harmonic tone that follows in the same voice, is called an _____________.

anticipation

8.63 The anticipation may also be approached from below.

Handel, *Suite in D Minor*

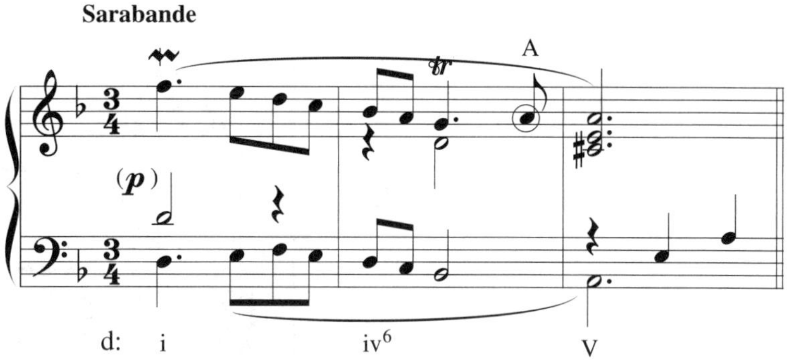

Anticipations may be approached from above or below, and they usually occupy a relatively weak rhythmic position. They ordinarily are of shorter time value than the tone that is anticipated.

The anticipation is a premature sounding of a ____________ tone.

harmonic
(or chord)

8.64 Although most anticipations are approached by step, they are occasionally approached by leap.

Bach, *Well-Tempered Clavier,* Vol. 1, Prelude XIII

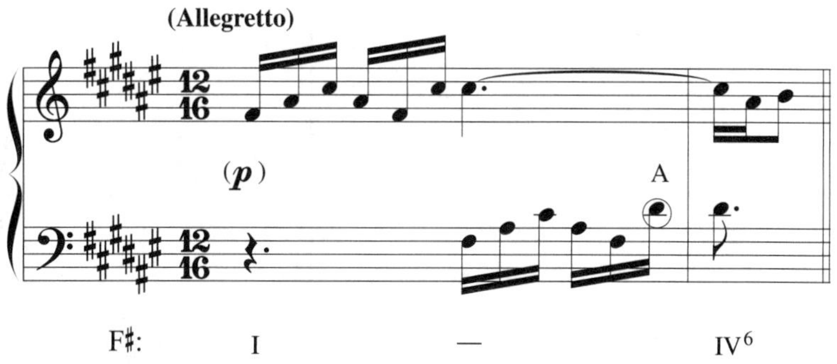

Regardless of the approach, the tone following the anticipation is always the ____________ pitch.

same

8.65 Most anticipations occur as part of a cadence pattern over the dominant chord. It is usually the tonic note that is anticipated.

Handel, *Sonata No. 1 for Oboe and Harpsichord*

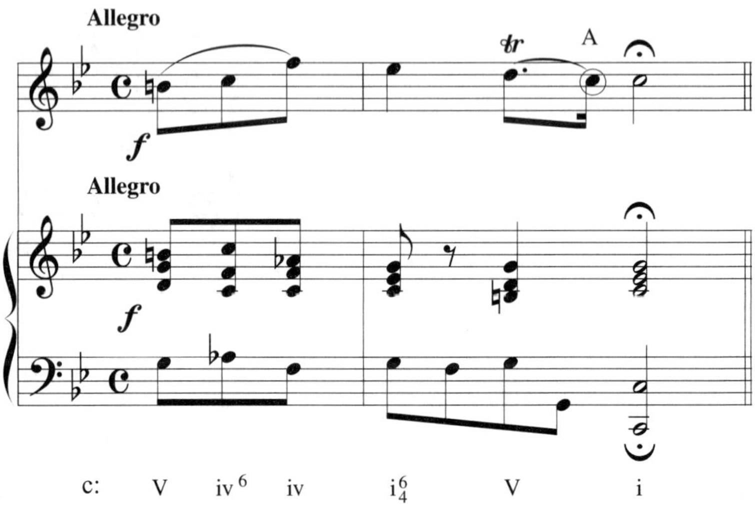

Anticipations may occur at any point in a phrase, but the majority are found at the _____________.

cadence

8.66 Check (✓) the type of nonharmonic tone shown in the example:

(1) Passing tone _____ (4) Escape tone _____

(2) Neighboring tone _____ (5) Anticipation _____

(3) Appoggiatura _____ (6) None of these _____

(4) ✓

8.67 Check (✓) the type of nonharmonic tone shown in the example:

(1) Passing tone	_____	(4) Escape tone	_____
(2) Neighboring tone	_____	(5) Anticipation	_____
(3) Appoggiatura	_____	(6) None of these	_____

(5) ✓

8.68 Check (✓) the type of nonharmonic tone shown in the example:

(1) Passing tone	_____	(4) Escape tone	_____
(2) Neighboring tone	_____	(5) Anticipation	_____
(3) Appoggiatura	_____	(6) None of these	_____

(3) ✓

8.69 In the first example below the nonharmonic tone approached by the same tone and left by step downward is called a SUSPENSION (symbol: S indicates point of suspension or tension). In the second example, although the tone leaves by step upward and is "suspended," it is sometimes called a RETARDATION.

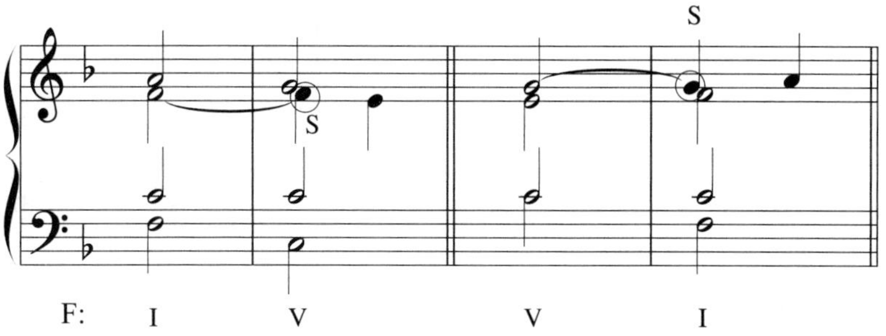

The approach to a suspension (or a retardation) is from a tone of the _____________ pitch.

same

step

8.70 The suspension is best understood as a figure composed of three parts; preparation, suspension, and resolution. Whether the motion is upward or downward, the suspension proceeds to the resolution by _____________.

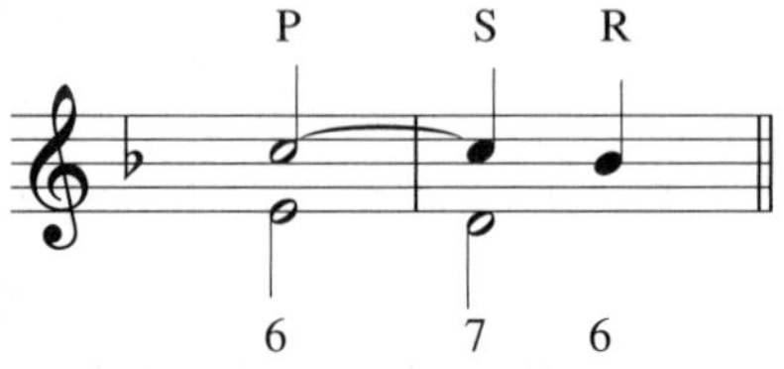

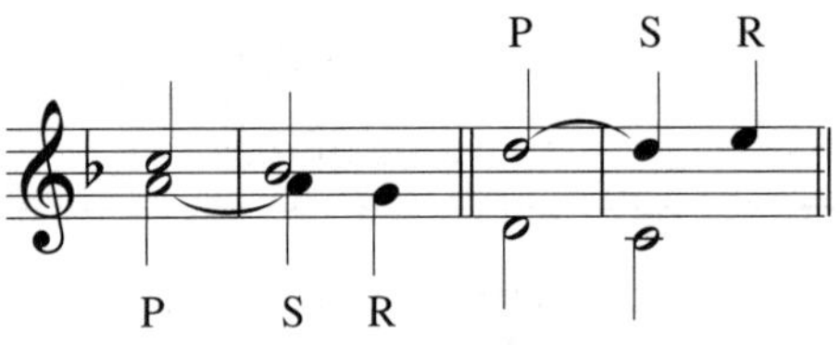

8.71 Label the three parts of each suspension figure. (P = Preparation, S = suspension, and R = resolution.)

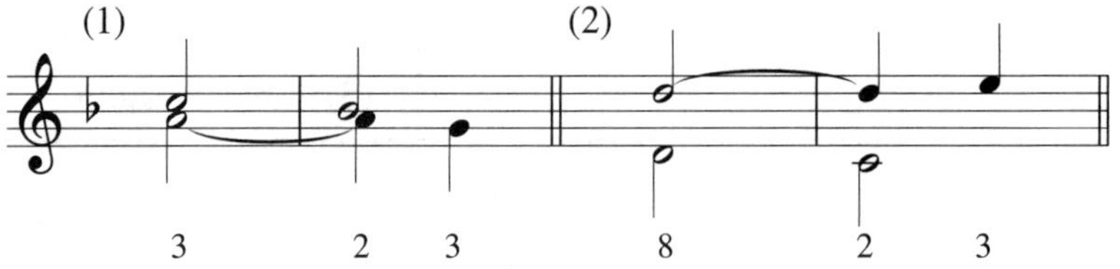

(1) ✓
(2) is incorrect because the resolution must be by STEP.

8.72 Check (✓) the correct option:

1. The suspension is prepared by a tone of the same pitch.
2. The suspension may resolve to any tone (higher or lower).

True statements:

(1) _______ (2) _______ Both _______ Neither _______

8.73 In most cases the preparation is sustained into the suspension by a tie or the note values used.

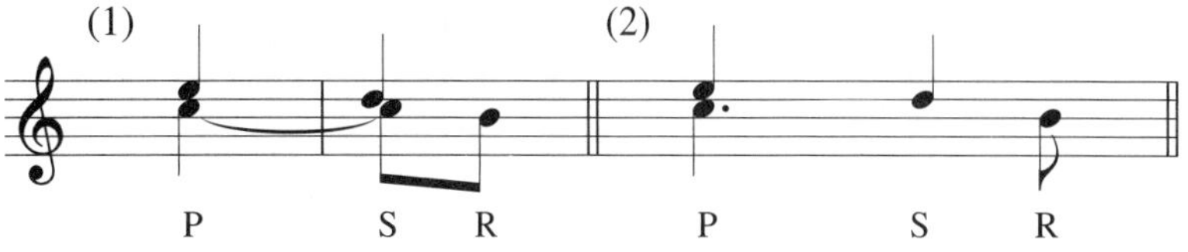

Continuous sounding (without repetition) of the preparation and suspension is considered by some to be an integral feature of the suspension. Current preference, however, is to classify nonharmonic tones according to the direction of movement preceding and following them. This approach simplifies terminology.

The preparation may be sustained into the suspension, or the suspension may be re-sounded. (True/False) _____________

True

Expository Frame

8.74 Suspensions not tied to their preparation are shown below:

Brahms, *Ein deutsches Requiem,* Op. 45, I

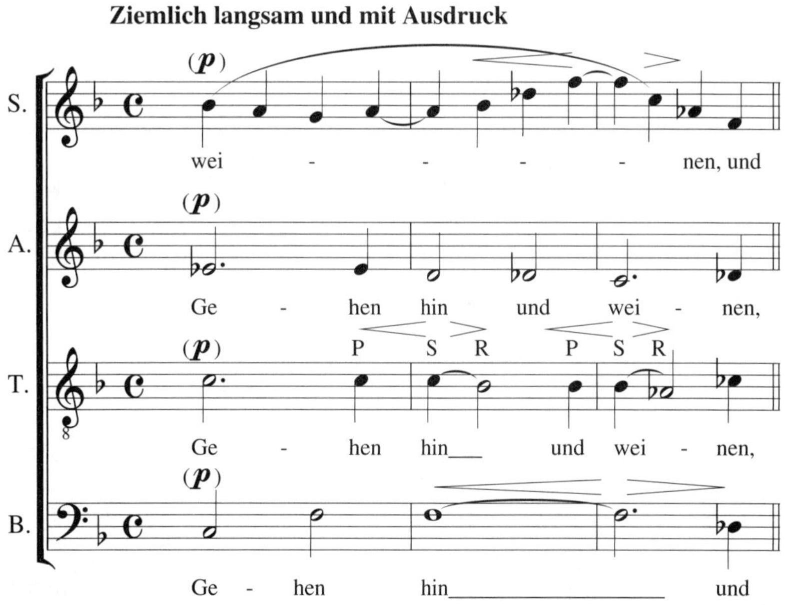

Suspensions such as these are sometimes called *appoggiaturas.* Be prepared to accept alternate terms for several nonharmonic tones, as terminology is not standardized in this area of music theory.

(No response required.)

8.75 As indicated before, most suspensions resolve DOWNWARD by step. Suspensions that resolve upward are relatively rare and are sometimes called RETARDATIONS.

Bach, *Well-Tempered Clavier,* Vol. 2, Prelude XII

(Moderato)

Since all of these suspensions are resounded, some theorists refer to them as appoggiaturas. The suspensions at the asterisks resolve upward. These also are known as ____________________.

retardations

Expository Frame

8.76 Because suspensions are handled the same whether they resolve upward or downward, are sustained or re-sounded, it seems unnecessary to apply different terms in each case.

To summarize:

The suspension is a nonharmonic tone that is approached by the same pitch and left by step (usually downward). The preparation may be sustained (usually by tie) into the suspension, or the suspension may be re-sounded. The term *retardation* refers to a suspension that resolves upward.

(No response required.)

8.77 Turning to a study of the rhythmic organization of the suspension figure:

Learn these principles:

1. The suspension occurs on an accented portion of the measure (or beat).
2. The resolution usually occurs on the weak beat (or portion of the beat) immediately following the suspension.
3. The preparation is usually equal to or longer than the time value of the suspension.

The metric organization of the suspension figure is in accordance with either the unit or the division of the unit, and there is notable consistency within a composition once a rate has been established.

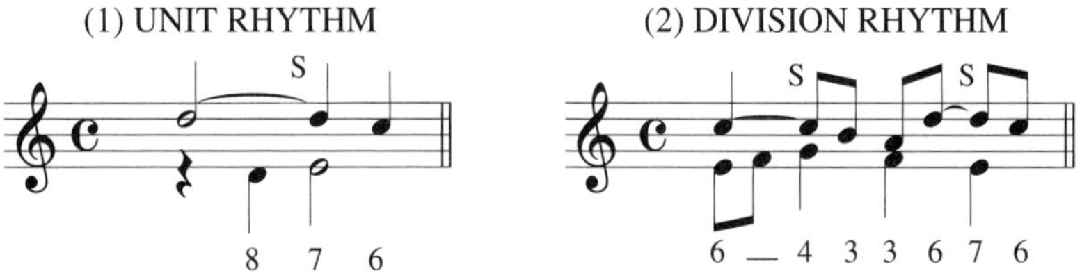

In (1) the rhythmic value of the preparation is double that of the suspension. Is this true in each case in (2)? _______

No

8.78 The preparation often is twice as long as the suspension; but, as shown by the second suspension in example (2) of the preceding frame, it may also be _____________ in value.

equal

8.79 Whereas the preparation is usually equal to or longer than the time value of the suspension, this is not a binding rule. The example below shows a suspension whose preparation is six times as long.

Bach, *Well-Tempered Clavier,* Vol. 2, Fugue I

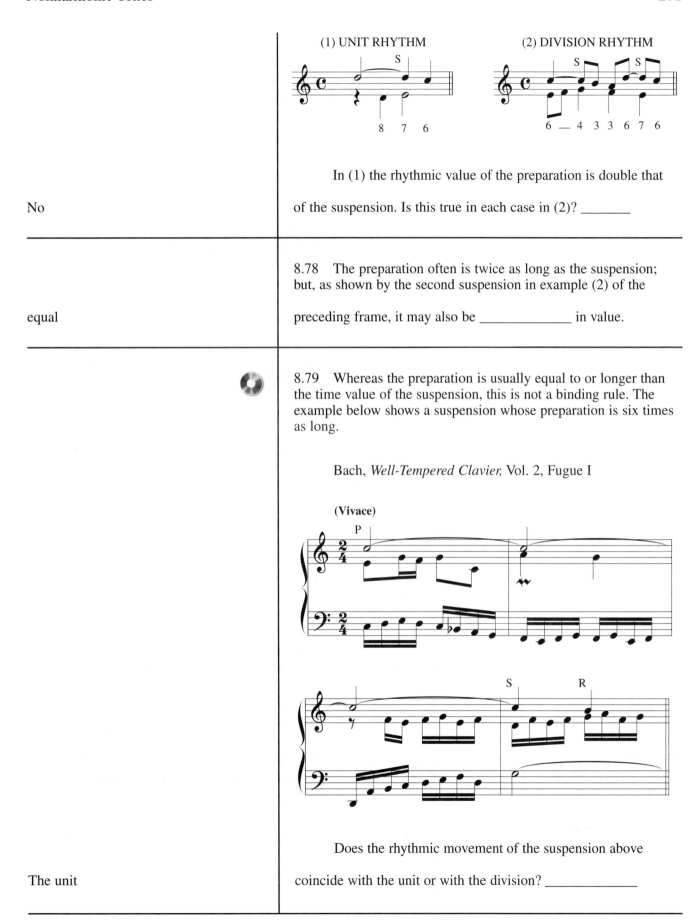

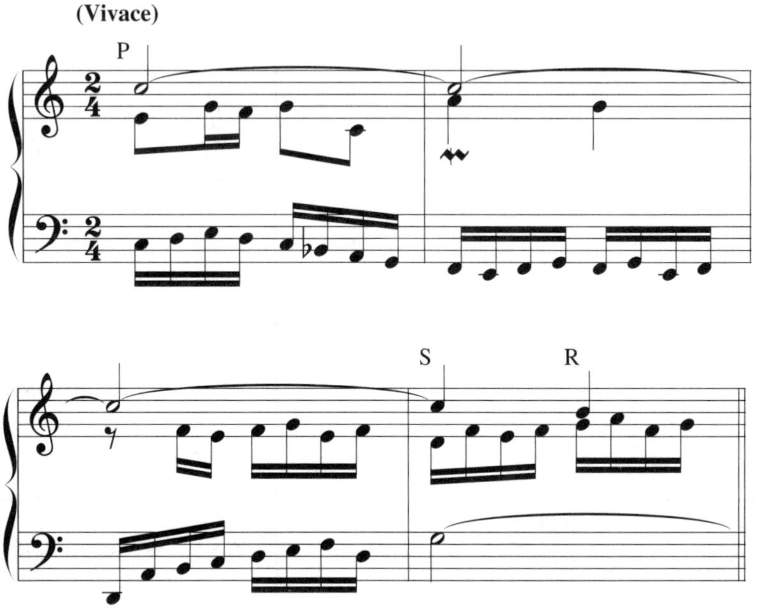

Does the rhythmic movement of the suspension above coincide with the unit or with the division? _____________

The unit

8.80 Below is an example of a suspension whose preparation is one-half as long.

Bach, *Well-Tempered Clavier,* Vol. 2, Fugue XI

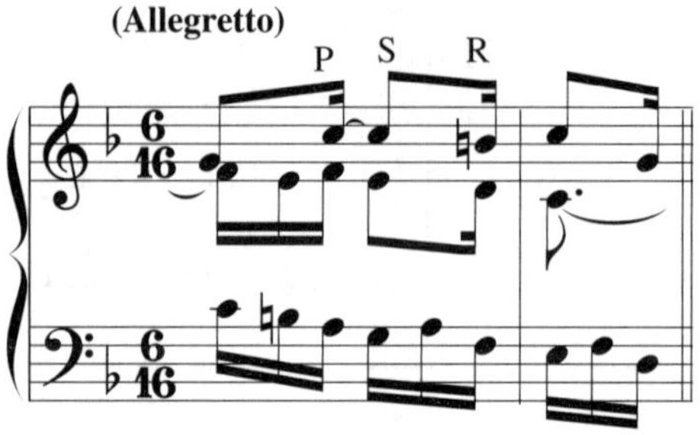

In all cases the resolution occupies a weaker rhythmic position than does the ___________________.

suspension

8.81 *Types of suspensions.* Suspensions are classified according to the figured bass symbols that are appropriate to each. Thus we speak of 4–3, 7–6, 2–1, and 2–3* suspensions. These are shown in two-part writing below.

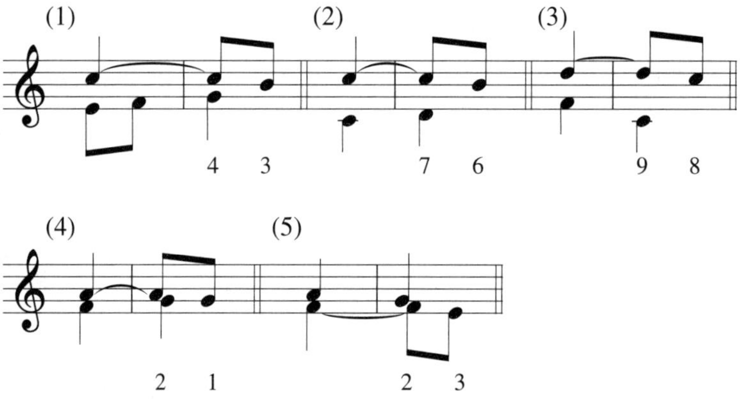

In a 7–6 suspension there is the interval of a seventh between the bass and suspension, and the interval of a sixth between the bass and the ___________________.

Note that the 2–3 suspension occurs in the lowest part (see [5] above).

resolution

8.82 Write suspensions as directed by the figured bass.

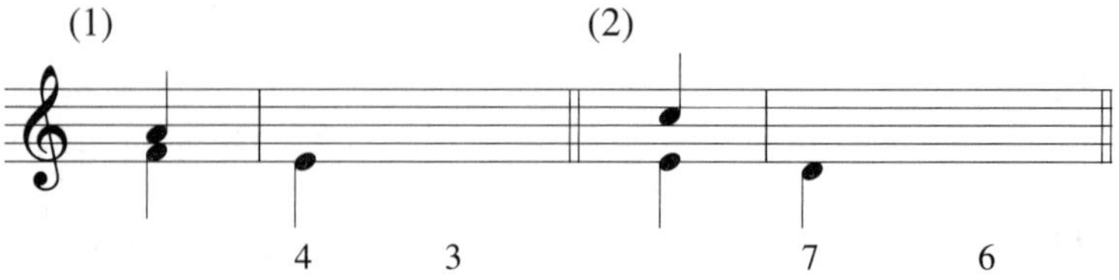

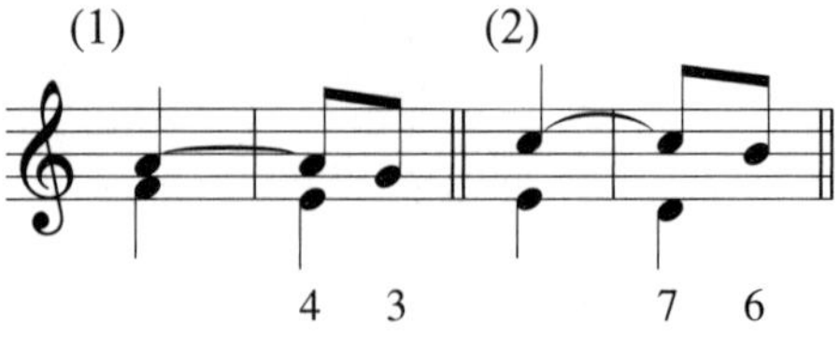

4 3 9 8

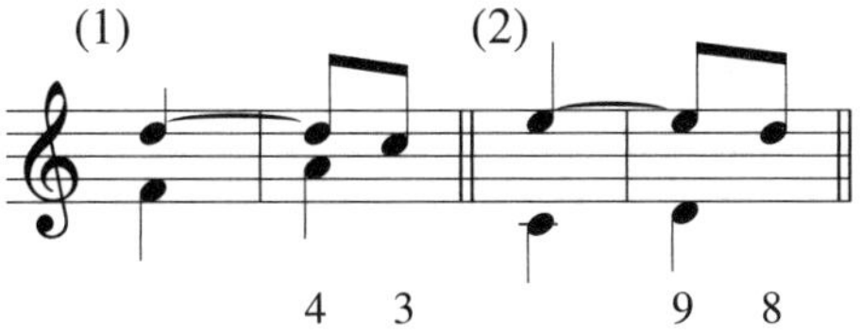

8.83 Continue as in the preceding frame.

(1) (2)

 4 3 9 8

(1) (2)

 2 1 2 3

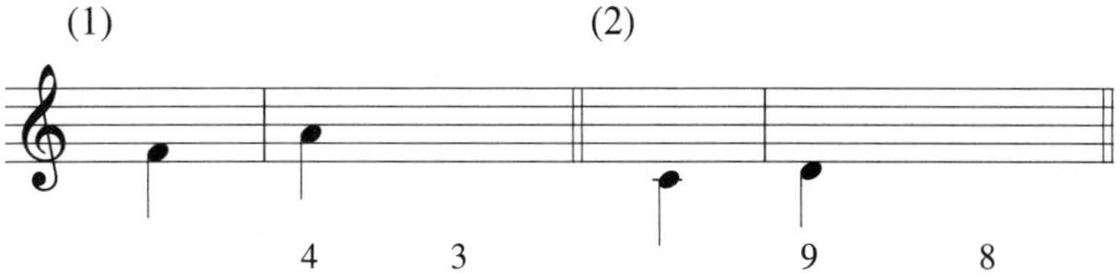

8.84 Continue as in the preceding frame.

(1) (2)

 2 1 2 3

D: I V ———— I

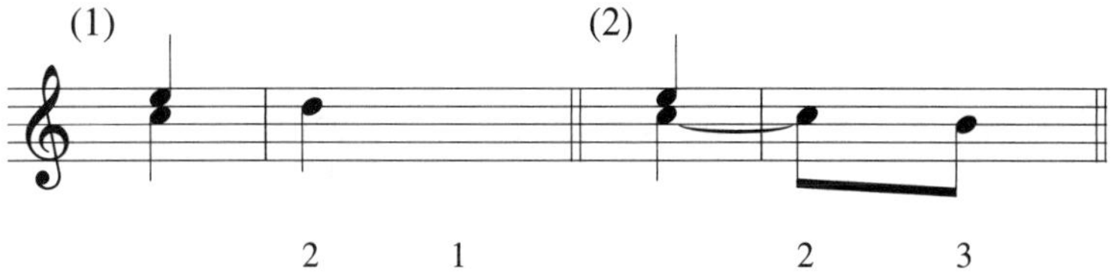

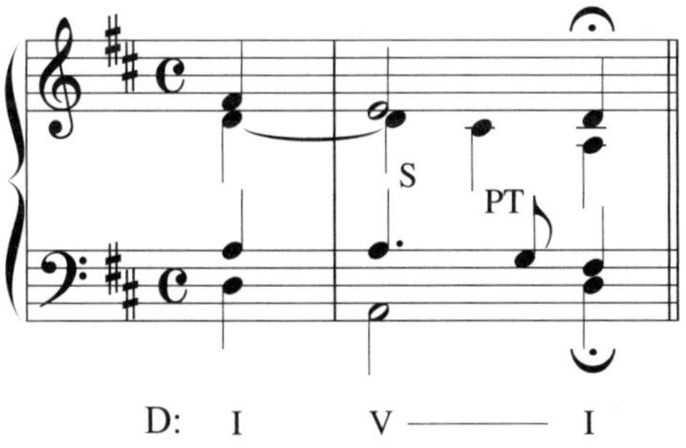

8.85 Complete the alto and tenor voices and label each
nonharmonic tone; analyze.

Bach, Chorale: *Wie schön leuchtet der Morgenstern*

 8 — 7
 4 3 —

D: ___ _____ ___

d: i vii°⁶ i⁶ V V i

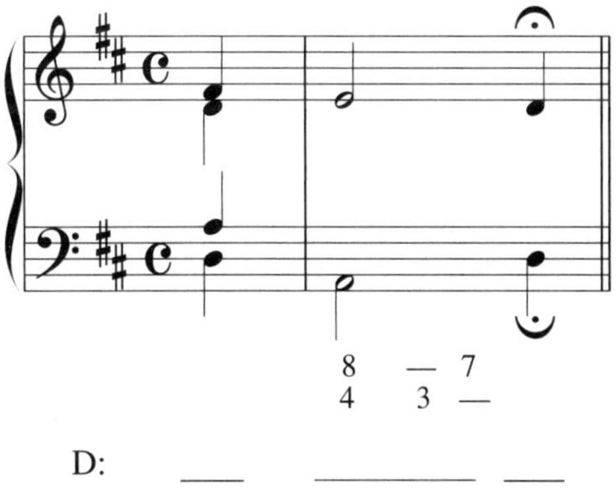

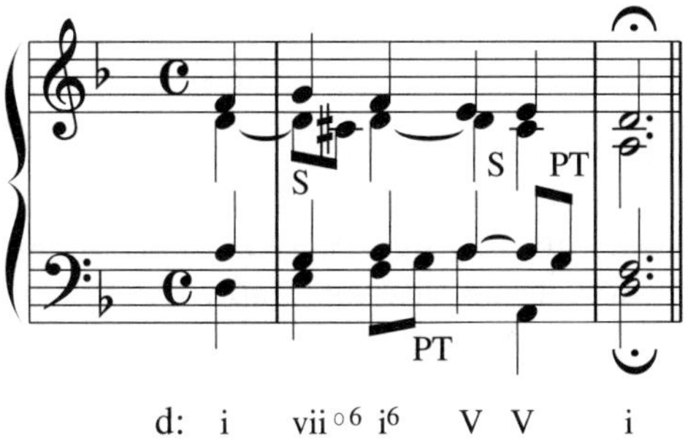

8.86 Continue as in the preceding frame.

Bach, Chorale: *Befiehl du deine Wege*

8 7
 7 ♯6 6 — 4 3 —

d: ___ _____ ___ ___

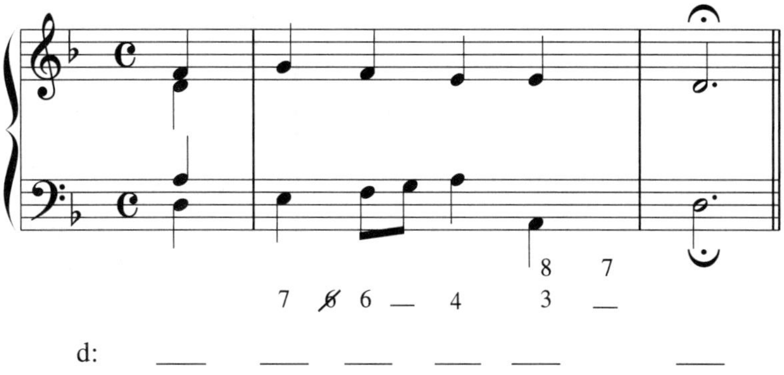

4–3

8.87 The first suspension in the preceding frame is a 7–6 suspension. Of what type is the second? _______

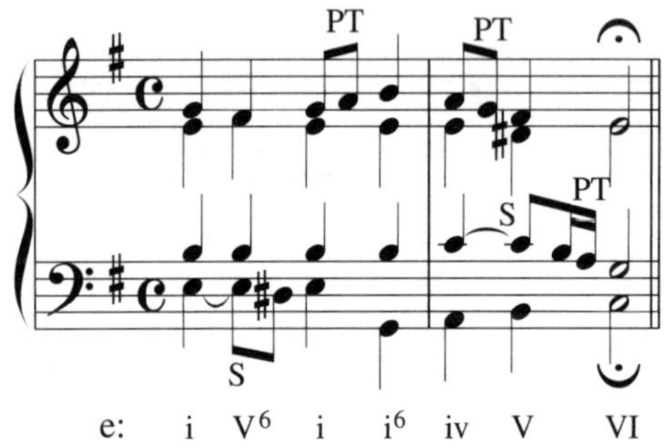

8.88 Complete the alto and tenor voices, label each nonharmonic tone and analyze.

Bach, Chorale: *Es wird schier der letzte Tag herkommen*

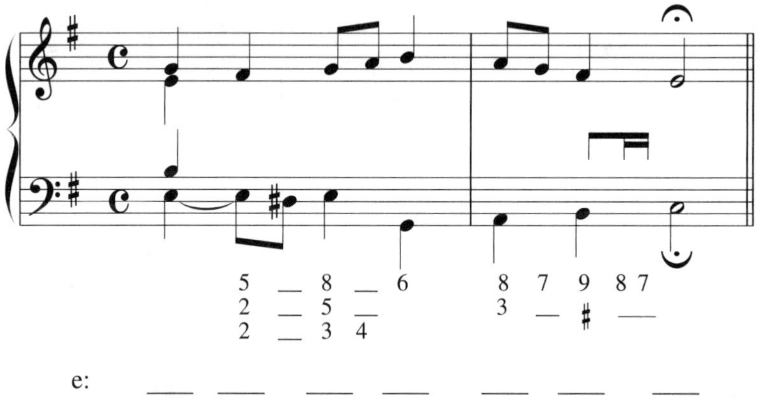

Expository Frame

8.89 Sometimes the resolution of one suspension becomes the preparation of another. This results in a "chain of suspensions."

Haydn, *Symphony No. 101 (The Clock)*

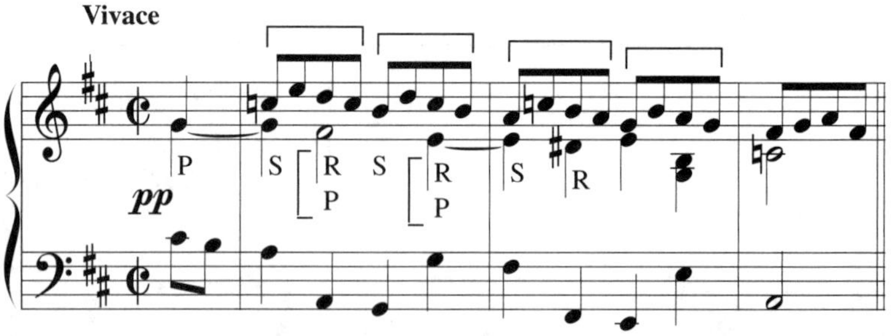

Chains of suspensions are usually part of a harmonic and/or melodic sequence.* The brackets in the above example identify the sequence pattern.

(No response required.)

*Sequence is the repetition of a musical pattern at a different pitch level.

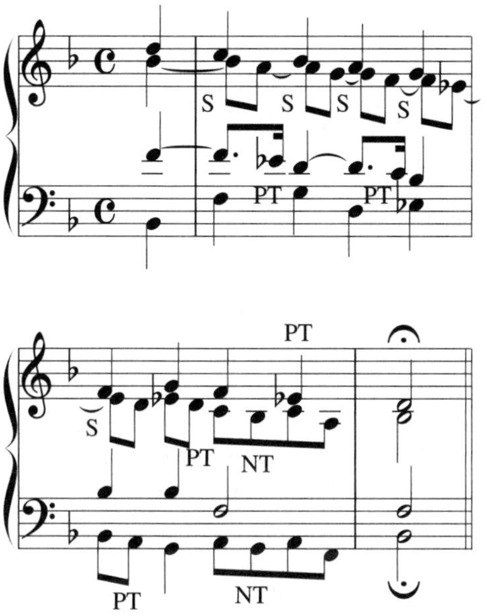

8.90 Complete the alto and tenor voices and label all nonharmonic tones.

Bach, Chorale: *Heut' ist, o Mensch ein Grosser Trauertag*

$$8 \; \underline{\quad} \; \flat 7 \; 9 \; 8 \; 8 \underline{\quad} 7 \; 9 \; 8 \quad 8 \underline{\quad} \flat 6 \; 5 \; 6 \underline{\quad\quad\quad}$$
$$4 \quad 3 \underline{\quad} \qquad 4 \; 3 \underline{\quad} \qquad 4 \; 4 \qquad 3 \; 3 \; 3 \; 3$$

Bb: V⁶___ V I

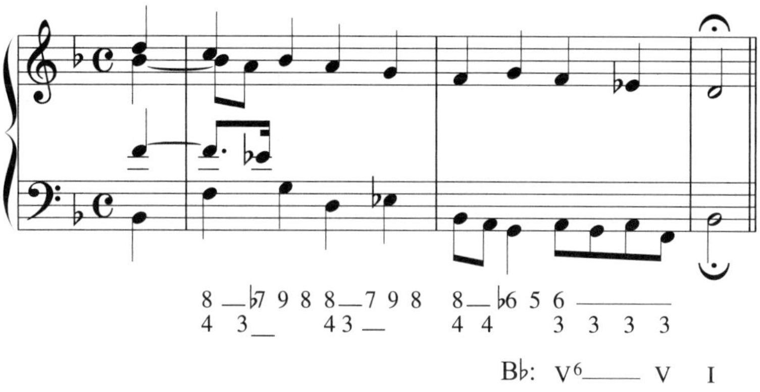

Note: This rather complicated phrase contains many nonharmonic tones (five suspensions, five passing tones, and two neighboring tones). See how many you can identify properly.

8.91 One or more notes may appear between a suspension and its resolution. These are called ORNAMENTATIONS and most take the form of nonharmonic tones.

SINGLE TONE ORNAMENTATIONS

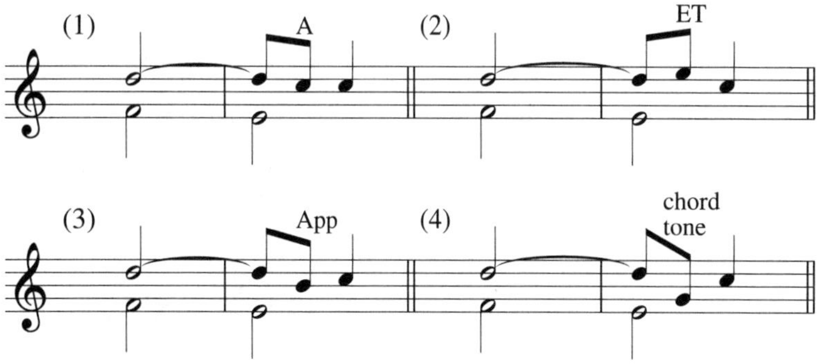

The ornament in (1) consists of an anticipation of the resolution; ornaments in the form of the escape tone and the appoggiatura are shown in (2) and (3); example (4) shows that a chord tone may be inserted between a suspension and its

resolution _____.

8.92 Ornamentations may consist of two or more tones.

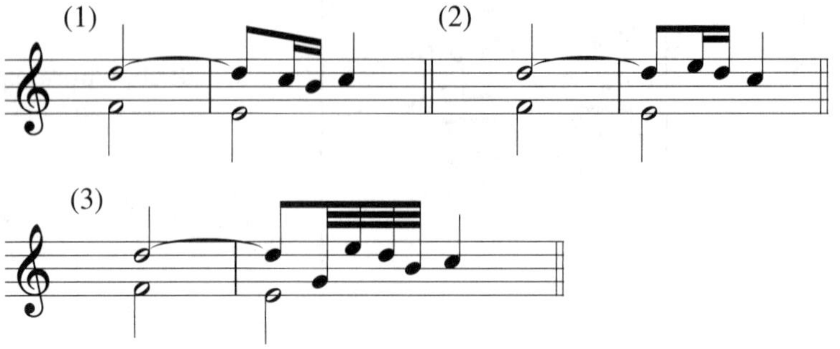

In (1) the B is a lower neighboring tone to the anticipation (C); the E in example (2) is an upper neighboring tone; although rare, florid ornamentations such as in (3) are sometimes encountered (see the following frame).

Ornamentations introduce melodic activity between a suspension and its resolution and may in some cases delay the resolution; but no matter how it is ornamented, the resolution (in relation to the suspension) is by step. Do the majority of suspensions resolve upward or downward? _______________

Downward

8.93 Ornamentations occur frequently when suspensions are woven into a complex contrapuntal fabric. Such a case is shown below where the florid ornamentation is part of the imitative procedure, as is shown by the brackets.

Bach, *Well-Tempered Clavier,* Vol. 1, Fugue XXIV

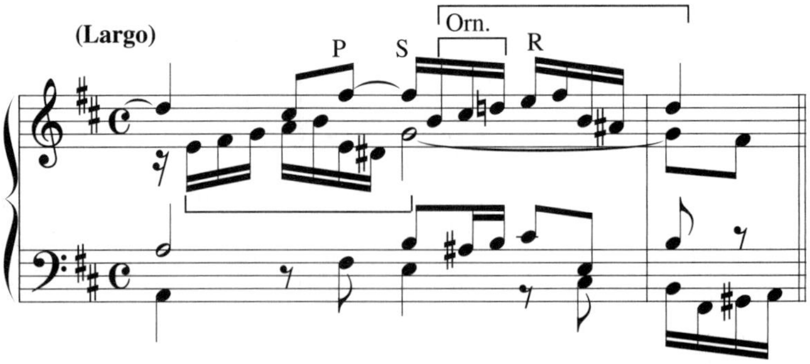

Ornamentation is used to increase melodic activity and give variety to suspension figures. Suspensions are ornamented by inserting a note (or notes) between the preparation and the suspension. (True/False) ___________

False
(Ornamentation occurs between the suspension and its resolution.)

8.94 Complete the alto and tenor voices and label each nonharmonic tone. In the case of suspensions indicate the preparation (P), suspension (S), and ornamentation (O).

Bach, Chorale: *Das alte Jahr vergangen ist*

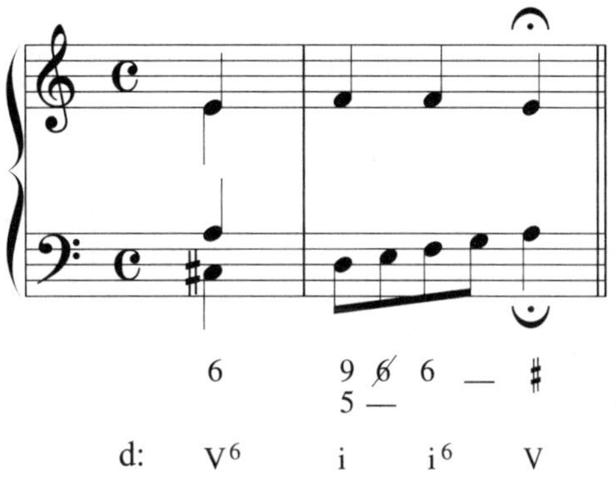

This example shows that the bass (as well as other voices) may move as the suspension resolves. The above is a 9–8 type suspension; but due to the movement in the bass, the result is actually a 9–6 suspension.

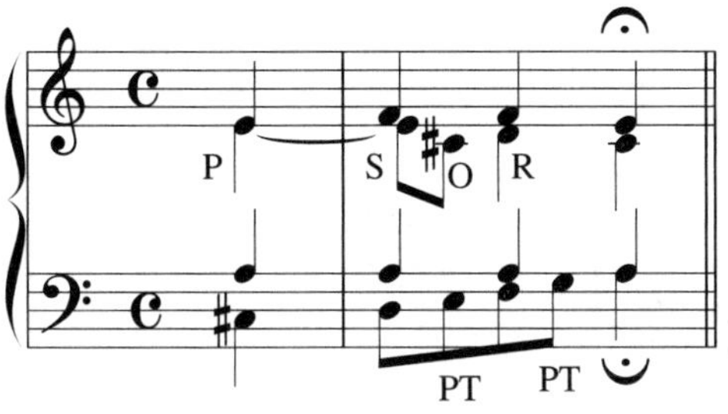

8.95 There may also be a change of harmony as the suspension resolves. This is shown at the asterisk.

Bach, Chorale: *Christ lag in Todesbanden*

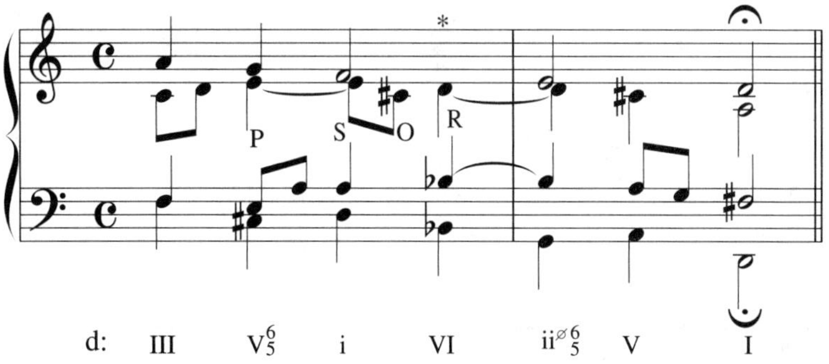

The suspension and its resolution do not always occur over the same ____________ note.

bass

8.96 In the following example, complete the alto and tenor voices and label each nonharmonic tone. In the case of suspensions indicate each part of the figure. (Use the symbol P, S, R, and O). Analyze.

Bach, Chorale: *Danket dem Herren, denn er ist sehr freundlich*

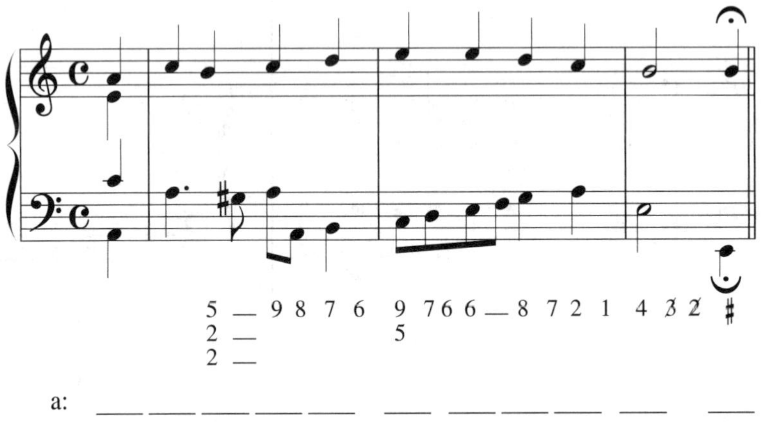

Note: This phrase contains six suspensions; label each carefully.

8.97 Continue as in the preceding frame.

Bach, Chorale: *Es spricht der Unweisen Mund*

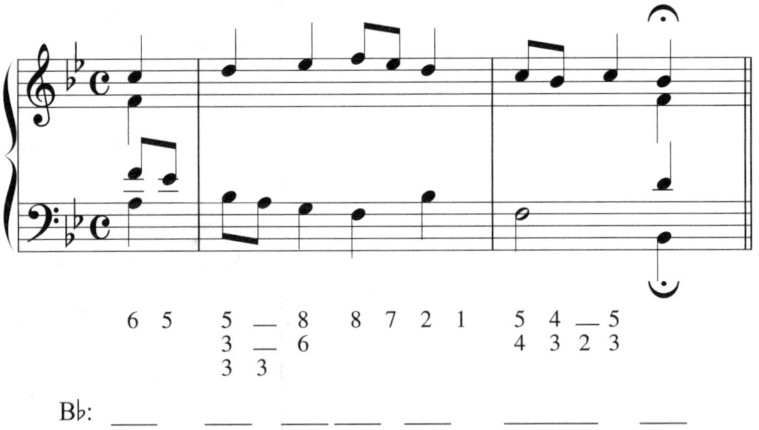

Expository Frame

8.98 Suspensions cause dissonance to occur on the accented portions of the beat or measure; thus they contribute to a higher level of tension than unaccented nonharmonic tones. But since suspensions resolve by step, the result is a smooth, satisfying release from tension. The suspension is the most complex nonharmonic tone, so review carefully the principles that govern its use as stated on the next page:

1. The suspension occurs on a *strong* beat or portion of a beat.

2. The resolution usually occurs on the *weak* beat (or portion of a beat) immediately following the suspension.

3. The preparation is the same pitch as the suspension and is usually equal to or longer than the time value of the suspension.

4. The majority of suspensions resolve downward. (Suspensions that resolve upward are sometimes called *retardations.*)

5. The preparation is usually sustained into the suspension (often by the use of a tie), but the suspension may also be re-sounded. (Some writers refer to such suspensions as *appoggiaturas.*)

6. Suspensions are classified according to the intervals that occur above the bass. The following types result: 4–3, 7–6, 9–8, 2–1, and 2–3.

7. Ornamentation consisting of one, two, or more tones may appear between the suspension and its resolution.

(No response required.)

Expository Frame

8.99 The example below shows nonharmonic tones that are called CHANGING TONES (symbol: CT):

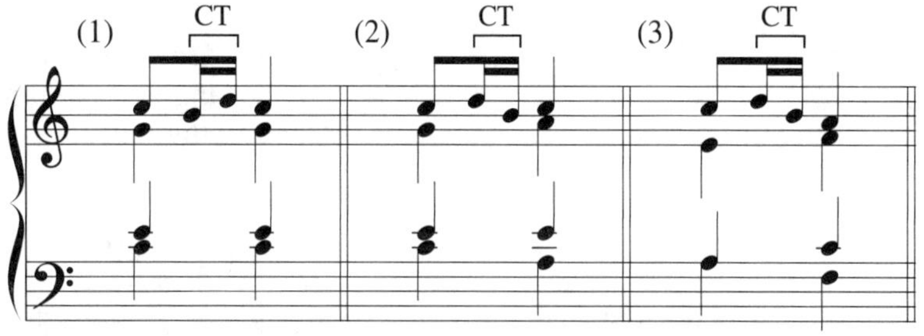

Changing tones fall into a pattern of four notes, *the first and last of which are harmonic.* The second tone of the figure is approached by step and is left by a leap of a third in the opposite direction. The third tone (also nonharmonic) resolves by step to the final tone of the figure.

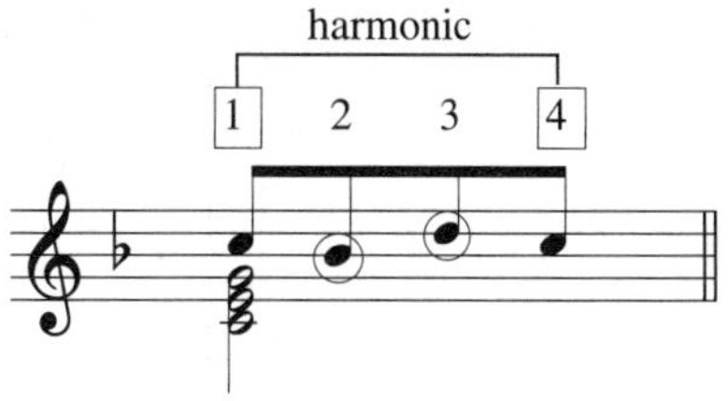

(No response required.)

leap	8.100 In the preceding frame the *first* nonharmonic tone is approached by step and the *second* by ______________.
step	8.101 The resolution of the *second* nonharmonic tone in the changing tone figure is by ______________.
(3)	8.102 Which example below shows changing tones? _______ 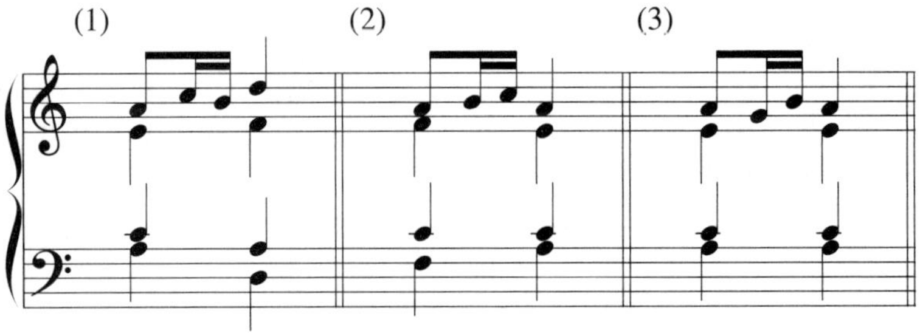
escape tone	8.103 One may wish to regard one of the nonharmonic tones of the changing tone figure as an ornamentation of a neighboring tone or passing tone.  The second of the two changing tones in both (1) and (2) is an ornamentation of a neighboring tone; in (3) the first changing tone is an ornamentation of a passing tone. The ornamentation in (1) and (2) is in the form of an appoggiatura; the ornamentation in (3) is in the form of a(n) ______________.

8.104 Circle and label all of the nonharmonic tones in the example below:

Berlioz, *Symphonie Fantastique*

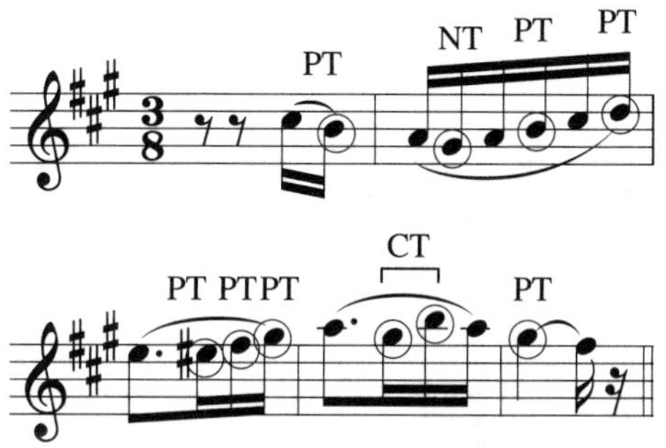

8.105 When a tone is retained in one part while harmonies that are foreign to it are produced by other parts the effect is called a PEDAL (symbol: Ped).*

Bach, *French Suite No. 1,* Allemande

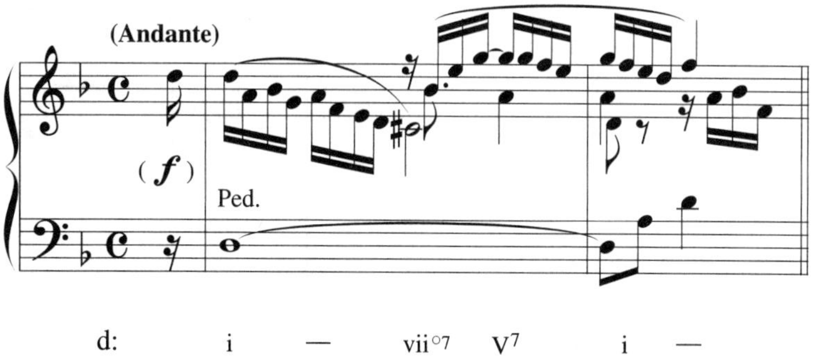

The tone D in the lowest part is sustained while the upper parts produce independent harmonies. What relation does the pedal (D) have to the tonality of this example? It is the __________.

tonic

*This device is also called *pedal point* or *organ point.*

8.106 The pedal device derives its name from the organist's technique of holding down a pedal while playing other harmonics above it. Pedals occur most frequently in the bass part. However, they may also occur in the upper or middle parts. The terms *inverted pedal* and *inner pedal* are sometimes used in such cases.

Bach, Chorale Prelude: *Vor deinen Thron tret' ich*

The pedal in the example above occurs in the highest voice. (True/False) _____________

True

8.107 The pedal may be any scale degree, but it is usually either the tonic or dominant. Occasionally both the tonic and dominant are used simultaneously. The result is a double pedal.

Schumann, *Album for the Young,* Op. 68, No. 18

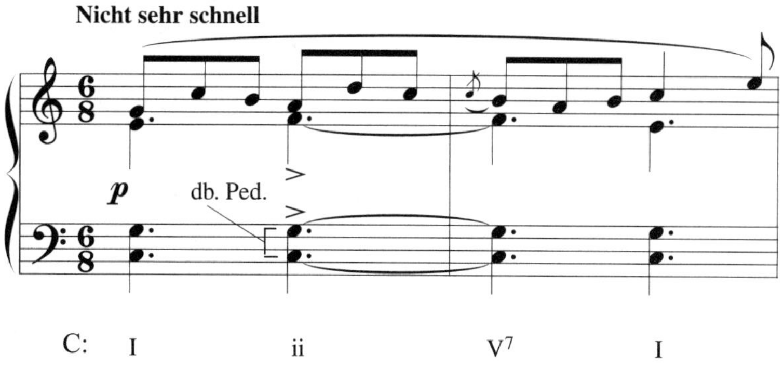

The pedal device gives a static quality in contrast to the harmonies with which it is associated. It tends to (strengthen/weaken) ____________________ the tonality.

strengthen

8.108 The pedal usually begins and ends as a harmonic tone. In this way its presence in the musical texture is "legitimized." Before proceeding to another tone, a pedal must be included once again as part of the harmony.

A nonharmonic tone that is approached and left by the same tone is called a pedal. (True/False) ____________

True

8.109 The pedal is sometimes more than just a sustained tone. The example below shows a double pedal (A–A) that is part of a melodic figure. Note that the higher pedal is embellished by lower neighbors (G♯s) to give added rhythmic interest.

Bach, *Well-Tempered Clavier,* Vol. 1, Prelude XX

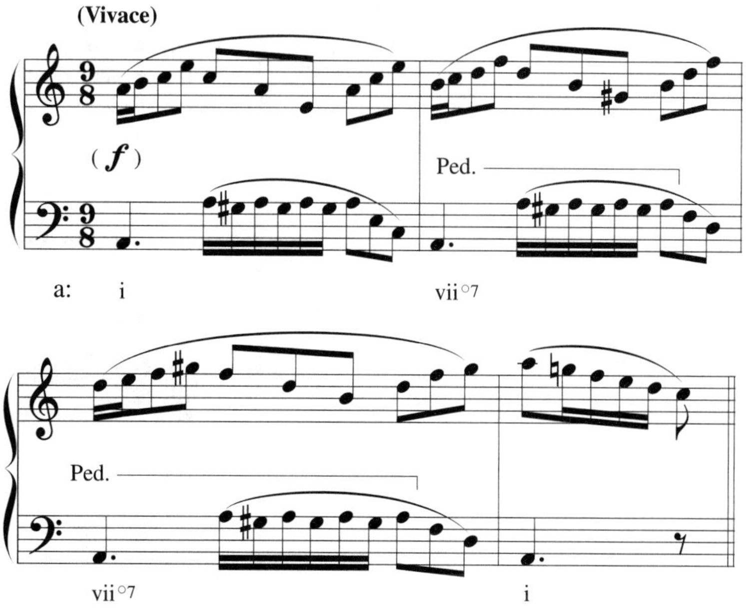

(Continued on the next page)

Rhythmic and melodic figuration is used to counteract the tonally static quality of the pedal.

Which scale degree is stressed by the double pedal in the above example? The _____________.

first

8.110 Since the pedal contributes greatly to tonal stability, accompanying harmony may be in sharp contrast to it. When double or triple pedals, or pedals with melodic significance are used, the effect is often of polyharmony or polytonality. Passages such as the one below are common in twentieth-century music.

Stravinsky, *Le Sacre du Printemps*

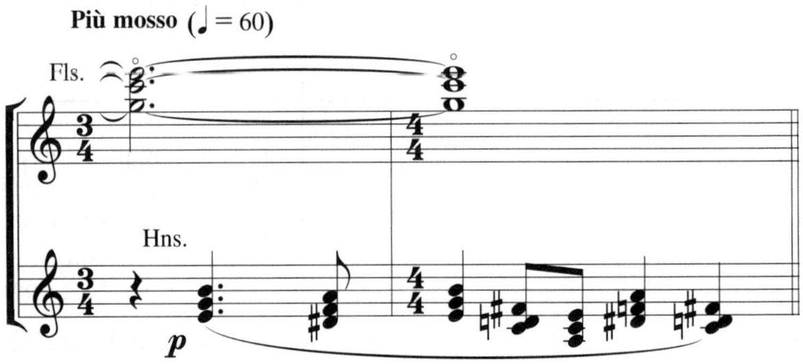

The triad sounded by the flutes is an example of a (single/double/triple) _____________ pedal.

triple

8.111 All of the nonharmonic tones presented thus far have been no more than a second away from either the preceding or succeeding tone. One nonharmonic tone, however, is both approached and left by leap. This type of nonharmonic tone is called a FREE TONE (symbol: FT).

Chopin, *Valse Brillante,* Op. 34, No. 2

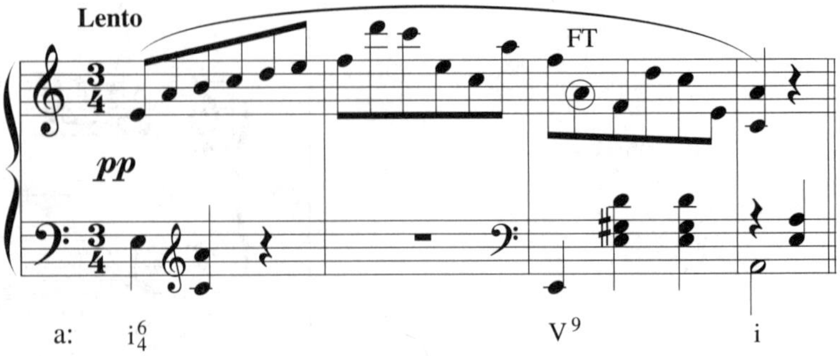

leap

The free tone is the only nonharmonic tone that is approached and left by _____________.

---

(3)

8.112 The free tone is the rarest of all nonharmonic tones so it will not be stressed here. In most cases it can be analyzed as part of a more complex sonority. The free tone in the preceding frame, for example, could be considered the eleventh of an expanded dominant sonority.

Which example below shows a free tone? _______

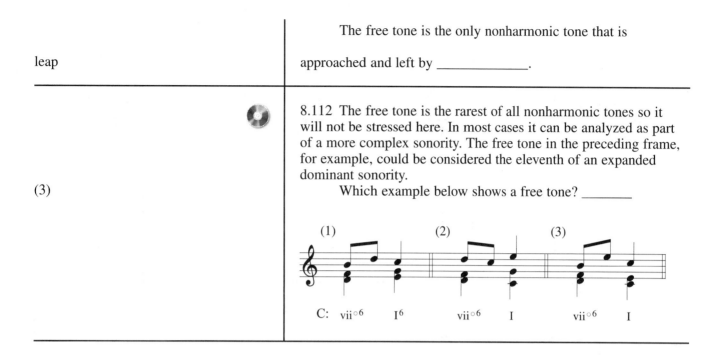

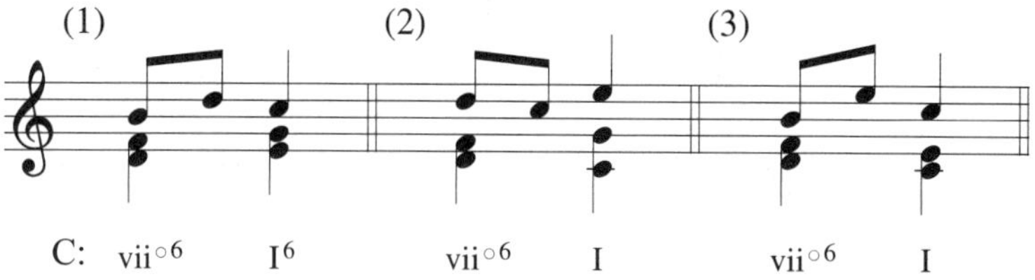

Summary

Nonharmonic tones are extraneous to the harmony. Most nonharmonic tones appear in such a way that chords retain their integrity. In other words, the nonharmonic tone cannot be mistaken for a chord tone. Some tones, however, can be analyzed as being either harmonic or nonharmonic. For this reason, the chord first should be identified clearly. Thus, any tone that does not fall into the chord as *analyzed* must be a nonharmonic tone.

Later on in *Harmonic Materials and Tonal Music: Part II*, Chapter 3.0 it will be found that nonharmonic tones also may be chromatically altered to supply further tonal color and variety. These "altered" nonharmonic tones are used to bring attention to particular harmonies as well. The most frequent alterations found are the *raised fourth* and the *lowered seventh* scale degrees.

The rhythmic activity that nonharmonic tones give to each part contributes to the independence of the melodic lines. Greater smoothness is another result of good nonharmonic tone usage. Of still greater importance, however, is the introduction of dissonance to the musical texture. Although not all nonharmonic tones are dissonant, most are. Dissonant tones that immediately resolve into more consonant ones cause an ebb and flow of tensions, which helps produce the effect of forward motion.

Nonharmonic tones provide the composer with the means of introducing dissonance into music to whatever degree desired. Nonharmonic dissonance, however, is fleeting; it is tightly controlled in accordance with established practice and is readily tolerated by the listener.

The terms that are explained or used in this chapter are listed below in chronological order:

harmonic tones	changing tone	retardation
nonharmonic tones	auxiliary tone	chain of suspensions
passing tone	appoggiatura	sequence
accented	escape tone	ornamentation
unaccented	*échappée*	changing tones
neighboring tone	anticipation	pedal (point or tone)
returning tone	suspension	free tone

The various types of nonharmonic tones are summarized and illustrated in the chart that follows:

SUMMARY OF NONHARMONIC TONES

Name	Symbol	Example	Approach	Left	Direction of Resolution
Passing tone (unaccented or accented)	PT		By step	By step	Same as approach
Neighboring tone (unaccented or accented)	NT		By step	By step	Opposite to approach
Appoggiatura (unaccented or accented)	App	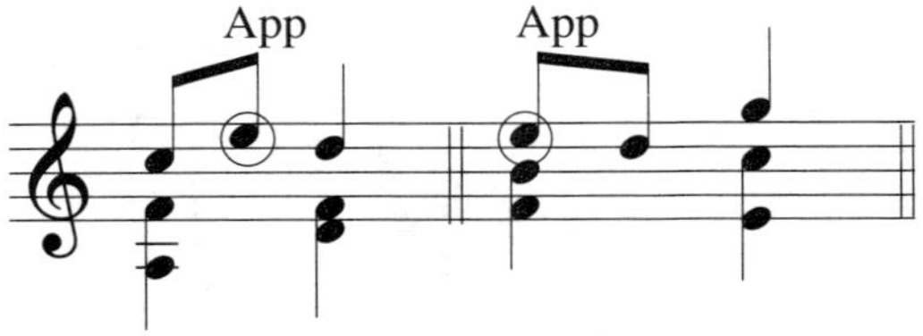	By leap (the App. may be the initial tone)	By step	Usually opposite to approach
Escape tone	ET		By step	By leap	Usually opposite to approach
Anticipation	A		Usually by step	By the same tone	Same tone

SUMMARY OF NONHARMONIC TONES

Name	Symbol	Example	Approach	Left	Direction of Resolution
Suspension	S		By the same tone (tied or reiterated)	By step	Up or down
Changing tones	CT	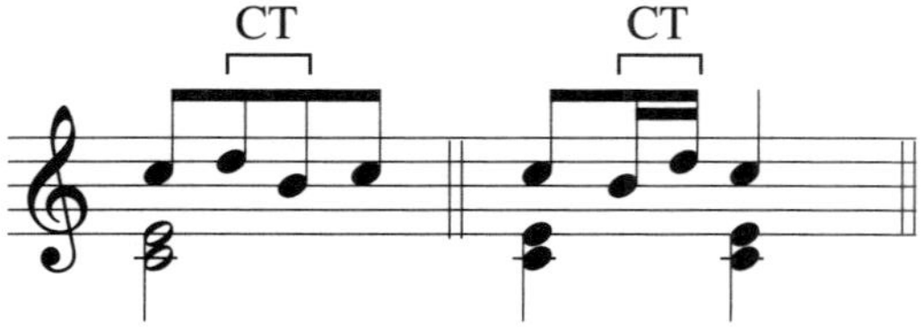	By step or leap	By step or leap	Usually the same tone as the approach
Pedal	Ped	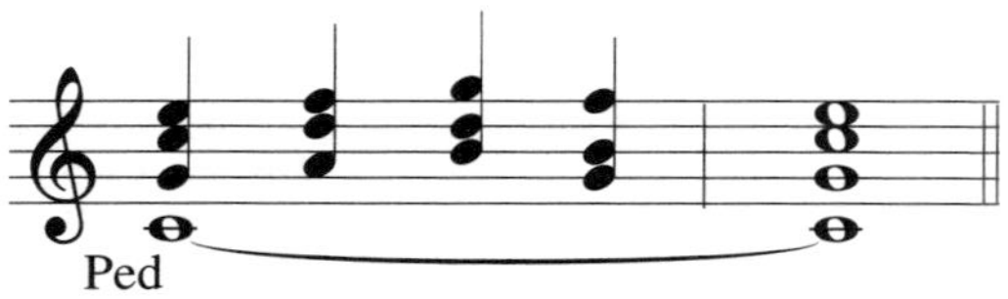	By the same tone	By the same tone	Same tone
Free tone	FT		By leap	By leap	Usually opposite to approach

Mastery Frames

8–1 Name the nonharmonic tone described in each case.

(1) Approached by step and left by repetition.

____

(2) Approached and left by step in the same direction.

____

(3) Approached by step and left by leap.

____

(4) Approached by leap and left by step.

____

(5) Approached and left by step with a change in direction.

____

(6) Approached by the same tone and left by step.

____

(1) Anticipation (8.61–.65)

(2) Passing tone (8.15–.33)

(3) Escape tone (8.50–.55)

(4) Appoggiatura (8.42–.49)

(5) Neighboring tone (8.34–.41)

(6) Suspension (8.69–.98)

8–2 Identify the three parts of the suspension figure shown below.

(1) ____________

(2) ____________

(3) ____________

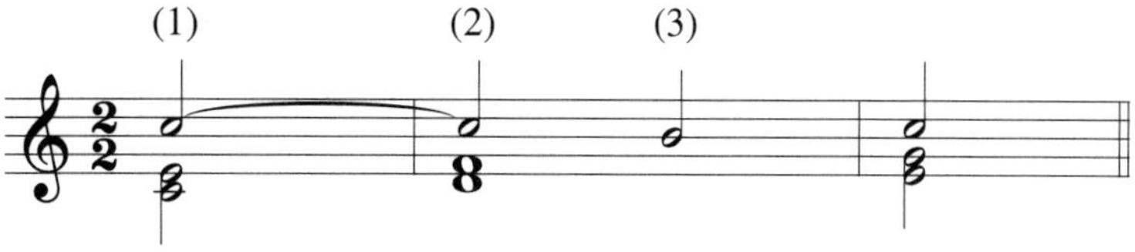

(1) Preparation

(2) Suspension

(3) Resolution

(8.70–.73)

2–3 (8.81)	8–3 Which of the suspension types (4–3, 7–6, 9–8, or 2–3) would be found in the bass voice? _______
(1) Changing tones (8.99–.104) (2) Free tone (8.111–.112) (3) Retardation (8.75)	8–4 Name the nonharmonic tones at the asterisks. (1) ____________ (2) ____________ (3) ____________ 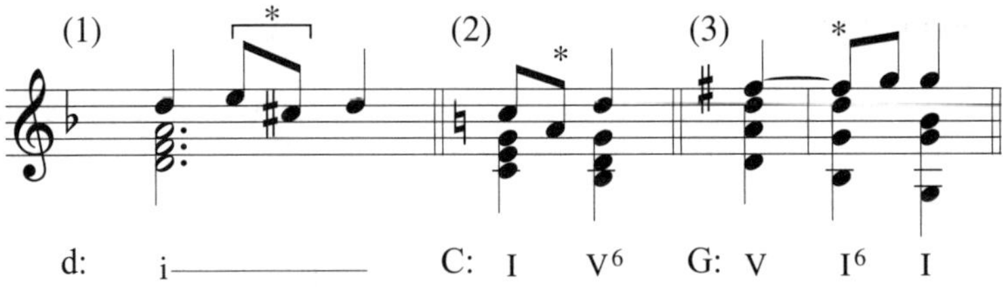
pedal (8.100–.110)	8–5 A tone that is retained in one part (usually the bass) while harmonies that are foreign to it are produced by other parts is called a ____________.

Supplementary Activities

1. Continue with the same activities as suggested in Chapter 7.0 but incorporate the addition of nonharmonic tones into the context. An ability to begin examining slightly more complex musical excerpts as well as to make more extensive comments about their musical contents should now be possible.

2. Continue to expand work in composition based on previous chapter experiences as well as suggestions found in Supplementary Assignment 8–1 or 2, No. 4.

Supplementary Assignments

ASSIGNMENTS 8–1 Name ______________________________

1. Circle all nonharmonic tones and label with abbreviations (PT, NT, etc.).

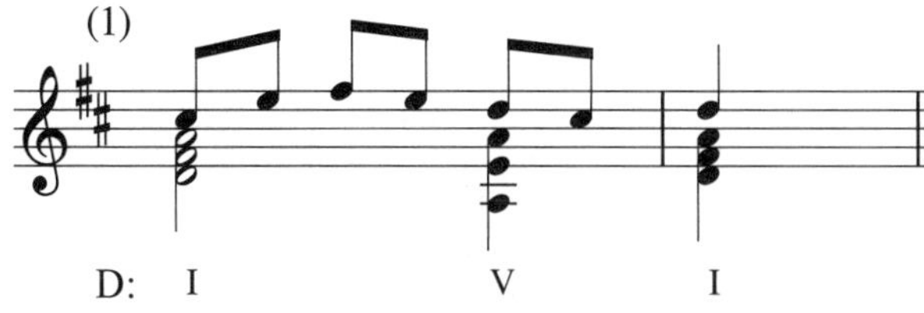

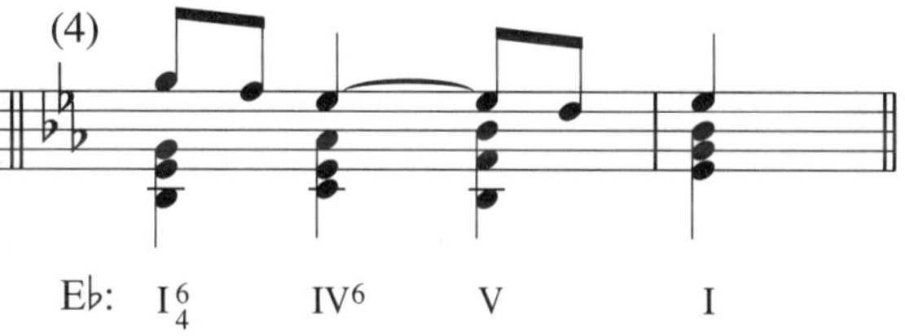

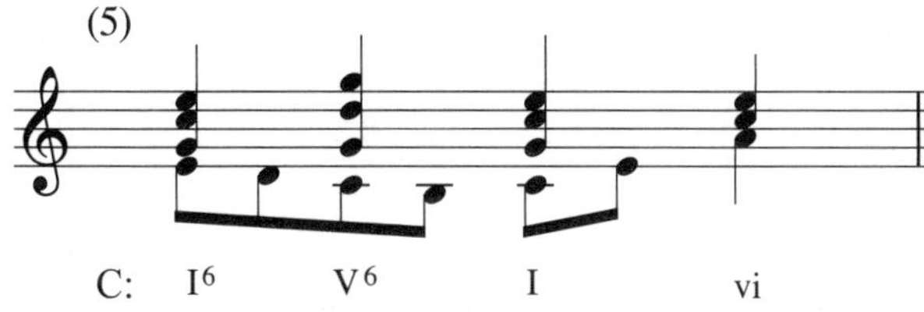

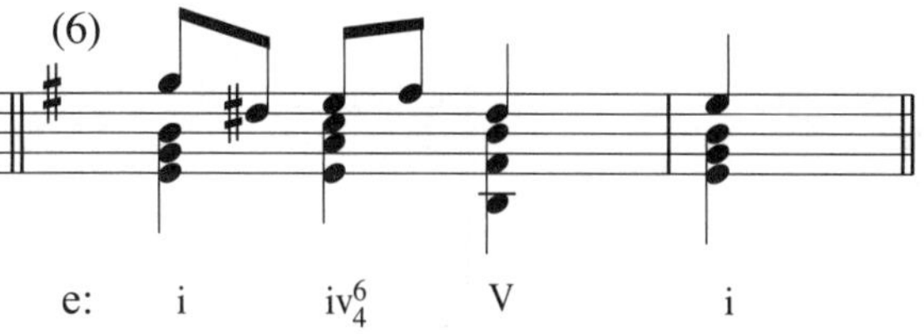

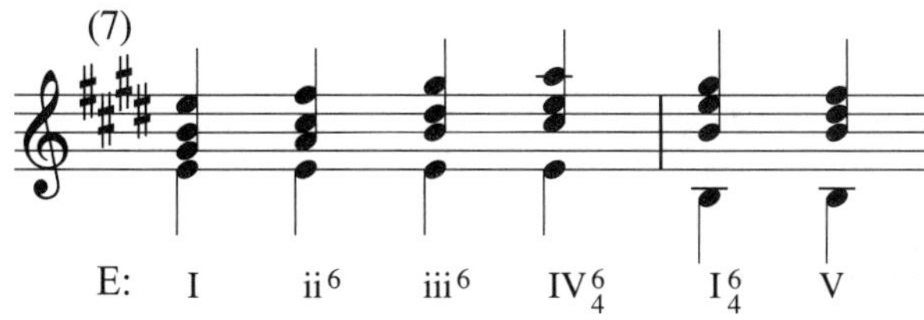

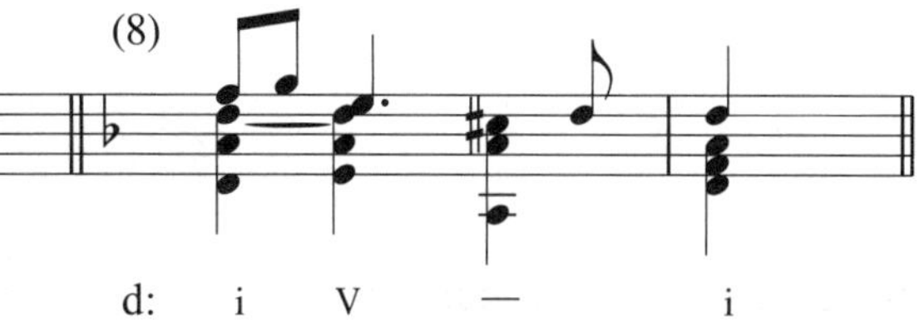

2. Write nonharmonic tones as directed. *(Notes may be added to the soprano or bass parts. Also, use accidentals when needed to produce the chord quality indicated by the roman numerals. Irregular doubling may be needed to facilitate creation of nonharmonic tones.)*

(1) PT (2) NT (3) ET (4) A

c: V I F: I vi G: I V a: V i

(5) App (6) 4–3 S (7) 7–6 S (8) FT

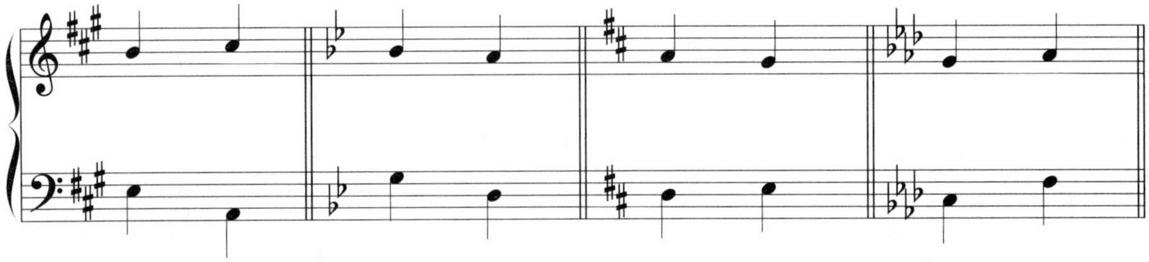

A: V I g: i V D: I vii°6 f: V i

3. Write the three upper voices to fulfill the requirements.

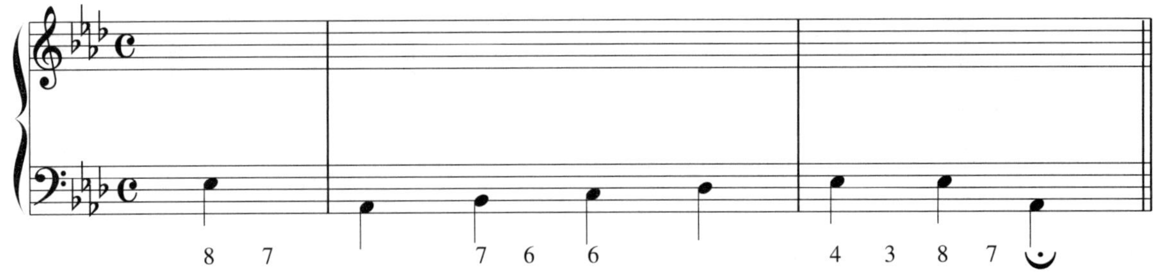

A♭: V I vii°6 I6 IV V ——— I

4. Compose a short work for four-part chorus (or other media, at the discretion of your instructor). Be guided by the items below.

(1) Length: at least 2 phrases
(2) Chorale style and texture (use “oo” or “ah” as singing syllables; or select/set a text of your own choosing or writing
(3) Meter and key of your choice
(4) Make liberal use of nonharmonic tones in the melody
(5) Identify all nonharmonic tones
(6) Do a harmonic analysis (either roman numeral or alternative or both)
(7) Use complete notation

ASSIGNMENTS 8–2 Name ______________________________

1. Rewrite the soprano part to show three different ornamentations of the suspension.

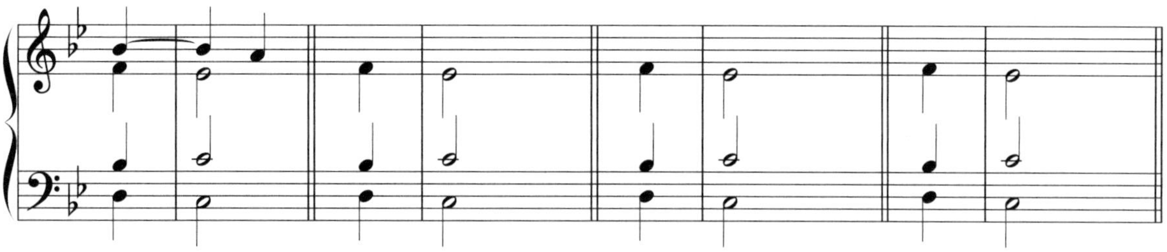

2. Write the alto and tenor voices according to the figured bass symbols. Label all nonharmonic tones and provide the roman numeral analysis.

(A)

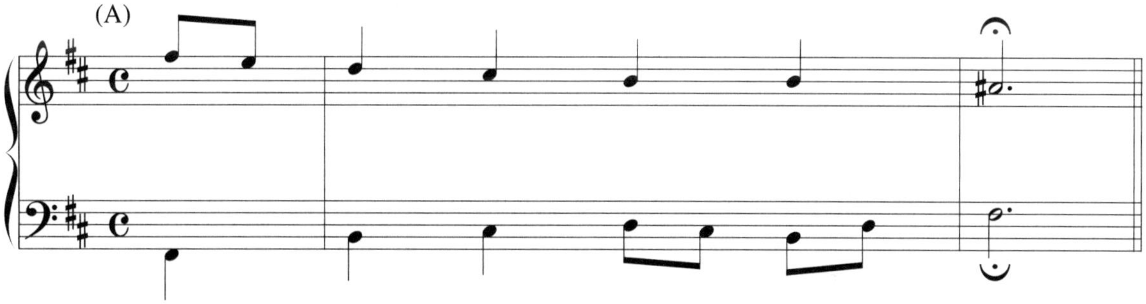

(B)

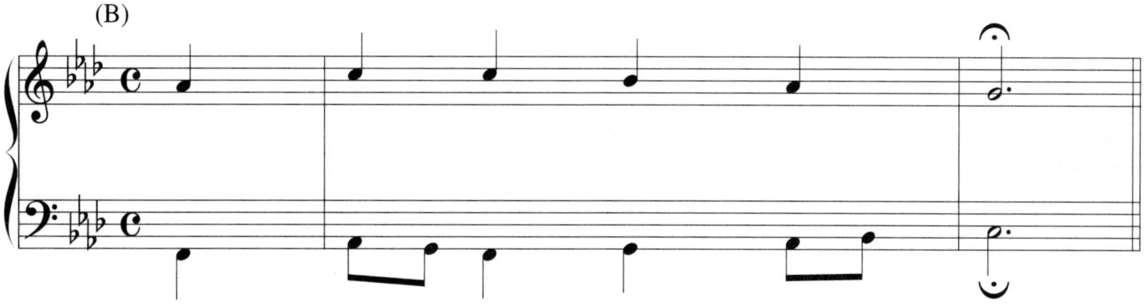

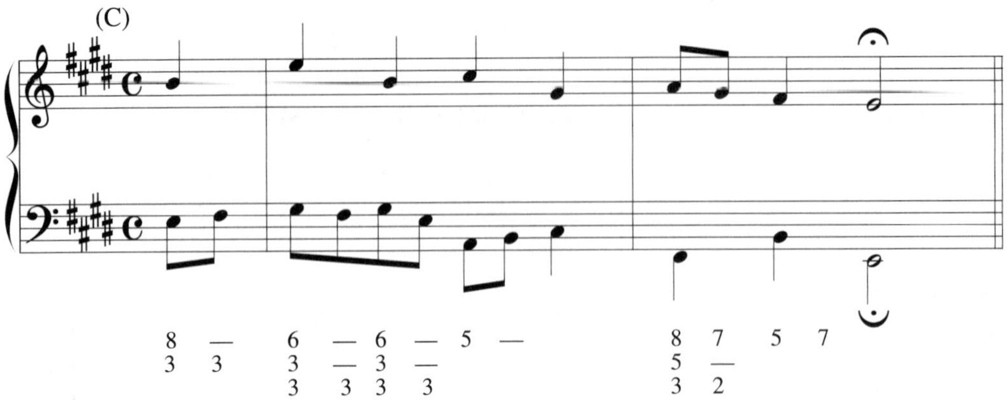

E: ___ ___ ___ ___ ___ ___ ___ ___

3. Supply four-voice harmonizations for the melodies below that include the nonharmonic tones indicated. Also provide the roman numeral analysis.

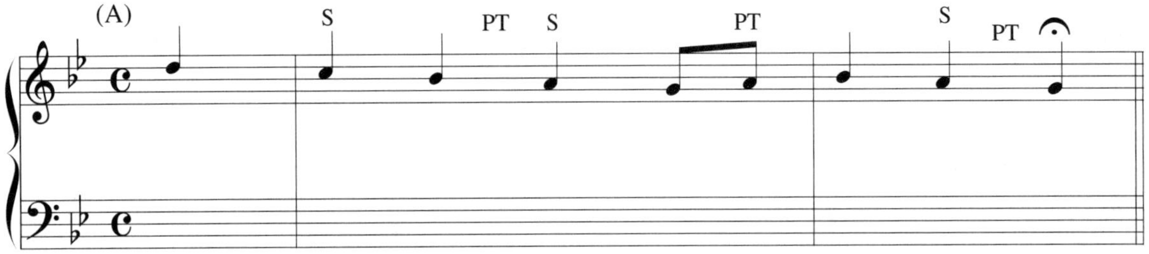

g: ___ ___ ___ ___ ___ ___ ___ ___

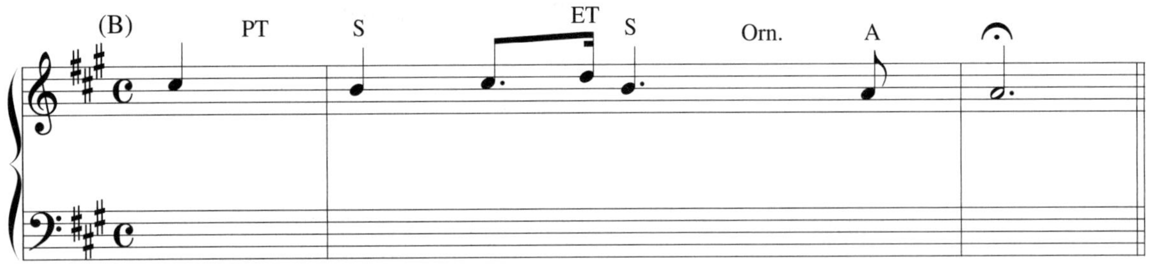

A: ___ ___ ___ ___ ___

4. Compose a short work for the piano (or other media, at the discretion of your instructor). Be guided by the items below.

(1) Length: 4–8 phrases
(2) Homophonic texture
(3) Meter and key of your choice
(4) Piano styles 2–18 are recommended
(5) Make liberal use of nonharmonic tones in the melody
(6) Identify all nonharmonic tones
(7) Do a harmonic analysis (either roman numeral or alternative or both)
(8) Use complete notation

Chapter 9.0
Harmonic Progression

The relation of chords to one another within the structure of tonality was treated in Chapter 2.0. The task now is to distinguish between progressive and retrogressive chord movement (movement of roots), and to examine various patterns of harmonic phrase structure (succession of harmonies within a phrase). The exercises in this chapter will shed additional light on the shaping function of harmony and prepare for the study of harmonization techniques that follows.

chords	9.1 The manner in which chords relate to one another lies at the heart of the study of tonal harmony. A series of chords is called a HARMONIC PROGRESSION. During the period of tonal harmony sufficient consistency in harmonic progression was shown that it is possible to refer to a "language of harmony." A language is established by consistent use, and it is the consistencies in the harmonic language that will be a chief concern. Even though the music of each composer in the period of tonal harmony speaks with a different "accent," the underlying principles are closely related. Harmonic progression is concerned with the way _________ relate to one another.
progression	9.2 The term *harmonic progression* refers in a general way to all harmonic movements. The term PROGRESSION, however, is applied to a particular type of harmonic action: one that gives a sense of "forward motion." Weaker harmonic relations, which sometimes give a sense of "backward motion" are called RETROGRESSIONS. The terms PROGRESSION and RETROGRESSION distinguish between relatively "strong" and "weak" harmonic movements. A "strong," "emphatic" harmonic movement is called a ____________.
progressions (and) retrogressions	9.3 "Strong" and "weak" are very subjective and inadequate words to describe the effect of various harmonic progressions. Above all, they should not be equated with "good" and "bad," since the expressive purpose of a particular passage may be served better by the use of retrogressions than by progressions. One of the ideals of harmony is variety, and too consistent a use of either progressions or retrogressions is undesirable. Harmonic variety is achieved by the use of both ____________ and ____________.

9.4 It is appropriate now to learn to distinguish between progressive and retrogressive harmonic movements.

The harmonic relationship of any two chords is classified according to the interval by which their roots are related.

Write in the space provided beneath each example the basic interval (2nd, 3rd, 4th, etc.) *between the roots* of the two chords.

(First determine the root of each chord.)

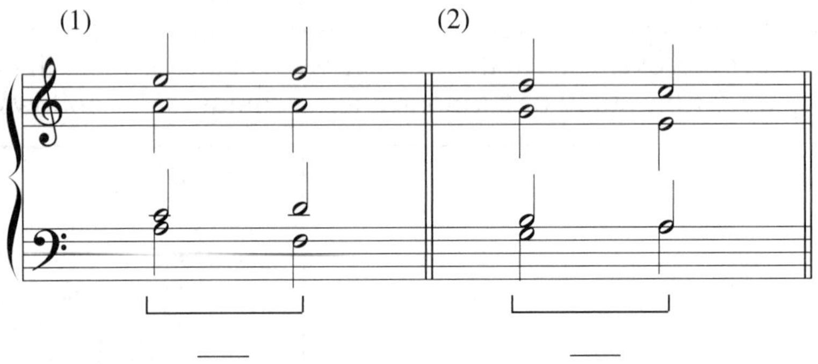

(1) 5th *(or 4th)*

(2) 2nd

9.5 Continue as in the preceding frame.

(First determine the root of each chord.)

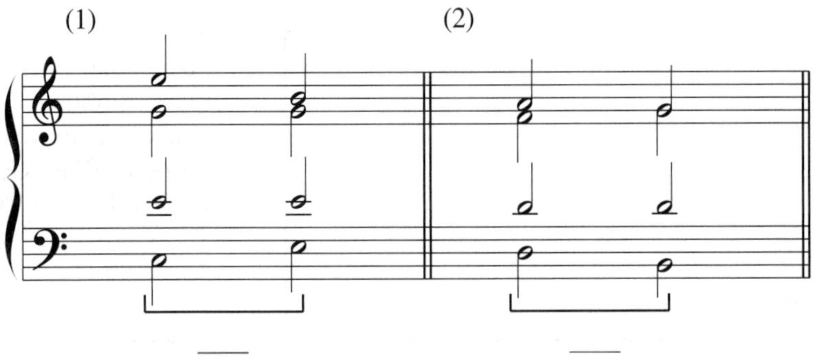

(1) 3rd

(2) 5th *(or 4th)*

9.6 In the preceding two frames the choice of analyzing some of the root movements as either down a fifth or up a fourth was given. Because of interval inversion, the root relationship in either case is the same.

The following example shows that the interval of a fourth up is the same as a fifth down, a sixth up is the same as a third down, and a seventh up is the same as a second down.

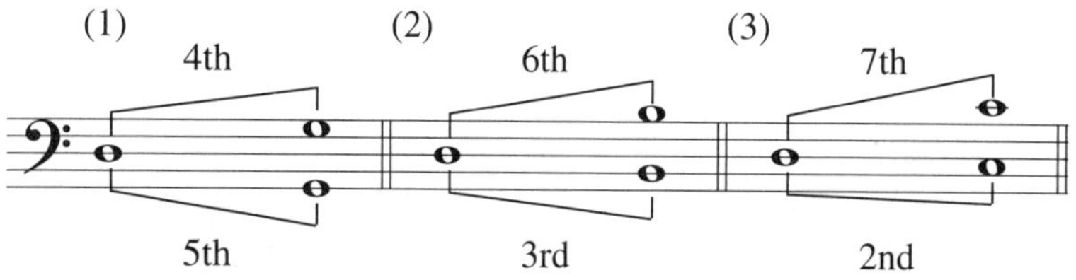

In order to simplify references to root movements, only three basic relationships will be discussed: fifths, thirds, and seconds.

third

Root movement up a sixth is the same as down a ____________.

---

second

9.7 Root movement up a seventh is the same as down a ____________.

---

fourth

9.8 Root movement down a fifth is the same as up a ____________.

---

up

9.9 Root movement down a seventh is the same as _______ a second.

---

(1) 2nd (2) 5th

9.10 Indicate the basic interval between the root of the chords in each case.

(Remember: The three relationships are fifths, thirds, and seconds.)

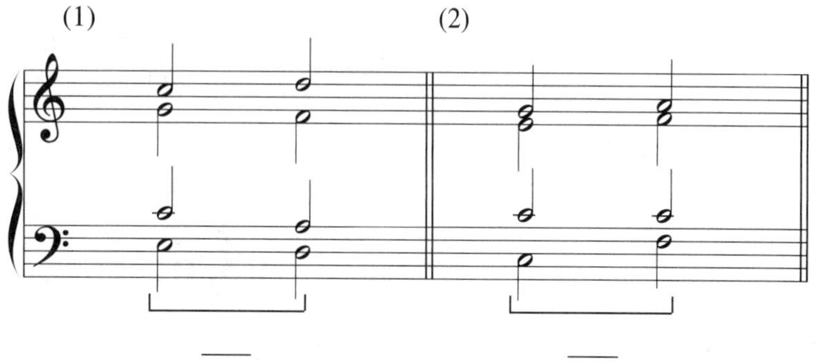

---

thirds, (or) seconds

9.11 If the answer for (2) in the preceding frame was "4th," remember that a fourth up is the same as a fifth down. In this study, basic root relationships are to be analyzed as fifths, ____________, or ____________.

(1) 3rd (2) 5th

9.12 Indicate the basic interval between the roots of the chords in each case.

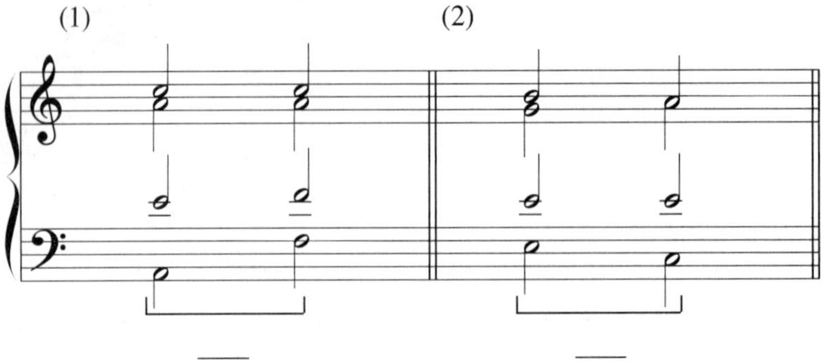

---

(1) 5th (2) 2nd

9.13 Continue as in the preceding frame.

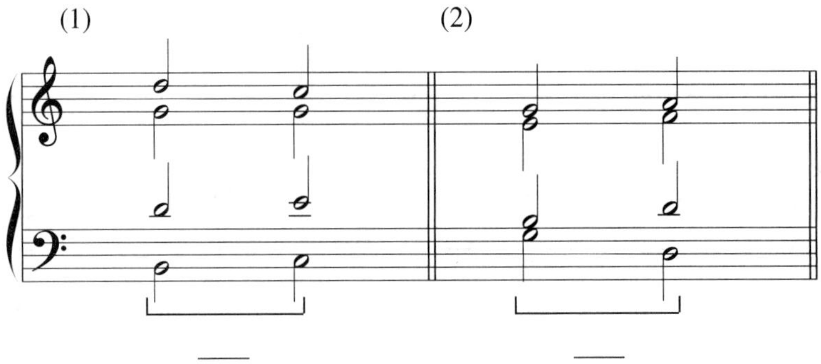

9.14 Do not confuse root movements with the melodic intervals shown in the bass voice.

Graun, Chorale: *Herzliebster Jesu, was hast du verbrochen*

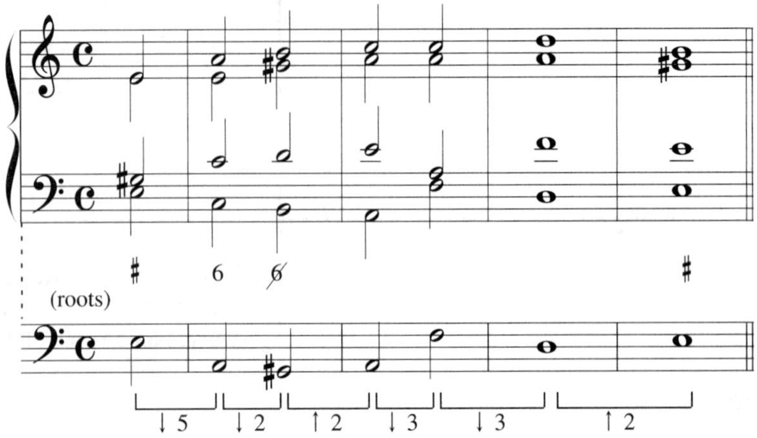

Down a second.

The arrows show the direction of the interval. The symbol ↓ 5, for example, means that the root movement is down a fifth. Notice, too, that the root movement between the fourth and fifth chords is actually *up a sixth.* This is classified as *down a third.*

How would root movement up a seventh be classified?

____

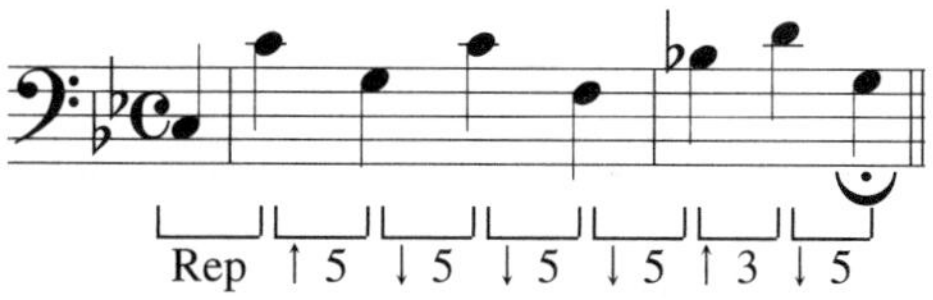

9.15 In order to classify root movements accurately, the root of each chord must be located. Do not be confused when some chords are in first or second inversion.

Write the roots and analyze with arrows and numbers (as in the preceding frame) each of the root movements in the example below.

(Remember: Up a fourth is classified as down a fifth.)

Bach, Chorale: *Von Gott will ich nicht lassen*

(Note: When the root is repeated, abbreviate "Rep.")

9.16 Continue as in the preceding frame.

(Continued on the next page)

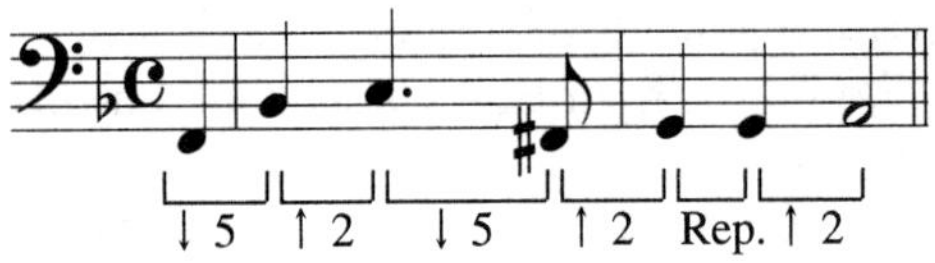

Schumann, *Album for the Young,* Op. 68, No. 41

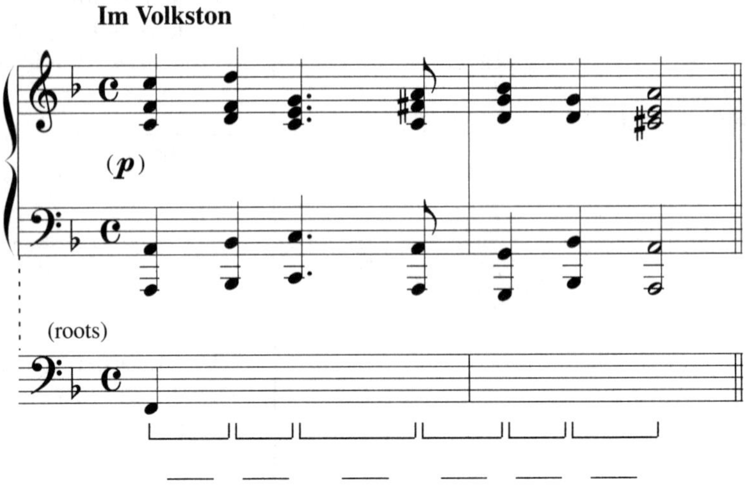

Down in fifths, up in seconds,

(and) down in thirds.

9.17 Chord movements are progressive or retrogressive depending upon the intervallic relation of their roots. Notice: *Inversions do not affect progression/retrogression classification; it is ROOT relations that count.*

Analysis of music from the eighteenth and nineteenth centuries reveals a predominance of root movements *down in fifths, up in seconds,* and *down in thirds.* The prevalence of these relationships has established a feeling of "progression," which contrasts with a feeling of "retrogression" when roots move otherwise.

List the root movements that result in PROGRESSIONS.

______________________, ______________________

and ______________________.

---

(3)

9.18 Which example below demonstrates a *progression*? ______

(Take care not to be fooled by inversions.)

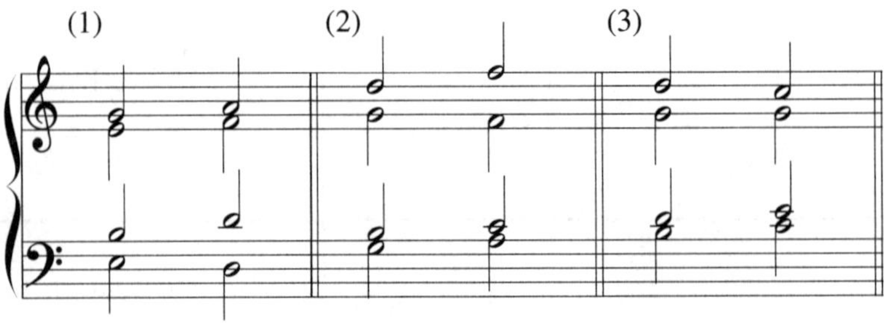

(2)

9.19 Which example below demonstrates a *progression*? _______

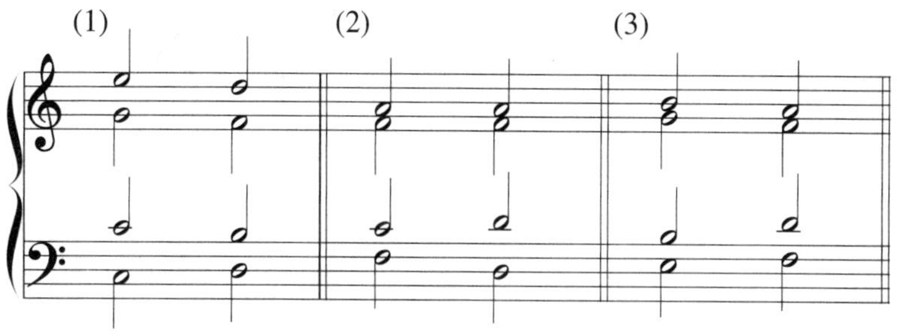

fifth

9.20 The diagram below may help you to remember the progressions that occur when roots move *down in fifths:*

ROOT MOVEMENT DOWN IN FIFTHS

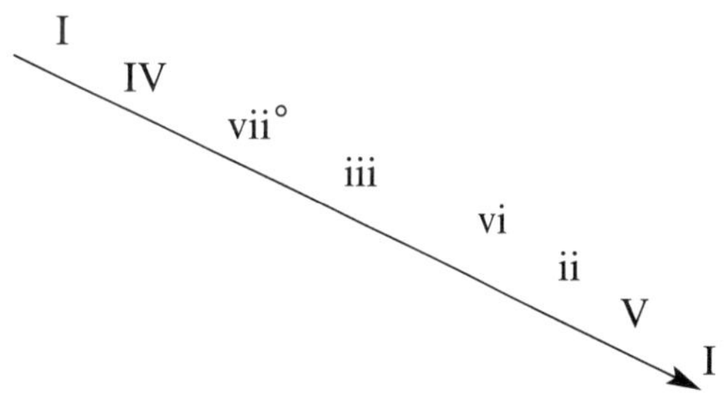

(Note: In this diagram, as in others elsewhere in this book, the roman numerals are given as for a major key. The progressions are equally valid in a minor key.)

The mediant chord followed by the submediant is a progression because the root movement is down a ____________.

1 (and) 2

4 (and) 5

9.21 In the following example there are two progressions in which roots move *down in fifths*. Between which chords do these occur?

Between chords _______ and _______, and between chords _______ and _______.

(You may wish to locate the root of each chord on the empty staff provided for this purpose.)

(Continued on the next page)

Brahms, *Symphony No. 1,* Op. 68

9.22 The diagram below shows progression of roots moving *up in seconds:*

ROOT MOVEMENT UP IN SECONDS

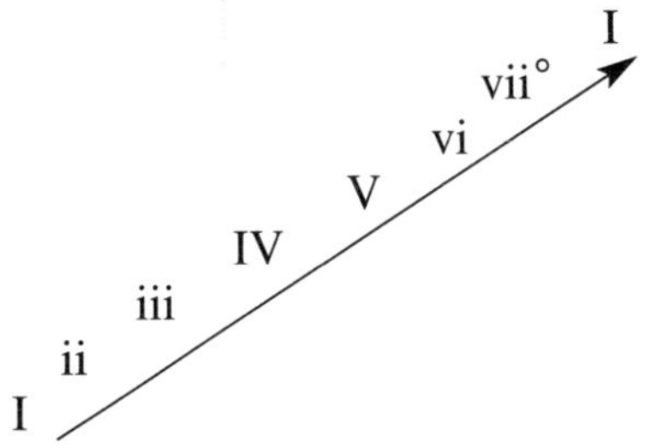

Is the subdominant chord followed by the dominant a progression or a retrogression? A ____________

progression

9.23 In the following example, roots move *up in seconds* twice. Between which chords do these progressions occur?

Between chords _______ and _______, and between chords _______ and _______.

(You may wish to locate the root of each chord on the empty staff provided for this purpose.)

3 (and) 4

5 (and) 6

Graun, Chorale: *O Traurigkeit, o Herzeleid*

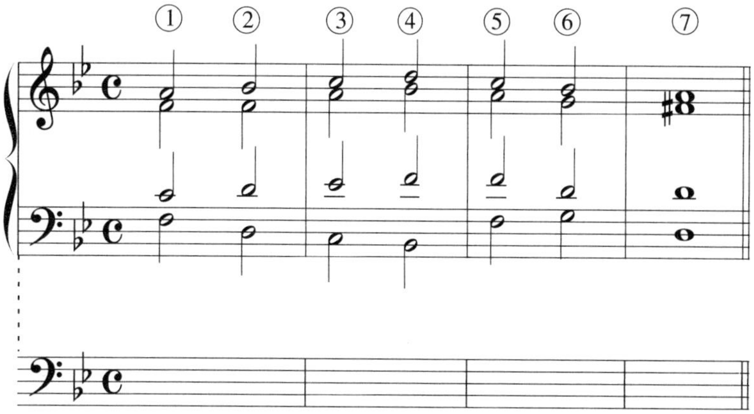

9.24 The diagram below shows progressions of roots moving *down in thirds.*

ROOT MOVEMENT DOWN IN THIRDS

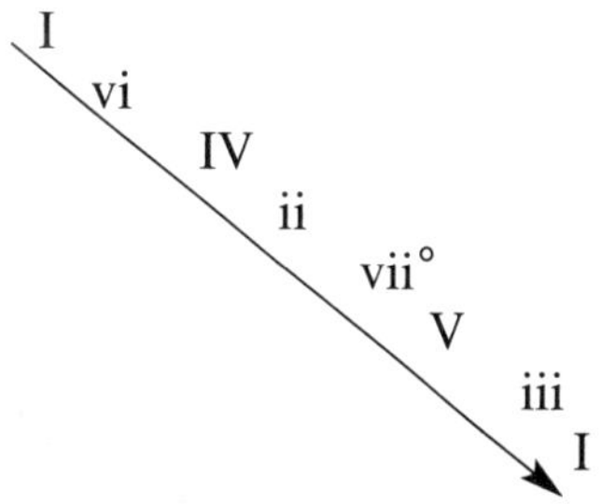

Roots moving down in thirds produce *progressions.* What term applies to root movements *UP in thirds*? ____________

Retrogression

9.25 When a chord moves to another chord whose root is a third higher, the new root is contained in the previous chord. This results in a weaker effect than when the root moves *down a third.* In this case the new root has not been heard previously; it is a new sound and the result is a "stronger" sense of progression.

(1) UP a 3rd (2) DOWN a 3rd

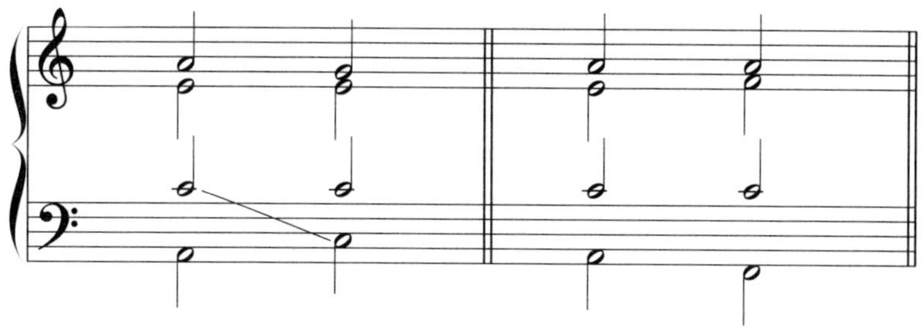

(Continued on the next page)

subdominant (IV)	What chord follows the submediant (vi) if the root moves down a third? The ______________
(1) ✓	9.26 Check (✓) the correct option: 1. Harmonic movement from one chord to another is classified as either a progression or a retrogression depending upon the root movement. 2. It is desirable that all harmonic movement should be progressions. True statements: (1) ______ (2) ______ Both ______ Neither ______
Both ✓	9.27 Check (✓) the correct option: (1) Root movement up a sixth is the same as down a third. (2) Root movement up a fourth is the same as down a fifth. True statement: (1) ______ (2) ______ Both ______ Neither ______
False. *(2) and (4) are retrogressions.*	9.28 All of the root movements listed below are progressions. (True/False) ____________ (1) up a 2nd (3) down a 3rd (2) down a 2nd (4) up a 5th
(2)	9.29 It has been learned that *progressive* harmonic movement occurs when roots move down in fifths, up in seconds, or down in thirds. One other important principle remains to be stated: *Harmonic movement from the tonic to any other chord is progressive regardless of the interval involved.* In view of this statement, which case below shows progressive harmonic movement? ______ KEY of D MAJOR 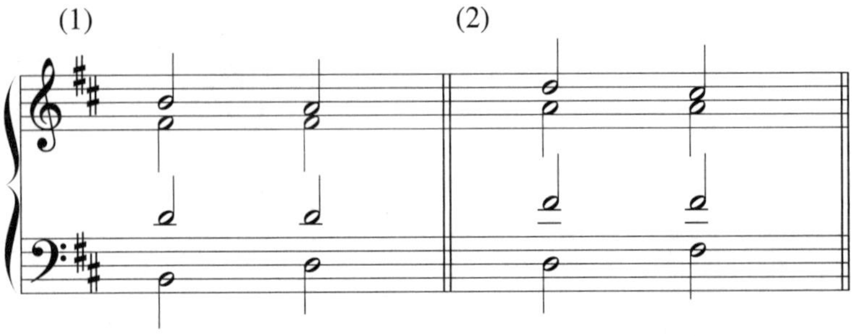

9.30 Because the tonic triad is built on the keynote it is the least active chord in any key. Thus, movement from the tonic to any other triad is movement to a *more active chord.*

Which example shows *retrogressive* harmonic movement? _______

KEY of G MINOR

(1) (2)

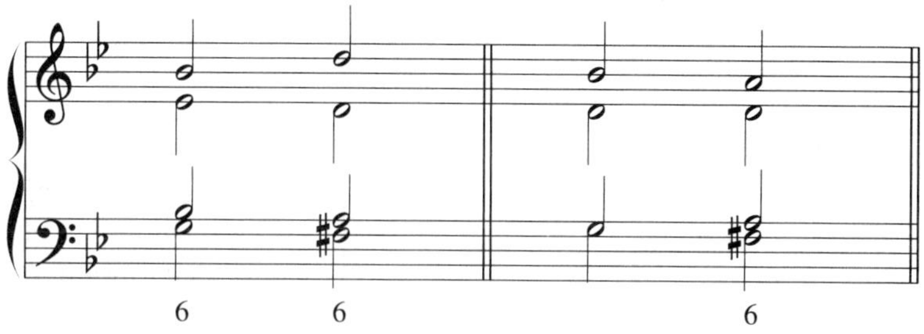

---

(1)
(2) is progressive because harmonic movement from the tonic to any other chord is progressive.

9.31 Which example shows *progressive* harmonic movement? _______

KEY of A MAJOR

(1) (2)

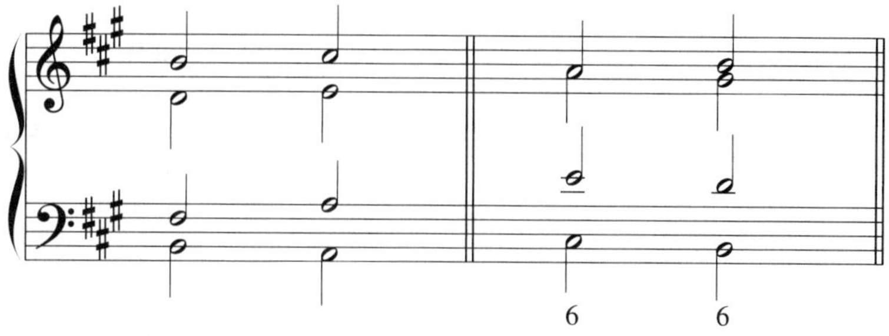

---

(2)
(Root movement down a 2nd as in [1] is retrogressive.)

9.32 No retrogression is possible when moving from the tonic chord. (True/False) _____________

True

9.33 The sequence of chords represented by roman numerals below contains progressions only. (True/False) _____________

I IV V vi IV ii V I

True

Expository Frame

9.34 Actually, no clear distinction between progression and retrogression can be made. Under most circumstances, harmony functions not as an isolated phenomenon, but in conjunction with rhythm and melody. The latter two elements may affect harmony so that a succession of chords sounds progressive in one case but retrogressive in another. Nevertheless, a sensitivity to various degrees of "progressiveness" in harmonic relations must be developed to acquire skill in selecting expressive harmonies.

Although the principles of harmonic progression are not absolutely clear, the tendency for roots to progress down in fifths, up in seconds, and down in thirds is prevalent enough in tonal music to serve as a guide in the choice of chords.

Few harmonic phrases consist entirely of either progressions or retrogressions. Fluctuation in the balance between these two types of harmonic movement provides the composer with an expressive tool. A passage in which stability and tonal clarity are desired calls for a large proportion of progressions, while more retrogressions might be used when the opposite effect is desired.

Harmony contributes to musical expression through the fluctuating balance between progressive and retrogressive harmonic movement.

(No response required.)

9.35 Another approach to harmonic progression can also be explored.

The structure of tonality rests upon the foundation of the three primary triads: the tonic, subdominant, and dominant. The remaining triads are called secondary triads and are related to the primary triads in the manner shown below.*

Primary triads:	I	IV	V
Secondary triads:	vi	ii	iii, vii°

Spell the primary triads in the key of E major.

I– _______

IV– _______

V– _______

*At this point you may wish to review Chapter 2.0: The Structure of Tonality.

I–E G♯ B

IV–A C♯ E

V–B D♯ F♯

9.36 Primary and secondary triads provide another approach to harmonic progressions.

Learn these two principles:

1. Movement from a primary triad to its secondary triad is *progressive.*
2. A secondary triad may be substituted for its primary triad.

With respect to (1) above, which case below is a progression? _______

(1) I–iii (2) vi–I 3) IV–ii (4) iii–V

(3)

9.37 Which case below is a progression? _______

(1) V–IV (2) I–vi (3) vii°–vi (4) vi–V

(2)

9.38 Applying the principle that primary triads tend to progress to their secondary triads rather than the reverse, show how each chord below would progress.

(1) I _______

(2) IV_______

(3) V _______ or _______

(1) vi

(2) ii

(3) iii (or) vii°

9.39 The harmonic relationships shown in the preceding frame are written out below:

(Play these progressions at the piano or listen to the recording.)

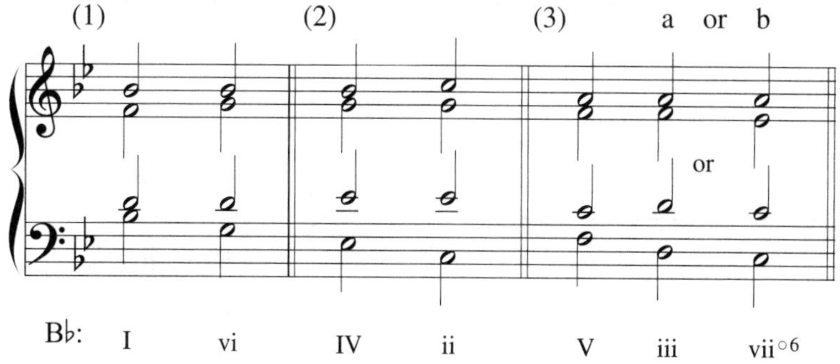

Are these progressions all equally effective?

____

Your opinion

True

9.40 Even when dealing with very simple musical material it is difficult to make absolute judgements; not only are all elements relative and easily influenced by other factors, but honest and perfectly valid differences of opinion may be held by all people.

Most will probably feel that all of the progressions shown in the preceding frame are effective with the possible exception of V–vii°. This is a relatively weak progression because the harmonic function of these two chords is so similar (vii° is considered by some to be an incomplete V^7) that little harmonic motion results when going from one to the other.*

Except for the progression V–vii°, movement from a primary triad to its secondary triad generally results in a strong harmonic effect. (True/False) _____________

*Note, too, that v–vii° is root movement up a third—a retrogression.

---

deceptive

9.41 A secondary triad may be substituted for its primary triad at any point in order to provide tonal variety and to prolong the harmonic motion.

Basic progression: [I [V [I

Substitutions: [I [vii° [vi

The basic progression (I–V–I) above is changed by substituting vii° for V, and vi for I. Further, the authentic cadence (V–I) has become a _____________ cadence (vii°–vi).

---

ii–vi–vii° or iii*

*Rarely used.

9.42 Applying the principle demonstrated in the preceding frame, show the chords that may be substituted where indicated below:

Basic progression: I [IV [I [V I

Substitutions: I [__ [__ [__ I

---

vi–ii–(V)–vi

9.43 Continue as in the preceding frame.

Basic progression: I V [I [IV V [I

Substitutions: I V [__ [__ V [__

---

vii° or iii*–(I)–vi–ii–(V)–vi

*Rarely used.

9.44 Continue as in the preceding frame.

Basic progression: I [V I [I [IV V [I

Substitutions: I [__ I [__ [__ V [__

(No response required.)	*Expository Frame* 9.45 The first principle stated in Frame 9.36 is that *movement from a primary triad to its secondary triad is progressive.* The second principle is that *a secondary triad may be substituted for its primary triad.* The application of these principles results in a wide variety of chord progressions. This is shown below: (1) (2) I vi IV vii° I Movement from a primary triad to its secondary triad is shown at (1); at (2), the leading tone triad (vii°) is substituted for the dominant (V).
(1) Principle 2 (2) Principle 1 (3) Principle 1 (4) Principle 2	9.46 Indicate which of the two principles is used at each of the points indicated. Principle 1. Movement from a primary triad to its secondary triad. Principle 2. Substitution of a secondary triad for its primary triad. (1) (2) (3) (4) I ii V iii IV I vi IV vii° I (1) ______________ (2) ______________ (3) ______________ (4) ______________
(1) Principle 1 (2) Principle 2 (3) Principle 1	9.47 Continue as in the preceding frame. (1) (2) (3) I iii IV ii V vi V iii I (1) ______________ (2) ______________ (3) ______________

Expository Frame

9.48 The primary triads (I, IV, and V) serve as the structural basis for harmonic progressions, but basic formulas such as I–V–I and I–IV–V–I can be expanded by the use of secondary triads. This is done by moving from a primary triad to its secondary triad before proceeding to the next chord in the basic formula (I–V–I expanded to I–vi–V–I); or by substituting a secondary triad for its primary triad (I–IV–V becomes I–ii–V). The result is greater tonal variety through a wider choice of chords and in some cases, prolongation of the harmonic activity.

As this study proceeds bear in mind that harmonic progression is not a science that can be presented in terms of precise laws. No attempt to relate harmony to natural acoustical phenomena will be made, even though much has been made of this approach in the past. This presentation is based on the observed practices of composers who use the traditional harmonic vocabulary.

In this text principles are not stated as rules, but are intended to serve as guides for the development of your own personal command of harmonic materials.

(No response required.)

9.49 An intimate relation exists between harmonic progression and phrase structure. A phrase has *shape* through melodic contour and *motion* through rhythm. Also it has a beginning, a sense of growth or movement in a particular direction, and finally a point of arrival at the cadence.

Harmonic progressions, like melody, tend to focus upon the cadence. The cadence to which a harmonic phrase moves has a strong influence on the choice of chords earlier in the phrase.

Cadences are structural points in a composition and the harmony at these points has special importance in the formal organization. Chords that appear at cadence points usually are chosen so that the tonal organization is stressed.

References have frequently been made to *melodic* phrases.

Would it be appropriate to speak of *harmonic* phrases? ______

Yes (certainly)

Expository Frame

9.50 Some chords in a harmonic phrase are more important to the formal organization of music than others. These include the following:

1. Chords that appear at structural points (cadences).
2. Chords that are stressed rhythmically (on strong beats or strong portions of beats, prolonged, or emphasized by being preceded by a rest).
3. Chords at important points in the phrase (at the peak of the melodic contour, for example).

Melodic contour, phrase structure, and rhythm all have an influence upon the choice of chords.

(No response required.)

9.51 Harmony that appears at strategic points and serves to establish the tonal organization is called STRUCTURAL HARMONY.

Examine the excerpt below:

Beethoven, *Sonatina in G Major*

The analysis above shows the basic "structural" harmonic movement from the tonic to the dominant in measure four. This is followed by a phrase that begins and ends with tonic harmony.

Show with roman numerals the *basic* harmonic organization of this excerpt. ____________

I–V–I

9.52 Referring again to the example in the preceding frame, notice that the chords at structural points of lesser importance (roman numerals in parentheses) also are primary triads (IV and V).

Harmony plays an important role in defining the tonal structure of music. As shown in the previous frame, this occurs at different levels even within the phrase itself. Harmony that is form-defining, and that helps to establish tonal coherence, is called ____________ harmony.

structural

9.53 Chords that occur more or less incidentally produce embellishing harmony. The first two measures of the excerpt in Frame 9.51 are shown below to illustrate this type of harmony.

Beethoven, *Sonatina in G Major*

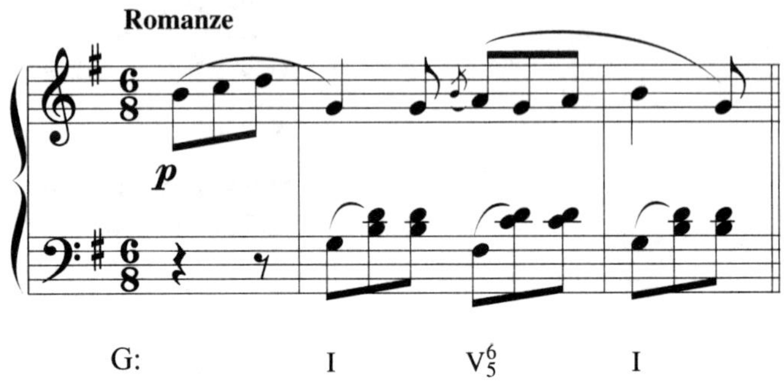

The dominant seventh chord on the second beat of the first measure is preceded and followed by tonic harmony. Thus, its function is clearly one of embellishment.

Is it likely that harmony at the end of a phrase would be embellishing? _______

No

9.54 *To achieve the delicate shades of nuance that fine performance demands, it is imperative that the difference between structural and embellishing harmony be recognized.* The larger units in the formal organization of a composition are defined, in part, by structural harmony. The importance of structural harmony as opposed to embellishing harmony cannot be understated. By phrasing, performers must make clear the formal design of the music being played. To do this, a sensitivity to the various roles of harmony is vital.

Harmony that is incidental and not form-defining is called _____________ harmony.

embellishing

9.55 In this frame the delicate task is that of distinguishing between structural and embellishing harmony. Examine carefully the example that follows and play it at the piano or from recording. Each chord is numbered and analyzed with a roman numeral. List in the space provided on the next page those chords that seem incidental to the basic harmonic scheme.

(Indicate your answer by recording the appropriate numbers.)

Beethoven, *Sonata,* Op. 49, No. 1

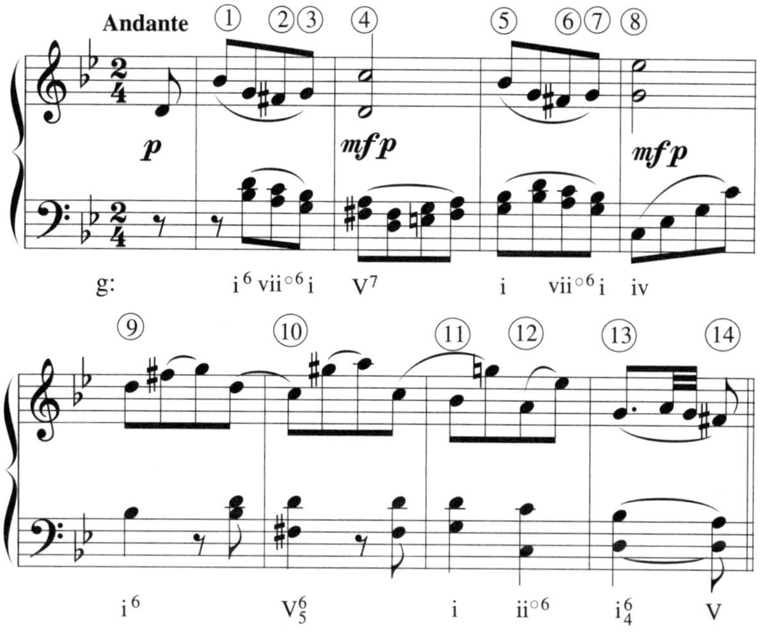

Embellishing harmony: Chords ____________________

2, 6, 10, 13
(There may be some difference of opinion, but the following frame justifies this list.)

9.56 A test that sometimes is useful to distinguish between structural and embellishing harmony is to play the passage omitting all embellishing harmony. Try the version below:

Beethoven, *Sonata,* Op. 49, No. 1 (altered)

Do you think the basic harmonic design of this passage has been affected by the elimination of chords 2, 6, 10, and 13? _______

Your answer is probably *No,* but you are entitled to your opinion.

9.57 Some may feel that in the preceding frame too many chords were retained. A further reduction of the harmony follows:

Beethoven, *Sonata,* Op. 49, No. 1 (altered)

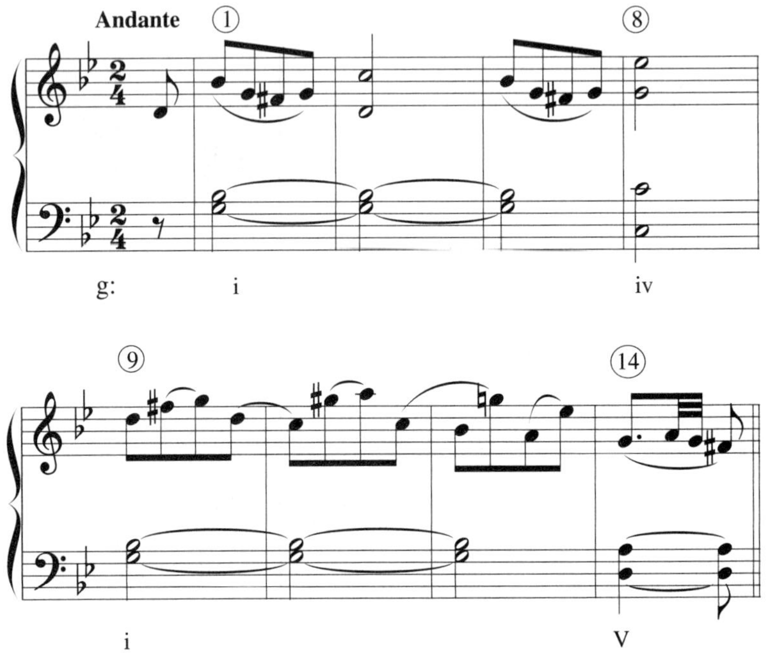

Now list (by number) all of the chords that have been deleted from the original version in Frame 9.55. Embellishing harmony:

2, 3, 4, 5, 6, 7, 10, 11, 12, 13

Chords ________________________________

9.58 In the preceding frame so many chords are deleted from the original version that not all of the melodic notes are accommodated by those that remain. Yet the basic structure of the harmonic phrase is preserved. Further reduction in the number of chords would destroy the sense of harmonic movement.

Structural harmony may be identified by eliminating

embellishing

all ____________ harmony.

(*No response.*)	*Expository Frame* 9.59 The structure of music is built up, in part, by harmonic relationships. Harmony operates at many levels, and even the tonal relationships between the parts of multimovement works are important. At the phrase level, harmony (along with cadences, melodic contour, rhythm, and motivic development) serves to define form and give coherence to music. The varying roles of harmony can be seen by stripping away the embellishing harmony layer by layer to reveal the different levels of the tonal structure. The harmony that remains is called *structural* harmony. A clear distinction between structural and embellishing harmony cannot always be made. This is a matter of personal opinion, and it also depends upon the purpose of the analysis. The language of harmony is full of subtleties, and there are few passages in music that are not open to a variety of interpretations.
cadence	9.60 There is an intimate relationship between harmonic progression and the phrase. An examination of this relationship will shed additional light upon the way chords are related, and will prepare for the technique of harmonization, which is the subject of Chapter 10.0. The harmony of the phrase is dominated by the CADENCE; it is the focal point—the "point of arrival"—toward which the melodic contour, rhythm, and harmony are directed. The focal point of the phrase is the ____________.
phrase	9.61 Although phrases seemingly may be harmonized in an infinite number of ways, a few simple practices are the most prevalent. These involve the extent to which the cadence formula dominates the phrase, and how the harmony leads into the cadence itself. Three types of phrases may be observed: 1. Phrases built on a single chord followed by a cadence. 2. Phrases with harmonic embellishment of a single chord followed by a cadence. 3. Phrases in which a basic progression is spread over the entire phrase. Harmonic progression is related to the structure of the ____________.

9.62 The example below shows a phrase that is built on a single chord (the tonic) followed by a cadence.

Verdi, *La Traviata,* Act III, No. 16

With what type of cadence does the above example close?

(Authentic/Plagal/Half/Deceptive) ______________

Authentic

9.63 Another example of a phrase that is built on a single chord followed by a cadence is shown on the next page.

Mozart, *Quartet,* K. 387

As in the preceding frame, it is the tonic chord that is prolonged.

What type of cadence is used to close the phrase? ____________

Authentic

9.64 The example below shows harmonic embellishment of the tonic followed by a cadence.

Haydn, *Capriccio*

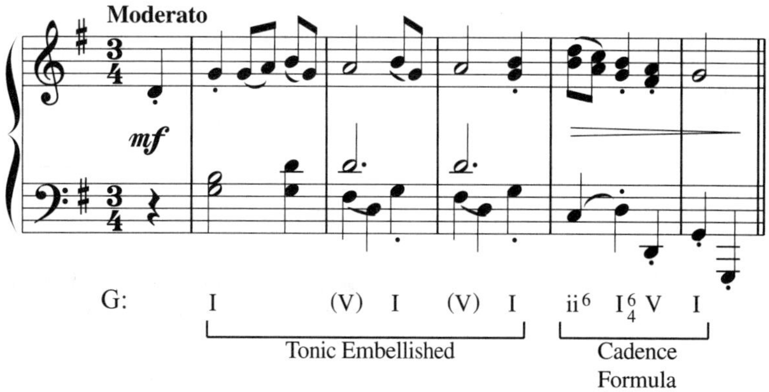

Are the dominant chords in the second and third measures examples of structural or embellishing harmony? ____________

Embellishing

9.65 A simple harmonic formula (I–IV–V–I) supplies the basis for the entire phrase in the example below. Note that the chords are spaced evenly throughout the phrase.

Boccherini, *Concerto for Violoncello in B♭ Major*

primary

In this phrase only (primary/secondary) ______________ triads are used.

9.66 Phrases based on the harmonic formula shown in the preceding frame (I–IV–V–I) are very numerous in the music of the classical period. Through chord substitution and harmonic embellishment, however, considerable variety can be achieved. In the example on the next page, the supertonic triad is substituted for the subdominant (measure 2), and the submediant triad is used as incidental harmony in the first measure.

Mozart, *Sonata,* K. 333

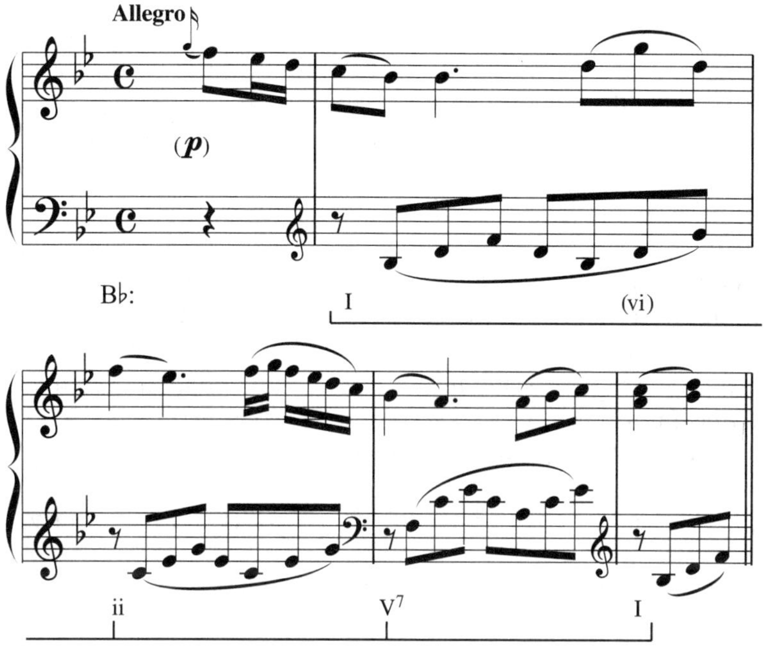

Variants of the progression I–IV–V–I often serve as the harmonic basis for an entire ____________.

phrase

Expository Frame

9.67 The harmonic basis of the phrase below is I–IV–V.

Mendelssohn, *Six Pieces for Children,* Op. 72, No. 3

The several chords that are indicated by the bracket above the staff do not serve a structural function; they appear more or less incidentally between those chords that provide the structural harmonic basis for the phrase.

(No response required.)

Summary

One of the variable factors in harmonic progression is the relation of the basic harmonic structure to the phrase as a whole. Three types of harmonic structure have been shown: phrases built on a single chord (usually the tonic) followed by a cadence, phrases with harmonic embellishment of a single chord followed by a cadence, and phrases in which a harmonic progression (such as I–IV–V–I) serves as the basis for the entire phrase.

But one must not think that all phrases fall into one of these three types. The harmonic element of music is subtle and the effect of chord relations is unpredictable. Harmonies are selected for their affective value, and the response they elicit eludes simple rationalization. Also, music resists being ordered into neat patterns of analysis; an approach that serves well for one period or composer may be useless for another. The information contained in this chapter is merely an introduction—the study of harmonic progression continues in the next chapter. Sensitivity to the language of harmony will increase not only by study and practice, but also through performing and listening experiences.

Some other helpful hints *(observations):*

1. The leading tone triad (vii°) is generally not used in root position in either a major or minor key.

2. The diminished supertonic (ii°) is also not generally used in root position in minor.

3. In general, iii probably resolves better to vi than to I, although both are technically "progressions."

4. The following chord progressions should probably be used with caution and within certain limited musical contexts in art music:

   vii^6–I or I^6; or $\text{vii}^{\circ 6}$–i^6

   ii^6–V; or $\text{ii}^{\circ 6}$–V

   (Note: In jazz the latter two progressions might enjoy more frequent occurrences.)

5. The constitution of a "good" progression is ultimately a matter of personal taste reconciled with musical style. One will find many times that theory instructors simply will never totally agree on these things, so it is necessary in the final analysis—pardon the pun—to find one's own way.

The terms that are explained or used in this chapter are listed below in chronological order:

harmonic phrase structure
harmonic progression:
  progression
  retrogression
root movement:
  by a fifth
  by a third
  by a second
structural harmony
structural harmonic movement
tonal structure of music
embellishing harmony
cadence

Mastery Frames

Up *Down* Fifths ✓ (Down) Seconds ✓ (Up) Thirds ✓ (Down) (9.20–.25)	9–1 Check (✓) the root movements that result in progressions. *Root Movement* *Up* *Down* Fifths ______ ______ Seconds ______ ______ Thirds ______ ______
(1) fifth (2) sixth (3) seventh (9.6–.9)	9–2 Complete each statement. (1) Root movement up a fourth is the same as down a ____________. (2) Root movement down a third is the same as up a ____________. (3) Root movement up a second is the same as down a ____________.
True (9.29–.32)	9–3 Root movement from the tonic to any other triad is progressive. (True/False) ____________
Secondary Triads Submediant Supertonic Mediant, Leading tone (9.35–.47)	9–4 Give the proper names of the secondary triad(s) related to each primary triad. *Primary Triads* *Secondary Triads* Tonic ____________ Subdominant ____________ Dominant ____________

Progressive (9.36–.38)	9–5 Is movement from a primary triad to its secondary triad progressive or retrogressive? ____________
structural (9.50–.59)	9–6 Harmony that appears at important points in the phrase such as at cadences is called ____________ harmony.
Embellishment of a single chord (I) followed by a cadence. (9.64)	9–7 Describe the harmonic structure of the phrase below. ______________________________ 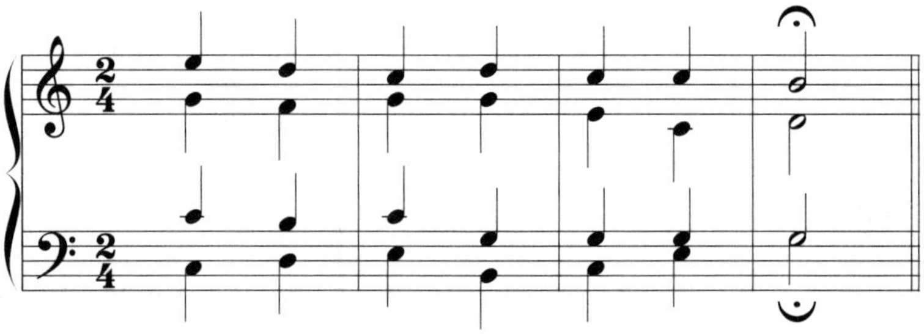 C:

Supplementary Activities

Concentrate on learning well the concepts presented here about harmonic progression and retrogression and the consistency that seems to underlay it all, even though the "accent" of a given composer leads to certain "twists" and "turns." Put this learning to use by analyzing, as formally as possible, musical examples of the so-called common practice period, c. 1750 to c. 1900. Beyond this, continue to compose short excerpts or whole compositions that explore and apply these principles to lead to a better understanding of the general principles underlying the creation of tonal music. Continued practice in ear training and listening, with a focus on the principles presented in the chapter, will help gain additional confidence in the mastery of these tonal concepts. Emphasize trying to clearly hear root movements and the relationships these root movements have to one another within a section of a piece and to one another within the larger dimensions of a composition.

Supplementary Assignments

ASSIGNMENT 9–1 Name ________________________________

1. Indicate the root movement in each case. Use the signs ↓ 5, ↑ 5, ↓ 2, ↑ 2, ↓ 3, and ↑ 3. *(Be alert for inversions.)*

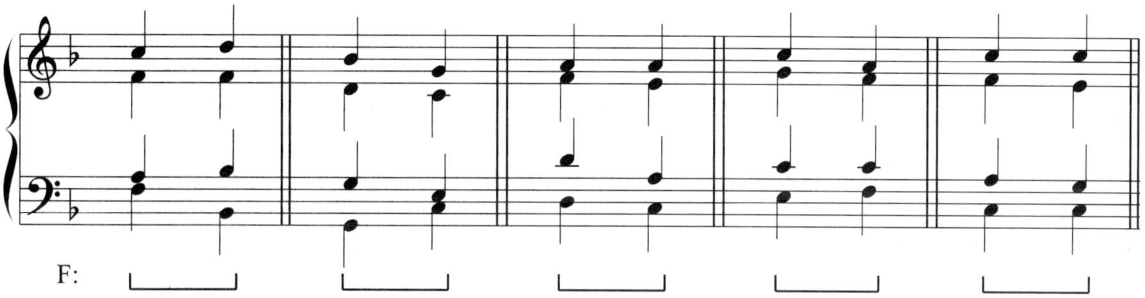

___ 1 ___ 2 ___ 3 ___ 4 ___ 5

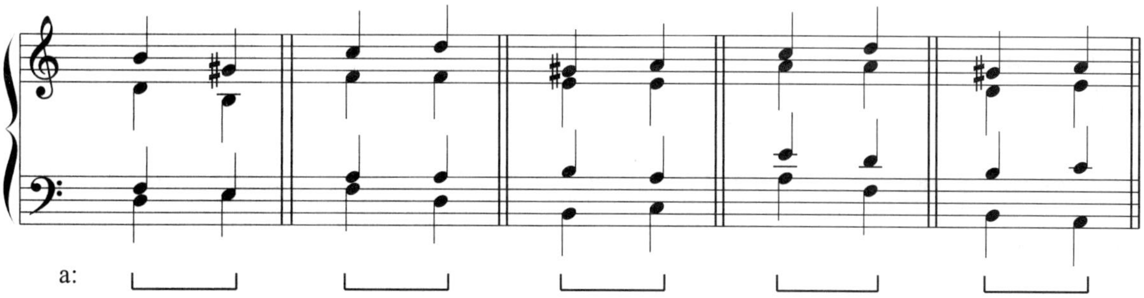

___ 6 ___ 7 ___ 8 ___ 9 ___ 10

2. Classify each root movement in question 1 as either a *progression* (P) or a *retrogression* (R). Remember: harmonic movement away from the tonic is *progressive* in all cases.

1 _______ 3 _______ 5 _______ 7 _______ 9 _______

2 _______ 4 _______ 6 _______ 8 _______ 10 _______

3. For each of the primary triads below write the secondary triad(s) to which they relate. Use correct part writing procedures and provide the roman numeral analysis.

(1) Tonic (2) Subdominant (3) Dominant (a) (b)

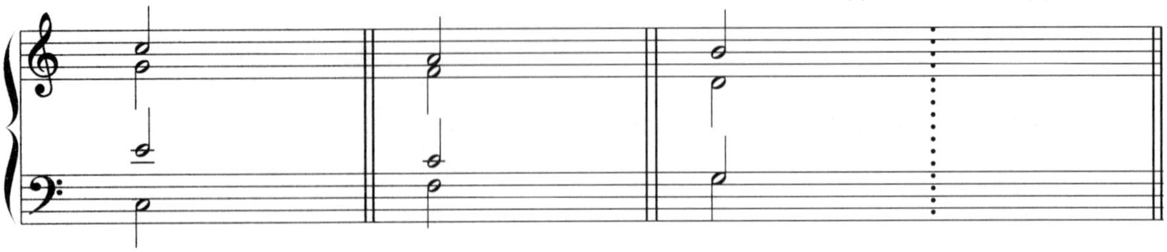

C: I ___ IV ___ V ___ ___

4. Indicate each case below as either *progressive* (P) or *retrogressive* (R).

(1) Movement from a primary triad to its secondary triad(s). ____________

(2) Movement from a secondary triad to its primary triad. ____________

5. Classify each of the harmonic movements below as a progression or retrogression.

V–vi ____________________

I–vii° ____________________

IV–iii ____________________

iii–V ____________________

6. The deceptive cadence is an example of a secondary triad substituted for its primary triad.

(True/False) ____________

7. Which example demonstrates movement from a primary triad to its secondary triad? ____________

(1) (2) (3)

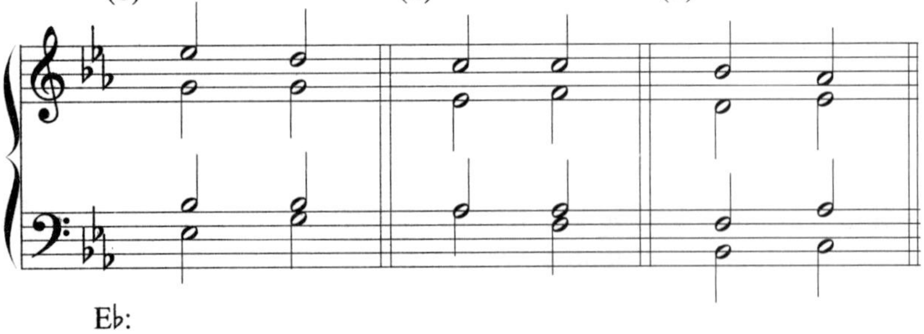

E♭:

8. Explain, in your own words, the distinction between structural and embellishing harmony.

____

____

ASSIGNMENT 9–2 Name ______________________________

1. Classify each of the harmonic movements below as a progression or retrogression.

   vii°–vi ____________________

   iii–IV ____________________

   ii–V ____________________

   IV–vii° ____________________

   I–iii ____________________

2. Revise the progression below to show substitution of secondary triads for primary triads.

I	V	I	ii	I	IV	V	I
I	__	__	ii	I	__	V	__

3. Which example demonstrates substitution of a secondary triad for its primary triad? ____________

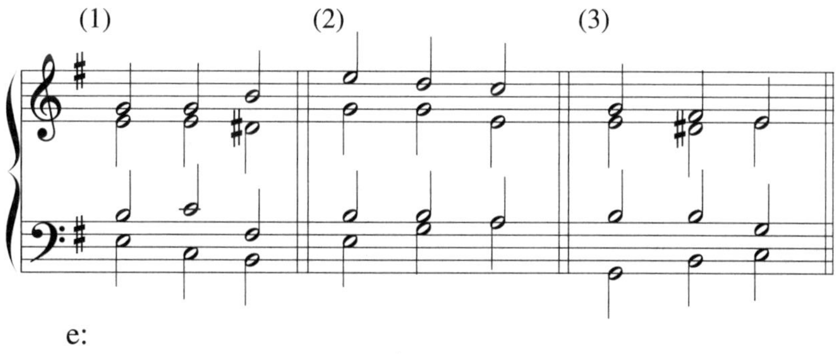

4. Compose a phrase for piano based on the given harmonic structure. Choose your own key and meter. Piano styles 2–12 are recommended (see Appendix B).

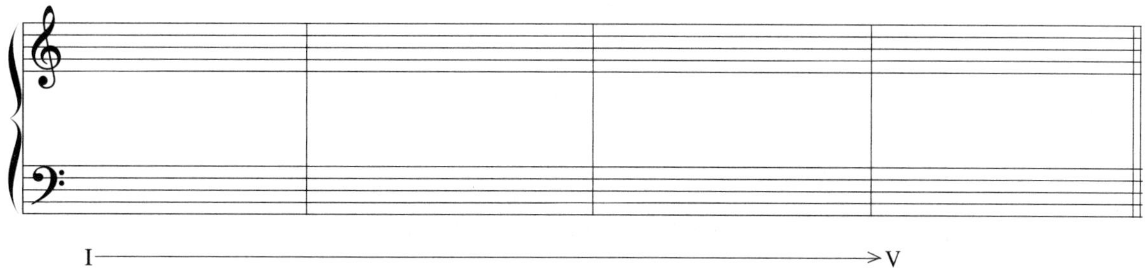

5. Describe the harmonic structure of the phrase above. ______________________________

____

____

6. Compose two phrases for piano based on the harmonic structures given below. Keys are given, but you may choose your own meters. Notate completely, including tempo, dynamics, and phrasing indications. Piano styles 13–18 for Example A and 19–25 for Example B are recommended.

(A)

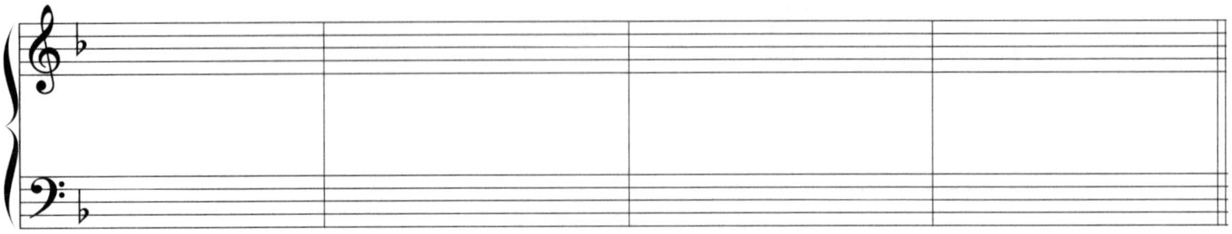

d: i V i iv i^6_4 V

(B)

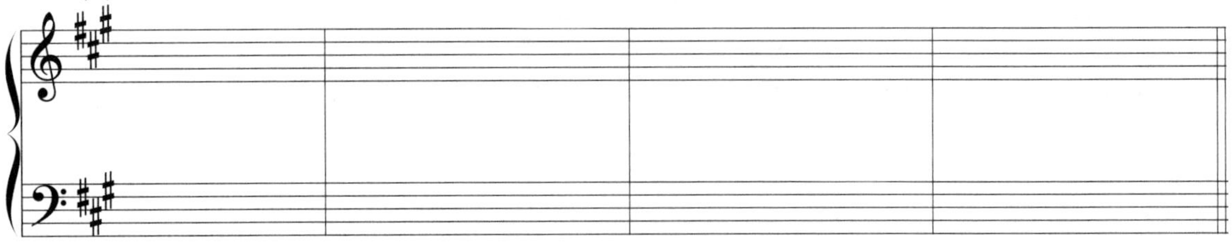

A: I ii^6 V I

7. Describe the harmonic structure of the phrases above. ____________________

____

____

8. Compose a short work for piano that embodies the features below:

(1) At least four phrases

(2) Each phrase should be based on one of the harmonic structures below:

(a) A single chord followed by a cadence

(b) A single chord embellished, followed by a cadence

(c) A harmonic progression spread evenly over the entire phrase

(3) Key and meter of your choice

(4) Piano style of your choice

(5) Complete notation (tempo, dynamic, and phrasing indications)

Chapter 10.0
The Technique of Harmonization

The harmonization of a melody involves selecting those chords from the available tonal material that realize the melody's harmonic implications. Even very simple melodies suggest more than one harmonization, so it is not a question of finding the "right" solution, but of selecting one of the alternatives that is stylistically consistent and appropriate to the function of the melody in the composition as a whole. There is no expectation to learn to harmonize just like Bach, Mozart, or Schubert, even though music by these and other composers is used to illustrate various points throughout the book. A "technique" of harmonization, not a specific harmonic style, is being learned. The lesson of this chapter should lead to the development of one's own mode of harmonic expression.

10.1 The study of the technique of harmonization is based on the tonal material that has been presented to this point. This limits us, therefore, to the triads of a single tonality; but these may be used in first and second inversions as well as in root position. The techniques learned in terms of this limited material will be equally valid when additional resources become available.

The melody below will be used to demonstrate the technique of harmonization.

Sing (or play) this melody to become familiar with its characteristics.

This melody is in the key of _______ major.

E♭

10.2 The first step in harmonizing a melody has just been taken: becoming familiar with its characteristics and identifying its tonality. Next, select an appropriate cadence. The last two notes of this melody suggest two cadences as shown with roman numerals.

KEY OF E♭ MAJOR

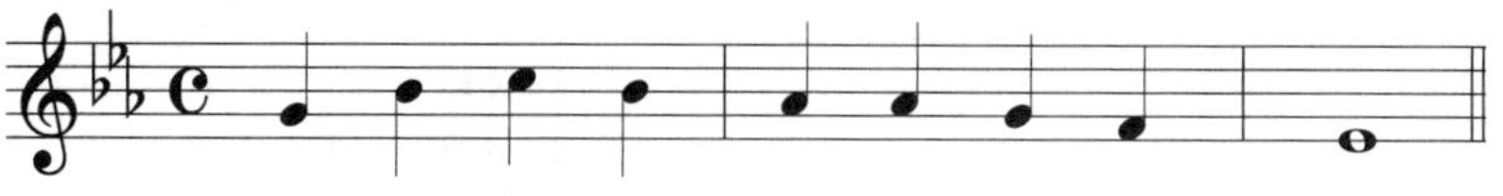

Cadences: 1. V I
2. V vi

(Continued on the next page)

	Name these cadences.
Authentic	Cadence No. 1 ______________
Deceptive	Cadence No. 2 ______________

10.3 Melodies often suggest more than one type of cadence. It is important to decide on the cadence that is appropriate for the end of a particular phrase.

Play the melody and try each of the two cadences as notated below:

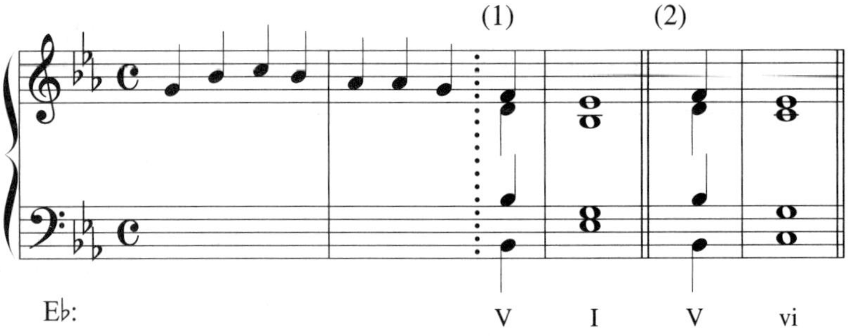

Which cadence gives the stronger sense of finality? (1) or (2) _______

Answer: (1)

10.4 This demonstration involves only a single phrase, so the authentic cadence is chosen for its stronger closing effect. The deceptive cadence would imply another phrase to carry forward and complete the musical idea of the first phrase. Contrasting cadences are highly desirable, so they should be chosen with care.

The choice of cadence is dictated entirely by the contour of the melody. (True/False) ______________

Answer: False *(The degree of finality desired is important.)*

10.5 The cadence has a strong influence on the harmonies that precede it. The harmonic destination must be known before the chords can be selected that will take one there. This is why it is so important to choose the cadence before starting to harmonize the first part of the melody.

The harmony of a phrase is strongly influenced by the ______________.

Answer: cadence

harmonic rhythm	10.6 The rate at which harmony changes—or, more succinctly, chords change—is referred to as HARMONIC RHYTHM. Harmonic rhythm contributes to the motivation of music and plays an important expressive role. Some passages are based on slow changes of harmony, others feature very rapid changes, still others have varying rates of harmonic changes that increase the rhythmic complexity of the composition. The temporal element of harmony is called _____________.
True	10.7 Returning to the melody that is being used to demonstrate the technique of harmonization, it is desirable at this point to settle upon an appropriate harmonic rhythm. The prevailing quarter note rhythm of the melody suggests the same rhythm for the harmony. This is not the only possibility; either one or two chords per measure could be employed to good effect. The limited material at our disposal, however, rules out these choices, since not all of the melodic notes could be included in such a harmonic scheme. Most melodies give rise to several possibilities of harmonic rhythm. (True/False) _____________.
chord	10.8 In completing the harmonization of the melody, the prevailing rate of chord change will be the quarter note. Two notes separated by a leap from a strong to a weak beat are frequently harmonized by the same chord. The first two notes (G and B♭), for example, are both members of the tonic triad. Since it is desirable to begin a phrase with tonic emphasis, it makes good sense to use the tonic triad for these two notes. The harmonization now stands as below:  Melodic leaps often give a clue to effective chord choice. The two tones of a melodic leap from a strong to a weak beat often are harmonized by the same _____________.

Expository Frame

10.9 To review the steps that have been taken to arrive at this point: (1) determined the tonality (E♭ major), (2) chosen an appropriate cadence (authentic), (3) chosen an appropriate harmonic rhythm (principally in quarter note rhythm), and (4) begun the harmonic phrase with tonic emphasis (suggested by the notes G and B♭, both of which are members of the tonic triad).

(No response required.)

10.10 Now play the phrase with the chords that already have been selected.

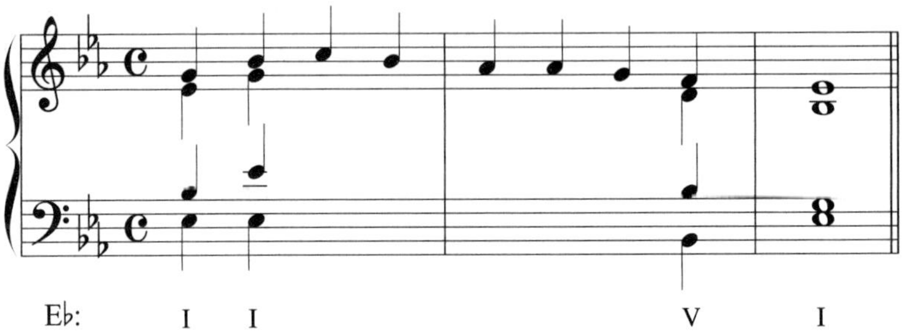

Three types of harmonic phrase structure were discussed in Chapter 9.0: (1) phrases consisting of a single chord followed by a cadence, (2) phrases consisting of the tonic embellished followed by a cadence, and (3) phrases based upon a harmonic formula such as I–IV–V–I.*

One's ear and imagination must be brought into play to decide which of these patterns is best suited to this melody.

Melodies usually are not harmonized by selecting a chord more or less independently for each successive note. The final choice evolves slowly, as a result of careful reference to the

cadence and to the _____________ as a whole.

*You may wish to review Chapter 9.0, especially Frames 9.61–.67

phrase *(or melody)*

10.11 Since the fourth scale degree (A♭) is stressed by appearing on both the first and second beats of the second measure, a subdominant emphasis is appropriate for these notes.

Play the phrase with the additions below:

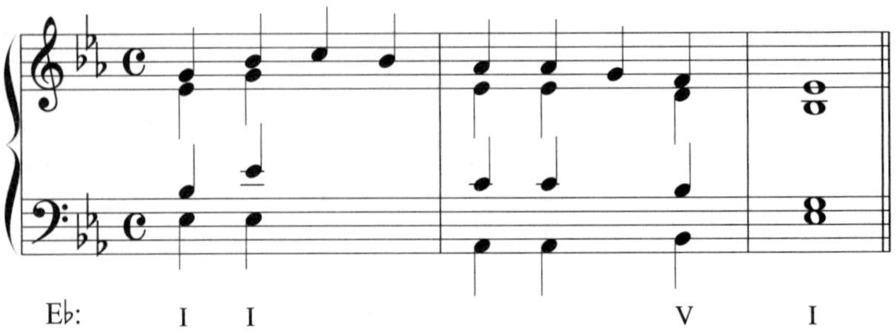

By now it is clear that the phrase is based on one of the simple harmonic formulas. Write the formula in roman numerals.

____

I–IV–V–I

10.12 Having come this far, and with only three notes yet to be harmonized, one's ear should help complete the harmonization. As an aid in making these final few choices, however, one may wish to list the possibilities for each note.

Since the tonal material is limited to triads, a given note can be harmonized by one of three triads. For example, the third note of the melody (C) may be the root of the submediant triad (C E♭ G), the third of the subdominant triad (A♭ C E♭), or the fifth of the supertonic triad (F A♭ C). Applying this method to the other remaining notes, the chords from which one may choose to complete the harmonization are listed below:

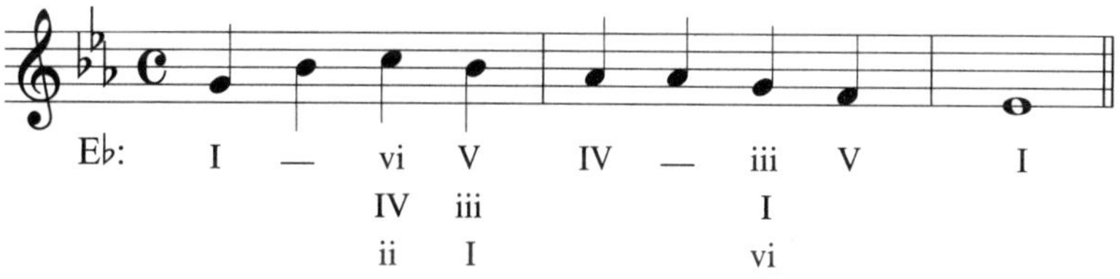

When the tonal material is limited to triads, any note may be harmonized by one of three triads. The note may be either the

____________, ____________, or ____________ of a triad.

root, third, (or) fifth
(Any order.)

10.13 The choice between the alternatives listed in the preceding frame is influenced by the balance between progressive and retrogressive harmonic movement that is desired, and also by practical necessities of part writing, which may not be revealed until later. But the final choice is based largely upon personal preference. *The basic underlying progression will hold the phrase together regardless of the decisions that are made at this point.*

The chords that will be used in this demonstration are shown below:

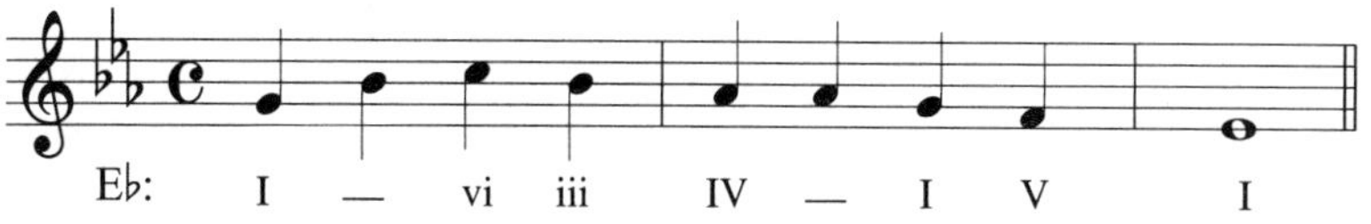

Although some choices may produce more effective results than others, the harmonic structure that practically guarantees the stability of this phrase consists of the progression

(roman numerals) ____________.

I–IV–V–I

10.14 It is vital that the bass be an effective melodic line that complements the soprano. The use of some contrary motion between the soprano and bass is desirable as it gives each a measure of independence. The outer voices (soprano and bass) define the "vertical" limits of music, and individuality in these voices contributes greatly to the musical interest.

Compare the soprano and bass in the harmonization as it now stands.

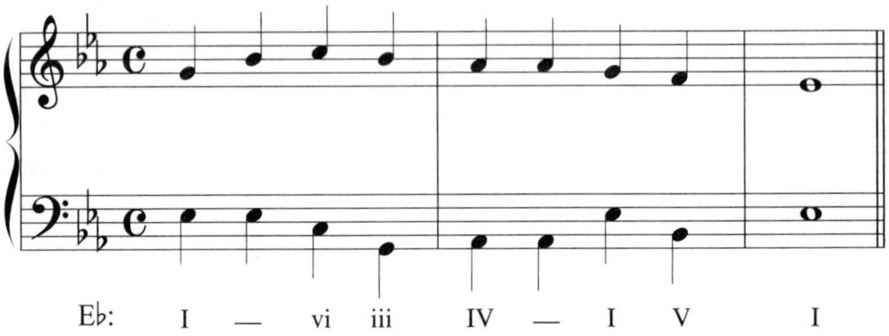

Evaluate each item.

1. Melodic contour of the bass (Good/Fair/Poor) ____________
2. Effectiveness of the bass in relationship to the soprano (Good/Fair/Poor) ____________

Your opinion

10.15 Regardless of how the bass was rated in the preceding frame, it can be improved as a melodic line by eliminating some of the large leaps. The bass usually contains a greater number of leaps than the other voices; but, even so, the angularity in the second measure is not especially good.

Observe the changes below:

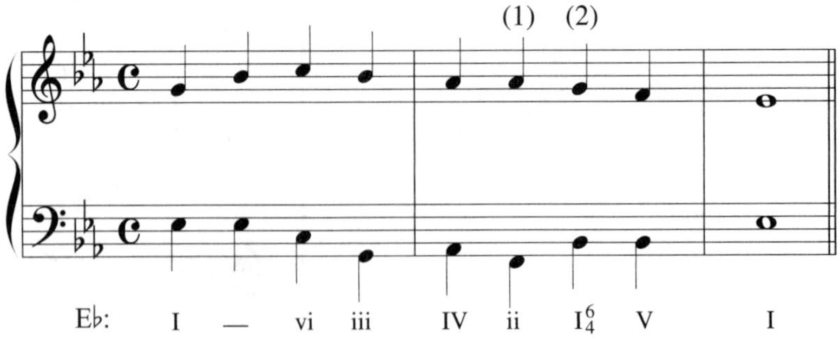

Two changes have been made: at (1) the supertonic has been substituted for its primary triad (the subdominant), and at (2) the tonic triad has been placed in second inversion. The cadence formula now includes the use of a ____________ six-four chord.

cadential

bass

10.16 Though slight, these changes bring greater tonal variety to the passage, reduce the angularity of the bass, and avoid the monotonous repetition of A♭ in both the soprano and bass simultaneously (beats one and two of the second measure, Frame 10.14).

Substitution of secondary for primary triads, and the use of inversions, helps refine the quality of the ____________ line.

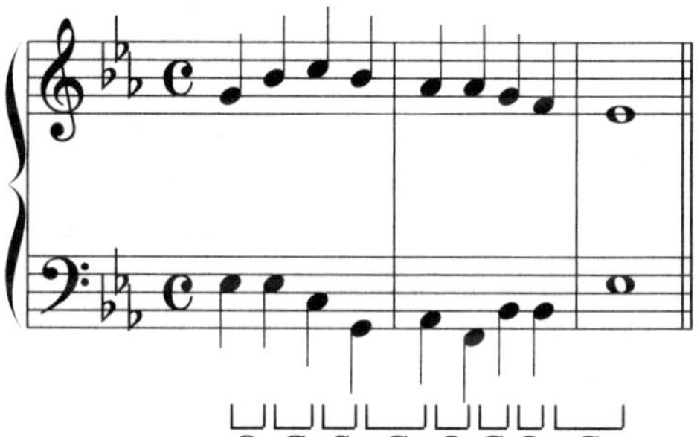

O C S C O C O C

10.17 Check the soprano and bass voices against one another for incorrect use of parallel motion. Such errors are easier to detect before the alto and tenor voices are written.

Indicate the type of motion in the spaces provided. Use the following abbreviations: O = oblique, C = contrary, S = similar, P = parallel.

No
(Parallel thirds and sixths are good.)

10.18 Since no parallel motion occurs between the soprano and bass, the possibility of incorrect parallel motion does not exist. Is all parallel motion between the soprano and bass forbidden? ______

(No response required.)

Expository Frame

10.19 The melodic quality of the bass line and its relation to the soprano is important, as much of the success of the harmonization depends on a good bass. An effective bass possesses the following features:

1. *Melodic contour.* The bass line should not be too angular even though more leaps are to be expected than in the upper parts.
2. *Contrapuntal interest with the soprano.* The bass and soprano together should make effective two-part writing—some contrary motion is desirable.
3. *Tonal variety.* Inversions help provide a more melodic bass line and contribute to tonal variety.
4. *Parallel motion.* Always check for parallel fifths and octaves between the bass and soprano before writing the remaining voices.

10.20 Complete the harmonization by writing the alto and tenor voices.

(Use close structure.)

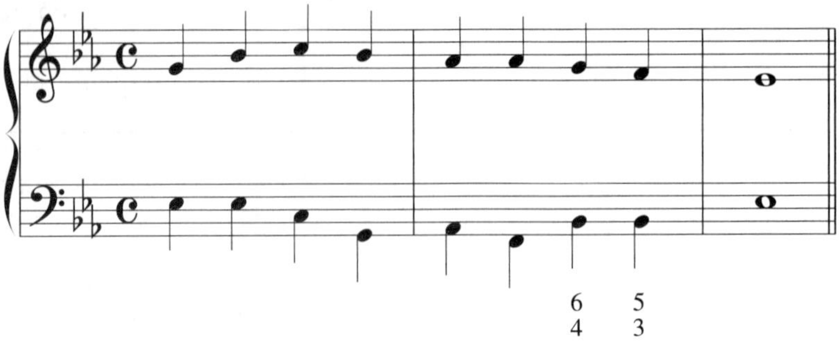

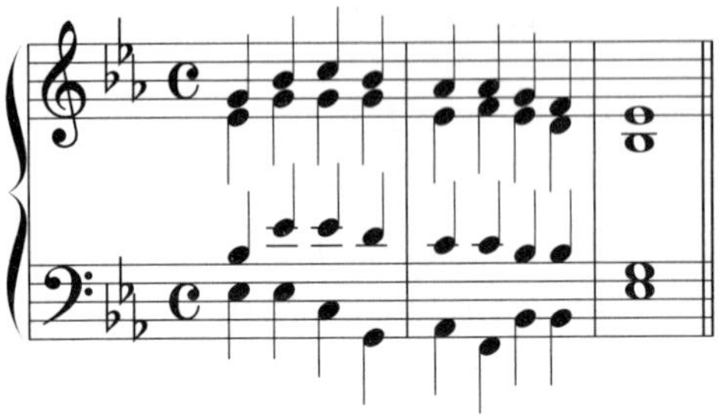

10.21 One should have had no trouble completing the harmonization as the alto and tenor voices fall neatly into place. Sometimes, however, part writing problems arise that cannot be solved. When this happens, changes in the bass line, such as the use of different inversions, or even the selection of new chords, will be necessary. Even with only limited harmonic material being utilized, there are many ways a melody can be harmonized. So, do not be reluctant to substitute one chord for another, no matter how enamored one is of a first choice.

Part writing difficulties sometimes are solved by the selection of a different chord, or by the use of ____________.

inversions

Expository Frame

10.22 One demonstration of the technique of harmonization has been completed. Before trying another, the principal steps taken should be reviewed:

1. Determine the tonality.
2. Choose an appropriate cadence.
3. Choose an appropriate harmonic rhythm.
4. Determine the basic harmonic structure of the phrase. (Look for notes that are emphasized by prolongation, contour, or rhythm.)
5. Select chords for notes that remain from the three possibilities for each.
6. Write the bass.
7. Write the alto and tenor.
8. Make adjustments if necessary.

(No response required.)

(2) ✓

10.23 Check (✓) the correct option:

1. Harmonic rhythm is always identical with the rhythm of the melody.
2. In four-part writing the bass is a melodic line nearly equal in importance to the soprano.

True statements:

(1) _______ (2) _______ Both _______ Neither _______

---

b minor

10.24 To continue with another demonstration of the technique of harmonization:

What is the tonality of the melody below? _____________.

Cruger, Chorale: *Herzliebster Jesu, was hast du verbrochen*

Half cadence
(See next frame.)

10.25 Notice that the melody in the preceding frame does not end on the keynote (tonic). What cadence is suggested by this phrase?

____

---

i–V, VI–V, or III–V

10.26 The melody in Frame 10.24 ends with the second scale degree. This note is not included in the tonic or submediant chords, so authentic, plagal, and deceptive cadences are not possible. The half cadence is the only one possible in this case.

Show with roman numerals two chords that produce a half cadence.

___ ___

The tonic (i)

10.27 The final dominant chord can be preceded by i, VI, or III. Try these three possibilities at the piano to get acquainted with the effect of each.

Under proper circumstances any one of these possibilities might be effective. The combination III–V, however, is probably the weakest, because in this case a primary triad (V) is preceded by its secondary triad (III). Our choice shall be i–V.

With what chord would you expect the harmonization to begin? _____________

10.28 The harmonization now has a beginning and an ending.

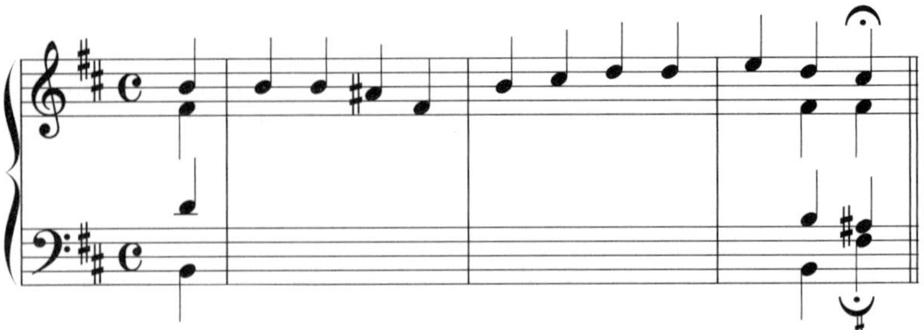

b: i i V

The cadence selected is a (final/nonfinal)

_____________ cadence.

nonfinal

10.29 Does the melody suggest a harmonic rhythm of the whole note, half note, or quarter note? _____________

The quarter note

10.30 Now sing (or play) the melody that is notated again below. Notice particularly the tones that suggest tonic harmony.

Draw a circle around each of the notes that could be harmonized with the tonic chord.

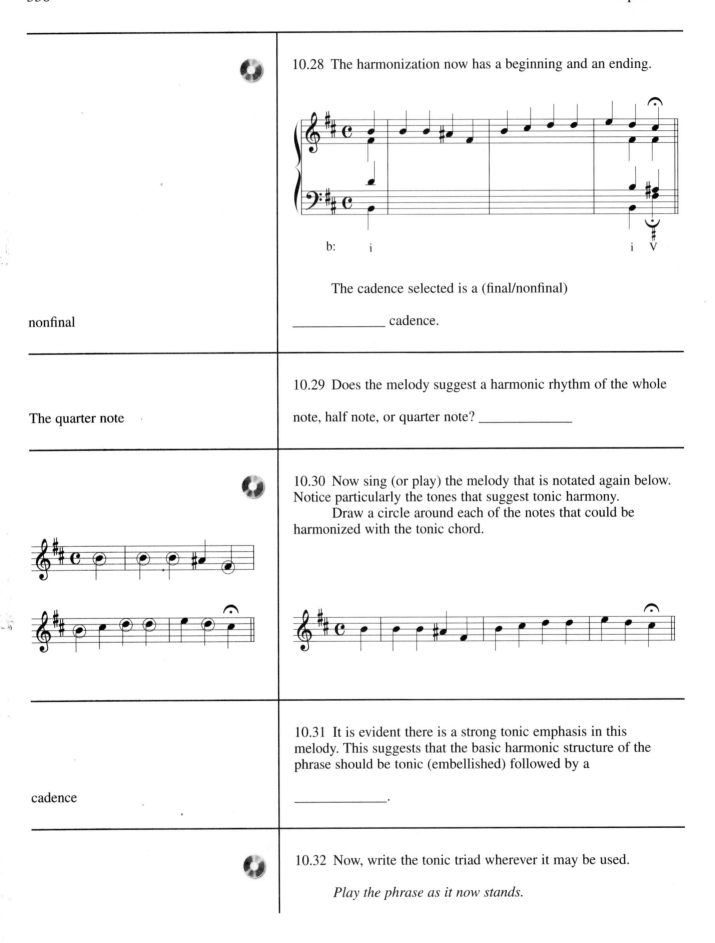

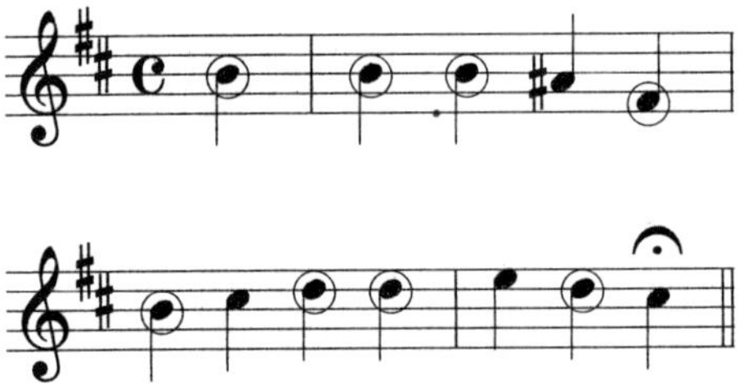

10.31 It is evident there is a strong tonic emphasis in this melody. This suggests that the basic harmonic structure of the phrase should be tonic (embellished) followed by a

_____________.

cadence

10.32 Now, write the tonic triad wherever it may be used.

Play the phrase as it now stands.

b: i i i i i i i i V

Do you find the effect of so many tonic triads to be rather monotonous? _______

Yes
(There should be little disagreement.)

10.33 The prevalence of implied tonic harmony was shown in the preceding frame to make clear the underlying harmonic design of this melody. Represented by roman numerals this is simply:

i ⟶ ____
↑
(Write the appropriate roman numeral here.)

V

10.34 The tonic triad need not be used as often as suggested in Frame 10.32. Some substitutions can be made and additional tonal variety can be obtained by the use of inversions. *But it is important to recognize the basic harmonic implications of a melody early in the processes of harmonization.*

Tonic harmony should be avoided except at the beginning and end of the phrase. (True/False) _____________

False
(Tonic harmony may occur at any point in the phrase.)

10.35 Proceed now to the selection of chords for those notes yet to be harmonized. Since each note may be the root, third, or fifth of a triad, there are three possibilities. The choices that exist for the first two of the remaining notes are shown below. Indicate the choices for the third remaining note (E).

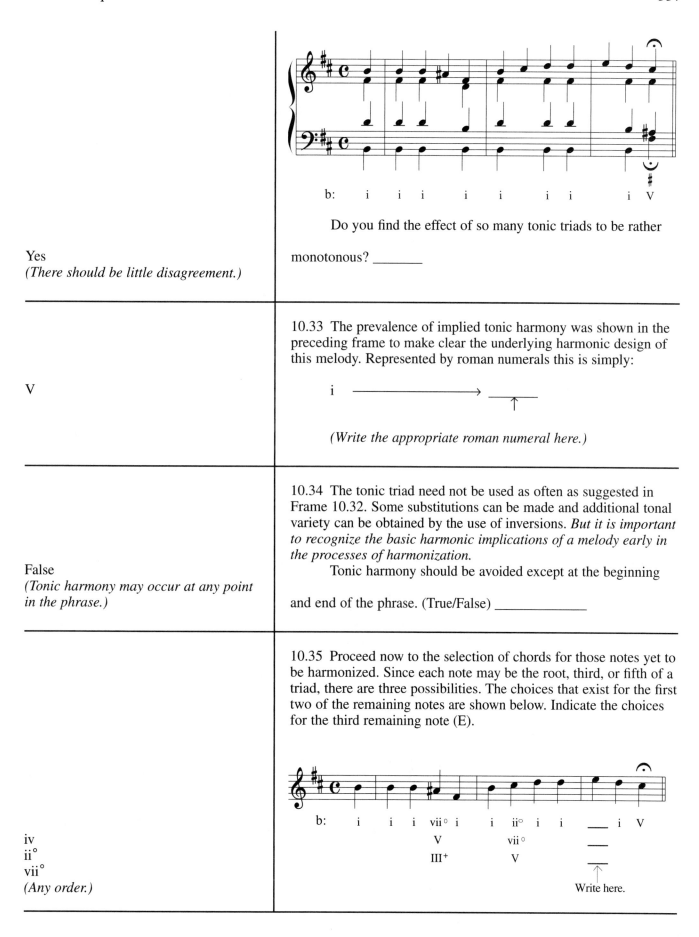

b: i i i vii° i i ii° i i ___ i V
V vii° ___
III^+ V ___
↑
Write here.

iv
ii°
vii°
(Any order.)

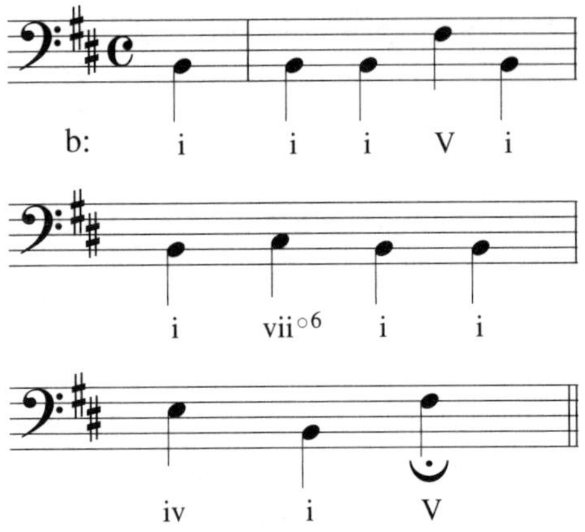

10.36 The choice between these possibilities is influenced by the changes made in the tonic harmonies. It is at this point that a sense of style and creative imagination must be brought to bear.

To continue the demonstration, the chords shown in the roman numeral analysis below will be used.

Complete the bass line in accordance with the roman numeral given.

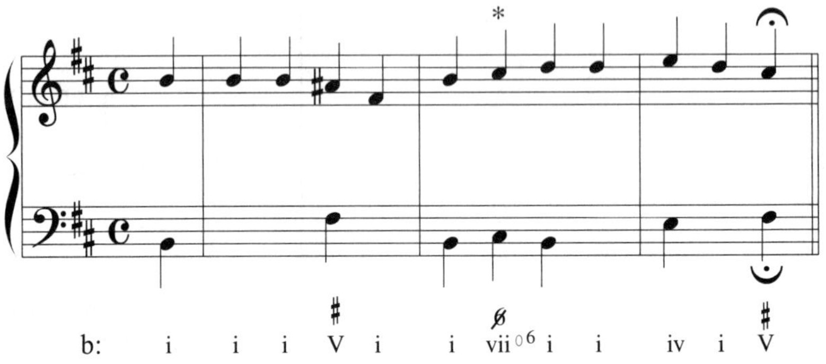

A diminished triad sounds best in first inversion.
(Or equivalent.)

10.37 There obviously is room for much improvement, both in the choice of chords and in the quality of the bass line. But don't expect a harmonization to take shape instantly; it usually develops slowly, with the final product the result of much experimentation and compromise.

Why is it necessary to place the chord at the asterisk in first inversion? ___________________________

10.38 Now follow the steps that are taken to refine the bass line and the choice of chords. Some of the tonic triads may be eliminated by substituting other chords and also providing greater tonal variety by the use of inversions. At the beginning of the phrase it would be desirable to have harmonic change to counter the monotony of the repeated notes in the soprano.

Two possibilities are shown below:

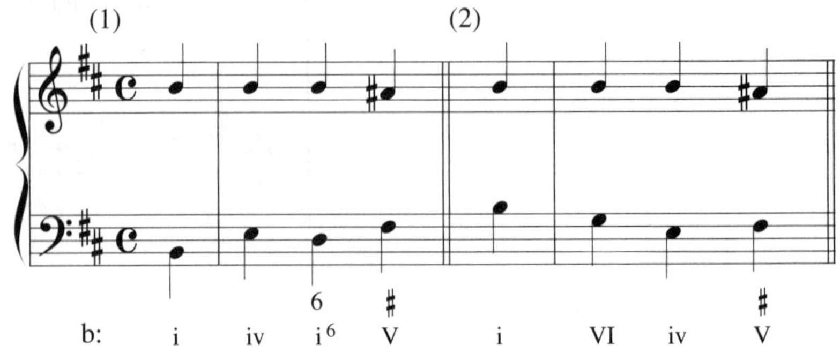

Repeated notes in the melody often call for harmonic changes or the use of ____________.

inversions

10.39 The possibility (1) of the preceding frame will be chosen. So now the harmonization looks like this:

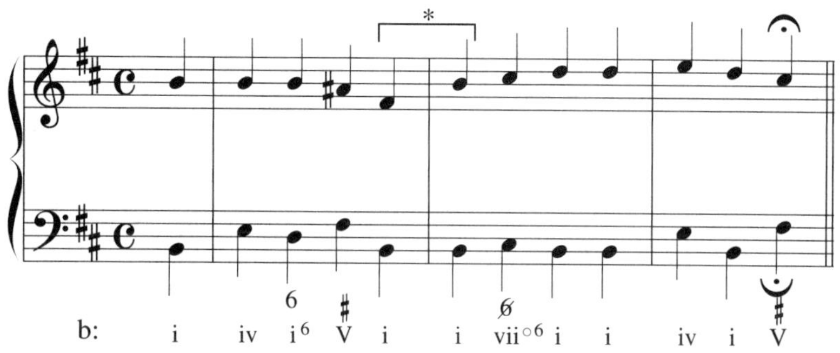

At the asterisk, the repetition of the tonic chord from the fourth beat of the first measure to the first beat of the second measure produces harmonic stagnation. It is usually desirable to have harmonic motion at a point of metric stress (such as the first beat of a measure), so some change is needed. What two chords other than the tonic can be used to harmonize the F♯?

(Use roman numerals.) _______ and _______.

V (and) III+

10.40 Since the leap from A♯ to F♯ at the asterisk defines the dominant triad, a repetition of this harmony on the fourth beat is also appropriate. By using the following tonic chord in first inversion the parallel octaves (B to C♯) are eliminated.

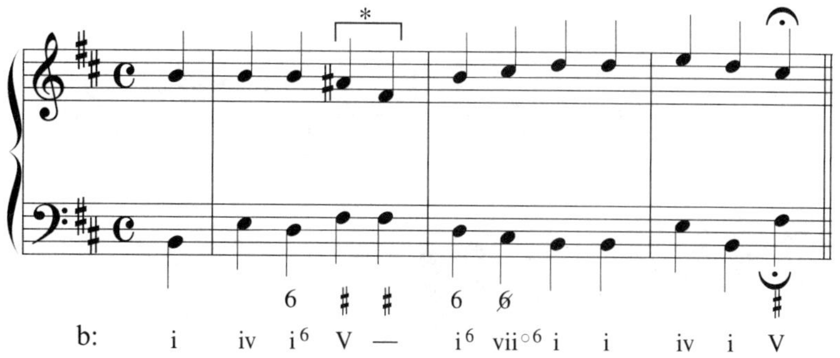

Incorrect use of parallel motion often is prevented by the use of ____________.

inversions

10.41 Now the first part of the harmonization has been greatly improved. One additional change that will add interest to the latter part is shown at the asterisk below:

b: i iv i6 V — i6 vii°6 i VI iv i V

The submediant triad (VI) may often be substituted for the tonic because it is the tonic's ____________ triad.

secondary

10.42 Now that all of the chords have been chosen, it is necessary to examine the bass line and its relationship to the soprano.

Evaluate the bass as written in the preceding frame.

1. Is the bass a good melodic line? ____________
2. Is there any incorrect parallel motion between the bass and soprano? _______
3. Does the bass complement the soprano (is there effective use of contrary motion)? _______

1. Your opinion
2. No
3. Yes

10.43 Write the alto and tenor voices.

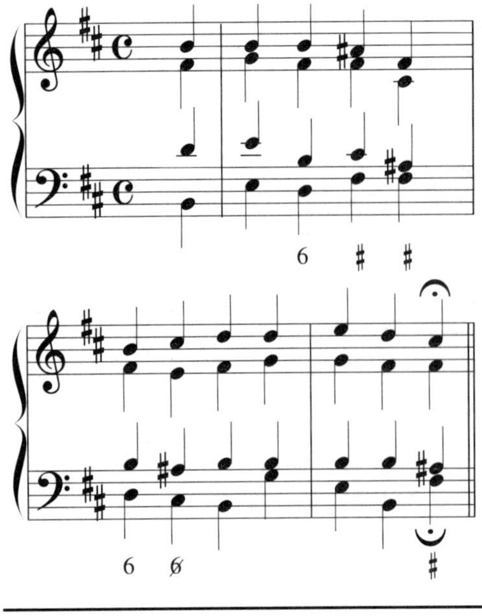

The fifths are not both perfect.
(A♯ to E is a diminished fifth.)
(Or equivalent.)

10.44 Notice in the solution given in the preceding frame that consecutive fifths occur in the second measure (beats two and three) between the alto and tenor voices. Why is this not an error? ____________

---

perfect

10.45 Consecutive fifths are incorrect only if both intervals are ____________.

(No response required.)

Expository Frame

10.46 An effective harmonization rarely appears instantly, but develops slowly and by successive stages. Compare, for example, the final version in the preceding frame with that of Frame 10.36. It is obvious that considerable improvement has taken place. Additional experience in harmonization will make it possible to proceed more quickly to the final version; *but until one's technique becomes more highly developed, it would be unwise to omit any of the steps that are demonstrated in this chapter.*

1st 3

2nd 1

3rd 5

4th 7

5th 4

6th 2

7th 6
(Unless all of your answers were correct review Frame 10.22.)

10.47 Some of the steps that are associated with the process of harmonization are listed at the left below. Arrange these steps in proper sequence by writing the number of each step in the appropriate space on the right.

1. Choose an appropriate cadence.
2. Write the bass.
3. Determine the tonality.
4. Select chords for notes not associated with the basic harmonic structure.
5. Choose an appropriate harmonic rhythm.
6. Check for incorrect parallel motion between bass and soprano.
7. Determine the basic harmonic structure of the phrase.

1st _______

2nd _______

3rd _______

4th _______

5th _______

6th _______

7th _______

---

authentic

10.48 The choice of chords is influenced by the cadence, so do not begin to harmonize until the cadence has been selected. If the melody consists of several phrases, there should be variety in the types of cadences used. The final cadence, of course, should be the most conclusive. For this reason the final cadence usually is a perfect ____________ cadence.

10.49 For the remainder of this chapter one must draw on the knowledge acquired regarding effective chord choice and part writing procedures. Which chord, (a), (b), or (c), most effectively continues the progression? ____________

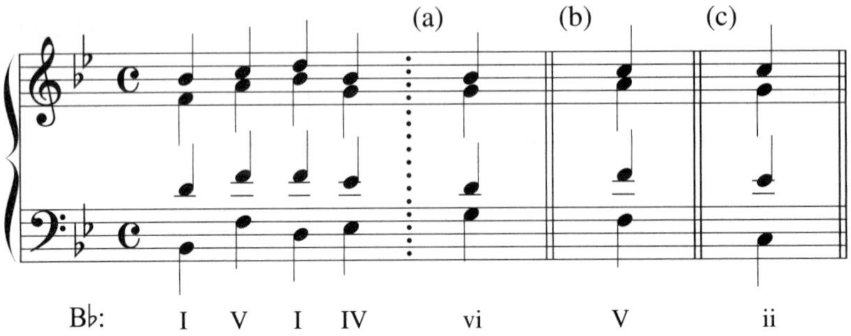

If choice was:

(a) go to Frame 10.50

(b) go to Frame 10.51

(c) go to Frame 10.52

Expository Frame

10.50 The harmonic movement IV–vi is a retrogression (the bass moves up a third). While retrogressions are not entirely ruled out, there is a better choice. *Return to Frame 10.49 and try again.*

(No response required.)

Expository Frame

10.51 The progression IV–V is very strong, but the parallel fifths and octaves (between the bass and soprano, and between the bass and tenor) make this a poor choice. *Return to Frame 10.49 and try again.*

(No response required.)

Expository Frame

10.52 This is the best choice. The harmonic movement IV–ii is a progression (the root moves down a third), and the part writing is correct. *Proceed with the next frame.*

(No response required.)

10.53 Which chord, (a), (b), or (c), most effectively continues the progression? ____________

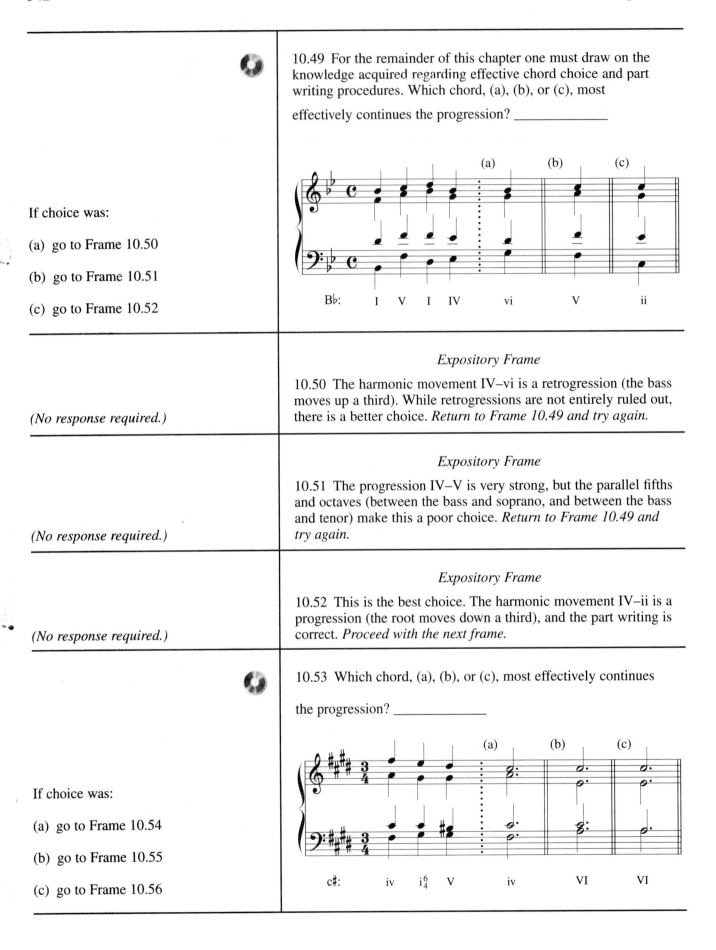

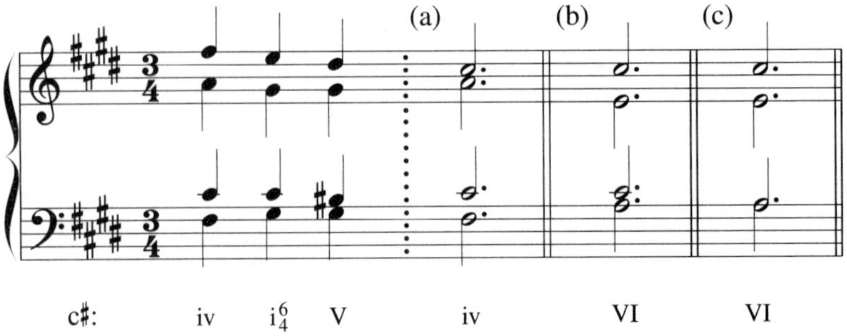

If choice was:

(a) go to Frame 10.54

(b) go to Frame 10.55

(c) go to Frame 10.56

Expository Frame

10.54 Several things are wrong with this choice. Not only is the harmonic movement V–iv weak, but there are parallel fifths between the bass and soprano. Notice, also, the incorrect doubling in the subdominant chord. *Return to Frame 10.53 and try again.*

(No response required.)

10.55 This is the best choice. Notice that the third is doubled in the submediant triad. This is to avoid the augmented second that would have occurred if the tenor had taken an A (as in chord (c)). What type of cadence is illustrated in this example?

A _____________ cadence

deceptive
(Skip to Frame 10.57.)

Expository Frame

10.56 The progression V–VI is good, but the augmented second between B♯ and A in the tenor makes this a bad choice. *Return to Frame 10.53 to find a better solution.*

(No response required.)

10.57 Which fragment, (a), (b), or (c), most effectively continues the progression? _____________

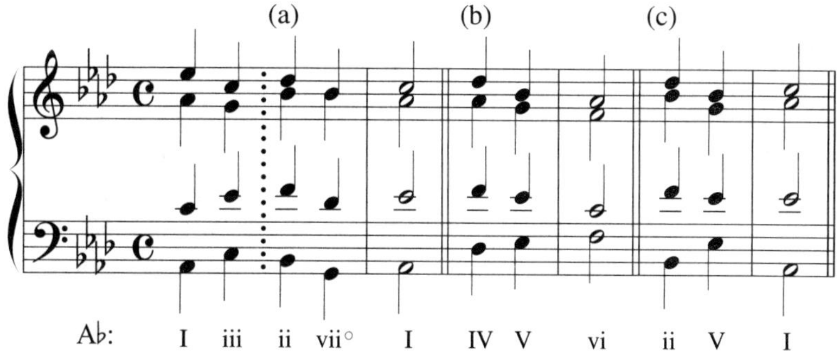

I choice was:

(a) go to Frame 10.58

(b) go to Frame 10.59

(c) go to Frame 10.60

Expository Frame

10.58 The use of the leading tone triad (vii°) in root position makes this a poor choice. *Return to Frame 10.57 and try again.*

(No response required.)

Expository Frame

10.59 The progression I–iii–IV–V–vi is a good one. Incorrect parallel motion between the second and third chords, however, makes this a bad choice. *Return to Frame 10.57 and try again.*

(No response required.)

10.60 This is the best choice. Identify the type of cadence used. *(Be specific.)* _____________

Imperfect authentic

The final chord does not have the keynote in the soprano. *(Or equivalent.)*	10.61 Why is the cadence in Frame 10.57 choice (c) not a perfect authentic cadence? ______________________
If choice was: (a) go to Frame 10.64 (b) go to Frame 10.63	10.62 Which fragment, (a) or (b), most effectively continues the progression? ____________

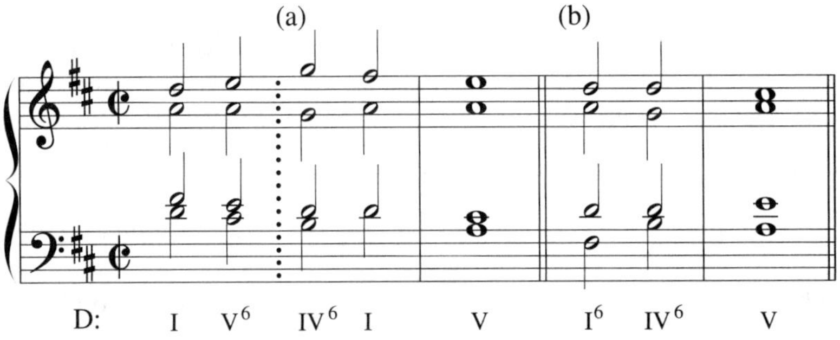

Expository Frame

10.63 The harmonic progression of (b) is a good one. There are, however, several flaws. The most serious of these is parallel octaves that occur between the second and third chords in the soprano and tenor voices (E to D). The bass line is excessively angular; also, it is undesirable to leap too often in the bass from triads in first inversion. *Continue with the next frame to learn why (a) was the better choice.*

(No response required.)

10.64 One may have been reluctant to make this choice because of the retrogression V–IV. Retrogressions, however, often provide good harmonic interest, and one should not be afraid to use them if good voice leading results.

Refer to Frame 10.63 to learn why (b) is weak.

If not used to excess, retrogressions are equal in effectiveness to progressions. (True/False) ____________

True

10.65 There should be an appropriate balance between progressions and retrogressions. This balance fluctuates drastically depending upon the wishes of the composer at a given moment. Merely as an arbitrary norm for an appropriate balance, two-thirds progression and one-third retrogression can be suggested as reasonable.

Does an excess of retrogressive harmonic relationships weaken or strengthen the sense of forward motion? ______________

Weaken

10.66 Which fragment, (a) or (b), most effectively continues the progression? ________

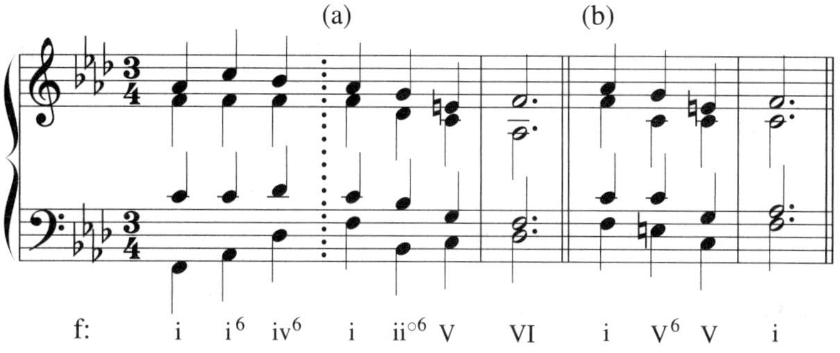

If your choice was:

(a) go to Frame 10.67

(b) go to Frame 10.68

Expository Frame

10.67 There is actually nothing wrong with either (a) or (b). This example is given to show that there are more ways than one to harmonize even a simple melodic line. The choice between these two possibilities is one of personal preference, as well as the type of cadence desired. Continue with Frame 10.68 for a comment on choice (b).

(No response required.)

Expository Frame

10.68 Although there is nothing wrong with this choice, many may prefer (a). The reason is that in (b) the dominant chord (V) is used on both the second and third beats immediately prior to the cadence chord. This reiteration of dominant harmony results in a stagnation of the harmonic rhythm. The greater sense of motion that results from the progression ii–V in (a) is desirable.

Read the comments in Frame 10.67 before continuing with Frame 10.69.

(No response required.)

10.69 Check (✓) the correct option:

1. Structural harmony occurs only at cadence points.
2. Relatively rapid chord changes produce animated harmonic rhythm.

True statements:
(1) ________ (2) ________ Both ________ Neither ________

(2) ✓

Expository Frame

10.70 To continue a study of harmonic materials (secondary dominants, modulation, chromatic harmony), please see the author's *Harmonic Materials in Tonal Music, Part II*, and after that *Bridge to 20th Century Music*, all published by Prentice Hall.

(No response required.)

Summary

The finished harmonization evolves from an assessment of the basic harmonic implications of the melody. Structural harmony—chords that constitute the tonal framework of the phrase—should be chosen first. Remember that tonal stability and modal clarity result chiefly from the use of primary triads in important structural positions. If used to excess, secondary triads weaken the tonality.

The steps to harmonizing a melody that are presented in this chapter are summarized below:

1. Familiarize oneself with the melody by singing or playing it.
2. Determine the key to be used. Some melodies may be harmonized in more than one key.
3. Select an appropriate cadence. If the phrase is one of a group of phrases, cadences should complement one another.
4. Choose an appropriate harmonic rhythm. The melody may suggest a particular rate of chord change, such as one or two per measure, or perhaps call for a chord for each note.
5. Determine the basic harmonic structure of the phrase. The three structures that have been presented are:
   a. A single chord followed by a cadence.
   b. Harmonic embellishment of a single chord followed by a cadence.
   c. A cadence formula (or a basic harmonic progression such as I–IV–V–I) spread over the entire phrase.
6. Select the remaining chords. Any note may be the root, third, or fifth of a triad. Progressions should predominate over retrogressions.
7. Write the bass voice. Produce an effective melodic line by using first and second inversions when appropriate. The bass should complement the melody. A variety of relative motion is desirable. Contrary motion contributes to the individuality of voices.
8. Check for incorrect parallel motion between the bass and soprano voices.
9. Write the alto and tenor voices. Each should produce an agreeable melodic line.
10. Check for part writing errors, including incorrect doubling, spacing, and parallel perfect intervals.

The terms that are explained or used in this chapter are listed below in chronological order:

harmonization
harmonic expression
melodic contour
chord (or triad) substitution
harmonic rhythm
contrapuntal interest
tonal variety
tonal framework
tonal stability
modal clarity

Mastery Frames

(3) ✓

(9.64–.67; 10.1–.5)

10–1 Check (✓) the cadence(s) that would be appropriate for the melody below:

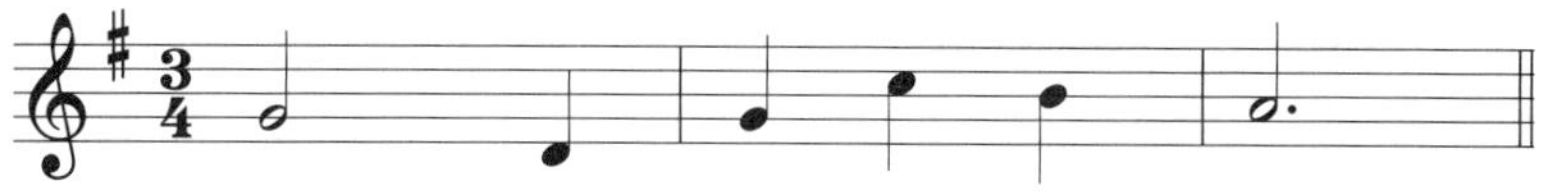

(1) Authentic _______ (3) Half _______

(2) Plagal _______ (4) Deceptive _______

(1) Authentic ✓

(4) Deceptive ✓

(9.64–.67; 10.1–.5)

10–2 Check (✓) the cadence(s) that would be appropriate for the melody below:

(1) Authentic _______ (3) Half _______

(2) Plagal _______ (4) Deceptive _______

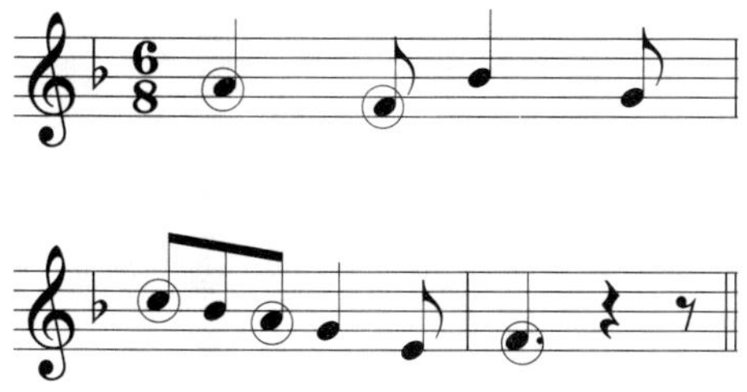

(10.30–.32)

10–3 Circle the notes that could be harmonized with the tonic triad.

(2) (10.10)	10–4 Which harmonic phrase structure is suggested by the melody in the preceding frame? _______ (1) A single chord followed by a cadence. (2) The tonic embellished followed by a cadence. (3) A harmonic formula spread over the entire phrase.
(1) (2) IV ii ii vii° vii° V (10.12)	10–5 Indicate with roman numerals the three triads that might be used at (1) and (2). (1) (2)  E♭: ___ ___ ___ ___ ___ ___

Supplementary Activities

Continue with all the activities suggested for previous chapters in terms of analysis, composition, and ear training. At this point, if those activities have been accomplished, there should now be the ability to develop larger-scale analyses and essays, compositions, and ear-training exercises. Work toward projects in these areas that attempt to synthesize and pull together the various materials presented in this volume. These will offer excellent preparation to continue with studies in Part II of *Harmonic Materials in Tonal Music.*

Supplementary Assignments

ASSIGNMENT 10–1 Name ______________________

1. Write chord symbols and identify the cadences that are appropriate for the melodic lines.

(A)

CADENCE TYPE

C: ___ ___ ______________________

___ ___ ______________________

(B)

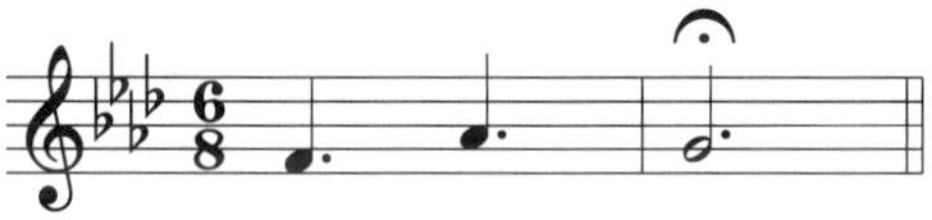

A♭: ___ ___ ______________________

(C)

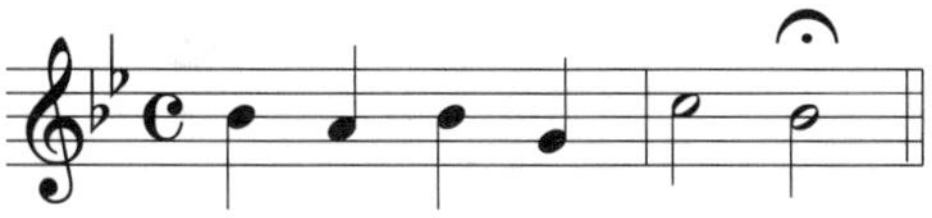

g: ___ ___ ______________________

(D)

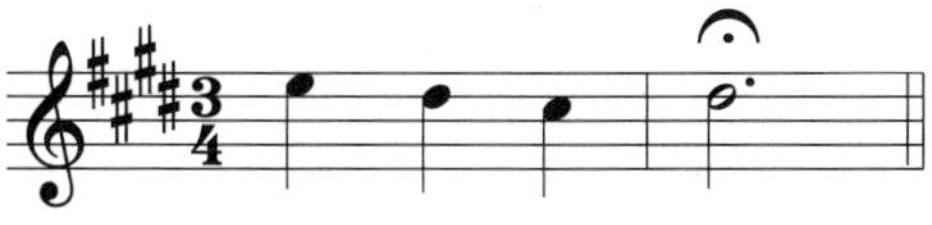

c♯: ___ ___ ______________________

(E)

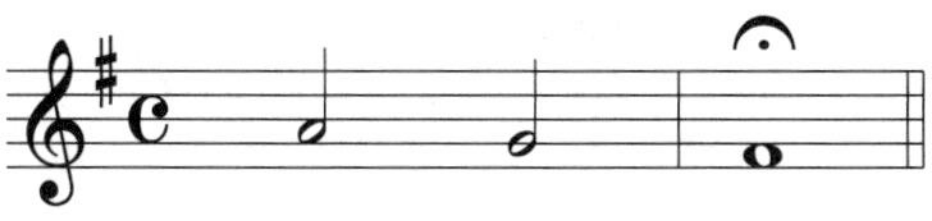

G: ___ ___ ______________________

2. Check (✓) the note value of the prevalent harmonic rhythm suggested by each of the melodies below.

3. The three chords provided in the example below indicate the basic harmonic structure of the phrase. Complete the harmonization by selecting chords for the remaining notes of the melody that produce mostly progressive harmonic movement. Use inversions and employ correct part writing procedures; supply the balance of the roman numeral analysis.

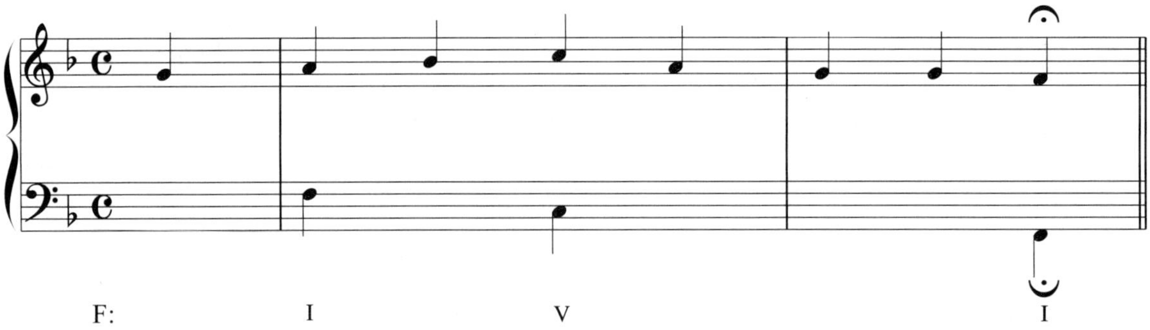

4. Complete the harmonization and supply the balance of the roman numeral analysis.

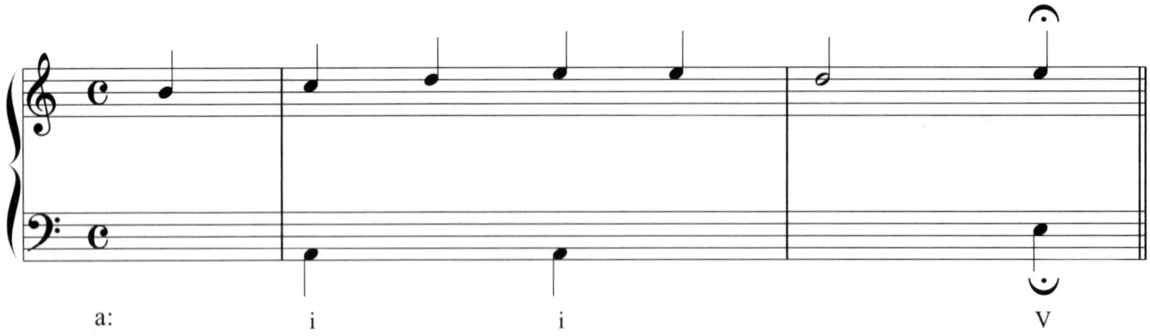

ASSIGNMENT 10–2 Name ________________________________

1. Show with roman numerals the three triads that may be used to harmonize each note of the major scale.

2. Show with roman numerals the three triads that may be used to harmonize each note of the minor scale.

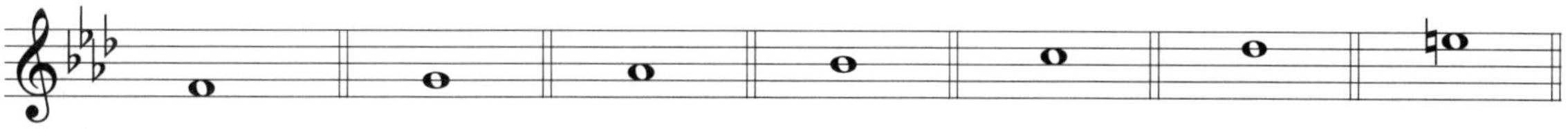

3. Complete the harmonization and supply the chord symbols.

(A)

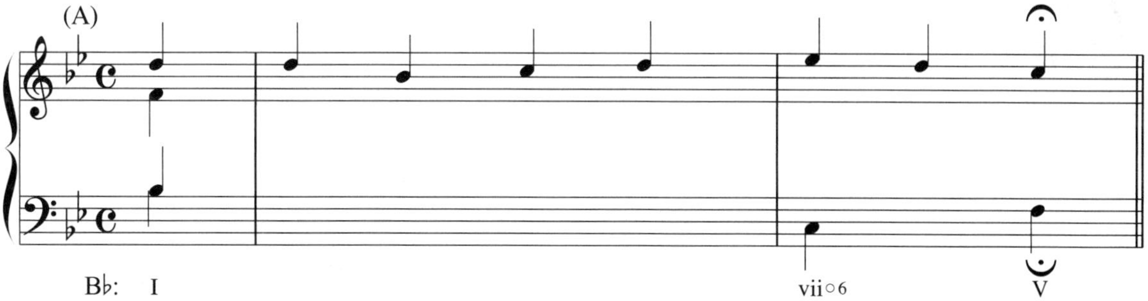

B♭: I vii○6 V

(B)

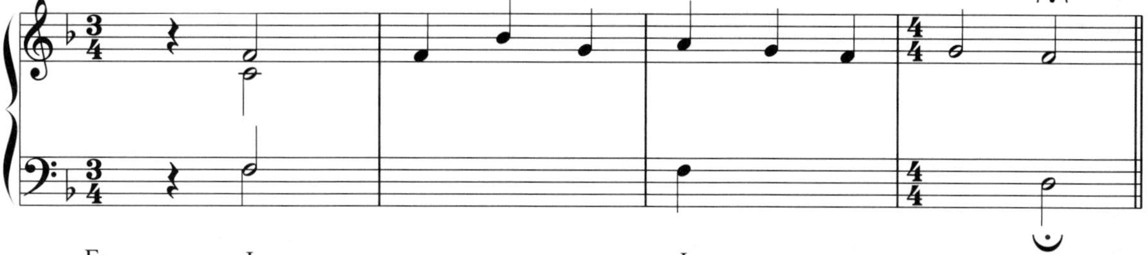

F: I I vi

4. Harmonize the melodies below using the method that is summarized in Frame 10.22. Analyze with roman numerals and complete 4 C and D with alternative analyses as well.

(A)

G:

(B)

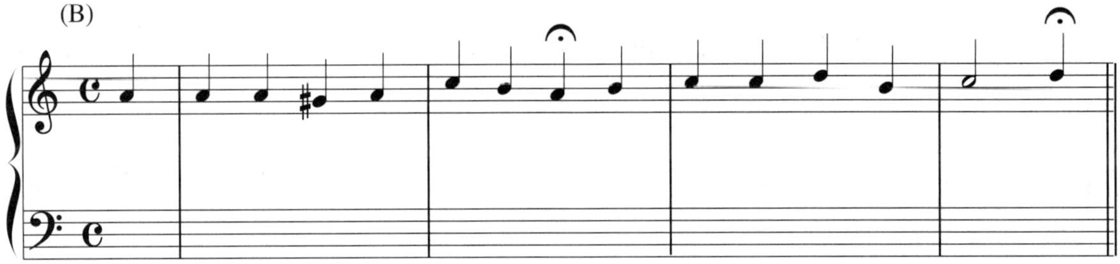

a:

(C)

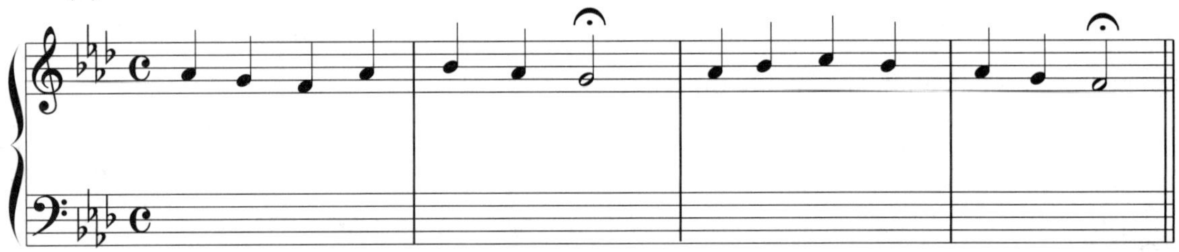

f:

Alternative:

(D)

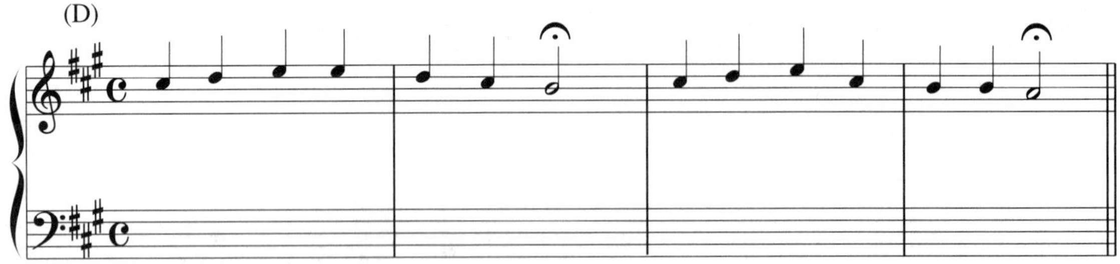

A:

Alternative:

5. Compose a short piece (4–8 phrases) for piano, instrumental or vocal ensemble (any style or utilize chorale style if a little unsure at this point) by creating a melody first, then creating an accompaniment utilizing the approach put forth in this chapter.

Appendix A: Chord Symbols

Since the early nineteenth century, symbols have been used to show the harmonic function of chords. These symbols consist of roman and arabic numerals as well as letters, accidentals, and figures such as the circle and plus sign. Chord symbols provide a vocabulary for verbal and written reference, and serve as a quick means of identifying not only a chord's relation to the tonal center, but also its quality and structure.

Musical analysis may take many forms, ranging from mere descriptive observation to complex interpretations made with reference to some explanatory system. Symbolism varies with the degree of exactness required by the analysis. The symbols used in this book are a compromise between simplicity and exactness; they may easily be adapted to serve the purpose of a particular type of analysis. Inversions, for example, generally are shown as part of the chord symbol; but, if the purpose of analysis is served merely by showing how chords function in a progression, symbols may be simplified by representing chords in root position only. Chord symbols are not precise enough to permit music to be reconstructed from them alone. They do, however, indicate the specific quality of diatonic triads and seventh chords (either directly or by inference) and usually show inversions. Thus the basic harmonic structure may readily be traced. In the case of certain altered chords, undue complexity is avoided at the expense of precision. To be completely consistent, logical, and devoid of ambiguity, chord symbols would be so complex that many no longer would serve as convenient references to harmonic entities.

As in many areas of music theory, there is a lack of standardization regarding chord symbols. Whenever possible, the most widely accepted practices have been observed. The following information summarizes the symbols used in this book.

DIATONIC TRIADS

Roman numerals are used to identify triads and are directly related to scale degrees. Further, the quality of triads is shown by the form of the symbols (capital letters = major, lowercase letters = minor, lowercase letters with circle = diminished, and capital letters with plus sign = augmented).

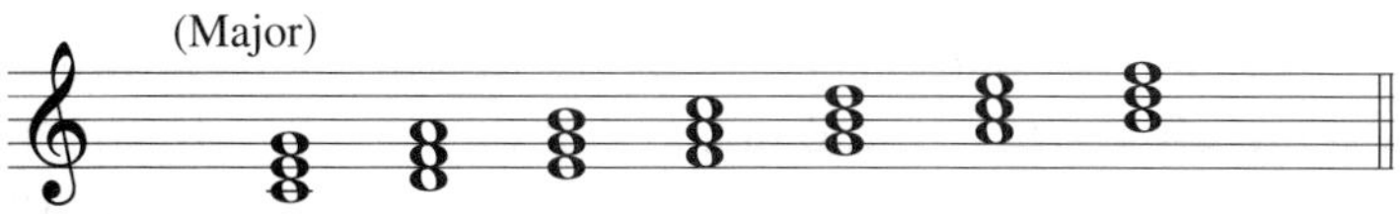

C: I ii iii IV V vi vii°

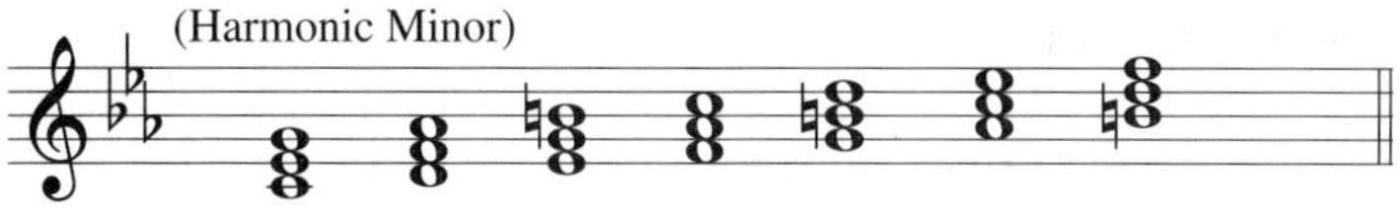

c: i ii° III+ iv V VI vii°

First and second inversions of triads are shown by adding the figured bass symbols 6 or $^{6}_{4}$ to the roman numerals.

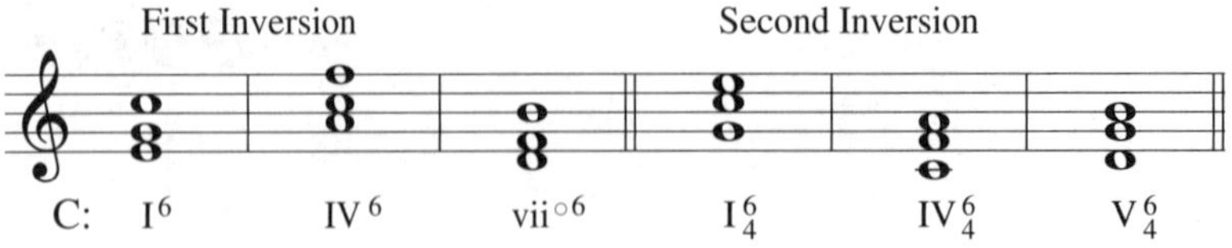

Notice that the figures are placed at the upper right-hand corner of the roman numerals. When more than one number is involved, the largest appears at the top and the remainder are placed in descending order.

SYMBOLS FOR CHORDS NOT PRESENTED IN THIS BOOK

Some of the examples in this book include chords that are not treated fully until *HMTM Part II.* In no case does comprehension of the material depend on an understanding of these chords.

DIATONIC SEVENTH CHORDS

The figure 7 added to the roman numeral indicates a seventh chord in root position. In a major key the form of the roman numeral is the same as for the corresponding triad.

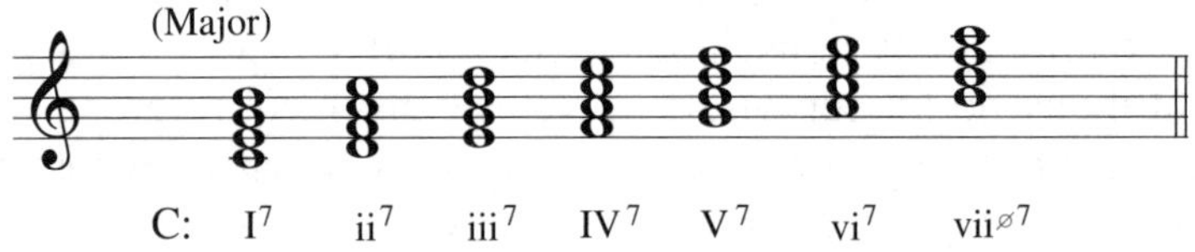

The symbols used in harmonic minor are shown below:

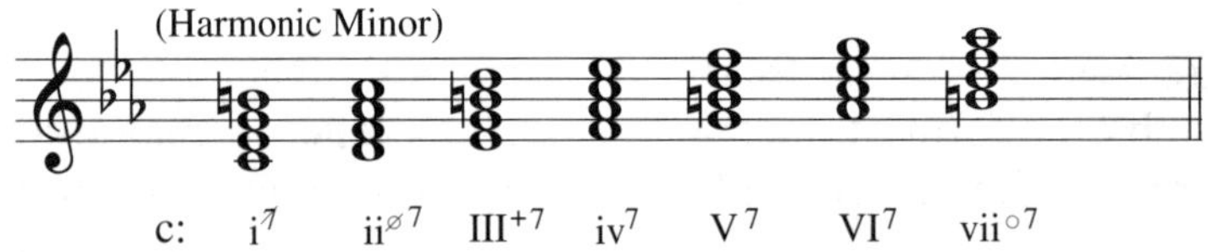

Notice that in the diminished minor, or so-called "half-diminished" seventh chord ($ii^{ø7}$, $vii^{ø7}$), the circle that denotes the diminished triad is replaced by a circle with a slash. For the fully diminished, or so-called "diminished" seventh chord ($vii^{\circ7}$), the circle that denotes the diminished triad is an indicator that the seventh is diminished as well. All half or fully diminished seventh chords are shown in these ways regardless of their use. This attempts to keep the nomenclature in conformity with that used by many writers and instructors. As somewhat traditional symbols, the circle and circle with a slash are appropriate in reflecting the theoretical practices currently in use.

Inversions of seventh chords are shown by figured bass symbols.

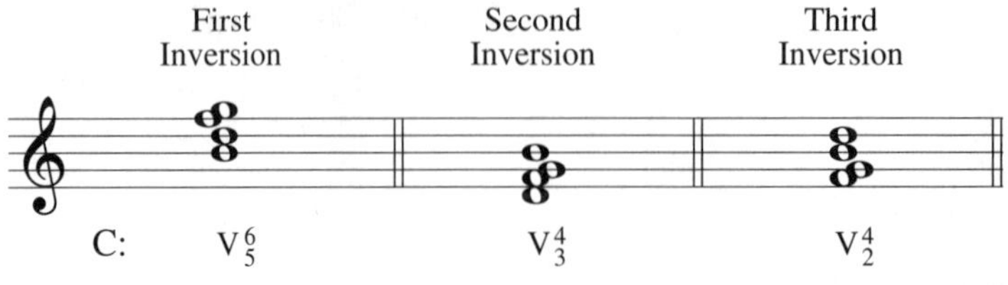

THE DOMINANT NINTH CHORD

The symbol V^9 is used to represent a dominant chord consisting of four superimposed thirds.

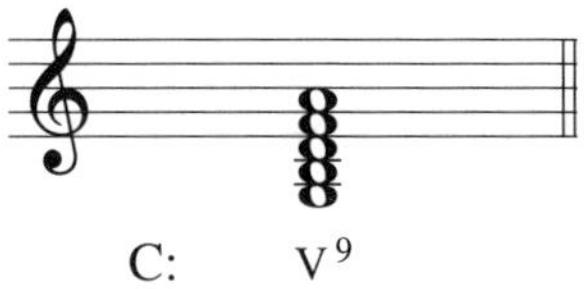

THE MEDIANT MAJOR TRIAD IN MINOR KEYS

The mediant generated by the descending form of the melodic minor scale is a major triad. The chord symbol is an uppercase roman numeral. For example:

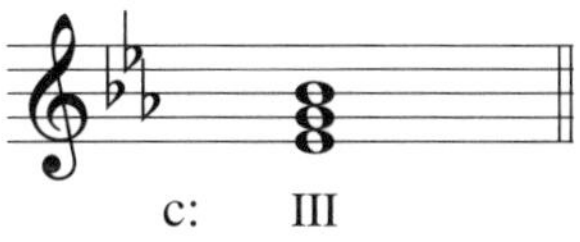

JAZZ-RELATED CHORDS AND CHORD SYMBOLS

The symbols below represent one way of representing chord symbols for some chords found in the Western jazz, commercial, and pop music fields. Actual practice will reveal that music symbology for these areas of music are far from standardized. It is hoped the following will assist in working with these areas of music. For more detailed information and also the vast array of the different ways chords are used for these areas of music please see this Web site from Wikipedia: http://en.wikipedia.org/wiki/Chord_%28music%29. For information on the Nashville Number System, which is yet another approach, please see these: www.nashvillenumbersystem.com (a Web site based on Chas Williams. *The Nashville Number System*, 7th ed. Chas Williams Publishing) or www.ducksdeluxe.com/opindex.html.

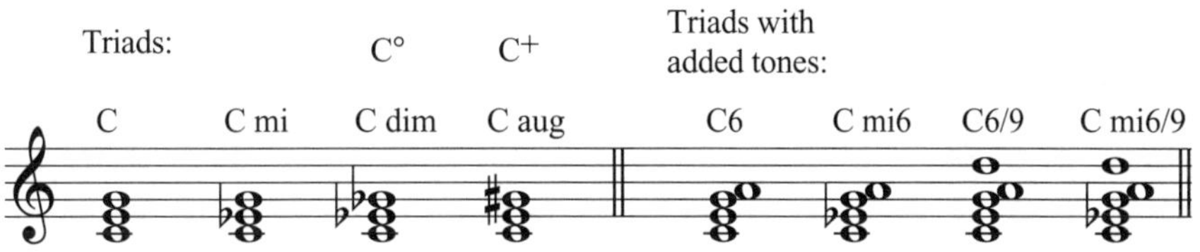

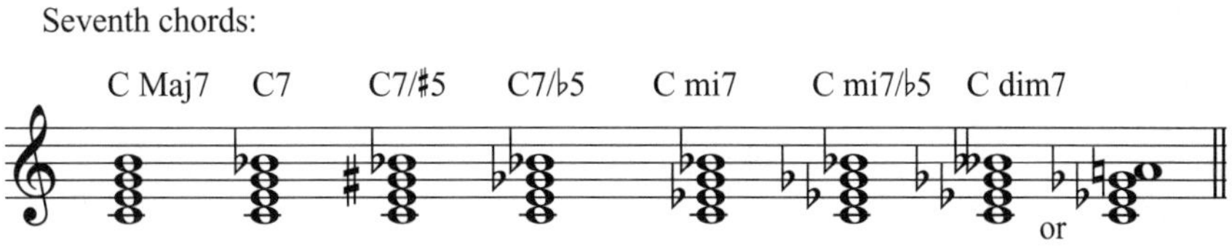

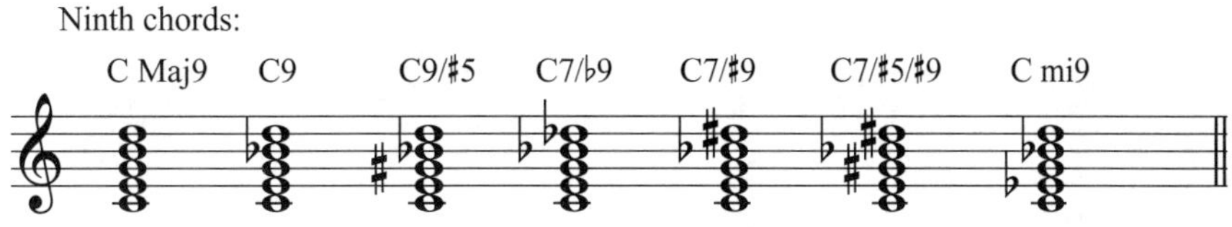

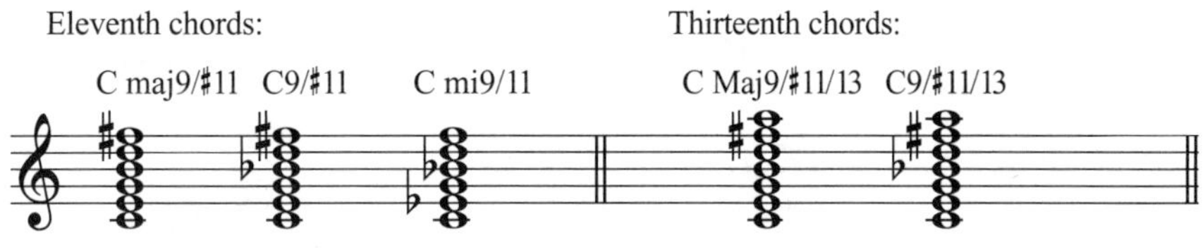

Appendix B: Piano Styles

Creative writing is possibly the best way to demonstrate command of the concepts and materials presented in this text. In original compositions students may apply the knowledge gained in terms of their own creativity. It is desirable that a variety of media (piano, voice, small ensembles, etc.) be used, but because of its availability, the piano is the most practical. The brief exposition of piano styles presented here provides a guide for those who have had little experience with keyboard techniques.* Effective writing is possible—even by non-pianists—if typical styles are utilized. The material that follows—used in conjunction with the suggested supplementary assignments—facilitates the creative work that helps develop a heightened sensitivity to the rhetoric of harmonic music.

There are three textures into which all music falls: *monophonic* (a single melodic line), *homophonic* (a melody with accompaniment), and *polyphonic* (several voices approximately equal in melodic interest). Of these, homophonic texture is the most practical for music in which the harmonic element is stressed. Thus we shall concentrate on various homophonic piano styles.

All of the following examples (**1–31**) are reproduced on the compact disc.

I. FIGURATED BLOCK CHORDS. In the example below, the melody is provided a simple accompaniment in block chords.

Mozart: *Sonata,* K. 545 (altered)

*Some of the examples contain harmonic materials presented in *HMTM Part II.*

Block chords are easy to play because the left hand does not move over the keyboard. Care should be taken that principles of doubling and voice leading are applied. Active tones (the leading tone and chord sevenths) should not be doubled, and should be resolved properly. Notice in measure two, for example, that the leading tone (B) is omitted from the left hand and also that the chord seventh (F) is resolved down by step to E.

Figuration patterns give rhythmic interest to block chords.

Mozart: *Sonata,* K. 545

(2)

The way that the three notes of the block chords are transcribed into the figuration pattern is clear.

(2A)

(2B)

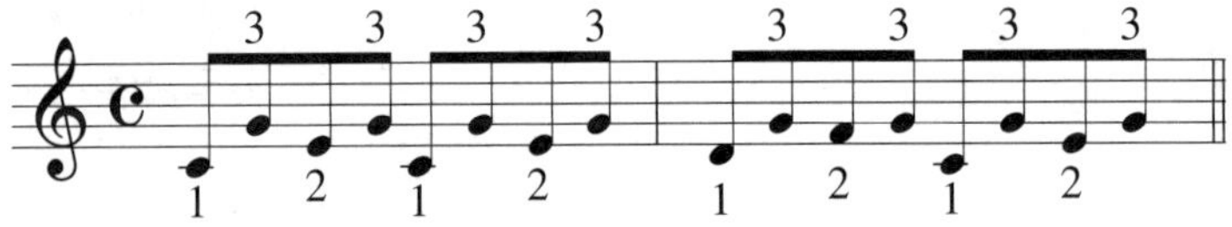

This technique of providing rhythmic animation for block chords is called "Alberti bass," after the Venetian composer Dominico Alberti (1710–1740?), who used such patterns extensively, perhaps even to excess.

Styles 3–12 show some of the many figurations that may be devised. The meter, as well as the degree of animation desired, affects the choice of pattern.

(3)

(4)

(5)

(6)

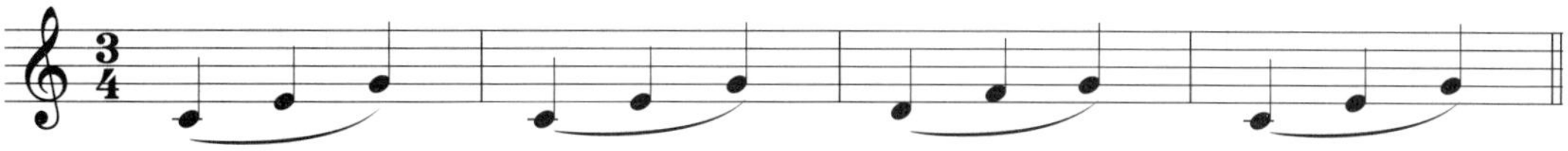

(7)

(8)

(9)

(10)

⑪ 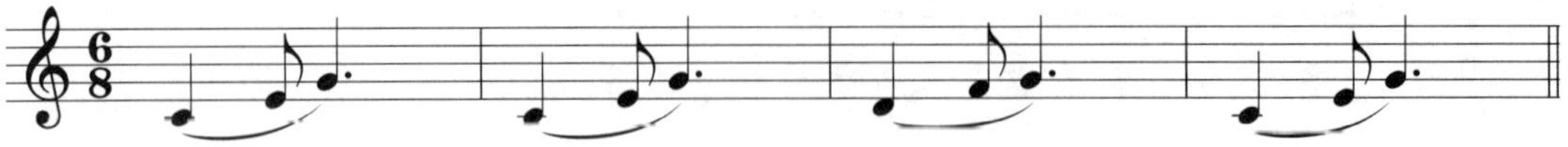

⑫ 

II. JUMP BASS (AFTERBEAT PATTERNS). In these styles the left hand jumps from bass notes to block chords. The best sonority results when the block chords are set in the vicinity of middle C.

Schubert: *Waltz in a minor*

⑬ 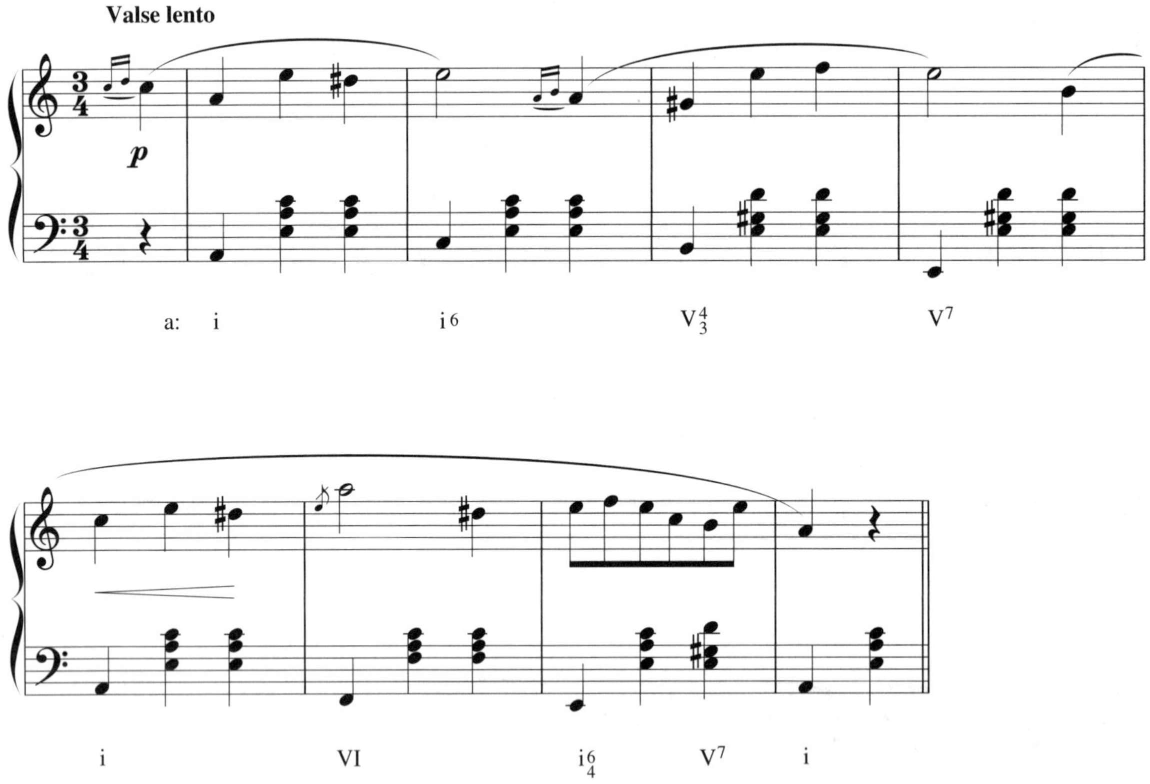

As in figured block chords, care must be taken that principles of part writing are observed. In the above example there are four voices in the left hand. Notice how each of these traces a smooth line, and also the way active tones resolve properly.

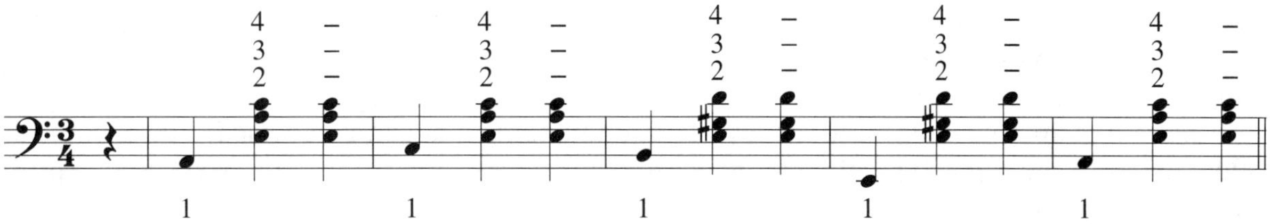

Of course the relation of the accompanying voices to the melody must also be considered. *Undesirable doubling and incorrect parallel motion must be avoided.*

Jump-bass patterns are exploited mostly in waltzes and mazurkas but are also useful in duple or quadruple meter for marchlike effects. Some typical patterns are shown in styles 14–18.

(14)

(15)

(16)

(17)

(18)

III. ARPEGGIATION. While being similar to the Alberti bass, the successive sounding of chord tones over a more or less extended range is called *arpeggiation.* Compared with previously presented styles, arpeggiation generally produces more sonorous effects. This is due to the vibration of more strings. Rhythmic animation and richer texture also result from arpeggiation.

There is scarcely any limit to the arpeggiation patterns that can be devised. The examples that follow demonstrate a few typical patterns; these may suggest others that satisfy specific expressive needs as they arise.

In style 19, arpeggiation is used exclusively throughout the entire composition. The effect is of figurated harmonies.

Schumann: *Album für die Jugend* ("Kleine Studie")

(19)
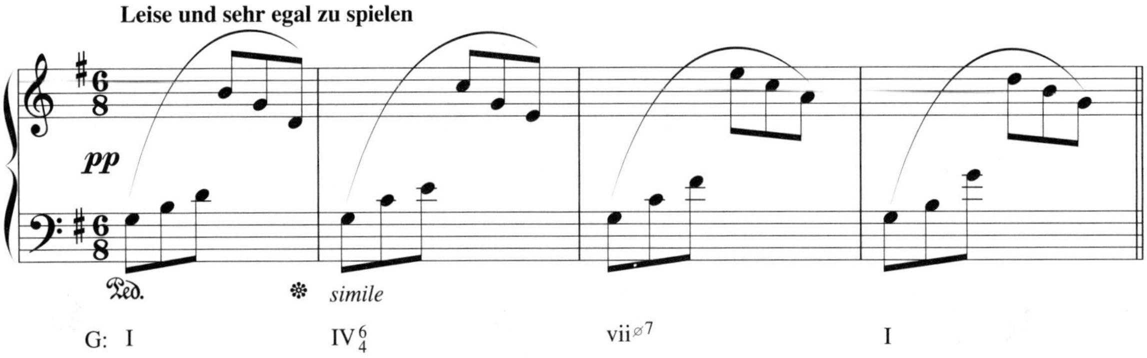

The example below shows fairly simple left hand arpeggiation, which supports a melody in the right hand.

Chopin: *Nocturne,* Posthumous

(20)

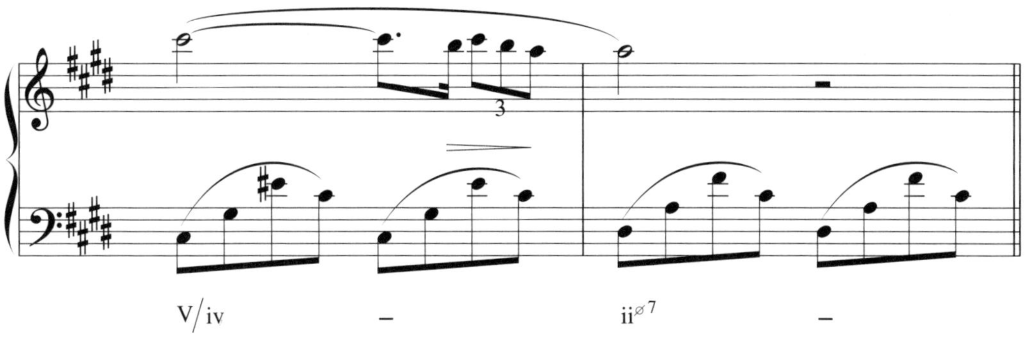

The arpeggiation in the next example is more extended in range.

Leybach: *Nocturne,* Op. 52

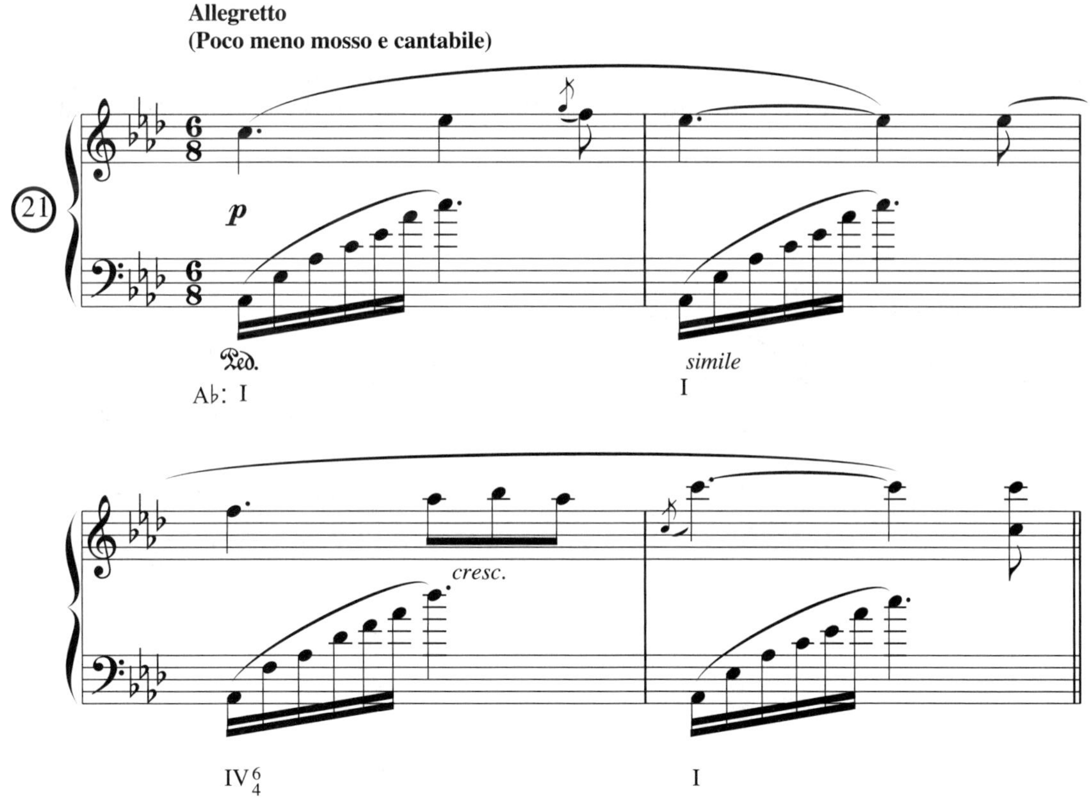

Style 22 has an arpeggiation pattern in the left hand while the right hand not only plays the melody but also fills in the harmony for additional sonority.

Brahms: *Intermezzo,* Op. 119, No. 2

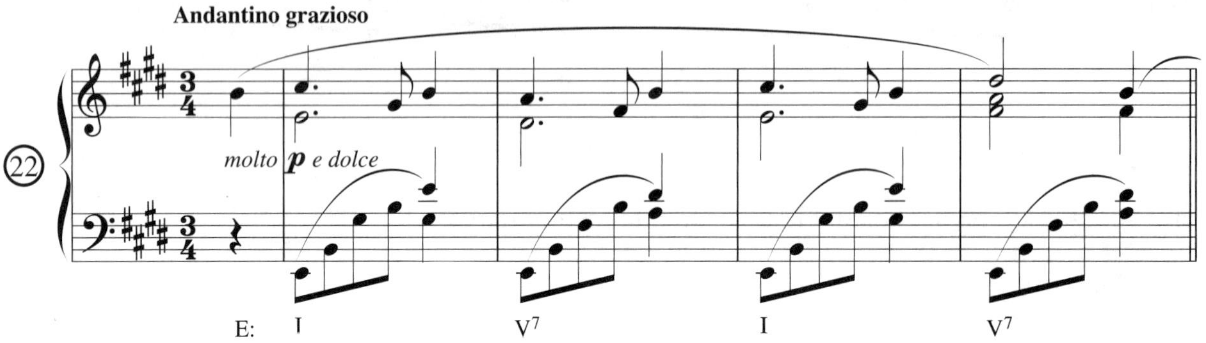

Arpeggiation takes a different form in the next example. The treble and bass move mostly in parallel tenths, while the middle voice completes the harmony, and fills in the eighth note rhythm.

Mendelssohn, *Lieder ohne Worte,* Op. 85, No. 2

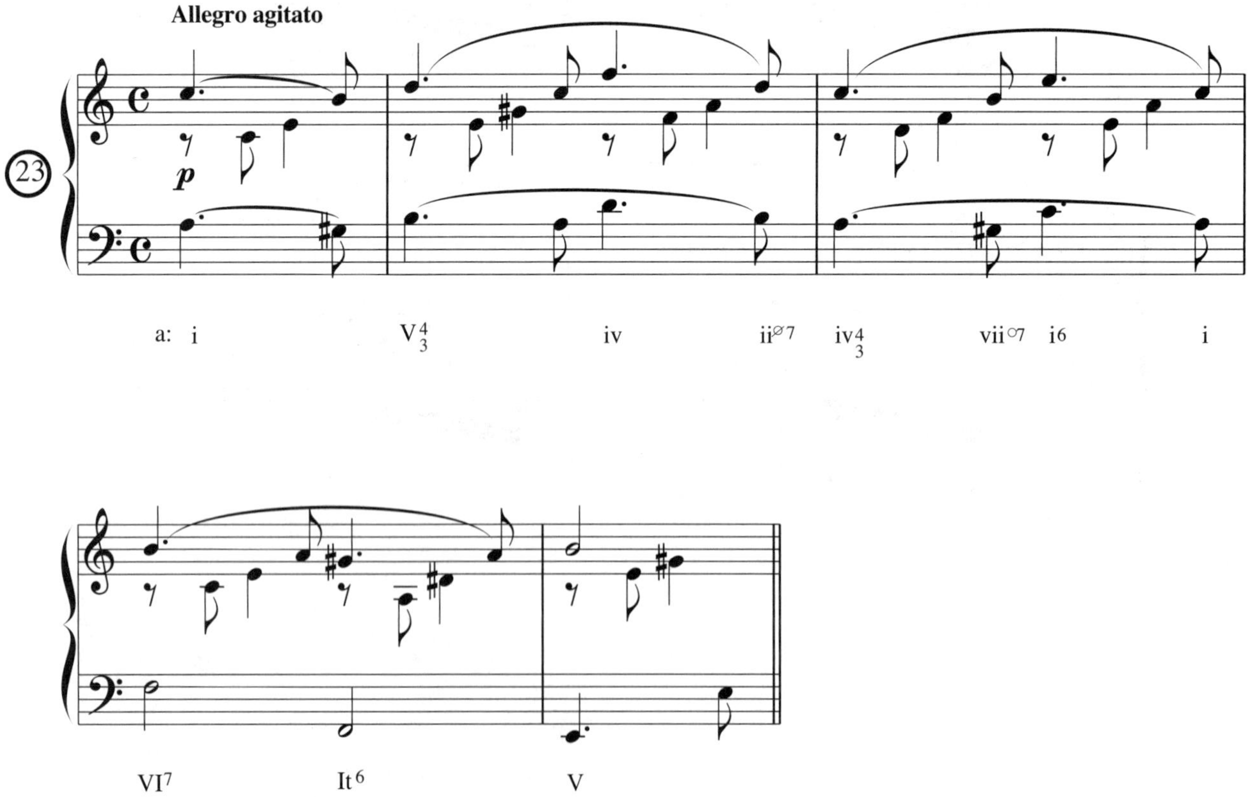

In style 24 the arpeggiation is in the tenor register, divided between the right and left hand.

Schumann: *Kinderscenen* ("Von Fremden Ländern und Menschen"), Op. 15

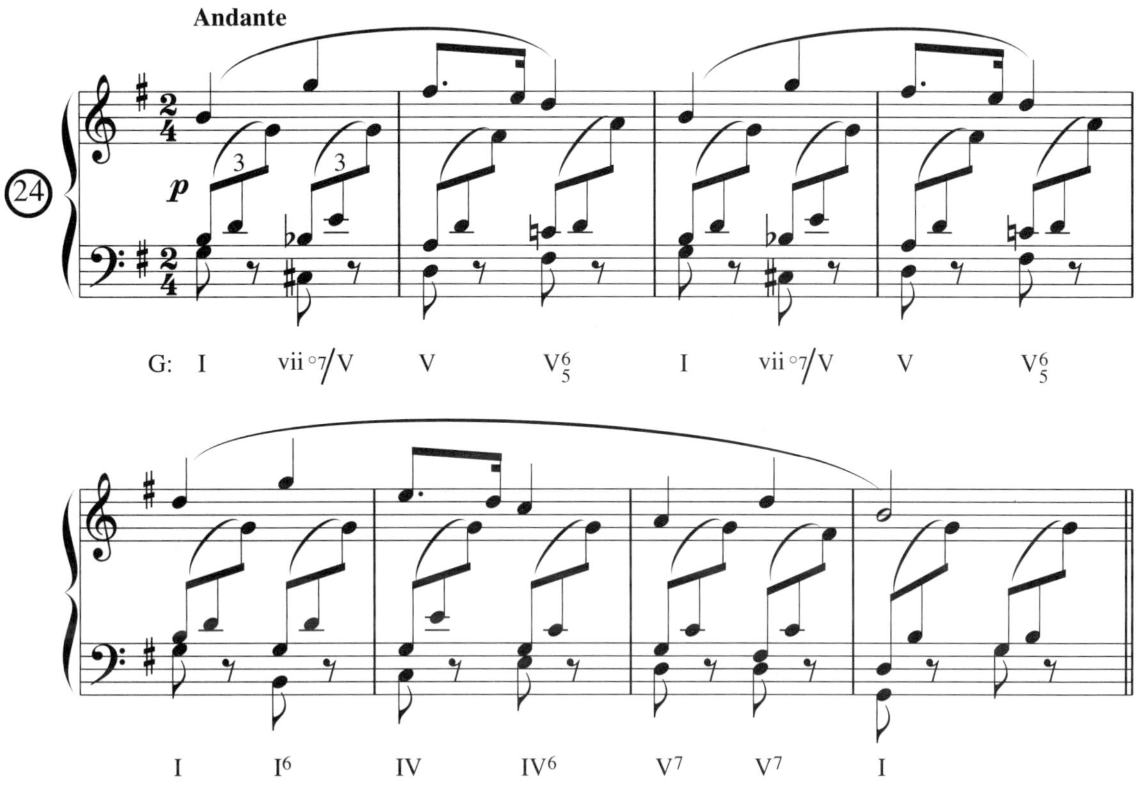

In the next example the arpeggiation is in descending motion, divided between the two hands.

Burgmüller: *Lullaby*

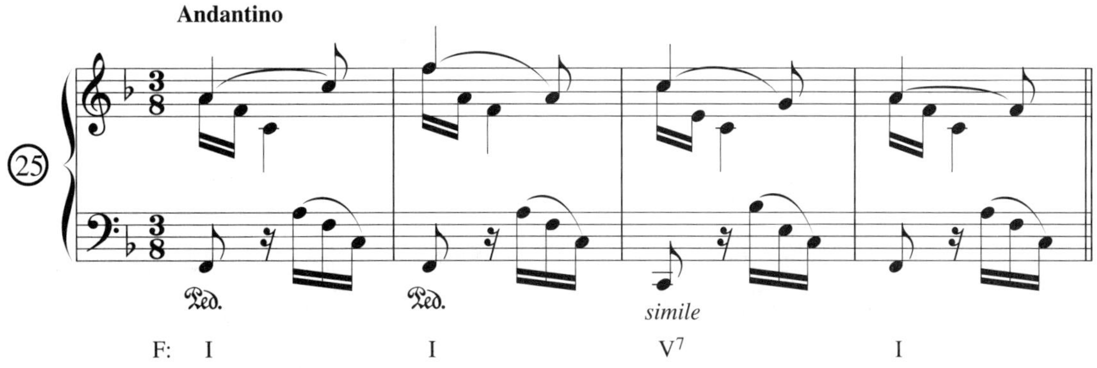

IV. HYMN STYLE. For serious, dignified or stately effects, melodies may be accompanied in a fashion similar to vocal settings of hymns. In this style chords change for almost every melody note. The resulting rapid harmonic rhythm makes figuration impractical. The number of voices may be consistent, or fluctuate to produce the desired sonorities.

Close style: The example below shows octave doubling of the bass, with the remaining voices in the right hand.

Schumann: *Album für die Jugend* ("Nordisches Lied"), Op. 26.

(26)

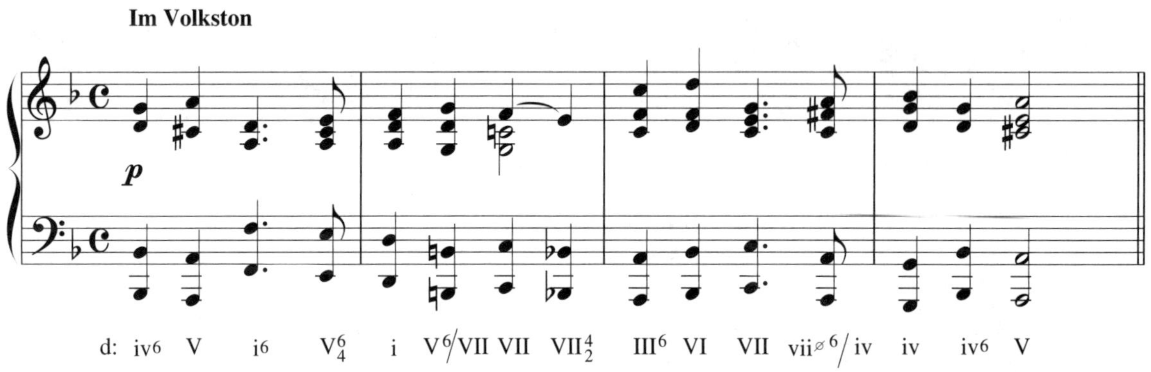

Open style: In this case the voices are divided equally between the two hands and open structure predominates. Only once is the four-part texture enriched by the addition of a fifth tone.

Chopin: *Mazurka,* Op. 68, No. 3

(27)

V. RIGHT-HAND PATTERNS. Of the several typical ways to treat the right hand, the single line melody is the simplest. This style has been amply demonstrated in previous examples (see styles 2, 13, 20, and 21). A few others are shown in the remaining examples.

Added alto in thirds and sixths:

Mozart: *Sonata,* K. 333

28

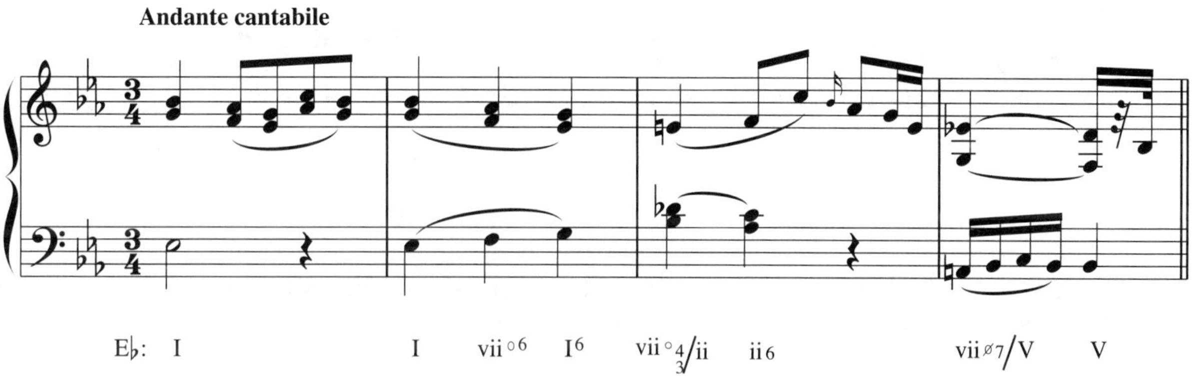

Schubert: *Waltz in B♭ Major*

29

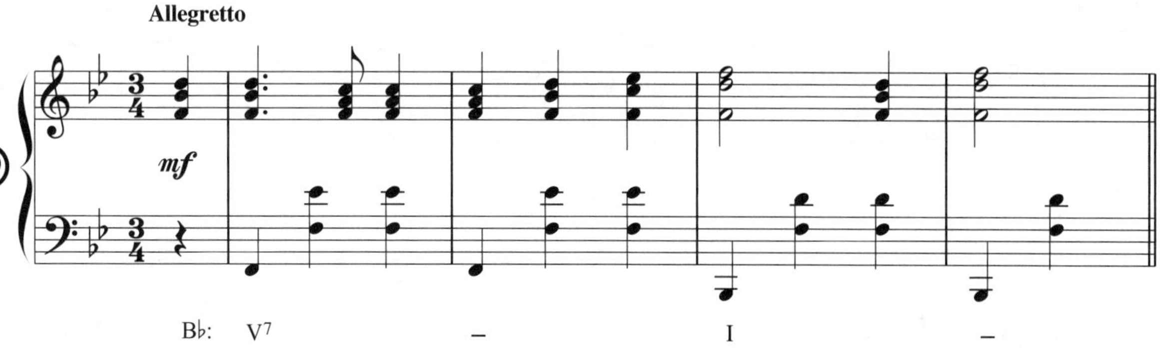

Melody in octaves: Increased sonority and prominence for the melodic line can be supplied by octave doubling.

Beethoven: *Sonata,* Op. 10, No. 1

(30)

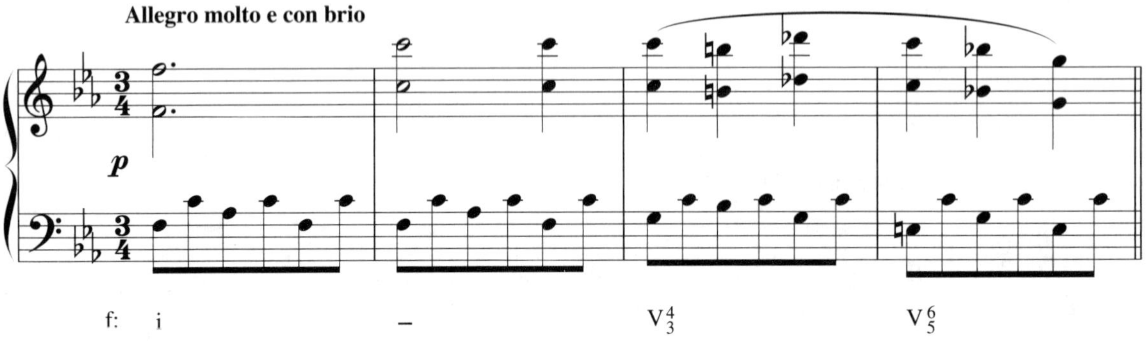

Melody with after beats: This technique is used when fuller sonorities are desired. Such patterns also produce a more intricate rhythmic texture.

Mendelssohn: *Lieder ohne Worte,* Op. 102, No. 1

(31)

Polyphonic texture has not been touched on here, but even casual use of imitation between melodic and accompaniment elements is effective. In addition, placement of the melody in the tenor or bass registers with the accompaniment above, provides variety. Above all, avoid using only a limited range. The compass of the piano is more than seven octaves, and effective writing requires that the hands range rather widely over the keyboard. In this way the color contrasts of the various registers are exploited.

Appendix C: Glossary of Terms

A

Accessory Tone *See* Nonharmonic tone.
Accidental A sign that affects the pitch of a note.
Acoustics The science that deals with sound.
Active tone A tone that has a strong tendency to resolve in a specific direction, *e.g*., the leading tone.
Altered chord A chord that contains one or more tones that are foreign to the prevailing tonality. Most altered chords fall into four classes: secondary dominants, borrowed chords, chromatic mediants, and augmented sixth chords.
Altered dominants Dominant triads or seventh chords with heightened activity due to chromatic alteration of the fifth.
Altered nonharmonic tone A nonharmonic tone that is inflected so as to be foreign to the prevailing tonality.
Altered tone A tone that is not included in the prevailing tonality.
Alto A low female voice. The next-to-the-highest voice of the four-part chorus.
Amen cadence *See* Plagal cadence.
Anticipation A nonharmonic tone that is approached by step and left by repetition.
Appoggiatura A nonharmonic tone that is approached by leap and left by step, usually with a change of direction.
Appoggiatura chord A chord that is used in a nonharmonic capacity similar to the appoggiatura.
Arpeggiation Sounding the tones of a chord in succession, rather than simultaneously.
Arpeggio six-four chord A second inversion chord formed by arpeggiated movement in the lowest voice.
Atonality The absence of a tonal center.
Augmented fourth An interval that is a half step larger than a perfect fourth.
Augmented major seventh chord A seventh chord consisting of an augmented triad plus a major seventh.
Augmented second An interval that is a half step larger than a major second.
Augmented six-five chord *See* German sixth chord.
Augmented six-four-three chord *See* French sixth chord.
Augmented six-three chord *See* Italian sixth chord.
Augmented sixth An interval that is a half step larger than a major sixth.
Augmented sixth chords A group of chords, all of which contain the interval of an augmented sixth (or diminished third). *See* French sixth chord, German sixth chord, and Italian sixth chord.
Augmented triad A chord consisting of two major thirds.
Authentic cadence A closing harmonic progression consisting of the dominant chord (sometimes the leading tone) followed by the tonic chord.
Auxilliary six-four chord *See* Pedal six-four chord.
Auxilliary tone *See* Neighboring tone.

B

Baroque era The musical period from 1600 to 1750 characterized by elaborate ornamentation, strict forms, and the establishment of functional harmonic tonality.
Bass A low male voice. Lowest voice of the four-part chorus.
Bass staff The staff modified by the bass clef sign, which designates F below middle C as occurring on the fourth line.
Borrowed chord A diatonic chord in one mode (major or minor), which appears as an altered chord in the opposite parallel mode. Most borrowed chords appear in major, borrowed from the parallel minor key.
Bytone *See* Nonharmonic tone.

C

Cadence A melodic-harmonic formula that brings a phrase to a more or less definite close.
Cadential six-four chord A second inversion chord that is part of a cadence formula—most frequently, the tonic chord in second inversion followed by the dominant.
Chain of suspensions Several suspensions in succession in which the resolution of one suspension becomes the preparation for the following.
Change of mode A change from major to minor (or the reverse) with the same tonal center retained.
Changing tone *See* Neighboring tone.
Changing tones The middle two notes of a four-note figure, of which the first and fourth are chord tones, and the second and third are nonharmonic tones.
Chord A combination of several tones, usually three or more, sounded simultaneously.
Chord changes Changes of harmony.
Chord function Chords function differently depending upon the relation of their root to the tonal center. The tonic chord, for example, is relatively static, whereas the dominant chord is active.
Chord of repose The tonic triad.
Chord quality Chords differ in quality according to their intervallic structure. Diatonic triads, for example, may be major, minor, diminished, or augmented.
Chord seventh The chord member that is a seventh above the root.
Chord spacing The placement of the various chord members in part writing. *See* Close structure; Open structure.
Chord symbol A figure composed of a Roman numeral and sometimes various figured bass symbols. Chord symbols identify the root of the chord in relation to the key center, as well as the quality.
Chord tone One of the tones that constitute a chord.
Chromatic (1) Melodic movement by half steps. (2) Music that incorporates many tones and chords foreign to the prevailing tonality.

Chromatic harmony Harmony that features many altered chords and frequent modulations to foreign keys.
Chromatic mediants Chords whose roots are related by the interval of a third and that contain one or more tones foreign to a single diatonic scale.
Chromatic modulation (1) Modulation in which not all voices move diatonically. (2) Modulation to a foreign key. (3) Modulation in which the common chord is an altered chord in one or both of the keys involved.
Chromatic movement Half-step movement that involves only one basic note.
Chromatic scale A scale consisting entirely of half steps.
Chromatic third relation *See* Chromatic mediants.
Chromatic third-relation harmony *See* Chromatic mediants.
Classical era The musical period from about 1750 to 1800, characterized by simplicity and order.
Close structure The spacing of voices so that no vacant chord members occur between the three upper voices.
Closely related keys Keys whose signatures differ by no more than one sharp or flat.
Color harmony *See* Nonfunctional harmony.
Common chord A chord that functions in two or more keys.
Common chord modulation A modulation that involves a common chord.
Common tone A tone that occurs in two or more chords.
Consecutive perfect intervals Perfect unisons, fourths, fifths, or octaves that occur in succession between the same two voices.
Contrary motion Two voices that move in opposite directions.
Cross relation *See* False relation.
Crossed voices The abnormal vertical distribution of voices in a chord, *e.g.*, the alto placed above the soprano.

D

Damper pedal The right-hand pedal of the piano, which, when depressed, allows the strings to continue vibrating.
Deceptive cadence A nonfinal cadence consisting of the dominant chord followed by the submediant chord.
Deceptive resolution An unexpected resolution of a chord. Typically, the resolution of the dominant chord to the submediant, rather than to the expected tonic.
Development section In sonata form, the section following the exposition. Previously stated themes undergo various types of variation and there is usually frequent modulation.
Diatonic Literally "by step"—having to do with scale tones; tonal material derived from a scale.
Diatonic modulation A modulation that involves diatonic melodic movement, and in which the common chord is a diatonic chord in both keys.
Diatonic scale A scale limited to the half and whole steps.
Diatonic seventh chords Seventh chords that are limited to tones of a diatonic scale.
Diatonic triad A triad consisting of tones included in a diatonic scale.
Diminished fifth An interval that is a half step smaller than a perfect fifth.
Diminished-minor seventh chord A seventh chord consisting of a diminished triad plus a minor seventh.
Diminished seventh chord A seventh chord consisting of a diminished triad plus a diminished seventh.
Diminished third An interval that is a half step smaller than a minor third.
Diminished triad A chord consisting of two minor thirds.
Dissonance Auditory tension produced by two or more tones when sounding intervals of the major or minor second, major or minor seventh, or tritone.
Dissonant elements A chord member or nonharmonic tone that creates a dissonance, *e.g.*, the chord seventh.
Distant keys *See* Foreign keys.
Dominant The fifth degree of the scale, or the chord built thereupon.
Dominant eleventh chord A chord of six tones built in thirds on the fifth scale degree.
Dominant function A chord that relates to the following chord as a dominant or leading tone triad, seventh, ninth, etc.
Dominant ninth chord A chord of five tones built in thirds on the fifth scale degree.
Dominant relation The relation between a dominant chord and its tonic.
Dominant seventh chord A chord of four tones built in thirds on the fifth scale degree, a major-minor seventh chord.
Dominant seventh chord with lowered fifth Equivalent to the French sixth chord built on the lowered second scale degree.
Dominant thirteenth chord A chord of seven tones built in thirds on the fifth scale degree.
Double flat A sign that causes a basic note to be lowered in pitch a whole step.
Double pedal Two tones (usually tonic and dominant) used simultaneously as a pedal.
Double sharp A sign that causes a basic note to be raised in pitch a whole step.
Doubled tones The same chord member sung by two or more voices.
Doubling The assignment of the same chord member to two or more voices. This is necessary when a triad is set for four or more voices.
Doubly augmented six-four-three chord A German sixth chord with the perfect fifth above the sounding root spelled enharmonically as a doubly augmented fourth.
Downward stem A stem that extends downward from a notehead. When the grand staff is used for the four-voice chorus, alto and bass stems go downward.
Dyad A two-note chord.
Dynamic indications Signs that indicate varying degrees of loudness (amplitude).
Dynamics The aspect of music concerning varying degrees of loudness and softness.

E

Echappée *See* Escape tone.
Elements of music The basic properties of music, which include rhythm, melody, timbre, texture, and harmony.
Eleventh chord A chord of six tones built in thirds.
Embellishing harmony The chords that are not vital to the stability of the phrase, in contrast to structural harmony.
Embellishing six-four chord *See* Pedal six-four chord.
Enharmonic change Alternate notation of the same pitch, *e.g.*, C♯ changed to D♭.
Enharmonic modulation Modulation in which there is an enharmonic change of one or more notes.
Enharmonic spelling A single pitch spelled differently, *e.g.*, G♯/A♭.
Equal temperament Tuning of the tones contained within an octave so that all half steps are of equal size.
Escape tone A nonharmonic tone that is approached by step and left by leap, usually with a change of direction.
Essential chord A chord that serves a structural function; often one of the three primary triads (tonic, subdominant, or dominant).

Essential dissonance Dissonance that is part of the harmony.
Expanded tertian sonorities Chords constructed by adding thirds above the triad (seventh, ninth, eleventh, and thirteenth chords).
Extended dominant chords Chords having a dominant function and including one or more higher dissonant tones—ninth, eleventh, and thirteenth.

F

False relation Chromaticism that occurs between two different voices.
Fifteenth The interval of a double octave.
Figured bass A shorthand notation widely used during the Baroque era. *See* Figured bass symbols.
Figured bass symbols Various signs, including numerals and accidentals, placed beneath the bass to indicate chords and melodic motion in the upper voices. Figured bass symbols basically show the intervals that occur above the lowest voice.
Final cadences The cadences that produce a sufficient sense of closure to conclude principal sections of the music. The two final cadences are the authentic and plagal.
First inversion A chord that employs the third in the lowest voice.
Flat A sign that causes a basic note to be lowered in pitch a half step.
Foreign keys Keys whose signatures differ by more than one sharp or flat.
Foreign tone *See* Nonharmonic tone.
Four-part texture Music set in four parts. *See* Four-voice chorus.
Four-part writing Music set in four parts.
Four-voice chorus A chorus consisting of soprano, alto, tenor, and bass.
Free tone A nonharmonic tone that is approached and left by leap.
French sixth chord An augmented sixth chord consisting of a major third, augmented fourth, and augmented sixth above a given note. The French sixth chord is sometimes called an augmented six-four-three chord.
Functional harmony The employment of chords and root progressions that serve to establish a tonality.

G

German sixth chord An augmented sixth chord consisting of a major third, perfect fifth, and augmented sixth above a given note. The German sixth chord is sometimes called an augmented six-five chord.
Grand staff Two staves joined together, usually with the treble clef sign on the upper and the bass clef sign on the lower.
Gregorian chant The monodic liturgical music of the Roman Catholic Church.

H

Half cadence A nonfinal cadence, usually terminating with the dominant chord.
Half step The smallest interval of the tempered scale, equivalent to a minor second.
Harmonic action The effect of chords moving from one to another.
Harmonic analysis The process of examining critically the harmonic element of music. The identification of tonalities and the labeling of chords are basic types of harmonic analysis.
Harmonic cadence Closure produced by harmonic action. The strong dominant-tonic progression, for example, contributes to the positive effect of the authentic cadence irrespective of the rhythmic and melodic elements.
Harmonic function The movement of chords to one another defines tonal space and delineates form. Harmonic function basically is either "structural" or "embellishing."
Harmonic interval The interval produced by two tones sounding simultaneously.
Harmonic minor scale A scale that consists of the following half- and whole-step pattern: W H W W H W+H H.
Harmonic phrase A succession of chords that constitutes a phrase.
Harmonic progression The movement from one chord to another.
Harmonic rhythm The rhythm defined by chord changes.
Harmonic sequence The successive repetition of a harmonic pattern at a different pitch.
Harmonic tension Tension created by the use of relatively dissonant chords.
Harmonic tonality The definition of a tonal center by means of chords relating in various ways to the tonic.
Harmonic tone A tone that is included as part of a chord.
Harmonization The technique of selecting chords to accompany a melody.
Harmony The element of music concerning chords and their relation to one another.
Horizontal aspect of harmony Successions of chords.

I

Imperfect cadence An authentic or plagal cadence that lacks a complete sense of finality. *See* Perfect cadence.
Impressionist music Music that utilizes techniques developed by impressionist composers, particularly Debussy and Ravel. Features of this music include liberal use of expanded tertian sonorities, unresolved dissonance, parallelism, the whole tone and pentatonic scales, and flexible rhythms.
Inactive tones Tones of the tonic triad are relatively inactive unless part of a dissonant sonority.
Inner pedal An alternate term for a pedal that occurs in an inner voice. *See* Pedal.
Interval The difference in pitch between two tones.
Inversion (1) Altering an interval so that the higher note becomes the lower. This is usually done by moving the upper note an octave lower, or vice versa. (2) Placing a chord member other than the root in the bass.
Inverted pedal An alternate term for a pedal that occurs in an upper voice. *See* Pedal.
Irregular doubling The exigencies of part writing sometimes make it necessary to employ an alternate doubling to avoid a more serious weakness.
Italian sixth chord An augmented sixth chord consisting of a major third and augmented sixth above a given note. The Italian sixth chord is sometimes called an augmented six-three chord.
Iteration Emphasis by repetition, immediate or delayed.

K

Key The tonality of a composition or segment thereof.
Key center The tonal center; the first degree of the scale upon which the music is based.
Key signature A group of sharps or flats that produce the desired half- and whole-step pattern of a given scale.
Keynote *See* Tonal center.

L

Leading tone The seventh scale degree (a half step below the tonic), or the chord built thereupon.
Leading tone relation A chord that relates to the following chord as a leading tone triad, seventh chord, etc.

Leading tone seventh chord A chord of four tones built in thirds on the seventh scale degree (a half step below the tonic).

M

Major key The tonality formed by a major scale.
Major-minor-major ninth chord A ninth chord consisting of a major triad, a minor seventh, and major ninth; a dominant ninth chord in a major key.
Major-minor seventh chord A seventh chord consisting of a major triad plus a minor seventh; the dominant seventh chord.
Major ninth chord Equivalent to a dominant ninth chord in a major key.
Major scale A scale that consists of the following half- and whole-step pattern: W W H W W W H.
Major seventh chord A seventh chord consisting of a major triad plus a major seventh.
Major triad A chord consisting of a major third and a superimposed minor third.
Mediant The third scale degree, or the chord built thereupon.
Mediant relationship Chords whose roots are the interval of a third apart are in a mediant relationship with one another.
Mediant seventh chord A seventh chord built on the third scale degree.
Melodic activity Interest created by the melodic element of music.
Melodic contour The shape defined by the rising and falling pitches of a melody.
Melodic function Performance of a linear, rather than a harmonic role.
Melodic line *See* Melodic contour.
Melodic minor scale A scale that consists of two forms:
Ascending: W H W W W W H
Descending: W W H W W H W
Melodic phrase A phrase etched by the melodic contour.
Melodic sequence The successive repetition of a melodic unit at a different pitch.
Melody A musical line produced by a series of single tones.
Minor-major seventh chord A seventh chord consisting of a minor triad plus a major seventh.
Minor ninth chord Equivalent to a dominant ninth chord in a minor key.
Minor seventh chord A seventh chord consisting of a minor triad plus a minor seventh.
Minor triad A chord consisting of a minor third and a superimposed major third.
Modal mixture The exchange of diatonic chords between parallel major and minor keys.
Mode (modal) Diatonic scale arrangements characteristic of classical Greek or medieval church scales.
Modulating sequence A melodic and/or harmonic pattern stated successively at different pitch levels and in different keys.
Modulation The act of establishing a new tonal center.

N

Natural minor scale A minor scale that uses the same tones as its relative major scale. It consists of the following half- and whole-step pattern: W H W W H W W.
Neapolitan sixth chord A major triad built on the lowered second scale degree, usually in the first inversion.
Neighboring tone A nonharmonic tone that is approached and left by step with a change of direction. Neighboring tones usually occur on an unaccented portion of the beat and may be either a step above or below the harmonic tone.
New key The tonal destination of a modulation.
Ninth chord A chord of five tones built in thirds.
Nonchord tone *See* Nonharmonic tone.
Nondominant seventh chord Any seventh chord other than the dominant seventh.
Nonfinal cadences Cadences that are incapable of bringing a composition to a close. The two nonfinal cadences are the half and the deceptive.
Nonfunctional Harmony that performs an embellishing, rather than a tonality-defining role.
Nonharmonic tone A tone that is extraneous to the harmony.
Normal resolution The usual, predictable movement of an active tone or chord.
Notehead The part of a note that indicates the pitch.

O

Oblique motion Movement of two voices, one of which remains stationary while the other moves either upward or downward.
Octave An interval in which the frequency of the higher note is double that of the lower.
Old key The original tonality of a modulation.
Open structure The spacing of voices so that there is a vacant chord member between the tenor and alto, and between the alto and soprano.
Opening progression Harmonic movement away from the tonic at the beginning of the phrase.
Organ point *See* Pedal.
Ornamentation One or more notes appearing between a suspension and its resolution.

P

Pandiatonicism The use of the tones of a diatonic scale without observing their usual functional idiosyncrasies.
Parallel fifths Movement in fifths between the same two voices. If both fifths are perfect, the individuality of the voices is diminished. Such movement is generally avoided.
Parallel keys Two keys (major and minor) that employ the same tonic.
Parallel motion Two or more voices moving by the same intervals in the same direction.
Parallel perfect fifths Movement in perfect fifths between the same two voices. Such movement is generally avoided.
Part writing The technique of writing chords and leading voices from one to another.
Passing chord A chord that performs a nonharmonic function similar to a passing tone.
Passing six-four chord A second-inversion chord that usually occurs between a triad in first inversion and the same triad in root position. Typical is the following: tonic in first inversion—dominant in second inversion—tonic in root position.
Passing tone A nonharmonic tone that is approached and left by step in the same direction. It may occur either ascending or descending, and may be either accented or unaccented.
Passive resolution The retention of an active tone, *e.g.*, the chord seventh, in the same voice in the following chord.
Pedal A nonharmonic tone that is sustained (usually in the bass and on the tonic or the dominant), against which other voices produce harmonies that are foreign to it.
Pedal point *See* Pedal.
Pedal six-four chord A second-inversion chord that occurs over the same (or repeated) bass note, *e.g.*, the subdominant six-four preceded and followed by the tonic in root position.
Perfect cadence An authentic or plagal cadence that meets the following conditions:

1. Both the final and penultimate chords must be in root position.
2. The final (tonic) chord must have the keynote in the highest voice.

Phrase A basic unit in the formal organization of music, usually four measures in length.

Phrase modulation A modulation that occurs at the beginning of a new phrase.

Phrase structure The underlying harmonies stripped of embellishing chords. Most phrases fall into one of three types:

1. A single chord followed by a cadence.
2. Harmonic embellishment of a single chord followed by a cadence.
3. A cadence formula (or basic harmonic progression) spread over the entire phrase.

Phrygian cadence In traditional harmony, a type of half cadence. The subdominant in first inversion moving to the dominant (in a minor key) is a typical example.

Picardy third The raised third in the tonic chord of a minor key. This effect is usually reserved for the final chord, to provide a more emphatic conclusion.

Pitch The "highness" or "lowness" of sound.

Pivot chord *See* Common chord.

Pivot tone A single tone that is common to two keys and serves as a link from one to the other.

Pivot tone modulation Modulation by means of a tone that is common to two keys.

Plagal cadence A closing harmonic progression consisting of the subdominant chord followed by the tonic chord.

Polychord Two or more chords sounding simultaneously.

Polyharmony Two or more chords that occur simultaneously.

Polytonality The simultaneous occurrence of two or more tonalities.

Preparation The initial note of the suspension figure. *See* Suspension.

Primary triads The tonic, subdominant, and dominant triads.

Progression (1) The movement from one chord to another. (2) More specifically, harmonic movement that creates a sense of forward motion. Root movements down in fifths, up in seconds, and down in thirds generally produce strong effects. *See also* Retrogression.

Pure minor scale *See* Natural scale.

Q

Quartal harmony Harmony based on combinations of the interval of a fourth.

R

Range The normal compass of a given voice or instrument.

Relative keys Major and minor keys that have the same signature, but different tonics.

Remote keys *See* Foreign keys.

Resolution (1) The movement from one chord to another; the term often denotes movement from an active chord to a less active one. (2) The final note of the suspension figure. *See also* Suspension.

Retardation Another term meaning an upward suspension. *See also* Suspension.

Retrogression A relatively weak harmonic movement. *See also* Progression.

Returning note *See* Neighboring tone.

Rhythm The temporal aspect of music. Involved is the division of time into beats, accent patterns of meter, and rhythmic figures.

Roman numeral analysis The use of Roman numerals and other figures associated with chord symbols to indicate the quality of chords and their position in relation to the key center.

Roman numerals Symbols used to identify chords built on the various degrees of the scale.

Romantic era The musical period from about 1800 to 1900 characterized by emphasis on emotional qualities, freedom of form, increased use of chromaticism, and expanded tonality.

Root The note on which a chord is built.

Root movement The intervallic relationship of the root of a chord to the root of an adjoining chord.

Root position The arrangement of a chord so that the root is in the lowest voice.

S

Scale A stepwise arrangement (ascending or descending) of the tones contained in an octave.

Scale degrees The tones contained in a scale.

Second inversion The arrangement of a triad so that the fifth is in the lowest voice.

Secondary dominant An altered chord that functions as dominant (a leading tone) to a diatonic triad other than the tonic.

Secondary seventh chord *See* Nondominant seventh chords.

Secondary triads Triads that are built on the second, third, sixth, and seventh scale degrees.

Sequence The successive statement or repetition of a melodic and/or harmonic unit at a different pitch level.

Sequence modulation Modulation caused by sequence units that move successively through different keys.

Sequential pattern A melodic and/or harmonic unit that is repeated successively at a different pitch.

Seventh (1) An interval encompassing seven basic notes. (2) The highest note of a seventh chord when in root position.

Seventh chord A chord consisting of four tones built in thirds.

Sharp A sign that causes a basic note to be raised a half step.

Signature *See* Key signature.

Similar motion Two voices that move in the same direction, but not by the same interval.

Six-four chord *See* Second inversion.

Slash (/) A sign that is used in connection with figured bass symbols. When drawn through a number, the note represented by the number is raised a half step.

Sonata form A form consisting of three principal sections: exposition, development, and recapitulation. Sometimes called "first movement" form because of its use in most opening movements of the classical symphony, sonata, and concerto.

Sonority The aural effect of a tone or group of tones.

Soprano A high female voice. The highest voice of the four-voice chorus.

Sounding root The chord member of the Italian and German sixth chords that has the aural effect of the root, as opposed to the "written" root. *See* Written root.

Spacing The placement of the various chord members in part writing. *See also* Chord spacing.

Staff The five parallel horizontal lines and intervening spaces upon which musical symbols are placed.

Stationary six-four chord *See* Pedal six-four chord.

Stem The vertical line attached to a notehead.
Stepwise motion Melodic movement to adjacent scale degrees.
Strong beat A beat that has relatively strong metric stress, *e.g.*, the first beat of the measure.
Structural harmony Harmony that appears at strategic formal points and serves to establish the tonal organization.
Structural points Locations that have special formal significance, *e.g.*, the beginning and end of the phrase.
Structural tones The first, fourth, and fifth tones of the scale are the roots of the three primary triads: tonic, subdominant, and dominant.
Structure of tonality The tonal pattern created by the three principal triads: the tonic, the dominant (a perfect fifth above), and the subdominant (a perfect fifth below).
Subdominant The fourth scale degree, or the chord built thereupon.
Subdominant seventh chord A seventh chord built on the fourth scale degree.
Submediant The sixth scale degree, or the chord built thereupon.
Submediant seventh chord A seventh chord built on the sixth scale degree.
Submediant seventh chord with raised root and third A diminished seventh chord built on the raised sixth scale degree in major. Resolution is usually to the dominant triad or seventh chord in first inversion.
Subtonic The tone a whole step below the tonic, or the chord built thereupon.
Supertonic The second scale degree, or the chord built thereupon.
Supertonic seventh chord A seventh chord built on the second scale degree.
Supertonic seventh chord with raised root and third A diminished seventh chord built on the raised second scale degree in major. Resolution is usually to the tonic chord in first inversion.
Suspended tonality The effect produced by a series of nonfunctional chords or rapid modulations.
Suspension A nonharmonic tone that is approached by the same note (usually tied) and left by step (usually downward).
Symmetrical chords Chords that incorporate some form of symmetry, *e.g.*, the augmented triad and the diminished seventh chords that divide the octave into equal intervals.
Symmetrical relationship Tones, chords, or rhythms that bear some kind of equal relationship to one another, *e.g.*, a passage of chords in which roots are related consistently by the interval of the third.

T

Tenor A high male voice. The next-to-the-lowest voice of the four-voice chorus.
Tension *See* Harmonic tension.
Tertian harmony Harmony based on combinations of the interval of the third.
Texture The general pattern of sound created by the elements of a musical work or passage.
Third inversion A chord that employs the seventh in the lowest voice.
Third relation Tones or chords related by the interval of the third.
Thirteenth chord A chord of seven tones built in thirds.
Timbre The quality of a sound determined by the number and relative intensity of its overtones.
Tonal center The first degree of the scale: the tonic.
Tonal harmony Harmony based on diatonic scales that demonstrates loyalty toward the tonic.
Tonal music Music that adheres to a central tone, the tonic.
Tonal spectrum The array of tones utilized in a given passage or composition.
Tonal system *See* Tonality.
Tonal vocabulary The tonal resources available within a particular style.
Tonality The organization of the tones and chords of a key with reference to the tonic.
Tone cluster A relatively dissonant chord produced by sounding several tones close together.
Tonic The first degree of the scale, or the chord built thereupon.
Tonic-dominant axis The tonality-defining relationship governed by the tonic and dominant chords, whose roots are a perfect fifth apart.
Tonic eleventh chord A chord of six tones built in thirds on the first scale degree.
Tonic seventh chord A chord of four tones built in thirds on the first scale degree.
Tonicization The emphasis of a particular diatonic chord by embellishing it with an altered chord that bears a dominant relationship to it.
Traditional music Music that is based on tonal, harmonic, rhythmic, and formal practices of the so-called common practice period—the baroque, classical, and romantic eras.
Transient modulation Modulation to a key that is passed through quickly on the way to another key.
Treble staff The staff modified by the treble clef sign, which designates G above middle C as occurring on the second line.
Triad A chord of three tones. Most triads are built in thirds.
Triad tone A tone that is part of a triad.
Triple pedal *See also* Pedal.
Tritone Three whole steps. The interval of the augmented fourth (or diminished fifth). The tritone divides the octave into two equal parts.

U

Unessential chord A chord that is not vital to the stability of the phrase. *See also* Embellishing harmony.
Unessential dissonance Dissonance that appears incidentally, as a nonharmonic tone.
Upper voices All voices other than the lowest.
Upward stem A stem that attaches to the right-hand side of the notehead and extends upward. When the grand staff is used for the four-voice chorus, soprano and tenor stems go upward.

V

Vertical aspect of harmony Chords, as opposed to chord progressions.
Voice leading The technique of moving the various voices from one chord to another.

W

Weak beat A beat that has relatively light metric stress.
Western music Music of Western Europe and music that has been derived therefrom.
Whole step The major second; two half steps.
Written root The lowest tone of a chord when arranged in thirds, as opposed to the sounding root in the case of the Italian and German sixth chords. *See* Sounding root.

Appendix D
Orchestration Chart; Note/Octave, MIDI Charts

Note that conservative, practical ranges have been given here. In compositional assignments the extreme ranges of the instruments would probably be best avoided to facilitate classroom performances. See orchestration books in the Bibliography for information on instruments not listed here. The sounding range of the instrument is given first in whole notes, followed by the written range in quarter notes. The transposition interval, if needed, is given just to the right of the range staff. (For more information on special performance techniques for any of the instruments, please see the Orchestration section of the *Bibliography for Further Study*, p. 384.)

WOODWINDS

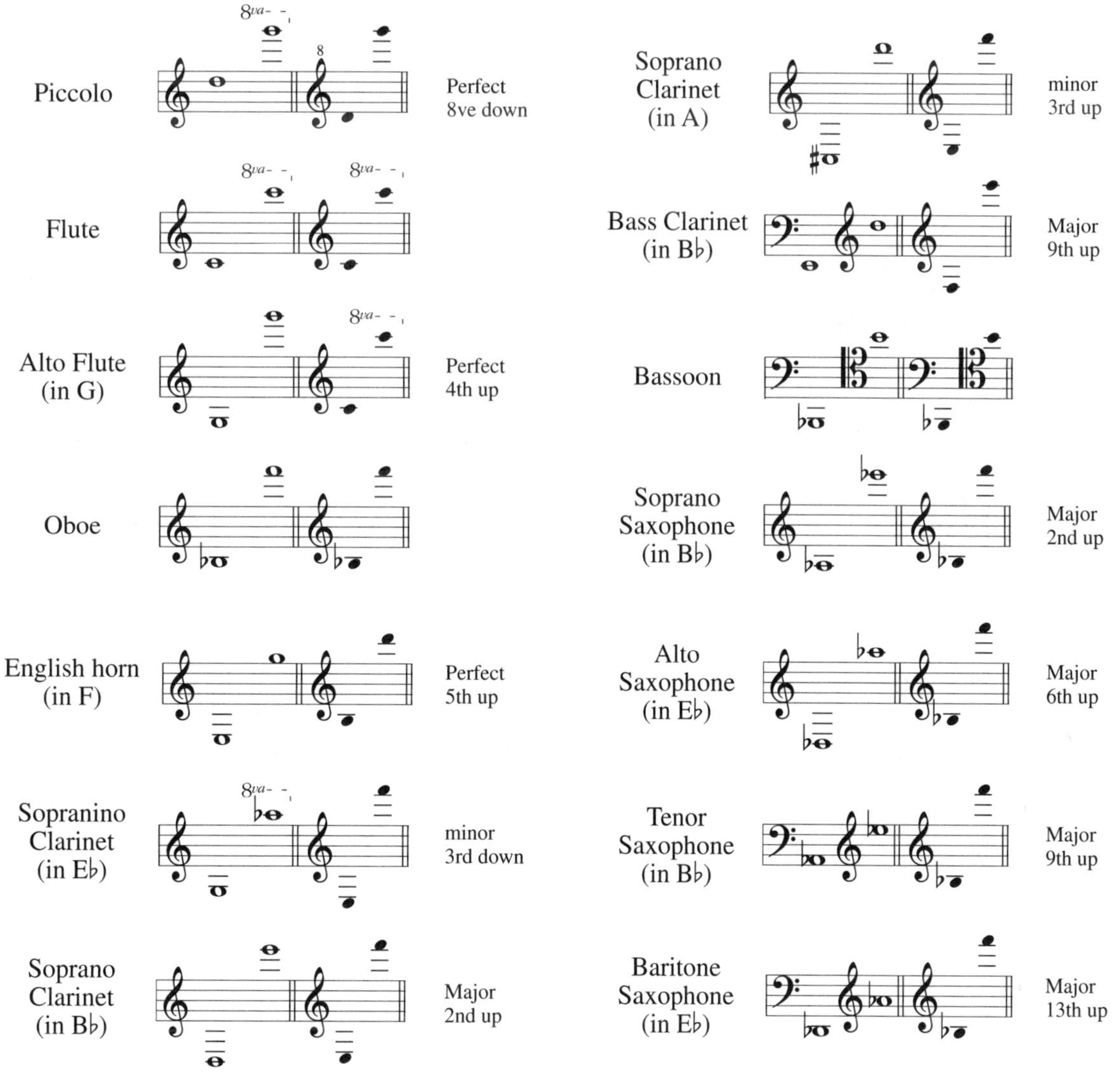

BRASS

Trumpet*
Cornet
Fluegelhorn
(in B♭)

Major
2nd up

Trombone
Baritone

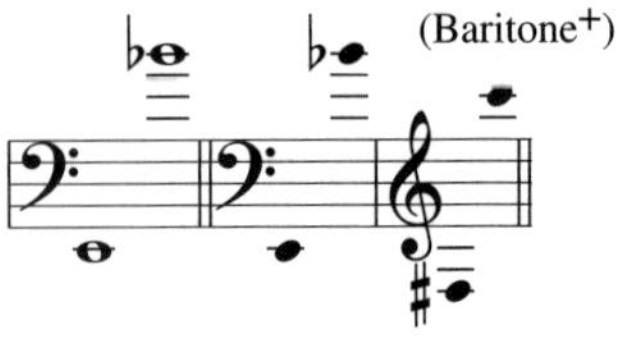

Horn
(in F)

Perfect
5th up

Tuba

The C trumpet's sounding and written range is the same as the B♭ trumpet's written range.

+ *If the baritone is written in treble clef, then it is written as a B♭ transposition; always check with your player to see which clef should be used for your part.*

STRINGS

Violin

Contrabass

Perfect
8ve up

Viola

Electric Bass

Perfect
8ve up

Violoncello

Guitar

Perfect
8ve up

KEYBOARD RELATED*

Piano+

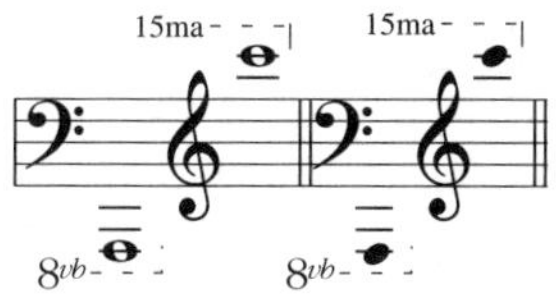

Xylophone

Perfect 8ve down

Celesta

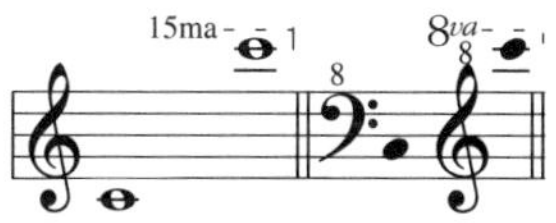

Perfect 8ve down

Marimba

Harp

Vibraphone

Harpsichord (single keyboard)

Accordion

* *For organ (pipe or electric) or synthesizers, check with instrument/performer available to you for ranges.*

+ *Electric or synthesized piano ranges may vary from this normal piano range.*

CHORAL VOICES*

Soprano

Tenor

Perfect 8ve down

Alto

Bass

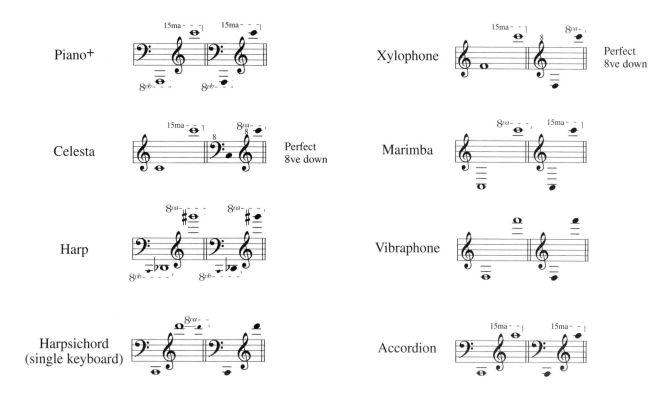

* *Less experienced singers may be limited to a range approximately a major second below the top notes and a major second above the low notes listed here.*

Octave Naming systems

Traditional	Shorthand 1	Shorthand 2	Numbered	MIDI nr	Frequency of A (Hz)
subsubcontra	$C_3 – B_3$	$C_{,,,} – B_{,}$ (CCCC–BBBB)	C-1 – B-1	0 – 11	13.75
sub-contra	$C_2 – B_2$	$C_{,,} – B_{,,}$(CCC–BBB)	C0 – B0	12 – 23	27.5
contra	$C_1 – B_1$	$C_{,} – B_{,}$ (CC – BB)	C1 – B1	24 – 35	55
great	C – B	C – B	C2 – B2	36 – 47	110
small	c – b	c – b	C3 – B3	48 – 59	220
one-lined	$c^1 – b^1$	c′ – b′	C4 – B4	60 – 71	440
two-lined	$c^2 – b^2$	c″ – b″	C5 – B5	72 – 83	880
three-lined	$c^3 – b^3$	c‴ – b‴	C6 – B6	84 – 95	1760
four-lined	$c^4 – b^3$	c⁗ – b⁗	C7 – B7	96 – 107	3520
five-lined	$c^5 – b^5$	c′′′′′ – b′′′′′	C8 – B8	108 – 119	7040
six-lined	$c^6 – b^6$	c′′′′′′ – b′′′′′′	C9 – G9	120 – 127	1408

Sample of World Note Names

Name	prime		second		third	fourth		fifth		sixth		seventh
Natural (English)	C		D		E	F		G		A		B
Sharp (symbol)		C♯		D♯			F♯		G♯		A♯	
Flat (symbol)		D♭		E♭			G♭		A♭		B♭	
Sharp (English name)		C sharp		D sharp			F sharp		G sharp		A sharp	
Flat (English name)		D flat		E flat			G flat		A flat		B flat	
Natural (No. European)	C		D		E	F		G		A		H
Sharp (Northern European)		Cis		Dis			Fis		Gis		Ais	
Flat (Northern European)		Des		Es			Ges		As		B	
Variant (Flat & Natural) (BE, NL)		-	-	-	-	-	-	-	-	-	Bes	B
Southern European	Do		Re		Mi	Fa		Sol		La		Si
Variant names	Ut		-		-	-		So		-		Ti
Indian style	Sa		Re		Ga	Ma		Pa		Da		Ni
Korean style	Da		Ra		Ma	Ba		Sa		Ga		Na
Approx. Frequency [Hz]	262	277	294	311	330	349	370	392	415	440	466	494
MIDI note number	60	61	62	63	64	65	66	67	68	69	70	71

Reprinted from
http://en.wikipedia.org/wiki/Note

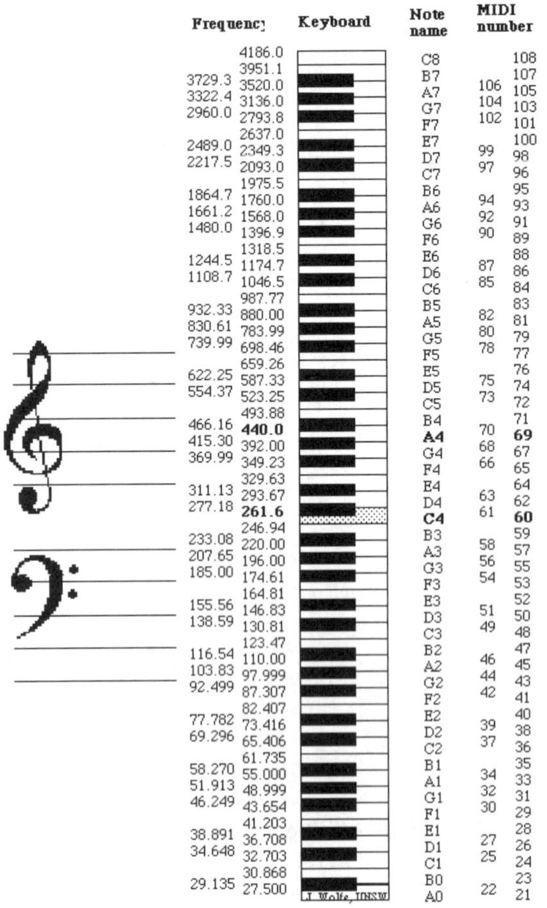

From "Music Acoustics,"
http://www.phys.unsw.edu.au/jw/notes.html.
Reprinted by permission

Bibliography for Further Study

ACOUSTICS

Backus, John. *Acoustical Foundations of Music.* 2nd ed. 1977. New York: W. W. Norton.

Benade, A. H. *Fundamentals of Musical Acoustics.* 2nd rev. ed. 1990. Mineaola, N.Y.: Dover Publications, Inc.

———. *Horns, Strings & Harmony.* 1992. Mineaola, N.Y.: Dover Publications, Inc.

Bienvenue, Gordon F. & Prout, James H. *Acoustics for You.* 1990. Malabar, Fla.: R. E. Krieger Pub. Co.

Campbell, D. W. & Greated, Clive A. *The Musicians Guide to Acoustics.* 1987. New York: Schirmer Books.

Erickson, Robert. *Sound Structure in Music.* 1975. Berkeley: University of California Press.

Moravcsik, Michael J. *Musical Sound. An Introduction to the Physics of Music.* 1987. New York: Paragon House.

Pierce, John R. *The Science of Musical Sound.* 1983. New York: W. H. Freeman.

Slawson, Wayne. *Sound Color.* 1985. Berkeley: University of California Press.

Wagner, Michael J. *Introductory Musical Acoustics.* 3rd ed. 1994. Raleigh, N.C.: Contemporary Publishing Company.

COMPOSITION

Adams, Robert T. *Electronic Music Composition for Beginners.* 2nd ed. 1992. Boston: McGraw-Hill Higher Ed.

Austin, Larry & Clark, Thomas. *Learning to Compose: Modes, Materials and Models of Musical Invention.* 1989. Madison, Wis.: WCB Brown & Benchmark.

Brindle, Reginald Smith. *Musical Composition.* 1986. New York: Oxford University Press.

———. *Serial Composition.* 1968. New York: Oxford University Press.

Carter, Elliott. *Harmony Book.* Nicholas, Hopkins & John F. Link, eds. 2002. Paoli, Penn.: Carl Fischer.

Cope, David. *New Music Composition.* 1977. New York: Schirmer Books.

———. *Techniques of the Contemporary Composer.* 1997. Belmont, Calif.: Schirmer/Thompson Learning.

Dallin, Leon. *Techniques of Twentieth Century Composition: A Guide to the Materials of Modern Music.* 3rd ed. 1974. Boston: McGraw-Hill Higher Ed.

Dodge, Charles & Jerse, Thomas A. *Computer Music: Synthesis, Composition, and Performance.* 1997. Belmont, Calif.: Schirmer/Thompson Learning.

Hanson, Howard. *Harmonic Materials of Modern Music: Resources of the Tempered Scale.* 1960. New York: Appleton-Century-Crofts.

Kohs, Ellis. *Musical Composition.* 1980. Lanham, Md.: Scarecrow Press.

Marquis, G. Welton. *Twentieth-Century Music Idioms.* Reprint of 1964 ed. 1981. Westport, Conn.: Greenwood Press.

Mitchell, Kevin M. *Essential Songwriters Rhyming Dictionary.* 1996. Van Nuys, Calif.: Alfred Publishing Company.

Pellman, Samuel. *An Introduction to the Creation of Electroacoustic Music.* 1994. Belmont, Calif.: Schirmer/Thompson Learning.

Persichetti, Vincent. *Twentieth-Century Harmony: Creative Aspects and Practice.* 1961. New York: W. W. Norton.

Russo, William & Ainis, Jeffrey. *Composing Music: A New Approach.* 1988. Chicago: University of Chicago Press.

Wuorinen, Charles. *Simple Composition.* 1979. New York: Longman.

COUNTERPOINT

Benjamin, Thomas. *Counterpoint in the Style of J. S. Bach.* 1986. New York: Schirmer Books.

———. *The Craft of Modal Counterpoint: A Practical Approach.* 1979. New York: Schirmer Books.

Counterpointer 1.0 (counterpoint software for MAC/ WIN) Redmond, Wash.: Ars Nova Software LLC, P.O. Box 3770, Redmond, WA 98073. (http://www.ars-nova.com)

Gauldin, Robert. *A Practical Approach to Sixteenth Century Counterpoint.* 1995. Prospect Heights, Ill.: Waveland Press, Inc.

———. *A Practical Approach to Eighteenth Century Counterpoint.* 1995. Prospect Heights, Ill.: Waveland Press, Inc.

Kennan, Kent. *Counterpoint.* 4th ed. 1999. Upper Saddle River, N.J.: Prentice Hall.

Mason, Neale B. *Essentials of Eighteenth-Century Counterpoint.* 1968. Madison, Wis.: WCB Brown & Benchmark.

Merriman, Margarita. *A New Look at Sixteenth-Century Counterpoint.* 1982. Lanham, Md.: University Press of America.

Owen, Harold. *Modal and Tonal Counterpoint.* 1992. Belmont, Calif.: Schirmer/Thompson Learning.

Parks, Richard S. *Eighteenth Century Counterpoint and Tonal Structure.* 1984. Englewood Cliffs, N.J.: Prentice Hall.

Piston, Walter. *Counterpoint.* 1947. New York: W. W. Norton.

Reed, H. Owen & Steinke, Greg A. *Basic Contrapuntal Techniques: An Introduction to Linear Style Through Creative Writing.* Rev. ed. 2003. Miami, Fla.: Alfred Publishing.

Schenker, Heinrich. *Counterpoint.* 2 Vols. Rothgeb, John & Thym, Jurgen, trans. 1986. New York: Schirmer Books.

Schoenberg, Arnold. *Preliminary Exercises in Counterpoint.* Stein, Leonard, ed. 1982. Winchester, Mass.: Faber & Faber.

Schubert, Peter. *Modal Counterpoint, Renaissance Style.* 1999. New York: Oxford University Press.

Schubert, Peter & Neidhöfer, Christolph. *Baroque Counterpoint.* 2006. Upper Saddle River, N.J.: Prentice Hall.

Searle, Humphrey. *Twentieth-Century Counterpoint: A Guide for Students.* Reprint of 1954 ed. 1986. Westport, Conn.: Hyperion Press.

Smith, Charlotte. *A Manual of Sixteenth-Century Contrapuntal Style.* 1989. Newark, N.J.: University of Delaware Press.

Stewart, Robert. *An Introduction to Sixteenth Century Counterpoint and Palestrina's Musical Style.* 1994. New York: Ardsley House Publishers, Inc.

Thakar, Markand. *Fundamentals of Music Making.* 1990. New Haven, Conn.: Yale University Press.

Trythall, H. Gilbert. *Eighteenth Century Counterpoint.* 1993. Boston: McGraw-Hill Higher Ed.

———. *Sixteenth Century Counterpoint.* 1993. Boston: McGraw-Hill Higher Ed.

Westergaard, Peter. *Introduction to Tonal Theory.* 1976. New York: W. W. Norton.

EAR TRAINING/SIGHT SINGING

Adler, Samuel. *Sight Singing: Pitch, Interval, Rhythm.* 2nd ed. 1997. New York: W. W. Norton.

Auralia 2 (MAC) 3 (WIN) (Interactive ear training for MAC/WIN) 2008. Walnut Creek, Calif.: Sibelius USA Inc., 1407 Oakland Blvd., Ste. 103, Walnut Creek, CA 94596. (http://www.sibelius.com/products/auralia/index.html)

Benjamin, Thomas E., Michael Horvit, & Robert Nelson. *Music for Sight Singing.* 3rd ed. 2000. Belmont, Calif.: Schirmer/Thompson Learning.

Benward, Bruce & Carr, Maureen. *Sight Singing Complete.* 7th ed. 2007. Boston: McGraw-Hill Higher Ed.

Benward, Bruce & Kolosick, J. Timothy. *Ear Training: A Technique for Listening.* 7th ed. 2005. Boston: McGraw-Hill Higher Ed.

Berkowitz, Sol, Gabriel Fontrier, & Leo Kraft. *A New Approach to Sight Singing.* 4th ed. 1997. New York: W. W. Norton.

Blombach, Ann K. *MacGAMUT 2000.* 2000. Columbus, Ohio: MacGAMUT Music Software International. (http://www.macgamut.com)

Campbell, Patricia Sheehan. *Lessons from the World.* 1st ed. 2001. Boston: McGraw-Hill Higher Ed.

D'Amante, Elvo S. *Ear Training* Series. 2002. Orinda, Calif.: Encore Music Publishing Company.

Damschroder, David. *Listen and Sing: Lessons in Ear-Training and Sight-Singing.* 1995. Belmont, Calif.: Schirmer/Thompson Learning.

Durham, Thomas. *Beginning Tonal Dictation.* 1994. Prospect Heights, Ill.: Waveland Press, Inc.

Fish, Arnold & Lloyd, Norman. *Fundamentals of Sight Singing and Ear Training.* 1994. Prospect Heights, Ill.: Waveland Press, Inc.

Friedmann, Michael L. *Ear Training for Twentieth-Century Music.* 1990. New Haven, Conn.: Yale University Press.

Ghezzo, Marta A. *Solfege, Ear Training, Rhythm, Dictation & Music Theory: A Comprehensive Course.* 1980. University (Tuscaloosa): University of Alabama Press.

Gregory, David. *Melodic Dictator* (Macintosh program). 1988. Ann Arbor: University of Michigan Center for Performing Arts and Technology.

Hall, Anne C. *Studying Rhythm.* 2005. Upper Saddle River, N.J.: Prentice Hall.

Henry, Earl. *Sight Singing.* 1997. Upper Saddle River, N.J.: Prentice Hall.

Hindemith, Paul. *Elementary Training for Musicians.* 2nd ed. 1949. New York: Associated Music Publishers.

Hoffman, Richard. *The Rhythm Book.* 2008. Nashville, Tenn.: Smith Creek Music. (http://www.smithcreekmusic.com).

Horvit, Michael, Timothy Koozin, & Robert Nelson. *Music for Ear Training: CD-ROM and Workbook.* 2001. Belmont, Calif.: Schirmer/Thompson Learning.

Karpinski, Gary S. *Aural Skills Acquisition, The Development of Listening, Reading, and Performing Skills in College-Level Musicians.* 2000. New York: Oxford University Press.

_______. *Manual for Ear Training and Sight Singing.* 2006. New York: W. W. Norton.

Karpinski, Gary S. & Kram, Richard. *Anthology for Sight Singing*. 2006. New York: W. W. Norton.

Kazez, Daniel. *Rhythm Reading: Elementary Through Advanced Training*. 1997. New York: W. W. Norton.

Kraft, Leo. *A New Approach to Ear Training*. 1999. New York: W. W. Norton.

Lund, Eric, Brett Terry, & David Bork. *Norton Interactive Aural Skills*. 2006. New York: W. W. Norton.

Marcozzi, Rudy T. *Strategies and Patterns for Ear Training*. 2009. Upper Saddle River, N.J.: Prentice Hall.

Ottman, Robert W. *Basic Ear Training Skills*. 1991. Upper Saddle River, N.J.: Prentice Hall.

———. *Music for Sight Singing*. 5th ed. 2001. Upper Saddle River, N.J.: Prentice Hall.

Practica Musica 5.0 (Ear Training Software for MAC/WIN). 2005. Redmond, Wash.: Ars Nova Software LLC, P.O. Box 3770, Redmond, WA 98073. (http://www.ars-nova.com)

Trubitt, Allen R. & Hines, Robert S. *Ear Training & Sight-Singing: An Integrated Approach*. 1979. New York: Schirmer Books.

FORM/ANALYSIS

Berry, Wallace. *Form in Music*. 2nd ed. 1986. Englewood Cliffs, N.J.: Prentice Hall.

Cadwallader, Allen & Gagné, David. *Analysis of Tonal Music: A Schenkerian Approach*. 1998. New York: Oxford University Press.

Caplin, William E. *Classical Form, A Theory of Formal Functions for the Instrumental Music of Haydn, Mozart, and Beethoven*. 2001. New York: Oxford University Press.

Cook, Nicholas. *A Guide to Musical Analysis*. 1987. New York: W. W. Norton.

———. *Analysing Musical Multimedia*. 1998. New York: Oxford University Press.

———. *Analysis Through Composition*. 1997. New York: Oxford University Press.

Cooper, Paul. *Perspectives in Music Theory: An Historical-Analytical Approach*. 1973. New York: Harper & Row.

Dunsby, Jonathan & Whittal, Arnold. *Musical Analysis*. 1987. New Haven, Conn.: Yale University Press.

Epstein, David. *Beyond Orpheus: Studies in Musical Structure*. 1987. Fairlawn, N.J.: Oxford University Press.

Forte, Allen & Gilbert, Steven E. *Introduction to Schenkerian Analysis: Form & Content in Tonal Music*. 1982. New York: W. W. Norton.

Gordon, Christopher. *Form and Content in Commercial Music*. 1992. New York: Ardsley House Publishers, Inc.

Green, Douglas M. *Form in Tonal Music: An Introduction to Analysis*. 2nd ed. 1979. New York: Holt, Rinehart & Winston.

Hutcheson, Jere T. *Musical Form & Analysis*. 2 vols. 1972, 1977. Boston: Taplinger.

Lester, Joel. *Analytic Approaches to Twentieth Century Music*. 1989. New York: W. W. Norton.

Mason, Robert M. *Modern Methods of Music Analysis Using Computers*. 1985. Peterborough, N.H.: Schoolhouse Press.

Mathes, James R. *The Analysis of Musical Form*. 2007. Upper Saddle River, N.J.: Prentice Hall.

Narmour, Eugene. *Beyond Schenkerism: The Need for Alternatives in Music Analysis*. 1980. Chicago: University of Chicago Press.

Neumeyer, David & Tepping, Susan. *A Guide to Schenkerian Analysis*. 1996. Upper Saddle River, N.J.: Prentice Hall.

Perone, James E. *Form and Analysis Theory: A Bibliography*. 1998. Westport, Conn.: Greenwood Press.

Spencer, Peter & Temko, Peter M. *A Practical Approach to the Study of Form in Music*. 1994. Prospect Heights, Ill.: Waveland Press, Inc.

Spring, Glenn & Hutcheson, Jere T. *Musical Form and Analysis*. 1995. Boston: McGraw-Hill Higher Ed.

Wade, Graham. *The Shape of Music: An Introduction to Musical Form*. 1982. New York: Schocken Books, Inc.

Walton, Charles W. *Basic Forms in Music*. 1974. Sherman Oaks, Calif.: Alfred Publishing.

Warfield, Gerald. *Layer Analysis: A Primer of Elementary Tonal Structures*. 1978. New York: Longman.

White, John D. *The Analysis of Music*. 2nd ed. 1984. Metuchen, N.J.: Scarecrow Press.

Williams, J. Kent. *Theories and Analyses of Twentieth-Century Music*. 1997. Fort Worth, Tex.: Harcourt Brace College Publishers.

GENERAL

Alten, Stanley R. *Audio in Media: The Recording Studio*. 1996. Belmont, Calif.: Schirmer/Thompson Learning.

Barra, Donald. *The Dynamic Performance: A Performer's Guide to Musical Expression and Interpretation*. 1983. Englewood Cliffs, N.J.: Prentice Hall.

Baur, John. *Music Theory Through Literature*. 2 Vols. 1985. Englewood Cliffs, N.J.: Prentice Hall.

Beach, David. *Aspects of Schenkerian Theory*. 1983. New Haven, Conn.: Yale University Press.

Boatwright, Howard. *Chromaticism: Theory and Practice*. 1995. Syracuse, N.Y.: Syracuse University Press.

Chadabe, Joel. *Electric Sound: The Past and Promise of Electronic Music*. 1997. Upper Saddle River, N.J.: Prentice Hall.

Clayton, Martin, Trevor Herbert, & Richard Middleton, eds. *The Cultural Study of Music*. 2003. New York: Routledge.

Cogan, Robert. *New Images of Musical Sound*. 1984. Cambridge: Harvard University Press.

Cogan, Robert & Escot, Pozzi. *Sonic Design: The Nature of Sound & Music.* 1976. Englewood Cliffs, N.J.: Prentice Hall; reprint Cambridge, Mass.: Publication Contact International, 1985.

Cohen, Allen. *Howard Hanson in Theory and Practice.* 2003. Westport, Conn.: Praeger Publishers.

Cook, Nicholas & Everist, Mark . *Rethinking Music.* 1998. New York: Oxford University Press.

Cooper, Grosvenor & Meyer, Leonard B. *The Rhythmic Structure of Music.* 1960. Chicago: University of Chicago Press.

Cope, David H. *New Directions in Music.* 7th ed. 1997. Prospect Heights, Ill.: Waveland Press, Inc.

Creston, Paul. *Principles of Rhythm.* 1964. New York: Franco Columbo.

Dell'Antonio, Andrew. *Beyond Structural Listening?: Postmodern Modes of Hearing.* 2004. Berkeley, Calif.: University of California Press.

Etler, Alvin. *Making Music: An Introduction to Theory.* 1974. New York: Harcourt Brace Jovanovich.

Fink, Michael. *Inside the Music Industry: Creativity, Process, and Business.* 2nd ed. 1996. Belmont, Calif.: Schirmer/Thompson Learning.

Forte, Allen. *The Structure of Atonal Music.* 1977. New Haven, Conn.: Yale University Press.

Fotine, Larry. *Contemporary Musician's Handbook & Dictionary.* 1984. Sepulveda, Calif.: Poly Tone Press.

Gordon, Christopher P. *Form and Content in Commercial Music.* 1992. New York: Ardsley House Publishers, Inc.

Halloran, Mark, ed. and comp. *The Musician's Business and Legal Guide.* 3rd ed. 2000. Upper Saddle River, N.J.: Prentice Hall.

Harnsberger, Lindsey C. *Essential Dictionary of Music.* 1997. Van Nuys, Calif.: Alfred Publishing Company.

Harrison, Lou. *Music Primer.* 1970. New York: C. F. Peters.

Helm, Eugene & Luper, Albert T. *Words and Music: Form and Procedure in Theses, Dissertations, Research Papers, Book Reports, Programs, and Theses in Composition.* 1971. Valley Forge, Pa.: European American Music.

Hofstetter, Fred T. *Computer Literacy for Musicians.* 1988. Englewood Cliffs, N.J.: Prentice Hall.

Jablonsky, Stephen. *Tonal Facts and Tonal Theories.* 2005. Dubuque, Iowa: Kendall/Hunt Publishing Company.

Karlin, Fred & Wright, Rayburn. *On the Track, A Guide to Contemporary Film Scoring.* 1990. New York: Schirmer Books.

Kostelanetz, Richard & Darby, Joseph. *Classic Essays on Twentieth-Century Music: A Continuing Symposium.* 1999. Belmont, Calif.: Schirmer/Thompson Learning.

Kostka, Steven. *Materials & Techniques of 20th Century Music.* 3rd ed. 2006. Upper Saddle River, N.J.: Prentice Hall.

Latarski, Don. *An Introduction to Chord Theory.* 1991. Van Nuys: Alfred Publishing Company.

Marin, Deborah S. & Wittlich, Gary E. *Tonal Harmony for the Keyboard: With an Introduction to Improvisation.* 1989. New York: Schirmer Books.

Middleton, Richard. *Reading Pop: Approaches to Textual Analysis in Popular Music.* 2000. New York: Oxford University Press.

______. *Studying Popular Music.* 1990. Berkshire, England: Open University Press, McGraw-Hill Education.

Middleton, Richard, & Horn, David, eds. *Popular Music 4. Performers and Audiences.* 1984. New York: Cambridge University Press.

Moore, F. Richard. *Elements of Computer Music.* 1990. Englewood Cliffs, N.J.: Prentice Hall.

Pratt, George. *The Dynamics of Harmony, Principles, and Practice.* 1997. New York: Oxford University Press.

Rahn, Jay. *A Theory for All Music: Problems and Solutions in the Analysis of Non-Western Forms.* 1983. Toronto: University of Toronto Press.

Rahn, John. *Basic Atonal Theory.* 1987. Belmont, Calif.: Schirmer/Thompson Learning.

Randel, Don Michael, ed. *The Harvard Dictionary of Music,* 4th ed. 2003. Cambridge, Mass.: The Belknap Press of Harvard University Press.

Rapaport, Diane. *How to Make and Sell Your Own Recording.* 5th ed. 2000. Upper Saddle River, N.J.: Prentice Hall.

Reti, Rudolph R. *The Thematic Process in Music.* Reprint of 1951 ed. 1978. Westport, Conn.: Greenwood Press, Inc.

———. *Tonality, Atonality, Pantonality: A Study of Some Trends in Twentieth-Century Music.* Reprint of 1958 ed. 1978. Westport, Conn.: Greenwood Press, Inc.

Roig-Francoli, Miguel A. *Understanding Post Tonal Music.* 1st ed. 2008. Boston: McGraw-Hill Higher Ed.

______. *Anthology of Post Tonal Music.* 2008. Boston: McGraw-Hill Higher Ed.

Salzman, Eric & Sahl, Michael. *Making Changes: A Practical Guide to Vernacular Harmony.* 1977. New York: McGraw-Hill.

Samson, Jim. *Music in Transition: A Study of Tonal Expansion and Atonality, 1900–1920.* 1995. New York: Oxford University Press.

Schafer, R. Murray. *The Thinking Ear.* 1986. (C86-093409-8). Arcana ed., Indian River, Ontario, Canada, K0L 2B0.

Schwartz, Elliott & Godfrey, Daniel. *Music Since 1945.* 1993. Belmont, Calif.: Schirmer/Thompson Learning.

Simms, Bryan R. *Composers on Modern Musical Culture: An Anthology of Source Readings on 20th Century*

Music. 1999. Belmont, Calif.: Schirmer/Thompson Learning.

———. *Music of the 20th Century.* 1996. Belmont, Calif.: Schirmer/Thompson Learning.

Sorce, Richard. *Music Theory for The Music Professional: A Comparison of Common-Practice and Popular Genres.* 1995. New York: Ardsley House Publishers.

Steinke, Greg A. *Basic Materials in Music Theory.* 12th ed., 2010. Upper Saddle River, N.J.: Prentice Hall.

Steinke, Greg A. *Bridge to 20th-Century Music,* rev. ed., 1999. Upper Saddle River, N.J.: Prentice Hall.

Strange, Allen. *Electronic Music*, 1st ed. 2000. Boston: McGraw-Hill Higher Ed.

Straus, Joseph N. *Introduction to Post-Tonal Theory.* 3rd ed. 2005. Upper Saddle River, N.J.: Prentice Hall.

Taylor, Clifford. *Musical Idea and the Design Aesthetic in Contemporary Music: A Text for Discerning Appraisal of Musical Thought in Western Culture.* 1990. Lewiston, N.Y.: Edwin Mellon Press.

Toch, Ernst. *The Shaping Forces in Music: An Inquiry into the Nature of Harmony, Melody, Counterpoint, Form.* 1977. Mineola, N.Y.: Dover Publications.

Watkins, Glenn. *Soundings: Music in the Twentieth Century.* 1995. Belmont, Calif.: Schirmer/Thompson Learning.

MUSICAL ANTHOLOGIES

Benjamin, Thomas E., Michael Horvit, & Robert Nelson. *Music for Analysis: Examples from the Common Practice Period and the Twentieth Century.* 5th ed. 2001. Belmont, Calif.: Schirmer/Thompson Learning.

Berry, Wallace & Chudacoff, Edward. *Eighteenth Century Imitative Counterpoint: Music for Analysis.* 1969. Englewood Cliffs, N.J.: Prentice Hall.

Bockmon, Guy A. & Starr, William J. *Scored for Listening: A Guide to Music.* 2nd ed. 1972. Records (ISBN 0-15-579056-0). San Diego, Calif.: Harcourt Brace Jovanovich.

Brandt, William, Arthur Corra, William Christ, Richard DeLone, & Allen Winold. *The Comprehensive Study of Music.* 1976. New York: Harper & Row.

Burkhart, Charles. *Anthology for Musical Analysis.* 6th ed. 2003. Belmont, Calif.: Schirmer/Thompson Learning.

De Lio, Thomas & Smith, Stuart Saunders. *Twentieth Century Music Scores.* 1989. Englewood Cliffs, N.J.: Prentice Hall.

DeVoto, Mark. *Mostly Short Pieces: An Anthology for Harmonic Analysis.* 1992. New York: W. W. Norton.

Forney, Kristine. ed. *The Norton Scores: An Anthology for Listening.* 8th ed. 2 Vols. [2000]. New York: W. W. Norton.

Hardy, Gordon & Fish, Arnold. *Music Literature: A Workbook for Analysis.* 2 Vols. 1966. New York: Harper & Row.

Melcher, Robert A., Willard F Warch, & Paul B. Mast. *Music for Study.* 3rd ed. 1988. Upper Saddle River, N.J.: Prentice Hall.

Owen, Harold. *Music Theory Resource Book.* 2000. New York: Oxford University Press.

Palisca, Claude V., ed. *Norton Anthology of Western Music.* 4th ed. 2 Vols. [2000]. New York: W. W. Norton.

Soderlund, Gustave & Scott, Samuel H. *Examples of Gregorian Chant and Sacred Music of the 16th Century.* 1996. Prospect Heights, Ill.: Waveland Press, Inc.

Straus, Joe. *Music by Women for Study and Analysis.* 1993. Upper Saddle River, N.J.: Prentice Hall.

Turek, Ralph. *Analytical Anthology of Music.* 2nd ed. 1992. Boston: McGraw-Hill Higher Ed.

Ward-Steinman, David & Ward-Steinman, Susan L. *Comparative Anthology of Musical Forms.* 2 Vols. Reprint of 1976 ed. 1987. Lanham, Md: University Press of America.

Wennerstrom, Mary H. *Anthology of Musical Structure and Style.* 2nd ed. 1988. Upper Saddle River, N.J.: Prentice Hall.

MUSICAL NOTATION

General listing site for notation programs: ace.acadiau.ca/score/others.htm#M

Finale 2009, Allegro, Print Music!, Smart Music Finale Notepad (computer programs for MAC/ WIN). 2009. Eden Prairie, Minn.: MakeMusic! Inc. (http://www.finalemusic.com).

Gerou, Tom & Lusk, Linda. *Essential Dictionary of Music Notation.* 1996. Van Nuys, Calif.: Alfred Publishing Company.

Harder, Paul O. *Music Manuscript Techniques, A Programmed Approach.* 2 Parts. 1984. Boston: Allyn & Bacon, Inc.

Heussenstamm, George. *Norton Manual of Music Notation.* 1987. New York: W. W. Norton.

Metronome and *MetTimes* (music fonts to use directly in word processing for MAC/WIN). 2008. Haverford, PA.: DVM Publications, 104 Woodside Rd., Haverford, PA 19041. (http://www.dvmpublications.com/)

Music Press 9.1 (computer program for MAC/WIN). 2003. Wilder, Vt.: Graphire Corp., 2706 NE 53rd St., Seattle, WA 98105-3114. (http://www.graphire.com)

NoteAbility Pro (MAC OSX). 2008. Vancouver, B.C., Canada.: Opus 1 Music, Inc., P.O. Box 39045, Vancouver, B.C., Canada V6R 1G0. (http://debussy.music.ubc.ca/download.html)

Notewriter II (computer program for MAC OS9.2). 2008. Vancouver, B.C., Canada: Opus 1 Music, Inc., P.O.

Box 39045, Vancouver, B.C., Canada V6R 1G0. (http://debussy.music.ubc.ca/ download.html)

Notion, Progression, Protege (computer programs for MAC/WIN). Greensboro, N.C.: Notion Music. (http://www.notionmusic.com)

Overture 4.1, Scorewriter 4.1 (computer programs for MAC/WIN). 2008. Mt. Pleasant, S.C.: Genie Soft, Inc., P.O. Box 1503, Mt. Pleasant, SC 29465. (http://www.geniesoft.com)

Powell, Steven. *Music Engraving Today*. 2nd ed. 2007. New York: Brichtmark Music, Inc.

Read, Gardner. *Music Notation.* 1979. Boston: Taplinger.

———. *Pictographic Score Notation: A Compendium.* 1998. Westport, Conn.: Greenwood Press.

Score (computer program for WIN). 2003. Palo Alto, Calif.: San Andreas Press, P.O. Box 60247, Palo Alto, CA 94306. (http://www.scoremus.com/)

Songworks II (computer program for MAC/WIN) Redmond, Wash.: Ars Nova Software LLC, P.O. Box 3770, Redmond, WA 98073. (http://www.ars-nova.com)

Stone, Kurt. *Music Notation in the Twentieth Century: A Practical Guidebook.* 1980. New York: W. W. Norton.

Warfield, Gerald. *How to Write Music Manuscript in Pencil.* 1977. New York: Longman.

MUSICAL TECHNOLOGY

Ballora, Mark. *Essentials of Music Technology*. 2003. Upper Saddle River, N.J.: Prentice Hall.

Hill, Brad. *Going Digital: A Musician's Guide to Technology*. 1998. Belmont, Calif.: Schirmer/ Thompson Learning.

Williams, David & Webster, Peter R. *Experiencing Music Technology: Software, Data, and Hardware*. 1999. Belmont, Calif.: Schirmer/Thompson Learning.

ORCHESTRATION

Adler, Samuel. *The Study of Orchestration.* 2nd ed. 1989. New York: W. W. Norton.

Black, Dave & Gerou, Tom. *Essential Dictionary of Orchestration.* 1998. Van Nuys, Calif.: Alfred Publishing Company.

Blatter, Alfred. *Instrumentation-Orchestration.* 2nd ed. 1985. Belmont, Calif.: Schirmer/Thompson Learning.

Burton, Steven D. *Orchestration.* 1982. Englewood Cliffs, N.J.: Prentice Hall.

Kennan, Kent & Grantham, Donald. *The Technique of Orchestration.* 6th ed. 2002. Upper Saddle River, N.J.: Prentice Hall.

Ostrander, Arthur E. & Wilson, Dana . *Contemporary Choral Arranging.* 1986. Upper Saddle River, N.J.: Prentice Hall.

Piston, Walter. *Orchestration.* 1955. New York: W. W. Norton.

Polansky, Larry. *New Instrumentation & Orchestration: An Outline for Study.* 1986. Oakland, Calif.: Frog Peak Music.

Ray, Don B. *The Orchestration Handbook.* 2000. Hal Leonard Pub. Corp.

Read, Gardner. *Contemporary Instrumental Techniques.* 1976. New York: Schirmer Books.

———. *Style & Orchestration.* 1979. Belmont, Calif.: Schirmer/Thompson Learning.

Rogers, Bernard. *The Art of Orchestration.* 1951. New York: Appleton-Century-Crofts.

Schotzkin, Merton. *Writing for the Orchestra: An Introduction to Orchestration.* 1992. Upper Saddle River, N.J.: Prentice Hall.

Stiller, Andrew. *Handbook of Instrumentation.* 1985. Berkeley: University of California Press.

White, Gary. *Instrumental Arranging.* 1992. Boston: McGraw-Hill Higher Ed.

Please note that there are many musical computer programs based on both Mac and Windows operating systems appearing all the time that may relate to one or more of the preceding bibliographical areas. Please check with an instructor or musical computer listings for what might be currently available.

Also note that there are many musical Web sites on the Internet that may provide many helpful resources. The primary resource is the Web site for the Society of Music Theory (SMT); use your Web browser search engine to seek out their latest correct site address and for other resources as well.

Musical Examples Index

(Numbers refer to frames, except where page numbers are indicated (p. or pp.), which refer to examples used for Supplementary Assignments.)

B

Bach, Johann Sebastian
  Chorale Prelude: *Vor deinen Thron Tret'ich,* 8.106
  Chorales:
    Ach Gott, wie manches Herzeleid, 8.5, 8.6, 8.52
    Allein, zu dir, Herr Jesu Christ, 8.16
    Aus meines Herzens Grunde, 8.21
    Befiehl du deine Wege, 4.36, 8.86
    Christ lag in Todesbanden, 8.95
    Dank sei Gott in der Höhe, 6.78
    Danket dem Herren, denn er ist sehr freundlich, 8.96
    Das alte Jahr vergangen ist, 8.94
    Das neugeborne Kindelein, 7.23
    Du grosser Schmerzensmann, 8.28, 8.30
    Es ist das Heil uns kommen her, 7.66
    Es spricht der Unweisen Mund, 8.97
    Es wird schier der letzte Tag herkommen, 8.88
    Gott des Himmels und der Erden, 8.55
    Gott lebet noch, 6.89
    Gott sei uns gnädig und barmherzig, 5.106
    Hast du denn, Jesu, seim Angesicht, 8.29
    Helft mir Gott's Güte preisen, 8.27
    Herr, nun lass in Friede, 8.38
    Herzlich lieb hab 'ich dich, o Herr, 8.31
    Heut'ist, o Mensch, ein Grosser Trauertag, #8.90
    In allen meinen Taten, 2.59
    Jesu, Deine tiefen Wunden, 6.84
    Jesu, nun sei gepreist, 8.49
    Komm, Gott Schöpfer, heiliger Geist, 7.33
    Nicht so traurig, nicht so sehr, 8.54
    O Ewigkeit, du Donnerwort, 8.24
    O Herre Gorr, dein göttlich Wort, 5.90
    Von Gorr well ich nicht lassen, 9.15
    Was mein Gott will, das g'scheh', 8.25
    Wer weiss, wie nahe mir, p. 165
    Wie schön leuchtet er Morgenstern, 8.85
  French Suite No. 1 (Allemande), 8.105
  French Suite No. 3 (Courante), 8.46
  Well-Tempered Clavier, Vol. 1:
    Fugue XXIV, 8.93
    Prelude XII, 4.47
    Prelude XIII, 8.64
    Prelude XX, 8.109
  Well-Tempered Clavier, Vol. 2:
    Fugue I, 8.97
    Fugue XI, 8.80
    Prelude XII, 8.75
Beethoven, Ludwig van
  Quartet, Op. 18, No. 2, 5.128
  Sonata, Op. 2, No. 3, 2.55, 2.56
  Sonata, Op. 10, No. 1, 8.42, p. 368
  Sonata, Op. 31, No. 3, p. 205
  Sonata, Op. 49, No. 1, 7.52, 9.55–9.57
  Sonata, Op. 49, No. 2, 8.34
  Sonata for Violin and Piano, Op. 24, 8.4
  Sonatina in F Major, 4.48
  Sonatina in G Major, 9.51, 9.53
  Symphony No. 7, Op. 92, 5.83
  Symphony No. 8, Op. 93, 7.16, p. 239
Berlioz, Hector
  Symphonie Fantastique, 9.104
Boccherini, Luigi
  Concert for 'Cello in B♭ Major, 9.65
Bourgeois, Loys
  "Old Hundredth," 7.40
Brahms, Johannes
  Ein deusches Requiem, Op. 45:
    I, 6.66
    IV, 5.111, 8.74
  Intermezzo, Op. 119, No. 2, p. 364
  Piano Concerto No. 2, Op. 83, 8.45
  Symphony No. 1, Op. 68, 7.39, 9.21
  Symphony No. 4, Op. 98, 7.7
Burgmüller, Johann
  Lullaby, p. 365

C

Carey, Henry
  America, 1.5
Chopin, Frédéric
  Etude, Op. 25, No. 8, 7.41
  Mazurka, Op. 68, No. 3, p. 366
  Nocturne, Posthumous, p. 362

(continued)

Prelude, Op. 28, No. 6, 5.129
Valse Brillante, Op. 34, No. 2, 7.67, 8.35, 8.111
Cruger, Johann
Chorale: *Herzliebster Jesu, was hast du verbrochen,* 10.24

D

Dvorák, Antonin
Symphony No. 9, Op. 95, 7.10

F

Frank, César
Symphonic Variations (1885), 7.4
Symphony in d minor, 8.51

G

Graun, Karl Heinrich
Chorales:
Herzliebster Jesu, was hast du verbrochen, 9.14
O Traurigkeit, o Herzeleid, 9.23

H

Handel, Georg Friedrich
Chorale: *Ach Gott und Herr, wir gross und schwer,* 7.31
Sarabande, 3.85
Sonata No. 1 for Oboe and Harpsichord, 8.65
Suite in d minor, 8.63
Haydn, Joseph
Capriccio, 9.64, 8.44
The Creation, No. 3, 7.15
String Quartet, Op. 3, No. 5, 7.9
String Quartet, Op. 76, No. 4, 6.87
Symphony No. 101 ("Clock"), 8.89

K

Kuhlau, Friedrich
Sonatina, p. 205
Sonatina, Op. 20, No. 1, 8.37

L

Leybach, Ignace
Nocturne, Op. 52, p. 363

M

Mendelssohn, Felix
Chorale: *Aus tiefer Noth schrei'ich zu dir,* 7.59
Lieder ohne Worte, Op. 85, No. 2, p. 364
Lieder ohne Worte, Op. 102, No. 1, p. 368
Six Pieces for Children, Op. 72, No. 3, 9.67
Songs Without Words, Op. 62, No. 4, 7.6
Mozart, Wolfgang Amadeus
Fantasia in c minor, K. 475, 6.82
Fantasia in d minor, K. 397, p. 206
Quartet, K. 387, 5.115, 9.63
Quartet, K. 575, 8.50
Sonata, K. 311, 2.57
Sonata, K. 331, 5.104
Sonata, K. 333, 9.66, p. 367
Sonata, K. 545, 5.125, p. 357, p. 358
Symphony No. 41, K. 551, 6.72

S

Schubert, Franz
Symphony No. 5 in B♭ Major, 7.73
Waltz in a minor, p. 360
Waltz in B♭ Major, p. 367
Schumann, Robert
Album for the Young, Op. 68:
No. 4, 7.51, 7.53
No. 8, p. 240
No. 10, 2.58
No. 11, 5.124, 9.15
No. 18, 8.107
No. 41, 9.16
Album für die Jugend
"Kleine Studie," p. 362
"Nordisches Lied," Op. 26, p. 366
Kinderscenen
"Von Fremden Ländern und Menschen," p. 365
Papillons, Op. 2, 6.86
Symphonic Studies, Op. 13, 8.3
Sibelius, Jean
Finlandia, Op. 26, 7.30, 8.62
Stravinsky, Igor
Le Sacre du Printemps, 8.110

T

Tchaikovsky, Peter Ilyich
Romeo and Juliet, Overture-Fantasy, 8.47
Symphony No. 4, Op. 36, 7.3
Symphony No. 5, Op. 64, 8.43

V

Verdi, Giuseppe
La Traviata, Act III, No. 16, 9.62

Subject Index

(Numbers refer to frames.)

A

Accessory tone, 8.14. *See also* Nonharmonic tones
Accidentals, 3.6–.22
Active tones, 5.91, 6.70–.72
Alto voices, 3.25–.26, 3.28
"Amen" cadence, 7.40–.41. *See also* Cadences, plagal
Anticipation, 8.62–.65
  double, 8.62
Appoggiatura, 8.42–.48, 8.50, 8.74–.75
  accented, 8.42–.43, 8.47
  double, 8.44–.45
  unaccented, 8.43, 8.47
  without preparation, 8.46–.48
Arpeggiation, 5.128–.129
Arpeggio six-four chord, 5.104, 5.128–.133
Augmented fourth interval, 4.38, 4.42–.46, 4.48
Augmented-major seventh chord, 6.19–.20
Augmented second interval, 4.38–.41, 4.46–.47, 4.92, 5.82, 5.101
Augmented triad, 1.35–.36, 1.39, 1.44
Authentic cadence, 7.13–.71, 7.41, 7.50, 7.64, 7.79–.81, 7.83, 9.62–.63, 10.2–.4, 10.48
Auxiliary six-four, 5.124. *See also* Pedal six-four chord
Auxiliary tone, 8.34. *See also* Neighboring tone

B

Bach, J. S., 4.36
Bass line, 5.29–.31, 10.14–.19, 10.23, 10.38, 10.42
Bass staff, 3.31
Bass voices, 3.25–.26, 3.30, 3.38
Borrowed chord, 5.106–.107
Bytone, 8.14. *See also* Nonharmonic tones

C

Cadences, 5.104, 7.11–.183, 8.65, 9.49–.50, 9.60–.64, 10.2–.5, 10.48
  authentic, 7.13–.38, 7.41, 7.50, 7.64, 7.79–.81, 7.83, 9.62–.63, 10.2–.4, 10.28
  deceptive, 7.13–.14, 7.64–.78, 10.2–.3
  final, 7.12–.13, 7.39, 7.48, 7.50, 7.83
  half, 7.13–.14, 7.51–.63, 10.25–.26
  imperfect, 7.17, 7.28, 7.30, 7.42–.43, 7.47, 7.49–.50
  nonfinal, 7.12–.13, 7.50–.51, 7.83
  perfect, 7.17–.22, 7.42–.43, 7.48–.50
  Phrygian, 7.59–.63
  plagal, 7.13–.14, 7.39–.50, 7.83
Cadential six-four chord, 5.104–.116, 7.15, 7.52
Chain of suspensions, 8.89–.90
Changing tones, 8.99–.104. *See also* Neighboring tone
Chord changes, 6.56, 6.58
Chord of repose. *See* Tonic triad
Chord spacing. *See* Spacing; Structure
Chord symbols, 1.34–.48, 1.60, 1.75; *See* Appendix A, Chord Symbols, pp. 353*ff.*
  inversions, 5.33–.37
Chords, 1.14–.19, 7.1
Chromatic inflection, 5.91
Close structure, 3.54–.55, 3.58, 3.83–.84, 3.86–.87
Common tones, 4.57–.71, 4.94–.97
Consecutive perfect intervals, 4.16, 4.24
Contour. *See* Melodic contour
Contrary motion, 4.1, 4.30–.35, 4.76–.78, 5.42, 10.14, 10.17
Crossed voices, 3.35–.61

D

Deceptive cadence, 6.13–.14, 6.64–.78, 10.2–.3
Diatonic seventh chords, 6.20–.23
Diatonic triad, 1.22–.33, 2.26
Diminished-minor seventh chord, 6.11–.12, 6.25, 6.35–.41, 6.60
Diminished seventh chord, 6.15, 6.17, 6.26–.27, 6.35–.43, 6.58–.60
Diminished triad, 1.35, 1.37, 1.39, 1.45
Dissonant elements, 6.67, 6.77
Distribution of voices, 3.31–.37, 9.8
Dominant seventh chord, 2.56, 2.78, 6.66–.92, 9.53
  dissonant elements, 6.67
  first inversion, 6.82–.85
  resolution, 6.66–.80
  second inversion, 6.86–.89
  third inversion, 6.90–.92

Dominant triad, 2.1, 2.3–.5, 2.16, 2.54–.57, 2.68, 2.78, 6.54, 7.51
Double pedal, 8.107, 8.109
Doubling, 3.23–.24, 8.8–.10
  irregular, 4.87–.94, 4.101–.108, 5.91, 7.55, 7.68–.71
  leading tone, 5.98
  triads. *See also* Part writing, doubling
  diminished, 5.74–.80
    first inversion, 5.38–.98
    major, 5.77
    minor, 5.77
    root position, 4.50, 5.38
    second inversion, 5.99–.103
Downward stem, 3.31–.34
Dyad, 1.15

E

Échappée, 8.50. *See also* Escape tone
Embellishing harmony, 9.53–.59, 9.61, 9.64, 9.66–.67
Embellishing six-four, 5.124. *See also* Pedal six-four chord
Escape tone, 8.50–.56
  double, 8.52, 8.56
  triple, 8.56
Essential chord. *See* Structural harmony

F

Figured bass symbols, 3.5–.22, 8.18–.22, 8.81
  accidentals, 3.6–.22, 5.16
  root position, 3.5–.22
  slash, 3.7–.12, 3.22
  triads:
    first inversion, 5.15–.20
    second inversion, 5.21–.25, 5.99–.103
Final cadence, 7.12–.13, 7.39, 7.48, 7.50, 7.83
First inversion, 5.15–.20, 5.38–.98
Foreign, 8.14. *See also* Nonharmonic tones
Four-part chorus, 3.25, 3.85
Four-part texture, 3.24–.25, 3.85

G

Grand staff, 3.31

H

Half cadence, 7.13–.14, 7.51–.63, 10.25–.26
Harmonic interval, 1.15–.16
Harmonic minor scale, 1.30–.32, 6.22–.23
Harmonic motion, 10.39
Harmonic movement, 2.55, 9.26. *See also* Harmonic progression; Progression; Retrogression from tonic, 9.29
Harmonic phrases, 9.49–.50
Harmonic progression, 9.1–.2, 9.36–.48. *See also* Progression
Harmonic rhythm, 8.3–.4, 10.6–.9, 10.23, 10.29
Harmonic structure, 9.48–.67, 10.31
Harmonization, 10.1–.69
  of melodic leaps, 10.8–.9

I

Imperfect cadences, 7.17, 7.28, 7.30, 7.42–.43, 7.47, 7.49–.50
Inactive tones, 6.70–.71
Inner pedal, 9.106
Intervals, 1.14–.16, 1.18, 1.33
  augmented fourth, 4.38, 4.42–.46, 4.48
  augmented second, 4.38–.41, 4.46–.47, 4.92, 5.82, 5.101
  diminished fifth, 5.71
  harmonic, 1.15–.16
  octave, 3.39, 3.42
  perfect fifth, 2.1, 2.3–.6, 2.68
  ratio of frequencies, 2.3
  seconds, 2.69, 2.75–.76
  thirds, 2.69, 2.71–.74, 2.77–.78
  twelfth, 3.42
Inversion, 5.1–.14, 5.29–.37, 10.21
  first, 5.15–.20, 5.38–.97
  second, 5.21–.29, 5.99–.133
Inverted pedal, 8.106
Irregular doubling, 4.87–.94, 4.101–.108, 5.91, 6.72, 6.76–.77, 7.55, 7.68–.71
Iteration, 1.6, 1.12

K

Key, 1.4–.77, 1.74
  identification, 1.61–.65, 1.74
Key center, 1.9, 1.11–.12
Keynote, 1.1–.6, 1.11–.12, 2.1–.3, 2.54, 6.82

L

Leading tone, 2.22–.30, 2.69, 2.76, 2.78, 5.91, 5.98, 7.32–.33

M

Major-minor seventh chord, 6.9–.10, 6.16, 6.67
Major scale, 1.1–.2, 1.4–.5, 1.13, 1.26–.29, 6.21, 6.23–.26
Major seventh chord, 6.16–.17
Major triad, 1.35, 1.39, 1.42, 1.46
Mediant triad, 2.16–.21, 2.69, 2.71, 2.73
Melodic activity, 8.93
Melodic contour, 7.3–.9, 9.49, 10.19
Melodic line, 8.5–.7
Melodic minor scale, 5.81–.83, 6.47, 7.36
Melodic motion, 4.36–.37
Melodic sequence, 8.89
Melodic tension, 7.5–.6
Metric stress, 10.39
Minor seventh chord, 6.13–.14, 6.16–.18, 6.24
Minor triad, 1.35, 1.38–.39, 1.43
Mode, 1.74
Motion:
  contrary, 4.1, 4.30–.35, 4.76–.78, 5.42, 10.14, 10.17
  oblique, 4.1, 4.26–.29, 4.35
  parallel, 4.1, 4.7–.12, 4.14–.18, 4.20–.25, 4.35, 5.46–.47, 5.98, 7.67–.69, 8.11, 10.40
  similar, 4.1–.7, 4.35, 10.171

N

Natural minor scale, 6.33–.34
Neighboring tone, 8.34–.41, 8.103, 8.109
  accented, 8.35–.36
  double, 8.38
  lower, 8.35–.36, 8.109
  unaccented, 8.34–.36
  upper, 8.35–.36
Nonchord tone, 8.14. *See also* Nonharmonic tones
Nonfinal cadences, 7.12–.13, 7.50–.51, 7.83
Nonharmonic tones, 5.105, 8.1–.14. *See also specific entries,* e.g., Passing tone; Suspension; etc.
  classification, 8.14

O

Oblique motion, 4.1, 4.26–.29, 4.35
Open structure, 3.54, 3.56–.57, 3.83–.84, 3.86–.87
Organ point, 8.105. *See also* Pedal
Ornamentation, 8.91–.98

P

Parallel fifths, 5.88
Parallel motion, 4.1, 4.7–.12, 4.14–.18, 4.20–.25, 4.35, 5.46–.47, 5.98, 8.11, 10.17–.19, 10.40
Parallel perfect intervals, 4.15–.25, 4.49, 4.74–.84, 5.88
Parallel triads, 4.24
Part writing:
  chord repetition, 4.50–.58
  doubling, 3.44–.48, 4.49
  roots a fifth apart, 4.59–.74
  roots a second apart, 4.75–.90
  roots a third apart, 4.95–.108
  spacing, 3.38–.43, 3.54, 3.83–.85, 4.49
  triads:
    consecutive first inversions, 5.88–.96
    diminished, 5.71–.77
    first inversion, 5.45–.98
    second inversion, 5.99–.133
Passing chord, 6.86
Passing six-four chord, 5.104, 5.117–.123
Passing tone, 8.15–.33, 8.13
  accented, 8.26–.29, 8.40
  ascending, 8.16
  descending, 8.16
  double, 8.16–.17, 8.32
  successive, 8.29–.30, 8.33
  unaccented, 8.26, 8.29
Pedal, 5.124, 8.105–.110
  double, 8.107, 8.109
  inner, 8.106
  inverted, 8.106
  triple, 8.110
Pedal point, 5.124, 8.105. *See also* Pedal
Pedal six-four chord, 5.104, 5.124–.127
Perfect cadences, 7.17–.22, 7.42–.43, 7.48–.50
Phrase, 7.1–.11
  shaping elements, 7.3
Phrase structure, 9.49–.67
Phrygian cadence, 7.59–.63
Phrygian mode, 7.59
Picardy third, 7.23–.29, 7.37
Plagal cadence, 7.13–.14, 7.39–.50, 7.83
Preparation. *See* Suspension
Primary triads, 2.7–.9, 2.54–.55, 2.63–.68, 2.70, 2.77–.82, 9.35–.48, 9.65
Progression, 8.13, 9.2–.50
  completion, 2.56, 2.58–.60
  opening, 2.55–.58, 2.60
Pure minor scale. *See* Natural minor scale

R

Range of voices, 3.25–.30
Resolution. *See* Suspension
Retardation, 8.75–.76
Retrogression, 9.2–.5, 9.17, 9.26, 9.34, 10.13
Returning note, 8.34. *See also* Neighboring tone
Rhythmic activity, 8.5
Roman numerals. *See* Chord symbols
Root, 1.20–.21
Root movements, 9.6–.17, 9.20–29
  down in fifths, 9.20–.21
  down in thirds, 9.24–.29
  up in seconds, 9.22–.23
Root position, 3.1–.5, 5.1–.2, 5.5, 5.8–.14

S

Scales:
  major, 1.1–.2, 1.4–.5, 1.13, 1.2–.29
  minor, 1.1, 1.3–.4, 1.13
    harmonic, 1.3–.32, 6.22–.23
    melodic, 5.81–.83, 6.47, 7.36
    natural, 6.33–.34
Secondary triads, 2.63–.65, 2.67, 2.69–.82, 9.35–.48, 10.41
Second inversion, 5.21–.29, 5.99–.133
Sequence, 8.89
Seventh chords, 6.1–.8
  approach to seventh, 6.94–.96
  chord symbols, 6.27–.60
  doubling, 6.61–.63
  figured bass symbols, 6.49–.54
  first inversion, 6.50, 6.53, 6.58
  in harmonic minor, 6.22–.23
  in major, 6.21
  inversion, 6.49–.65
  irregular resolution of seventh, 6.93–.94
  quality, 6.9–.22, 6.31, 6.48
  resolution of seventh, 6.78–.80
  root position, 6.49, 6.58
  second inversion, 6.51, 6.53, 6.58
  terminology, 6.9–.19
  third inversion, 6.52–.53, 6.58
  types, 6.20
Similar motion, 4.1–.7, 4.35, 8.17
Six-four chord. *See* Second inversion

Slash, 3.7–.12, 3.22, 6.30–.32, 6.35, 6.38. *See also* Figured bass symbols
Soprano voice, 3.25–.27
Spacing:
first inversion, 5.43
root position, 3.38–.43
Stationary six-four, 5.124. *See also* Pedal six-four chord
Stems, direction of, 3.31–.34
Structural harmony, 9.51–.67, 10.69
Structure:
close, 3.54–.55, 3.58, 3.83–.84, 3.86–.87
open, 3.54, 3.56–.57, 3.83–.84, 3.86–.87
Subdominant triad, 2.1, 2.5–.8, 2.16, 2.54, 2.57–.60, 2.68, 7.36, 7.51, 7.54
Submediant triad, 2.16–.21, 2.69, 2.72, 2.74, 7.65, 7.67–.68, 10.41
Subtonic triad, 2.26–.31
Supertonic triad, 2.22–.23, 2.32–.34, 2.69, 2.75
Suspension, 8.69–.98
ornamentation, 8.91–.98
preparation, 8.71–.74, 8.76–.80, 8.93, 8.98
resolution, 8.71–.72, 8.75–.77, 8.91–.93, 8.98
types, 8.81–.87, 8.98

T

Tenor voice, 3.25–.26, 3.29
Texture. *See* Four-part texture
Tonal center, 1.74. *See also* Key center
Tonal harmony, 1.13, 7.1
Tonal music, 1.1, 1.6–.12
Tonality, 1.7–.8, 1.12
structure, 2.8–.9, 2.57, 2.68
Tonic triad, 2.1–.2, 2.7–.9, 2.16, 2.54–.60, 2.78, 10.27, 10.30–.34
Treble staff, 3.31
Triads, 1.14, 1.19–.60, 1.66–.73. *See specific entries;* e.g., Dominant triad; Tonic triad
augmented, 1.35–.36, 1.39, 1.44
diatonic, 1.22–.33, 2.26
diminished, 1.35, 1.37, 1.39, 1.45
dominant, 2.1, 2.3–.5, 2.16, 2.54–.57, 2.68, 2.78, 7.51, 7.54
first inversion, 5.2–.20
inverted, 5.1
leading tone, 2.22–.30, 2.69, 2.76, 2.78, 6.32–.33
major, 1.35, 1.39, 1.42, 1.46
mediant, 2.16–.21, 2.69, 2.71, 2.73
minor, 1.35, 1.38–.39, 1.43
primary, 2.7–.9, 2.54–.55, 2.63–.68, 2.70, 2.77–.82, 9.35–.48, 9.65
proper names, 2.1–.39, 2.53
quality, 1.49–.57
root position, 3.1–.5, 3.83, 5.1–.2, 5.8–.9, 5.31–.32
second inversion, 5.2, 5.9, 5.21–.28
secondary, 2.63–.65, 2.67, 2.69–.82, 9.35–.48, 10.41
subdominant, 2.1, 2.5–.9, 2.16, 2.54, 2.57–.60, 2.68, 7.36, 7.51, 7.54
submediant, 2.16–.21, 2.69, 2.72, 2.74, 7.65, 7.67–.68, 10.41
subtonic, 2.26–.31
supertonic, 2.22–.23, 2.32–.34, 2.69, 2.75
tonic, 2.1–.2, 2.7–.9, 2.16, 2.54–.60, 2.78, 10.27, 10.30–.34
Triple pedal, 8.110
Tritone, 6.67–.72, 6.79

U

Unessential chord. *See* Embellishing harmony
Upper voices, 3.38, 3.40–.43, 3.54–.58, 3.83, 4.49, 4.77–.78, 4.90
Upward stem, 3.31–.32

V

Vertical limits of music, 10.14
Vocal music, 4.46
Voice leading, 4.36–.37, 4.49–.108
Voices:
adjacent, 3.39–.42
alto, 3.25–.26, 3.28
bass, 3.25–.26, 3.30, 3.38
crossed, 3.35–.36
distribution, 3.31–.37, 9.8
range, 3.26–.30
soprano, 3.25–.27
tenor, 3.25–.26, 3.29
upper, 3.38, 3.40–.43, 3.54–.58, 3.83, 4.49, 4.77–.78, 4.90

NOTES

NOTES